107

WITHDRAWN

CHANCE AND CIRCUMSTANCE

CHANCE AND

TWENTY YEARS WITH

CIRCUMSTANCE

CAGE AND CUNNINGHAM

CAROLYN BROWN

ALFRED A. KNOPF   NEW YORK 2007

THIS IS A BORZOI BOOK PUBLISHED BY ALFRED A. KNOPF

www.aaknopf.com

Owing to limitations of space, all permissions to reprint previously
published material will be found following the index.

Library of Congress Cataloging-in-Publication Data
Brown, Carolyn.
Chance and circumstance : twenty years with Cage and
Cunningham / by Carolyn Brown.—1st ed.
p. cm.
ISBN 978-0-394-40191-1 (alk. paper)
1. Brown, Carolyn, ballet-dancer.   2. Cunningham, Merce.
3. Cage, John.   4. Dancers—United States—Biography.   I. Title.
GV1785.B755A3 2007
792.802'80922—dc22
[B]   2006048799

Manufactured in the United States of America

FIRST EDITION

CONTENTS

to Jim

for all the reasons he knows and a few he doesn't

Everything in the universe is the fruit of chance or necessity.

— DEMOCRITUS, c. 460–370 B.C.

One day, a year or two after I'd stopped performing with the Merce Cunningham Dance Company, I received a phone call from Maxine Groffsky, who had left her position as the Paris editor of the *Paris Review* and had returned to New York. "I want to be your agent?" she said. Astonished, I asked, "For what?" "Your book." "What book" "The one John Cage says you're going to write." "Well, maybe, someday." "No, now." I resisted; she persisted. So I wrote a sample chapter and Maxine presented it to Bob Gottlieb, then editor in chief at Knopf, and suddenly I found myself committed to the daunting project of writing a book. That was over thirty years ago. The writing and the *not* writing took that long.

The book chronicles a twenty-year period in the life of the company based on voluminous journals and letters—admittedly self-referential— that I'd written during that time. It is just one version of the story, but surely there are as many other versions as there were people involved— plus that impossible, truly objective one.

With rare exception, books I've read—describing events I've experienced firsthand—have had factual errors. No doubt there will be errors here as well, but facts are not the essence of this book so much as feeling.

CHANCE AND CIRCUMSTANCE

The taxi moved slowly along the rue du Bac and across the Pont Royal. Hazy, late morning sunlight filtered through the remaining chestnut leaves, spilling on damp cobblestones and the darkly glinting waters of the Seine. Paris. Autumn. October 29, to be exact, a Sunday, with scarcely another automobile on the boulevard, and only an occasional pedestrian walking by the river. I held hard the hand of my friend Jim Klosty in the hope that it would relieve the knot thickening in my throat and quiet the fear that I wouldn't be able to control the excess of feeling that had been steadily mounting since the first day of our weeklong run at the Théâtre de la Ville. For the Merce Cunningham Dance Company, this day, with a matinee performance, was the end of the Paris season and the end of the 1972 tour begun in Iran in early September. For me, it was the end of a twenty-year way of life.

I had deliberately chosen to end that life abruptly, telling no one but those most intimately concerned, and to end it where I loved performing most—in Europe. A romantic gesture, certainly, but one that insured a happy ending to a life I cherished and had been nourished by. Most of all, I wanted to leave "well." Only one of Merce's dancers had managed that in the past: Marianne Preger. With grace and good humor and abundant love, she managed to depart the company, having chosen motherhood and family after more than eight years dancing with Merce. Without feeling rejected, Merce was able to accept her decision. Like Marianne, I wanted to leave without ill feeling, rancor, or bitterness. I believe I managed it, though certainly not without pain on both sides. One cannot leave, after dancing in the company of Merce Cunningham and John Cage for any number of years, without suffering enormous loss. A loss never to be retrieved. But I knew, and had known for several years, that I needed to move on; perhaps what is surprising is that I stayed so long.

It was shortly after graduating from Wheaton College in Norton, Massachusetts, marrying Earle Brown, my childhood sweetheart, and moving to

Denver, Colorado, that I first saw Merce Cunningham dance—not perform, I hasten to add, but dance, in a master class that he taught and I took in April 1951. He was slender and tall, with a long spine, long neck, and sloping shoulders; a bit pigeon-breasted. There was a lightness of the upper body which contrasted with the solid legs, so beautifully shaped, and the heavy, massive feet. The body was a blue-period Picasso *saltimbanque*, though the face and head were not. I remember Merce most clearly demonstrating a fall that began with him rising onto three-quarter point in parallel position, swiftly arching back like a bow as he raised his left arm overhead and sinking quietly to the floor on his left hand, curving his body over his knees, rising on his knees to fall flat out like a priest at the foot of the cross, rolling over quickly and arriving on his feet again in parallel position—all done with such speed and elegance, suppressed passion and catlike stealth that my imitative dancer's mind was caught short. I could not repeat it. I could only marvel at what I hadn't really seen. His dancing was airborne then; critics and audiences of that time still cannot forget his extraordinary gift for jumping. An Aries, born April 16, 1919, about one month before and in the same year as Margot Fonteyn, Merce Cunningham had an appetite for dancing that seemed to me then, as it does today, to be his sole reason for living.

I was brought up on dancing; for fourteen years or more my mother, Marion Stevens Rice, had taken me to dance events in Boston—ballet, modern, ethnic. I'd watched her take class from Ted Shawn and members of the Braggiotti Denishawn school, caught glimpses of Miss Ruth (Ruth St. Denis) through open studio doors, sat mesmerized in a box in the old Boston Opera House for scores of performances of Ballets Russes and later Ballet Theatre, and each summer we went faithfully to Ted Shawn's Jacob's Pillow for every new program. Despite that exposure, I'd never seen anyone move like Merce: he was a strange, disturbing mixture of Greek god, panther, and madman.

But seeing Merce move and experiencing vicariously his hungry passion for dancing in the two classes he taught was not a reason to pack up, leave Denver, and follow him back to New York. It would never have occurred to me to do that. I had no intention of becoming a dancer. Born to a dancing mother, having danced since I was three, I had rejected life as a dancer or dancing teacher. I wanted to write, and with that in mind, I went off to college for four years to major in philosophy, taking no tights or leotards, convinced that my dancing days were over. My mother said nothing, but she admits to an "I knew it!" smile at my frantic letter two weeks later requesting my practice clothes by return mail. I danced and choreographed all four years at college, but refused to write my honors thesis on dance aesthetics as my philosophy professor Holcombe Austin suggested. Dance wasn't serious enough. I needed a reason—a philosophical raison d'être—for a life in dance to which to devote myself. It was John Cage who provided that, though I didn't realize it at the time.

John and Merce were on a tour of the United States. Just the two of them. John performed his *Sonatas and Interludes* for prepared piano[1] and Merce gave master classes. Together they gave concerts with Merce performing an evening of solos and John playing the piano or percussion for Merce's dances, although in Denver there was no dance concert. John's *Sonatas and Interludes* were exquisite; beautiful, quiet, gently percussive, rhythmically tantalizing music, seductively and hypnotically easy to listen to. Earle found them "pretty" but not compelling. His own interests at the time were the works of Arnold Schoenberg and Anton von Webern, and the ideas of Joseph Schillinger.[2] In Denver, where he taught the Schillinger System of arranging and composition, Earle found no one to talk with except his students, most of them jazz musicians (Broadway and Hollywood composers had been prominent among Schillinger's students), and Eric Johnson, a young pianist-composer who accompanied dancers and composed for Jane McLean. It was Jane who had arranged for Cunningham and Cage to appear in Denver, although she could not afford to present them in a dance concert, and it was Jane (a dancer formerly with Martha Graham and thereby an acquaintance of Merce) with whom I was then studying and performing. Johnson, her pianist, had met John Cage in New York and reported back to us that John was charming but completely crazy, a common consensus in those years. Charming John Cage most certainly could be; completely crazy he was not, had never been.

At each of two parties given for Cage and Cunningham that weekend, Earle and I "rather cornered John" (as I wrote home) "and talked the evening away." The first real question Earle asked him was "Do you feel there is an affinity between your music and the music of Anton Webern?" It was still rare in the United States in 1951 for anyone to know Webern's work. Cage looked quickly toward Earle and replied, "What do you know about Webern?" The conversation took off from there. We heard for the first time the names Pierre Boulez, a young French composer whom Cage had met two years earlier in Paris; David Tudor, an extraordinary young pianist; Morton Feldman, a young New York composer writing graph music. All these young men, more than a decade younger than Cage, were born within a year or two of each other and were Earle's immediate contemporaries. Cage told us about his own *Music of Changes*, which he was then writing, and about his use of "chance operations" in composing. Eventually the talk moved away from music to art in general, and to philosophy and religion; specifically to Zen Buddhism and the I Ching. I was tremendously disturbed by much that he said.

The second night, we talked again—just Earle and John and I, for the most part—and in a letter to my parents describing that weekend I wrote: "John Cage is *more* than a startlingly original musician—he is living his philosophy of life which is a vital and free one. His philosophy of life *is* the thing I wrote my paper about last year!" (In my senior year at Wheaton College, I'd written an honors thesis on "Creativity in Ethics" that had not been understood by my New England–born Episcopalian mother and Baptist father. For some reason they had taken it to be a criticism of their values and philosophies. It wasn't.) After our second evening with John Cage, Earle wrote down all that he and I could remember of our conversation. I believe we both understood then that the weekend had altered our lives, that we had to leave Denver and go to New York. But we had no money to make such a move; it wasn't until August 1952 that we packed our belongings in a wagon trailer hitched behind our Ford station wagon and headed east.

In April 1951, Earle was already working at three jobs daily. From nine to five he worked at Cabaniss, a contemporary furniture store and interior design shop that sold Eames, Saarinen, Mies van der Rohe, Herman Miller, the Knoll line, and Schiffer prints. Earle got the job when we were down to our last dollar—a silver keepsake. He used the dollar for a haircut and got the job the same afternoon. From that job, he went to his own studio in a midtown professional building where he gave private lessons to four young jazz musicians and also taught a class with five students. After that he came home to compose. In the early hours of the morning he wrote a string quartet, a passacaglia (for Jane McLean and me to dance to), and a trio. When he finally did go to bed he had trouble sleeping, music still on his mind.

I, too, had been trying to write. A few short stories. A review of Martha Graham's performance of *Judith* with the Denver Symphony. Dutifully I sent them off, hoping for publication. They were returned—sometimes with a few kind encouraging words attached, but returned nonetheless. I was utterly lost. I suppose I was not unlike many young married female college graduates in the fifties who despite their love for their husbands, felt as though they had dropped into a void. It was Earle, not I, who sensed that I missed dancing. His boss, Mrs. Adelaide Cabaniss, told him about Jane McLean, and he encouraged me to seek her out; he even took me to her studio the first time! Partly, I'm sure, this was self-defense on Earle's part: with so much to do, so much he wanted to do, he must have felt suffocated by my attempting to live vicariously through his activities.

It was with a sense of relief that I stopped trying to write and started again to dance. I took daily classes with Jane McLean and performed in her concerts and lecture demonstrations. Her classes were my first exposure to "real" Graham technique after fifteen years of studying and performing Denishawn and ballet, plus four years of the usual hodgepodge taught in the dance classes of liberal arts colleges' physical education departments at that time.

Before meeting Cage and Cunningham, Earle and I had enrolled at Colorado College Summer School, Earle to study with Arnold Schoenberg and I with Hanya Holm. On our honeymoon the previous summer, we had made a pilgrimage to 116 North Rockingham Avenue in Los Angeles, parked our battered but beloved '42 station wagon in front of Schoenberg's home and, for about an hour, just sat there quietly. Ten years later, when we met Schoenberg's daughter Nuria in Venice, we told her of our silent homage. "Oh, you should have come in! He would have been so pleased to meet you," was the gist of her reply as she expressed her sorrow over the reticence of those who truly respected her father and the audacity of those who came merely sightseeing.

John Cage had been Schoenberg's pupil from around 1934 to 1936, both privately and at the University of California, Los Angeles. Music critic Peter Yates quotes Schoenberg on Cage: "He is not a composer, but an inventor of genius."[3] In May 1951, we learned that Schoenberg would not come to Colorado. Earle was deeply disappointed and decided to ask Schoenberg if he could study with him later that summer, privately. On June 27, 1951, Schoenberg replied:

Dear Mr. Brown:
If it is not too expensive for you to pay $25.00 per lesson and if I am well enough to teach you, I could suggest that you come to Los Angeles for a number of weeks. I hope I will be able to teach you, but I cannot guaranty it. Anyway, in a space of several weeks there will probably be a possibility once or twice a week.
    Let me hear from you.

Sincerely yours, Arnold Schoenberg

And so of course we would go to Los Angeles.

In the early part of the summer of '51, we met David Tudor at the University of Colorado in Boulder, where Jean Erdman's dance company was in residence. David played for her concerts and also gave solo concerts of his own. We'd been told by John Cage to be sure to meet him. On July 5 we attended his concert of contemporary music where he performed for the first time anywhere Part I of Cage's *Music of Changes*, the work Cage had discussed with us a few months earlier. Afterward, Earle went up to speak to David, who quickly responded: "So you're the one John told me to look out for." Immediately warm and friendly, he invited us to join him at a party being given in his honor. We happily tagged along. David introduced us to Jean Erdman and her erudite, extremely handsome husband, Joseph Campbell (not then of world renown but certainly well known in academic circles for his *The Hero with a Thousand Faces*, published in 1949). We discovered that both Jean and Joe were friends of Merce and John. Jean had been a member of Martha Graham's company in the same period (late thirties, early forties), as had Merce. In 1942, at Bennington College in Vermont, she and Merce had presented a joint concert of solos and duets with their own choreography. Earle and I went several times to Boulder. Jean allowed me to take her technique class and to observe her composition workshop, and Earle spent hours with David or in David's room studying manuscripts and taking notes, and after each visit David, Earle, and I would have dinner together, continuing conversations begun earlier in the day. I was obviously impressed: "David has been so very generous and helpful—he's gone out of his way to be nice to us. He is such an interesting person—really a genius, I guess. He is the only pianist who can play contemporary music[4] (which is unbelievably difficult), and not only plays this music, but studies the aesthetics of the composers, and their philosophies of life as well, in order to do true justice to what they express in music. An amazing person. And probably not over twenty-five years old."

And that is exactly what he was. Born in Philadelphia on January 20, 1926, he was not even a year older than Earle, who was born on December 26, 1926, in Lunenburg, Massachusetts. David had been living in New York City for about four years and, through Morton Feldman, he'd met John Cage just at the time Cage had returned from Paris bearing with him Pierre Boulez's *Second Piano Sonata*. Cage was looking for someone to play it. David expressed interest and his interest became total commitment: he memorized it, mastered it; studied French so that he could read Boulez's articles as well as the French authors René Char and Antonin Artaud, both of whom Boulez himself was reading at the time he composed the work. Tudor gave the first American performance in 1950. It's been reported that Henry Cowell (composer, musicologist, teacher) was at the concert, score in hand, and said, "He played it with fantastic accuracy. I couldn't think of a living pianist who could have done it!"

The sense of awe David produced in both Earle and me is something I've witnessed in others all the years since then. Cage himself usually deferred to this man fourteen years his junior, setting him up as a kind of omniscient deity, even in areas in which David didn't presume to be an authority. At that time he chain-smoked cigarettes (often hand-rolled, and often mistaken for marijuana), leaving the cigarettes burning between his thin lips until his own saliva put them out. His brown eyes were soft and gentle with just a bit of mystery and mischief in them. Medium height, high-browed, with thick, dark, lustrous hair; he was slightly overweight that summer, I remember, because he gave Earle, who was reed-slender, a pair of trousers that no longer fit him.

For a few days we happily chauffeured him around Denver and into the mountains. David never had a driver's license that I was aware of, and wherever the Cunningham Dance Company toured in the years to follow there was always someone who wanted to drive David Tudor around in search of his many curious diversions: exotic spices, homeopathic herbs and medicines, fruit wines and liquors, gadgets for music-making of unimaginable variety (and eventually electronic hardware), bookshops of every description, and out-of-the-ordinary restaurants. How he loved to eat! And how terrified I was to cook for him, although I did when he stayed with us for a few days before taking a train to Black Mountain College in North Carolina. It was David Tudor who turned me into a label-reader; it took twice as long to get through a shopping expedition with David because he bought nothing without checking out the ingredients on every item. He checked out restaurants in similar fashion and truly appreciated our favorite restaurant, a hideous dump with garish fluorescent lighting on Larimer Street, Denver's skid row, but the best Mexican eatery in town. Before leaving, David gave us two gifts: a list of his preferred New York restaurants and a private piano recital in Earle's tiny studio, on Earle's secondhand upright (purchased on the installment plan at $6.50 a month). It was a hot summer night. We opened wide both window and door. Strange music by John Cage, Pierre Boulez, Morton Feldman, Anton von Webern, and Stefan Wolpe echoed in the long corridor of the empty professional building and out to the empty streets. David's concert for a rapt audience of two was one more reason Earle had to move to New York.

On July 14, Earle and I received a telegram from my brother, Parker: "Bad break Schoenberg. If heading east let us know pronto." We didn't understand it until the Sunday *New York Times* arrived the following Wednesday. The headline read: "Schoenberg Composer Dies at 76. His Atonal Music Caused a Furor." For us, Schoenberg's death meant, literally, a new direction: going east instead of west. Possibly, East instead of West philosophically as well. For Earle, Schoenberg was not dead aesthetically as Boulez once dogmatically stated. Earle never agreed with either Cage or Boulez on the necessity of destroying the past for the revolution of the present (Boulez later changed his mind), and Schoenberg's death truly saddened him. He realized that Schoenberg had written that simple, brief letter to him when he was very ill, and yet he had expressed a willingness to teach an eager student, probably out of financial need as well as the desire to share his musical ideas, and Earle was touched anew by the sad paradox of Schoenberg's always difficult life.

After a quick visit with both our families in Massachusetts, we headed directly to 326 Monroe Street, a tenement building on the Lower East Side of Manhattan in the shadow of the Williamsburg Bridge, where John Cage lived on the top floor in two small apartments he'd made into one. The shabby building, almost on the East River, also housed Morton Feldman and the painter-collagist Ray Johnson, who shared his tiny work space with the sculptor Richard Lippold. They called the place the "Bozza Mansion," Bozza being their landlord's name. John's apartment made a great impression on me: walls, ceiling, woodwork painted flat white; cocoa matting wall-to-wall; a baby grand piano surrounded by huge avocado trees in big pots; on the floor against two adjacent walls, long narrow cushions—church-pew cushions covered in white corduroy—and just off the floor in front of them, a long slab of gray-white marble, rescued, I believe, from the stairway of some deserted tenement building. Suspended high above the cushion on the west wall were delicate wire sculptures by Richard Lippold. There was a closet near the entrance that held Cage's library and musical instruments; probably his clothes as well, though I don't remember seeing any. Windows faced east and south—out to the East River and across to Brooklyn and down to the Statue of Liberty and Staten Island. In the next room, which had windows to the south and west, there were three pieces of furniture: a bed covered in the same white corduroy, a wood draftsman's table, and a stool. Nothing else. There was a tiny kitchen, and off it, the bathroom. The views from each window were breathtaking. The rooms were airy, spare, serene. Surely this was the home of an ascetic, not a revolutionary. The place seemed to accurately reflect the man who lived there. Outside was a constantly varying parade of random events—a whole world teeming with activity—barges, boats, buses, taxis, trucks, cars, and pedestrians; even a playground; changing light in sky and water; and of course the constant ever-varying soundscape in a seeming chaos of sound-full splendor that intrigued and delighted him. Inside was his retreat, monastic in its restraint and quiet, geared to dawn-'til-dusk disciplined work and a certain amount of self-denial.

John greeted us with that well-documented remarkable open-mouthed half-chuckle/half-laugh that exposed a large fleshy tongue lolling on lower teeth. He seemed genuinely delighted to see us. Although taller than he appeared, his peculiar posture—a spine aligned in such a way that the body from the waist up and the body from the waist down seemed to be heading in opposing diagonal directions—disguised his height. In 1951, he was clean-shaven and his thick, wiry, dark-brown hair bristled in an over-grown GI haircut. Even before registering these details, I noticed his ears—large protuberances jutting out on each side of his long face, alert and almost aquiver, like those of a deer in hunting season who hears things most of us don't. Cage made lunch for us and we talked into the late after-noon during the course of which he introduced us to his next door neigh-bors, Ray and Richard, just recently moved to the Bozza Mansion. Theirs was a small irregular space with one view, equally spare but lacking the exquisite refinement of John's quarters. Lippold showed us a scale model of his newest project, *Sun,* which would one day hang in the Metropolitan Museum of Art.

Toward evening, John took us downstairs to Morton Feldman's apart-ment, where we met Morty for the first time. Just a few weeks earlier, David Tudor had played his piano pieces in Earle's studio in Denver. Now we were having dinner in his apartment. Who would have guessed from hear-ing that exquisite, spare, precise, and jewel-like music what his physical presence would be? The large, heavyset man peering out from behind extra-thick lenses who greeted us so affably at the door was a surprise. So was his pronounced New York Jewish accent. Friends of Morty's were already there: Danny Stern, a writer and jazz saxophonist; and Herbert and Mercedes Matter, he a slender quiet man, a photographer, and she an ani-mated, wildly beautiful woman with a curious gravelly voice, a painter. Herbert Matter was planning a film of the New York skyline as seen from the rooftop of the Saint George Hotel in Brooklyn Heights, so after dinner, Matter, his wife, John Cage, Earle, and I drove over the Brooklyn Bridge to check out the location. John was to write the music for the project. While Herbert took test shots, both still and motion, the rest of us watched the blood-red sun set behind Manhattan's skyscrapers. Sky-blue faded to lavender, then gray, then turned to black as the buildings began another kind of light show from within.

So ended our first day with John Cage in New York. It was only a hint, a tiny preview of John's generosity, of the many new faces, new thoughts, new foods, new adventures I would encounter because of him. In a single afternoon and evening, prefaced by our two meetings in Denver, I'd made John Cage my guru and probably my hero as well. It took a while before I was able to free him of that burden and try to become his friend. In 1951, I was looking for a reason and a way to live my life that I could believe in. I caught a glimpse of a way, if not a reason, through Cage.

The next day, we visited the Bozza Mansion once again—a shorter stay this time. Earle brought his most recent compositions to show Cage and we talked of future New York plans. Cage was encouraging. We were elated. I didn't see Merce Cunningham in New York that August, though I'd tried to find him in his studio. John told me that Merce was in New England recovering from a back injury.

By the end of August, Earle and I had made a decision: stay one more year in Denver, work to save as much money as possible, then move to New York. I had decided to apply for admission to Columbia University's graduate school to get a master's degree in philosophy with the idea of eventually teaching in a college. Earle hoped, once in New York, to be included in a project for the making of music directly onto magnetic tape for which Cage was attempting to raise funds. Our decision meant I must get a job, and at the last minute I did, at the Kent School for Girls, where they indentured me: I was to teach dance to the entire school, first grade through high school; to teach drama; the eighth-grade speech classes; an elective appreciation course in dance and drama to juniors and seniors; to serve as substitute teacher for eighth-grade history (a disaster!); to be bus proctor, study-hall proctor, librarian, and drama coach—all for two thousand dollars a year! Each school day began and ended with me proctoring a busload of giggling girls to and from school; when the school day was over, I was completely wiped out and still had more homework to do than the kids. I barely managed to keep one step ahead of them. Even so, I tried to continue taking classes with Jane McLean because I was discovering how much it meant to me to dance, even though teaching dance at the Kent School was an exasperating task that I loathed. I took it far too seriously, and the girls' completely normal unprofessional attitude toward studying dance pained me. I hated teaching dance as fun and games, and in silly arrogance, I refused to do so. More than once I retreated to the faculty changing room to cry, moving the headmistress to lecture the rowdy young ladies that dance was a serious art for Mrs. Brown and that they should be more respectful.

Earle continued his three jobs, and added another: teaching and conducting an ensemble class of twenty to thirty young men who met to play original arrangements by his students. This was particularly enjoyable for him; he'd played trumpet in jazz bands and in his own dance band in high school (my brother Parker played drums); and later, at the end of the Second World War, he played trumpet in Army Air Corps bands. During the year, letters went back and forth between Earle and John Cage. "Glad to hear we are about to receive your new work. Full of anticipation," Cage wrote. The letter was signed, "Very affectionately to you both, John." Our spirits soared. The next letter, postmarked November 7, 1951, was written after Cage had received Earle's music:

Dear Earle,
I had little time with your music because David was about to leave and I sent it along with him. I went through it however and liked it very much. David will be gone now until around xmas so I won't be able to hear it until then. I wd. like to propose it for publishing in the New Music Edition. It seems to me that you are working very well and the only thing one can say in such a situation is "Walk on!" . . . Thank you for the music. More please.
Yours, John

Less than two months passed; in the mail came a flyer addressed to us in John's own beautiful hand. Inside, elegantly spaced and lettered, was the announcement that the Living Theatre, Inc., would present two recitals by David Tudor at the Cherry Lane Theatre, 38 Commerce Street, in New York. At the first, Tudor would play Boulez's *2ème Sonate* and for the first time anywhere the complete *Music of Changes* by Cage, as well as a work by Christian Wolff and one by Morton Feldman. The next month, Tudor would play music by Webern, Cage, Wladimir Woronoff, Henry Cowell, Stefan Wolpe, Josef M. Hauer, Lou Harrison, Wolff, Feldman, and *Earle Brown*! The flyer was designed by Cage. In the forties and much of the fifties, Cage and Cunningham (and often Tudor) concerts were usually graced with simple, elegant, handsome flyers, posters, programs, and sometimes tickets that Cage himself designed; when possible he chose the paper as well as the type, layout, colors, etc. Earle and I were about two thousand miles away and felt wretched to be missing it, but his parents and his sister Marilyn drove to New York for the occasion of the first New York performance of a composition by Earle Brown. It wasn't until late

March that there was a brief note from John: "Dear Earle, Your music was beautiful and should have told you sooner. It was good too to meet your family. What are you writing? And when do you come to New York?"

David Tudor wrote: "Lots of people liked your pieces, said they were very fresh-sounding, and I wish you would send some more, there are opportunities and a dearth of material."

Excitement about our move to New York escalated. Earle worked at full speed, never seeming to tire, composing new works for solo piano and for piano, cello, and violin. By the end of my year at the Kent School, I'd choreographed for an Egyptian play and for Carnival; written and directed a history play for the eighth grade; and choreographed and directed an adaptation of Edna St. Vincent Millay's "The Princess Marries the Page," which was presented in a garden. For me, it was the kind of year one describes to others as "good experience" and prays to oneself will never have to be repeated.

A letter to my parents mentioned the Brandeis Creative Arts Festival, which had commissioned Merce Cunningham to choreograph Stravinsky's *Les Noces* and *Symphonie pour un homme seul,* musique concrète composed by Pierre Schaeffer with the collaboration of Pierre Henry. I wrote: "Hope you plan to go. . . . Don't miss it!! . . . be interested to know what you think of Merce Cunningham's choreography. I have never seen any— but know that as a dancer he is *tremendous!*"

The teaching job over, I took a job as a car-hop at the Terrace Drive-In for five weeks (relishing, with a perverse reverse snobbery, the shocked faces of my former students' parents when they discovered a faculty member of the very expensive, exclusive upper-class Kent School working as a carhop in such a place). With the money earned I took the University of Colorado Summer Dance Course with Jean Erdman. "Dance classes are fun and stimulating," I wrote home in July 1952, "so stimulating, in fact, that I'm now contemplating going to Juilliard for my M.A. in dance." Juilliard's new dance department had an astonishingly stellar faculty that included Martha Graham, Doris Humphrey, José Limón, Agnes de Mille, Jerome Robbins, and Antony Tudor. Somehow the thought of studying dance with these people seemed far more compelling than the prospect of scholarly pursuits at Columbia. Again, it was Earle who gave the deciding shove: he knew me much better than I knew myself.

Unfortunately for Earle, David Tudor had not returned to Boulder with Jean Erdman. He had been working on the electronic music project with Cage and in August was going again to Black Mountain, this time with Cage and Cunningham. He wrote:

So why don't you two use my place till you get settled. 69 East 4th Street, between 2nd and 3rd Ave. 5th floor front, Apt. 22, no glass visible in door. It is a dump, you have to walk up, no ice, etc. but will hold you and yours for a while. Use anything you see. I will leave the key with Morty Feldman, 326 Monroe Street (GR3-2109) or at work (till 2:30 IL8-7460), or at the Cedar Bar, 8th St. & University Place.

P.S. Take care of your car, lock it and try not to leave it on the street with a lot of baggage inside. Mine is a pretty tough neighborhood.

John wrote us, too:

Will be in North Carolina (Black Mtn. College) during August, otherwise on the lookout for you and room for you. Started project for music on tape in May, goes through October (that is raised enough money for that much time). The Brandeis business is unfortunately not Boulez but a lousy piece by Schaeffer and Henry. Boulez will be here in November! Perhaps early September concerts (Tudor) near New York.

Black Mountain College? Neither Earle nor I had ever heard of it.

lack Mountain College, situated in the foothills of North Carolina, has become a legend and like most legends has suffered a confusion of contradictory histories, but as one Black Mountain member put it twenty years after it closed, "The kind of interest Black Mountain attracts now indicates that its spirit continues to stimulate ways of thinking imaginatively about the arts, about community, about education."[1] For those of us who went to Black Mountain only in the summer, it was a kind of paradise. Little of Black Mountain's struggles was known to us. It didn't seem to be a place of competition or aggression, but a true community of easy ebullient sharing. But I've learned since that Black Mountain from September to June was something quite different. In the school's twenty-three-year existence, attempts were made and remade and made yet again to define "community" and to discover what teaching is, what balance should be struck between giving information and developing character. There was a continuous struggle to clarify and evaluate aims, with the inevitable anguish that accompanies heartfelt disagreement within a family.

M. C. Richards, a professor of English and writing at Black Mountain for six years, was deeply involved in the spiritual well-being of the college and was eventually profoundly disillusioned by her experience there. "The Black Mountain community of artists, scholars, and scientists were torn apart time and time again by schism, secession, mutinies, expulsions. Power politics, empire building, territorial combat existed there as elsewhere," she wrote in her book *The Crossing Point,* and she went on to ask, "Why is it, if we are so well-educated and brilliant and gifted and artistic and idealistic and distinguished in scholarship, that we are so selfish and scheming and dishonest and begrudging and impatient and arrogant and disrespectful of others?"[2] What M. C. Richards says she learned at Black Mountain was "that university education had not equipped its faculty for self-government nor for cooperation nor with social imagination."[3] Nonetheless, Black Mountain was willing to try new ideas; unfortunately, the administrative gifts of the faculty and students, who together owned, operated, and governed in a kind of quasi-Quaker democracy, rarely matched the cultural and artistic ones. Close to poverty at all times, Black Mountain opened its doors to artists equally poverty-stricken, artists often unwelcome elsewhere due to the radical or experimental nature of their work. Josef Albers and Charles Olson are probably the two most important to Black Mountain's history, but the list includes Ernst Krenek, Edward Steuerman, Walter Gropius, Lionel Feininger, Ossip Zadkine, Robert Motherwell, Willem de Kooning, Elaine de Kooning, Richard Lippold, Buckminster Fuller, John Cage, Merce Cunningham, Paul Goodman, Robert Duncan, Robert Creeley, Esteban Vicente, Theodoras Stamos, Katherine Litz, Bernard Leach, Karen Karnes, David Weinrib, Peter Voulkos, John Chamberlain, David Tudor, Lou Harrison, Ben Shahn, Franz Kline, Jack Tworkov, Stefan Wolpe—the majority of whom were in residence only in summer sessions. (Artists emerged from Black Mountain's student body as well: James Leo Herlihy, Arthur Penn, Nicola Cernovich, Kenneth Noland, Robert Rauschenberg, Cy Twombly, Francine du Plessix Gray, Dorothea Rockburne, and Viola Farber, to name a few.) The college offered its faculty the freedom to work and teach unrestricted (or almost), albeit for little to nothing more than room and board. The father of Black Mountain College, John Andrew Rice, believed that music, art, and drama should be central to Black Mountain's curriculum, not necessarily to produce artists but to develop individuals capable of choosing. "We are all artists," said Rice, "everyone of us: we are free to create the kind of world in which we choose to live, and we're equal in that freedom."[4]

Black Mountain's reputation reached all the way to Seattle, Washington, where, in 1937, John Cage was accompanying dance classes for Bonnie Bird at the Cornish School, and where for the first time he met Merce Cunningham, a student at the school. Cage wrote to Black Mountain hoping to be offered a position, but he was not. He wrote again in 1942, offering to establish a Center for Experimental Music. This offer was not accepted, either. John Cage was not yet known. In any case, there were no funds for such a project. But in April 1948, while touring with Merce Cunningham, Cage did finally get invited to the college. The two men spent about a week there, giving performances and lectures and talking with the faculty and students. The Black Mountain community loved them and they loved Black Mountain, and they enthusiastically agreed to return for the next summer session.

The summer of 1948 brought together Willem and Elaine de Kooning, Richard and Louise Lippold, Buckminster Fuller, Arthur Penn, Mary Caroline (M.C.) Richards, John Cage, and Merce Cunningham, and brought them together not only as artists sharing a summer but as collaborators in what turned out to be the hit of the summer, John Cage's production of *Le Piège de Méduse* (The Ruse of Meduse) by the French composer Erik Satie. Cage was indelibly influenced by Satie, and in 1948 was in the heat of the first stages of his love affair with Satie's music, thoughts, and legend. Satie had ridiculed the pompous in German music; he was concerned with the reduction of music to its essential elements, to form that was nondevelopmental, and to sonority for its own sake. His music was both sardonic and witty, brief and unpretentious. *Le Piège de Méduse* (1913) was one of Satie's first works for the theater, and to quote Rollo Myers's biography, *Erik Satie*, "might easily and appropriately be described as 'Dada' except the 'Dadaist' movement in the arts had not yet been invented."[5] Cage's production at Black Mountain was the climax to a series of twenty-five concerts devoted to the music of Satie. Three nights a week for about half an hour, Cage worked his way through thirteen hours of Satie's compositions.

That summer, Black Mountain was peopled with many German refugees. Asked by Josef Albers, who was the rector of the college then, to give lectures on Satie prior to performing the music, Cage managed to infuriate a large number of these Germans with his inflammatory remarks on Beethoven. (Albers was himself a German who'd come to Black Mountain from Berlin, from the Bauhaus, which had closed its doors rather than submit to Nazi directives.) In one of his lectures, ostensibly on Satie, Cage said:

> With Beethoven the parts of the composition were defined by means of harmony. With Satie and Webern they are defined by means of time lengths. The question of structure is so basic, and it is so important to be in agreement about it, that one must now ask: Was Beethoven right or are Webern and Satie right? I answer immediately and unequivocally, Beethoven was in error, and his influence, which has been as extensive as it is lamentable, has been deadening to the art of music.[6]

The harmony-versus-duration question (Beethoven versus Satie, according to Cage) was a central argument in Cage's philosophy of music: he abandoned harmony (he said he had no gift for it), the traditional means of structuring Western nineteenth- and twentieth-century music, and in its place he defined the structure of his own compositions by time lengths— by duration—which he considered to be the most fundamental of the four characteristics of sound, the others being pitch, loudness, and timbre. According to Cage, it took a Satie and a Webern to rediscover this musical truth. Having freed himself of the musical habits of scales, modes, and theories of counterpoint and harmony, Cage determined that music was simply a matter of sound and its opposite and necessary coexistent, silence,[7] though, as Cage discovered, "Try as we may to make a silence, we cannot." Even in an anechoic chamber, designed to be as silent as possible, one hears two sounds—a high one, one's own nervous system in operation, and a low one, one's own blood circulating. Having determined that the barest definition of music is sound and silence, Cage then arrived at a corollary in dance: movement and stillness. From that premise he resolved that the common denominator of music and dance is time. Following Cage's lead, Cunningham structured his dances by time lengths. Said Cage: "I freed the dancers from the necessity to interpret music on the level of feeling; they could make a dance in the same structure that a musician was using. They could do it independently of one another, bringing their results together as pure hypothetical meaning."[8] Cage was in sync with the American artist Barnett Newman, who wrote in 1947: "It is only the pure idea that has meaning. Everything else has everything else."[9]

Despite the hostility aroused by Cage's remarks about Beethoven, everyone was apparently in agreement that the performance of Satie's *Le Piège de Méduse* was an enormous delight and an unqualified success— such a success that its sets and costumes were taken to New York in the hope of future performances there. But neither Cage nor any of the other participants had access to large funds,[10] so *The Ruse of Méduse* had only a one-night stand in the dining hall at Black Mountain College on August 14, 1948. In the very best Black Mountain spirit of community, the faculty joined Cage's effort: the translation was by M. C. Richards; it was directed by Arthur Penn, with sets by Willem de Kooning, assisted by his wife, Elaine; the play starred Buckminster Fuller as the Baron and Elaine de Kooning as his foster daughter or "*fille de lait*" Frisette; Merce Cunningham choreographed and danced the role of the monkey Jonas "stuffed by a master hand," whose tail was designed by Richard Lippold; Cage, of course, was at the piano.

Relatively few people beyond Black Mountain ever knew of *Le Piège de Méduse*. The same cannot be said of a theatrical evening presented during the summer of 1952. Many art history books now credit this particular evening with being the prototype of the "Happenings" that took place in the late fifties and early sixties. Claes Oldenburg demurs, writing in *Store Days,* "It should have been made clear that Happenings came about when painters and sculptors crossed into theater taking with them their way of looking and doing things." Oldenburg may not have known about Antonin Artaud's *The Theatre and Its Double;* Cage certainly did, and his Black Mountain theater event was clearly influenced by it. It was Artaud who wanted *une sorte d'événement,* which can also be translated as a kind of Happening, and who postulated that the theater should merge with real life to form a genuine Event. Excluding Cage, Oldenburg was correct in his declaration that it was the painters and sculptors who were the first to cross into theater and come out with the Happening. However, Cage had taught a class at the New School attended by many of those who would become Happening artists—George Brecht, Al Hansen, Dick Higgins, and Allan Kaprow—and his class was an extremely important seed-sower and fertilizer, as its participants have readily acknowledged. Dick Higgins stated: "The best thing that happened to us in Cage's class was the sense that 'anything goes,' at least potentially."[11] But Cage was horrified by an anything-goes attitude toward the making of music or dance or theater. Rigorously disciplined himself, he more often experienced pain than pleasure in observing what he considered the misapplication of the ideas of openness and freedom that he extolled.

Cage's recipe for theater-music-art included a wild mix: Eastern philosophy; Antonin Artaud's ideas of a nonliterary theater involving all the senses, devoid of narrative, rich with sound, movement, and light; a dash of Duchamp ("All in all, the creative act is not performed by the artist alone; the spectator brings the work in contact with the external world by deciphering and interpreting its inner qualifications and thus adds his contribution to the creative act.")[12]; a sprinkle of Dada ("When art is brought into line with everyday life and individual experience, it is exposed to the same risks, the same unforeseeable laws of chance, the same interplay of living forces. Art is no longer a 'serious and weighty' emotional stimulus, nor a sentimental tragedy, but the fruit of experience and joy in life."[13]); plus a dollop or two of Cage's own deadly-earnest moralizing ("Nothing is accomplished by writing a piece of music . . . nothing is accomplished by hearing a piece of music . . . nothing is accomplished by playing a piece of music . . . our ears are now in excellent condition.")[14] This whole concoction was served up to the Black Mountain community in its dining hall in a collaborative non-collaboration that involved John Cage, David Tudor, M. C. Richards, Charles Olson, Merce Cunningham, a dog, and a twenty-six-year-old painter named Bob Rauschenberg. Cage delivered a timed lecture, with silences, on a ladder; Richards and Olsen read their own poetry from another ladder at different times; David Tudor played the piano; Rauschenberg played old records on an antique wind-up phono-graph, and his white paintings were suspended at various angles above the audience; Cunningham danced in the aisles and around the audience, improvising his material—all the while being followed by a barking dog (whose presence was completely fortuitous).

Like Artaud, Cage was interested in the dislocation of sensibility through the juxtaposition of heterogeneous elements, which turns the expected order of things upside down. These separate and unrelated activities were structured into time brackets, which were determined by Cage's use of chance operations, and the collage of events was presented in an unusual seating and performance-area arrangement devised by Cage, although, in fact, the idea originated with Artaud: "In the 'theatre of cruelty' the spectator is in the middle and the spectacle surrounds him."[15] Cage had the people in the audience face one another in four triangular blocks whose apexes pointed in to the center, with four aisles between them; the performance took place for the most part outside and around the audience, as well as in the aisles and center section. Central focus was eliminated. There were no "best seats"; members of the audience were thus invited to be omni-attentive or selective, as they chose. As Cage explained it, "More pertinent to our daily experience is a theatre in which we ourselves are in the round . . . in which the activity takes place around us."[16] It was Artaud who wrote: "We are eliminating the stage and the auditorium and replacing them with a single site, without partition or barrier of any kind . . . A direct communication will be reestablished between the spectator and the spectacle, between the actor and the spectator, because the spectator, by being placed in the middle of the action, is enveloped by it and caught in its crossfire . . . In effect, the absence of a stage in the ordinary sense of the word will allow the action to spread out to the four corners of the room."[17] It's clear that Cage responded to new stimuli quickly and decisively.

The evening did not have the unqualified success that *Le Piège de Méduse* had four summers earlier. Reactions were mixed; some people thought of it as a joke, others as a party, or a three-ring circus, a bore, an outrage, an interesting experience, or, as Cunningham so characteristically put it, "just an evening of theatre." Whatever it was, it was seminal, containing as it did a half-dozen or so separate idées fixes, leitmotifs that appeared and reappeared in Cage and Cunningham works for the twenty years I worked with them and afterward.

n the summer of 1952, Black Mountain meant nothing more to Earle and me than some place where David Tudor would be spending the month of August, thereby enabling us to use his vacant flat in New York City while we searched for an apartment of our own. We went directly to Morty Feldman's apartment. He gave us the key to David's cold-water flat but warned us not to spend our first night there, it would be too depressing, he said. He recommended we stay in John's airy rooms upstairs, and we accepted gratefully. My most vivid memory of that evening in New York is walking in the summer twilight with Morty and Danny Stern across Washington Square to the Cedar Tavern and listening to Morty's steady stream of kindly advice, which began with: "The first thing you have to do after you find a pad is to get yourself a shrink. Everybody who's somebody has an analyst." I was five feet eight inches tall, and only a few years younger than Morty, but next to his height and bulk and his infinite savvy about the New York art scene, I felt myself a bewildered Alice in Wonderland, shrinking and full of trepidation. Going into the Cedar Tavern didn't help any: it was noisy, murky with smoke, jammed with rugged-looking men and women talking in a vernacular dismayingly unfamiliar to me, all of whom seemed to know one another on the easiest of intimate terms. At least one or two of the people standing five-deep at the bar were unpleasantly, hostilely drunk. Since I didn't smoke, didn't drink, and had never heard of any contemporary American painter other than Jackson Pollock, I felt like a guppy in a dolphin tank. No doubt Pollock was there, if not that night, then the next, or the one after that. So, too, at one time or another, were Willem de Kooning, Franz Kline, Philip Guston, Jack Tworkov, Joan Mitchell, Mike Goldberg, Milton Resnick, Norman Bluhm, Paul and Mimi (Shapiro) Brach, Herman Cherry, Robert Motherwell, Mark Rothko, Grace Hartigan, Helen Frankenthaler, and dozens of others. The whole abstract expressionist movement could have been blasted off the face of the earth on almost any given evening in the early fifties had a bomb fallen on the

Cedar. Though Earle felt immediately comfortable, I was unprepared and awkwardly unfit for that hot, tumbling artists' world and felt enormous relief when we finally returned to John's monastic rooms and I could remember why we'd come to New York in the first place.

It was a relief as well to remember John's words about psychoanalysis, which until that evening I'd naively supposed to be only for the mentally ill, certainly not a required activity in order to be in step with the times. A year earlier, John had told us he had considered analysis at a particularly troubling time in his life, but had decided against it. Fortunately, into his life just then had come a young Indian woman named Gita Sarabhai, who was in New York for a brief period to learn something about Western music, whose influence on traditional Indian music troubled her. She planned to study for six months and then return to India to do what she could to preserve the Indian traditions.[1] She'd asked John to teach her about contemporary Western music. He agreed, if in exchange for his lessons she would teach him about Indian music and philosophy. It was Gita who told John that "the purpose of music is to sober and quiet the mind, thus making it susceptible to divine influences." This had powerful meaning for John. He would quote it often. They were together almost every day for six months; soon after she returned to India, John started to study Zen Buddhism with Daisetz T. Suzuki. Eventually I, too, began reading Suzuki's books on Zen, and since John was the "somebody" I cared about, for better or for worse, I disregarded Morty's counsel about getting myself a shrink.

Cage's interest and deep involvement with Zen and the philosophies of the East anticipated by a good many years the West's rush to religions of the Orient. Cage never pursued the meditative life with its central breath-awareness exercises, choosing instead to employ different mechanical, chance procedures that required endless hours of disciplined, painstaking, repetitive work in an attempt to exclude his ego and thus his preferences and any vestiges of personal taste from his music. Nor did Cage ever take hallucinogenic drugs, wishing to achieve an enlightened consciousness through conscious effort. Curiously, it's a kind of puritan work ethic that he practiced and revered. Apparently, he was permanently dissuaded from following the inward path because his close friend Lou Harrison had experienced a frightening state of imbalance when meditating without a spiritual master or even guidance, becoming self-hypnotized and auto-intoxicated. He had to be taken away in a straitjacket, an incident that Cage witnessed. Cunningham, on the other hand, taught himself the physical exercises of hatha yoga from Yogi Vithaldas's book *The Yoga System of*

Health and Relief from Tension and practices it to this day, but after one disquieting experience when the force of energy known as *kundalini* rose like a fiery serpent from the base of his spine, he avoided the special exercises whose goal is the brain, the mind, and the discerning of things on a spiritual plane, recognizing instantly the dangers that might befall him without a spiritual master. Though Cunningham tried for more than thirty years to teach Cage physical exercises, yoga, even the most rudimentary body-maintenance movements, it wasn't until Cage was almost sixty-five years old and visiting the latest in an endless string of doctors that he finally agreed to exercise. Cage always seemed to me to be a stranger to his body, in conflict with it, inhabiting it in some sort of awkward truce, but never trusting what it might do to him next. Of course I didn't know any of this in 1952. I was just glad to recall John's own escape from psychoanalysis, and hoped I'd be as lucky.

The next day, when we reluctantly left John's cloistered chambers and moved into David Tudor's place, I wondered what madness had possessed us to leave the cool, clean, crisp spaces of Colorado for the sweaty, dank, musty filth of Manhattan's Lower East Side. I was appalled and scared. Up five flights, down a long hallway—dimly lit, smelling of yesterday's cabbage and stale sausage and the rotting garbage that oozed putrescence from the brown paper bags outside each door—to Apartment 22, which lay behind an ugly metal door, front right. We opened it gingerly. In the dark kitchen that also housed the bathtub, a battered, half-chewed sneaker lay in the middle of the floor, where, we supposed, a rat who'd found nothing else to eat had left it. (In fact, it was a puppy's toy.) The kitchen window looked out on an air shaft. Double doors opened to a small living room, a great deal of which was occupied by an upright piano; two windows looked out on the southern sky above Fourth Street and another grimy tenement building across the way. In the other direction was the bedroom, little more than a closet on the air shaft. We found the toilet outside, down the hall. As David had written, it *was* a dump, but it did provide a home base for us, for free, and that we appreciated. An additional advantage was the sharp jolt of reality it provided to whatever romantic notions about artists' living quarters in New York City I may have had. A note to my parents read: "David's apartment is a god-awful dump. Worse than I imagined. Don't see how anyone could stand it."

We apartment-hunted from early morning into the night for four days. Forty dollars for a flat worse than David's uptown in Hell's Kitchen; sixty-five for a six-room place we'd have loved but couldn't afford on Sixth Avenue near Bleecker Street. We got *The Villager* (no *Village Voice* in

1952) on Thursdays; it led nowhere. A charming, barefoot poet-boy who'd befriended us in Café Reggio, a coffeehouse on MacDougal Street, led us on innumerable wild-goose chases. By Friday night I was thoroughly discouraged and we escaped back to New England. Earle returned to New York on Sunday, alone, and the next day he phoned gleefully: he'd found an apartment! It was lilliputian, in the West Village, just off Sixth Avenue and Fourth Street, at 11 Cornelia Street, in the rear building at the end of a long, very narrow alley: third floor, two and a half tiny rooms with a tinier bathroom with everything in it (not down the hall!) for $54.75. The living room, with a working fireplace, was nine feet square and looked out on a little cobblestone courtyard that boasted a stonework fountain and a single living tree. In order to put a double bed in the bedroom we had to remove the bathroom door, the bedroom being about five by seven, but what matter! Earle was jubilant—he'd not only found a place we could maybe afford, he'd found a place that would satisfy his concerns for my safety and my perpetual desire for some, however modest, charm.

Five days later, David Tudor was to accompany Katherine Litz in a program of solo dances at Jacob's Pillow in Lee, Massachusetts. We drove out, and it was there we met, for the first time, Mary Caroline Richards, who'd just given up her position at Black Mountain College—discouraged and disillusioned by its factionalism—to begin a new life with David Tudor in New York City. David, in a letter to us, had mentioned "my girl" (it had a Humphrey Bogart forties-movie resonance), but we knew nothing whatever about her and were completely unprepared to meet this woman whose strength and bearing were, for me at least, intimidating and utterly arresting. Her directness with others and her strict honesty with herself, coupled with a genuine sense of caring, seemed antithetical to small talk and the superficiality of ordinary social discourse. Yet there we were between matinee and evening performances—M. C. Richards, Katherine Litz, David Tudor, Earle, and I—exchanging pleasantries with Ted Shawn and John Christian (our hosts) and a number of other Jacob's Pillow guests. While sipping sherry and making small talk (Shawn was a master of the art) under the huge shade trees in Shawn's garden where I'd been so often as a child with my mother, I wondered at this curious meeting of my old familiar world and the beginnings of my intriguing new one.

Soon afterward, Earle and I transferred our first load of belongings from Massachusetts to New York, but we left again almost immediately, this time with Cage, Tudor, and M. C. Richards, for a trip to Woodstock, New York. It was the first of dozens of festive jaunts with Cage acting as tour guide: discovering a delightful fish restaurant tucked away under a bridge near the Hudson River, or taking a scenic route that took an hour longer to anywhere but was always worth it, or who knows what else he'd seek out, the better to enchant and edify us all. The reason for this particular journey was a concert of contemporary music: the Woodstock Artists' Association was presenting John Cage and David Tudor on August 29 at Maverick Concert Hall. Tudor played music by Boulez, Brown, Cage, Cowell, Feldman, and Wolff. This was our first opportunity to hear David play Earle's *Three Pieces for Piano,* which we'd missed in its first performance in New York, and we were thrilled. For everyone else, the real excitement of the evening was being present at the first performance of Cage's soon-to-be-infamous piece, *4′33″.* In Cage's own words, "This is a piece in three movements during all three of which no sounds are intentionally produced. The lengths of time were determined by chance operations but could be any others."[2]

The piece was next-to-last on the program. David came out onstage, sat down at the grand piano, and after waiting for absolute stillness from the audience, he raised the lid of the keyboard. He sat there immobile and impassive for a specified number of seconds, at which moment he closed the lid; this was repeated for the second and third movements. The audience's stillness changed to restlessness: a rustle of programs, bodies shifting uneasily in the seats, shuffling feet, the inevitable self-conscious giggle, the nervous cough, and one thoroughly outraged soul stomping up the aisle and out of the building, protesting aloud. There was a sudden sprinkle of rain on the tin roof, and the wind brushed a branch across a windowpane. (Aural haiku?) Other sounds could be heard, too, if one relaxed the mind and paid attention. Most people didn't and were angry, put out, and put off.

In Cage's book *Silence,* he stated: "To whom it may concern: the white paintings came first; my silent piece came later."[3] The white paintings John referred to were Rauschenberg's, made at Black Mountain College in 1951. When first shown in New York they were misunderstood as gestures and anti-paintings, but Bob described them as "open compositions responding to the activity within their reach."

While in Woodstock, Cage took us along on his visit to Philip Guston's studio. Guston was in the process of moving away from representational painting to what eventually was labeled abstract expressionism (in his case, abstract *im*pressionism, although he disliked labels). He was in the throes of forging a new style and way of working. He told John about a revelatory experience. Applying a stroke of paint here, there, wherever, then standing back for long periods of time to look and consider, Guston suddenly said to himself, "What is it that I am deciding?" He was beginning to question the agonizing decisions he'd been forcing upon himself and to distrust his previous intellectualization. He began to experiment with switching off his will and letting things just happen, letting the subconscious determine his actions. For Cage this was electrifying: a reaffirmation of his belief that in composition, one should give up one's desire to control sounds and to set about discovering means to let them be themselves. Actually, Cage and Guston were still worlds apart. Cage was leery of *any* human intervention, even that of the subconscious, in composing his music, yet there's no escaping that he'd made a personal decision: he *chose* chance.

In the forties, before John's exposure to Eastern religions and philosophies, he met Max Ernst, one of the surrealists who had explored semi-automatic methods in creating new forms—even inventing a machine for randomly spotting the canvas with paint[4]—but John parted philosophical company with the surrealists in their use of random occurrences, even accidents, as a means of achieving spontaneity: this was Rauschenberg's way, but not Cage's. John's application of strict chance procedures precluded spontaneity of this kind.

After that weekend in Woodstock, Earle and I went back to Massachusetts, where I set to work choreographing a solo for my Juilliard audition. Earle composed some music for it. We worked in my mother's studio, where I'd spent fifteen years dancing the dances of Ruth St. Denis and Ted Shawn to music by Beethoven, Schumann, Schubert, Grieg, Chopin, and Rachmaninoff. I can still remember many of those dances, but I have not the faintest idea what I made for the Juilliard audition, nor what became of the tape recording of Earle's music. We didn't return to New York until mid-September, just in time for the hottest day in New York's recorded history. For six sticky, sweating days I studied dance history and music for my Juilliard entrance exams in our tiny, airless apartment and rehearsed in Jean Erdman's Fifth Avenue studio for the audition. In all those weeks, we never saw Merce Cunningham. We heard he'd had his appendix removed after a summer of misery when he'd been too busy to take the time for an operation. During the late spring and early summer, while choreographing the two works that were premiered at the Brandeis Festival in June and then teaching and performing at Black Mountain, he'd held an ice pack to his ailing gut to get him through the worst times. Finally, in the autumn, with the pressures eased, he submitted to surgery. Cage told us that when Merce was fit again he might go to Black Mountain to teach for the winter. An enormous disappointment! I'd hoped to study with him whether or not I was accepted at Juilliard.

A three-day wait after three days of exams and auditions to learn that I'd been accepted, and one more day to receive the special-delivery letter notifying me that I'd been given a small scholarship. On October 2, classes at Juilliard began. Being placed in Ballet III (advanced) and Modern II (intermediate) was the reverse of what I'd hoped for, but the modern technique was Graham and my two years with Jane McLean in Denver simply wasn't sufficient background for the most advanced level. Graham technique had changed since Jane had studied it, and most of the first exercises in the advanced class were performed by rote in a set sequence with scarcely any interruption. Martha Graham was scheduled to teach our class once a week, with Robert Cohan and Helen McGehee teaching the rest, but Graham came rarely. By midyear, the wails and outcries of complaining, disappointed students finally sent Martha Hill, Juilliard's director of dance, scurrying to the Graham classes to quell the uprising. I've never forgotten her lecture to us—it made a lot of sense—which was, in essence: "How dare you complain? Why don't you appreciate how fortunate you are? Music students at Juilliard have one weekly lesson with their teacher and must practice alone the rest of the week. You dancers are pampered six days a week with daily classes and constant personal attention." And, of course, this was true.

In the ballet division we were extremely fortunate. Antony Tudor rarely, if ever, missed his classes; he taught the advanced students four technique classes weekly, plus a class in supported adagio/pas de deux. On Fridays, Margaret Craske taught, and on Wednesday mornings at the ghastly hour of nine, Mattlyn Gavers gave the girls pointe class. Pointe class, following as it did Tudor's Tuesday late afternoon pas de deux class, was excruciating torture for me. I hadn't worn pointe shoes in about ten years, and I'd never expected to again.

Louis Horst—the massive, sloe-eyed, gentle yet ever so devastatingly and perceptively critical Louis Horst—was the dance composition instructor at Juilliard, beloved by the generations of modern dancers he had initiated into the mysteries of pavanes and sarabandes, minuets and gigues, earth and air primitive, religious and secular medieval, archaic, cerebral, and introspective dance forms. By the time Louis Horst came to Juilliard, this man who was at one time Martha Graham's mentor, composer, accompanist, lover, and relentless Svengali, had taught Pre-Classic Forms, Modern Forms, and Group Forms for so many years that there surely could have been no surprises, good or bad, no matter who the student; that he managed to look at the trite, insufferable drivel we all meted out most of the time would qualify him for a Purple Heart. (Actually, he always seemed to be more asleep than awake.) The miracle was in what he saw. Incisive, witty, encouraging, disparaging, and insistent, he goaded us on. The content of these classes (I took Pre-Classic and Modern Forms) seemed ridiculous to me at the time, based as they were primarily on forms of old music and old art (Satie and Picasso were about as modern as he got), but their value was in the discipline: a weekly problem to be met and solved; a small dance constructed according to his specific requirements that had to be (1) performed exactly again and again ("What did you do on count 'two-and' of the fourth measure?" Louis would ask) and (2) explained rationally ("How does that movement relate to your original 'A'?"). Louis missed nothing, and by missing nothing he taught us to see. The Juilliard workweek was five full days plus Saturday mornings. I was often there from nine in the morning until nine at night. Other classes were in dance notation and literature and materials of music. My Wheaton College degree exempted me from academic courses, but I took extra lower-level ballet classes because I felt as unfamiliar with the Cecchetti technique as I did with the Graham, and I loved the classes taught by Alfredo Corvino. Fifteen years of Denishawn training can develop "a dancer," but not a Graham dancer or a ballet dancer. Specific skills, quite different skills, are required for both. When my cousin Barbara Stevens (my mother, my sister-in-law, two nieces, and at least two cousins all dance, and my mother taught us all) came to watch classes before Thanksgiving, she exclaimed in surprise: "Carol, you can dance better than that! What's the matter with you?" But I couldn't. Until I understood the basic groundwork of those two techniques, the one so very different from the other, I felt completely inhibited. Even years of ballet study with a Russian émigré when I was a kid had not prepared me for Cecchetti's approach to ballet training. As Margaret Craske said to me: "It takes five years just to become a good student. Another five to become a dancer, and who knows how long, if ever, to become an artist." And then with a twinkle in her eye, she added, "But what else is there to do?" Actually it hadn't occurred to me that I would be studying ballet at all.

My biggest disappointment at Juilliard was being rejected by Doris Humphrey, who was restaging "Desert Gods" from her work *Song of the West* with music by Roy Harris. At the audition I was dismissed as "too balletic." I didn't have the courage to protest: "Miss Humphrey, *please*! For years I danced *Soaring* and *Sonata pathétique,* dances you choreographed with Miss Ruth; I performed your roles in Miss Ruth's *Mana-Zucca Waltz* and *Second Arabesque,* even danced the solo Ted Shawn made for you to music by Louis Moreau Gottschalk. I'm really a barefoot Denishawn dancer, not a ballet dancer at all!" But I suppose it is just as well that I didn't tell her, since her parting with Shawn and Miss Ruth was not a happy one, and perhaps even her own early work with them displeased her. And so, almost by default, it was Antony Tudor and Margaret Craske who became my true teachers, and after I left Juilliard they continued to be my teachers. I studied with Tudor from 1952 until 1967, when they tore down the old Metropolitan Opera House, and with Craske from 1952 until 1976 — even after I'd stopped performing in 1972.

What a fabulous combination—Craske and Tudor! Margaret Craske, born in England in 1898, danced with the Diaghilev company and was one of a very few chosen by Enrico Cecchetti to teach his system. At Antony Tudor's invitation, she later came to America to become ballet mistress of (American) Ballet Theatre in the mid-forties. Miss Craske taught a strict, pure, exquisitely shaped classical ballet class, often choreographing her own beautiful adagios based on Cecchetti material. But in the twenty-three years I studied with her, there was never a formula class that exactly followed the Cecchetti manual of day-by-day classes. Although we learned Maestro Cecchetti's set steps, it was never merely by rote. It was the principles behind them, applicable to many, many kinds of movement, that Miss Craske wanted us to understand, and it was Miss Craske who regularly admonished any attempts at self-expression with: "The meaning is in the movement. The movement is expressive of itself."

Antony Tudor, also English-born, was ten years Miss Craske's junior; he'd studied with her in London and was responsible for bringing her to New York to be ballet mistress with the company producing his ballets. Tudor as teacher was brilliant, sometimes quixotic, sometimes cruel, often breathtaking, often just plain naughty, occasionally outrageous, and always inspiring. He experimented, he choreographed. He extended the Cecchetti technique, himself, and his students. His class was an adventure, almost like a dare, but it was usually at least barely possible to do what he asked for if one kept one's wits (he enjoyed testing them) and if one had absorbed Miss Craske's words of wisdom (especially those about placement) into the muscles, and joints, and along the entire skeletal framework—remembered, too, her scathing words, clipped and sharply articulated in her high-pitched British voice, spoken to a student splashing around in the rosin box: "What you need, my dear, is rhythm, not rosin!" I believe Craske and Tudor were in complete accord regarding self-expression. Tudor speaking: "I want my dancers to grow into their roles through the movements of those roles. Understanding, development, and growth must always come through the movement. Otherwise, it's only veneer."[5]

Although both Graham and Tudor created intensely dramatic ballets, the American chose to create her own vocabulary of movement, while the Englishman worked from the basic classical ballet tradition. As *The Village Voice* dance critic Deborah Jowitt put it: "Ballet was impersonal in origin and, as a technique, it remains impersonal. Graham wrenched her 'technique' out of her own body and psyche. Everything about it is passionate and individual."[6] I felt extremely uncomfortable in Graham's very personal technique; it was so deeply hers and could never be organically mine. During one of her rare visits to teach our intermediate class at Juilliard, Graham had us form a large circle around her. Then she glided clockwise round the circle—slipping silent-footed across the floor on thick-soled, calloused, near-deformed bare feet, with her hands writhing like exotic snakes—and as she approached she hissed menacingly and each of us in turn was to twist, curve, and spiral down to the floor in a quicksilver sensuous serpentine fall. How unspeakably foolish I felt! Mirth rose in me as I sank; how thankful I was to be able to hide the giggles bubbling unbidden in my throat, and yet how fascinated I was, as I peeked out from under my arms, to catch a glimpse of the extraordinary feet of this extraordinary witch-lady as she passed just inches from my nose. For me, the Graham classes were always an alien experience; they seemed to demand a kind of emotional hype that felt dishonest, extraneous, external, and artificial—unrelated to my understanding of Dance (with a capital "D"). Tudor and Craske, on the other hand, were developing in their students the tools and skills, the framework from which dance (any kind!) could emerge; the difference seemed to be similar to the difference between psychology and mathematics—the difference between an imprecise science and a precise one.

Philosophically, it was a very short distance from Craske and Tudor's teaching uptown at Juilliard to Cunningham's teaching in Greenwich Village. Although Merce spent five years in Martha Graham's company, when he began to develop his own technique it was, like ballet, an "impersonal" one. He unplugged the highly charged passionate cords connected to Graham's "contraction and release" and composed exercises for the back— lower, middle, upper—which, in their bare execution, were devoid of emotional connotation. His technique evolved out of his personal explorations in determining the primary needs necessary to train the whole body so that it could be ready to move in the many ways possible to it, without adhering to any one rigid style. Some exercises he made after injuring his back, basing them on therapeutic strengthening exercises that his doctor had recommended to him. Some of it came from Graham, certainly, but she herself had told him to go to George Balanchine's School of American Ballet, because she said she could not provide him with a complete training—especially in aerial work and in the development of strength and speed in the feet and legs. (Cunningham was the second male dancer to work with Graham; the first, Erick Hawkins, was already a trained ballet dancer when he joined her company.) On the other hand, ballet, at least as it was then taught (and usually still is), did not train the torso to twist, curve, tilt, attack percussively, or train the dancer to move various parts in isolation, nor did it train a dancer to fall and recover from a fall in a variety of ways. Cunningham's own classes attempt to teach all these moves, but until his work with *Life Forms* (computer-generated choreography) in the nineties, the strong emphasis in his classes was on the workings of the spine, the legs, and the feet, and he practically ignored the use of the arms and hands. Until the 1990s, Cunningham's choreography rarely, except in his own solos and movement he created for himself in the group works, defined the use of the arms and hands other than in a kind of semi-balletic or free-floating natural style. There were few classroom exercises designed especially to train the arms and hands as do, for example, Cecchetti's eight port de bras.

Although I never thought about it then, Cecchetti and Cunningham have much in common, as Richard Glasstone, director of the Cecchetti Centre in London, pointed out in an article in *Dancing Times* nearly forty years later:

> The exciting thing about so much of Cecchetti's work is the way it *can* and *does* transcend its time and its stylistic boundaries. What more convincing proof of this can there be than the fact that many of Merce Cunningham's dancers were Margaret Craske's greatest devotees? Some people express surprise when I remark on the similarities between Cunningham's use of dance movement and that of Cecchetti. But look beneath the *avant-garde* astringency of the one, and the 19th Century Romanticism of the other, and you will find the same core of superlative rhythmic coordination, combined with absolute precision in the placement and positioning of the whole body. The rapid changes of direction, the finely tuned sense of balance—as well as the mastery of off-balance movements—the incredible bursts of speed so characteristic of Cunningham's choreography, all these are amazingly similar to the demands made by that of Cecchetti.[7]

About three weeks after starting classes at Juilliard, I began studying with Merce Cunningham. He hadn't gone to Black Mountain after all, and he'd begun teaching in a dingy little loft building on Eighth Street between Broadway and University Place, which he rented by the hour. It was a dark, cheerless studio: the grimy windows were covered with even grimier sheets of plastic to keep out the cold; there was no central heating; the dressing areas were partitioned off with dusty draperies; Merce dressed behind a couple of screens. He always had a curious dry cough in that studio—probably an allergic reaction to the dirt and the smelly gas space heater. There was seldom any piano accompaniment unless Cage happened to come by, in which case he'd disrupt everything by playing "The Star-Spangled Banner" or "My Country, 'Tis of Thee" in the wrong key and the wrong rhythms and often the wrong notes as well and make us all laugh and Merce furious, but helpless to fight John's infectious grin and mischievous shenanigans. The classes were small. I remember Jo Anne Melsher, Marianne Preger, Remy Charlip, Viola Farber, Sudie Bond, Dorothea Berea, and occasionally two wonderful dancers who had performed fairly often with Merce: Joan Skinner and Anneliese Widman. Joan and Anneliese had played the mothers in Cunningham's *Les Noces* at the Brandeis Festival the previous June; Jo Anne, Marianne, and Remy had been in it, too, and all five had also performed in *Excerpts from Symphonie pour un homme seul,* the other work Cunningham choreographed for the Brandeis Festival. Sudie Bond was essentially an actress, but along with Marianne and Remy, she'd danced *Ragtime Parade* to music by Satie at Cooper Union in November 1950. Viola had been at Black Mountain the previous summer, where she'd studied with Merce and seen Cage's theater piece. Almost everyone in the class (except me) had danced or studied with Merce for a year or so. If they weren't accomplished in or comfortable with his work, they were at least familiar with it, but I don't think it was easy for any of us, even though Joan and Anneliese were already fine dancers.

Unlike Graham classes, which begin sitting on the floor, Cunningham's start with the class on its feet standing in parallel position, looking directly ahead into the mirror (provided there is a mirror). That experience alone is enough to deter one forever. Cunningham looked as if he was born in parallel position. It is absolutely right for him. But people, women especially, with wide pelvises, broad hips, and (heaven forbid!) "saddle thighs" look hopelessly wrong. And then there's the problem of knock-knees or bowlegs. But standing thus is not, after all, a peculiar idiosyncrasy of Merce Cunningham. Once off all fours, the human animal should be able to stand straight, with feet forward and body lifted, both alert and at ease. But how many years it takes to do just that! In those first classes, standing behind Merce, seeing first his reflection—solid and straight as an arrow—and then my own, with my hips and my legs' curves and hollows all seeming to be in the wrong places, was utterly discouraging.

Merce turned, tilted, twisted, curved, and arched his torso above a solid, centered base, but when we tried to imitate him, our hips wiggled, our knees knocked, our ankles wobbled, and our insteps dropped, and his simple, beautiful movements disintegrated into the grotesque, devoid even of the grace of awkwardness. When he reached the slow, adagio part of the class—about midway through—he'd demonstrate a long, complicated phrase while standing on one leg, extending the working leg here and there, and using the torso in opposition, the arms and head going their separate ways as well. As we all attempted to repeat it, tears burned my eyes from the pain and frustration of being too weak to do it properly. Of course I was usually exhausted before I got to the studio (if excuses need be found), having already taken at least two technique classes at Juilliard as well as all the other classes. Just the dash from Juilliard (then at Claremont Avenue and 120th Street) to Eighth Street via two subways plus negotiating the mad crush at rush hour between the IRT and BMT lines at Forty-second Street was debilitating. Apparently, during those first classes with Merce, I looked anguished and miserable. After several weeks, Merce told John to tell Earle to tell me that I needn't come if I was unhappy there. The curiously circuitous route that Merce's message to me took in the fall of 1952 remained typical of his communications with his dancers. I'm told it still is.

Sore and aching for much of my first year in New York, by sundown I wanted only to eat my dinner and fall into bed. A social life, any other life, seemed beyond my capabilities. But while I danced from morning until night, Earle sat at a worktable with John Cage producing musique concrète. Cage had finally gotten financial assistance for his project from a young student architect named Paul Williams, whom he'd met at Black Mountain College. For about twelve hours a day, Earle and John spliced magnetic tape, a painstaking and tedious occupation that used neither physical nor intellectual energy to any great degree. By evening, Earle was ready to begin "living" just as I was ready to collapse. But I couldn't turn my back on the activity bursting from every quarter of the neighborhood we lived in. Fortunately, even if I had wanted to, Earle wouldn't let me.

Most important, perhaps, even though its greatest years were past, was the Artists' Club, which had been started by Robert Motherwell in the 1940s and carried on by Philip Pavia, Willem de Kooning, and Franz Kline, among others. In the forties the central meeting place for the artists was the Waldorf Cafeteria on Sixth Avenue at Eighth Street, but by the early fifties the atmosphere there began to change to one of sordidness and even danger. Longshoremen and local toughs started beating people up. The artists decided then to form their own club, where they could gather for serious discussion and exchange ideas. They met on Wednesdays and Fridays on West Eighth Street near Broadway, a few doors away from where Cunningham was teaching classes. The Eighth Street area became the art center not only of New York but of the world (although the world didn't acknowledge this for a number of years). Hans Hofmann's school, Robert Motherwell's school, and the club were on Eighth Street, the Cedar Tavern was just north of Eighth on University Place, and eventually a number of galleries opened on Tenth Street between Third and Fourth avenues. In these few Village blocks was born the art revolution that humbled Paris into second place after centuries of European domination of painting and sculpture. Ideas were now flowing across the Atlantic in the opposite direction, and this was no less true in the worlds of music and dance. Wherever the artists gathered, one inhaled the heady air of revolution; there was excitement brewing and a self-congratulatory air of knowing beyond a doubt that you were on the right train going to the right place with the right people: people who were true to their personal convictions and who gave each other permission to be daringly different and to thumb their noses at the status quo. In the forties, de Kooning, Kline, Gottlieb, Rothko, Gorky, and many others were made to feel like outcasts, even derelicts, not part of the proper artistic society. Everything changed in the fifties: the painters sensed themselves differently; they'd become powerful and strong because they believed in themselves now that *they* were the *rarae aves* of the art world! Not that the general public knew or cared. Not that their work sold particularly well. But the artists knew. An undercurrent of optimism swept through the community, and it *was* a community then, a real family, a brotherhood. Work was everything. Perhaps most important of all, they cared about one another's work, and this caring was generously and warmly expressed. There was no expectation of monetary gain or of worldly reward in the form of power or prestige. This community of artists, in which art was still thought to possess an ethical content, attracted a whole new generation of painters, as well as writers, composers, and dancers (Earle and myself among them).

The quality of the life of the spirit—this was of serious concern. The beliefs: "Dancing is a spiritual exercise in physical form" (Merce Cunningham) and "Painting at its highest level should reveal spiritual reality" (Hans Hofmann) touched a responsive chord deep down in my psyche, reaffirming certain aspects of my early Denishawn training. The older painters were inspirational, especially de Kooning, who was revered for his integrity, for his artistic honesty, for producing "emotionally genuine" work, and for perpetually taking risks and venturing courageously beyond the already known, as Cage and Cunningham were also striving to do.

At Juilliard I sensed no such life. Quite the opposite. A retrenchment had begun—a setting up of academy rules and bylaws. Worse, the world of modern dance was split with petty jealousies and tired aesthetics. It was at least ten years too late to experience even a vestige of the American modern dance revolution brought about separately by Graham and Humphrey when they rejected the eclecticism of Denishawn in the late twenties and early thirties for a more rigorous and personal statement. Of course, this could not have been as clear to me then as it is now looking back on it decades later; nevertheless I was not aware of any undercurrent of real adventure or purpose at Juilliard; the liveliest modern dance teacher in the place, to my mind, was Yuriko, fresh from her triumph in *The King and I* and willing to share with her students her enthusiasm for dancing. Thus it was my extreme good fortune to be included in the Cage-Cunningham world with its ever-expanding vision of new possibilities.

Only Earle, among our closest friends, had a useful, functioning automobile—Richard Lippold had a hearse and Cage had a Model-A Ford Roadster, neither exactly a practical vehicle for long journeys—so our Ford station wagon was usually filled to overcapacity on our trips out of the city. One Sunday afternoon late in October, David gave a concert at Princeton. Nine of us piled in and drove over—Tudor, M. C. Richards, Cage, Cunningham, Feldman, painters Joan Mitchell and Mike Goldberg, Earle, and I. Among other works, David played Cage's *Water Music*, a six-minute piece that employs a grand piano, a radio, whistles, water containers, and a deck of cards. During the rehearsal—it was a beautiful fall day—M.C. and I talked as we walked the rolling green lawns near the church where David was working. We were both happy to be out of New York City, to be breathing unfetid air and catching a glimpse of autumn's splendors. I was terribly shy with this woman whom I regarded with total awe. How relieved I was to hear her express her misgivings and doubts about the strange music our new friends wrote; she was finding it difficult to listen to, to understand, to like, to comprehend the "why" of it. It was reassuring to know that my confusion with these peculiar—and to my ears often unpleasant-sounding—works was shared by someone so intelligent. David's performance of Cage's *Water Music* astonished us equally. Executed with the meticulous care of a Japanese monk presiding over a tea ceremony, he handled each incongruous extramusical instrument with the same respect Rubinstein gives to his piano. He compelled one's admiration. Had *Water Music* been performed by Harpo Marx with the same minute attention to detail, it would have been hilarious, but it was unthinkable to laugh when David performed it. David dedicated himself to performing Cage's music at a time when no one except Cage himself was willing or able to perform it. For this, Cage was profoundly in his debt and knew it. Immediately after David's afternoon performance at Princeton, we all rushed back to Manhattan to attend yet another concert. This one—a birthday retrospective of music by Cage's friend Lou Harrison—took place at the Museum of Modern Art.

Thus did Cage befriend us—not only by introducing us to his painter, sculptor, and composer friends but by directing our attention to events and places, thoughts and things in which he himself was vitally interested. His influence was all-encompassing. Earle and I attended a few of Daisetz Suzuki's lectures on Zen Buddhism at Columbia with him. On his recommendation, we began reading *The Huang Po Doctrine of Universal Mind*. (I still have the dog-eared paper copy I read every day on my way to Juilliard, from Sheridan Square to 125th Street and back again. There were days when I couldn't understand a single sentence without rereading it a dozen times.) Because of John we began frequenting Orientalia, a bookstore on Twelfth Street off Fifth Avenue devoted to Oriental art, philosophy, religion, and language, becoming friendly with the two very dear elderly women—Elsie Becker and Helen Pinkerton—who owned and ran the shop. Orientalia was much more than a bookstore. It was a gathering place (coincidentally, some years later, Antony Tudor could be found there) where one was invited to have tea, browse, ask questions, or simply sit in a corner and read any book of one's choosing. There was never any pressure to purchase anything. But Earle and I began acquiring a library: Suzuki books, haiku books edited by Blythe, books on Tibet. At the same time that we were buying, Cage was selling his—a book or two or three at a time. Extremely poor yet generous to a fault, he often fed his friends at his Monroe Street apartment with the proceeds, and sometimes if the books were especially valuable and brought a good price, he would treat a friend or two at a restaurant. At Merce and John's suggestion, we ventured uptown to see the Balinese Theater, which had, decades earlier, so profoundly affected Antonin Artaud (and Debussy and Ravel, among others), and by extension Cage and Cunningham: "In Oriental theater with its metaphysical tendencies, in contrast to Western theater with its psychological tendencies . . . vibrations are not received on a single level, but on all levels at once."[8]

To read Artaud is to comprehend just how profoundly his writings on theater affected Cage. Cage was a true eclectic: he borrowed ideas as easily as he changed his socks. An all-inclusive list of influences would consume far too many pages but here's a sample in no particular order of importance: Antonin Artaud, Henry Cowell, Edgard Varèse, Daisetz Suzuki, Gertrude Stein, Buckminster Fuller, Meister Eckhart, Norman O. Brown, Marshall McLuhan, Erik Satie, Marcel Duchamp, Max Ernst, Morton Feldman, Robert Rauschenberg, Earle Brown, David Tudor, Gordon Mumma . . . John took in their ideas like a hummingbird flitting at high speed from flower to flower sipping precious nectar on the wing. In his own unique and perhaps intellectually outrageous fashion, he made their ideas his own, now blunderingly, now brilliantly synthesizing—but always with an ingenuous freshness and spontaneity. I think he often forgot where a particular idea initially came from, sometimes even believing it to be original to himself, and furthermore he enthusiastically believed every word he uttered, at least at the time of "his" conception. And so did I. He was a hero to me. His openness, his appetite for new ideas, his enormous pleasure in life, his overwhelming generosity, and his genuine delight in being a guru of sorts were irresistible. I had no reason to doubt that what he preached he practiced.

During the fall, Cunningham was working on new choreography with some of the students in his class—Sudie Bond, Remy Charlip, Jo Anne Melsher, and Marianne Preger. This new work, *Suite by Chance,* was the first dance in which he used chance means to structure an entire work. It had taken him several months working several hours a day to make a series of charts: one chart listed a gamut of movement possibilities—phrases and positions selected by Cunningham, plus the possibility of stillness; another indicated the possible directions in space; still another gave the durations that movement or stillness would take. Cunningham purposely chose movements "as unadorned and flat" as he could make them. They were simple, direct, unconnected, precise movements linked together not by habit or physical ease or by the demands of a rhythmic pulse or for reasons of expressiveness but by the flip of a coin: when the dancers entered and when they exited, whether they were moving or still, what directions they moved in, where they faced, how many dancers were in the space at one time—all determined by the flip of a coin. Some of these charts may be seen in Cunningham's book *Changes: Notes on Choreography.* They are far more complicated than I have explained here.

The original cast presented the four movements of *Suite by Chance* one Sunday afternoon in the studio on Eighth Street where Merce taught. It was the first dance of Merce's I'd seen, and I didn't know what to think. Certainly, Christian Wolff's music, commissioned especially for the dance, was difficult—even unpleasant—to listen to. Composed for magnetic tape, it was one of the pieces that John, David, and Earle had cut and spliced together. To my ears, its sounds were unrelentingly harsh and ugly. Christian Wolff appeared to be an extremely sensitive, gentle, somewhat shy young man. This music offered no evidence of such qualities, and he admitted that he was both surprised and disquieted upon hearing his own composition for the first time. Since the dancers, excluding Merce, were neither experienced performers nor, as yet, technically proficient, the work as a whole seemed incongruous and inscrutable but at the same time excruciatingly honest. It was this naked honesty that was arresting. And curiously, there was a similarity to the work of the abstract expressionists—in the taking of risks, the venturing beyond the already known, the naked exposure of the self—despite the fact that the chance means that Cunningham employed were the complete antithesis of the subjective, inner-searching creative process used by abstract expressionist artists. It was not, however, the self-exposure of the choreographer that was offered but that of each of the dancers, including Cunningham himself. He didn't ask for or want conformity either to his way of moving or to some abstract ideal; he wanted the individuality of each dancer revealed through the movement material itself, and in this I believe he succeeded, although the dance itself was austere and uncompromising, and exceedingly difficult to simply enjoy.

I was baffled and disappointed. And yet, when I learned the dance and eventually performed it (it was the first work of Merce's that I danced), I loved the space and time it allowed me to be myself, even those parts of the fourth movement that have difficult and exhausting (for all of us at the time) turning, jumping, and leaping high-speed unison dancing, made all the more difficult because there was no unifying pulse provided in the musical accompaniment. Chance procedures can produce fiendishly arduous combinations of movement; the dancers' stamina is neither considered nor questioned. I don't think we often, if ever, executed the difficult unison parts of the fourth movement with the straightforward clarity that they require. (Of course, compared with the mind-bogglingly difficult and complex movement Merce devised through the *Life Forms* computer program in the 1990s, even the most difficult material in *Suite by Chance* now seems like child's play.)

But in 1953, Merce was breaking new ground. *Suite by Chance* is an important work in the Cunningham oeuvre for one reason: in its elaborate schema lies the embryonic nucleus of his search for and discovery of a new choreographic process. Although he had used chance procedures before, it was in far more rudimentary ways. *Suite by Chance* was the first work whose raison d'être was the desire to explore the use of chance procedures in the making of a dance from its inception, and, in Cunningham's own words, "its composition was unprompted by references other than its own life." Just as Cage was interested in letting sounds be themselves, Cunningham was interested in letting movements be themselves, unfettered by content derived from literature, history, psychology, mythology, mood, or music.

With this spare, intractable, yet classical choreography, Merce Cunningham embarked on a journey that has continued to fascinate him for over fifty years—and, at this writing, still does. The chance procedures opened up possibilities he'd never considered before and led to different ways of seeing. Certain decisions arrived at in the early fifties still inform the work he produces today: (1) the relationship between dance and music is one of coexistence: dance and music are unrelated in the majority of his works; they simply exist at the same time; (2) the choreography is constructed in time, not on or opposed to a metric beat (though often, for practicality's sake, phrases are rehearsed to counts); (3) space is decentralized and becomes a field of multidirectional activity that lacks the audience-facing "front" prescribed by the conventional proscenium arch of the Renaissance theater. *Suite by Chance* was for many viewers an unappealing work, bare to its very bones. Nothing Merce has choreographed since then has been so rigorously austere. Merce himself felt that it "let the individual quality of each [dancer] appear naked, powerful and unashamed."[9] There were no roles to play, no specified emotions to convey, no sensually gratifying movements, and no music to be in step with. The plainness of the movement and the stoic stillnesses revealed the dancer utterly.

Suite by Chance was followed by *Solo Suite in Space and Time.* In 1952, Merce's working methods—that is, his chance procedures for both these dances—paralleled Cage's chance experiments in, respectively, *Music of Changes* and *Music for Piano. Music of Changes* had charts for tempi, duration, sounds, dynamics, and superimpositions (how many events happen at once during a given structural space). Cage's next experiment with chance procedures was to have the notes for the music correspond to the slight imperfections on a piece of ordinary paper (seen when the paper is held up to the light) upon which the piece was to be written. When Cunningham choreographed *Solo Suite in Space and Time,* he, too, used paper imperfections, to determine certain elements of his dance: space and lengths of time for each brief solo and the sequence of movements. During this period, Cage gave a weekly composition workshop for Merce's students, and those of us who attended made dances in similar fashion. We choreographed the movement, but the sequence of steps, the space, and the time (which we discovered by measuring the distances between paper imperfections and equating them with clock time, i.e., inches equals minutes) was "found," as it were. I made *Trio for Five Dancers.* Using my space plan, Earle composed music for it. At Juilliard, we were making "Horstian" allemandes and sarabandes, "cerebrals" and "introspectives." The distance between the two studios was closer to one hundred light-years than to the one hundred or so city blocks that separated them. Not that the resulting dances in either place were particularly distinguished. Far from it.

December 1952. Pierre Boulez was in America for the first time. He'd come earlier in the fall, as conductor with the Jean-Louis Barrault–Madeleine Renaud Theatre Company. I think it was probably the last time that Cage and Boulez were genuinely friendly. While Cage was systematically abandoning conscious control over the music he made, Boulez was seeking a means of total control. The serial process originating with Schoenberg and refined by Webern had pointed the way. In his *Second Piano Sonata* (the one Cage had given David Tudor on his return from Paris in 1949), Boulez had extended the serial treatment of pitch to the duration of notes, making the decisive step toward an integral serial work in which all the musical parameters would be encompassed. As Boulez told an interviewer: "What we were doing, by total serialization, was to annihilate the will of the composer in favor of a predetermining system."[10] Annihilating the will was expressly what Cage had set out to accomplish. But for Cage it was an ethical decision relating to his entire philosophy of life, not only an aesthetic one relating to his music; for Boulez, as it turned out, gaining total control was merely a step in his development and filled his need to transmute his musical heritage. Once he reached the zero point as a composer, he was ready to begin. As the young revolutionary of that time, Boulez has been quoted as saying: "I believe a civilization that conserves is one that will decay because it is afraid of going forward and attributes more importance to memory than to the future."[11] With this Cage was in perfect agreement. But later Boulez said he wished to gain freedom through conquest, not merely through a laissez-faire approach, and he retracted much of what he'd professed in the heat of his revolt from the past: "The highest goal is to combine innovation with memory, to build with a consciousness of the past. That way one can create something new through an act of will, not merely by accident."[12]

This last statement was, perhaps, Boulez's not-so-subtle means of rebuking Cage. The philosophical disagreement between them resulted in a social break as well, much to Cage's surprise and disappointment. Although Boulez could understand—though not completely accept—Cage's basic desire for "a music free of one's memory and imagination," he could not accept Cage's determination to relinquish the desire to control sound, to clear the mind of music, and to set about discovering means to let sounds be themselves rather than be the vehicles for theories or for expressions of human sentiment. Boulez could not envisage chance as a serious compositional device. Furthermore, Cage had rejected the dualistic notion of right or wrong. Boulez disagreed with him entirely. When asked if he was conscious of a battle line drawn between conservative and radical tendencies, Boulez stated unequivocally: "No. The only line I recognize is between right and wrong. It is just as possible to be wrong in avant-garde circles as in conservatism. Easier perhaps."[13] Thus the lines between Cage and Boulez were drawn, and the earlier friendship disintegrated.

In 1949, after Cage returned from Paris—where he had met and become quite friendly with Boulez—the two men began to correspond. It might be said that Cage was smitten with Boulez, even in awe of him, although he was the elder by twelve years. Immediately upon his return to New York he began working on Boulez's behalf, trying to find pianists to play his music, publishers to publish it, magazines to print his articles, and places for Boulez to lecture and perform with proper remuneration. When Boulez finally did come to the States in the autumn of 1952, Cage, characteristically, was extraordinarily generous to him; not only did he move out of his own Monroe Street living-working quarters so that Boulez might have the place to himself, he did everything he could to promote Boulez; to arrange concerts; to introduce him to artists, writers, musicians, and composers; and to show him something of New York and environs.

On Pierre Boulez's last night in New York, December 26, Cage gave a farewell party for him in the Monroe Street apartment. The two rooms overflowed with John's friends. The party went on all night and into the morning. In the early hours, sometime between midnight and dawn, I remember seeing Pierre and Earle sitting on John's bed bent over scores, deep in conversation. The music of Earle's that Pierre liked was in the tradition of the Schoenberg/Webern aesthetic and thus nearer his own. "He had no patience with my *Folio* stuff," Earle recalled, any more than he'd had with Cage's chance methods of composition, but Earle's germinal concepts set forth in *Folio*—graphic notation, collective improvisation, and open form—would eventually influence not only composers—including Boulez—on both sides of the Atlantic, but also dancers, especially the Judson generation of choreographers, and Earle's "open form" concept would be taken up by Cunningham long before Cage ventured there himself.

My most vivid recollection of that all-night party is not of Boulez at all. What I recall, with no little regret, was missing an opportunity to know better the crowned prince of the abstract-expressionist painters—Willem de Kooning. At forty-eight, still ruggedly handsome and a devastating ladies' man, he took a great fancy (or so he claimed) to my bare dancer's feet and wooed me enchantingly. I still blush remembering my idiotically prim reply to his invitation to join him for dinner sometime soon: "If my husband could come too, I'd be pleased to . . ." His beautiful blue eyes crinkled in amusement and he laughed aloud—not unkindly, but with almost fatherly solicitude. Needless to relate, the invitation was never renewed.

As dawn crept over the Brooklyn skyline, someone suggested that Earle drive Boulez across the Brooklyn Bridge and along the Narrows for a sunrise glimpse of Manhattan. As many as would fit crowded into Earle's station wagon for this sentimental journey before taking Boulez to the boat dock, where we made our farewells. Waving him off were John Cage, David Tudor, M. C. Richards, Ray Johnson, Remy Charlip, Nicola Cernovich, Norman Solomon, Sari Dienes, Earle, and myself. Certainly Boulez and Cage would continue to greet each other cordially, but their true friendship seems to have ended right there, although John was not aware of it at the time. Boulez did not write to John, not even the most perfunctory thank-you note, for at least six months.

Perhaps friendship was not the issue. What was very probably at stake was power. The music world, like any other, was rife with politics. Neither Cage nor Boulez was ignorant of this fact. Virgil Thomson, both as composer and as music critic for the *New York Herald Tribune,* wielded considerable political clout in the music circles of those years; he championed first Cage and then Boulez. In fact, it was he who had suggested that Cage, when he went to Paris in 1949, look up Pierre Boulez. For years the musical battle waged had been between the followers of Schoenberg and Webern and the followers of Stravinsky. But soon, among younger composers on both sides of the Atlantic, everyone would begin to sense that this was last year's struggle. A new one was to begin. Yet between Cage and Boulez the problem was not simply one of power or ego. The schism had its true origins in the fundamental and crucial differences in personality, manifested quite simply by the way each man perceived the world and his role in it. These differences were philosophical. And they were profound.

What is odd, as I look back on that time, is how important all this was to my own life. Boulez was to introduce Earle and his work to conductors, composers, and musicians in Europe, which eventually resulted in Earle's spending more time abroad than at home. My life began to be centered on Merce Cunningham's world, and at the center of that world was John Cage. Boulez/Europe and Cage/USA became magnetic poles slowly pulling Earle and me apart.

It was the composers and painters who were providing the palette of possibilities for future experimentation in the early fifties. Merce Cunningham followed their lead. He was no exception to what seems always to have been true: dance has but rarely been the harbinger of a radically different aesthetic of sufficient power to influence and change the other arts and perhaps even life itself with the force of its innovativeness. As shocking as Merce's choreography may have seemed to both dancers and the minuscule dance public that saw it, the aesthetic ground, the philosophical foundations for his explorations had been worked by composers and artists—some his contemporaries, others younger or older than himself. In the early fifties, Cunningham the choreographer was still insecure, finding his way. John Cage and his composer and painter friends walked just ahead of him, opening the gates to a field freshly sown with the seeds of revolution.

My first experience performing in a work choreographed by Merce Cunningham consisted of dancing a maximum of two minutes in the official first performance of *Suite by Chance*, which took place in Lincoln Hall Theater at the University of Illinois on March 24, 1953. Oddly, I have no recollection of how or when Merce invited me to learn the dance and perform it with him, Jo Anne Melsher, Natanya Neumann, Marianne Preger (who at the last minute developed double pneumonia and couldn't go), and Joan Skinner. From Illinois I wrote my parents: "I dance for not more than a minute or so in the whole concert! But it's fun and gives me a legitimate excuse for being out here."

Merce's concert at the University of Illinois was part of the Sixth Annual Festival of Contemporary Arts, which included, among other events, a piano concert by David Tudor and a lecture-demonstration presented by John entitled *Music for Magnetic Tape*. Earle's *Perspectives* for piano, and the three works for magnetic tape that John, David, and Earle had worked on for the past year, would all have first performances. Naturally, I wanted to be there. By giving me a minute or two of dancing to do, Merce made it possible for me to leave Juilliard (for more than a week) in order to attend the festival with Earle. It was a favor Merce was granting me, and I knew it. He certainly didn't need me, but I think he may have been auditioning me. I traveled by automobile with Earle, John, and M. C. Richards. Five days later, Merce and the other dancers arrived by plane. Our auto trip to Urbana, Illinois, and back, via Chicago both ways, contained all the best things about life with John Cage on the road: (1) wildly utopian conversation, (2) the meeting of un-ordinary people, (3) the opening of one's senses to sights and sounds, to the natural world through John's eyes and ears, and (4) adventures in food, fun, and laughter. It was this life *combined* with the intensity of commitment to work (music, painting, dance) that enthralled me—a holistic approach to living each hour of the day that, without John, dwindled as the years went by because managers and assistant managers, unions, Merce's own practicality, and the hovering specter of the company's economic survival began to rule our lives, and John's appetite for life became something to be smiled at but prudently (though, for me, oh-so-wistfully) ignored.

The indignant reaction to Cage's presentation by much of the public and most of the critics in Urbana, Illinois, in 1953 was typical of the response Cage received fairly consistently throughout most of his composing life, but particularly in regard to his role as music director for the Cunningham company. Merce's concert at the University of Illinois, by contrast, aroused little anguish. In the words of one local reviewer, it "was well-received . . . despite the efforts of a few bores and boo-ers left over from Sunday." It was the first time I'd seen Merce perform except for the informal studio showing. I wrote home: "The audience started out by laughing but they were compelled to silence simply by the power of the dance. The *Sixteen Dances* are magnificent. Merce is really a tremendous dancer!"

Merce had no stage manager or lighting designer who toured with him in those years, so he had to do both jobs himself. All the dancers worked the night before and the entire day of the concert ironing costumes, arranging props, setting light cues, and spacing and rehearsing the dances. I was flushed with pleasure being backstage again, involved once more with the theater that I'd apparently taken for granted all those years I'd danced in my mother's concerts in her programs for women's clubs, for disabled veterans in army hospitals, for churches, and for summer camps, plus four years in college dance and drama productions and in Jane McLean's company in Denver. Merce seemed both amused and pleased with my unabashed delight in being a part of it all. I felt more like a mascot or a theatrical au pair than a bona fide member of the company, but that didn't diminish my excitement.

The company presented *Suite by Chance* (1952), using Christian Wolff's music for magnetic tape, part of which had been heard two days before and which was apparently the reason for the audience's first fit of giggles, followed by *Sixteen Dances for Soloist and Company of Three* (1950), which had Cage's music written for conventional instruments, with Cage conducting an ensemble of university musicians. At the intermission, after my grand total of less than two minutes onstage in *Suite by Chance,* I rushed down to the dressing room to help paint the soles of the feet of the three women in *Sixteen Dances* with a red pigment mixed with water, a holy Hindu ritual, and then backstage to assist Merce by calling light cues to the single stagehand available to us—a kindly old man who moved with the speed of a box turtle looking for a nesting site. Though willing and even eager to do well, he was inevitably at least five light cues behind, no matter what my strategy to keep up with the dance.

Of *Sixteen Dances* Merce wrote in his book *Changes: Notes on Choreography:* "It was the first time the use of chance entered into the compositional technique. It dealt with expressive qualities, the nine permanent emotions of the Indian classical theatre—four light [the Erotic, the Heroic, the Mirthful and the Wondrous] and four dark [Fear, the Odious, Anger and Sorrow] with Tranquility the ninth and pervading one—in image form and not personal."[1] Trying to decide upon the sequence of solos, duets, trios, and quartets, Merce came to the conclusion that it was possible for any dance to follow any other and could find no reason why a specific Indian "permanent emotion" (light or dark) should follow any other, so he chanced rather than choose the order. In the final quartet he gave each dancer a small gamut of movements whose direction in space, length of time, and sequence he discovered by tossing coins. It must be emphasized, because there has been so much confusion about this, that once the coins had been tossed the order was permanent. Chance was a part of the *choreographic* process only: the dancers were never involved in the chance procedure. Two performances were as alike (or unalike) as any two performances of *Symphony in C* might be. Still, the overriding formal concept in *Sixteen Dances* was the rhythmic structure that linked choreography and music, not chance.

Several years earlier, Cage had written *Sonatas and Interludes* (1946–48), a seventy-minute work for prepared piano, and it, too, was described as an attempt to express in music the "permanent emotions" of Indian tradition. This is another instance in which Cunningham's choreography follows a path traveled originally by Cage's music. Musically, Cage's *Sonatas and Interludes* and *The Seasons* (1947) (a fifteen-minute ballet Cunningham choreographed for Ballet Society, later to become New York City Ballet) and *Sixteen Dances* were all the expressions of Cage's then-pervading interest in rhythm—not rhythm defined as individual rhythmic patterns but rhythm as structure—and it is here that Cage's music and Cunningham's choreography were joined. In the 1940s, Cage viewed composition as an activity integrating the opposites, the rational, and the irrational, bringing about, ideally, a freely moving continuity within a strict division of parts. They based their common structure on the use of arithmetical proportions—the whole divided into parts, large and small; it was an "empty" structure agreed upon by composer and choreographer, who then set about filling it, independently of each other, with sound and silence, movement and stillness.

By the time he was writing *Music for Piano* in 1953, Cage had taken the view that composition "is not an activity the purpose of which is to integrate the opposites, but rather an activity characterized by process and essentially purposeless."[2] He had, he wrote, "affirmed the absence of mind as a ruling agent of structure and method," something, I would hazard to guess, that Cunningham has never completely done. But before stripping his mind of its right to control, Cage was interested in the study of numbers with which he found it congenial to begin a musical composition. Cunningham wanted *The Seasons* to be cyclical and concise, so Cage devised a rhythmic structure that corresponded to the sections of the dance—Prelude: Winter; Prelude: Spring; Prelude: Summer; Prelude: Fall; and ending with a repeat of Winter's prelude. In Cage's words, "*The Seasons* was an attempt to express the traditional Indian view of the seasons as quiescence (winter), creation (spring), preservation (summer), and destruction (fall). Of *The Seasons* Cunningham wrote: "If time and the seasons are inseparable, it seems to me that time and dancing are hardly less so."

Beyond this concern with rhythm as structure, *Sonatas and Interludes*—Cage's seminal work for prepared piano—and *The Seasons*, and *Sixteen Dances*, all reflect the Cage-Cunningham preoccupation at that time with Indian thought and the Oriental theory that art represents a continuous condition, rather than the European one, which depicts a moment of time or an arrested action. In Ananda K. Coomaraswamy's book *The Transformation of Nature in Art* Cage found a philosophical basis for his and Cunningham's work: "Asiatic art is ideal in the mathematical sense: like Nature (*natura naturans*), not in appearance (viz. that of *ens naturata*), but in operation."[3] Cage translated that concept into: "The highest purpose is to have no purpose at all. This puts one in accord with nature in her manner of operation."[4] Born to the ministry as he was (his grandfather was a Methodist minister, and at one time he had intended to become one, too), Cage was never shy about expressing himself in a highly moralistic tone that could range freely from mere calm didacticism to a squealingly and occasionally thunderous righteousness. But in those statements he was referring to the writing of music: "And what is the purpose of writing music? One is, of course, not dealing with purposes but dealing with sounds. Or the answer must take the form of paradox: a purposeful purposelessness or a purposeless play. This play, however, is an affirmation of life—not an attempt to bring order out of chaos nor to suggest improvements in creation, but simply a way of waking up to the very life we're living which is so excellent once one gets one's mind and one's ideas out of its way and lets it act of its own accord."[5]

And so Cage began to move away from controlling his music by devising rhythmic structures; he stopped choosing the sounds and no longer submitted his music to his own taste, mind, and will. Nor did he attempt to express in the content of his work Oriental views *about* specific things, choosing instead to have his work be, in and of itself, an expression of the Eastern, specifically the Zen Buddhist, attitude toward art and life as he perceived it. He encouraged Cunningham to do the same.

Suite by Chance, which was described in a previous chapter, was probably the purest chance work Cunningham ever attempted in the years I worked with him. Performing it was both perplexing and frightening. My very first dance performance at the age of three took place in a beautiful garden during my mother's first recital. I was Maia, the Flower Fairy, and I created the dance myself. My father carried me onstage in something resembling a giant May basket, a pink and green crêpe-paper flower from which I emerged to reach for the sun, open my petals, bend and sway, and sink slowly back inside. Over the years I danced a flower fairy, a raindrop, Minnie Mouse, a Puritan child, a hobgoblin, a splinter of broken mirror, morning mist, lightning, a sailor, a flirt, an ice cream soda, a coolie, an American Indian, an East Indian, a Hawaiian hula girl, an African-American slave, and an Egyptian slave. Later I was allowed to do the "pure" dances from the Denishawn repertoire, musical visualizations requiring a fluid torso, softness, continuous flow, and both spiritual and musical awareness. Still later, in college, I choreographed Joan of Arc (Graham hadn't done hers yet) and works to poems of Robert Frost and Walt Whitman, and I had the naive audacity to do a one-act ballet based on *The Brothers Karamazov.* (Dr. Vakar, my Russian teacher, a beautiful, elegant White Russian refugee, cringed when I invited him to see it, but he did come and later offered to introduce me to his friends in the Ballet Russe de Monte Carlo.) Thus, in the light of my performance background, *Suite by Chance* was, quite obviously, a foreign language to me. There was only one way for me to approach its abruptness, the going from one isolated movement to another without flow or intended continuity, without a rhythmic pulse dictated by the music, divested of all the dramatic, romantic, sentimental, or sensuous artifices that theatrical dance usually offers as protection from revealing the self, and that was with absolute concentration on each single moment, as though the movements were *objets trouvés,* and in a sense, of course, they were. Did I realize that then? Not in the first performance, certainly. But without knowledge, without thinking about it, and with no direction from Merce, there was no other way I knew how to do it.

Suite by Chance was choreographed and rehearsed in silence. Dance and music met, as if by accident, in the performance space. But by sheer force of habit, I suppose, Cunningham constructed and originally rehearsed it to a metric beat. However, because music for magnetic tape is constructed not in measures but in inches per second, it made sense to unpin the movement from a metric pulse and use instead a stopwatch to relate to the music by means of time units alone. This was, in fact, a giant step forward for dance; or, one might see it as a giant step backward toward the origins of dance. By abandoning meter, rhythmic nuances—complex and capable of enormous variation from dancer to dancer—could be expressed freely if the choreographer so desired and if the choreographer was sufficiently skilled. So it was not, as so many Cunningham detractors thought at the time, an arbitrary, dehumanizing act, this use of the stopwatch, but rather a practical means of functioning with the new music so that dance and music might, if desired, at least start and end together, meanwhile releasing the dance and the dancer from the beat-for-beat or phrase-for-phrase (or the decision to go against the beat or phrase) kind of synchronization most choreographers had accepted as law. One must, of course, admit that this release from the beat could validly be called deprivation.

The most musical of choreographers—in my humble opinion, Frederick Ashton and Antony Tudor—move through, over, around, and against, as well as *with* their music with subtlety, brilliance, wit, even daring, and what seems to be a profound intuitive perception. There is no one-to-one relationship. George Balanchine, on the other hand, widely acclaimed as *the* most brilliant musician-choreographer, seems to me to be dealing mostly in musical surfaces, occasionally coming uncomfortably close to the Mickey Mouse–*Fantasia* aesthetic. Heresy, I know; so I must quickly confess that throughout two or three decades of almost universal Balanchinemania, though I have appreciated his greatness, acknowledged his genius, and been impressed both by his personal charm in interviews and by the fervent loyalty his dancers have shown him, I have remained, with a number of important exceptions, unmoved by his work and all too often angered, even insulted by his peculiar brand of sexism, which strikes me not only as anti-woman but anti-man as well. He may have said and meant "Ballet is woman!" but his definition of "woman" must have been a very different one from mine. I seldom saw a woman dancing in a Balanchine ballet—girls, nymphettes, high-prancing fillies, yes, by the dozens, but women (despite exceptions like Diana Adams, Violette Verdy, Maria Tallchief, and Danilova) rarely. As for his movement vocabulary, how often when choreographing contemporary music did Mr. B. resort to the flexed wrist and splayed fingers, flexed foot and thrust pelvis, pirouettes on bent knees and daisy-chain contortionist acrobatics, or Tin Pan Alley, girlie-show kitsch from old Broadway to signify "This is modern!"? I wonder what his considerations were when he choreographed to the music of Schoenberg, Webern, Ives, Xenakis, beyond the obvious idiosyncrasies of the sounds and the irregular rhythms? And yet in those early years Balanchine's influence on Merce's work was far greater than Graham's, because Balanchine had moved away from dependence on story and message. "Ballet is like a rose; it's beautiful and you admire it, but you don't ask what it means," Balanchine said, but when asked if ballet reflected life, he answered, "No. It's a fantasy. It has nothing to do with life."[6] Cage might have responded: "Theatre takes place all the time wherever one is and art simply facilitates persuading one this is the case."[7] One suspects that both Balanchine and Cunningham would have happily dispensed with spectacle, scenery, and costumes if left entirely to their own interest, which is: the movement of bodies in time. And—in Cunningham's work, at least—in space. It's my observation that Balanchine's choreographic gifts were not significant regarding his use of space, which was for the most part conventional, geared to the proportions and seeing habits of the Renaissance theater.

The most obvious difference between Balanchine and Cunningham is in their attitude toward the relationship of dance to music. Said Mr. B.: "Our movements have to be performed in the composer's time. That's what makes ballet so exciting—this movement of bodies in time. That's why I call Stravinsky 'an architect of time.' His music provides the dancer's floor. It's the reason we move. Without the music we don't want to move."[8] But for Cunningham, the dancer's floor is literally the dancer's floor. He wants to move because he wants to move. It's that simple. In Cunningham's choreography since 1953—though there have been exceptions—it is the choreographer, not the composer, who is "the architect of time." Merce knows that it is hard for many people to accept that dancing has nothing in common with music other than the element of time (and the division of time). But he believes that choreography equated predictably beat-for-beat on the musical pulse may, for the spectator anyway, rob both the dancer and the dance of the subtle rhythms unique to each human body in much the same way as the music imposed on the movements of wild animals (in Disney films, for example) robs them of their instinctual rhythms and leaves them as caricatures.

In order to begin rehearsing for the American Dance Festival performances at the Alvin Theater in April, Merce and his company had to return to New York by plane the day after the University of Illinois performance. John, David, M.C. Earle, and I took a circuitous route home via

Chicago, Terre Haute, and Louisville, Bardstown, and Lexington, Kentucky, before returning to New York City at 4:30 in the morning five days later, feeling only slightly guilty for having had such a rip-roaring good time. In Chicago, David gave a command performance in a spectacular Mies van der Rohe apartment. In Bardstown we spent the most hilarious night of the trip, camped out together in one room at Ye Old Talbott Tavern, eating dinner, tippling Kentucky moonshine, playing cards into the wee hours of the morning, and hatching giddy plans to tour like this forever. It was during these five days of intimate proximity that I first heard John speak about his feelings for Merce, about the sexual passion that Merce the dancer, whom he likened to a Greek god, aroused in him. Because their public behavior was always so circumspect, I don't think it had occurred to me before this time that theirs was a sexual relationship. At no time has Merce ever spoken of such matters with me. John has always been more open with his feelings.

Returning to classes at Juilliard, I received comments from fellow students and even some faculty on the change in my dancing. I doubt that my dancing had changed much, but my attitude certainly had. Stimulated and cheered by ten days of diversified activities highlighted by performing with Merce, I was out of the doldrums after a long, difficult winter of endless classes in which I'd felt technically inadequate and embarrassingly insecure about what I was doing and why I was doing it. John's appetite for adventure in both work and play, and his crazy, outlandish ideas about theater and life, enlivened everyone around him. They were irresistible, and like a delicious spring tonic, they had revived my flagging spirits.

On April 15, 1953, shortly after we'd all returned to New York, Merce presented a lecture-demonstration in the Lecture Hall of the Brooklyn Academy of Music and invited his students to take part. Merce is quoted by *Dance Observer* as saying during his lecture that he got the idea of using chance procedures "while watching the chance relationships of people in the street, through a high window."[9] This was certainly not the only time that Merce explained aspects of his work in this way. Years later, in his book *Changes*, he wrote that the movements for *Minutiae* (1954) "were found by watching people out the window of the studio."[10] Merce would have us believe, it seems, that watching street activity has been an endlessly fecund source of choreographic ideas. Or is this simply an explanation that he felt could be easily grasped and understood by the general public? Certainly no one who has ever worked or studied at the various Cunningham studios over the years would deny that staring out the studio window appeared to be a principal preoccupation of the artist-in-residence. However, I doubt that much of the movement vocabulary or many of the choreographic ideas present in his work actually derived from this activity. Merce must forgive my doubt, since in *Changes*, after soberly explaining the window-gazing origins of the *Minutiae* movements, he himself adds in the most disarming manner, "At least that's what I replied when asked."[11] Leaving aside conjecture about the precise amount of influence street observation played in the finished work, the point to be made here is that the fundamental (*true*) origins of Merce's use of chance procedures and everyday gestures as a part of his movement vocabulary should be attributed to John Cage, not to staring out of studio windows. On the other hand, I'm sure that once imbued with John's ideas about art and life and the use of chance (as a reflection of John's belief that art should imitate nature *in her manner of operation*), Merce indeed applied them often to his favorite pastime.

In the question-and-answer session in Brooklyn in 1953, there were some antagonistic questions from disapproving audience members who found fault with both Merce's approach to dance and Christian Wolff's music. When asked if *Suite by Chance* was "an abstract dance," Merce is quoted as saying that he did not see how humans could be abstract. This response has remained an organic and oft-repeated premise in Merce's long history of verbal self-defense. "The meaning of the dance exists in the activity of the dance. A jump means nothing more than a jump. Dancing is an expression of life—if this is not valid, life is not valid."[12]

It's interesting that both Balanchine and Cunningham were accused of making "abstract" dances in those years. Balanchine's answer to this (expressed in *Dance Index* in 1947): "No piece of music, no dance can in itself be abstract. You hear a physical sound, humanly organized, performed by people, or see moving before you dancers in flesh and blood in a living relation to one another. What you hear and see is completely real. But the after image that remains with the observer may have for him the quality of an abstraction."[13] Cunningham, writing a few years later, agreed: "What the dancer does is the most realistic of all possible things."[14] Neither choreographer considered the storyless ballet "abstract." For Balanchine, the dance had its own means of telling a story: "Two dancers on stage are enough material for a story; for me, they are already a story in themselves."[15] He saw the basic elements of the dance in the movement, not in meaning or interpretation. Even Frederick Ashton, surely one of the greatest story-ballet choreographers who has ever lived, has said that "if ballet is to survive, it must survive through its dancing qualities . . . it is the dance that must be paramount."[16] Words spoken by Merce in his lecture-demonstration in 1953 sound very much like echoes of words spoken by his onetime mentor, Martha Graham, in 1935: "My dancing is just dancing. It is not an attempt to interpret life in a literary sense. It is the affirmation of life through movement. Its only aim is to impart the sensation of living, to energize the spectator into keener awareness of the vigor, of the mystery, the humor, the variety and wonder of life."[17]

In fact, had I not read that these were Martha Graham's own words, I would have guessed they were Merce's. For almost five years, Martha Graham's and Merce's dancing lives were entwined, but under John's influence the strands had frayed and come unraveled and the two dancer-choreographers were pulled in unreconcilably divergent directions. Still, the tiny threads of Martha's early influence continued to run through Merce's work and even his words, while she moved ever closer to dramatic exposition of psychological and literary themes.

With very rare exceptions, Merce was alone and undoubtedly lonely among his modern-dance peers. In his desire for the movement to be self-expressive (*not* expressive of the self or anything else), he was far closer in spirit and intent to the choreographic principles of Balanchine and Ashton than to the doctrines espoused by Graham, Humphrey, Weidman, or Limón and their disciples. But Balanchine repeatedly states that the controlling image comes from the music, and Ashton wrote: "Through [music] one gets the purity of the dance expressing nothing but itself, and thereby expressing a thousand degrees and facets of emotion, and the mystery and poetry of movement, leaving the audience to respond at will and to bring their own poetic reactions to the work before them."[18] Of the three, Merce alone begins with movement, not music, so that the purity of the dance *truly* expresses nothing but itself.

"A jump means nothing more than a jump." Had I unequivocally believed that, had I truly believed that Merce himself honestly believed that, I doubt that I could have spent so many years of my life rehearsing and performing his dances. But it was also Merce who once defined dance as "a spiritual exercise in physical form,"[19] and that I did and do believe. That definition of dance was the link that made it possible for me to do the dances of Ruth St. Denis and Ted Shawn in my mother's Denishawn studio for fifteen years and work with Merce and John for twenty.

After seeing my mother's first New York concert of Denishawn dances (she made her New York debut at the age of seventy-two in January 1977, about five years *after* I'd stopped performing!), Richard Alston, the British choreographer, who was in New York studying with Merce, asked me in undisguised amazement how on earth I'd gone from Denishawn to Cunningham. I don't remember what I told him at the time. The question shouldn't have surprised me, but it did. I'd never stopped to analyze it, but the answer is simple enough. In both my mother's studio and in Merce's, steps are danced for their own sake, and dancing is an activity that is allowed to be expressive of itself. More important, the *reason* for dancing all those steps, whether they were Denishawn or Cunningham, was for me the same: "spiritual exercise in physical form." But I know this only now, in retrospect.

Can anyone look at those early photographs of Merce jumping, his head thrown back and his throat exposed in a kind of orgiastic ecstasy, and believe that "a jump means nothing more than a jump"? Even in a dance as dry and austere as *Suite by Chance,* more is revealed than the mere existence and mechanics of movement. "Let the movement speak for itself!" Margaret Craske admonished her students. "We give ourselves away at every moment. We do not, therefore, have to try to do it,"[20] says Merce. To paraphrase François Delsarte, each gesture or movement is expressive of something. Or, as the popular song from the 1910 musical comedy *Madame Sherry* put it, "Every little movement has a meaning all its own." But while most modern dancers in the forties and fifties were attempting to create meaningful movement by plumbing the depths of their subconsciouses in search of images, convinced that dance *should* express something primordial and truthful, Merce was convinced that the meaning was already in the movement. "If it is there, we do not need to pretend that we have to put it there."[21] Merce believed it essential that the dancer allow whatever quality is there to *happen,* rather than force it. It was the "tranquility" of the actor or dancer that seemed to him essential. A tranquility that allows the dancer to detach himself and thereby to *present* freely and liberally.[22] Maybe this explains Merce's own dancing—why it is that he can appear to be possessed by both Apollo and Dionysus, by both Pan and deadpan Buster Keaton in turn. As Ashton said, "expressing a thousand degrees and facets of emotion, and the mystery and poetry of movement." *This* is what I believed, and wanted to believe that Merce believed. But in John's zeal to wrest, through chance procedures, the single sound and single movement from concepts of continuity and context and emotional connotation, in his desperate attempt to reject the weighty message ballets—the sociopolitical, religious, psychological, dramaturgical dance essays being created in the 1950s—and in order to get audiences to see and hear what Merce and he *were* doing rather than faulting them for what they *weren't,* John (and Merce), perhaps unintentionally, caused Merce's work to be viewed as mere surface, thereby encouraging people to believe that what they saw was *all* there was and *nothing* more. When Cage and Cunningham were taken at their word in this most literal-minded sense, misunderstanding was inevitable: the lazy among the critics and the gullible among his audience swallowed the simplistic propaganda that states that Merce's dances have no meaning (thus, goes the logic, they're meaningless, right?), and they sat back complacently to look at the choreography as though it were so much wallpaper. There's never been a single work in Merce's entire oeuvre that could or should be looked at with such indolence.

When the Brooklyn lecture-demonstration was over, Merce gave each of us five dollars. That took us by surprise. We hadn't expected to be paid, were thrilled just to have the opportunity to perform his work, on a stage, for an audience, with him. We pleaded with him to keep the money, but he refused. Undaunted, when he was in the bathroom Marianne and I crept into his dressing room and stuffed the bills into his jacket pocket. How times have changed! In the sixties, the Cunningham company had the union (AGMA) forced upon it, against the wishes of just about everyone. Insidiously, the union worked its polarizing poison into the tiny cracks of discontent, dividing what had been a family into the dualism of employer/employee; worse than that—employer *versus* employee. It's only recently that I've heard of dancers who join the Cunningham company because it's a paying job. In the early fifties, no matter what modern-dance group one danced with, it was a privilege one paid *for;* paid for by outside work, any kind one could get that would allow time for daily classes and rehearsals and the infrequent performance. Rarely was anything paid beyond a token fee. In those days, because the dancers (and, of course, the choreographers) themselves subsidized modern dance—not the NEA, NYSCA, the Ford Foundation, Exxon, Phillip Morris, or any other establishment Santa Claus—the climate was radically different. The passion to dance was what sustained them.

Once we were back in New York, Earle was without a job. The Project for Magnetic Tape had to be disbanded due to lack of funds. After many days of studying the classified want-ads, much walking and searching, he walked into Brentano's bookstore one morning and got a job in about five minutes. Someone had just quit. He ended up as the "Head of the Philosophy Section" in the big store on Fifth Avenue. Salary for five days a week, eight hours a day, was forty dollars. After taxes and paying the rent, we had about twenty dollars a week to live on. I wasn't earning anything and needed subway fare, thirty cents daily, to get to and from Juilliard, plus lunch money. Earle ate his lunch—coffee and a danish—for fifteen cents in the Automat, and he often walked the forty-five or so blocks home after work. Our Denver savings from my job at the Kent School were fast disappearing. My parents helped with strategically timed "gifts" that we used mostly for tickets to performances of dance and music. John was almost parental in his concern for our well-being. Merce never charged me for classes. Not that John or Merce, David or M.C., or for that matter, any of our friends were any better off financially than we were. But somehow we all managed. Our one big meal of the week was usually on Sunday evening, when John's mother and father would feed John, Merce, Earle, and me, and often David and M.C. as well. John's parents lived in a state of fluctuating fortune. In those years they had a large apartment on Fifth Avenue, and the weekly dinner party was always a jolly occasion ending with us gathered around the dining table playing Scrabble or Oh, Pshaw. John adored games, became addicted to them, and his parents seemed to share his enthusiasm.

John Milton Cage Sr. was a slightly eccentric, lovable, voluble, visionary inventor, an electrical engineer by profession. *Harper's* magazine described him "cut to a pattern often thought obsolete—independent, devoted to a dozen unorthodoxies, and completely alien to a smooth, public relations *persona*."[23] In 1912, the year John Jr. was born, his father invented, among other things, a submarine run by a gasoline engine. (It was useless to our government for wartime purposes because its location was easily detected by the rising bubbles.) That same year, obstinate and persevering, he came close to drowning when he set the world record for a submarine staying underwater. He also invented an extraordinary panacea (almost straight alcohol, I've heard—Henry Cowell was reported to have preferred it to whiskey) that we called Cage's Cure-All. John Jr. swore by it for colds, skin problems, dandruff, you name it, and his father insisted it was a sure cure for severe burns. The AMA, however, would never permit it to be licensed. Toward the end of his life, Mr. Cage's luck was down, but he continued to work, in a cluttered and dingy room on the third floor of a Union Square loft building, this time on a wall-size projected television system he'd fully patented, but which was ahead of its time and never completely realized. A true loner, he refused to work within the establishment for any company and was usually without the funds to realize his dreams, although this never stopped him from trying.

John's mother, Crete, was eccentric in her own way. Twice married before marrying John's father, she'd been a journalist; but still she seemed to me an innocent. A story John tells about his mother that ends with her statement, "Now, John, you know perfectly well that I've never enjoyed having a good time," may sound apocryphal, but it's actually very telling. Unerringly devoted and loyal to John, she was unquestionably baffled, and a little distressed, by his life, his work, and his friends. When I'd help out in the kitchen before or after dinner (the dishes were washed twice—before we ate off them as well as after—because Crete had an utter loathing for dust, dirt, and especially cockroaches, even the thought of them), she would tell me stories about John as a baby or a little boy. Listening to her, I perceived that she still looked upon him as a little boy; the man I knew as John Cage was an enigma to her, almost a stranger, someone she didn't really want to recognize. Her response to the dozens of autobiographical stories in John's lecture, *Indeterminacy*, recorded by Folkways, was this: "After hearing all those stories about your childhood, I keep asking myself, 'Where is it that I failed?' "

Eighth Street in 1953 was no longer in its bohemian heyday, but neither had it degenerated into the tawdry, tacky place it is today. I was a New Englander, raised in the country, and had loved it. I warmed to the city slowly. But by spring, I was smitten. Washington Square, suddenly greened over, was a candy box full of lovers; a stampede of kids on roller skates, on bikes, in the sandboxes, on the swings, straddling the seesaws; a maze of pigeons and nurses with prams; a leafy synagogue of chess players. Along the Village streets, carts brimmed over with flowers, fruits, and vegetables; the fragrance of crusty Italian bread mingled with the odors of newly worked leather from the sandal shops. Suddenly I felt that there was a joyous, wonderful unknown just around the next corner. I felt it climbing the stairs to the second balcony of the New York City Center to see Balanchine's company, or sneaking into the Alvin Theater with someone else's pass to see Graham or Limón; I sensed it attending a Buddhist festival near Harlem with John Cage, or walking into a Suzuki lecture at Columbia, or—heart in the mouth—auditioning for summer stock or a Broadway musical summer replacement job. Everything was new, exciting; everything held promise.

I saw the New York City Ballet as often as I could, sometimes sneaking in, with the aid of sympathetic ushers, to a seat high up in the second balcony, from which I looked through railing and bars down to a tiny stage and tinier dancers. From there I first saw Jerome Robbins's *Age of Anxiety, The Cage, Interplay,* and *The Pied Piper;* Antony Tudor's *Lilac Garden,* and Balanchine's *La Valse, Serenade, Firebird,* and *Bourrée fantasque.* At the Ziegfeld Theatre in March, a modern-dance festival featured works by Sophie Maslow, Jane Dudley, William Bales, and Donald McKayle. I went mostly to see Remy Charlip performing in McKayle's *Games,* a delightful dance about street kids, with Remy looking like the kid from Brooklyn he

once was. At the Alvin Theatre in April, Martha Graham's company performed *Letter to the World, Night Journey, Appalachian Spring,* and *Canti-
cle for Innocent Comedians;* José Limón's company danced Doris
Humphrey's *Night Spell, Fantasy and Fugue,* and *Deep Rhythm,* plus
Limón's own *The Moor's Pavane* and *The Visitation.* In addition to the two
major modern-dance companies, four former and current Graham company members—Merce Cunningham (*Sixteen Dances*), Pearl Lang (*Rites*),
Helen McGehee (*La Intrusa*), and May O'Donnell (*Dance Sonata*)—each
presented one work. I attended six performances and saw most of the
dances twice.

On one of these evenings, Cunningham's *Sixteen Dances* was performed
between Limón's *The Moor's Pavane* and Graham's *Appalachian Spring.*
Without question Merce's work was the most controversial of the season.
Simultaneously roars of "bravo" and thunderous boos greeted Merce and
his three dancers as they took their bows. Audience members were on
their feet shouting; in the balcony, I was amazed to see people actually hitting each other over the head with their programs. I suppose it is difficult
today to comprehend the partisanship, the fierce loyalties, the strident
fanaticism of that evening. But I think it was a genuine reflection of the
barely hidden hostilities harbored by the choreographers themselves.
They were suspicious and intolerant of one another, and the audiences,
made up in large part of each choreographer's own self-appointed claque
of student-disciples, fractured itself into three uneven camps of turbulent
opposition. Graham, Limón, and Cunningham spoke different languages,
and few people thought it possible or proper to be conversant in all three.
I was as excited as everyone else, but called upon to choose sides, I had no
problem, intellectually, aligning myself with Cunningham and Cage,
although I was uneasy. About Merce Cunningham the dancer there was not
a doubt. Quite simply and in the strictest sense of the word, I thought he
was a *great* dancer. But Merce Cunningham the choreographer puzzled
me. Though I could and did defend his work from Cage's philosophical
position, I was inwardly disquieted by my own ambivalent feelings.

On May 7 and 8 of that year Juilliard presented "A Demonstration in
Dance" with Antony Tudor and Doris Humphrey, performed by students
from Juilliard's dance division. Tudor's lecture was in fact an apology—an
apology for us, none of whom, he said, would become professional dancers.
I know at least five of the twenty-six dancers in that performance of Tudor's
Exercise Piece (music by Arriaga y Balzola) who proved him wrong: Paul
Taylor, Richard Englund, Nancy King, William Aubry, and myself. I'm
fairly certain there are others. In rehearsals Tudor kept repeating: "What

are you people worried about? I'm the one to worry. You have no reputation to lose. I may be out of a job after this!" The week before performance he was still choreographing and changing the ballet. "We haven't really been *rehearsed* in it once!" I wailed, panic-stricken, in a letter to my mother. Tudor had given me a pas de deux on pointe, as well as a pas de quatre. I was terrified of them both, and I didn't know how to go about working on pointe steps I couldn't do. It wasn't even a question of doing the parts well, it was a question of being able to do them at all, in a week's time.

Tudor had no interest in coaching us, no patience for it, either. He worked with us as though we were professionals, setting some movement one day and expecting it to be in performance shape the next so he could move on. We never rehearsed yesterday's steps, just ran through them and then we went on to new ones. Or he'd change yesterday's steps, and change them so often, we couldn't remember which ones he'd kept. Few of us could cope with the material this way. Confused and shaken, I finally went to him and asked to be taken out of the pas de deux and the pas de quatre; off pointe I could have managed, on pointe it was unthinkable. I was disappointed in myself, but took solace from the fact that Tudor had wanted me to do them in the first place. I remember Paul Taylor—"Big Pete," we called him at Juilliard—not understanding that I had chosen to relinquish the parts, and being aghast at what he interpreted as my complacence in losing them. "Why aren't you angry?" My answer: "Because I couldn't do them justice." His reply: "Nonsense!" But it really wasn't nonsense. As Paul told me many years later, he was brimming with self-confidence in those years and had an absolute conviction that he would succeed. I felt no equivalent self-esteem. For the week before the performance I concentrated on those parts I thought I could do without shaming myself and Tudor—a brief solo variation, the six-couple supported adagio section, and the finale, all on pointe. Miss Craske kindly offered to help us and gave us advice about the most useful exercises to do as a warm-up before performance. Tudor suffered through the ordeal. His ballet, at least as we performed it, seemed to be an embarrassment to him. Even so, people said they enjoyed it, and Hugh Laing, Tudor's friend and formerly a powerful interpreter of his ballets, was there to proffer kind and encouraging words. I never knew if Merce came. He never mentioned it. I never asked.

It's interesting to compare my first working experience with Cunningham to the one with Tudor. Merce gave me the tiniest morsel to chew on, a mere taste from the feast of possibilities. Tudor gave me a banquet. Merce seemed to have no definite expectations, leaving me free to prove myself in whatever way I could. Tudor seemed to expect ballerina-caliber work because his ballet required it, but he, too, left me free to prove myself, although it felt more like being thrown overboard in a rough sea and not knowing which way the land lay. Both dances, in this case, were without a story. *Exercise Piece* was a plotless, neoclassical ballet with Tudor vocabulary, rhythms, and musicality, but otherwise unlike any of his previous ballets. I do recall he made a few wry movement "jokes." One involved Paul Taylor: in the midst of a large group sedately executing a classical port de bras Tudor had Big Pete do an exaggerated Graham contraction, fall heavily to the floor, and, as I recall, roll offstage.

I first really took notice of Paul Taylor in a Graham technique class during the early autumn of that school year at Juilliard. Martha Graham herself was teaching. As we went across the floor on the diagonal doing a leaping combination, Graham shouted a correction at Paul, adding in ominous tones, "Young man, I'm grooming you!" And everyone stopped to stare at this very tall, broad-chested, athletic fellow who had just been singled out by America's high priestess of the modern dance. Something not unlike this had happened to Merce, Martha Hill recalled:

> The first view anybody had of Merce outside of Washington [state] was when we went to Mills in '39. . . . Arch Lauterer and I taught Experimental Production together. . . . This tall young man went across the stage and I nudged Arch and said, "We have something there." It was Merce Cunningham. There was something in the turn of his head—something almost Nijinsky-like. So I went to Martha [Graham] immediately and said, "Martha, we have someone you must look at." Martha put her finger on Merce, and that's when he came to New York with Martha.[24]

Paul had come to Juilliard without much more than a summer's worth of dance training, but with a natural and unique gift for moving. Every one of the choreographers on the faculty was interested in him, though none of us students quite understood why. He looked more like an Olympic athlete than a dancer. He was chosen by both Tudor and Doris Humphrey to be in their dances in the spring concert. Graham had demonstrated her interest even earlier. And rumor had it that José Limón wanted Paul to work with him. But Paul had heard about Merce Cunningham, seen his *Sixteen Dances* at the Alvin, and was curious to know more about him and his work. Eventually he went with me one afternoon to take Merce's class. Anita Dencks, another Juilliard student in our class, came, too. They both liked Merce's classes and began attending them several times a week.

With spring came talk of auditions for summer stock, Radio City Music

Hall replacements, and Broadway musicals. I asked Merce what he thought about that kind of dance job, beyond the obvious advantage of a weekly paycheck. In his actual words there was no attempt to dissuade me from auditioning, but between the lines, in the hesitations, I read a certain disapproval. Not too many weeks after that conversation, we learned that he was going to Black Mountain College for six weeks, from July 13 to August 22, to teach daily technique and composition courses as a part of Black Mountain's ten-week Summer Institute of the Arts. The best part of the news was that in addition to giving classes, Merce had been invited to give performances at the end of the summer session, and for these he was allowed to bring with him, for the last three weeks only, a company of four.

Merce had no permanent company. The dancers with whom he'd worked in the past—Dorothy Berea, Mili Churchill, Natanya Neumann, Joan Skinner, and Annaliese Widman—had been his contemporaries at the Graham School. They were trained dancers with strongly developed tastes and points of view. Apparently Merce sensed from one or two of these dancers aesthetic opposition as well as an inflexible devotion to the style and manner of Graham's technique. He felt the need for unformed (open) minds and bodies, so he decided to invite his own students to join him at Black Mountain. Those of us who had had some performing experience with him—Jo Anne, Marianne, Remy, and myself—were invited to come down for the last three weeks. We had to pay our own bus fare in order to get there, but once at Black Mountain we would be housed and fed, and our dance classes would be free. Merce also invited Viola Farber, Paul Taylor, and Anita Dencks. A work scholarship had been arranged for Viola, but after a few days, someone at Black Mountain, who remains to this day anonymous, paid her tuition so that she could devote herself full-time to classes and rehearsals. To his surprise, Paul got a bill at the end of the summer. He thought he had been given a full scholarship, and in the end, he had, since he could not afford to pay the bill. So, of the seven of us, it was only Anita who actually paid anything to attend the summer session. Or perhaps it should be stated that it was Merce himself who paid for our presence, because in order to have us at Black Mountain, he gave up any fee or salary he might otherwise have been paid. Like the rest of us, he received room and board only. But he leapt at the opportunity to work undisturbed with a small group of dancers of his own choosing, and we leapt at the chance to work full-time with Merce.

Thus, in the summer of 1953, at Black Mountain College, in the back hills of North Carolina, Merce Cunningham formed his own company.

Black Mountain held its last Summer Institute of the Arts from June 22 through August 29, 1953. Its faculty included ceramicists Peter Voulkos, Daniel Rhodes, Warren MacKenzie, Karen Karnes, and David Weinrib; composers and musicians Stefan Wolpe, Mme. Irma Wolpe, Josef Marx, and David Tudor; painters Esteban Vicente and Joseph Fiore; dancer/choreographer Merce Cunningham; and for theater, Wesley Hus. In addition, not listed on the brochure but palpably present in every way, was the poet Charles Olson, who was, as it turned out, Black Mountain's last rector. The college itself survived less than three more years. For Black Mountain, the summer of '53 was the beginning of the end, but for Merce Cunningham, it was the birth of his dance company that would continue into the twenty-first century. It, too, would become a community of sorts, and like Black Mountain it would weather poverty, change, calamity, struggle, and upheaval. Unlike Black Mountain, and despite John Cage's professed belief in anarchy, its existence was predicated upon the presence of one man, Merce Cunningham, who ruled it like an eccentric prince. Everyone played by his rules, willingly or unwillingly. The trick, often, was discovering what they were.

For us, Black Mountain was a kind of paradise: the paradise of being able to be dancers twenty-four hours a day, freed from the dreary little jobs most of us needed to pay the rent and grocery bills, freed from the hassles of scheduling rehearsals to accommodate the peculiar hours of seven or more people's dreary little jobs, and freed, too, from hours wasted on subways and buses shuttling back and forth to classes, rehearsals, jobs, cold-water flats, and unheated lofts. At Black Mountain we walked dirt roads, breathed clean air, heard birds at dawn. We were fed good plain fare from the college's farm, were housed in comfortable, rustic simplicity, and were surrounded by artists and students of other disciplines equally free to do nothing else but their work.

Marianne, Jo Anne, and I arrived in Asheville, North Carolina, on Sunday, August 2, at about seven in the morning after twenty-two hours on three different buses. The bus ride from New York to Washington, D.C., had been okay. After Washington and a bus change, we got our first glimpse of the 1953-style WHITE ONLY apartheid practices of the "Land of the Free," and the trip turned sour. We whites got dirty buses, dirtier bus stops and coffee shops, filthy restrooms. God knows what the blacks got. We jounced and jostled all night in miserable broken seats. No dinner stop and no sleep. A bus change at 3:10 a.m. Our bodies began to atrophy and turn numb. Since we'd been told we would be met in Asheville, we waited for an hour, stiff and dizzy with fatigue, before finally hiring a taxi to deliver us to Black Mountain. It deposited us, in a swirl of dust, in front of a large wooden building surrounded by porches. A tall, bearded, wonderfully handsome Carolinian farmer fellow (who under the woolly beard turned out to be a very healthy, thriving Paul Taylor) greeted us with the news that we'd be rehearsing that very afternoon. Remy had just arrived separately, from Boulder, Colorado, where he'd been performing with Jean Erdman. Before our taxi's dust had settled, the three of us were asleep in the guesthouse until lunchtime, too tired to look at our new surroundings.

Thus did Merce set the pace for the intensive workweeks that followed: for at least eight hours a day, seven days a week, with only Saturday and Sunday nights and Sunday mornings free, we danced and kept dancing until around 10:30 at night, when we'd wearily stumble up the dirt road in the inky blackness of the North Carolina summer night to Meadow Lodge, a rustic cottage that housed all the dancers. Recuperating in a hot bath or shower, as we desperately longed to do, was not an option; by that hour the hot water was used up. Each morning I opted to rise at six so that I could soak my sore leg muscles in the three available inches of really hot water. Never before had I worked so hard and been so happy.

This is not to say there weren't awful moments. In the first few days I learned the hard way that a dancer cannot stop training, even for a week, without losing resiliency, speed, and ease. I'd done just that; I'd given myself a three-week vacation when Merce left for Black Mountain. I'd have spared myself both physical agony and mental anguish had I been able to read Alfred Kahn's book *Days with Ulanova* (it wasn't published for another ten years), in which Galina Ulanova speaks about getting back into dancing condition after a vacation: however many days or weeks she'd rested, it took her an equal number of days or weeks to recoup the losses. And that was how long it took one of the greatest ballerinas of all time! My payback for three weeks of beach-bumming inactivity was nightly muscle cramps in my calves and excruciating shin splints twenty-four hours a day. I'd been a damned fool. But far worse than the pain was enduring Merce's reaction to it, to all the aches and pains, injuries and illnesses his dancers suffered. Glum, moody, not at all given to sympathy, he seemed barely able to contain his disapproval and an almost resentful anger. It was a lesson I had to learn only once. Fortunately for me, although unfortunately for Merce, I was not the only casualty. Anita Dencks caught the mumps; Jo Anne Melsher, upon arrival, developed a mysterious malady diagnosed by a local doctor as some form of hysteria; Viola Farber injured her shoulder; Marianne Preger sprained her ankle. But despite fatigue and injuries, all the dancers were high as kites buoyed up by the joyous feel of freedom that dancing can sometimes give.

The Black Mountain community appeared genuinely amazed by Merce and his fledgling company. Few, if any, of the other artists and students had been in close working proximity with dancers before. Initial curiosity about our activities gave way at first to shock at the rigorous demands Merce made on himself and us, but that shock eventually gave way to universal admiration, even awe, for the strenuous, nonstop, totally committed way in which we conducted our lives.

Our class and rehearsal space was in the dining hall, and although summer meals were taken on the outside porches overlooking Lake Eden, the dining hall remained a kind of thoroughfare for students and staff working in the kitchen, setting or clearing the table, and performing other necessary KP duties. Our dancing was accompanied by a symphony of clanging pots and pans, the clatter of plates and cups and the clinking of utensils and cutlery, and, in addition, a continuous flow of traffic in and out of administrative offices in the front of the building. Rarely, except for an hour or two in midafternoon and at night, did Merce have a work space that was either private or quiet. There were compensations: the space was large, the floor was excellent (wood, with a nice springy give-and-take), and the ceiling was reasonably high. But the piano wasn't great and the phonograph was lousy.

If Merce's schedule was frantically busy, David Tudor's was no less so. We rarely had an opportunity to see the rest of the campus in action, but I doubt there were others at Black Mountain that August who worked as hard as Merce and David. Like woodstoves stoked by demons, they radiated a white heat of endless energy. David gave classes in piano, taught a survey course in piano literature, and rehearsed with Black Mountain resident musicians for concerts of classical and contemporary music, and on top of this he had to prepare his own solo concerts. His repertory was astonishing: Bach, Beethoven, Mozart, and Brahms; Ravel, Debussy, Stravinsky, Webern, and Messiaen; and new music by Brown, Boulez, Cage, Feldman, Wolpe, and Wolff. For rehearsals of Merce's new work *Dime-a-Dance* he played a potpourri of nineteenth-century piano music that he selected from "Music the Whole World Loves," as well as music by Cage, Feldman, Satie, Wolff, and Louis Moreau Gottschalk. I still wonder that Merce and David survived not just the workloads they'd given themselves but the high standards they had set. Merce, in just six weeks, developed a small repertory of dances, and in only three, a company (of sorts) to perform it. The repertory consisted of four new works—*Banjo, Dime-a-Dance, Untitled Solo,* and *Septet*—and five old works—*Ragtime Parade* (1950), *Variation* (1951), *Collage (Excerpts from Symphonie pour un homme seul)* (1952), the first two movements of *Suite by Chance* (1953), and *Solo Suite in Space and Time* (1953). Although the old dances had been choreographed by Merce before he'd come to Black Mountain, three were group works that had to be taught and rehearsed with new dancers. In some ways that was more difficult—and it was certainly more time-consuming—than starting from scratch.

In New York in June and early July, Merce began to work on material for *Septet.* What a joy to be learning a part made directly on me, for the dancer I was then, the dancer he saw in me, rather than learning a role made for someone else, assimilating movement information made special by another dancer. *Septet*'s music was Erik Satie's *Trois Morceaux en forme de poire,*[1] and the dance seemed to be *about* something—wistful, tender, sad, and romantic. I adored it—we all did. A brief trio he made for Jo Anne, Marianne, and me was gently playful, girlishly innocent; the three of us responded to it like kittens given a saucer of cream. Via the grapevine we learned that Merce was pleased with us, delighted we'd brought something more to the work than the correct execution of the steps. What he meant by this, as I understand it, is not that we altered the steps or added to them but that we contributed another dimension through our imaginations and spirit, which illuminated the dance as well as revealed aspects of ourselves.

At Black Mountain it was impossible for David Tudor to come to all of our rehearsals, and Merce was forced to use the college's wretched record player while choreographing *Septet.* Mechanical, Merce was not. He loathed machines in those days, and machines appeared to reciprocate in kind. One day, when nothing was working including phonograph and dancers (we couldn't hear the cues, even after repeated listening), Merce, exasperated beyond control, or so it seemed, marched over to the machine, grabbed the record, and flung it the length of the dining hall, where it hit the wall, fell to the floor and broke into pieces. Then he stalked out of the room. Utter silence. No one breathed. No one moved. I fought back tears; I was terrified by his anger and miserable to think he might abandon *Septet.* Marianne, much more sensible and savvy than I in her responses to Merce's peculiarities, rarely lost her sense of humor or capacity for understanding. After a second or two, in the panicked silence, she walked across the hall and picked up the shards of the ruined record. Suddenly a merry peal of laughter broke the stillness: "This record isn't *Septet!*" However furious and frustrated, Merce had not been completely out of control. He'd just thrown a bit of a tantrum and demonstrated some old-fashioned theatrics to vent his exasperation. We fell to the floor laughing. Our next rehearsal was a joy; David Tudor was there playing the four-hands Satie with his amazing two. He cleared up all the cues and rhythms we'd been struggling with in vain.

Septet, like so many of Cunningham's works, is a suite of dances, but unlike most of them, it seems to have a slender thread of narrative, a poetic tale to tell, though only Cunningham knows precisely what it is. It opens on three women poised in stillness along a long diagonal, like statuary in a French garden. Merce bursts into the placid space with an energy both passionate and disquieting, and one by one, on musical cue, the women move, change position, as though stirred to life by his dynamic presence. I suppose all of us were a little in love with Merce. I suspect he knew it, even wanted it that way. Though at times he could be genuinely friendly, even courtly in his manner toward his female dancers, Merce, the man, outside the studio or theater environment, was inaccessible. He was thirty-four years old; we, in our late teens or early twenties, were still young enough to mix awe—born of respect—with wistful romantic fantasy. For eleven years, following the summer of its creation, *Septet* was performed throughout the United States and around the world. Dancing it, there was always for me a fragile erotic sensibility tinged with innocence, nostalgic sadness, and an unexplainable sense of loss. For Merce, though, I've always thought *Septet* related to some earlier personal experience, perhaps to a beloved whose death he'd suffered in his own youth—a romantic fantasy, based on fragments of hearsay, gossip whispered in the dark walking home under the North Carolina stars at night and, much later, fed by

Merce's own titles for the seven parts of the dance. Marianne and I loved making up stories about some of his dances, peopling them with characters, and chronicling their chimerical adventures. Merce, inscrutably sphinxlike, told us absolutely nothing. When teaching us a part, he rarely used images to evoke a particular quality of movement. Occasionally in class he might use images related to the movements of animals, but never to emotional or psychological states of being. In refusing to tell us anything about his dances, he left us free to our imaginings. Marianne and I, at least, delighted in exploring them. We gave each dance no one fixed story; we continually made new ones, altered old ones. How much they affected the way we danced the dances I'm not sure. In one way or another, even the simplest of Merce's dances challenged our technical resources sufficiently to keep us focused on the physical aspects of the dances. We certainly did not intend to act out our story-fantasies, but because they enriched the life of the dance in us, I can't deny the possibility of their effect on our performances on the stage.

Not until two years later did we learn that "In the Garden," "In the Music Hall," "In the Tea House," "In the Playground," "In the Morgue," "In the Distance," and "In the End" were the titles for the seven parts of *Septet.* And even then we only learned it by reading the program notes for a performance we gave at Sarah Lawrence College in Bronxville, New York, which also contained this astonishing sentence: "The poetic ambiguity of the music and dance titles express the character of the ballet, whose subject is Eros, and whose occurrence is at the intersection of joy and sorrow."

Where did the titles come from? David Vaughan asked Merce this question when interviewing him for his book. Merce responded, "They're from me," but then went on to explain that he'd invented the titles to identify the various sections for rehearsal purposes, and that they did not necessarily reflect their content.[2] To which I say, poppycock! They most certainly do reflect their content as well as the Satie music—"now sprightly and gay, now tender and melancholy; always poetical, imaginative."[3] In rehearsing the dance, Merce had never used those program titles and always referred to the sections as the solo, duet, girls' trio, quartet, couple dance, etc. Here was just one of many instances throughout Merce's choreographic career when he would obfuscate his true intentions. In any case, Merce's disingenuousness was only following the precedent established by Satie, who is widely known to have titled and structured the music in reaction to Debussy's remark that his work was lacking in formal cohesion. Satie titled the work "*Trois Morceaux* . . ." when it was in fact seven pieces, and "*en forme de poire*" so that Debussy could not call it "formless"! Added to this bit of mischievous cheek, given that the colloquial or slang meaning of *poire* is "dupe" or "sucker," "it seems likely that Satie in his choice of title was slyly poking fun not only at Debussy but at himself—the '*poire.*' "[4]

"In the Tea House" was my first duet with Merce. When he told me I was to do a duet with him I was blissfully happy but also extremely nervous. Curiously formal, static, reserved, "In the Tea House" is a tranquil dance with little happening except subtle shifts of weight and changes of positions and long stillnesses. In the silence, after his solo "In the Music Hall," Merce comes to the wings and swiftly leads me by the hand to center stage, where we hold, facing the audience in curiously off-center positions, he slightly behind and to my left. Cautiously, slipping his right hand behind my back and around my waist, Merce proffers it, palm upturned. Carefully, I slide my palm over his. Lifting me off the floor (like a rigid doll) and holding me against his chest, he walks deliberately downstage, sets me down onto three-quarter *relevé*. Again, he picks me up (our positions change), tilts me, rocks me, lowers me, kneels and puts his arm around my waist; I slip my hand around his neck; he lifts me to his shoulder, and as he carries me offstage, I turn my head to look at him and slowly touch his cheek with my palm and fingertips, then look away—into the distance. Throughout this brief dance, my actions respond to his; I initiate nothing. My movement concerns were stillness and balance and inflecting the stillness with life, with a sense of yielding and being moved. Despite its static, quiet reserve, I always considered "In the Tea House" to be lyrical, a tender male-female duet, all soft curves and voluptuous angles, made the more erotic by its understatement and Merce's gentleness. For "In the Morgue" (or "the couple dance" as we called it), Merce is said to have wanted candelabra as decor; clearly he'd had romantic notions about *Septet*. It was one of the last times, he says, that he used a wholly intuitive procedure in choreographing a work.[5]

And what a contrast to the working procedures of *Untitled Solo*, which he was making at the same time! For this work, Merce devised a large gamut of movements for the head, the torso, the arms, and the legs. He describes the movements as "essentially tensile in character and off the normal or tranquil body-balance." Each had its own rhythm and time length. By tossing coins, he then determined the continuity of these movements, allowing for the superimposition of one or more of the different actions. Mastering in his own body the complexities of the physically unfamiliar coordinations—some of them close to impossible to perform—was the next task; following that, he had to cope with the space, also derived from chance operations, as was the time, i.e., how long a given sequence should take. As he puts it, the time "was left approximate, as the complexity of the movement was great enough to make some kind of elastic time necessary." Christian Wolff's music presented its own difficulties. Merce tells the story of trying to practice it in the dining hall on one of those hot, muggy North Carolina afternoons, with David Tudor at the piano. He had stopped in exhaustion and despair, and David said to him, "This is clearly impossible, but we're going right ahead and do it anyway." And they did. Merce also had three other long solos, plus several short ones, to rehearse. His only opportunity to work alone with David was time squeezed between class and lunch, or rehearsal and dinner, or late at night. In a letter to Earle, I wrote: "Watched Merce dance yesterday. It brought tears he was so beautiful. What a waste! He should be dancing, performing all over the world—not sweating it out with a bunch of kids in this place. It is *no place* for him!'"

Repeatedly, in letters to Earle and my parents, I wrote: "Merce is *magnificent.* Such a beautiful, beautiful dancer," etc., etc. Equally often I mentioned his moods: "Poor Merce is almost constantly in a state of depression. It's frightening to me." "Merce is moody—his dancers all have aches and pains." "Merce is pooped." "Merce was limping last night—hurt his hip. This schedule is pretty rough. I love it though, but WOW!'"

Even so, Black Mountain wasn't all work and no play. Eight of us would pile into Merce's ancient little Ford, and he'd drive us to Asheville to the movies, or for an ice cream soda, or to hear a concert by David Tudor. Occasionally we swam in a creek not far from Meadow Lodge and had picnic suppers in M. C. Richards's backyard. Charles Olson would read to the community from his *Maximus Poems.* Like almost everyone else, I enjoyed Olson enormously, while comprehending little of what he read to us. Viola and I loved to mimic—nonsensically, no disrespect intended—the curious cadences, the rhetoric, the peculiar sentences that seemed to end with prepositions dangling in midair. Olson was as out of the mainstream in his field as Cage and Cunningham were in theirs. All three were rebels, rejecting for themselves the traditional forms, questioning the separation of art and life. Though their means, even their reasons differed radically, they met on the common ground of search and experimentation.

Dancing from morning to night felt right. But it was more than that. I'm fairly certain that dancing from morning to night in one of the ballet companies of the fifties would not have generated the same quality of intense involvement that I experienced dancing with Merce at Black Mountain. There was more than dance and dancing to think about; there were other arts and other artists to consider—all nonconformists, searching in a world of changing ideas. It was a three-week education in engagement and discovery. As Walter Gropius (architect, founder of the Bauhaus, and closely connected to Black Mountain over the years) said about education, "You educate someone to come to himself. If you only bring him to imitate you, then you destroy him. We should cultivate the strongest individualism but also the attitude that we all enrich one another."[7] For me, surrounded by Black Mountain's highest ideals and homespun humanity, Cunningham and Cage seemed to offer just this possibility.

Cage arrived for our last week. He, Earle, and Helen Pinkerton, co-owner of the New York book shop *Orientalia,* had driven twenty-eight hours, with John and Earle taking turns at the wheel. Much passed between them. Earle remembered John confessing that he was suspicious of what he considered Earle's too-easy acceptance of Cage's most recent compositional ideas, as well as those of Morton Feldman and Pierre Boulez. Earle was surprised by John's mistrust. In Earle's case, it wasn't just the generation gap that made their ideas quite natural but also his years of studying the Schillinger technique. Yes, he had ideas about freedom and spontaneity *not* shared by Cage, which had developed from Earle's longtime association with jazz, but perhaps stronger than any musical influence were the mobiles of Alexander Calder (open form) and the paintings of Jackson Pollock (spontaneity), which had had a profound effect on Earle's thinking several years before his meeting with Cage in Denver in 1951. Like Morton Feldman's, Earle's musical ideas were his own, original and different from Cage's. The relationship of these three men was founded on their expressed interest in one another's work. Certainly the younger men had tremendous admiration and respect for Cage in those years, and were honored by his friendship, but they were not, as Virgil Thomson glibly and rather insultingly labeled them "Cage's Boys." Nor were they Cage's "disciples," as characterized by countless others.

Although Cage and Cunningham had begun using chance means for composing their works, the final results were still as fixed in their final form as a Beethoven symphony. Earle's ideas about open form changed all that. His *Twenty-Five Pages,* which he began writing in the spring of 1953 and completed while I was at Black Mountain, provides one or more (up to twenty-five) pianists with twenty-five loose pages of music, and then allows the performer to play any number of the pages in any order, spontaneously, in performance. The mathematical possibilities are nearly endless, guaranteeing that no performance is ever likely to repeat another. In *Twenty-Five Pages,* all the sound material is composed, but the final form—the organization of the given material—is left open. Open form. Cage declared upon seeing the score of *Twenty-Five Pages,* "It's an epoch-making piece!" and the concept of "open form" was to have an enormous impact on Cunningham's work in the years to follow.

In the summer of 1953, in *Dime-a-Dance,* Cunningham experimented playfully with having the sequence of the thirteen separate dances determined by chance: a member of the audience paid a dime, then picked a card from a deck of thirteen cards. Each card designated one of the dances to be performed. Hence the title of the dance. However, this indeterminate element was decided upon *after* the choreography was completed; it was not integral to it. Merce was simply allowing chance to determine the continuity of a collection of short, discrete dances that he'd made as classroom exercises for his advanced class. It wasn't until 1956, with *Galaxy,* that he attempted to make a dance in which "open form" was a central choreographic concern, and for this dance, fittingly, he chose music by Earle Brown. Another three years later, he tried it again in a limited way with *Rune* (1959), whose five parts of five minutes each could be performed in any order. In *Changes: Notes on Choreography* he wrote: "I had become interested in not having a fixed order to a piece. *Rune,* made at Connecticut College, reflected this for the first time." Apparently he'd forgotten about *Dime-a-Dance,* and, more importantly, *Galaxy.* But neither of these dances stayed in the repertory very long. Other open-form pieces, from extremely simple to relatively complex, followed: *Field Dances* and *Story* in 1963; *Paired* in 1964; *Scramble* in 1967; *Canfield* in 1969; *Signals* in 1970; *Landrover* and *TV Re-Run,* both in 1972, to name only those created during my years with the company. But *only* in *Field Dances* and *Paired* was the form *wholly* determined spontaneously in performance. In the others, the form could change, but with a very few exceptions, the change was determined before the performance and almost always rigorously rehearsed.

At the end of the long drive from New York to Black Mountain and after hours and hours of conversation, Earle felt that John's mistrust had finally been dispelled when John exclaimed, in one of his typical Americanisms: "You're the real McCoy!" The two of them immediately set about helping with Merce's performances by designing and printing the programs together. At first glance, members of the audience thought they had been given blank pieces of heavyweight paper. Closer inspection revealed that the information was there all right, but that it had been engraved without ink. White on white: the words pressed into the paper rather than printed on it. If that wasn't difficult enough to read, John and Earle provided other stumbling blocks for the audience to cope with. The program for the two evenings was printed in two parts, on two separate pieces of paper, which required matching at odd angles in order to make a whole. Once that was done, there was a code of letters and numbers that indicated dancers, composers, musicians, instruments, and choreographers: "x" preceding a number meant "choreographed by"; A through J listed composers; 1 through 11, names of the dancers; a through d, musicians; I through III, instruments. Here is an example: *SEPTET* x-1, 1,2,4,8,10,11 H, a, d, II. To find out what all that meant, the program had to be turned every which way—sideways, upside down, and on the diagonal—because each code was printed with a different "top" of the paper; if one didn't find it amusing, the program was guaranteed to madden and frustrate the most tolerant of audiences.

While John and Earle entertained themselves making the programs, Remy Charlip, who is listed on the program as "Entrepreneur and in charge of Spectacle," was dyeing and sewing huge sheets of cloth to make a backdrop or cyclorama of sorts. Remy was in charge of production, costume coordination, and design, in addition to his role as dancer. Costumes, of course, were minimal. No funds. Merce had brought boxes of old costumes. We all, including the dance students, contributed whatever leotards and tights we had, and proffered our street clothes as well. From this hodgepodge of garments Remy selected our apparel for all the dances: street clothes for *Collage;* wonderful, full-skirted, bare-shouldered nylon jersey dresses in different colors for the women, found in Merce's costume box, in *Banjo;* bright-colored wool leotards and black tights (new for the University of Illinois concert of *Suite by Chance*); practice clothes for *Dime-a-Dance;* and, hilarious flea-market stuff (a feather boa; a long, skinny crushed-velvet dress; crazy pantaloons) for *Ragtime Parade.* For *Septet* (and to set the record straight about this—it was Remy Charlip who did the original costumes for this dance, not Bob Rauschenberg, who, much later, redesigned them for the 1964 world tour), Remy chose sleeveless, square-necked, shirred-elastic cotton leotards for the women because by chance three women happened to have them. I was given white, Marianne turquoise, and Jo Anne lavender. Somehow Remy, who had his own kind of visual alchemy, managed to dress each dance so that it had its own specific character, different from the others.

On Sunday of that final week, Marianne sprained her ankle, badly. It swelled up like a pumpkin. There was no way she could dance on it, which is why the Black Mountain program listed seven dancers in *Septet* instead of six. With such short notice, and so many other dances to replace her in, two dancers shared her part in *Septet,* and another shirred-elastic cotton leotard had to be found. Where it was feasible, Merce omitted Marianne's part, and where it wasn't, Viola and/or Anita jumped in to replace her. Everyone was frantic. Marianne was devastated. Double pneumonia had caused her to miss the University of Illinois performance in March; now she'd miss out on the culmination of weeks and weeks of spring and summer rehearsals. Performance meant a lot to her. Endless rehearsing without any performances was, she remarked more than once, like masturbating; but she accepted her fate with good nature. At least she was able to perform the music for guitar that she'd composed for Paul Taylor's choreography.

The first part of Friday's program was made up of student work choreographed for Merce's composition class. Paul and Viola danced his *Mother and Son Duet* (from *Jack and the Bean Stalk*) for which Marianne had composed the music. (Paul later performed *Jack and the Bean Stalk* in New York with a specially commissioned score by Hy Gubernick and design by Bob Rauschenberg, and he lists it as his very first dance in the chronology of his works. But in his autobiography, *Private Domain,* he seems to have forgotten that he made the duet in Merce's composition class at Black Mountain in the summer of 1953.)

Remy transformed Black Mountain's dining hall into some semblance of a theater. His hand-dyed and -sewn back-cloth and wings shaped a stage space. Lights were ferreted out, hung, and focused. Dining-room chairs became audience seating. Except for the fact that there was no front curtain, the performance space in which Merce first presented his new repertory was made to resemble that of any conventional theater. During the last intermission of the second performance, the seating was rearranged in a large rectangle around the performance space and the first two movements of *Suite by Chance* were danced with the audience surrounding the dancers. (Without Marianne, we couldn't do the last two movements. Her part was long, complex, and technically difficult, and there simply wasn't time for someone else to learn it.)

In all, Merce presented nine dances and danced in every piece but one, *Ragtime Parade.* On both evenings he did two long solos, as well as brief solos within group works. The company appeared in three dances each evening. Three summer students joined the company in *Collage* and *Dime-a-Dance.* One couldn't easily forget the first performance of *Dime-a-Dance:* it involved audience participation and felt more like playing a game than presenting a dance, making it fun for audience and dancers alike. *Ragtime Parade,* a crazy, funny dance full of movement gags and non sequiturs and silliness, performed absolutely straight-faced in our flea-market attire, was a smashing success with the audience; they applauded, whistled, hooted, and begged for a repeat. In the wings we hopped up and down with pleasure, asking each other if we should do it again; then Merce appeared and settled the issue. He was adamant that we should *not* do an encore. He didn't trust us to perform it straight a second time. He said as much. He feared we might play it for the laughs we hadn't expected the first time around. It had been a delightful, surprising experience to hear the packed house explode in spontaneous laughter, so naturally we were disappointed not to reap those wonderful rewards all over again, and disappointed, too, to discover that Merce felt he couldn't trust us. Both *Ragtime* and *Banjo* were exhilarating dances to perform (and rehearse); truth be told, much of the pleasure derived from dancing to the joyous music of Satie and Gottschalk. Though we played *Ragtime* absolutely deadpan, in *Banjo,* a brisk and breezy romp to David's thunderous simile of forty-five banjos playing simultaneously, we were all smiles as we cavorted cakewalk/Cunningham-style in undisguised enjoyment. Both were unabashedly fun dances, entertainment pure and simple, that we loved doing, and that the audience—yes, the Black Mountain avant-garde community—loved seeing. In fact, the Black Mountain community was not a sophisticated dance audience and probably as a group had as much difficulty with the Cage, Feldman, and Wolff music they heard in our two performances, as did most of the dance audiences who saw Merce's company in the fifties, the sixties, and even the seventies. No matter—the whole community turned out to celebrate our modest success with a wine- and beer-drinking, dancing, living-it-up party after the second performance.

Merce needed only a beer or two to get happily tipsy. Amazing all of us, he took to the ballroom dance floor. His long body held erect, almost stiff in a curious kind of formality, he danced with the women in his company, with a student or two, and with some of the women faculty. A beer or two later, he turned clown and let loose alone in a wild and daffy soft-shoe caper that seemed to amuse and delight just about everyone—everyone but me, anyway. His behavior, so unexpected, so unlike any of the personae that he'd revealed so far, wasn't dignified! Silly, prudish goose that I was, I was unable to allow him a minute's respite from being the Noble and Exalted Teacher, Choreographer, Director, Artist. It was usually Marianne who gently taught me to grow up.

Three weeks of the hardest work I'd ever known were over; both Merce and John seemed pleased with us all. It was a time for rejoicing, for spinning fantasies about the future. John, in a crescendo of optimism, outdid us all with glorious pipe dreams about Broadway seasons, national and international tours. Merce, of course, wasn't present; had he been, he would not have joined in. Great expectations, if Merce had them, were private sentiments, not to be shared.

The day following our last performance at Black Mountain, the company—and suddenly there was a feeling that we were indeed a company—split into various small groups and wended its way north. Earle drove a carload to New York and continued on to Massachusetts to deposit me at my childhood dentist's office, where my impacted wisdom tooth had an appointment with oblivion. I was back in New York shortly after Labor Day. Merce was still away. I headed immediately to the Metropolitan Opera Ballet School, where Antony Tudor and Margaret Craske taught daily. Miss Craske greeted me with "How nice to see you! You came at just the proper time. How tall are you? Do you have a job? Well, how would you like to be a walk-on in *Sleeping Beauty* with the Sadler's Wells?" My answer to her last question was a breathless "Yes! I'd love to!" And then, on second thought, I asked, "Would it mean I'd have to miss classes?" Miss Craske chided me, quite seriously: "You'll learn much more as a walk-on with the Wells than you'd learn in the few classes you may have to miss."

Supering with the Wells had many bonuses. We were allowed to watch the company take class, to observe rehearsals of the whole repertory, to see couples—even Margot Fonteyn and Michael Somes—work together on their pas de deux. I was demolished with admiration. "These English girls are so lovely. And some very young, beautiful girls are already such exquisite dancers! It takes one's breath away." So did I rhapsodize in a letter to my mother. Our ballet mistress—a trim, coolly efficient, kind gentlewoman named Jill Gregory—was resolutely meticulous in the care of her supernumeraries; it was her job to teach us our parts and our court-lady demeanor, to see to it that we wore our costumes properly, and to give us careful instruction in makeup. But she did much more than that. Her calm, sensible way of coping with backstage theater life exemplified for me a code of behavior that in future I would try to emulate, and for this I shall always be indebted. Watching Fonteyn, hour after hour, day by day, I saw Jill Gregory's standards perfectly realized.

In 1953, Fonteyn was modest (almost to a fault), utterly disciplined, self-critical, generous, and never given to histrionics or temper tantrums backstage, and she seemed to be incapable of making a flashy or applause-catching gesture onstage. Her kindheartedness extended to stagehands, even to the lowliest super. Everyone in the Sadler's Wells with whom I came in contact—administrators, stage people, dancers—treated the walk-ons with exceptional consideration and respect, giving us every opportunity to learn as much as we had a desire to learn. One of my fellow court ladies was Sallie Wilson, later to become a principal with American Ballet Theatre and an eloquent dancer whose performances in Antony Tudor's *Pillar of Fire* and Agnes de Mille's *Fall River Legend* remain, for me, the definitive ones, unmatched in their depth and clarity by those who attempted those ballets before and after. Not even Nora Kaye, who created the original roles, could wrench such feeling from them and still dance the steps with such lucid purity. Sallie had supered with the Wells on its first triumphant New York season in 1949. She told me she had been unable to sleep for a week after seeing her first *Sleeping Beauty* with Fonteyn and Robert Helpmann.

The court ladies had been chosen from the tallest girls in the professional and advanced classes at the Met. As court ladies, we had the good fortune to be onstage for the Prologue, Aurora's sixteenth-birthday celebration, which includes the Rose Adagio, and the last act, with the divertissement and the wedding finale. In the beginning of the last act we actually got to dance. Partnered by men from the Sadler's Wells corps de ballet, we polonaised in a grand swoop around the stage and straight down center stage, looking out on the great glittering diamond horseshoe of the glamorous, seedy, beloved old Met. What intoxicating fun! I took part in nine performances of *The Sleeping Beauty* with Fonteyn, Violetta Elvin, and Nadia Nerina alternating in the title role.

Among the younger dancers, soloist Svetlana Beriosova and corps de ballet members Anya Linden and Valerie Taylor were my favorites and those from whom I learned the most. Except for Fonteyn and Elvin, all were at least one or two years younger than I. The experience of seeing them take class, rehearse, and perform was both inspirational and, if I dared to compare myself to them, terribly depressing. All except Fonteyn affected me this way. With her, comparison was unthinkable. When Fonteyn danced, I awaited her entrance with a sense of acute anticipation, a sensation close to pain—my heart pounding in my constricted chest, my eyes riveted on the spot where she would first appear. My whole being went out to her with a complicated mixture of emotions that added up to overwhelming adoration.

No dancer has ever made me care so terribly, moved me so deeply. More than once I had to turn my face upstage to hide tears and trembling lips. How amazed I was to discover veteran dancers in the company similarly moved. On the nights Fonteyn danced the role of Aurora, the company excelled; and no matter how many dozens of performances of *The Sleeping Beauty* they'd danced or seen, no matter how much the ballet may have bored them (and it did), when Fonteyn danced, all eyes were on her, filled with more than admiration, just as mine were.

As Richard Buckle has written, Fonteyn possessed a spiritual technique as opposed to a physical one. Simplicity, purity, being one with the music and the movement, graced with the humility to let the dancing speak through her—this was the Fonteyn of 1953 whom I idolized, who could move me to the depths of my being, whose dancing of the spirit has never been surpassed. When Fonteyn came back behind the curtain, she was greeted with more applause from the starry-eyed walk-ons and the dozen or so wing-watchers. After the last bow of the final performance I rushed to change clothes and remove makeup in order to join my parents and throngs of Fonteyn fans outside the stage door on Fortieth Street for one more glimpse of the woman who'd given me a new vision of what dancing could be.

The morning after my last performance in *Sleeping Beauty*, Merce held his first rehearsal since we'd left Black Mountain. For the four weeks that the Sadler's Wells was in residence, the old Metropolitan Opera House— between Thirty-ninth and Fortieth streets—was where I wanted to be. Fortunately there had been no schedule conflicts, since Merce had spent September searching for and finally finding a studio space of his own, and then getting it painted, mirrors hung, a piano installed, and dressing rooms arranged. The new studio, on the second floor at 224 West Fourth Street in Sheridan Square, consisted of one not very large room with an alcove that, by hanging up yards of gray corduroy, became three tiny dressing rooms— women's, men's, Merce's, respectively: tiny, tinier, tiniest, except that Merce's did have a window looking out on Sheridan Square. The dressing rooms were so cramped that when the women bent over to put on their tights, they'd often bump bottoms with the men on the other side of the curtain, and of course, every word spoken was audible to all.

We were happy to be back to work, full of anticipation and eager to believe rumors about a fall dance concert, possibly even a real season at the Ziegfeld Theatre in November. There were other exciting rumors: a music concert of works by Brown, Cage, Feldman, and Wolff, etc., at the Museum of Modern Art; a grand tour of the Package Festival—music and dance concerts, lectures on Artaud, master classes, panel discussions—as concocted by John, M. C. Richards, David Tudor, Earle, and me on that frolicking journey home from the University of Illinois the previous spring. Perhaps the concept was a bit ahead of its time. "You may choose your own schedule of events for a three, two or one day festival of the contemporary arts. For further information write to Package Festival c/o John Cage 326 Monroe Street New York City 2 N.Y.," read John's elegantly designed yet simple brochure, printed on one sheet of newsprint-weight paper, cleverly folded. The artists involved were John Cage, Merce Cunningham and Dance Company, M. C. Richards, and David Tudor. M.C. offered two lectures: "Artaud and New Theatre" and "Poetry: Lecture and Reading." David would present a Recital of Contemporary Music for Piano. John offered both a Recital of Music for Prepared Piano and an Illustrated Lecture on Contemporary Music. Together, John and David would present a Performance of Music for Magnetic Tape. Merce offered a Program of Dance as well as a Master Class in Dance. A Panel Discussion was offered by all. Nothing ever came of the plans for the Ziegfeld or the concert at MoMA, just as nothing ever came of the Package Festival, despite much letter-writing, brochure-mailing, and stamp-licking.

The one date that was definite was kept secret—only Merce knew about it. His company learned about it by reading the *New York Times,* which announced that the Brooklyn Academy of Music would present "Prominent soloists in contemporary dance, many of them with their companies and assisting artists." On Wednesday, January 20, Merce Cunningham was to be the prominent soloist. Since he hadn't told us anything about it, none of us dared ask whether it was to be a solo or a company performance. Shortly after we began rehearsals in the new studio, John held a company meeting to inform us that tentative plans were being made for a season between Christmas and New Year's Eve at the Theatre de Lys, a tiny theater on Christopher Street in the West Village, and that, yes, the company would perform with Merce in Brooklyn.

This was the first time that it became uncomfortably obvious to me that Merce couldn't (or didn't want to) communicate with his company about future plans. Every so often over the years he tried, but he never could make a go of it. This personality trait of his has always perplexed me and any number of other people who have worked with him. Did we threaten him? Make him feel trapped, vulnerable, insecure, afraid? I've never been sure. What troubled me, when I let myself think about it, was the possibility that his attitude was a manifestation of a lack of respect for us. I don't know. It was an unfortunate predicament. Merce needed a group of dancers to realize his choreography, yet he didn't want to assume any directorial responsibility for the day-to-day functioning of these dancers and at that time he hadn't the financial resources for administrative personnel. Most days, I'm sure he would have been content never to set eyes on any of his dancers outside the rehearsal room and the stage. Perhaps his antisocial behavior was a strong reaction to his five-year experience with Martha Graham, who, as choreographer and director of her company, was notorious for meddling in the private lives of her dancers; her example probably induced Merce to reject any shred of an authoritarian relationship with his own company members. Though many choreographers seem to thrive on such role-playing, Merce, understandably, did not want to become a father figure, hero, spiritual advisor, psychiatrist, or surrogate lover to his dancers. Nor should he have to have been. Yet, I think he felt (and sometimes he was justified in his feeling) that all these roles, from one company member or another, might be demanded of him.

John went to the other extreme: he was open, frank, ready to reveal all his most optimistic utopian schemes and dreams, willing to be a friend to any who sought him out. He enjoyed being a guru, or just a playmate at chess, Scrabble, word games, or cards. Most important, he was able to talk to us as a company, and usually he treated us as adults. If Merce attended John's meetings with us, he'd hover in the background, all but ignoring the proceedings, seeming to be totally preoccupied as he scribbled in his notebook. But he was articulate enough about work at rehearsals. And that October, he let us know that there was an enormous amount to be accomplished between then and the end of December. The repertory for the Theater de Lys season would include: the nine dances we had done at Black Mountain, plus *Sixteen Dances for Soloist and Company of Three;* three of Merce's older solos—*Totem Ancestor* (1942), *Root of an Unfocus* (1944), and *Two Step* (1949); a trio and a duet he'd choreographed in Paris in 1949; and a new work called *Fragments* for full company, with music by Pierre Boulez.

After the departure of the Sadler's Wells Ballet, the Met seemed a quiet and unexciting place. Although I adored ballet classes with Miss Craske and Mr. Tudor and continued taking one, two, and sometimes three a day, my focus swiftly shifted downtown. There was so much new choreography to learn and so much I wanted to improve in my parts in the Black Mountain repertory. And I would be learning *Amores,* a brief duet Merce had made for himself and Tanaquil LeClercq, the archetypical Balanchine dancer (and one of Mr. B.'s several wives) who danced with New York City Ballet from 1946 to 1956, when she contracted poliomyelitis and was forced to retire at the age of twenty-seven. The duet was first performed in Paris at the Théâtre du Vieux-Colombier in simple black-and-white practice clothes to *Amores I* and *IV*, music for prepared piano by Cage, part of a suite for percussion that Cage had written in 1943. "If you have three days to make a duet (this happened once in Paris with Tanaquil LeClercq), do you worry about ideas, or do you make a dance involving two people, a man and a woman?"[1] Merce wrote in *Changes*. "The work is an attempt to express in combination the erotic and the tranquil, two of the permanent emotions of Indian tradition,"[2] wrote Cage about the music. Erotic and tranquil—so many of Merce's man-woman duets that I performed with him seem to embody these qualities. Certainly, the duet in *Septet*, the first he made specifically for the two of us, could be so described.

Typically, though the rehearsal workload was great, Merce still wanted to choreograph something new. It's making new work that intrigues him, that seems to sustain his unswerving interest in dance. *Fragments* was just what the title implies. Structured in three parts, the middle one in silence, it consisted of brief fragments of movement phrases tossed haphazardly into the arena like small firecrackers—the kind that fizz and the kind that pop. I remember floor work, falls, big skips and leaps, no unison passages at all. It was a dance that felt both spare and spartan, yet curiously busy. Each one of us (the dance was for seven dancers, including Merce) had many entrances and exits with individual movement material—like assigned tasks—to perform. Though we often danced at the same time, I felt unrelated to any other dancer in the space, cut off from everyone and everything, a bit like one of seven molecules bouncing around in a void. "The sounds (*Deux Études* by Boulez) and sights of this dance occur in the contemporary work of magnetic tape, fables of science, and atomic research. The silence of the middle part marks the extremity of the dance's contrasts." Fables of science and atomic research? This program note, like the one for *Septet*, did not appear until our West Coast concert tour in 1955, and it struck me then, as it does now, as funny: that is, both odd and laughable. Remy Charlip dressed us in elasticized cotton leotards, each with a different neckline, in somber shades of gray. *Fragments* may have been a serviceable dance, but, I suspect, it wasn't a particularly distinguished one; it stayed in the repertory for about two years.

Scheduling rehearsals became a problem: gone was that brief Black Mountain luxury of being dancers twenty-four hours a day. Merce couldn't afford to pay us, of course, so among us we held a crazy assortment of jobs. Working as a spy for Chock Full o' Nuts was probably the nuttiest (forgive the pun), but this was indeed how Jo Anne Melsher was employed. She was paid to check out the caliber of the service at Chock Full o' Nuts quick-lunch counters around town. It meant ordering food and eating it in four or five locations around Manhattan from 11:30 a.m. to 2:30 p.m. five days a week with much getting around by foot, bus, or subway, and, in Jo Anne's case, a constant battle with weight gain. What an incongruous job for a dancer! Just eighteen, with a High School of Performing Arts diploma, she could find nothing better. None of us wanted night rehearsals, but they were inevitable. We'd start with an hour-and-a-half class and then rehearse as long as we could last. Merce always knew when it was ten o'clock. That's when the giggling began, and the mistakes. The silly hour, we called it, when fatigue in various guises betrayed everyone and Merce knew it was best to stop.

Rehearsals were free from judgment and criticism. There was a working atmosphere that gave us freedom to err, to find our own way. There was never any personal pressure put on us. Merce gave us our steps, clearly articulated and phrased, unembellished. He moved at a considerate pace in those first years. He accepted our inexperience, and built it into his teaching methods and rehearsal procedures. He set the example. He never marked the dances then—never—so we didn't, either. Over and over again we danced them full-out, pushing beyond anything we thought our-selves capable of. He was developing stamina, testing our resiliency, because he had to build not only a repertory but dancers to perform it, and he had an uncanny sense of how that should be done.

Bob Rauschenberg began coming to rehearsals to take photographs of the company at work. He developed and printed the photos himself, and they were used—pasted on hand-lettered cardboard posters designed and executed by Remy Charlip—to advertise the Theater de Lys season. The posters appeared in the windows of Village drugstores, bookshops, art gal-leries, and clothing emporiums just as my mother's recital posters did in Fitchburg, Massachusetts. No slick printed flyers slapped up by the hun-dreds on vacant walls and lampposts in those years. Bob's photographs were poorly printed on inexpensive paper and slightly blurry. They caught the dancers off-center, in motion, touchingly vulnerable, the expressions on our faces a mingling of intensity and innocence. A dozen years later that kind of innocence, so perishable, was gone. Bob captured that ephemeral virginality with his camera and preserved it on film, and somewhere in the process I think he fell in love with the company. In the immediacy of the dancing (as opposed to painting), in the physicality and discipline it required, and in the familial spirit of our work atmosphere, he saw something he wanted to be a part of. He says he was always stagestruck, but Merce and John's brand of theater struck a special chord and loosed vibrations that powerfully affected his life and the life of the company for the next eleven years.

Rauschenberg wasn't at Black Mountain in the summer of '53 when Merce's company was born. His history with the company had begun at the college the previous summer, when he met Cage and participated in Cage's collaborative Event/Happening/theater piece. Theirs was by no means a one-sided relationship. Rauschenberg made as strong an impression on Cage as Cage had made on him, despite their thirteen-year age difference. The mainspring of influence vibrated back and forth between them. When Rauschenberg said, "I'm trying to be unfamiliar with what I'm doing," he was on common ground with Cage. However, while Rauschenberg accepted accident, adopting a permissive aesthetic that let the world into his work, Cage chose chance.

Earle and I had first met Bob earlier that year on one of those mysterious excursions in which Ray Johnson (Cage's painter friend and next-door neighbor in the Bozza Mansion) delighted. Ray arrived at our door one sunny Sunday morning and lured us out for a leisurely walk downtown to the Battery. As far as we knew, he was taking us on another of his footpath jaunts to show us the scenic wonders of his *ville trouvée,* and he gave no hint of our destination until we found ourselves on Fulton Street staring up at the rooftop of an ancient derelict building and Ray began bawling, "Bob Rauschenberg!" in a voice loud enough to stir the dead. After a dozen or more calls, the bolts were thrown on the door at street level and a fellow, who looked like my idea of a bookish, diffident male librarian, peered out at us. Ray made very formal introductions and then we all climbed the many dark, narrow wooden stairs to the sound of boards creaking underfoot. Eventually we arrived, out of breath, in Rauschenberg's newly acquired studio. At last: a place that met my most romantic, storybook conception of an artist's garret! It could have been a stage set for Ashton's *The Two Pigeons* ballet: plain wide-board plank floor, partially whitewashed brick walls, dark wooden beams jutting skyward to support a steeply sloped cathedral roof. Canvases were stacked neatly against one wall, their surfaces hidden from view. On another wall, a horizontal beam displayed a host of small treasures and mementos; above and below were drawings and sketches, framed and unframed. At the street end of the loft was a curious sort of "island," a slightly raised wooden platform, made out of salvaged boxes from the nearby fish market, which served as Bob's domestic living space—as bed, table, bench, desk, or whatever need he might have for it.

In the back, through a kind of sky-door, one could see an eerily green-lit pinnacle, the tip of a Wall Street skyscraper. This green scepter of the financial world hovering over his lodgings amused Bob. He subsisted on pennies a day; what money he had went to purchase paints and supplies and the ill-stretched cloth (he rarely had good canvas or decent wood for stretching it) that he used and reused and used again in a whirlwind fury of endeavor, painting over earlier pictures as some new idea consumed his attention and obliterated any concern for the immediate past.

From the very beginning I was slightly uneasy around Bob. There seemed to be a curious contradiction in his personality: he was sensitive, gentle, and wildly generous, but he was also tough, impassioned, and wildly competitive. By nature a non-competer, I was unable to see how constructively competition worked for him: presenting Bob with a little competition is like throwing gasoline on a steady flame. It fires his energy, his resolve, his ingenuity, and he races into the situation not just to win but to play, to have fun. At the age of seventy-eight, answering an interviewer's question, "Didn't you want to be a great American artist?" he responded: "Not particularly, I just didn't want any other artist to be better than I was."[3]

His physical appearance belied his personality. Though Rauschenberg was then actually six feet tall, his usual stoop-shouldered posture gave the impression of a man much shorter. In 1953 he was thin and reedy, he wore his short hair plastered down from a side part revealing an extremely high, broad forehead; and his odd metal-rimmed glasses (Navy issue) gave a rather prim, reticent appearance to his face. It was his hands that gave him away. Rauschenberg's hands fascinated me: almost awkward in repose, they were eloquent, masterful hands, agile and cunning as a cat whether hammering a nail, opening a can of chili, clutching a double Jack Daniel's, gripping a paintbrush, or leafing through a magazine. They're all fingers—extremely long, slender, bony fingers—and thumbs, widely flaring double-jointed thumbs bespeaking (truthfully) his outrageously generous nature. Rauschenberg's hands appeared to me to be a graphic expression of his personality—grappler and gentleman, genius and congenial contender who set about his life as though it were a medieval tournament to be fought and won, heroically.

That autumn, Rauschenberg was having his second New York exhibition. The first, in 1951, was a one-man show at Betty Parson's gallery. His second was to be at the Stable Gallery, which was then on Seventh Avenue and Fifty-eighth Street. Eleanor Ward ran the gallery; she'd invited Cy Twombly (with whom Bob had gone to Europe in the fall of 1952) to show his recent paintings, and Twombly had introduced her to Rauschenberg.

She saw his work, became intrigued by what she saw, and an exhibition of both artists' work resulted. Earle helped Bob and Cy move their paintings and Bob's large, cumbersome sculptures to the gallery. (Earle's station wagon was still the only useful automobile in our group.)

The show was a shocker: black paintings—flat black and glossy black paint splattered and stroked and dripped across yesterday's newspapers collaged onto unstretched canvas stapled to rough wood supports; plain white paintings—almost completely devoid of texture, squares and rectangles in singles or in groups; a dirt painting that in time sprouted tiny green shoots; and peculiar sculptures of rock and rope and wood. Artists, art critics, and viewing public alike were flabbergasted, outraged, or mystified—often all three. Nothing sold: at least nothing sold through the gallery. On the day the show came down, a few of Bob's friends bought paintings, but unfortunately for Bob, his friends were as poor as he was. When we asked the prices, Bob's answer was "I'll take whatever you have in your pocket." I think Morty Feldman had seven dollars. Earle had a rebate check from the phone company—our twenty-five-dollar deposit plus interest, a total of $26.30—which had come in that day's mail. When it came to selecting a painting, we had to consider our $9' \times 9'$ living room, so we couldn't choose any of the large or paneled pieces. Earle especially liked one of the black oil-and-newsprint-on-canvas collage paintings, which was approximately $72'' \times 53''$, but I had a problem with a shiny black rectangle rising up in the middle of the picture. "It keeps looking like a door to me," I apologized stubbornly, despite my embarrassment. Immediately Bob took the painting off the wall, turned it on its side, and said, "How's that?" "You don't mind?" I asked incredulously. He said he didn't. So the painting was purchased for twenty-six dollars and thirty cents and has hung sideways ever since. (Except in much later years when it was exhibited publicly. Its final home will be the San Francisco Museum of Modern Art.) Bob gave several paintings away to friends—to David Tudor, to Merce and John, probably to others as well.

In our first year in New York, Earle and I had met many artists, made many friends. Almost everyone we knew was poor, some poorer than others—it was only a matter of degree. The grants machines hadn't churned into being yet. Artists survived without the government and corporate funding, which began to flourish in the seventies and eighties. Tenacity and the willingness to work for work's sake—that's what kept artists alive, that and the undercurrent of excitement and enthusiasm shared with fellow artists and friends. No one expected financial support from any quarter; it was peer support that counted, and that was plentiful. We had

Merce, 1969

LEFT: *Suite for Five*
BELOW: *Antic Meet*

LEFT: *Untitled Solo*
BELOW: *Suite for Five*

RIGHT : *How to Pass,*
Kick, Fall and Run
BELOW : *Story*

Canfield

ABOVE: *Walkaround Time*
BELOW: *How to Pass, Kick, Fall and Run.*
Left to right: Valda Setterfield, Sandra Neels, me, Merce

ABOVE: *How to Pass, Kick, Fall and Run:* Merce . . .
BELOW: and me with Chase Robinson

LEFT: *Crises*
BELOW: Merce with me,
Bill Davis, and Steve
Paxton in *Story*

RIGHT: *Tread*
BELOW: *Place*

Gambit for Dancers and Orchestra (*Suite for Five* costumes)

"Extended Moment" duet from *Suite for Five*

With Jeff Slayton in *Canfield*

dozens of ways of entertaining ourselves while spending little cash. Movies were cheap, and the art cinema was thriving in numerous theaters all over town. Most of us were movie addicts, but especially Nicola Cernovich, who was known to spend eight hours or more on Forty-second Street seeing one double bill after another.

Nick had been a true Black Mountain-eer, which is to say that he was a full-time student and deeply involved in the inner workings of the college and its politics. When the board of directors tried to have M. C. Richards fired, Nick led a student protest that got her reinstated. In June 1951, the college presented a play he'd written after the Noh tradition, and it was published in the first issue of the *Black Mountain Review.* Like Bob Rauschenberg, Nick first met Cage and Cunningham and David Tudor at Black Mountain. Via Cambridge and Boston, he eventually moved to New York and into a loft he shared with Remy Charlip and Norman Solomon.

Nick and Remy and Norman. What a threesome! In the years when they seemed inseparable I called them "The Brothers K" (Karamazov); Earle called them "The Mad Russians." Nick, a six-foot-plus Serbo-Croatian (not Russian at all) from the Midwest, was well-read and caustically witty, and he had a bitter brilliance that frightened me. His interest in things Oriental led him to find work at Orientalia Bookshop, and he was the only one of the three who was regularly employed. There was a story that Norman, the shortest Brother, had been declared 75 percent insane by the United States Army. All that really meant, at least to him, was that he was able to collect the maximum veteran's disability allowance. Not a bad stipend for an artist at a time when few painters sold their work. No doubt the Battle of the Bulge did leave its scars—Norman occasionally behaved in a peculiar fashion—but I never thought of him as much more insane than any of the rest of us. He was a student and disciple of Franz Kline; he painted in black and white, took black-and-white photographs, adored beautiful women, and at one time lived in a loft he painted white—white floor, white walls, white window panes, white ceiling. Living there, he wore only white, ate only white. I never knew if he was an Erik Satie copycat or had arrived at this all-white fixation on his own. I don't think he was Russian, either.

Remy Charlip was. At least, his parents or his parents' parents had come from Russia. Born and raised in Brooklyn, Remy walked the Village streets with his bouncy, lopsided lilting gait, his eyes twinkling, with a smile on his lips, and every third person he passed would greet him. He seemed to know everyone and everyone seemed to love him. Remy had been an art student at Cooper Union. He first saw Merce dance in January 1949 in a performance of Merce's ballet *The Seasons* with the New York

City Ballet at City Center. Through Lou Harrison, a mutual friend, Remy met Merce and John that same year. In December 1949, Remy again saw Merce dance at the City Center, this time performing a solo, *Two Step*, to Satie. Remy remembers that when Merce leapt onstage, from upstage left on the diagonal into center stage, the entire audience gasped. Remy was enthralled and soon found his way to the studio on lower Fifth Avenue where Merce was teaching. By the fall of 1950, he was performing Merce's choreography and beginning to design costumes and properties, to make masks, and to perform any task of an artistic nature that needed doing. Merce and John became substitute family and had an almost parental authority for Remy, though I'm not sure they ever realized just how deeply they had influenced him, or how important they were in his life.

Remy, Nick, and Norman shared an enormous floor-through loft at 30 Suffolk Street on the Lower East Side. A doll factory before they moved in, it continued to offer up sawdust and doll body parts for most of the years they lived there. On the ground floor of their building someone raised chickens, commercially, and coincidentally raised vermin and bad, bad smells, both of which made their way upward to "The Mad Russians" on the top floor, where windows on three sides looked out on a wonderful Lower Manhattan rooftop panorama. The windows were a joy in summer but permitted a cruel onslaught of chilling winds the rest of the year. There was no heat. In the freezing winter months the guys camped in a peculiar Arabian Nights tentlike structure they rigged up in the middle of the space. Inside were mattresses and a lethal little stove that threatened asphyxiation by fumes as well as immolation by flame. Their clothing was usually as exotic as their living quarters. They presaged the layered look, the army-navy surplus look, and a number of other looks by twenty years. Oversized ankle-length army-surplus coats, looking more like those worn by peasants from the Russian steppes than GI issue, sported custom-made pockets that opened into cavernous inner linings ready to receive cart-loads of produce from local grocery stores. Only Remy had the guts and fearless fingers to actually take the stuff, but Nick and Norman hid it in their coats and the rest of us, asking no questions, were felonious accomplices since we ate the filched food at gatherings in one person's loft or another's flat, everyone sharing whatever they had brought. We felt guilty, but none of us ever said no to two-inch slabs of sirloin steak! Sometimes the three of them would arrive at 11 Cornelia Street (as we were one of the few who had heat and hot water) bearing edible gifts of dubious origin, and take turns using our bathtub and shower and all the towels in the place. Our bathtub was also commandeered by Rauschenberg to develop his blueprints. I served as model for some of the blueprints used in store windows. Bob would spread out the blueprint paper on our living-room floor. I'd lie on it in whatever position he selected while he used a sun lamp to trace the image he wanted. We also did some blueprints with leaves and grasses and nature objects, without any human model.

We spent many an evening at the movies—Merce and John, M.C. and David, Earle and I, Remy, Nick, and Norman, and any number of others. In July and August we went to escape the furnace blasts of New York's summer heat. In winter we went even more often to escape the miserable cold of unheated living quarters. Woolen hats pulled over ears and down to the bridges of their noses, Remy, Nick, and Norman would arrive breathless, the winds whipping their long coattails and mufflers, and they'd dance around Merce and John, laughing, hugging, and kissing everyone as we fled into the dark, comforting warmth of the movie house. With a group that large, we usually met outside and went in together—we bought fewer tickets that way, and "The Brothers K" usually managed to slip past the ticket-taker gratis. In the Vietnam sixties there was much talk about "beating the system," operating underground. Painters, composers, poets, and dancers in the early fifties didn't talk about it, they simply did it.

We spent other cold evenings together, too. Everyone was interested in food, and, by extension, cooking; those who weren't, learned to be. Some nights we'd crowd into M.C. and David's sixth-floor walk-up on East Fourth Street off Third Avenue. M.C. would cook kasha and bake whole-grain bread, and after dinner David would sometimes play—Stefan Wolpe, Pierre Boulez, Morton Feldman, John Cage, and Earle Brown. But what many of us loved best was when he'd open the thick green book of *What the Whole World Loves to Play* (the *Dime-a-Dance* musical resource book) and entertain himself and us with the musical literature of the nineteenth century. David took a witty delight in performing this music—cigarette between his lips, chain-smoking, chortling his amusement at certain passages—never finishing one work before starting the next.

Once a week for a month or two one winter, we gathered for dinner at 12 East Seventeenth Street in Merce's top-floor loft. A five-pound T-bone steak, brazenly dropped into the caverns of Remy's greatcoat, fed us all. Merce and John cooked, with everyone contributing something and crowding into the little cubicle that served as kitchen (and shower room). Remy's idea that Merce bill his company as "The World's Best-Fed Dance Company" was no joke, despite the poverty we all shared. The weekly gathering had been arranged so that M. C. Richards could read aloud her in-progress translation of Artaud's *Theatre of Cruelty*. After dinner, she would sit on Merce's bed, knees drawn up, back propped against the wall, and the rest of us would sprawl around her. James Leo Herlihy joined us those evenings. While M.C. read, he sat on a small stool, hunched over the sweater he was knitting, looking up every so often to interrupt M.C. with an incisive question. Herlihy, who had recently moved to New York, was another Black Mountain alumnus and devoted student of M.C.'s. In the following years he wrote plays and novels that became Hollywood motion pictures and/or Broadway plays (*Blue Denim, All Fall Down,* and *Midnight Cowboy*), attaining a kind of popular success that few of his Black Mountain peers or teachers achieved. He was exceedingly bright and perceptive, and M.C. welcomed his questions; in fact, she welcomed everyone's questions, thoughts, and criticisms pertaining to her translation of Artaud, and she encouraged a free-for-all discussion after reading each chapter. My French was not strong enough to participate in these exchanges and my provincial New England childhood and college life had ill prepared me for the shock of Artaud's ideas. We'd seen the Living Theatre, but it was still in its formative years in the early fifties, and though its production of Pirandello's *Six Characters in Search of an Author* in a loft theater at 100th Street and Broadway had a stunning set by Julian Beck and disturbingly original direction by Judith Malina, the Living Theatre was still a long way from Artaud.

Merce rarely joined in the Artaud discussions. In fact, I'm not at all sure he even listened. He usually puttered about his loft, busying himself with countless trips to the small potbellied stove, feeding it milk cartons and paper refuse, and bit by bit allocating the precious sticks of wood we'd brought—gathered on the streets along our way—as offerings. Merce lived for many years on the south side of Seventeenth Street between Fifth Avenue and Union Square. I can't remember a time when the hall lights weren't burned out, and in winter, arriving at Merce's building, we'd leave the cold street only to enter another, bitter, more penetrating cold as we'd grope up the stairways, feeling our way along the icy walls. The roof leaked in the rainy season. The place was a furnace in summer. But for at least on that one day in spring when the trees burst into feathery green in Union Square, it wasn't a bad place to live. The building housed a printing press, and, one floor below Merce, Grete Sultan, pianist extraordinaire, her mother (both were refugees from Nazi Germany), and Merce's cat, who'd moved downstairs for the loving attention and abundant food the two gentle ladies lavished upon it. The cat was no vegetarian and he had made that fact known. One day, fed only peas from table leftovers, he took one sniff, then disappeared. Returning a few minutes later, he deposited a mouse neatly on his plate beside the peas. Merce told that story—a per-petual favorite—at least once a week for months on end.

The subject of starting a community was an issue that involved any number of dinner gatherings. It all began with a phone call to John, Merce, M.C., and David from Paul Williams at Black Mountain. More than once Paul had bailed the school out of financial disaster; and he'd come to John's aid by supporting John's tape-music project when no one else would. Black Mountain was in its death throes. Paul wondered if it could be saved. Would the New Yorkers come back as permanent faculty? If not, did they think he should continue to help Black Mountain with financial and moral support, or should he try to start an artists' community else-where, and if he did, would they participate, and if they would, where should it be located? Finding out how each one of us honestly felt about these questions involved much discussion and an attempt to visualize our-selves as a viable community. Merce was quieter than usual; the few thoughts he expressed on the subject were judiciously negative: he firmly believed that a dance studio and a serious company could not function in the country, and commuting for him would be wasteful of his time and energy. But no one really paid any attention to his lack of enthusiasm. Despite M.C.'s disillusionment with Black Mountain, she was willing, even eager, to try again with a group of committed artists, and David appeared to be willing to go along with her. John, gazing ahead into a utopian dream of his own making, was keen to try it. Earle and I were included in these talks, and we were mildly interested but a bit wary, too. My real commitment now was to dancing with Merce, not to communal liv-ing, so Merce's decision would be crucial to us. There was general agree-ment that no one wanted to be at Black Mountain year-round, and that any community should be located within easy driving distance of New York City. Further than that, no one committed him- or herself, and nothing was decided for months, but the discussions went on week after week, and a tiny advertisement appeared in the pages of Merce's Theater de Lys sea-son program that read: WANTED: about 100 acres, hilly, mostly wooded, with stream or lake and house, up to 50 miles N.Y.C. Call Williams, WA6-4744.

I was once again dancing at least five or six hours a day—two classes at the Met, plus class and rehearsal with Merce. In November, Merce added Saturday and Sunday rehearsals. No one complained or wanted to. Those of us who didn't have outside jobs—and I was one of the lucky ones who didn't, that fall—worked on publicity for the de Lys, typing releases for newspapers and magazines. Remy decided that what was needed was an article in *Dance Magazine,* so he wrote "Composing by Chance" and the magazine accepted it for its January issue, which was on the stands by the time the company opened at the Theater de Lys on December 29. In mid-November Merce got the flu, but it didn't keep him away from work except for one day, and that day we rehearsed ourselves. We rehearsed Thanksgiving Day, then a dozen or so people went to Merce's loft to address flyers for the season while John and M.C. and Nick made a glorious dinner. The Thanksgiving turkey—mammoth size—was a gift from Remy and the A&P. The design for the flyers was a gift from Remy, too, and everyone was delighted with them: they were 17″ × 5½″, on heavy, high-gloss colored paper (orange, green, yellow, turquoise, sea foam) with bold type and a clean, clear layout. Seeing the printed flyer was a sudden jarring confirmation of the reality that lay ahead; reading it made me weak in the legs and caused my innards to heave up against my diaphragm. For the month that followed, a horrible feeling of fright and near-paralysis alternated with happier, more positive emotions. Working really hard alleviated the stage fright, but when I was away from the studio, should my eye fall on a poster or newspaper advertisement or a sheaf of flyers, my panic would return. At Black Mountain classes, rehearsals and performances were in the same familiar space in the midst of an audience of people we saw and conversed with every day. There was a sense of wholeness about that experience, a sense that art and life were really one. But the Theater de Lys was alien territory: its stage proportions were radically different from our studio's proportions, the surface was unfamiliar and slightly treacherous, and the audience—for the most part—was that unknown enigmatic thing, the New York Audience, which holds nameless terrors for all performers from whatever discipline, of whatever nationality.

I felt our professional status even more when, on December 10, I signed my first dancers' Standard Artists Agreement, an AGMA (American Guild of Musical Artists) contract. "The DANCER shall be paid $87.50 per week for performance week and $47.00 for the first five rehearsal weeks . . ." We rehearsed for at least ten weeks before the season, but there was no way Merce and John could pay us union wages (or *any* wages) for that length of time, so our contract—one week of rehearsals, one week of performances—met the barest, most minimal union requirements and still allowed us to play the Theater de Lys, a union house. Once again Paul Williams appeared, like a benevolent genie, to provide the necessary funds. Without him the season could not have taken place. John took on the job of administrative director and fund-raiser, even going door-to-door to get advertisers for the program. He'd arrive in the middle of rehearsal, beaming, jubilant over the newest catch: Pantheon Books or Salabert Music Publishers or Tibor de Nagy Gallery. It was an elegant group of advertisers that John succeeded in enlisting. It included art galleries, bookstores, book publishers, music publishers, dancers, a couple of Village restaurants and specialty shops, and Morty Feldman, whose advertisement simply gave his name and phone number.

The flu went the rounds of the company. For a while David Tudor was sick, unable to play for our rehearsals, but by mid-December my letters to my parents were reassuring: "All goes well. We rehearse daily—work very hard—but things are going smoothly," but they also included words of warning: "Have no doubt you and [your students] will be *shocked* by the music for some of the dances. I don't think you'll have much trouble with the dancing itself—although you may be shocked there too. I've grown so accustomed to this kind of movement that it is no longer strange to me."

The stage for the Theater de Lys was minuscule. Merce's dances couldn't possibly be seen to advantage in such a cramped space, so it was decided to build an extension, a large apron jutting out into the house, which would give us more depth, even though it meant losing some of the three hundred seats. We had almost no rehearsal time in the theater and everyone was uneasy about the two different floors under our bare feet. Not only were the two surfaces unfamiliar, but the sense of solidity changed from backstage to front, and each floor resonated differently, too. On the day of opening night, I woke up with a stiff neck and an upset stomach, and spent the predawn hours throwing up or huddled shivering uncontrollably under the covers. Earle was more amused than worried; he was sure I was suffering from nothing more serious than a case of stage fright. That infuriated me! *I* blamed Simple Simon, the hamburger restaurant in Sheridan Square where the company often went after rehearsal. I'd never had stage fright of that sort before, not even as a college sophomore when I'd done the lead role in two versions of *Antigone* in a single day: Sophocles' at the matinee and Jean Anouilh's French adaptation in the evening. This *had* to be mild food poisoning! I would not accept any other explanation! By noon I rallied and made my way to the theater. Though my skin was ashen, my knees were weak, and I was thoroughly frightened, I was also angry at my body for letting me down, and this anger roused my determination to get through rehearsal and the performance without revealing my malady to Merce. For the next twenty years, I rarely performed without experiencing some degree of stage fright, but I was never again physically ill with it as I was, apparently, on the day that Merce's fledgling company made its New York debut in 1953.

The week flew by. I remember almost nothing. The essence of performing is its "now-ness"—no mind, no memory. Just that brief time when one has the chance to be whole, when seemingly disconnected threads of one's being are woven and intertwined into the complete present. No other. No past. No future. No mind as an entity distinct from the body. Certainly I've experienced memorable performances—but what made them memorable was extraneous to the dancing. And, unfortunately, there are all too many remembered performances—the ones I call "supermarket performances"—when one's mind and body are functioning, but separately, each on a different course, the mind preoccupied with dreary details as mundane as today's grocery list or as self-involved as a catalogue of criticisms of one's own dancing, while the body goes through the motions, executing the steps like a windup toy.

What I best remember about that week is sitting out in the house watching Merce rehearse his solos. Until then, he had always rehearsed them when the company was absent. *Two Step. Root of an Unfocus. Totem Ancestor. Collage. Solo Suite in Space and Time. Untitled Solo. Variations.* A solo in *Suite by Chance.* Plus the brief, hilarious solo in *Dime-a-Dance* called "The Eclectic," set to Beethoven's *Bagatelle* (opus 126, no. 4) which was a sendup of modern dance and dancers and a parody of current mannerisms. These solos encompassed an enormous range of physical and emotional expression. The early ones, *Totem Ancestor* (1942) and *Root of an Unfocus* (1944), appeared to be narratives—"telling" specific stories. *Untitled Solo* (1953), so powerful in its dramatic intensity, was not *about* something, it *was* that thing—raw, direct, immediate, in itself dynamically real. When Viola Farber, Paul Taylor, and I were reminiscing about the early days some twenty-seven years later, we all agreed that *Untitled Solo* was, of all Merce's solos, still our favorite. *Solo Suite in Space and Time* (1953) was just that, but no Cunningham solo is ever devoid of drama. *Two Step* was a tour de force of mercurial exuberance, breathtaking to watch and looking as if it was fun to do. I think *Variations* was an attempt to present basic academic ballet vocabulary in a new way, by reordering the rhythms and phrasing and continuity that one comes to expect in conventional ballet, but it never succeeded with me—it lacked the clarity of truly *classical* ballet, so the intentions of the dance were never satisfactorily realized. I quite agreed with Louis Horst, who wrote that *Variations* "was disappointing and seemed to have no place on a modern dance program. While it showed that Mr. Cunningham knows his ballet principles, it also showed that performance of a dance such as this should be left to some great ballet virtuoso."[4] The *Collage* solo, I read as a kind of medley of personae, contrarily heroic as it celebrated the ordinary and the commonplace: James Joyce's "H.C.E." in motion.

For Merce the de Lys season was a grueling labor of love: eight performances, including matinee and evening on both Saturday and Sunday. In addition to the six group works and our duet, *Amores,* Merce danced eight different solos, at least two at each performance, with each solo performed at least twice during the week's run. By the middle of the week he'd injured himself. He kept rubbing or feeling his foot and ankle in rehearsal, and he limped noticeably when he taught company class, but I saw no indication of any injury when he performed. Thinking about it now, reading over the program and realizing what fierce demands he'd made on himself, I was made acutely aware that the Theater de Lys season was very nearly a one-man show, with Merce onstage dancing nonstop from the moment the curtain rose at 8:40 p.m. until it fell at the end of each performance about two hours later. But he showed little pleasure, as I recall, and for most of that week he seemed depressed. On the last evening, when it was over, I saw him sitting motionless, alone in the men's dressing room after everyone else had cleared out; he looked dispirited and hollow-eyed. I asked if he was all right; his reply was direct and devastating: "My jump is gone. I'll never be able to jump again as I used to." He was thirty-four years old, and for him at that moment, this was a tragedy. It was his nimble-footed jump that had won him accolades in Martha Graham's company ("Dear March, come in!" in *Letter to the World*). It was his phenomenal bounding elevation when he leapt halfway across the City Center stage in *Two Step* that had made the audience gasp in amazement. Now he was convinced that he'd never jump like that again. Merce had been onstage at least 95 percent of the time in all eight performances of the de Lys season. For someone with such a voracious appetite for performing, an appetite that abated only slightly in the succeeding forty-plus years, the loss of any movement possibility would seem a calamity. And he was right about his jump. That special aeriality he'd become famous for did not return. But he didn't stop jumping; he found other ways, new accents, and different rhythms when choreographing for himself.

The 1953–54 season was neither a great success nor a dismal failure. We had full houses, even SRO houses at a few performances. With seats removed in order to enlarge the stage, the theater held fewer than three hundred people, not a very large house to fill. Our audiences were often enthusiastic. Artists made up the faithful regulars who attended more than one performance—Richard Lippold, Bill and Elaine de Kooning, Jack and Wally Tworkov and their two daughters, Esteban Vicente, and Paul and

Mimi Brach, to name only a few. Virgil Thomson came at least once, and a few musicians and composers came, prompted by curiosity about the musique concrète. Most of the dancers and choreographers who came—Katherine Litz, Merle Marsicano, Louise Lippold, Jean Erdman, Midi Garth, James Waring—were modern-dance experimentalists. Few from the Establishment Modern Dance (Graham, Humphrey, Weidman, Limón, Holm) attended, and equally few from the ballet world were seen in the audience, although Jerome Robbins was reported to have attended more than once. The Black Mountain College contingent came often.

Pre-performance publicity had been excellent, thanks to John's efforts and a lot of hard work by Remy and some of the other dancers. Both the *New York Times* and the *New York Herald Tribune* printed news releases that we sent out over a span of three or four weeks, but neither John Martin from the *Times* nor Walter Terry from the *Tribune* reviewed a single performance! Why? Was it callous indifference or calculated slight? I've never heard a satisfactory explanation for this negligence. John Cage had devoted three months—his entire time and energy—to producing this week of performances. He was stunned, disbelieving. Each day he would buy the papers. Each day there was nothing. Not a single mention. Merce was tight-lipped and silent; although he didn't admit it, I think he was keenly disappointed.

It was usual in the 1940s and '50s for modern dancer/choreographers to work a year to present their dances in concert for one evening or, at the most, two. With the exception of Martha Graham's company, which had Bethsabée de Rothschild's patronage, no modern-dance company could afford to attempt a weeklong season on or off Broadway, not even José Limón, whose company did give six performances that year, but on two successive weekends under the auspices of the Juilliard School in its theater at 120th Street. For the dance critics of New York's major daily newspapers to turn their backs on a week of performances of fifteen dances, nine of them new to New York, presented in an off-Broadway professional theater by a young choreographer whose work had been considered of sufficient interest to be presented by Ballet Society would be unheard-of today. It was preposterous then. The *New York Times,* especially, wields awesome power that tends to influence theater managers and bookers of tours in the States and abroad. The financial risks of a week's run in a New York theater are balanced against bookings that might be gained through coverage in New York's most prestigious newspapers, but as luck (or something more sinister?) would have it, Merce was denied this. For years afterward he had to prove himself in college auditoriums, in small towns and large in at least twenty states, and in a dozen or more countries around the world before

New York City gave him serious recognition in the major dailies. And with-out New York press, getting bookings was not easy. In fact, it was nearly impossible. Merce had no booking agent, no manager, not even a secretary to write letters. He and John did the work themselves, with some help from their friends. Eventually, in subsequent years, Walter Terry did write about Merce. John Martin did not. If Martin bore Merce a private grudge, and I'm convinced that he did, he never relinquished it and remained steadfast in his resolve never to review Merce from 1954 until he retired in 1962.

The specialized dance publications, with a very small readership, did take Merce seriously, and eventually, weeks after the season, reviews appeared in *Dance Observer, Dance News,* and *Dance Magazine.* General journals also considered the performances of sufficient interest to evalu-ate them critically: the *Christian Science Monitor,* and even *Newsweek,* printed comments. The season, after all, *was* controversial. In 1953 chance dances and musique concrète—whether or not aesthetically acceptable—were new and certainly newsworthy, even if the *Times* and the *Herald Tri-bune* failed to acknowledge them. The "official" publication reviewing modern dance in those years was *Dance Observer,* whose managing editor and principal reviewer was Louis Horst. Louis's was a formidable critical presence—not only visually, with his portly figure and lion's head of white hair, but audibly. Muttering and mumbling, loudly snorting and sniffling, he never failed to let it be known, to audience and performers alike, that he was there, passing judgment from his seat on the aisle. But whatever his personal preference, Louis was usually fair; he believed in the artist as a radical: "If he is an artist he is progressive and if he is progressive he must break with tradition."[5] Louis respected Merce's efforts (though he didn't always like the results) and assigned three reviewers—Robert Sabin, Nick Krevitsky, and himself (he came twice)—to cover the de Lys performances. Three separate, seriously considered reviews appeared in the February 1954 issue of *Dance Observer.*

Margaret Lloyd, dance critic for the *Christian Science Monitor,* thought the season important enough to make the trip from Boston to New York to see several programs. For her, as for many people in Merce's audiences throughout his life, "It is the music that complicates things, particularly when it goes into the field of electronics or magnetic tape recording."[6] The *Musical Courier* writer Rosalyn Krokover admitted in print that she had not gone to see the company herself but had sent "a trusted and knowl-edgeable substitute" who was never named, nor was it revealed in her "review" what music had been heard or which choreography had been seen! Despite this, Miss Krokover still had the audacity to write, and *Musi-*

cal Courier to print: "It is very doubtful if anything permanent will emerge from [musique concrète], just as it is equally doubtful if the Cunningham choreography and methodology will have anything valid to offer."[7] Admittedly, this view was also held by many who *did* attend performances. Anatole Chujoy in *Dance News* was not enthusiastic: "To us," he wrote, " 'choreography by chance' and 'music for magnetic tape' are private jokes, improvisatory in nature and exceedingly boring when presented in a public performance."[8] Improvisatory? Neither Merce's choreography nor musique concrète is "improvisatory" in *any* way. But this was a common misconception for decades. *Dance Magazine* also got it wrong: "According to the tenets of chance composition, this method is supposed to disclose the spontaneity missing in conventionally composed works and to establish a freedom from all but the most basic rhythmic requirements."[9] But it was not spontaneity that Cunningham and Cage were seeking through chance means; it was an attempt to free their imaginations from their own clichés, to go beyond their own likes and dislikes.

Newsweek ignored both the choreography and the dancing. Their article discussed only the musique concrète, reporting that to the layman's ear most of the music for magnetic tape sounded "pretty strange" and likened Christian Wolff's music for *Suite by Chance* to Dennis the Menace let loose with an amateur shortwave set.[10] Few who read *Newsweek* had heard the name Merce Cunningham, but John Cage had made a national name for himself as early as 1943 when a program of his percussion music that he conducted at the Museum of Modern Art had garnered much publicity, including several pages in *Life* magazine (March 15, 1943) and an article in *Time* magazine (February 22, 1943). Even though the de Lys season was a dance event, *Newsweek* would have the world believe it was a week of deranged music. Little attempt was made to understand the Cage/Cunningham ideas. The work was judged by the cultural biases of the day, by the conventional standards and artistic values that were familiar. Naturally, it was found wanting.

There were two critics, however, who, despite personal reservations about particular works seen and heard, revealed an openmindedness not common to their trade in those years. Robert Sabin, in *Dance Observer*, wrote: "This [chance] method [of choreography] . . . represents a bold and promising experiment with new forms of dance . . . I left this concert . . . with the conviction that some valuable experimentation had been performed."[11] And Margaret Lloyd, in the *Christian Science Monitor*, wrote: "This new world of dance and music invites inquiry. The spirit of play, of adventure, carries one along with it, and induces a desire to know more."[12]

But if much of the new choreography and most of the new music were judged to be of questionable value, at least Merce's dancing was highly praised: "a magnificently gifted dancer . . . whenever he is on stage, one is held with the magnetism of his performance,"[13] and even his neophyte company fared quite well: "a fine company, all of whom performed with devotion and with a remarkable approximation of the choreographer's own highly refined style."[14] Thrilling for me was receiving my very first New York notice:

> A true delight was *Amores* (not a new work) to Cage's music, played by the composer, and danced by Carolyn Brown and Cunningham. It is a romantic pas de deux of delicate tenderness and exquisite in form, and it makes one forget many of the things which Cunningham and his entourage would like one to remember. Miss Brown, incidentally, has a beautiful line, moves extraordinarily well in any arrangement and is another dancer, along with Cunningham, who is not to be defeated by a patina of avant-garde'ism at all cost.[15]

Dances like *Septet*/Satie and *Banjo*/Gottschalk, along with Merce's earlier dramatic solos, won the warmest applause from the majority of critics and audiences. The dance that aroused the most antipathy was, not surprisingly, *Suite by Chance,* described by one reviewer as "This nihilistic excursion . . . to a series of silences and squeals that set the teeth on edge . . . an ordeal"[16] and by another as "Inert, static, almost chaotic at times . . . the music proved more disappointing than the dance. The sounds that were produced resembled the groan and squeals of faulty plumbing."[17] Almost everyone seemed to have trouble with that dance. John Cage's father and my father joined forces in boyish glee, agreeing that they both made better music in the "water-closet," and with a merry twinkle in his eye, John's father would henceforth call this music "chamber music." Merce was not originally aware of the juxtaposition of music and movement in his *Suite by Chance* solo that prompted this scatological humor. As Merce did a slow, deep plié in second position, a sound, as close to a prolonged, resounding fart as electronics were then capable of, scorched the stage space and set the audience atwitter. Both John's mother and mine were truly offended. But the flatulent sound juxtaposed to deep plié occurred completely by chance and took Merce (and the composer!) by surprise the first time the dance was performed. In subsequent performances, although Merce could have adjusted the timing of his plié if he so chose, he rarely did. I think he took a perverse delight in what chance procedures had wrought.

For my parents, the music and dancing were shocking enough. Still, it didn't prepare them for seeing Rauschenberg's painting hanging on the wall of their daughter and son-in-law's apartment. I never knew how bad they felt until I read my mother's journal more than three decades later: "Had discussions about the hideous painting Earle paid $26.00 for—black paint, newspapers, torn, etc. Awful. Frightening. To think Earle likes it. Calls it 'free spirit.' Is he really unwell mentally? It's horrifying. I wept. Jim did too on the way home. Our spirits low, miserable."[18]

Well, my loving parents had gotten a taste of my life, all right: Merce's dancing and choreography; music by Cage, Feldman, Wolff, and musique concrète; and Rauschenberg's painting. Gentle warnings had not prepared them, hadn't even softened the blow. The Cage/Cunningham/Rauschenberg aesthetic was anathema to them, and they felt terrible about their daughter in "such company." But what they suffered so keenly they kept to themselves. They made no attempt to influence me. They saw that my excitement was too great, my appetite too strongly whetted. And only three weeks later, after the company had performed at the Brooklyn Academy of Music on January 20, 1954, dancing *Suite by Chance, Fragments, Septet, Banjo,* and *Dime-a-Dance,* my mother's diary reported a change of attitude: "The tape music (?) was not as offensive this time—perhaps I'm getting used to it. I love the *Banjo* and *Septet* dances especially, though tonight I liked all the dances better than I did before."[19]

For the rest of my performing years with Merce, my mother's ability to grow, to look, to really see and appreciate never ceased to amaze me. Although the music continued to be a problem throughout her twenty years of active Cunningham company audience participation, she often astonished me with her willingness to try to experience it without prejudice. It was simply there as part of the theatrical experience of Merce's work.

I don't know what Merce expected of his dancers, but he certainly seemed pleased when most of us showed up for class as usual the day after the de Lys season ended. Marianne and I arrived early to find him alone in the studio, sitting by the window with all the gray corduroy dressing-room draperies pulled aside, as though he had no plans to teach that afternoon.

"What are *you* doing here?" he asked gruffly, though mock-gruff it was, probably to hide his own pleasure. Perhaps our faithful attendance at the daily class gave him evidence of our commitment to his work and to him. Perhaps he really wished we hadn't come so that he could enjoy a day of rest. But then, he could have closed the studio for the day, even for the whole week, if he'd wanted to. So often with Merce one felt one was being tested. We never knew, firsthand, whether we had passed or failed.

Nineteen fifty-four. It seemed as though everyone was on the move. Everyone, that is, except the Merce Cunningham Dance Company. Only two dates materialized, both at the Academy of Music in Brooklyn—one in January, a few weeks after the Theatre de Lys season, the other in December, nearly eleven months later, with not a single performance in between. Rehearsals ceased after the January 20 concert, but the company continued to take class with Merce four days a week and I continued ballet classes at the Met with Margaret Craske. Tudor had informed me that I was not ready for his morning professional classes, and his evening classes met at the same time as Merce's. Forced to choose, there was never a question where I would go, but I missed the hours with that ornery, brilliant, sarcastic Englishman. Mixed with a certain amount of fear and awe was an affinity, an almost filial bond (present until his death) that I felt for Antony Tudor and his work. He never called me "Carolyn" until long after I'd stopped studying with him. It was always "Caroline," as in his *Jardin aux Lilas*. When at Juilliard he first learned my name, he sneered "How affected!" I was surprised. " Carolyn" affected? "Caroline" not? I'd always thought it the other way around! But Tudor was always encouraging young dancers to change their names as he, William Cook, had changed his, and confessing how deeply bothered I was by his accusation of affectation would have been a mistake. Willingly exposing one's vulnerabilities to Tudor was asking for trouble, and I kept a certain distance from this Svengali, sensing he could be dangerous. Always a disrupter of the peace, he was forever creating difficulties for Miss Craske at the Metropolitan Opera Ballet School by tangling situations instead of untangling them. At times, it seemed as if there was an undeclared state of war between them, except that Miss Craske was the pacifist, unwilling to fight him or to be disloyal. Her love was stronger than his deviltry.

Most of Merce's company began studying at the Met, joining Paul Taylor and Anita Dencks, who had gone there from Juilliard as I had, and all of us continued Cecchetti ballet classes for the next few years. If Merce objected, he never said so, but I know he would have preferred that we study the Russian technique as taught at Balanchine's school by Anatole Oboukhoff, Pierre Vladimirov, Felia Doubrovska, and Muriel Stuart just as he had done some years earlier. Merce believed that the Cecchetti technique emphasized small, neat movement, and he wanted us to move big. In my case, my unfortunate tendency to want always to be "correct" did limit the breadth and scope of my movement, and Merce quite rightly wanted to counteract this. But I'd found a teacher—a true teacher—and I wasn't ready to try another. I didn't then nor do I now believe in playing musical chairs with one's technique classes. It isn't merely a class that a dancer needs every day; it's a teacher, and teachers are hard to find. Anyone can give a class. Many can give a good class. But a teacher who is dedicated to serving dance, who plays no destructive or cruel power games, nor indulges in self-admiring ego trips, one who has a method and a point of view and can communicate with consistency and caring, always allowing for the students' personal idiosyncrasies in body build and temperament and always demanding growth—that person is rare, and that person I found in Margaret Craske.

Merce lost Paul Taylor that winter. Paul's last performance with us was in the January Brooklyn Academy of Music concert. Blaming *Dime-a-Dance*, he says he left because he "had no assurance we were not always to be cast by chance," admitting parenthetically, "What I did not know was that a large part of my whole career was to be due to chance in one form or another."[1] Actually, it's doubtful that chance ever played any part in Merce's casting. *Dime-a-Dance* had thirteen brief dances. We learned all of them in class, but Merce eventually, for performance purposes, assigned specific dances to specific dancers. In a given performance, out of the thirteen dances, only seven were performed, which ones and in what order supposedly determined by chance, but be assured that whether or not Merce's solo *The Eclectic* came up, he always performed it! At the Theater de Lys, instead of members of the audience paying a dime for a card that would determine the next dance (the procedure used at Black Mountain), each dance was identified by its own colorful prop, which was selected at random out of a basket in seven brief pantomimic episodes. The best episode—actually the only one I remember—was Viola being carried aloft on the shoulders of Remy and Paul, then reaching into the basket with her extraordinarily arched and supple foot to withdraw a red rose for—what else?—*The Tango*! But who was to dance *The Tango* was never a matter of chance. It was always Jo Anne Melsher. *Dime-a-Dance* was dropped from the repertory after only five performances.

I suspect the real reasons Paul left Merce's company were far more complex. Earle remembers complimenting Paul with genuine enthusiasm after the de Lys season, saying, "You've improved tremendously!" Paul, apparently offended, replied coldly, "That's certainly a backhanded compliment if ever I heard one." Did he honestly not think there was room for improvement, even though he'd been dancing for less than two years? Paul was, as he readily admits, supremely self-confident. He was also supremely gifted, and impatient. He was quick to recognize that there wasn't a place in Merce's company in those years for another featured male dancer. The company at that time was billed, for good reason, Merce Cunningham *and* Dance Company, and it stayed that way well into the seventies, when the "and" was dropped, coinciding with the moment when Merce's physical limitations forced him to dance less and less and consequently his male dancers began to dance more and more, including some of Merce's own parts. Merce's loss was Martha's gain. Paul joined the Graham Company in 1955. He'd already begun making dances on his own.

Paul met Bob Rauschenberg during the autumn of 1953, when Bob was photographing Merce's company for the de Lys posters. There was a mutual attraction between these two Southerners, and a long-lasting friendship began. *Jack and the Bean Stalk,* the first work Paul presented in New York (begun in Merce's composition class at Black Mountain), had Rauschenberg's designs, and from 1954 through 1962, ending with *Tracer,* Bob designed costumes and/or sets and sometimes even sound for Paul's work—twelve dances in all. Paul seemed to be, like the rest of us, very nearly penniless in those years. His small loft on Sixth Avenue, not far from the old Metropolitan Opera House, had no shower or bathtub, so Paul took his showers at the Met. As he put it, it got him to ballet class, if only to do the barre. I think Tudor must have given Paul a full scholarship. Not a bad deal: free ballet classes and unlimited access to the plumbing facilities. Anyway, that's where I went on seeing Paul after he left Merce's company. There were nights when I was just hanging around the Met, working on my own in the big studio, waiting to go on in some super's role, and Paul would amble in, after a full day of rehearsing in his own studio, to take a shower and chat. He hadn't bothered to come to class at all. But he was choreographing in earnest, and two of Merce's dancers (Viola Farber and Anita Dencks) danced with him in his earliest concerts. For a while, what little money Paul earned came from assisting Rauschenberg and Jasper

Johns, who were attempting to support their painting by working with Gene Moore preparing window displays for Tiffany and Bonwit Teller.

The Brooklyn Academy of Music performance (Paul's last with Merce) took place on David Tudor's twenty-eighth birthday, January 20. Following the performance, Merce gave a party at his Sheridan Square studio in David's honor. The studio was jammed wall-to-wall with people associated by love and/or marriage, blood, or artistic sympathies—who can say which of these ties are the closest? Marianne Preger, in charming French, gave a carefully enunciated, brief, pedantic lecture on time and space, making sport of the current Cage/Cunningham obsession, ending with a mock serious, beguilingly flirtatious question addressed to David: "Si tu as le temps, moi, j'ai l'espace." M. C. Richards, in high spirits, decided that what Merce needed was a woman to look after him, so with all the women in cahoots, Marianne was chosen to seduce him. She managed to sit on his lap, ruffle his hair, and provoke his laughter and mildly pleased embarrassment, but I think we all knew, even if M.C. didn't want to believe it, that he'd never be available to any of us.

David's birthday party marked, in a sense, the end of the beginning. The company had scarcely been formed and already it was changing. Losing Paul Taylor put the repertory in jeopardy. Male dancers were scarce in the mid-fifties, and none of any real promise was then studying with Merce. The best male dancers were in ballet companies or working with Graham and Limón. Merce was tired and discouraged, feeling ignored by the New York papers and betrayed by his own body. But that spring, he received a psychological boost as well as a financial one—a John Simon Guggenheim Fellowship to the tune of three thousand dollars! It seemed like a fortune at the time, and although we only learned of it by reading the *New York Times*, it helped to bolster our faith in the continued existence of his company through those many, many months without performances or even rehearsals.

John received notice that his beloved Monroe Street tenement building—the "Bozza Mansion"—was to be razed, the whole area to be replaced by a city housing project. It was the first time I'd had any inkling that John was not the perfect Zen-enlightened being that I'd foolishly imagined him to be. He was greatly saddened by the prospect of losing his wonderful aerie perched high above the East River and upper New York Bay, and I, without intending impudence, had the bad sense to remind him of his beliefs in the Zen Buddhist philosophy of non-attachment. "Don't you *ever* parrot my words back at me!" he hissed. The ferocity of his anger startled me. In John's lectures, his writings, his everyday conversations, in

fact anywhere he had an audience, he preached "non-attachment"—
"What is possessed is nothing"[2]—but putting his beliefs into practice in
everyday living wasn't always easy for him. I hadn't guessed how very
attached, in fact, John Cage was—to people, situations, relationships,
though rarely to things.

John got angry with me a second time that year. Having done a lot of
thinking about John's "silent piece," *4′33,″* which I'd heard in the fall of
'52, and then again in its first New York performance in the spring of '54, I
had the temerity to tell him that what he was doing in that piece was sermonizing, and that as a member of the audience I resented being lectured in
this manner. How could he profess to compose purposeless music and at
the same time claim that the purpose of this purposeless music would be
achieved if people learned to listen[3]? I hoped I was opening up a discussion, but he perceived my response to his silent piece as an attack on him
personally and an act of disloyalty. On another occasion, after dinner in our
apartment, John, David, and Earle embroiled themselves in a very serious
musical discussion and David began to question what John was saying.
John left the room and did not return. We found him sitting on our bed, close
to tears. Neither Earle nor I could console him. "David attacked me. Didn't
you hear him? He attacked me!" "No, no, John, he's only disagreeing with
something you said," Earle replied. But for John, disagreeing with his ideas
was equivalent to attacking his person, and his ego—the one he so valiantly
tried to obliterate—was bruised. Incongruously, John hated change. He
had tenacious loyalties to people and to ideas. The disruption of deeply valued friendships reduced him to misery. What saved him, eventually, was
his own unsquelchable optimism, which would reliably surface just in time.

Fortunately the loss of the Bozza Mansion coincided with his renewed
curiosity about nature. Although he had an aversion to the sun and loathed
mosquitoes, snakes, spiders, and other creepy-crawly things associated
with country living, he was firmly committed to Saint Thomas Aquinas's
precept (as quoted by Ananda K. Coomaraswamy) that "Art is the imitation of Nature in her manner of operation"[3] and thought perhaps it was
time to observe Nature more closely than New York City living would
allow. Paul and Vera Williams were seriously searching for "The Land"
where they could start a community of artists. John, David, M.C., Earle,
and I joined the Williamses on a number of forays into the country north of
New York, and eventually we found a tract of land in Stony Point that
almost perfectly matched the little advertisement Paul had placed in
Merce's Theater de Lys program. It was hilly and mostly wooded, had a
stream, waterfalls, and a house, and was within fifty miles of the city. The

clapboard house, desperately in need of a paint job, not unlike the kind of derelict shanties one sees in the poverty-stricken South, had four small rooms downstairs and two attic spaces under the eaves. No bathroom. An outhouse in the back. A hand pump for water. (Eventually there was running water in the kitchen sink.) Into this cottage moved M. C. Richards and David Tudor, Karen Karnes and David Weinrib—potters from Black Mountain—and John. Each of the two couples had a tiny bedroom downstairs; upstairs, in one of the spaces under the eaves, John had his. He moved from the serene and spartan elegance of his relatively spacious Monroe Street flat with its exquisite city views twenty-four hours a day to this little attic space, under a pitched roof, with room for only a mattress on the floor and a few books, and no view at all unless one got down on all fours to look out the window into a small, unkempt field bordering the woods. For more than a year the five of them lived together in this cramped and awkwardly intimate proximity while Paul set to work designing their houses. They were the pioneers who began "The Community on The Land." The Williamses, who had children, rented a larger house down the road. Paul's dream was to build a quasi-Italian hillside village with houses built around squares and most of the land left free and wild for all to enjoy.

When it came time to build, everyone lent a hand to help Paul and the one or two hired construction men. Although Earle and I had decided not to join the community, Earle occasionally drove out to help in the building of the pottery studio, which was the first to go up because the Weinribs depended upon it for their income. Their house eventually rose next to it— both buildings nestled close to the brook on flat land fairly close to the road, making it accessible to future customers. Also built on the flat, although off by itself in the woods—out of hearing range—was David's studio. It's a curious-looking triangular structure built on stilts to prevent ground moisture and floods from damaging the baby grand piano that had once been in Cage's Monroe Street apartment. On a kind of permanent loan, this piano was for years the only furniture in the studio, although David sometimes camped out there, sleeping under the piano on a mat and cooking his meals over a Bunsen burner in the corner. Piles of manuscripts, many of them piano scores dedicated to David by young composers from all over the world, lined the walls along with cartons of the required gadgets and odd bits of paraphernalia that David used to produce the sounds of new music. (Long after the others had left The Community on The Land, David Tudor went on living there until 1995, when several strokes and blindness made it impossible for him to live alone.)

John's house didn't go up until the summer of '55. It was built into the hillside and shared a floor-to-ceiling stone wall with the Williamses' two-storey house adjoining it. John built the wall himself—selecting each rock with loving care. On the Williamses' side the stones fit smoothly; on his side the wall was jagged and uneven, providing niches for a candle, or a recently foraged mushroom, or some ancient musical instrument, or a single blossom in a discarded wine bottle. The opposite wall was an enormous sliding glass door that opened onto the wooded, steeply ascending hillside covered with massive boulders and lush undergrowth beneath a canopy of trees. As in his New York apartment, John's living arrangements were spare and monklike. A small kitchen area, a shower, a toilet. No furniture. He slept on the floor. He'd given away or sold most of his books and his art. But he began collecting books again—mushroom books.

In the beginning, there was talk of a theater (for Merce), and for years, long after the dream had been forgotten, the only large field on the property was called "The Theater Field," but few people remembered why. Merce never moved to The Land. I don't think he ever seriously considered it. In fact, he only rarely visited John out there, and when he did, he complained of allergies to flora and fauna, mosses and molds and dampness from the brook. Although Merce didn't move that year, or the next, almost everyone else we knew changed addresses in 1954 or 1955.

Cage's parents moved to an apartment hotel on Riverside Drive with a glorious view of the Hudson. Viola Farber moved into David Tudor's Fourth Street tenement; Anita Dencks got a small loft on University Place that was so cold she wore a sweater in the bathtub when she wanted to soak her aching legs; Jasper Johns took a loft at 278 Pearl Street in a condemned building discovered by Rachel Rosenthal, an extraordinarily vivacious redheaded Frenchwoman, the daughter of a Russian "Pearl King," who had met Merce in Paris, moved to New York, and for a brief time studied and performed with Merce, but by 1954 had quit dancing and was trying her hand at sculpture. A plaster cast of her face appears in Jasper's *Untitled 1954*. When Rachel moved to California in 1955, Rauschenberg moved from Fulton Street into her loft, and for six years Bob and Jap were nearly inseparable. Our friends Fance and Louis Stevenson also headed downtown, leaving their elegant East Side river-view apartment for a small downtown loft, not far from Johns and Rauschenberg, and Fance's face became the face in Jasper's 1955 *Target with Four Faces*. Louis Stevenson, a shy, brilliant research engineer, had fallen in love with Merce's company, become a kind of camp follower, and frequently photographed us in rehearsal and performance.

Our Cornelia Street apartment, airless in summer, cramped and claustrophobic year-round, had no room for Earle to compose. His newest work for orchestra had 175 pages that he needed to work on simultaneously. We had to find a loft and found one in a block of mostly three-storey buildings on the west side of Third Avenue between Ninth and Tenth Streets. It was an area of pawnshops, bars, and liquor stores. The street level of our building was a classic example of the unsavory, gloomy bar/restaurant frequented by Bowery bums and a peculiar variety of S&M hoods and tarts. The second floor—meant for light manufacturing—was empty, but we couldn't afford it. The third floor-through rented for forty-five dollars. Although no longer a legal living space, it had a tiled bathroom with an enormous bathtub (a dancer's dream!), although no sink. No hot water was provided by the landlord, but the crummy bar agreed to supply us for five dollars a month. There was nothing to supply any sort of heat. Except for a double white-enameled kitchen sink, there were no appliances—we had to provide for ourselves.

After moving in, we discovered that most of our neighbors were artists: among them Mary and Robert Frank, then married (she a sculptress, he a photographer and filmmaker), and John Cohen, a visual artist and filmmaker. Out the back windows, across a large open lot, was Willem de Kooning's studio on the top floor of 88 Tenth Street. Our loft was only about forty feet long, but compared to Cornelia Street it felt luxuriously spacious. The six large windows—three facing east onto Third Avenue, three facing west—flooded it with light. Best of all was the open space we called the "bum's garden" between us and de Kooning's building, which boasted several large ailanthus trees, wild grasses, wilder cats, and an assortment of disheveled, indolent bums sleeping it off at any time of day or night in almost any kind of weather. Most amazing of all was a rose of Sharon that actually bloomed every summer. For a time, a family of Gypsies from the fortune-telling salon on Third Avenue had picnics and exotic-smelling cookouts in the garden.

Sunlight! Trees! Sky, clouds, stars, and moon! Once again I was able to witness the changing of the seasons from my window. I was overjoyed. What appealed most to Earle was a workroom all his own (in what would have been the hall bedroom, I suppose). True, it overlooked Third Avenue and the decrepit elevated train that stopped right outside our windows, disgorging and engorging passengers who paced the platforms, some furtively glancing, others brazenly staring into our loft, which was directly opposite them. But we got used to the sound of the El—the trains ran from seven in the morning until six in the evening—and eventually I stopped hearing them at all. When the El was abandoned and finally torn down, I actually missed it. But the unaccustomed light that poured into our living-room window was compensation.

A distant friendship of waved hellos and shouted good mornings developed across the tangle of leaves and branches, weeds and litter of the bum's garden. From our kitchen and bathroom windows we could observe Bill de Kooning working, pacing, standing immobile staring out of his windows, or entertaining visitors, who we imagined to be prestigious collectors, gallery owners, and museum directors. De Kooning never again asked me out as he had that night at John's Bozza Mansion party for Boulez, but we maintained a neighborly acquaintance and he remained a loyal fan of Merce's company. According to his wife, Elaine, "Artists seemed to be the built-in audience for modern dancers, poets, composers in the forties—and even more so in the fifties. Harold Rosenberg put it in a nutshell in 1954 when he surveyed a full house before a Cage/Cunningham concert and said in his booming voice, 'Here it is almost curtain time and the Lassaws aren't here yet.' Everyone doubled up laughing. We all attended every event and everyone in the audience knew everyone else. 'There's a stranger in the third row,' continued Harold, 'Throw him out!' "[4]

Tenth Street between Third and Fourth Avenues had not only de Kooning and other artists in its lofts but several galleries, including the Tanager Gallery (where I first saw a work by Jasper Johns—*Construction with Toy Piano*), a bookstore, and a tiny coffeehouse run by Mickey Rudkin, who opened The Ninth Circle and Max's Kansas City—favorite haunts of the art crowd. His first place on Tenth Street had no liquor license, but for poets, playwrights, musicians, and artists who wanted a change from the booze and bull being thrown at the Cedar bar it was a welcome hangout. For Earle it was a place to take a break when composing late at night, a place where he was sure to find good conversation, maybe a poetry reading by LeRoi Jones, Diane Di Prima, Kenneth Koch, or Jackson Mac Low, and a good cup of coffee. On Friday nights Tenth Street was like a street fair, with all of the New York modern-art world crowding into the gallery openings on both sides of the street, drinking the free cheap wine, spilling out onto the sidewalks, continuing heated discussions as they headed off to the Cedar bar or the Tenth Street Coffee House, the Sagamore Cafeteria at Third Avenue and St. Mark's, the Hansa Gallery on Twelfth Street, a concert at Cooper Union, or to Ratner's deli on Second Avenue.

Our neighborhood horrified our parents. They couldn't see how the dank gloom under the El was dispelled for us by the lively goings-on of the artists who had appropriated the area and been assimilated by it as easily as one adds another patch to an already crazy quilt. Actually, I pretended a bravery and nonchalance I never felt. The slimy cobblestones and rank odors made me queasy, and the bizarre cast of characters hanging around the underbelly of the El scared me plenty. I never got used to finding a bum asleep in our doorway, or in a heap on the second- or third-floor landing reeking of stale booze, urine, and acrid sweat: was he dead or merely dead drunk? Negotiate the street, quickly insert keys into the several locks, warily climb the stairs; more keys. Once inside our loft, I'd lean against the door, drained and relieved as I slid the bolt back into the lock. Home. Safe. I felt as though I'd crossed through a war zone, especially in the years that I lived there alone for weeks at a time, with Earle away in Europe. Always, when jolted awake in the middle of the night by screaming and shouting, street fights and police sirens, my heart would pound violently and fear clutch at my throat. Worse still was seeing some man or woman forced up against a streetlight or the hood of a car and roughed up by a couple of cops. But the loft itself, its space, its light, and the bum's garden, I loved and wouldn't have considered trading for the tiny but safer Cornelia Street apartment. Earle set to work on his new and exciting project—an orchestral composition that Merce had commissioned. Years later, Earle wrote: "While sketching, it occurred to John and Merce and me this could be a commission from Merce that would be in payment for all of Carol's lessons with Merce before she became a member of his company . . . we still (technically) owed for the past. Given that Merce had no money to pay for my score and we had no money to pay for classes, it was 'good thinking' all the way around."[5]

Throughout the miserably hot New York summer months of 1954, Earle worked on *Indices,* the score for Merce's new dance. They had together agreed on twenty-nine minutes as the length of the dance. Then Earle—using tables of random sampling numbers—determined the "intricate and terribly complex" program that included the characteristics of each sound event and when it would appear within the twenty-nine minutes. The sounds were dropped into the overall time. "The piece is not written from left to right (start to finish) but the 'program' [of composing] was such that each sound was a completely self-contained 'event' . . . There were 175 pages of ruled score paper which equalled twenty-nine minutes at mm 120. According to the 'program' the first sound composed might have entered on page 107; the second on page 22, the third on page 136, etc."[6] The music used a discontinuous compositional process that John likened to dropping pebbles into a lake. When the orchestral version was finished, Earle got to work making not a transcription but a literal piano reduction for David to play on those hoped-for but yet-to-materialize tours that John kept doggedly working on.

While Earle slaved away, Merce's own activities came to a standstill. Rumored performance dates fell through. Even classes stopped. We didn't return to work with him until the end of September, just shortly before John and David left on a whirlwind tour of Europe, where they performed the new piano and tape music of Brown, Cage, Feldman, and Wolff in Donaueschingen, Cologne, Paris, Brussels, Zurich, and London. With great fanfare we waved them off on the *Maasdam* on a Saturday in early October. Imagine our surprise when the next evening they walked in on Merce, Earle, and me as we were having dinner at Peter McManus's pub. "What are *you* doing here?" we screamed. In the fog, somewhere off the coast of Nantucket, their ship had collided with a French freighter. Could this be an omen? We speculated on the possible interpretations of this event, only half-joking. Two days later they flew from Idlewild (now JFK) and arrived safely, without further mishap. It's no exaggeration to state that their performances influenced the course of Europe's musical history, though many Europeans would be reluctant to admit it. The Donaueschingen Festival in Germany had invited Cage to present a program of new American music and to write a new work expressly for the festival, and it was there that a new generation of European avant-garde composers—Luciano Berio, Pierre Boulez, Bruno Maderna, Luigi Nono, Henri Pousseur, and Karlheinz Stockhausen—first heard music composed by chance means, open form music, and compositions that explored indeterminacy in performance, utterly new concepts to these composers, most of whom were embroiled in the problems of applying Arnold Schoenberg's "serialism" to all the parameters of sound. The Cage/Tudor performances of new American avant-garde music, predating all aleatoric and open form experiments by European composers, drove a wedge deep into the grain of Europe's well-seasoned wood, splitting asunder the belief that Europeans were at the forefront of musical innovation. The split generated controversy, endless discussion, heated argument, and, for some, a change of mind.

Back in New York, Merce had at last begun working on a new dance. The torpor of August abruptly ended. Life became hectic once again. My schedule included professional ballet classes at the Met every morning with Craske, or with Antony Tudor, who now allowed me to take his professional class. I even wrote to my parents, "Classes with Tudor are great fun! I'm not in a panic at all, anymore. *Really wonderful!*" There was class with Merce every afternoon; rehearsals several days a week; and on Saturdays I taught two children's classes at Merce's studio. Viola played for them, and for a while my only students were the two daughters of Louise and Richard Lippold and the two daughters of Wally and Jack Tworkov. Supering at the Met for the Opera—essentially standing around doing nothing—added a few more dollars to our weekly till at the cost of many tedious hours of rehearsals and performances. Cast in the part of Madame Le Gray with a bit of silent acting to do in a new production of *Andrea Chénier,* I was fitted several times at Brooks Costumes for a gorgeous costume of blue-gray silk, exquisitely made to my measure, only to be fired at the dress rehearsal. I had notified the assistant manager that I would be late for the one o'clock call, but he forgot, put someone too short in *my* costume, which had to be pinned up—a sacrilege!—and sent her on, unrehearsed, in my place. I arrived in ample time to put on makeup, dress, and be onstage on cue but that, he said, was irrelevant. I lost my beloved costume and the part forever.

My few paying jobs were actually beginning to interfere with one another. The Met paid only a minimum of four dollars for the first two hours, and two dollars an hour after that, but the meager wages still helped to pay the grocery bills. To make matters worse, Met rehearsals sometimes conflicted with Merce's. And the performances themselves were extraordinarily time-consuming and exhausting. *Die Meistersinger,* for example, didn't finish until after midnight. I was in the Act II fight scene and then had to hang around to be a bridesmaid in the procession and finale. Over the years, I supered or danced in *Andrea Chénier* (though never again as Madame Le Gray), *Die Meistersinger, Orfeo and Eurydice* (Alicia Markova, guest ballerina), *Cavalleria Rusticana, Pagliacci, Salome,* and *La Gioconda.* Zachary Solov was the resident choreographer.

If you're not particularly fond of opera, and I was not, supering at the old Met in the 1950s would be enough to guarantee a lifelong antipathy to the art form. Supering for the opera was a completely different experience from supering for the Sadler's Wells/Royal Ballet. Even if one got to dance, as I did in *Orfeo, Salome,* and *Gioconda,* one learned next to nothing. At least of artistic merit. What one did learn was to have eyes in the back of one's head, to be on guard at all times against fanny-pinchers, mashers, inebriates, and the inevitable assortment of conceited, self-appointed lady-killers who seemed to consider the opera supers fair game—to be molested at will. Even the opera ballet company's own dancers (both male and female) were often treated as sexual objects, up for grabs by just about everyone from exalted members of the board of directors and the management (most of them married) on down to the singers (the famous and the not-so-famous) and the stagehands. Whether the seduction began with flowers and champagne in the dressing room or a vulgar pass in the wings, it often appeared to me, with my strongly negative bias against the art form, that what was happening onstage was merely an excuse for the intrigues and debauchery going on backstage. With the regional ballet movement still a number of years in the future, the Met Opera Ballet, in the fifties, was one of the few places offering steady employment to ballet dancers. I doubt it was *ever* a first choice for any serious dancer, but many young hopefuls looked to it as a place to get experience, as a stepping-stone to Ballet Theatre or New York City Ballet. All too often they discovered it was a quagmire leading nowhere.

From bordello to monastery—that's what I thought as I went from my opera job (which I disdained) and the faded opulence of the seedy old Met (which I adored) to rehearsals with Merce in the spartan little studio at 224 West Fourth Street in the Village. Merce was making two new pieces for full company. *Minutiae,* the one to be premiered in Brooklyn, struck all of us, including Merce, as quirky and odd in the extreme. Alone in his second-floor studio above Sheridan Square—where Seventh Avenue, Fourth Street, Christopher Street, Grove Street, and West Tenth Street all meet in a complicated intersection—Merce observed the haphazard confluence of individuals crisscrossing the space, each person with his or her own reason for being there, in pursuit of who knows what destination, moving in a unique rhythm, using an obscure, totally personal, adapted-for-the-street body language that both disguised and revealed. This was the raw material for Merce's newest choreography. "This dance uses small, short abrupt movements arising from an observation over periods of time of people walking in the streets." So reads the program note that appeared after the first two performances. But Merce, remember, in his book, tells us, "at least that's what I replied when asked. [The movements] were, mostly, movements anyone does when getting set to do a larger movement . . . the movements before the effort . . . small in scale, details only. The procedure was by chance, with each dancer [there were six] being given a separate line, like a separate life, occasionally coming together."[7]

I remember: scrunching along the floor on my behind; slow repetitive slinky walks in unison with two other women; hurried movement with peculiar little gestures; odd jabbing with elbows; isolated head, shoulder, and hand movements; a little floor duet with Merce; but most of all I remember Marianne and me facing each other, holding right hands as though in greeting or farewell, traveling across the stage in a slow amble, all the while conversing, and all the while on our knees! I suppose Merce *must* have told us to talk to each other, but I don't recall. In any event, we did, making up a story in turns, weaving it into an ever-more-elaborate tale with each rehearsal. Our story got so interesting we couldn't wait until the next rehearsal to continue it. Our rule was to tell the tale only while on our knees during the actual dancing. The story was our secret and we never told it to anyone.

Merce, as usual, didn't discuss the dance in terms of his intentions, its meaning, or what he wished us to convey. We had to assume the meaning was in the movement, that the choreography was the message, and that it communicated simply by us doing as well as we could what he had given us to do. If the dance was meant to be funny, we never knew it, and we certainly didn't play it that way. We performed it deadpan, like earnest schoolchildren. As it happens, *Minutiae was* funny. It was also poignant, oddly commonplace, and uncommonly peculiar, and Rauschenberg's set added a startling dimension. When Merce asked him to make something for *Minutiae,* the dance was not finished. Merce recalled: "I did not tell him what to make, only that it could be something that was in the dance area, that we could move through it, around it and with it if he so liked. He made an object and beautiful as it was, I knew it couldn't work because it needed a pipe to hang on."[8] Merce could never count on having a proper theater with fly space, and he wanted all his dances to be tourable. So, undaunted, Bob made another object, an easily dismantled three-paneled screen that stood on its own legs.

By late 1953, Bob had moved away from his all-black period. One day he invited some friends, including John, Merce, Earle, and me, to his Fulton Street loft to see his newest paintings. He was strangely ill at ease, even though we were among the few people who had liked his earlier white and black paintings. Leaning against the walls were several very large predominately red paintings. Surprised? We were thunderstruck. The new work was garish, giddy, Gypsy caravan-esque. There was an audible, almost communal intake of breath. No one said a word. What an eyeful! Suddenly the energy from those paintings seemed to explode in us and everyone started talking and laughing at once. Affirmation, joy, some animating spirit that was contagious and intoxicating overwhelmed any reservations or doubts. There was no question of liking or disliking. The red paintings had lives of their own; they could not be denied. Most critics and many older artists had rejected Bob's earlier paintings, calling them jokes or crude insults to the art of painting. As Calvin Tomkins explains in his book about Bob: "The white and black paintings, which the artist himself had thought rather modest and quiet, had evidently impressed a lot of people (other artists included) as aggressive, ugly, and full of the anger of negation; that being the case, Rauschenberg thought he'd better find out whether there was any truth to these charges. He would test his own motives by turning from black and white to red, for him the most aggressive, the most difficult, the least austere color in the spectrum."[9]

Bob hadn't been sure if we would be able to accept the startling change in his work. Later that day, quite seriously, he said to us, "I didn't want to lose my friends." Friends had always been important to Bob; he had very few in those years, and of those few, John Cage, thirteen years Bob's senior, was perhaps the most valued. He needn't have worried. Both John and Merce saw in these lively, astonishing paintings Bob's strikingly original sense of the theatrical, and a vital working friendship was begun that would last ten years: Bob would design sets, costumes, and eventually the lighting as well, working on more than twenty dances before leaving the company in 1964. (He returned in 1977 to design the extravagant *Travelogue* sets and costumes, in 1994 to paint a stunning back cloth for Events, and in 2000 to create both the decor—two identical painted back cloths, one in black and white, the other in glorious technicolor—and the costumes for *Interscape*.)

Minutiae was Bob's first work for the company, and his set was, in its own way, every bit as strange as the dance itself. Closely related to his sudden change of style, it was predominately red, constructed of fabric, paper, metal, plastic, wood, and oil, with a round metal-rimmed shaving mirror hung from a string in the middle of the tall center panel. Just before the curtain opened, the mirror was set spinning. A doorway between the two rear panels was hung with sewn-together rectangles of China silk in many colors. Collage elements included old lace, ribbon, comic strips, patterned cloth, and newspaper. Gaudy and mysterious, the *Minutiae* set evoked carnivals and circuses, the world of honky-tonk and Gypsies. P. W. Manchester called it "a sort of thing . . . something like a Victorian scrap screen and something like a fortune telling booth and a bit like a photograph yourself kiosk."[10] Louis Horst described it as "a most fantastic and wildly colored set piece with a sort of peep-hole in front which strongly suggested a huge kaleidoscope."[11] One might have supposed that Merce would want street clothes for *Minutiae* costumes, but Remy Charlip worked off Bob's set rather than taking clues from the choreography, tie-dyeing plain tights and leotards himself in a complicated collage of rich, vibrant colors that complemented the Rauschenberg construction.

Minutiae was the only new work on the December 8 Brooklyn Academy of Music concert. The dance was not well received by the two critics who reviewed it. P. W. Manchester scolded:

A dance which has every appearance of being intended to mean something and yet is utterly meaningless must surely be accounted a failure . . . the pity of it is that Merce Cunningham is a stupendous dancer and was in stupendous form all through the evening. He has a marvelously trained company of accomplished dancers and, in Carolyn Brown, a partner of extraordinary beauty and skill. But so long as he remains faithful to magnetic tape and the noises with which John Cage debases a noble instrument, it seems to me he is defeating himself in his essays toward creative dance.[12]

Louis Horst, who was far more skilled in fathoming works by modern-dance choreographers than Miss Manchester, wrote that *Minutiae* "depicted the busy but aimless and directionless and quasi-insane scurrying of man through life," but he didn't like it any better than she did: "Some of it was funny and some of it was just silly, but none of it seemed significant or visually interesting. Maybe that is what life is although one does stubbornly think that man occasionally rises above the hectic and grubbing activity of insects and creates some illusions of beauty and plan, if but for an instant now and then."[13] Louis probably saw in *Minutiae* exactly what was there to see, but he seemed unwilling to consider that the activity of insects often is both highly ordered and remarkably beautiful. The illustrious "Dean of American [Modern] Dance" said no to two other dances on the program: "*Fragments* and *Collage,* done to noisy and tasteless sound scores by Pierre Boulez and Pierre Schaeffer, were dadaistic and incomprehensible, and, way over (or under) this old white head."[14] But he said yes to Merce as "a truly great dancer . . . a dancer with a perfect command of a fabulous technical equipment." So, little had changed since the Theatre de Lys season. There was no breakthrough in the critical response. It was still no! to Merce the choreographer, yes! to Merce the dancer.

At the same time that Merce was rehearsing the repertoire for Brooklyn, he was choreographing *Springweather and People.* The Brooklyn concert over, he devoted all our rehearsals to *Springweather,* a wonderfully "dance-y" and lyrical ballet—the very antithesis of *Minutiae.* It had duet sections with big space-devouring musical phrases and strange lifts for Merce and me that, quite naturally, I adored and felt challenged and excited by. Perhaps, inevitably, the pleasure in being given special solo or duet material was always tempered by the awareness that my good fortune could be the cause of someone else's bitter disappointment. And so it was when Jo Anne Melsher quit the company in the winter of 1955. Jo Anne had begun studying with Merce while still in high school; she'd approached his work with an astonishingly quick, no-nonsense intelligence and had become his strongest dancer, with an extraordinary rhythmic acuity, a lovely sense of phrasing, plus a natural jump and a bubbly, bouncy *ballon* that we all envied. But this lively dance sensibility was coupled with a very difficult body, tending to overweight, with slightly awkward proportions, bowed legs (wonderful for jumping!), and poor (flat) feet. Like all the women in the company, she hoped to be cast in romantic duets with Merce, but he didn't envision her that way, and in the midst of the making of *Springweather*, Jo Anne became disillusioned and decided to leave the company, which saddened all of us. Only a few years later she was killed as she stepped off a curb directly into the path of an oncoming Fifth Avenue bus. She was barely twenty. Inevitably, troubling questions haunt one: would it have been different if only . . . ? Jo Anne was not replaced. Merce rearranged her part into the already-choreographed sections of *Springweather*, dividing them among Marianne, Viola, Anita, Remy, me, and himself; he did the same with her roles in the repertory.

John, in a mood of unflappable optimism, set madly to work once again, writing hundreds of letters a week striving to get performance dates for the company. It was the fourth letter-writing campaign in less than three years. Remy and John began designing a brochure; I helped with the text and the typing. In March 1955, I wrote to my mother asking if she would consider writing a note to Ted Shawn: "You don't have to 'recommend' Merce on *your* personal likes or dislikes [knowing the reservations she had about the work and especially the music]. It is just that Merce IS, and what he does *deserves* to be looked at *now*, while he is at his peak."

Merce had a more immediate goal. In early May, Bethsabée de Rothschild planned to present another American Dance Festival in a Broadway theater. Merce wanted to present *Springweather and People* at that festival. We auditioned the dance on a Sunday afternoon in mid-March at Martha Graham's studio on East Sixty-third Street for a viewing committee made up of de Rothschild, Doris Humphrey, Don Duncan (publicity representative), and an elderly gentleman who was then the secretary of the Bethsabée de Rothschild Foundation of Arts and Sciences. Martha Graham was not on the committee, but she was there at the studio to greet Merce when he arrived and to press an exotic little talisman into his hand while murmuring almost inaudible words of encouragement. She greeted the rest of us most cordially, then mysteriously slipped away. I'd never been to her studio before and was properly impressed by the three studios, the beautiful wood floors and sparkling mirrors, the office and dressing-room facilities, and such amenities as kitchen, wardrobe room, and a little courtyard garden. Relating this event to my parents, I stated: "We weren't very nervous and we danced it well, I think. David played Parts II and III of the music. We danced in silence Parts I and IV. David hadn't practiced I and Earle hadn't 'reduced' IV to piano yet. We wore black tights and bright colored leotards—our *Suite by Chance* costumes." If we weren't "very nervous," we were certainly nervous enough. I remember feeling alien and stared at in the dressing rooms we shared with a few Graham company regulars who were there for their own rehearsal. Once in the large, elegant studio, the familiar faces of Nick Cernovich, John, and Earle, who'd come to silently cheer us through our ordeal, eased the tension somewhat. But there was a distance, unbridged, and a coolness, which remained, in the space between the area where the people in straight-backed chairs sat judging us and the dancing arena where we danced our hearts out. Afterward, politely, they told Merce that they would call him. Not so politely, they never did. Merce waited. We waited while Merce waited. But the call never came. We were left with dashed hopes and the feeling that we'd been treated badly.

In late April 1955, the company auditioned for Ted Shawn. "He seemed to like *Amores* and *Banjo*, but he didn't like the new piece with Earle's music," I told my mother. "I doubt if he'll use us, but he might." He did. Shawn not only called, he booked us for four performances the following July at Jacob's Pillow. As if in anticipation of being at Papa Shawn's Pillow, the performing life of the company began to liven up a bit. We gave two performances in the last week in May: the first at Bard College, Annandale-on-Hudson, about two and a half hours north of the city, where *Springweather and People* was given its first performance, though not with orchestra or costumes; and the second at the Henry Street Playhouse in New York, sponsored by the Japan Society. It must have been at the request of the Japan Society that the program copy for this concert included brief notes on each dance (something that had not occurred before), plus an attached one-page "Note on 'Modern' Dance and the Work of Merce Cunningham," written, no doubt, by John Cage. The last two paragraphs, in which the Cage/Cunningham philosophy is thoroughly, succinctly, and lucidly presented, should be read as written, not paraphrased by me:

> Merce Cunningham, who was for several years a soloist in the company of Martha Graham, and a member of the faculty of the American School of Ballet, has, since 1944, developed his own school of dancing and choreography, the continuity of which no longer relies on linear elements, be they narrative or psychological, nor does it rely on a movement towards and away

from climax. As in abstract painting, it is assumed that an element (a movement, a sound, a change of light) is in and of itself expressive; what it communicates is in large part determined by the observer himself. It is assumed
that the dance supports itself and does not need support from the music.
The two arts take place in a common rhythmic structure, but each art
expresses this structure in its own way. The result is an activity of interpen-
etrations in time and space, not counterpoints, or controlled relationships,
but flexibilities as are known from the mobiles of Alexander Calder. By not
relying on psychology, the "modern" dance is freed from the concerns of
most such dancing. What comes through, though different for each
observer, is clear (since one can approach it directly—not through any
other conception), brilliant (the dancers can move unencumbered, not covering themselves with disguising costumes), and serene (the absence of an
emotionally-driven continuity brings about an over-all sense of tranquillity,
illuminated from time to time by feelings which are in turn heroic, mirthful,
wondrous, erotic, fearful, disgusting, sorrowful and angry). As for individual movements, they are both derived and discovered; in being derived,
they stem as much from the ballet as from modern dance; in being discovered, they represent the findings of Cunningham himself, who has constantly searched and refined his sense of movement. Where other music
and dance generally attempt to "say" something, this theater is one which
"presents" activity. This can be said to affirm life, to introduce an audience,
not to a specialized world of art, but to the open, unpredictably changing
world of everyday living.[15]

This Cage/Cunningham philosophy never altered, but after nearly fifty
years it's been taken for granted that audiences understand it. No one
expresses these ideas as well as John did, and he got very tired of repeating himself over the years, thus they were expressed less and less frequently. Today's audiences are often as baffled by Merce's work as
audiences were years ago, and they have no easy access to the ideas that
could illuminate and augment their own perceptions. No matter what is
said by publicists or written by critics, and no matter what Merce himself
says publicly (as we've seen, he admits to devious behavior when it comes
to discussing his own work), there *is* more to see (perceive) than steps. For
John, the proselytizer, opening eyes and ears through his work was a lifelong crusade. For Merce, the effector, his work was always a matter of
necessity: he did what he had to do and could not do without. Willy-nilly,
they were beginning to change the way people look and listen.

Changing the way people look. That is what Bob Rauschenberg was doing with paintings like *Charlene* (1954) and *Rebus* (1955) and the notorious *Bed* (1955). The poverty that was the status quo for all of us in the mid-fifties was never a deterrent to creativity, and this was nowhere more evident than in Bob's loft on Pearl Street. As Calvin Tomkins tells the story, Bob woke up one spring morning eager to paint, had no canvas and no money to buy any, so decided to make a stretcher for an old hand-me-down quilt and paint on it. "Any incentive to paint is as good as another,"[1] says Bob. The quilt had been given to him by a fellow student at Black Mountain, and was, by this time, well worn and beyond its intended use. Says Bob, "There is no poor subject."[2] But he discovered that the quilt pattern was too strong, so he attached his pillow and a piece of sheet to the top, giving him a white area to paint on, and the quilt (in his words) "gave up and became a bed, stopped insisting on itself."[3] A real bed? A painting of a bed? Both. Neither. Whatever it was, it "was to become one of the *objets de scandale* of American art,"[4] shocking and out-raging almost everyone who saw it. According to art critic John Russell, "The case of Rauschenberg's *Bed* is comparatively simple, though few works of art have caused so much exasperation. . . . *Bed* . . . asserts that the eloquence of paint can be bestowed on the apparatus of everyday life."[5] As Rauschenberg put it, his "paintings became awkwardly physi-cal."[6] He coined the term "combine" to describe the new works that incor-porated real objects: not merely paintings, more than collage, and not really sculpture. As Jasper Johns said years later, "It was a fantastically prolific conception of what art was."[7] Although Jasper recently recalled that the term "combine" was his suggestion, Bob told an interviewer: "Instead of actually *looking* at the work of art, people would argue why it looked more like sculpture or painting . . . so I had to start calling the work I was doing something. Then I remembered a story, which may or may not be true, about Calder, who struggled to be considered a sculptor. He made up the word "mobiles." [Actually, Duchamp coined the term for Calder's sculptures in 1931.] So I thought that I'd try such a thing. My work was sculpture and painting, a combination of the two."[8]

"Combines." The objects Bob used were of every description: other people's discarded junk found in the streets and back alleys of Manhattan and on the beaches and wharves of Staten Island (only a nickel ferry-boat ride away); occasionally, things given him by friends (the quilt, and the tailless pheasant used in *Satellite*). In the case of the stuffed white rooster strutting on top of his free-standing *Odalisque* and the elegant stuffed angora goat with a tire around its belly in *Monogram*, they were purchases that he couldn't afford, made on the installment plan. The rooster and the goat were irresistible because, he said, they reminded him of the animals he'd had as a child. His love of animals never languished, but in 1955 he was frustrated by lack of money to feed pets of his own. Temporarily, the love was transferred to the stuffed ones he put into his combines—a pheasant, a hen, a rooster, a goat, an eagle. He had little fear of losing his animal friends since nothing he made at that time sold. The combines were offensive to me when I first saw them. I associated them with trophies hanging over the mantelpieces of macho "great" white hunters. When I got to know Bob better, I learned that he, too, hated hunting and the arrogance of land developers who destroyed precious wildlife habitats for personal profit.

In any case, the stuffed animals were atypical compared to the commonplace objects that usually found their way into his work of that period: buckets, doors, signs, automobile parts, electric lights, old radios, old tires, rope, chain, tin cans, worn and weathered wood, mirror, and glass, as well as cheap, printed reproductions of works by the great artists of the past, and more personal stuff like old socks, cast-off neckties, paint-spattered pants, photographs, fabric, umbrellas, postcards, newspaper and magazine clippings—public and private "junk"—put together with bravado and glue, hammer and nails, screws and screwdriver; painted by drip, splash, and brush; scribbled on with pencil, in what he called "random order." No representation. No illusionistic transcriptions of reality. No hierarchies of importance. No judgments about what is beautiful or what is ugly. What did it signify? For me—a gleeful acceptance of the multiplicity of things in the environment in which he lived and his affirmation of Cage's philosophy that "the use of art was to 'change ways of seeing [and hearing], to open up one's eyes to just seeing what there was to see."[9] In the mid-fifties, Rauschenberg realized "that raw material can be served up raw and that art and life could be made to interlock as they had never quite interlocked before."[10] If, on first viewing, Bob's combines often appeared capricious, willfully clumsy, jumbled, chaotic, and maddeningly perverse they also gave evidence of a prodigious talent, and, to quote John Russell again, "the application of an acrobatic intelligence to the situation of painting as it presented itself in the 1950's."[11] Less than twenty-five years later, the combines were considered sensuous, poetic, graceful, and highly evocative masterpieces. They had moved from the obscurity of Bob's Battery lofts into the major museums of the world, and just as suddenly the enfant terrible who made them had become "a protean genius,"[12] the producer of "some of the finest art that has been made in our lifetime."[13]

Although Cage's ideas influenced Bob profoundly, these ideas were transformed in Bob's hands into an ardently permissive, explosively energetic aesthetic far freer and far more personally passionate than anything Cage wanted for himself as a composer or indeed was capable of. Bob says that when he is working he tries to disappear, to stop thinking about his own existence, but he makes no attempt to negate the self or the ego by using complex, calculated, chance procedures as Cage did in composing music. John's puritanism wasn't suited to Bob's extravagant nature. Bob's found materials were allowed to be themselves in much the same spirit as Cage's found sounds and Cunningham's found movements but, ironically, Cage's philosophy found a purer realization in Bob's combines than in Cage's live music or—particularly—in Cunningham's choreography. Dance, like all performance arts, depends upon human beings to present the material, and the dancer's presence cannot fail but muddy the waters, so to speak. The same movement performed by two different dancers is inevitably different, and even the same movement performed by the same dancer on two different occasions can never be exactly the same. It cannot be otherwise. We see the dance through the dancer. Not so with Rauschenberg's combines. There the materials can be themselves, can have a life of their own, separate from the artist who put them together. No need for a middleman, i.e., a performer, to bring the work to life. But it was just this human element, this complex and unpredictable interaction of people in art and life, that Bob so loved in theater and especially in Merce's dance company, and sorely missed in the solitary act of painting. Ironic! While Merce's temperament is ideally suited to the isolated existence of the painter, Bob's is best fitted to coexistence in a community of artists as found in Merce's company.

A visit to Bob's Pearl Street studio in 1955 was charged with almost unbearable excitement: "What will we find this time?" He was riding the crest of a wave of inventive energy, and to jump aboard with him at that speed was dizzying. Passage from his black to his red paintings hadn't been too difficult due to the exhilarating sense of joy that swept one along with him, but the combines struck me as downright aggressive in their visual overload. I was always uncomfortable with excess, so it was calming to go downstairs, where Jasper Johns—a man as reticent as Bob was irrepressible—painted American flags, targets, and numbers. I scarcely knew Jasper. Earle and I first met him at Sari Dienes's studio on Fifty-seventh Street near Carnegie Hall when he was clerking in a Marboro bookstore nearby. I didn't like him then; he seemed cold, aloof to the point of rudeness, sullen and monosyllabic. His personality couldn't have been more unlike Bob's, so it was a shock to learn some months later that they'd developed a strong, intimate relationship, and a pleasant surprise to discover that Jasper could be very polite and thoughtful. What I'd thought was coldness was really extreme reserve, the manifestation of a meticulously precise intellect.

But flags? targets? numbers? Strange paintings this man made. Commonplace images. Said Jasper: "Things the mind already knows . . . that gave me room to work on other levels."[14] What levels? The most accessible were pure painting. Bold and arresting. The others—intellectual investigations in perception, illusion and reality, abstraction and representation, ambiguity—were not so easy to grasp. I had no comprehension of what Jasper was really doing, but of course that didn't stop me from having preferences. Flags and targets as subject or symbol were puzzling and unappealing, but the numbers moved me instantly, intuitively. It was something to do with the conjunction of the unexplainably simple and the obviously complex, and the precise yet lyrical way in which they were painted in a thin milky white wax on newsprint. These paintings were remote, with nothing of the slapdash tumultuousness of Bob's combines. Despite the surprising subject/object, one could peruse the work peacefully—observe and ruminate, and allow oneself to be totally bewitched by the painterliness, by the exquisite use of encaustic (hot wax with which pigments are combined, applied quickly, and fixed with a hot iron). It was an unusual, ancient technique that he had discovered in a book on one of those jumbled remainders tables in the Marboro shop where he worked. If I felt more at ease with Jap's work at that moment, it was because I could identify with his painstaking attention to minute detail—even though I wasn't always happy with this approach in my own work, where it seemed constricting to my growth as a performer. I envied Bob's openness and daring at the same time that I felt threatened by his voracious exuberance. I wonder . . . did Jap feel this, too?

On June 6, while I was in Fitchburg, Massachusetts, helping my mother

with her twenty-fifth annual dance concert, I received a telegram:
TOASTED SUZIE IS OUR ICECREAM. HAPPY DANCING AND LOVE. EARLE. The
slightly altered quote from Gertrude Stein translated: "I got the job! We
eat!" The job was recording engineer for Capitol Records, by our standards an extremely well-paid position, but difficult, extremely tiring, leaving him little energy for his own work. That Earle should support my
dancing at the expense of his composing troubled me deeply and would be
a problem for me (for both of us, although he never complained) for several
years. Although I had some intermittent modeling work, and a five-week
job teaching and staging a spring dance concert for a private school in New
Jersey, I still wasn't able to support my dancing in 1955, and I owed a
whole year's tuition to the Metropolitan Opera Ballet School, which I was
determined to pay myself. Paul Taylor suggested I go to television and
Broadway dance auditions: he had made $197 in one week doing a televi-
sion show. So off I went to auditions: the Fred Waring show; Rod Alexander show; Broadway musical summer replacement auditions; Jones Beach.
I was always petrified, but at each audition I did a little better and lasted a
little longer, but never long enough. Alas, a showgirl I wasn't. Taken seriously, auditioning was a dehumanizing ordeal. Not taken seriously, it
could be educational, even fun, but being rejected usually left me demor-
alized. It happened a lot that season—not only to me, out on my own, but
to the Cunningham company in its attempt to get bookings. Remy suggested that I try high-fashion photographic modeling. He got a friend of
his—Saul Leiter, a painter who supported himself by doing commercial
photography—to take some photos of me. Saul's studio was, as I recall, in
the same building as de Kooning's. My father gave me a huge leather port-
folio and I began to trudge the streets looking for work, despite the fact
that I needed all my time and energy for dancing. Merce desperately
wanted to be able to support his dance company, but he could barely support himself. He was often in debt and took teaching jobs all over the
country whenever he could in order to pay his own bills. That summer, he
closed his studio and went out to California to teach at the Idyllwild Summer Institute. John stayed in Stony Point building the stone wall for his
house. In early July, Merce returned to rehearse for Jacob's Pillow and
invited Bruce King, who'd been taking Merce's advanced class regularly
for some time, to replace Paul Taylor in our Pillow performances of *Septet.*

Jacob's Pillow! Scene of countless performances attended with my
mother. In the 1930s, sitting on straw mats on the barn studio floor, we
watched Shawn and his men dancers (my mother's distant cousin by marriage, Wilbur McCormack, among them) perform works-in-progress. In the

forties, with the building of the Ted Shawn Dance Festival Theatre, we sat in proper seats to see a mix of ballet, modern, and ethnic dance that became the standard bill of fare at the Pillow for years to come. The Cunningham company shared the bill with Alicia Alonso and Erik Bruhn and La Mariquita. Our repertory included *Septet, Banjo,* and Merce's Satie solo *Two Step,* all with recognizably tuneful accompaniment guaranteed to tax the audience not at all. Walter Terry, reviewing us at long last, apparently agreed: "Three of [Cunningham's] most engaging and theatrically pursuable [?] numbers . . . If Miss Alonso and Mr. Bruhn shone brightly on this bill, they by no means obscured excellent dancing of quite another nature, the dancing of Merce Cunningham and his fine company."[15]

While the choice of dances also pleased my mother, who came with several carloads of her students, Shawn's pre-performance curtain speech was an especially delightful treat for her. He said he was proud to present his " 'grand-daughter' Carolyn Brown, daughter of his pupil Marion Rice of Fitchburg, the best dance teacher in Massachusetts!" In her diary, she wrote, "My kids were proud and joyous."

Being on a program with Alicia Alonso and Erik Bruhn was thrilling and intimidating. Instructive, too. At every performance we watched them from the wings. Ballet's focus is frontal and its practitioners are trained with that perspective foremost in mind. If a dancer isn't blessed with ideal proportions, good turnout, perfect line, and beautiful feet, he or she can all too quickly learn to cheat the position in order to achieve the desired look from the audience's perspective. I saw that in Alonso's performance. From where we stood, her feet appeared to be "sickled" and her line in certain positions almost awkward, yet from out front, these faults were adroitly disguised. Bruhn's technique from whatever angle was impeccable. Only because he shared a dressing room with Merce did we learn that this eloquent, technically incomparable Danish dancer, whose every performance seemed flawless, was suffering excruciating pain from a repeated injury sustained when he landed on his knee out of a double *tour en l'air.* The pain was so acute that, at the age of twenty-six, he was seriously considering retiring from the stage. He believed that the vocabulary and *enchaînement* of the classical ballet repertoire must be performed as written, not adjusted to suit the foibles of injured dancers, and that his audience, at least the knowledgeable ballet audience that he cared about, had expectations that must be met, if not exceeded.

Harnessed to an ever-rising, more challenging, increasingly difficult standard of technical excellence, the male ballet dancer's body often burns out before he has reached maturity as an artist. Male modern dancer-choreographers can last longer because their vocabulary is their own, can be flexible and can change. They aren't competing Olympic-style. Even the expectations of the audience are somewhat different. After injuries suffered during the de Lys season, Merce asked himself questions such as, If not that way of jumping, then what else? prompting him to explore other ways and other qualities of jumping. The development of the new movement could be subtle, complex, but not necessarily easier. For Erik Bruhn, other options did not exist. He would have to find a doctor to cure him—he was trying acupuncture next—or quit. He must have found one, because he didn't officially retire until 1973, at the age of forty-four.

When we left the Pillow after the last performance late Saturday night, Merce already had an invitation from Shawn to return with the company the following summer, and I had a tiny sterling-silver charm—a likeness of Shawn in a Denishawn *pas de basque* pose. On the envelope he'd written: "To Carolyn Brown from her proud 'Grandpa Shawn.' "

Back in the city, I received a phone call from Merce instructing me to start passport proceedings. All those letters John had been writing were producing results! But less than two weeks later, John's application to the Asiatic Institute for funds for the tour was turned down, and coincidentally we learned that the United States government was going to send Martha Graham and Company to the Orient. John refused to give up. He insisted that no matter what happened about the tour abroad, the pre-Oriental tour on the West Coast was definitely ON! Classes and rehearsals with Merce resumed in August.

In September, the Sadler's Wells returned for five weeks. Again it was pure joy, and I actually got to dance a bit, in *Sleeping Beauty, Swan Lake, Firebird,* and *Coppélia.* Twenty-six performances. A day when Fonteyn danced only the matinee, I chose to forgo my super's job in the evening's *Swan Lake* in order to allow her performance to sink indelibly into my memory. If anything, I was more worshipful, more acutely aware of her unassuming artistry than I had been two years earlier. Little offstage glimpses revealed a person who was genuinely kind, thoughtful, generous. Not attributes characteristically found in stars. But as one biographer wrote, "Fonteyn is a great artist by design and a great star by accident. It is well to remember that many a celebrity answers to this description in reverse. The artist develops from within and the star assimilates from without . . . the sources [of the artist] are spiritual, intangible."[16]

Once again, the management of the Sadler's Wells treated the supers with remarkable generosity, allowing us to stand in the wings as long as we stood with our backs pressed against the flats and did not move. Occasionally, VIP guests were also allowed into the wings for some ballets, and when Fonteyn danced, the wings were usually packed. It was astonishing to me that she permitted it.

In the opening section of Fokine's *Firebird,* the firebird—as though in flight—makes a number of swift leaping diagonals across the stage, exiting and entering from different wings several times. In order to make the next entrance on musical cue, the dancer must dash from downstage to upstage, often making a quick stop at the rosin box on her way. One night when Fonteyn was dancing the role, a tiny girl, not more than five years old, stepped away from the flat and into the wing to get a better view. At just that moment Fonteyn flew offstage, knocked the little girl down and sent her thudding across the floor. The child's mother was panic-stricken, not so much for her daughter's safety as for Fonteyn's. The rest of us held our breath. Fonteyn rushed to the child, knelt beside her, apologized (!), asked if she was hurt, if she was *sure* she hadn't been injured; then, reassured by the wide-eyed mute child who kept vigorously shaking her head no to each question, Fonteyn touched her gently, then dashed upstage into the entrance wing and onto the stage on cue. At the end of the scene she went back to see the little girl, to make sure that she really was all right. Another dancer would have lashed out in fury. It could have been much more serious than a missed entrance; she might have broken bones or torn cartilage. Of course, that is what concerned us, but her concern was only for the child. Fonteyn's instantaneous response in that moment of crisis revealed the human being within the artist.

For the five weeks that the Sadler's Wells was in residence at the old Met I took class there every morning, rehearsed with Merce or the Wells every afternoon, took a class every evening with Merce or at the Met, supered most nights and weekends (matinees and evening performances), and was rarely in bed before one in the morning. I loved, cherished every minute of those five weeks. In the midst of all this, Miss Craske asked me and seven others to audition for the Metropolitan Opera Ballet. I had to explain to her that I expected to be performing with Merce in the fall. After the final auditions, Zachary Solov's assistant approached me after class and asked me why I hadn't auditioned, and would I be interested in joining the company? The eighty-seven dollars a week would have been very welcome, but truthfully I did not want to dance in that company, and I would have appeared ungrateful and lacking in humility if I'd told anyone that I just couldn't start as a corps dancer in the Metropolitan Opera Ballet. There wasn't time for that! Although most people there thought I was about eighteen, I had just turned twenty-eight. At one of Merce's rehearsals, shortly after I'd turned down the Met offer, I attacked my parts with a kind of wildcat ferocity, dancing as though possessed. "I've never seen you dance so wildly! What's gotten into you?" I recall Viola asking. "There's not much time left!" was my answer. The exquisitely trained English dancers had once again inspired and depressed me. I wanted to work harder and improve faster, but how? Miss Craske said I needed to perform, and of course dancing in the Opera Ballet would have fulfilled this need as well as the financial one. As luck would have it, Merce's West Coast tour did materialize in November and was preceded by two performance dates outside New York City.

The first one, *A Program of Music and Dance,* presented by the Rockland Foundation in New City, New York, took place despite torrential rains and gale-force winds that began early in the morning before we left New York. For the first time, Nicola Cernovich was with us to design lighting. Should the company's Far East tour materialize, Merce would certainly need a lighting designer and a stage manager, and there lay Nick's opportunity.

That night *Springweather* had its own costumes, credited in the program to the artistic collaboration of Remy Charlip, Bob Rauschenberg, Ray Johnson, and Vera Williams, but exactly who did what was never clear to me. Up to curtain time the costumes were still being put together. Vera did the sewing while Remy, Bob, and Ray hovered and kibitzed. While Vera sewed, we rehearsed and Nick desperately tried to learn the complicated science of lighting design in the space of an afternoon. Actually he appeared to be more interested in experimenting with effects—for instance, what happens when bottles of water are shaken in front of gelled light? M.C. and Fance Stevenson were dashing around after him to do his bidding and learn their cues. The place was lunatic. "Is it still raining?" John would inevitably ask whenever anyone came in out of the storm. The answer was always "Yes!" from the soaked-to-the-skin person who stood dripping into a puddle of his own making. We heard new rumors of catastrophes—cars stuck, bridges out, detours, evacuations. The bridge to The Land did wash out, and there were fears the dam above would burst, release torrents of water, and sweep away the little Community on The Land.

As the downpour continued, we entertained serious doubts about having any audience at all. At curtain time—8:40 p.m.—less than a dozen people had arrived. "Hold the curtain," Nick was told. So he held. Ten minutes. Fifteen. Twenty. Thirty. By 9:15, five hundred people had shown up—among them Franz Kline, Willem de Kooning, Philip Guston, Jasper

Johns, Alan Hovhaness, and Morton Feldman. Our reliable fans. By the time we danced the twenty-nine-minute *Springweather and People* it was very late and we were exceedingly tired. A post-performance party still lay ahead at a de Rothschild mansion (not Bethsabée's). The extraordinarily considerate hostess bundled us off to an elegantly laid table and a lavish four-course dinner in her kitchen while the other guests were kept out until we had finished—a blessing, because discussing the Cage/Cunningham aesthetic while holding a drink in one hand and a plate in the other turned most parties into an ordeal. We didn't leave until three in the morning and, with washouts, detours, and getting lost several times, didn't arrive home until six. That afternoon I had a matinee of *Sleeping Beauty*, followed by the last performance of the season that evening. I wouldn't have considered missing them.

On November 2, the company assembled at Forty-first and Broadway to take the limousine to the Marine Terminal at La Guardia Airport: Merce and John, M.C. and David, Remy, Nick, new company member Bruce King, and the four women dancers—Anita Dencks, Viola Farber, Marianne Preger, and me. It was *really* happening: we were on our way to California, Oregon, and Washington. Merce Cunningham and Dance Company ON TOUR! John had managed to secure nine dance performances, two music concerts, a number of master classes and demonstrations, and, for himself, some seminars and lectures, spread over the space of a month. Such a leisurely tour would not be economically feasible today, but in 1955, our housing was arranged through friends and relatives; we rarely stayed in hotels. We cooked our own meals wherever there was a kitchen available to us and accepted *every* invitation to dine—be it for breakfast, lunch, dinner, or after-performance parties. No one was paid a salary. We traveled as one big, slightly unwieldy family, John and Merce playing the parental roles. They organized travel and the sleeping and eating arrangements, planned the schedule, and paid the bills. We were completely dependent upon their decisions. Although a few chafed at this lack of independence, I think most of us felt well cared for and enjoyed being free to concentrate on just dancing. Our responsibilities included taking company class and occasionally teaching it; caring for our costumes (laundering, ironing, and mending); and, of course, rehearsing and performing. Oh, we sometimes took turns with the cooking and the washing up, but usually John, Nick, and M.C. took over in the kitchen. In fact, John coddled us, overextending himself to make sure that everyone was happy and well provided for. Merce did *not* coddle us. Not then. Not ever.

The first hardship occurred at the very beginning of the tour, in Santa

Barbara, where we stayed in the guesthouse of a luxurious rambling adobe villa nestled high in the side of a mountain: outside our door was a magnificent swimming pool, and we hadn't brought our swimsuits! Of course that didn't stop us. Merce wasn't amused. In fact, he was worried that we would be seduced by such luxury and that the company work ethic would be subverted. He didn't actually tell us not to sunbathe, except by example—he didn't go near the pool himself until after the performance. We were there five days. With only one performance, Merce scheduled class and rehearsal every day, thus carefully restricting the time we could spend lolling about in the sun.

The Lobero Theatre was small, charming, and quasi-Spanish in architecture. An audience of about 325 people attended, which was, we were told, a good size for dance events in Santa Barbara, the town where Martha Graham spent her teenage years. The audience responded warmly, and the review in the local newspaper was informed and interesting. The reviewer ended his review with these observations: "The intellectual preoccupations and the amazing newness of Cunningham's conceptions offer some barrier to full and immediate understanding of his work. Its full emotional impact, its thorough craftsmanship and its refreshing ingenuity sufficiently attest to its validity."[17]

Midway through the first movement of *Springweather and People*, the piano pedals fell off. David sent a frantic SOS to John, out in the audience, who came running back to help. For the rest of the twenty-nine-minute dance, John lay flat on his back under the piano holding the pedals in place; every time David pressed on a pedal his hands got pinched, painfully. "One has to pedal that piece like a bicycle," was Earle's response to this bit of news. "John's hands must look like hamburger!" Said John after the ordeal was over: "With this, I'm ready to give up the art of the dance." In fact, with this exception, John was having a wonderful time, absolutely brimming over with enthusiasm and good cheer. At dinner parties, he and Nick and M.C. entertained everyone with their hilarious version of the Japanese tea ceremony, but the wildest hilarity was earned by John's *spécialité*—a sort of theater of the absurd in which he set up an improvised puppet theater, without the puppets, by draping a tablecloth or sheet over a table or two chairs. He, hidden from view, was the "puppeteer." Curtain up. There, "onstage," would be an object—a shoe, perhaps. Curtain down. Curtain up. Shoe gone. In its place, a rumpled handkerchief. Curtain down. On and on he'd go, juxtaposing ordinary objects, sometimes adding one or more at a time, always in total silence. At first it seemed just plain silly, but the longer it went on, and the more absurd the incongruities, the funnier it became—until he had his audience collapsed on the floor, groaning with laughter.

Nights at the Morgans' mountainside villa were magical: hot, balmy, desert breezes blew in from the land every now and then, setting the foliage to rustling and murmuring. Then deep silence. Below, the lights of Santa Barbara twinkled at the edge of the sea, and above, out of the still blackness, falling stars plummeted earthward. On our last night we women couldn't resist a midnight skinny-dip in the pool. Remy and Merce followed (without) suit. And our magnanimous host appeared with a bottle of champagne and a toast to the continuing success of our tour. "What a *fantastic* beginning!!!! It is really hard to believe that it is all true," I gushed in a letter home.

Next stop: Los Angeles—John's hometown. The Sadler's Wells Ballet was touring the West Coast at the same time, and in L.A. we were in direct competition with each other. We feared we would have no audience, but we did just fine, and to our amazement, the Los Angeles correspondent of the *Musical Courier* wrote: "More rewarding [than the Sadler's Wells] was the agile athleticism of Merce Cunningham and his company seen at UCLA. His program had good contrast, with music by Satie and Gottschalk balanced with modern scores by John Cage and Christian Wolff. Above all, Cunningham's work had real style and 'bite,' which was too often missing from the offering of the larger troupe."[18]

Arriving at night in San Diego on a train from Los Angeles, we were met by a group of people with station wagons. A good-looking man approached Marianne and me as the company milled about waiting to be assigned to particular hosts. He introduced himself and quickly led us to his automobile, saying to the person in charge, "I'll take these two," and drove us off into the hills to the most fabulous contemporary *Arts and Architecture*–type house we'd ever seen except in magazines. Our abductor turned out to be the house's architect, Lloyd Ruoco. Marianne and I couldn't believe our good fortune. We learned later that we were not the intended guests! It was *Mrs.* Ruoco's intention to have Merce and John as her celebrity guests, but her husband, with an eye for pretty young women, ignored her wishes and whisked us off before she had a chance to protest. She could barely suppress her anger and disappointment. Merce and John were only amused. Mr. Ruoco was smugly triumphant. And Marianne and I took to living like queens-for-a-day with irrepressible exuberance. Another good audience greeted us in San Diego, the performance went without a glitch, and we were entertained lavishly. Hurrah for the touring life!

Beginning with our stay in San Francisco, my letters home became a bit giddy, with an embarrassing abundance of exclamation points, underlinings, capital letters, and strings of superlatives like marvelous, glorious, incredible, magnificent, delightful, unbelievable, and the like. As had thousands before us, we fell in love with San Francisco and did all the touristy things we could squeeze in.

It was my turn to teach company class on the day of the performance. Merce took the class, an unnerving experience for me. Afterward he gave me a critique of sorts. It was the only time I can remember in the nearly forty years I taught his technique that he ever said one word to me about my teaching, so I valued that brief discussion and never forgot it. His principal correction had to do with the overall pace of my class and specifically with the speed of each exercise or phrase within the context of the whole class. It was something I had never thought about. From that time on, whenever Merce taught I observed his pacing—the way the rhythms varied and the speeds shifted and how important these changes were to developing strength and flexibility.

In San Francisco, Anita and I stayed in a $2.50-a-night, very old, small, seedy hotel—the Taylor—that proffered its own sort of luxury: privacy. Being a guest in someone's home, particularly if one is working hard, presents certain difficulties. No matter how comfortable the accommodations or how kind the hosts, there are always social obligations that can't be graciously avoided. Remy and Nick were given a different option: the choice of staying at the Taylor Hotel or in a defunct "house of pleasure." They opted for the brothel. There was still the huge sunken pool where the Ziegfeld Follies' beauty Anna Held was supposed to have taken milk baths; beaded curtains still jangled in doorways; dark plush velvets, dust-laden, still hung on walls and windows. Nick and Remy couldn't resist the tawdry fascination of the place and camped out under magnificent chandeliers in the midst of building materials and plaster dust and the faded opulence that still hinted of decadent orgies and illicit intrigues past.

We were having too much fun—not a single hardship so far. San Francisco was such a temptress that even Merce succumbed a bit to its enticements. We had to remind ourselves that we were there to work, although in the years that John "managed" the company, work and play always seemed to be happily mixed. Sometimes even the work was play, as it was for John and David in San Francisco, where all the music, with the exception of the Satie two-piano score for *Septet,* was composed for magnetic tape, and John had managed to borrow eight excellent new tape machines and loudspeakers from Ampex Corporation. David and John were like two kids at

Christmas, with eight new Tinkertoys. They fussed and fiddled over the equipment all day long right up until curtain.

John and Merce had chosen a daring and difficult program to present at the Marine's Memorial Theatre: three compositions for magnetic tape—by Brown, Cage, and Feldman—and three dances with tape music: *Collage I* (Pierre Schaeffer), *Fragments* (Pierre Boulez), and *Suite by Chance* (Christian Wolff). *Septet* was the only offering that used a conventional musical instrument. But what a night! Everyone agreed: the music pieces were marvelous, each one surprisingly distinctive. The audience laughed aloud with pleasure, apparently finding them amusing and delightful. Merce danced magnificently, as though something crucial was at stake, and the audience, quite enthusiastic throughout the evening, seemed to adore him especially. John was ecstatic.

A day and a half later, as the company gathered on the ferry about to embark across the bay to Oakland, Nick came prancing aboard—jubilant, grinning, chortling—waving a bunch of newspapers over his head. Reviews by Alfred Frankenstein in the *San Francisco Chronicle*, Alexander Fried in the *San Francisco Examiner*, and Marjorie Fisher in the *San Francisco News*. Instant gratification! This was the experience John had expected but was inexplicably denied in New York during the Theatre de Lys season. What a spectacular ending to the fabulous San Francisco leg of our journey: while the city's skyline, rosy-hued in the early morning sun, receded into the snake of fog curling slowly across the bay, Nick read the reviews aloud while the rest of us danced deliriously around the deck, hollering, whooping, and hugging one another.

If you like to keep track of what's brand new in the arts you have a right to kick yourself for not coming out to the Marine's Memorial Theatre last Tuesday evening. What took place was a recital of strikingly novel dancing by Merce Cunningham and his New York troupe. Cunningham is a fine, lively and graceful dancer. What's more, he has ideas. . . . All his numbers had a stimulating, and often really expressive new approach.[19]

Dancing as far removed from Russian ballet as the jet age is from the Pony Express delighted a Marine's Memorial Theatre audience last night. The stark simplicity of the modern contrasted with the artificiality of the other. And while Merce Cunningham could certainly outdo any male dancer at his own game we have yet to see a classic male dancer who could match the incredible balance, poise, and precision by Mr. Cunningham in his modern dance program. . . . He and his excellent associates have made their bodies such precision instruments that they seemed able to do the impossible. Moreover, there was a naturalness and buoyancy in their movements and rhythmic flow that kept rhythmic patterns going steadily and projecting themselves across the footlights even when there was no music to define or carry it.[20]

Alfred Frankenstein, the music critic for the *San Francisco Chronicle* since 1934, was held in high regard by John and Merce; what he thought about the company meant a great deal to them: "Cunningham's company, like their director, possess both an incomparable range of technique and personalities well worth projecting by means of it."[21] Personalities well worth projecting? What indescribable pleasure that gave us after so many reviewers seemed to agree with P. W. Manchester, who had described us as "so completely dehumanized as to seem almost inhuman."[22] And if all these reviews weren't sufficient good news, John then announced that the San Francisco Ballet had commissioned Merce to choreograph a new work for them, with music by John, set and costumes by Rauschenberg. In a state of total euphoria we boarded the Southern Pacific Railroad's *Shasta Daylight* for the sixteen-hour trip to Portland and our next engagement.

After San Francisco, Portland seemed a sad, dull place; damp and dreary. There were no friends to wine and dine us. The few people whom John knew seemed to be avoiding us, so the whole company had to stay in a hotel for six days—a worrisome expense. Adding to the gloom, John received word that ANTA definitely would not sponsor the company's trip to the Orient. He told us that he'd received a hideous letter from ANTA, which he described as "very mean." I started to wire Earle—"Orient Trip Canceled"—but John wouldn't let me. He said he hadn't given up all hope yet, even with the latest setback, but he needed to raise the astronomical sum of fifty thousand dollars in a few days. He and Merce dictated the telegram that I finally did send to Earle:

ORIENT TRIP EXTREMELY DOUBTFUL. DO NOTHING SUBVERSIVE. NO FUNDS. NO FUTURE FUN. WE LOVE YOU.

The message was delivered by telephone at three in the morning, a little more than twelve hours too late! Thinking optimistically, Earle had just had all the required inoculations—typhoid, cholera, and smallpox shots— *at once,* ignoring common sense and his doctor's warnings, because as the Cunningham company "Advance Man," he wanted to be ready for as speedy a departure to the Far East as possible once the ANTA funding was confirmed. He'd also ignored his doctor's advice to go straight home to bed after getting the shots. Instead, he went to hear the premiere of a Luigi Nono piece played by the Modern Jazz Quartet and an orchestra conducted by Gunther Schuller. By the end of the concert he was utterly miserable; by the time he got home he couldn't move his arms even to get out of his jacket. He fell into bed fully clothed only to be awakened at three a.m. by our telegram, to learn that his misery was to be endured for nought.

But perhaps not. Suddenly things began looking optimistic again. Isadora Bennett,[23] the company's press representative in New York, was excited by the San Francisco reviews and renewed her efforts on Merce's behalf. Senators and congressmen were telephoned. Emile de Antonio[24] phoned Chester Bowles. Morris Ernst, the lawyer who helped James Joyce's *Ulysses into* the United States, was trying to get the Cunningham company *out.* Ten days remained before John would have to admit defeat and cancel the bookings in India and Japan, and to sadly decline the invitation extended to the whole company to be guests of the Balinese government for two weeks. John fought valiantly for our Asian tour right up to the last second. A last-ditch try-everything/try-anything frenzy of activity seized his every waking moment when he wasn't running around meeting the demands of the present tour, which required him to function as company manager, performer, and lecturer.

We became quite fond of Portland by the end of our stay. Merce bloomed under a shower of attention and adoration. His pleasure actually showed. John was positively, unabashedly rapturous. He seemed to be in a state of perpetual intoxication. Whether from joy, beer, or both, he never stopped laughing, and he kept dreaming up ever more exalted adventures for the company's future.

The Thanksgiving holiday was spent in Centralia, Washington, Merce's hometown. Merce's father put us up in the Lewis-Clark Hotel for two nights as his guests. What a dear, charming, elegant gentleman was Merce's dad. Mr. Clifford Cunningham was a country lawyer of the old school whose practice included cases as diverse as homesteading, murder, and kidnapping. He wore dapper gray spats and very proper suits and spoke unaffectedly in a kindly, wise, and courteous manner—my idea of a classic Old World barrister. "He contends he wore spats to keep warm," Merce explained, "but he had an eye as to how he looked." One of three sons, Merce was the only one who chose not to become a lawyer. I asked Merce, had his parents wanted him to be a lawyer, too? And did they mind him becoming a dancer? About becoming a lawyer he remembered no specific mention. As to dancing, he said, "They were undoubtedly dubious about the enterprise, but game." He quotes his father: "I don't know any-thing about your theater game, but you certainly work at it."

Merce was the middle son. His brothers, Dorwin (the eldest and a judge) and Jack, were both married and between them had seven children. At the party given by Dorwin and his wife on our first evening in Centralia, I got the impression that Merce, christened "Mercier" and called that by his family, was something of an embarrassment to his quite conventional brothers. They didn't seem to know what to make of this dancer-brother who let his curly hair grow long enough to show the curls, or this oddball, goofy composer friend of his who was always laughing. They were friendly to us all, but in a guarded, uneasy sort of way.

Mayne Cunningham, Merce's mother, was something else entirely. Although Merce often claimed to be "a changeling," there were definite family resemblances between mother—of Czechoslovakian descent—and son. Certainly Merce's facial features could be traced to his mother's genes. Mrs. Cunningham was overjoyed to have us all in her home, and she loved talking about her Mercier as a little boy. Merce squirmed. If he seemed to be an embarrassment to his straitlaced brothers, his effusive mother also seemed to be an embarrassment to him. On Thanksgiving Day she got out old scrapbooks, photographs, and clippings from Merce's grade school and high school years that Marianne and I were dying to pore over from cover to cover, but Merce, groaning with displeasure over this unseemly violation of his privacy, quickly spirited the stuff away. By this time, Mrs. Cunningham had found "Wilhelmina," a life-size girl-doll attached by its shoes to a second, much larger pair of shoes. Merce's, of course. Wearing them, Merce had an ideally responsive "partner" with whom he used to perform a kind of "exhibition ballroom act as a high-jinks." He doesn't remember why he named her Wilhelmina, but he thinks it probably came out of a book he was reading. "Her feet were tied to mine so we wouldn't step on each other," he explained, with dry, understated humor. This wonderfully floppy stuffed doll caused a sensation with all of us—we wanted to dance with her—but I fear Merce was cross with his overly enthusiastic mother for revealing this bit of his past, and Wil-helmina was swiftly returned to the closet.

The seven grandchildren came over after dinner; they appeared to be delighted, if a bit shy, with their New York uncle, whom they talked into playing games with them. We all joined in. Years later, when I asked Merce about that day, all he could remember was "my mother worrying about how the biscuits did or didn't turn out, and Remy playing Scrabble with one of *mes frères.*" The Cunningham family home was old-fashioned and comfortable, with dark woodwork and large, overstuffed chairs; the architecture reminded me of my grandparents' home in Fitchburg.

After the holiday there was only one week remaining, with just three performances. Luckily, no one had sustained a serious injury and no illness had prevented anyone from missing a performance, although at the onset of the tour Bruce developed a misery-making strep throat with high fever that slowly worked its way through the company. Our morale was uneven. Not all the dancers were as ecstatic as I was. Anita and Viola, for example, were in the unenviable position of being the only dancers on that tour to share a role. Bruce was in only three of the six company dances and spent much of his time sitting on the sidelines. These situations understandably caused some edginess. Although Merce complained of not sleeping well and having little appetite, he was, for the most part, in excellent spirits. The extraordinarily warm reception from audiences and critics everywhere we went couldn't help but thaw his habitually cool reserve. In Tacoma, a reviewer thought it worthwhile to mention that, "Following the program a horde of young autograph-seekers crowded backstage and were graciously received by Cunningham and his dancers and the musicians. Having danced to packed houses on their tour up from California, the group may have become accustomed to an enthusiastic response."[25] But we had not become accustomed to it. Each time, we were surprised and grateful. Merce included.

Until Bellingham, the biggest flap I can recall was over a parking ticket Merce received in front of Grauman's Chinese Theatre in Hollywood, while he waited for us to look at Marilyn Monroe's handprints preserved in cement. But in Bellingham, the company morale was badly shaken when Merce behaved in a churlish and cantankerous fashion, thus alienating all of his dancers for a day or two.

In the fifties and early sixties, whenever Merce became unaccountably withdrawn or black with pent-up fury, any attempts to communicate with him were useless, so some of the dancers would turn to John to discover and, if possible, to solve the problem. John was always completely loyal to Merce, finding reasons for his conduct, reminding us of extenuating circumstances and telling us how much improved Merce's moods were compared to some years earlier when, for instance, he would lock himself in his dressing room and refuse to see or talk to anyone, including John. But John also managed to see our side; he'd attempt to soothe the hurt, make us laugh, and if Merce had offended someone for reasons John felt were undeserved, John would even offer to apologize in Merce's stead, which of course would accomplish little. But it revealed how deeply troubled John was by the disruption of company morale.

In Seattle, the last stop of the West Coast tour, John's own optimism and cheerful disposition faltered. Finally forced to accept defeat, he announced at a company gathering that his desperate efforts to get the company to the Orient had failed. He blamed himself. Then it was Merce who came to the rescue. Telling us how very, very sad John was, Merce tried to reassure us and to console him. It couldn't have been easy. Merce had given up his Sheridan Square studio on the strength of John's dogged determination to keep the company touring for several months. Neither Merce nor John had a penny; both were in debt, with no reliable source of steady income. Since this predicament was common to most of us, they both felt responsible, and John felt horribly guilty. John didn't live long enough to know the disheartening story of just why the company was rejected by the Dance Panel (part of the cultural diplomacy arm of the State Department) that year. But in 1998, formerly classified documents revealed the partisan politics practiced by some members of that panel (especially Martha Hill and Doris Humphrey[26]), and these were exposed in *Dance for Export: Cultural Diplomacy and the Cold War* (Wesleyan University Press) by Naima Prevots. Equally partisan politics had played a decisive role in providing Balanchine's company and six N.Y.C. Ballet–related companies with a ten-year grant of $6,765,750, totally bypassing modern dance, causing outrage in the American dance community, and prompting Robert Sabin in *Dance Observer* to ask: "Creatively speaking, what has ballet in America to offer to compare with the work of Martha Graham, Doris Humphrey, José Limón, Anna Sokolow, Merce Cunningham, and a host of other native choreographers we could mention?" How our little company could have used just a minuscule portion of that grant to continue on to the Orient. But it was the Graham company, picking up many of John's tentative engagements for the Cunningham company, that got State Department funding.

Tour expenses, mailing costs, printing for the New City concert, and Isadora Bennett's fee came to over seven thousand dollars. The income from the tour (performances, master classes, and lecture demonstrations) plus subsidies from Paul Williams ($1,800) and Nancy Oakes (a beautiful red-haired woman who had been a friend of Merce's when both were students at Balanchine's School of American Ballet and who would come to Merce's aid in financial crises again and again) also came to over seven thousand dollars. We'd broken even—a remarkable achievement! We'd been royally fed, wined, housed, and transported, and had even received weekly pocket money. "It is just amazing," I wrote to my parents, "John has managed superbly, *lavishly,* generously!" At the final meeting of the company before everyone went off in different directions, John gave each of us plane fare home plus one hundred dollars in cash as an "honorarium." "Does anyone insist on more money?" he asked apologetically. We were surprised to be given so much. I wrote to my parents: "The company is disbanded as of last night. The concert went pretty well, but I felt three times removed watching myself think about dancing it. An awful experience. So awful to have been the last concert. . . . Poor John is heartsick about the orient tour. . . . Thank heavens he was here. He smoothed the ruffled, cheered the weary and was unendingly working for our good. *Such a guy!* He says he intends to withdraw as manager, and get us a professional one . . . but NO ONE will be so loving and devoted as John has been."

I was especially grateful. At tour's end, John cared enough to take the time to talk to me alone about my dancing. Perhaps he did this with everyone. I had many doubts about my own performing. As much as I loved the dancing, as ecstatic as I was about the touring life, only twice on the tour (in *Septet* in Tacoma and *Springweather* in Portland, when I felt very much "there" and complete) did I perform as fully as I felt I should. Merce was silent about these matters. I never knew what he thought or whether he and John discussed the dancers' strengths and weaknesses or if John's expressed opinions reflected their discussions. In any case, it was John who spoke to me about my dancing, not Merce. From Seattle, in my last letter of the tour, I wrote to Earle:

> John was so sweet to me. Said that I was a fulfilled dancer now. That my whole body was expressive, and my shoulder-chest problem was gone! How happy this makes me. He said that before I danced with reserve and detachment but that now I danced completely. I hope so. I'm never so happy as when I dance—in class, rehearsal or performance. I still don't feel that I perform as fully as I might . . . It is more and more exciting to discover what it is to really dance. Much much more to learn . . . wish we could continue performing . . . I don't feel "let down" after the tour (except annoyed to be sick) and look forward to everything ahead, *whatever* it may be.

Mark Tobey, a painter friend of John's from 1937 to 1938 when John was the composer-accompanist for Bonnie Bird's classes at the Cornish School in Seattle, came to our last performance. Later he told John it was the best dance concert he'd ever seen and that he thought me "the most beautiful dancer since Pavlova." How could I not have felt honored? I knew Tobey only through the exquisite drawing, on loan from John, that hung on the wall of Earle's and my loft at 40 Third Avenue. Soon after the tour, John had to sell it to survive. I think John's willingness to repeat Tobey's extravagant praise must have come from his desire to bolster my self-confidence and to encourage me to stick with it. John was desperately anxious to keep Merce's company together.

It would have been gratifying if the company, buoyed by enthusiastic audiences and the critical acclaim garnered in five weeks of mostly happy touring, could have returned triumphantly to New York in a spirit of solidarity and togetherness, reasonably expecting Merce's creative activity to flourish and requests for bookings to pour in. But it didn't work out that way. After Seattle, each of us went off to follow purely personal pursuits without any plans to reassemble in the near future. To make matters worse, the *only* negative review received by the company on the entire tour appeared in *Dance News* after our return to New York. A cruel irony: that the only words about our tour read by the dance world at large should be these, written by Maxine Cushing Gray, the Seattle correspondent for *Dance News:* "The dreadful thought that this group was on its way to the Far East to represent current American stage art was chilling enough, but the self-indulgence in movement which was served up in the name of modern dance (excepting the quite charming and direct *Banjo,* to music by Gottschalk) left us quite numb. We respect the right of the ticket holder and we think he deserves to have something communicated to him."[27]

The company could no longer afford Isadora Bennett; her fee had been too steep, and she'd done precious little to deserve it. With the collapse of the Oriental tour and not a single booking in sight, John returned to the job of booking agent and publicist. He wasted no time in getting handsome brochure material made up, with seven reviews from West Coast newspapers reprinted in their entirety, and on the back in bold capital letters: "FOR DETAILED INFORMATION WRITE TO JOHN CAGE WILLOW BROOK ROAD RFD STONYPOINT, NEW YORK." He didn't throw in the manager's towel. Far from it. More doggedly and determinedly than ever, he launched a new campaign. It wasn't long before I was writing home about a possible tour in April and May, of spending a whole month in San Francisco, of a series of Monday-night music and dance concerts in a small theater in Carnegie Hall. John's optimism, that rare thing—a true-blue perennial—was flowering once again.

For the next two and a half years the existence of the company was more often a matter of faith than fact. Largely John's faith. In 1956, there were eleven performances, six of them—thanks to Ted Shawn—at Jacob's Pillow, and none in New York. In 1957 there were only five and one-quarter performances. Even worse was the first half of 1958, with a total of two and one-third performances. It was all too clear that there was going to be no way for any of us to make a living dancing with Merce. Morale was unsteady. Merce suffered most of all, I'm sure. His low spirits were the norm, his highs were rare and brief. For the rest of us it became a matter of priorities. Marianne married and began to think about having children. The conundrum remained: how to get and keep a job that would feed and house one and still accommodate the necessary technique classes, rehearsals, and the occasional out-of-town performance. Both Marianne and Bruce had part-time jobs teaching dancing to children. Viola got a series of jobs—as pianist accompanying dance classes, waitress, dance teacher. Anita, with the benefit of an art education, was able to do some freelance fabric designing, and I think, like one or two others of us, received some financial assistance from parents. Remy, an artist who'd trained at Cooper Union before becoming a dancer, was able to solve the problem in a way that was both creatively and financially rewarding. He designed book jackets and began writing and illustrating children's books. It was an ideal second occupation for a dancer—not physically taxing (at least compared to being a waiter at Schrafft's, which is what Merce had been when he first came to New York) and allowing him flexibility in arranging his work schedule around Merce's. Once Earle began to work at Capitol Records, and especially after his promotion to mixer, I was spared the basic financial worries as well as the terrible scheduling problems faced by most of Merce's other dancers. But I couldn't pursue my dancing life without guilt, since Earle's new job left him with little time or energy to compose. For many years I'd wake each morning uneasy, the unreality between sleep and waking inhabited by a disquietingly persistent voice, asking me, "What do you really want?"

Merce didn't teach or rehearse until mid-January 1956. Meanwhile, I took two ballet classes a day with either Mr. Tudor or Miss Craske and danced in Zachary Solov's rather tacky, run-of-the-mill bacchanal-orgy choreography for Saint-Saëns's *Samson and Delilah* at the Met. I was filling in for one of two dancers who were suffering second-degree burns from hot steam jets ("atmosphere"). Many of the dancers in the Metropolitan Opera Ballet had injuries—fractured toes, sprained ankles, knee problems. They were worked very hard. My friends in the company couldn't believe I'd been away five weeks; for them, time had stood still. Those not injured were bored and discouraged. Buoyed by Merce's West Coast tour and John's loving encouragement, I was neither bored nor discouraged. It was great fun performing again with orchestra on the opera-house stage in a glamorous costume: body paint from the waist up, tight blue metallic cloth trousers, the tiniest of bras, gold headgear, eyelids drooping under heavy shadow and blue sequins, lips ablaze under layers of blood-red lipstick and smarting from still more dazzling sequins. ("We looked ready to do a burly-show," I told my parents.) And yet surely *this* wasn't what I really wanted! Nor was the modeling job with Saul Leiter, this time a magazine advertisement in which I was seen leaping across the screen of a Sylvania television set (hoping I wouldn't be recognized but happy to be earning enough money to buy a hot-water heater for our loft, an item desperately desired, since the hot-water supply by the bar downstairs had become less and less reliable).

After the West Coast tour, Merce could no longer afford a studio of his own. When he did begin to teach, in a fourth-floor walk-up studio he sublet by the hour from the modern dancer Edith Stephen at 430 Sixth Avenue, hardly anyone was in class. Mostly, there was just Remy and me. Marianne and Bruce could come only twice a week. Viola came occasionally and Anita didn't come at all. (We didn't know it yet, but we'd lost Anita.) The studio was a dreary, untidy place with dusty burlap draperies hanging everywhere and a terrible floor, uneven and splintery. There was no decent mirror, so Merce rented one for six dollars a month. What a depressing time for him: no money, no performance dates in the offing, no studio of his own, few paying students (no one in the company paid for class), an accumulation of debts, and a company whose loyalty seemed to him uncertain. When he received an invitation from the Arts Ministry to teach in Mexico, he had no choice but to accept. There were endless delays with the contracts and working papers, but finally, in the second week of March, he left for Mexico and was gone five weeks. I received one postcard: "Living here is like walking thru water. I miss everyone." And one letter: "Life here is too luxurious and pleasurable. And Mexican dancers are equally interested in personal glory on stage and the cha-cha-cha. Many tales. . . . Miss you all. Conversations here are humerous [*sic*], but ideas of what-to-do-about-dance (or any art) are pre-Conquest in origin. And the art is awful. Love to both of you. You are the best dancer I've seen in Mexico. M."

With Merce away, my dance life revolved once again around classes at the Met, at least two a day plus pointe with Miss Craske and pas de deux with Mr. Tudor. I was getting strong encouragement from my ballet teachers and ballet friends, and I began to realize that if I was going to support myself and continue to dance, it might have to be as a ballet dancer. In February, at the Brooklyn Academy of Music, the National Ballet of Canada danced Tudor's *Dark Elegies,* based upon Mahler's *Kindertotenlieder.* Stark. Emotional power through a kind of imploding quiet. Soul-wrenching depth of feeling—in this case, grief—expressed through movement, not mime. Such simple eloquence. . . . if I could dance *that* kind of ballet . . . At the intermission, I found Tudor. "Would you like to be in it?" he asked after I had tried to put into words how much his ballet had moved me. "Yes." (Could there be any other answer?) "Get into the company and you can have the part." He was teasing me, but later that same evening both Miss Craske and Mattlyn Gavers said quite seriously that I should dance the first solo, and several friends said I was right for Tudor ballets. I went home unreasonably happy. As I write this, decades later, I'm still hoping—should chance have me born a dancer in some other reincarnation—that I'll get to dance, above all other ballets I've ever seen, *Dark Elegies.* Several times in the next few years I came very close to working with Tudor, but fate had it otherwise. While Merce was still in Mexico, Tudor sent me, along with four female dancers from the Met Opera Ballet, to audition for Lucia Chase at Ballet Theatre. None of us was taken into the company. Dancers who interested Tudor did not fit the mold of the typical Ballet Theatre corps de ballet dancer Miss Chase seemed to favor in the fifties: i.e., about five feet four inches tall, blond and blandly pretty in an All-American girl-next-door sort of way. About a year later, I was again sent off to audition for Miss Chase, and again nothing came of it. At Tudor's instigation and with the hope of performing his ballets, I continued to audition for Miss Chase off and on for about ten years, when at last, and finally, I decided that it was too late to realize that dream. There were other dreams, but they were passing fancies compared to the never-to-be-realized yearning to dance *Dark Elegies* and *Lilac Garden*.

For several years I was open to most possibilities, and there always seemed to be some surprising opportunity presenting itself that could have led me on a very different path from the Cage/Cunningham one I followed. It seems to me, in retrospect, that my life "happened" to me—it was mostly a matter of chance, kismet, or karma. Of course, faced with alternatives, I had to make decisions, to choose this or that, but those choices almost always seemed inevitable. When forced to choose, I chose Merce and John. The strongest dreams were John's, and I was swept up in them, pulled along in their bubbling wake; occasionally I'd protest and try to hold back if he was too domineering, but usually I was happy to be caught up in the current of his energy and ideas.

Few of his dreams were realized in 1956. The first major disappointment was to discover that the verbal agreement made by the San Francisco Ballet to commission a work by Cunningham, Cage, and Rauschenberg was just talk. No contract was ever forthcoming. Then, the spring tour for the dance company never materialized; no firm bookings. The Monday-night series of music and dance concerts planned for May and June in a little theater at Carnegie Hall also came to nought; John couldn't raise the money fast enough.

In the seven-month period between December 2, 1955, and July 11, 1956, the dance company had just one performance date. During that time, Merce choreographed four dances: *Lavish Escapade, Galaxy, Suite for Five,* and *Nocturnes.* Even when it was absolutely certain that Anita was not coming back, Merce made no attempt to replace her, although he'd now lost two of the five women from the original company he'd formed at Black Mountain only two summers before. Instead, he made new dances for the people who were there and rearranged some of the "old" ones for a company of six. Always practical, he accepted the fact that a smaller group costs less—fewer costumes, fewer mouths to feed, fewer rooms to rent—making touring more economically feasible and somewhat simplifying rehearsal scheduling. For a time he was able to resolve the maddeningly difficult scheduling problems that continually plagued us by choreographing a quartet of solos for Viola, Marianne, Remy, and me and working with each of us individually. It was in this quartet, titled *Galaxy,* that Merce first used the open-form ideas pioneered by Earle in compositions such as *Folio* (1952–53), *Twenty-Five Pages* (1953), and *Four Systems* (1954). The last, written especially for David Tudor's twenty-ninth birthday, was the music Merce had so admired in its first performance in the spring of 1954, and it was this music he chose to accompany the new quartet.

Quite aside from Merce's keen interest in the concept of open form as applied to choreography, he saw its use as a practical means of making a relatively complex dance that need never be the same twice despite a severely restricted rehearsal situation. As in Earle's open-form pieces, *Galaxy* had a "mobile score" that permitted an unknown number of different, integral, and "valid" realizations. But the "mobile" elements of *Galaxy* were very limited compared to those in *Four Systems*. Theoretically, the four solos in *Galaxy* could be performed separately in any order, or simultaneously, or split into sections. *Galaxy* could be a trio, duet, or solo, as well as a quartet. Usually, however, we performed the solos simultaneously, with our entrances and exits staggered so that the solos overlapped and intersected. In Earle's *Four Systems*, the open form is realized by the performer, who is free to respond spontaneously to the fixed graphic elements of the score. Merce did not allow us this freedom in *Galaxy*. The movement material was fixed, and he allowed no spontaneous action on our part. It was he who determined the order and timing of the four solos, but from performance to performance the dance could appear to be very different if he changed the order and timing of our entrances and exits, which would then alter the density, the spacial configuration, and the sense of interaction between the dancers. The continuity of each solo, however, remained the same; it could be fragmented, but it was always performed sequentially. Merce told Earle at the time that the reason he didn't allow us the freedoms that Earle specifies in *Four Systems* was that while musicians could respond spontaneously in performance without fear of bodily harm, dancers were in danger of crashing into each other, of being injured, or causing injury. Seven years later, in *Field Dances*, he tried again, and this time he used the open-form concept more fully and granted the dancers the freedom to make spontaneous decisions in performance.

The program note for *Galaxy:* "The complexity of this dance and its music is in imitation of complex situations in nature, where for instance, air, earth, fire and water act at one and the same time." Merce cast it, Remy costumed it: Air/Carolyn, Earth/Marianne, Fire/Remy, and Water/Viola. The movement vocabulary was distinctive for each of us. There was no movement common to all, no movement even shared by any two dancers. *Galaxy* was technically difficult for each of us. Merce tried to challenge us and extend our range in the direction of whatever element he had chosen for us. I'm fairly certain he did *not* toss any pennies when determining which dancer was to represent which element, and if he said otherwise I don't think I'd believe him, but certainly it was the Water solo for Viola that was the most unusual and interesting of the four, and it marks the beginning of a very special collaboration between Merce and Viola, between choreographer and dancer, which was further developed in *Nocturnes* (1956), came to full flower in *Crises* (1960), and reached a kind of crazy zenith in their duet *Paired* (1964). For these dances especially, Merce invented movement that is hers alone, only for her body, its astonishing ability to be not of a piece; to be oddly, fascinatingly disjointed, extravagantly sensuous, even exotic, and to quote *The Village Voice*'s dance critic (from 1959 to 1970) Jill Johnston, "divinely awkward." "Her body often had the look of one part being in balance, and the rest extremely off. Now and again it was like two persons, another just ahead or behind the first. This coupled with an "acute rhythmic sense,"[1] so Merce described her in *Changes*. The way her body was put together, the quirks of heredity, temperament, and personality, created an astonishing dancer whose most unusual gifts were unschooled and impossible to imitate.

Although starting from what was becoming the Cunningham company's basic uniform—footless tights and a leotard—Remy created four completely distinct images for the elements suggested in *Galaxy*. Viola's— strange and beautiful—was mauve and gray-green, tie-dyed in watery ribbons of color with plain purple, green, and red buttons sewn in a random pattern all over her abdomen. In motion and under light the many "belly buttons" were curiously provocative—fish eyes glimpsed in a slow-moving eddy, or stones just visible on the bottom of a riverbed. On her head she wore an exotic many-tasseled headdress of pearlescent plastic on a lanyard that Remy had netted into a cap. The shoulder-length tassels of blue, purple, and green—a metaphor for the glinting, shimmering flash and tumult of a waterfall—swirled and bobbed, dancing their own dance in response to Viola's movements.

For Earth/Marianne, Remy dyed leotard and tights in descending shades from white to gold. Resting on her hip bones and covering only her derrière was a flashy deep-gold satin half-skirt lined with gold lamé. Fire/Remy skipped the leotard and went bare-chested (the only time, I believe, this has ever occurred in a Cunningham dance); he wore cuffs of Indian embroidered mirror cloth and red tights. Air/Carolyn's tights and leotards were solid "bluebird blue." Over hands, arms, and shoulders Remy had me wear a pair of black elastic mesh tights, the kind Radio City Music Hall Rockettes used to wear on their legs, into which were interlaced dozens upon dozens of single, six-inch blue feathers that had to be inserted one at a time before every performance of *Galaxy*. Remy usually laced me with feathers himself because he wanted it done a particular way. I know I was supposed to look airy, but I felt horribly bound and constricted. Trying to be or to project the real or imagined qualities of air in a straitjacket was surely a contradiction—and Merce's choreography was challenge enough. I fear that if any sense of airiness was achieved, it was due to the feathers that let loose and fluttered to the ground as I tried to fly through my steps. Both Viola and Marianne had trouble with their costumes, too: Viola's tassels were long and sometimes swatted her painfully in the face, and Marianne's skirt occasionally tripped her up due to its weight and length.

Merce has never cared very much about costumes, so there was almost never any real collaboration between him and the costume designer. Rarely did the dance steps get made with any thought about what the costumes might be. Anyone designing costumes for Merce had to work within very strict limitations; the nearly inflexible rule was: body unencumbered, body visible. For the women, Merce wanted something as classical as the short classical ballet tutu, which he claimed was ideal for revealing the whole body, yet still covering that troublesome area—the female derrière. He never found a consistently satisfactory solution to that problem, although both Remy and Bob tried. Eventually, I think Merce gave up seeing it as a problem. In any case, clothed so often in unisex outfits, we began to exercise and diet and dance away our "unsightly" bottoms. Usually our costumes were designed and constructed after the choreography was completed (or almost) and were not seen by us from the last fitting until the moment we put them on for performance. We never rehearsed in them unless the lighting designer requested it.

Confronted with the inevitable tights and leotards, a designer's range of creativity was confined to color (skills in tie-dyeing developed quickly), choosing necklines and sleeve lengths, and fabric, although the choices were limited to wool, elasticized cotton, and nylon (until the creation of milliskin—after I'd left the company, thank heaven). Of course, tights and leotards were also extremely economical compared to any other sort of costume, and they were easily replaced and packed, took up little space, required no ironing, and could be washed by the dancers themselves. Remy and later Bob experimented constantly with what variations, modifications, and additions to this basic Cunningham stage uniform were possible—sometimes with delightfully surprising results. When they slightly broke the rules and difficulties arose, we dancers hated to complain, because we were as bored with tights and leotards as the designers were. Truth is, the company women would have been happy to wear skirts a lot more often than we did.

Costumes for *Suite for Five,* the first dance to be costumed by Rauschenberg, were simple in the extreme. From the painter's palette, Bob chose two primary colors—blue for Merce, yellow for me (he omitted red, which, as we've seen, he considered "the most aggressive and the most difficult" color in the spectrum), and the three secondary colors—purple, orange, and green—for Marianne, Viola, and Remy. To the tank-top leotards for the women, Bob's only addition was some thread tied around the straps to narrow them and secure them to the bra straps underneath. (No bra-less boobs in those days!) The men wore custom-made long-sleeved shirts. The simplicity and straightforwardness of the costumes were elegantly appropriate for *Suite for Five,* which is perhaps the most purely classical work of Merce's entire oeuvre up until 1971.

Formal. Refined. Simple. Unequivocal. Elegant. Reposeful. Understated. Clear. An expanded version of the 1953 *Solo Suite in Space and Time, Suite for Five* became one of Merce's signature works; it was in the repertory continuously for sixteen years. (After 1972, parts of *Suite for Five* continued on in *Events.* In 2002, it was revived for the company's fiftieth-anniversary celebration at Lincoln Center.) To the original five solos, Merce added a trio for Marianne, Viola, and Remy, a duet for himself and me, and a quintet. After the first performance, two of his original solos were omitted. Two years later, in 1958, he added a solo for me, and for the next fourteen years the definitive version of *Suite for Five* was:

SOLO:	At Random	**(MC)**
SOLO:	A Meander	**(CB)**
TRIO:	Transition	**(MP, VF, RC)**
SOLO:	Stillness	**(MC)**
DUET:	Extended Moment	**(MC, CB)**
SOLO:	Excursion	**(MC)**
QUINTET:	Meetings	**(MC, CB, MP, VF, RC)**

In the new material for the expanded version, Merce continued to explore pure movement in relation to time and space. The trio—which I was able to watch hundreds of times in sixteen years—is, I think, a marvel for its economy of means and subtle spacial and rhythmic complexity. The movement continuity goes forward to a point and then retreats in a kind of retrograde to the end. The three dancers change in perspective, appearing to alter in size; their relationships to one another and to the total space are constantly shifting. And yet at each moment, each of the three is central; that is, no one is ever subordinate to another. Time is extremely important. As Merce explains, the trio simply does not work unless it is performed precisely in the given time. I should guess that this brief dance—two minutes and forty-five seconds—had more rehearsal hours, proportionate to its length, than any other in the entire repertory in the twenty years I danced with Merce.

Suite for Five, according to Merce, "was one of the first [of his] dances where meter was completely abandoned, and [the] dancers had to rely on [their] own dance timing to guard the length of any phrase, and the timing of the complete dance."[2] Spacial patterns and time lengths were determined by means of chance procedures, similar to those used by Cage in composing the music, using imperfections on white paper as points in space. *Suite for Five* was the quintessential embodiment of Merce's 1952 definition of dance, "Dancing is a spiritual exercise in physical form."[3] For me it became a kind of rite—deeply experienced, richly rewarding, and never, ever losing its meaning. If I had to choose one dance with which I most identify out of the forty-four in Merce's repertory I performed between 1953 and 1973, it would be, unquestionably, *Suite for Five.*

"Serenity" is a word John had once used to describe my performance presence. If I ever achieved the appearance of serenity, the means to that end I discovered through working, above all, on *Suite for Five.* I think it suited my temperament, and it satisfied my deepest and highest expectations about the power that dance can exert over the performer. Merce in his own writing states that dance is not "feeling about something" but "is a whipping of the mind and body into an action that is so intense that for the one brief moment involved, the mind and body are one. The dancer knows how solidly he must be aware of this centering when he dances. And it is just this very fusion at a white heat that gives the look of objectivity and serenity that a fine dancer has."[4]

Suite for Five is what might be considered "Cunningham classical," and though not without dramatic intensity, the form, the movement in space and time, is like pure water: clear, transparent, and reflective. Our duet, "Extended Moment," was spare, cool, and fine-tuned, but no duet between a man and a woman can entirely escape certain human references. Our relationship to each other was far more sculptural than suggestive of sexual or romantic attachment, yet the resonances were there. As I experienced it, a steady, sure white flame of intensity burned beneath the tranquility. Fire and ice, fused. And there in the choreography—crystalized, yet fluid—was an unstated emotional content. Dancing that work in whatever guise—as *Suite for Five* or *Suite for Two* (a duet version made in 1958) or out of context in *Events*, whether in or out of its proper costume, with or without its intended music, on tiny stages, on raked stages, on magnificent opera-house stages, in dingy college auditoriums, in gymnasiums, museums, field houses, in the Piazza San Marco in Venice, by the River Sabarmati in Ahmedabad, India—wherever and whatever the circumstances, I became a supplicant, a celebrant, part of some ritual invocation to a god or gods I could barely imagine, but whose presence was unquestionable and powerful.

Lavish Escapade ("An adventure into an uncharted territory"), a solo Merce made for himself, was the most strikingly original of the dances he made in 1956. Occasionally, before or after company rehearsals, we'd hear him groaning and muttering somewhat incoherently to no one in particular about the difficulties he was having in realizing his new solo. But beyond that it was a mystery; he worked on it, if not actually in secret, in total privacy, allowing no one to watch, even weeks after it was finished. When finally John and Christian Wolff were permitted to see a rehearsal, with David playing Christian's *For Piano II*, they were flabbergasted.

The dance was hideously difficult to perform, far more difficult than *Untitled Solo*, the dance about which David had said one day at Black Mountain when Merce had stopped practicing in fatigue and despair, "This is clearly impossible, but we're going right ahead and do it anyway." The second of three solos with music by Christian Wolff, *Lavish Escapade* was, like the other two, composed by chance means from "a large gamut of movements, (separate for each of the three dances), devised for the arms, the legs, the head and the torso which were separate and essentially tensile in character, and off the normal or tranquil body-balance . . . All were concerned with the possibility of containment and explosion being instantaneous."[5] The continuity of the separate movements was arrived at by chance means, with the added complexity of the random superimposition of one or more movements, each having its own rhythm and time length. Imagine tackling such a feat! Unheard-of coordinations. Superhuman patience, not to mention endurance. Why would anyone choose such a thorny, encumbered, irksome path in order to rid himself of habitual ways of moving and disorient his predilections? The result was grotesque, bizarre, and frightening, and I think even Merce himself was startled by it, by the impact it had on him as well as on his audience. When at last he was able to perform it all the way through (it took hours and hours of exasperating, exhausting, painstaking work), he appeared to be possessed by demons, crazed, as though he'd been inflicted with an altogether crippling

My mother, Marion Rice,
at twenty-eight . . .

. . . and at seventy-two

BELOW LEFT: "The Great Chief"—me at age ten
BELOW RIGHT: Marion Rice Denishawn Dancers at Jacob's Pillow, 1972.
Left to right: Anne Marie Bell; me; my niece, Robin Rice; Barton Mumaw;
my mother; and my niece, Rebecca Rice

ABOVE: John: delight in sound
BELOW: In contemplation

ABOVE: The mushroom expert
BELOW: The philosopher/teacher

ABOVE: With Earle at Tanglewood, 1962
BELOW: Earle with his score for
Springweather and People, 1955

ABOVE: On the film set for *Variations V* in Hamburg, Germany, 1966.
Left to right: John, David Tudor, Gordon Mumma, and me
BELOW LEFT: John improvising a sound system at St. Paul de Vence, 1966
BELOW RIGHT: David Tudor with his bandoneon

ABOVE: *Back row, left to right:* Merce, John, M. C. Richards, Jasper
Johns. *Seated:* Bob Rauschenberg and Bob Cato [?], 1958
BELOW: Bob with his "combines," 1958

ABOVE: Jasper working on Duchamp's set for
Walkaround Time, 1968
BELOW: The New York School composers. *Left to right:*
Christian Wolff, Earle Brown, John Cage, and Morton Feldman

With Bob at Tanya Grossman's Universal Limited lithography studio on Long Island. On the near right is the sculptor Maurice Grossman.

mental disorder. When we first saw *Lavish Escapade* we were truly shocked, and Remy whispered to John, "Is he really going to do that in public?"

In an earlier chapter, I confessed that *Untitled Solo*, the first of Merce's three Christian Wolff solos, was a dance I coveted. I've always wanted to learn it, to perform it, to know it in my own body. There was absolutely no question of that with *Lavish Escapade*. Quite the contrary—it was beyond anything I could or would want to attempt. *Suite for Five* and *Lavish Escapade* were worlds apart—the contrast could not have been more extreme—but oh how much I envied Merce his escape into madness in those intensely dramatic solos. He wrote: "The dance as performed seems to have an unmistakable dramatic intensity in its bones, so to speak. it seems to me that it was simply a question of 'allowing' this quality to happen rather than 'forcing' it. It is this 'tranquility' of the actor or dancer which seems to me essential. A tranquility which allows him to detach himself and thereby to *present* freely and liberally."[6]

But no matter what Merce has said or written about tranquility and serenity, in those three solos, in a few later dances such as *Place*, but especially in *Lavish Escapade*, I'm convinced that his dancing was an ecstatic and passionate act, and he was inflamed—just as Martha Graham was by her Greek heroines—and consumed by the dance. Says Merce: "Our ecstasy in dance comes from the possible gift of freedom, the exhilarating moment that this exposing of the bare energy can give us. What is meant is not license, but freedom, that is, a complete awareness of the world and at the same time a detachment from it."[7]

The three new works—*Lavish Escapade, Galaxy,* and *Suite for Five in Space and Time*—were given their first performances at the University of Notre Dame on May 18, 1956. It was our first performance since the West Coast tour. We hadn't been together on a stage as a company for five and a half months, far too long for the lessons learned on the tour to be applied effortlessly. We were starting all over again—at least, it felt that way. An ancient, rusty, falling-apart station wagon with one of its doors tied shut (on loan from friends of John's who had recently moved to The Land in Stony Point) got us to Michigan. Some of us, anyway. Viola, Marianne, and Bruce—unable to take so much time from their jobs—had to be flown one or both ways. Not economical, but unavoidable. This trip was the precursor of hundreds to follow: an arduous two-day haul each way to present a single performance.

At Washington Hall, where we performed, a sober-faced youngish monk in a long brown robe had been assigned to help our lighting designer, Nick

Cernovich. By the way the monk kept his head slightly lowered, not daring to look at us straight-on, we guessed he'd never seen a woman in leotard and tights before. Or a man, for that matter. From the beginning we'd thought it odd that an all-male Catholic university, most famous (at least to us) for its football team, should have invited Merce and company to present a concert of dance, but we thought it odder still when told we probably wouldn't have much of an audience.

"There's no one out there!" we whispered to one another as the curtain opened for Merce's solo. But we were wrong. Halfway back, slightly off to the left of center, sat two brown-robed gentlemen, and in the very last row in nearly total blackness, a barely discernible line of white peaked caps revealed the presence of fewer than a dozen nuns! Whether it was the religious constituency or the size of our audience or the fact that there were three new untried works on the program, Merce was rattled. And I knew it for certain during our duet in *Suite*. He was supposed to catch my weight in a kind of embrace by putting his right arm around my waist as I looked up at him, sort of cradled on his knees. Imagine my expression (and his!) as his right arm shot between my legs encircling my crotch, *not* my waist. In this compromising position I glimpsed our shy, kindly, sober-faced monk standing in the wings ready to pull the curtain, his mouth agape, his eyes—like saucers—aghast, whether from shock or mortification I couldn't tell. The grab-and-grope school of choreography so popular with third-rate choreographers in the late sixties and the seventies (and ever onward into the twenty-first century) was, in the fifties, unheard-of. Surely monks and nuns had not been expecting such maneuvers from the high-minded modern dance!

To make matters worse for us, getting out of this unrehearsed position into the next choreographed one wasn't easy. Where his hand should have helped, it was now only a hindrance. Verbal communication was of course impossible. We both heaved ourselves clumsily into what we each hoped the other thought was the next move and staggered on from there, salvaging the rest of the duet somehow. Marianne, Viola, and Remy, in the wings, had to stifle their laughter and try to maintain some decorum in front of our poor scandalized curtain-puller.

I was utterly dejected by the whole evening. That little episode merely compounded the misery, although I wasn't *so* depressed that I failed to appreciate how ludicrously funny it had been. But as far as I was concerned, my entire performance had been a disaster. I'd danced badly, lost whatever it was I thought I'd gained on the West Coast tour, and, with no more performances on the horizon until July, felt that the situation was hopeless. How were any of us to improve with only these single anxiety-ridden first performances spaced months and months apart? As always, Marianne came to the rescue. She lectured me, lovingly, on the useless-ness of my idiotic perfectionism; she was convinced that Merce suffered no such self-destructive trait. And although she, too, felt discouraged by how few performances there were, she loved performing and enjoyed it when it happened. The problem was, I didn't. Merce did. If, in perfor-mance I came up short of my expectations for myself, and this was the rule rather than the exception, I could enjoy nothing. All too often, performing was a terror, accompanied by a sense of failing—the work, Merce, Dance with a capital "D," and most of all, I guess, myself. It was rehearsals I loved. Working at things. Discovering. Exploring. Growing. Learning. Being a part of the creative process. But if I couldn't carry that joy and commitment onto the stage and share it, then didn't that mean I was not a performer? Merce never discussed performing as separate from dancing. It was not a problem for him. He became *more* onstage, not less. His dancing in performance was almost always more alive, more brilliant, more pas-sionate. "Our ecstasy in dance comes from the possible gift of freedom." And there was the problem: how is one to obtain this "gift of freedom"? Merce said freedom is "a complete awareness of the world and at the same time a detachment from it." Yet even that synthesis of awareness and detachment, pertinent as it is to Merce's approach to his art, does not com-pletely explain that singular phenomenon—Merce Cunningham, the per-former.

Before Notre Dame, Merce had begun work on *Nocturnes*, a new piece for six dancers set to music by Satie. He'd experimented briefly with me on some slightly erotic duet material, but I couldn't make myself do what he asked—for instance, undulate my upper body. I froze. After a few more attempts, he gave up. Before long I realized he was making a duet for him-self and Viola, and I knew there was no one to blame but my own prissy, overly chaste self. "You can't be a lady onstage if you're going to be a dancer!" It was with words to that effect that Margaret Craske once admon-ished a perfectly lovely young dancer whose deportment was demure, prim, utterly correct; what she lacked was the willingness to abandon her-self in the movement. The girl blushed deeply. Miss Craske smiled: "You don't have to stop *being* a lady, my dear child, just behaving like one." And then she added, "Onstage, my dear, *onstage*! Unless, of course, the part calls for it." Unfortunately, I heard Miss Craske make those remarks many years after the *Nocturnes* episode. I marked them ruefully; I had learned the lesson the hard way. In any case, after the initial disappointment I discovered that I didn't really mind not being cast in the *Nocturnes* duet. I would have been a fool to covet Viola's role. I couldn't have done it as she did, even if I could have rid myself of my prudery. And the part Merce made for me was wonderful: full of small high jumps, fast turns, long stretched positions, and solemn gestures. I was grateful. I didn't feel punished for my inabilities. I felt that Merce understood me, and I came to appreciate that what he had made for me was special, too, developing what I could do then, yet pushing me in a direction where I could grow even as he realized how incapable I was at that time of jettisoning certain of my puritanical notions about movement.

Enhanced by Satie's haunting and evocative music of the same name and Rauschenberg's magical set and costumes, *Nocturnes* turned out to be one of Merce's most fanciful and romantic works and one that became richer and more rewarding to dance the more we did it. Eventually it became a favorite with everyone—dancers and audiences. Critics, bless them, eventually warmed up to it, too, but it took them longer. "In five parts from dusk to the witching hour." That was the subtitle, although the dancers knew nothing of this beforehand. As usual, Merce said nothing about it. For me, *Nocturnes* evoked the mystery of a summer night flooded with moonlight and fireflies, peopled with eccentric ghosts attending a midnight garden party.

The days before our opening performance at the Pillow were fraught. Fance and Louis Stevenson had deserted the Battery loft scene and moved to a huge, handsome apartment on Riverside Drive that was the envy of all, with its high-ceilinged rooms and spectacular view of the Hudson River. It cost a spectacular $180 a month, but it had a maid's room that Louis could use as a darkroom. Both Fance and Louis were now thoroughly enamored of the company, Louis donating his services as company photographer, and before we left for the Pillow they threw us a celebratory party. In the midst of the festivities, Remy complained of feeling truly rotten. A doctor was sent for, and he diagnosed glandular fever and insisted that Remy be put to bed right there and then in the Stevensons' apartment. For a week or so it was uncertain whether he would be well enough to perform at the Pillow. He had no understudy. No one did.

Then came Problem #2: as chance would have it, the day of Merce's technical rehearsal in the Ted Shawn Theatre happened to coincide with "Silent Day," a day observed by those who follow the teachings of the Indian master Meher Baba, and Viola had recently become one of these through Miss Craske. Margaret Craske first met Meher Baba in 1931 and became one of his first Western disciples. Eventually, she gave up her life in London, where she had her own school of ballet, taught for the Sadler's Wells Company, and choreographed for the Carl Rosa Opera, in order to obey Baba's order: "If war breaks out involving England, you come immediately to me here."[8] "Here" was India. With great difficulty, since no civilians were allowed to leave England after war was declared, she managed to wangle a passport and passage, arriving penniless in India after a rather harrowing six-week journey. She didn't expect ever to return. But seven years later, at war's end, Baba told her "to go back to England, and then to go on to the USA and there to teach ballet."[9] She did exactly as he instructed her.

Several of my Metropolitan Opera Ballet School friends were also followers of Meher Baba, and they had urged me to speak to Miss Craske about him. Unfortunately, they made it seem as if I would be joining some terribly exclusive club, which was not appealing, but I made an appointment with Miss Craske at her apartment because I was drawn to the aura surrounding *her*—one of wisdom and compassion—and I wanted to know more about her relationship to Baba. In vivid contrast with my friends' enthusiasms, she spoke of him with the utmost simplicity, using commonsense language and an utterly down-to-earth manner. She gave me several books about his life and teaching. Reading them left me unmoved and puzzled. I was hesitant to pursue it further. Miss Craske invited me to meet Baba when he came to New York later in the summer of '56. We left it at that.

As it happened, Miss Craske was teaching at the Pillow that summer, as she had for many summers, and she needed someone to teach her two ballet classes on Silent Day, a day she usually spent alone in her room or walking in the woods. When she asked me if I would hold her classes for her, I felt truly honored. Of all my dance teachers, Miss Craske is the one whose way of teaching I have most aspired to. I learned afterward that she sat in the shadows of the tiny unlit balcony above the studio watching me. Thank god I didn't know it at the time!

No one, however, could fill in for Viola on Silent Day. Rehearsals required that she be present to try out a new prop that Bob Rauschenberg had devised for the trio in *Suite,* to cope with the set and costumes for *Nocturnes,* learn sight cues, give Nick light cues, to adjust spacing and determine crossovers. The situation was maddeningly awkward and, at the same time, marvelously comic. Merce was wonderful. He made not a single complaint regarding the inconveniences wrought by Viola's observance of Silent Day, handling the whole thing with patient good humor, and showing a special courtesy and affection for her throughout her ordeal.

Since none of us was conversant with "signing," Viola kept a pencil and pad of paper offstage in order to communicate with us. We, of course, could speak to her but, more often than not, we didn't. Her silence was infectious. We began scribbling messages back to her on her pad or attempted some primitive form of sign language. "*You* can talk!" she'd scribble, and then we'd resort to whispering.

The basic *Nocturnes* costume for the women—white tights and white turtleneck leotards—included peculiar headdresses, exotic constructs of Rauschenbergian originality. Viola's headdress was a curious meld of images that reminded one simultaneously of a covered wagon, an arbor, and a nun's habit. Bob constructed a double hoop of wire that rested on her shoulders, and he covered it with a length of transparent white nylon that fell to the floor on each side. On her right thigh she wore two garters of blood-red glass beads. (Perhaps a tribute to the god Hymen?) Marianne's headdress was reminiscent of a mortarboard in shape—a taut square of wired transparent white nylon that seemed to float atop her head. Rhinestones sparkled from a centerpiece. From the four corners hung ropes of silky white cord ending in tassels. Around her wrists she wore one-inch-wide rhinestone bracelets. My headdress consisted of a round mirror set into a frame of braided hair that seemed to grow out of the top of my head. A full, gathered, circular veil of translucent white nylon slipped over the base of the mirror, covering my face and chest. The mirror, like a huge glittering diamond, or one great glittering eye, refracted the light with my slightest movement. Our headdresses were not worn all the time, although I kept my mirror on throughout. For Viola, getting in and out of her "covered wagon" was difficult. There was no time for written messages. Mishaps and missed entrances ensued before a routine could be established for how best to secure her to or release her from her contraption.

The set, which we'd never seen, consisted of a large, tall, square column—framed in wood and paneled in white. Attached to it was a transparent white scrim that stretched about twelve feet across and disappeared into the upstage left wing. Some of the action took place behind this scrim at different times throughout the ballet. Timing and spacing problems had to be identified and sorted out with inevitable fumbling and mess-ups, which Merce had to view as funny since there was no point in getting cross.

The difficulties caused by Silent Day were exacerbated by the fact that Nick Cernovich and Bob Rauschenberg weren't getting along. It was not a clash of personalities so much as a matter of differing aesthetics. Bob didn't like what was happening to his costumes and set in Nick's lighting.

It was here at Jacob's Pillow in 1956 that Bob realized he'd have to learn lighting himself if he was ever to be satisfied with the way his work looked onstage. *Nocturnes* was especially problematic. Decor and costumes were white. The dance was truly a *ballet blanc*—that is, a Cunningham/ Rauschenberg version of a *ballet blanc*. Bob wanted the white light of moonlight in all its variety, changed through intensity and direction of light, even by shadows, but *not* by colored gels. Nick envisioned how beautiful the whiteness would look bathed in a myriad of colored lights. Bob had already supplied the only color he wanted: red "drops of blood" on Viola's right thigh and the bizarre, masklike makeup he had devised for the men, which divided their faces down the middle, one side chalk-white, the other a vibrant, almost lurid color. Merce might have settled the argument by stating his own wishes, but he avoided the fray, leaving Bob and Nick to sort it out between themselves. Their dispute was *sotto voce,* but we knew it was going on by the kind of wary edginess in their voices.

Compounding the tension and anxiety during rehearsal was Ted Shawn's obvious displeasure upon first viewing a run-through of *Nocturnes,* which he had commissioned. Confronting Merce with a look of puzzled irritation, he said, "But I asked for a light work!" Merce's rather flippant rejoinder—"It's all in white; how much lighter could it be?"—was not appreciated. Merce was defensive. Maybe even hurt. He believed that he had made a "light work" in the spirit Shawn had intended. But the form and substance of its poetry, the simple, elegant beauty of the piece—gossamer light—were, I think, too original for Shawn to comprehend. People look for what they are already familiar with and, as usual, Merce disappointed.

Poor Shawn! The final outrage was the hole we burned in the stage floor. Blame Rauschenberg for that one. Bob suddenly got it into his head that a smoking ball should be passed from hand to hand throughout the trio in *Suite for Five.* It hadn't been rehearsed, of course. The smoking ball was awkward to transfer and hot to handle. Several times it clattered to the floor, once denting and burning a hole in it, but when, during a performance, it rolled off the stage and into the audience, from where it had to be retrieved and tossed back onto the stage, Merce nixed it forever. In a way, it's too bad—it was a striking image. But of course it upstaged the choreography. Upstaging—unintentional—was something Bob was adept at doing and something Merce was quick to spot and quash when it happened.

The mixed bill of fare during our week at the 1956 Jacob's Pillow Dance Festival included Sonia Arova and Job Sanders (from Ballet Theatre) and Carola Goya and Matteo (ethnic dancers). The ballet portion of each performance was considerably less illustrious than on our previous visit; the ethnic was somewhat more. As for Merce's portion, it was far riskier than the *Two Step, Septet,* and *Banjo* program we'd done in 1955. Even so, the reception by critics was better than expected. Reviewing the mixed bill, Walter Terry wrote: "At the top, I would place Mr. Cunningham and his company. . . . There is little of heart or overt passions (although latent emotions are indicated) about either [*Suite for Five* or *Nocturnes*] but the strangely isolated phrases, the swift sculptural lines of certain passages, the writhings and ebbings of action added up to something which was pretty fascinating if one could be content with merely watching movement."[10]

Apparently he could not see, as Sir Frederick Ashton had so beautifully expressed it, "the purity of the dance expressing nothing but itself, and thereby expressing a thousand degrees and facets of emotion, and the mystery of poetry and movement."[11]

Nocturnes was our Pillow swan song. It wasn't until 1984, twenty-eight years later and twelve years after Shawn's death, that the Cunningham company would be invited back. When Liz Thompson, the new executive director, was interviewed for the position, one of the members of the Jacob's Pillow board of directors warned her in no uncertain terms, "Just don't *ever* invite Merce Cunningham!" Merce's reputation with Shawn and no doubt the reputation he acquired after setting his notoriously controversial work *Winterbranch* on the Boston Ballet must have irrevocably branded him with certain conservative Boston Brahmins as *the* avantgarde "untouchable." Liz Thompson held her tongue, kept her own council, and, several years after becoming director, invited Merce back to the Pillow. There was no mixed bill of fare that time. The Merce Cunningham Dance Company was the only attraction, and the houses were sold out for the entire week.

In July 1956, Meher Baba made his fourth trip to the United States, and Miss Craske invited a number of her students to the Hotel Delmonico, where he was staying, to meet him. Those who had already become followers of Baba spent many hours on several days in attendance. Remy and I went just once for a brief audience. When we arrived, the outer waiting room was jammed with people. We found Miss Craske with her students clustered around her, a safe haven in the middle of the noisy, chaotic crush of bodies. Eventually, Baba called for Miss Craske and her group. I remember a dark, cavernous room—probably a ballroom—that had been partially curtained off to give Baba and his closest disciples a place in which to retire. This room was also crowded with people, but far fewer than in the antechamber. Here there was no babble of conversation, only the hush one expects in a cathedral before a service with whispers or all-but-inaudible voices murmuring now and then, but mainly quiet and a compelling sense of anticipation.

Meeting a Perfect Master in the ballroom of New York City's Hotel Delmonico seemed to me a curious anomaly, but when I finally saw Baba, the surroundings melted away. His eyes dissolved space and time. And animated them. I remember little else. Remy had to fill me in on the details afterward. The scene struck him as sweetly silly and he had to struggle not to laugh aloud. There was Baba, center stage, so to speak, in front of the curtained-off section of the room, enthroned upon a chaise lounge that had been covered with a rather tacky white chenille bedspread. His closest Indian disciples clustered behind him in a semicircle. At Baba's side was a table with a bowl of grapes and a carafe of water. Our little group stayed close together. Eventually, Miss Craske was called to Baba's side. I don't know how long we stood there, or what communication took place. Suddenly, or so it seemed, I was called forward and told to sit on the foot of the chaise. No words were spoken that I recall. (In 1925, Baba had taken a vow of silence, which he observed until his death in 1969.) I looked into Baba's eyes. He into mine. As he placed a grape between my lips he made some sort of sign, which his disciple translated almost instantaneously and which I perceived as if Baba himself had spoken: "You will come to love me very much." That was all. I wasn't certain that I'd actually heard it— I was truly lost in his gaze. The "interview" over, I must have been instructed to return to our group. I remember nothing about what happened after that until we were all out in the hotel hallway and everyone was talking at once. Remy, with cheeky innocence and charm, went up to Miss Craske, gave her a big kiss, and said, "He's a living doll!" There was a sucking-in of breath, a furrowing of brows; our friends pulled back, scandalized. Miss Craske just smiled. Wise, patient, loving, she did not appear to be scandalized. Remy's breezy flippancy cut right through the idolatry, the breathless, weighty solemnity of the occasion.

Remy and I fled from the Delmonico. Neither of us could get out of there fast enough—out of the oppressively sacrosanct hothouse (air-conditioned) atmosphere into the blinding light and sweltering heat of a New York City sidewalk at noon in July, where reality was tawdry and differently oppressive yet had a feeling of authenticity. I don't mean to imply that Baba was bogus. It was the atmosphere surrounding him, the making of a cult and the setting up of a shrine, the venerating of inequalities and dualistic structures: High/low, God/man. Perhaps the trouble lay in "confusing the finger with the moon." Baba's way, as least as I perceived it to be practiced by most Westerners, was not the way for me or for Remy, even though our experience of meeting him had been very different. Baba's presence had genuinely moved me. Remy, I think, was only amused.

While Meher Baba's discourses were often compatible with Zen Buddhism, his style was radically different. To quote Suzuki, "Zen is more daringly concrete in its paradoxes than other mystical teachings. The latter are more or less confined to general statements concerning life or God or the world, but Zen carries its paradoxical assertions into every detail of our daily life."[12] Baba's writings abound with the terminology of love, such as "Baba's love is with his lovers always, helping and guiding them. And they? They should keep their love for him alive and aglow, by making him their constant companion in all their thoughts, words and actions."[13] In the Zen experience, there is no reference whatever to such personal relationships.

> It is all too easy for ideas and concepts to conceal rather than reveal Reality. Thus the Zen master says that ideas are fingers pointing at the moon of Reality, but that most people mistake the finger for the moon. . . . It is quite impossible for ideas to describe or convey the deepest truth of life, since ideas are forms and Reality is too living to be held in any form. Zen does not consist in acquiring ideas about Reality and our relation to it; it consists in getting rid of ideas and feeling *about* life in order that we may get to life itself.[14]

Here was the Zen of John and Merce, at least as I saw it—in their work and in their working, and it called up responses deep within me. I was not called to Baba in this way. It was the Zen connection that made the life with John and Merce such a powerful experience. I needed to believe in the beliefs of the people with whom I worked, to feel that what I was doing was a way of life, not a career.

But even so, since I was now determined to support at least my dancing, my belief, strong as it was, didn't prevent continually wavering uncertainty about how I would continue with Merce. In August, I was invited to join the Marquis de Cuevas Ballet in France for the upcoming season. Forty dollars a week, fifty on the road. Pay my own way to Europe. One or two of my Met friends would be going. I wrote to my parents, "I said no. Don't know why exactly, except that I feel I have so much to learn *immediately* in a good classroom, at the same time that I learn in performance *and* make a salary. I think for the next year, the Met [Opera Ballet] is the best place for me to do all that—*if* I can get the job!" In this same letter I wrote: "If I can't support my dancing *myself* after this, I shall give it up." "This" referred to yet another embarrassed request to borrow money in order to pay up my long-overdue bill at the Met Opera Ballet School. I already owed my mother five hundred dollars. I needed another two hundred to cover classes from the previous spring. My decision to audition for the Met company was an about-face from the year before, but I was now more realistic about Merce's chances of supporting a company, even part-time. When I talked with him about the Opera Ballet, to my surprise, he seemed not the least bit perturbed about me joining, saying he'd fly me out to whatever performances he had lined up. But I heard from Remy that John was terribly upset and was going around asking whether he ought to throw in the towel.

For the ten days before the auditions I felt unhinged: classes every morning with Mr. Tudor or Miss Craske, rehearsals every afternoon with Merce, then Merce's class, and a mad dash back again to the Met to take (or watch if I arrived late) yet another class. While I was in the midst of that schedule, Merce managed to whisk me off to an elegant reception for the Royal Danish Ballet in the oak-paneled trustees room of the New York Public Library, where he whirled me through the stellar gathering, either introducing me or being himself introduced to everyone who was anyone in the dance world. It was glamorous and fun, and we had a lovely time together. As Viola once commented after being wined and dined by Merce, he could, upon occasion, summon up the beguiling gallantry and courtliness of a noble swain, especially when he wished to discourage one of his women dancers from leaving his company. But I didn't want to leave him. I needed no convincing on that score. What I needed was help in keeping my resolve to earn my way, even if *that* meant leaving him.

The first audition was on a Thursday. If I got through that one, the final was the following Monday. On the Tuesday before, Miss Craske stopped me as I was leaving class and said, "I'd give it a lot of thought, my dear, before I'd audition for the Met. You've become known as a soloist—in the Met you'll be nothing but a chorine." Oh, God! I *had* given it a lot of thought. But I couldn't think about it anymore. I went to the first audition. It was brutal, a real stinger. I got through it, but not as well as I should have. Tudor kept me anyway. I went home and threw up. The next evening in class, Tudor made a lengthy speech about auditioning. Turning to me, he said that I was nervous and tense because I wanted the job too much. He was partly correct. The job was both wanted and *not* wanted—too much. After class I asked if I might have a talk with him. It was the only

truly personal conversation I ever had with Antony Tudor. It took place in
the tiny faculty dressing room he and Miss Craske shared in alternation.
He was aloof, rather stern but not unkind. Hoping that I might have the
best of both worlds, I needed to know—should I be accepted into the
Opera Ballet—whether I would be allowed to do the five performances for
which Merce had already signed contracts. (The first engagement was only
two and a half weeks away!) "Absolutely not," he said. "The Met will not
excuse you for even one day." It was then that I explained that I really did
not want to be in the Met but saw no alternative at the moment, that
although I wanted to work with Merce, there was no money and I would not
continue dancing without some income. "Never dance for money. Better to
starve doing something one loves." For those words he still has my heartfelt thanks and overwhelming respect. At the time, I was stunned. I hadn't
expected to hear words like those from Tudor. The cynical, caustic side of
his nature was what he mostly showed us in the classroom, and I'd
expected him to tell me to stop coddling myself, to face up to the harsh
realities of the profession in the real world. I had been prepared for him to
laugh at me, not to hear him say quite seriously, "Better to starve doing
something one loves." I found Remy waiting for me. Seeing my stricken
face, my eyes brimming with tears, he put his arms around me; that simple, affectionate gesture of understanding undid me. He held me while I
sobbed. The next morning, I visited the little faculty dressing room once
again, this time for another talk with Miss Craske. She threw up her hands,
saying, "It's terribly difficult to advise you. I can't take the responsibility
for another person's life. But you won't like doing Zachary's [Solov] choreography, you know. You like Merce's work. Wait another year—perhaps
Tudor will be choreographing then." Before I left, she said she'd talk to
Tudor about me teaching at Juilliard, and that she'd be willing to help me
through the Cecchetti syllabus.

Tudor and Craske had reenforced my deepest feelings. I didn't want to
leave Merce. Or John. But my resolve, my promise to my parents and to
myself that I would support my dancing or quit—*that* had been completely
undermined. For the next week I was wretched, confused, full of doubt and
self-recrimination. I walked around Manhattan like a traumatized zom-
bie—not always aware that tears were spilling from my eyes and down my
cheeks. By midweek I had a bad cold, and I missed all my classes for the
rest of the week, although I still staggered through Merce's rehearsals and
there, at least, I managed not to cry, or, if I did, to hide my tears behind the
façade of a runny nose and rasping cough. By Friday night I could scarcely
breathe and felt seriously ill. Earle was working the late shift at Capitol

Records and didn't get home until four in the morning. I hadn't slept. I could breathe only if I sat up and concentrated on it: inhale, exhale, inhale, exhale . . . through the wee hours I huddled in a corner of the couch wrapped in blankets, very scared, but still not wanting to awaken Earle. Waiting for dawn was an eternity. At nine I discovered that my doctor was on vacation. I waited until ten to phone Remy. His doctor wouldn't see me until two in the afternoon. Earle drove me to the office. In the waiting room I was afraid I'd pass out. When at last the doctor saw me, took my temperature, and listened to my breathing, she apologized again and again for not agreeing to see me sooner. An hour later I was in Manhattan General Hospital. I was there a week. Diagnosis: pneumonia, but later it was rediagnosed as "traumatic bronchitis," which smacked strongly, I thought, of an illness of psychosomatic origins carefully incubated during those seven days of walking the city in tears and numb with misery, all brought on, I have little doubt, by making a promise I wouldn't be able to keep.

Merce arranged for me to fly to Cornell College, Mount Vernon, Iowa, to give me an extra two days to recuperate and get my strength back once I was out of the hospital. I was ecstatic to be there. It was a small college set amid cornfields, surrounded by big lovely old trees ablaze with fall foliage. I felt liberated being out of New York City, being able to breathe freely, having the tangy, crisp country air sing in my lungs like a benediction. And it felt so good being on tour again, however briefly. The crushing weight on my chest that I'd borne for the past few weeks was relieved by a glorious sense of deliverance. I was where I belonged. With my own family. Dancing the work I loved to dance. The idea of joining the Metropolitan Opera Ballet was jettisoned, forever.

November 1956. John and Merce borrowed money to buy a Volkswagen Microbus, the vehicle that defined—willy-nilly—a classic era of the dance company's history: the VW years. Our first VW-bus jaunt was crazily impractical, but according to a postcard sent to my parents, "a very happy trip." To give two performances we drove for two days and one-third of the way across the country and, although I don't know how Merce was able to afford it, we stayed, for all the world like a professional dance company, in a big city hotel—the Roosevelt in downtown St. Louis. We performed on two separate campuses of a Christian Science college called the Principia, one in St. Louis and the other forty miles away, across the Missouri and Mississippi rivers, in Elsah, Illinois. The Illinois campus, situated high on the bluffs of the Mississippi, with its handsome buildings of English-style architecture connected by brick paths and separated by apple orchards and gardens, remains to this day the most beautiful college campus I've seen. Even though it was early November, the fall foliage was still in full splendor, and at sunset the sky, reflecting on the surface of the mighty Mississippi, was like molten fire. Lights flickered from a village at the river's edge, and on the horizon a tiny thumbnail moon ensnared the glimmering of the departed sun. It was time to make up, warm up, and get on with the show, but I was reluctant to leave the bluff.

Living in theaters, being so apart, so out of step with nature, was in many ways like being blind, deaf, and numb. I was always to feel this pull: away from the artificial agenda and intransigent timetable imposed on us by our theater life, and toward life where time is defined by nature's clock, by the seasons, by sunup/sundown instead of curtain up/curtain down. Almost always I felt resentment when plunging into the unnatural darkness of a theater in the middle of a sunny day in order to rehearse by artificial light. John's way of touring tried not to shut out the sun; it embraced wholeness, inclusiveness. But when John was no longer in the driver's seat, he was often treated like a fool by those who were, and his ideas about touring were scoffed at and usually ignored in the cause of efficiency and economy. It began to happen as soon as he stopped being the company manager.

For the Principia audiences, at our sponsor's request, John gave a curtain-raiser talk (later printed in *Dance Observer*) that began: "In this day of TV-darkened homes, a live performance has become something of a rarity, so much so that Aaron Copland recently said, 'a concert is a thing of the past.' "[1] In explaining the most unusual aspect of the Cage/Cunningham ideas—the independence of the music and the dance—John stated that "a rhythm results which is not that of . . . regular beats but which reminds us of a multiplicity of events in time and space, stars, for instance, in the sky, or activities of earth viewed from the air."[2]

Ever since John first spoke them on November 9, 1956, words from this talk have been quoted repeatedly (although few people who quote them today know their source). They are still apt because little changed in Merce's or John's aesthetic to warrant John having said anything different later on, even though what he said then was only partly true and continued to be only partly true (in *my* opinion) forever after:

> We are not, in these dances and music, saying something. We are simple-minded enough to think that if we were saying something we would use words. We are rather doing something. The meaning of what we do is determined by each one who sees and hears it . . . there are no stories and no psychological problems. There is simply an activity of movement, sound and light.
>
> The activity of movement, sound and light, we believe, is expressive, but what it expresses is determined by each one of you who is right, as Pirandello's title has it, if he thinks he is.
>
> The novelty of our work derives therefore from our having moved away from simply private concerns towards the world of nature and society of which all of us is a part. Our intention is to affirm this life, not to bring order out of chaos nor to suggest improvements in creation, but simply to wake up to the very life we're living, which is so excellent once one gets one's mind and one's desires out of its way and lets it act of its own accord.[3]

Actually, although John may have done so in his own work, and certainly wanted Merce to do so in his, I don't believe Merce ever moved completely away from "private concerns." Whatever John believed, I'm convinced that there are "stories" and "psychological problems" hidden away in a secret subtext in many of Merce's dances. Merce relishes conundrums and riddles, and his skills in deception are Promethean. He's like a fox, agile and sly, unexcelled at putting people off his scent.

We had no more out-of-town performance dates after the Principia until mid-May 1957. Our first trip in the new VW bus would also be our last for six months. Faced with a bleak schedule, John, Remy, and I once again set to work writing letters and publicity material; this time our focus was Europe. Shortly after Principia, David Tudor went off to Europe alone to play solo concerts of John's *Music of Changes* and compositions by Earle, Morty, and Christian in Cologne, Paris, Milan, Venice, London, Zurich, and Vienna. About one month later, on December 22, Earle boarded the United States Lines' *America*, bound for Le Havre, carrying with him hand-written manuscripts of the scores he'd composed since 1950. Although Earle's music had reached European audiences, this was his first voyage abroad.

Everywhere he went there were receptive, sympathetic ears. In six weeks he met with and showed his work to Pierre Boulez, Heinrich Strobel, Hans Rosbaud, Bruno Maderna, Luciano Berio, Wolfgang Steinecke, Karlheinz Stockhausen, Otto Tomek, and William Glock, among others. He went from Paris to Baden-Baden and on to Milan, Vienna, Munich, Darmstadt, Cologne, Hamburg, back to Cologne, and to Paris again, and finally to London. He wrote: "The reception in every case has been much better than I expected . . . the modern music climate here is amazing compared to America . . . [they are] making extraordinary technical progress via electronic experiments."

He found Boulez quickly, and their conversations spanned several evenings. While their ideas and methods were similar, there existed a basic aesthetic disagreement that Earle felt made for a very vital kind of situation. Boulez was particularly interested in Earle's use of instruments and kept checking in his reference books to see if they really were possible. (They were.) In Milan, Earle met Bruno Maderna for the first time and reestablished an acquaintance with Luciano Berio, whom he'd met in New York. Maderna brought his students to look over Earle's scores. They were "quite astonished" by *Indices*, and Maderna himself was so excited about it that he wanted to conduct it that coming summer at Darmstadt. In Cologne, Earle took an instant liking to Karlheinz Stockhausen and his wife, Doris. His first impression of Stockhausen was that "his mind is better than his music—[he] seems to have everything figured out except why he figured it out."

Shortly after David Tudor's return from Europe, he appeared at a Cunningham rehearsal with Stockhausen's newest piece for piano—

Klavierstücke XI—to show it to John and Christian and Merce. The score was "indeterminate," or "aleatoric"—the term preferred by Europeans. I gasped, exclaiming, "Great minds meet across the sea!" but nobody seemed to notice how remarkably similar it was to Earle's work of a few years earlier, which David had performed in Europe on his concert tours. Only David responded, with one of his sly, enigmatic smiles.

Fortunately, from the time Earle left for Europe in late December until mid-January I was so busy preparing for our single performance at the Brooklyn Academy of Music on January 12 that there was scarcely time to feel lonely. Happily, the sleazy bar on the street level had been closed by the cops; unhappily, our new neighbor, the artist David Budd, who'd moved into the floor-through loft below us, had escaped the winter and gone to Sarasota, Florida, to join his wife, Corky, a bareback rider of the illustrious Christiani Circus family. Being the sole tenant meant that no heat rose from the floors below me to ward off the bitter January chill. I dared not leave the gas on in our tiny cast-iron cooking stove or in the small space heater while I was away most of the day, so returning to my frigid empty loft was not something to look forward to. Still, I preferred being there alone to being lonely with other people, and I actually enjoyed the solitude: I read, I listened to music, and despite having done little else all day long, I danced . . . to music. Usually the Modern Jazz Quartet. Remy says that more than once, as he walked home on the east side of Third Avenue, he caught a glimpse of my silhouette careering madly around the loft behind bamboo "blinds." Well, it was a terrific way to keep warm.

The Brooklyn program included four New York first performances—*Suite for Five, Galaxy, Lavish Escapade,* and *Nocturnes*—plus two repertory works, *Septet* and *Minutiae.* In addition, John's most recent composition, *Winter Music,* had its first performance anywhere as a musical interlude. We performed in the smaller of the academy's two theaters: the notion that a modern-dance audience could fill the large opera house was unheard-of. Yet eleven hundred people arrived for our performance, and the curtain had to be held until almost nine o'clock because few of them had bought tickets in advance. Backstage, we were told that the lobby was a madhouse and that we must wait. So we kept warming up, pacing, warming up over and over again, becoming more and more nervous and frustrated by the delay. The early birds who'd bought tickets ahead of time and were already seated were impatient, too, and showed it with sporadic bouts of rhythmic clapping.

Once the delay was forgotten, everyone on both sides of the curtain agreed that the concert was a great success. It was the most enthusiastic and responsive audience we'd had since Black Mountain. This time, however, most of the people in the audience were unknown to us. Whoever they were, they set the tone of the evening with the opening curtain when they warmly applauded Merce at the beginning of *Suite,* and clapped so long and loudly after our new duet section that Merce was forced to delay his next solo. Later, they clapped thunderously and bravoed Merce's *Lavish Escapade.* And when the curtain opened on both *Minutiae* and *Nocturnes,* before a single step of either dance had been taken they applauded Rauschenberg's sets. They seemed to love everything. Everything, that is, except *Winter Music,* which they only loved to hate. They booed vociferously at the end of the music, but then, unappeased, they applauded wildly until John and David reappeared for a second bow, when again they booed and hissed, with gusto! David licked his lips with pleasure after bowing to booing. Not John. He was pale and tremulous, and it was my impression that he was shocked and deeply hurt, but P. W. Manchester, reviewing the concert for *Dance News,* wrote: "I wish I did not feel that the composer accepted boos with greater complacency than the applause." I believe her "feeling" was incorrect. I've never agreed with those of John's critics who thought he enjoyed being hated. In fact, John craved adulation and always seemed surprised when the music he'd written, which he found "amazing" and "interesting" and "beautiful," was found by others to be abhorrent and unendurable. *Winter Music* was played just before *Nocturnes*—the last dance of the evening—and we were told that some people walked out during the musical interlude and didn't return, which wasn't really surprising, since, due to its late start, the concert went on until nearly 11:30 p.m.

What was surprising, and very disappointing, was to learn that Edwin Denby (America's most revered, respected, and best-loved dance critic)[4] had left at the first intermission, having seen only *Suite for Five, Septet,* and *Minutiae.* The next day he telephoned Merce with profuse apologies, expressing genuine regret at having missed three of the four new dances. It seems he had invited Lincoln Kirstein (or been invited by Kirstein) to attend, and Kirstein (the director of the New York City Ballet and one of the most influential men in American ballet) was determined to leave the concert before it was half over. Edwin had allowed himself to be swept out of the theater in Kirstein's wake. Dear, kind, gentle Edwin—the man who always went out of his way to see all the new dance work being produced anywhere in the city! Even though he was no longer writing dance criticism on a regular basis, he was abjectly ashamed of his moral cowardice and felt compelled by conscience to explain his predicament to Merce.

The *New York Times*'s dance critic, John Martin, suffered no such pangs; he hadn't bothered to come at all. Considered (in 1957) the dean of American dance critics, he claimed to have been "too busy." At least that's what he told Remy. And since he didn't deem the event of sufficient interest to send someone in his place (there were no second- or third-string staff dance writers on the *Times* in those days), once again there was no review in New York's most distinguished newspaper. When it came to Merce's work, John Martin would always be, in my view, thoroughly unprofessional. Of course the de Lys season had prepared us, so we weren't surprised, but it still rankled—though not enough to cast a pall on the good feeling the concert had generated.

Crowds from the remarkably demonstrative audience came around to the stage door to congratulate Merce and the rest of the company—so many, in fact, that the management was forced to refuse entry to most of them. One person who did get backstage to see Merce was Muriel Stuart. Formerly a dancer with Anna Pavlova's company (1916–1921), Miss Stuart had become one of the principal teachers at Balanchine's School of American Ballet, and she had gotten to know Merce when he studied there. After telling Merce that she really loved the program, she made a point of asking him where the women's dressing room was and searched us out to tell us that she thought we'd danced beautifully and that all of us had made great advances since she'd last seen the company. As she left, she kissed me on the cheek and said some lovely complimentary words about my dancing, and then "Keep it up, stick with it!" Stick with dancing, or stick with Merce? I wasn't sure, but my intuition told me she meant "stick with Merce." Although Miss Craske didn't come backstage, she, too, was extremely enthusiastic about the performance: she thought the program "excellent," Merce's movement "fabulous," the way he danced "marvelous," and that the company was now "a unit." She particularly liked *Suite for Five* and *Nocturnes*. Antony Tudor, however, was baffled and disappointed by the direction Merce was taking. He'd expected "greater things." At least, that's the information I gleaned secondhand, and I was too timid to find out firsthand what he thought. Elsie Becker at Orientalia Bookshop (where Tudor shopped for books on Zen Buddhism) reported that he liked the *Suite* duet and my dancing, but to me Tudor said absolutely nothing. In subsequent classes he made a number of comments about my rigid head and matchstick arms. Miss Craske agreed with him; not only was my head stiff, she said, but the stiffness was present in my whole muscle structure. I needed "to flow more," she said, and then—no doubt to soften the blow—she said I was much better about these things than before, that there had been improvement ever since the Jacob's Pillow performances in July. "So I guess I see the direction for me to work in," I wrote my parents after hearing Tudor's and Craske's comments.

To my surprise and pleasure, Merce actually spoke to me about my dancing. Since it was one of the rare times that I felt I'd danced well, at least as well as I was then capable of, having Merce corroborate this feeling meant a great deal. It was also one of the rare times that I can remember Merce being visibly, unguardedly happy, even exuberant about a performance. And when, after the final reckoning (his expenses for costumes, dancers, musicians, and designers, and even the monthly VW Microbus installment), he discovered he'd made thirty-five dollars for himself—clear—his spirits were positively jovial!

But not everyone was rosy. Right after the concert, Viola was confined to bed with viral pneumonia. Karen Kanner, the dancer chosen to do Anita Dencks's part in *Minutiae*, decided she didn't want to continue with the company after her very first performance. Rumor was that her parents were outraged by the music and apparently more baffled than Antony Tudor by the choreography. Or maybe it was Walter Terry's rather nasty review that influenced her decision. Terry, as usual, praised Merce the dancer—"one of the finest dancers of our day, a superb technician and arresting stage personality"—but went on to castigate much of the choreography with these words: "appalling," "insulting," "worse than idiotic," "frighteningly barren."[5] For me, the post-performance glow turned swiftly to gloom. Despite the success of that one New York concert, the company's future appeared to be pretty miserable. While Merce kept smiling delightedly, saying, "Wasn't it nice?" I kept wondering, "What now?"

According to the letter I sent off to Earle in Europe, "Merce's concert set off a real furor—as usual, much discussion, excitement. Someone said there hasn't been this much controversy since Diaghilev was around."

But only Walter Sorell, writing in the *Providence Sunday Journal*, gave any indication that a radically new aesthetic was being explored:

> An evening with Merce Cunningham is a unique experience, puzzling here and perplexing there, but an exploration of time and space in a new fashion. He seems to have done for the dance what Bert Brecht did for the theatre: He has created an epic theatre dance. Brecht and Cunningham do not want us to identify ourselves with anyone or anything happening on stage. They want to shock us into an awareness of reality. The choreography is objective, the dancer's self-expression reduced to a minimum . . . Merce Cunningham delights in a tormenting simplicity by cutting away all extraneous

movement and dares to freeze a phrase in a static pose and to hold it at will. But only a dancer utterly conscious of movements and inner dynamics of the body can successfully challenge all convention and create his own independent art.[6]

David Vaughan, in Britain's *Dance and Dancers*, characterized *Lavish Escapade* as "one of Cunningham's most violent and disturbing dances . . . its initial impact is powerful indeed. It has the terrifying and inescapable intensity of a nightmare."[7] Vaughan, who would eventually play a crucial role in the Cunningham company's history, was an English dancer, actor, singer, choreographer, and writer whom Lincoln Kirstein had helped bring to New York to study at the School of American Ballet. There he'd met dancer-choreographer James Waring, and through him he was introduced to Merce's work. The July 1956 issue of *Dance and Dancers* included an article—"Transatlantic View: More American Dancers and Their Work"—in which Vaughan wrote: "I think he [Merce Cunningham] is the finest male dancer the modern dance has produced." For the April 1957 issue of *Dance and Dancers* he wrote, about *Suite for Five*, "What takes place before our eyes is arresting and brilliant: the duet in particular . . . explores the possibilities of supported adagio in a plastique idiom of astonishing originality."[8]

Is it possible that Walter Terry was writing about the same piece when he wrote:

The results, in my opinion, were appalling and, I would say, insulting. The music (which is hardly the right word) provided by Mr. Cage was primarily silence occasionally interrupted by a limited number of noises of varying pitch and timbre. As choreographer, Mr. Cunningham went right along with this idea and gave us vast stretches of inaction interrupted by rather dull movements.[9]

I think one can detect in David's commentary the voice of someone who was coming to Merce's work freshly, without any of the historical hangups or prejudices that seemed to afflict so many American dance critics when writing about modern dance in the 1950s. When confronted with something intrinsically different from the aesthetic premise of Martha Graham, or of Doris Humphrey, Charles Weidman, Hanya Holm, or Helen Tamiris—those remarkable pioneers of the 1920s, '30s, and '40s—Terry and most other dance critics simply failed to realize that a new language was being spoken, a language they would have to learn; instead, they went on using the standards they'd devised for judging the pioneers. For David Vaughan, coming from a British ballet and musical-theater background, all American modern dance was a relatively new experience; he had no ax to grind, no preconceptions, no attachment to any ideas about what modern dance *should* be.

I won't attempt to defend the music. Certainly some of it I disliked intensely, and among the company dancers I was not alone. If I found it unbearable, I tried to "turn it off," tried to *not hear it,* because it could be disruptive, painful, even violating. For me, those pieces did not coexist with the choreography, they competed with it, even attempted to annihilate it, like an insanely jealous lover. But I think there is no denying the paradox that some of the music, without having much distinction on its own, made a definite contribution to the work *as a whole.* And occasionally the music was truly extraordinary—dynamic and multifaceted.

In order to approach Merce's work sympathetically, one has no choice but to come to terms with the Cage/Cunningham premise regarding the coexistence of the music and the dance. One doesn't have to like it, or agree with it, but one has to, in some way, accept it.

Getting beyond the music/sound in order to appreciate the dance and dancing has remained an ongoing problem for a great many people, and the professional dance critics were no exception. This is unfortunate, for it prevented Merce's work from being seriously analyzed or even properly *seen.* It was so much easier to rant and rail about the music than to write intelligently about the dance, which would have required *serious* consideration of the implications of Merce's chance procedures. Ponder this: *Suite for Five* and *Lavish Escapade* produced strikingly diverse audience and critical reactions, and they are in fact entirely different from each other in form, style, movement vocabulary, continuity, and performance quality. Yet both were composed by chance means. They exemplify the richness, depth, and variety that Merce was able to create through the chance process. And it should be clearly understood: Merce *did* create them. No one else could have or would have made those particular dances, with or without chance methods. They prove—unequivocally—the validity of Merce's use of chance as a choreographic tool . . . for *him.*

The company did not perform again until April 27, when Merce joined Shirley Broughton, Katherine Litz, and Merle Marsicano in a symposium entitled "Four Dancers Speak and Dance: at the Henry Street Playhouse." In the first half of the symposium, moderated by David Vaughan, each of the choreographers read a statement, a kind of manifesto of beliefs. Much of what they had to say, though focused and presented differently, concerned ideas they held in common. The second part of the evening opened with a performance of Merce's *Suite for Five,* which seemed an apt demonstration of Merce's spoken words: "The nature of dancing is stillness in movement and movement in stillness. . . . No stillness exists without movement, and no movement is fully expressed without stillness. But stillness acts of itself, not hampered by before or after. It is not a pause or a premonition. . . . the liveliness that dancing can have is *not* in what the movement comes from, but in what it actually *is* as the dancer does it, and how it is surrounded and inhabited by stillness."[10]

Space and time. Movement and stillness. Meaning found in the movement itself. The process of discovery. Here were Merce's immediate concerns. When expressing themselves verbally, the four choreographers seemed to have similar views, and one might easily imagine from hearing them talk that one would see similarities in the physical expression of their ideas. But this was not the case. Rather, each choreographer appeared to be coming from a distinctly individual ideology, none common to any other. Similar concerns, filtered through the unique personal histories of these four unusual choreographers, had produced totally dissimilar dances. The idea for the symposium, according to Vaughan, was Merce's. Perhaps Merce hoped that his choreography, when seen on a program of dances by others who were also working outside modern dance's mainstream, would be perceived as less of an aberration and would be given more serious attention. At least, the backstage ambience at Henry Street that evening was one of mutual respect and admiration, but even in this congenial company, I sensed that Merce felt the odd man out.

Our brief moments on the Henry Street stage (less than ten minutes of dancing for Marianne, Remy, Viola, and me) was the only performing the company did during the four months before an engagement at Antioch College in Yellow Springs, Ohio, on May 14. The Antioch "tour" (as we named any performance not reachable by subway) was another one of those times when we spent far more hours in the Volkswagen minibus on the road than we did onstage rehearsing and dancing, but at least it was a two-day "residency" instead of a one-night stand, and it included a music concert by John and David, a master class by Merce, and a seminar, as well as a performance. Then came an even longer hiatus, until November 30. In nine and a half months, the company performed one full program plus a single dance at the Henry Street symposium. Merce's cheer following our Brooklyn Academy success descended into gloom far, far gloomier than mine had been.

Mine, by this time, had dissipated. Prompted by Merce's suggestion that the breadth of my dancing would benefit from studying at Balanchine's School of American Ballet, I auditioned at the school, was accepted as a professional student, and began classes with Anatole Oboukhoff, with whom Merce had studied while he was dancing in Martha Graham's company. Oboukhoff was born in Czarist Russia in 1896 and trained at the Imperial Ballet School in St. Petersburg. A soloist with the legendary Maryinsky Theatre before leaving Russia in 1920, he was considered "one of the best *danseurs nobles* of his time."[11] He'd begun teaching at the school in 1940 and was now known as one of the great teachers of Russian classical dancing. I'd heard all sorts of wild and humorous tales about his classes and fully expected to be intimidated both by him and the prowess of my classmates, but the worst intimidation took place in the chilly silence of the women's dressing room, where I was looked over from head to toe, like some filly at a racetrack. Not a single civil word was ever spoken to me there except by Diana Adams, then one of City Ballet's most beautiful, warm, and womanly principal dancers. There was a mutual sense of acquaintanceship, since she often came to the Met to study with Mr. Tudor and Miss Craske. At SAB she always greeted me with a smile. From most of the others, my timid hello received only icy stares. But Oboukhoff's class was so exhilarating that it more than made up for any discomfort suffered in the dressing room. Extremely demanding physically (far more rigorous for the body than the mind), his classes were nonetheless a little disappointing because there wasn't much teaching as I'd come to understand that word while studying Cecchetti technique with Craske and Tudor. Oboukhoff's was a do-or-die class, in some ways much the same as Merce's. To the question, "How do I do this movement?" Merce would answer, "The only way to do it is to do it." True, of course, but Zen simplicity isn't always helpful. It was clear to me through my studies with Craske and Tudor that certain anatomically insightful rules *can* be learned, and, if applied correctly, will protect the body from injury, will meld mind and muscle into a oneness of good habits rather than poor ones, and can actually hasten the doing. Yet, from my own experience as a student and later as a teacher, I also know that sometimes no matter how many dozens of times one is told or one tells a student how best to accomplish a certain difficult step, the student is able to apply that information *only* when he or she is ready; and then, *suddenly*, it becomes a revelation, an act of self-discovery, rather than something learned. One finds oneself simply doing it, struck, as if by lightning. When that happened to me, I'd think, "Why didn't anyone ever tell me that before?" (knowing perfectly well that someone had—dozens of times) because it *felt* as though I'd just that moment figured it out myself. I suspect it often takes a certain amount of time, different for each of us, for verbally transmitted information to connect between mind and body before one can execute difficult coordinations correctly. If one always bypasses that interconnection and goes the route of brute force (the "just do it!" philosophy), the body too easily develops habits that can get it into trouble along the way, particularly near the end of the road, when accreted bad habits that youthful resilience has held at bay finally lead to chronic and often serious injuries.

Oboukhoff's combinations in the center and across the floor were space-eaters, big movements in the lush, romantic, grand manner of Imperial Russia. It was precisely this bigness, this devouring of space and lack of finicky detail (*not* the grand manner), that Merce wanted me to experience. In every exercise in every class, the energy level was extremely high, yet Oboukhoff kept pushing for more. I needed those classes, no question about it, and I enjoyed them immensely, but I couldn't give up Miss Craske or Mr. Tudor. During that period I often took three classes a day. Since Merce was teaching only three times a week and wasn't working on anything new with the company, I had time and energy and a strong appetite for taking class.

Later on, I also took classes with Muriel Stuart, Pierre Vladimirov, and his wife, Felia Doubrovska, another St. Petersburg Imperial Academy graduate and member of the Maryinsky Theatre (before joining Diaghilev's company in 1920). Regal to the bone, tall (for a dancer of that period), yet so delicately feminine, Doubrovska at sixty-two was ageless and exquisitely glamorous in her softly draped pink chiffon skirt and gossamer wool shawl. Like so many hundreds of dancers, I was utterly smitten by her. "She is fantastic!" I gushed, in a letter to my parents, "Such beautiful legs and elegant neck and shoulders!" I was touched by her attention and kindness to me, which always dissipated the chilly reception I'd received in the dressing room. Her classes, like Oboukhoff's, were doubly inspiring because they were peopled with New York City Ballet principals, soloists, and corps. In the hope of absorbing her elegance of phrasing and the musicality of her port de bras, top-rank professional dancers from around the country and even from abroad also attended her classes when they were in town.

Near the end of May, Remy and I, grateful for every performance experience, journeyed to Fitchburg, Massachusetts, to dance in my mother's annual spring concert. In June, with nothing in the offing for Merce's company until November, I auditioned for Radio City Music Hall's corps de ballet. Margaret Sande was the resident choreographer and Bettina Rose was her assistant. The audition was all on pointe, with the inevitable thirty-two *fouettés* required. I was accepted, joined AGVA (American Guild of Variety Artists—the circus union!), signed my contract on July 2, began rehearsals on July 9, and on July 11 went into a show that had been running for several weeks.

Merce left for California and a five-week teaching engagement at Idyllwild. Just before he left, he began work on two new dances. That brief rehearsal period seemed a last-ditch effort on his part to keep the company together. He wasn't giving up, but the poor man still hadn't surfaced from his despairing sense of the hopelessness of it all. Once again the company split up. Marianne, now married, rented a summerhouse on Long Island and did some teaching. Viola went home to her parents in Washington, D.C. Remy, along with several of our Met Ballet School classmates, danced in Alfredo Corvino's choreography for *Die Fledermaus* at the Amato Opera House in the Village. It was *demi-caractère* work; Remy adored it, and everyone who saw him said he was terrific. Remy was thriving. Two of his children's books—*Dress Up and Let's Have a Party* (written in 1956 and featuring many of his friends, including Marianne, Viola, and me) and *Where Is Everybody?* (1957) had been published and received excellent reviews. Two others for which he'd done the illustrations were also in the bookstores. Encouraged by his recent success as author/illustrator, he'd begun work on four more children's books. Remy was the only company member I saw all summer, and I scarcely had time to see him, or even Earle, during those crazy weeks when I danced four shows a day at the Music Hall.

For seventy dollars a week (fifty-seven take-home), new members of the corps de ballet danced four shows a day, seven days a week, three weeks out of four, and along with that performance schedule, they rehearsed up to an additional six hours when preparing for a new show, plus attending the obligatory costume, shoe, and wig fittings! Working at Radio City Music Hall pretty much meant living there. For many of the old-timers who'd persevered ten, fifteen, even twenty years, it was more like being part of an institution than holding down a job, and they suffered the conflicting feelings of passionate loyalty and carping disgruntlement that such situations spawn. The loyalty was from pride in the place itself: who isn't impressed by the Music Hall, that Art Deco marvel? Not only the auditorium, but the lobbies, the restrooms, and the staircases that connect them are astonishing. The auditorium—6,200 seats!—is awe-inspiring, with vast, gilded arches framing the stage and the boxes. In the theater's heyday, a heroic organ materialized out of the wall, and the orchestra seemed to levitate by magic as it floated into view on an elevator platform. This was everything a movie theater ought to be. It made moviegoing a real event, embodying the Hollywood world of luxury, elegance, and glamour that people could only read or dream about. At the Music Hall it was all theirs for three hours. "The 1950's were a golden age for the Music Hall," declared the *New York Times* (January 6, 1968), when "the stage was filled with dazzling pageants produced by Leon Leonidoff."

Backstage at the Music Hall was pretty amazing, too. Everything was provided: cafeteria, infirmary, lounges, smoking rooms, an auditorium just for the personnel to view the latest movies, a roof deck for sunning (although it was absolutely verboten for the dancers to get a tan), a dormitory for sleepovers or catnaps, administrative offices, scene shops, costume shops, music and dance rehearsal rooms, even places for live animals to be housed. The stage was a vast expanse 144 feet wide and 60 feet high. But the stage floor, at least from a dancer's point of view, was terrible—a cruel infliction of cement, sectioned off (with treacherous metal edges) so that each section could be raised or lowered at any time. Running along the entire front edge of the stage was a double metal rail that provided a wall of steam—a "steam curtain"—at the flick of a switch. Looking up into the flies, out to the wings, or into the auditorium at the thousands of lighting instruments was like trying to count the stars in the Milky Way. Had the Music Hall given Merce every light he might *ever* have needed, I'm sure no one would have missed even one of them. I couldn't stop wondering what Merce and John might have done with only a fraction of those fabulous resources. And hardly a day went by that summer that I didn't question the inequity represented by those two organizations: the one a lavish monument to popular culture, and the other a little modern-dance company struggling to exist on the most meager of terms. Obviously, I had no crystal ball to tell me that by the eighties the Music Hall's golden age would be over and the former marvel would become a white elephant fighting to survive while the little modern-dance company, grown a little larger, would be thriving, operating with a budget in the millions of dollars, its creator nationally recognized at the 1985 Kennedy Center Honors as "an individual who throughout his lifetime has made a significant contribution to American culture through the performing arts." Even if I could have envisioned that curious twist of history it wouldn't have made any sense to me; it hardly makes sense to me now, because the real question is not Merce's lifetime contribution to American culture through his art, but how many people know about it, or care? He's always worked outside the glittering entertainment hub, apart from trends and fashion, alone even among artists, and in the popular sense he continues to be unrecognized, despite grants and international honors that would extend longer than this page were I to list them all. Of those people who paid $2,500 to attend the Kennedy Center Honors Gala on December 8, 1985, or who watched the edited CBS-TV version a few weeks later, how many had ever seen Merce Cunningham dance, had ever seen his choreography in a theater, or, for that matter, ever heard of him at all?

Although it was the crème de la crème of first-run Hollywood movies that kept the Music Hall so popular for so long, the stage shows were what gave it its unique prestige, enticing thousands of people to line up around the block for several hours to gain entrance. Along with the Statue of Liberty and the Empire State Building, Radio City Music Hall was a tourist "must." The main attraction, unquestionably, was the Rockettes—all-American, tap-dancing women, all 5'5" to 5'8", most of them pretty, whose thirty-six pairs of shapely legs were trained to execute routines beyond any military drill-sergeant's wildest dreams. The dancers in the ballet couldn't help feeling like second-class citizens, knowing full well that it wasn't the corps de ballet that the audience lined up to see. Even so, the ballet added a certain cachet to the extravaganza of each pageant, a cut above the jugglers and acrobats, dog acts, barbershop quartets, and bareback riders.

Backstage, the hierarchy was absolute: at the very top (*and how well they knew it*) were the Rockettes. Somewhere close to the bottom was the corps de ballet. Even the animals (via their trainers) had more clout. After my very first show, I was chagrined to receive a note from the corps de ballet dance captain, who'd received a note from the Rockettes' dance captain to the effect that one of the senior members of the Rockettes (fifty if she was a day, but—despite a haggard face and too many inches around the middle—still the possessor of a gorgeous pair of legs) had complained bitterly that I had put too much pressure on her shoulder in the "figure-eight bourrée section." My god. She couldn't turn around and tell me so herself? Ah! I had to remember, queens do not speak directly to parlor maids! The distance between us was that great; not imagined, terribly real.

I had the rotten misfortune of going into the current show one week before the new one was to open. So, having barely assimilated the material and the spacing for the show that I was performing four times a day, I had also to learn the material for the upcoming show. This meant starting rehearsals at eight in the morning and rehearsing constantly between shows, except during the dinner break. There were moments during that first week when I didn't think I'd make it. I wasn't used to doing that much pointe work, and especially not on such an immense bone-crushing cement floor, the hardest surface I can remember working on. It was a week of exquisite torture. My left leg, knee, calf, foot, and groin felt nearly paralyzed with pain. I had to spend every free second I had in the hospital-infirmary soaking my muscles, joints, and tendons and fighting back tears. There might have been some consolation (I felt none) in knowing that several other new girls and even a couple of the old-timers were in similar straits. If a dancer had made it through the audition, it was assumed that she could dance sufficiently well to do the choreography correctly. I never received a single note about my dancing, only about being on my mark. The vast reaches of stage and auditorium meant that for most of the 6,200 people in the audience the things clearly visible were pattern and spacing, not steps, not facial expression, and, heaven forbid, not quality. Being in the right place at the right time—i.e., "on your mark"—was *all*. For that amazingly streamlined race of beings called the Rockettes, the unforgivable breach of conduct was getting even the faintest blush of a sunburn, a sin punishable by a fine, and if it happened very often, it could mean getting sacked. The same rule applied to us in the ballet, but, since we were second-class citizens, the rule was less zealously enforced.

Within the well-appointed dressing room there was also a pecking order. We were ranked according to unwritten laws established by the senior members. Where one sat, which row and beside whom, was dictated to and accepted by the newest of us without question. There were always twenty-eight dancers working in the corps at any one time. We were a crazy mix: from sixteen to thirty years old, from the most eager, fresh, and starry-eyed would-be ballerinas to the most cynical, tough, lazy and disillusioned regulars who aspired to nothing beyond the weekly paycheck that came with the job. Those of us who looked upon the job as a training ground and a road to something better worked hard and took advantage of the available studio space to give ourselves class, practice, even choreograph a little. The cynical members never bothered even to warm up. What amazed me was that they rarely seemed to hurt themselves. There were also a dozen or so very talented, hardworking young dancers in both the Rockettes and the ballet who honestly believed they'd reached the zenith of their careers. They'd come from little dance studios in tiny provincial towns in far-off states where, in the fifties, dancing in the stage show at Radio City Music Hall meant one had gone as far as one could go, one had attained the very pinnacle of success.

I worked at the Music Hall for nine weeks, and in that time I did three different stage shows. The first, which I performed for only one week, had a rather sappy romantic ballet, set to Chopin. We wore long tutus, rhinestones around wrists and neck, and wigs with coronets of artificial flowers. The guest ballerina was New York City Ballet's Melissa Hayden, who, thirteen years earlier, had been a member of the corps there. That gave a number of us hope. But otherwise Melissa Hayden was more dismaying than she was impressive—at least for me. After having witnessed the regal courtesy of Margot Fonteyn, watching Hayden strut around like a little tough off the streets of Brooklyn and curse in language that might make a longshoreman shudder was a shocker. When Conrad Ludlow (then a soloist with the San Francisco Ballet, later with NYCB) replaced her, his manner couldn't have been more different. He was shy, soft-spoken, self-effacing, and very much a gentleman.

The stage show ran only as long as the motion picture it accompanied drew a house. As soon as audience attendance began to dwindle, a new film and a totally new show went on. The changeover happened on Thursdays, but we never knew which Thursday, and no one backstage ever seemed quite prepared for it. The week before each show opened was known as "Hell Week." As I've said, my first "hell week" was also my first week on the job, which made it hell and purgatory all rolled into one. The new show, "Blue Yonder," was one of those "dazzling pageants produced by Leon Leonidoff." It was advertised as "a gloriously exciting celebration of the golden anniversary of the United States Air Force." The Rockettes appeared as dancing WAFs. The corps danced in a "unique 'Space' spectacle." There were comedy acts, the Radio City Music Hall Glee Club singing patriotic Air Force songs, the full Radio City Music Hall Symphony Orchestra and "Special Added Attraction—the thrilling Air Force Drum and Bugle Corps and crack precision Air Force Ceremonial Drill Team." At the end, *everyone* appeared onstage in a humongous flag-waving finale, with huge projections of planes flashing across a giant screen. Posed a bit like the Statue of Liberty in a lipstick-red, sequined, strapless gown, I and two of my compatriots from the corps (one in silver, the other in blue) ascended out of the orchestra pit. The whole glee club, in Air Force uniforms, singing "Off we go, into the wild blue yonder" ascended with us—a stirring scene in which I felt utterly ridiculous. On the opening day of "Blue Yonder," we were up at 5:15 a.m., in makeup and onstage at

7 a.m. for a lighting rehearsal, which was followed by a studio rehearsal of the ballet, which was followed by the first performance of the usual four per day. At every rehearsal, including final dress, the dance was changed. Except when dancing for Antony Tudor (at his most quixotic) I'd never worked this way, certainly not with Merce, who rarely changed anything once he'd set a sequence of movement. The first performance was a mess. In the second, I came close to breaking a leg when someone let go of her wooden-paddle-with-two-yard-streamer-attached (all twenty-eight of us had them!) and the streamer wound twice around my leg while the paddle banged noisily on the floor behind me. I had to hobble off the stage to avert catastrophe.

But these trifling discomforts were nothing compared to my last Hell Week, which was rated by corps de ballet regulars who had been employed at the Music Hall six years or more as the very worst Hell Week in memory. On opening morning, after two weeks of rehearsals that had begun at seven or eight in the morning and gone on between performances, we still had no ballet. Poor Margaret Sande. We'd been told that she was unable to work well unless under pressure. Instead of creating a new ballet during the run of the current show, it was tradition for her to wait until the very last hours and hope for a heaven-sent ray of inspiration. But on this occasion, heaven—apparently—withheld its beneficence. The ballet was "The Dance of the Hours" from Ponchielli's opera *La Gioconda.* The previous April I'd been suddenly thrown into two performances of Zachary Solov's choreography for *La Gioconda* at the Met, replacing a badly injured company member who'd been shoved into an oncoming subway train at rush hour. At the time, I'd thought his choreography quite nice; four months later it seemed a work of genius! Running out of time, backed into a corner and desperate for inspiration that never came, Miss Sande got it into her head to have all twenty-eight of her dancers execute thirty-two *fouettés, in unison!* Now, it is rare to see even the most technically accomplished dancer perform thirty-two *fouettés en place,* without moving some slight degree to the side or forward. To expect twenty-eight Music Hall dancers to stay on their marks throughout thirty-two *fouettés* was lunacy. Of course she knew this, but, obviously desperate, she was adamant and kept us practicing them until our toes were bruised and bloody; only after the disastrous dress rehearsal, when it was abundantly clear that we would never get it right, were those accursed *fouettés* scrapped. We continued to rehearse between shows even after the opening, and *still* the steps were changed and we were threatened with still *more* rehearsals (into the wee hours of the morning, if necessary) if we didn't do well.

To add to our distress, Russell Markert, the founder of the Rockettes, had made an additional tap number just for the corps de ballet. Actually, most of us were thrilled to be working with him. My tap experience consisted of not-very-serious lessons in my mother's studio (not taught by my mother) when I was about ten years old. All I'd retained from those lessons was the basic time step, and that was exceedingly rusty. But working for Mr. Markert was really fun, even though his choreography seemed to me a bit tacky. He taught us our whole routine in three hours and never changed a step of it. We all wanted to do well for him, and on our own we practiced his routine assiduously right up until showtime. To our huge disappointment, the number was cut after the dress rehearsal. Mr. Markert assured us that he hadn't been displeased with our efforts; quite the contrary, but the whole show was too long, and our tap number was the only thing that could be cut. Rumor circulated that we'd shown up the Rockettes (if not in clarity, certainly in enthusiasm), and of course we wanted to believe it. We still had a short tap sequence with the Rockettes in the finale—vulgar, corny stuff standing on a staircase, Busby Berkeley style, costumed in tiny black velveteen bathing suits, cut low in the bust and high in the leg, a blue sequined strip from crotch to bust, and a black velveteen, blue-sequined tail attached to our bottoms and one wrist, black elastic mesh hose, and blue feathers in our hair. We did a series of bumps and grinds, high leg-kicks, plus a couple of rudimentary tap steps. In the front row center on opening morning were Jimmy Waring (who made almost a fetish of attending *every* Music Hall Thursday-morning opening) and Remy Charlip. I fully expected them to hoot with laughter, but Remy told me afterward that when he saw me in the finale, bumping and grinding and flicking my sequined tail, he cried. Backstage, I cried, too. And a couple of motherly corps senior members embraced me, patted me sympathetically on the back, and then proceeded to scold me for caring so much. "It's just a job, honey! It's not art. It's not worth crying about!" I knew they were right, but nevertheless, I wrote to my parents, "I don't think I'll ever forget the sense of frustration and shame of that week."

In any case, my days at Radio City Music Hall were numbered. On September 3, Merce—back from California—was to come after the show to take me to dinner. By this time, the choreography had finally been set, and I was beginning to relax and enjoy it, at least to enjoy dancing to Ponchielli's music played by the huge Music Hall orchestra. Perhaps I was enjoying it too much, because while executing my favorite step in the ballet (it was straight out of Cecchetti's manual) I tripped on one of the warped boards on the apron in front of the steam curtain's metal rail and fell sprawling. As I tripped I heard a terrible, ominous crunch. Fortunately I was close to the wings and could hop offstage quickly. Once off, I collapsed on the floor and wept. All I could think about was Merce witnessing my clumsy fall. Within seconds, stagehands and stage managers surrounded me, gently placed me in a wheelchair, and whisked me by elevator to the in-house hospital, where a flustered nurse put ice on my ankle and tried to give me a glass of Bromo-Seltzer; I suppose the bromo was to quiet my seemingly inconsolable weeping. I felt like an idiot and even more so when a lovely bouquet of miniature roses arrived for me. They'd been sent up from Merce, who was waiting for me at the stage door. Oh, God! He *had* seen my ignominious fall! I began to laugh and cry at once. Later on, he said he hadn't seen the performance. But if not, why the roses? I didn't dare ask him that. Still, I've never been quite sure whether he told me the truth or whether he was simply sparing me further embarrassment. Later I learned that I wasn't the only casualty from that Hell Week—there were at least a half-dozen others.

How wonderful Merce was. He took me in a cab to Roosevelt Hospital for X-rays (no broken bones; a severe sprain, that was all); then in another cab back to the Music Hall so I could collect my belongings; yet another cab to meet Remy at a favorite Italian restaurant in the East Village, and still another cab to take me home. So ended my Radio City Music Hall "career"—a month earlier than planned, but not a moment too soon as far as I was concerned. I had earned enough money to pay off my entire debt at the Metropolitan Opera Ballet School—a year's worth of classes!—and, thanks to my sprained ankle, I collected enough money through workman's compensation to be ahead of the game for the next year, and maybe, just maybe, if the opportunity ever presented itself, to go to Europe someday. I had no regrets about working at the Music Hall. There had been one lesson worth learning: be in the right space at the right time—be On Your Mark! And one lesson I never wanted to learn: "Don't care so much. It's not worth it." I knew for certain that I wanted to do something I cared about profoundly; then, whatever the difficulties, it *would* be worth it.

n mid-September, Merce began teaching again. This time he rented space at Dance Players Studio, just a block or two from Radio City, but he taught only an intermediate-level class on Monday, Wednesday, and Friday evenings. For company rehearsals he continued to rent Edith Stephen's studio in the West Village, where we recommenced work on the two dances he'd begun in the early summer. The first, *Labyrinthian Dances,* would eventually be accompanied by a relatively obscure piece of music rediscovered by David Tudor and written by Josef Matthias Hauer (1889–1959), a self-taught Austrian composer still living at the time, who had developed a twelve-tone system of musical composition independently of Arnold Schoenberg; the second, *Picnic Polka,* was a companion piece to *Banjo,* set to Gottschalk's *Ses Yeux.* The company now included Viola Farber, Marianne Preger-Simon, Remy Charlip, Bruce King, myself, and newcomer Cynthia Stone, whom Merce had invited to dance Anita Dencks's part in *Springweather and People.* At last, *Springweather* was to have its New York premiere and would be performed, finally, with Earle's original orchestral version of the score.

Rehearsals began without me. My ankle had taken much longer to heal than I'd expected, even with all the whirlpool and massage treatments. After several weeks and several doctors, I went to yet another doctor (this one recommended by Miss Craske), who told me that my ankle had healed incorrectly and gave me heat and "violent" massage to increase the circulation. Walking on it was just bearable, but class and rehearsal were excruciating, so I decided to use my unexpected free time and the money I'd earned modeling for Saul Leiter the previous spring[1] to see as much dance and theater as I could.

I managed quite an eclectic education. While still working at Radio City, knowing that I wouldn't be free to super with the Royal Ballet that autumn, I'd bought tickets for six performances, and, as luck would have it, Fonteyn danced five out of the six. I saw her in *Firebird, Swan Lake, The*

Sleeping Beauty, Petrouchka, and *Birthday Offering.* Once again I was completely swept away by her, especially her *Firebird* and *Swan Lake.* But on closing night, an emotional occasion on both sides of the curtain whenever the Royal Ballet performed at the old Met in the fifties and sixties, Fonteyn's performance in *The Sleeping Beauty* did not seem true. The wide-eyed innocence, the guileless radiance of Fonteyn's Aurora appeared forced for the first time in my experience, and her serenity and regal composure looked cosmetically applied rather than, as always before, her natural birthright. I thought she forced her technique as well—something I had never seen her do. Perhaps this was a case of someone caring too much. She'd become an idol, and the weight of that responsibility must have been genuinely terrifying, not unlike feeling as though she'd been blackmailed.

By 1957, Fonteyn's artistry had grown far beyond that of her male partners. Although she was only thirty-eight, it seemed that perhaps the time for her to retire was imminent—not because her dancing was in any way less than it had been (quite the contrary, that closing-night tension was the exception, not the rule) but because she was so alone. It hadn't occurred to me until then that being without peers could have real disadvantages: aside from the professional loneliness she must have felt, having to bear the burden of reigniting the fires wholly out of her own resources night after night, performance after performance, must have become harrowing, threatening to rob her of spontaneity and joy. Once more I feared I was seeing her dance for the last time.

My remaining dance/theater education of that autumn included a Ruth St. Denis solo concert, two performances of Shanta Rao and Dancers of India, the Dancers of Bali, a Viennese dancer named Cilli Wang, the New York City Ballet's all-Stravinsky program, O'Neill's *Long Day's Journey into Night* (with Jason Robards, whom Earle and I had seen earlier that year in *The Iceman Cometh*—a shattering experience both times), Dylan Thomas's *Under Milk Wood,* Jean-Louis Barrault in Marcel Carné's film *Les Enfants du Paradis,* lots of Charlie Chaplin films, and—never to be forgotten—Paul Taylor's most wonderful and infamous concert, which prompted Louis Horst's wonderful and infamous "blank" review. Paul's program at the 92nd Street YM-YWHA on October 20, 1957, was his very first company concert. He presented an evening of works entitled *Seven New Dances.* The designs were by Bob Rauschenberg and Jasper Johns, and, in my opinion at least, so was the aesthetic influence. There was a John Cage influence as well. The scores for *Seven New Dances* included commissioned music by Cage, plus a collaged tape-recording by Rauschenberg of

wind sounds, rain sounds, and "noise," as well as that anonymous telephone voice that announces the time every fifteen seconds. Paul's solo,
made up of a series of curious, static poses, was accompanied by the telephone voice ("The correct time is . . . exactly . . ." ad infinitum). Electric
fans stirred the air, gently blowing the women's dresses. A dog sauntered
onstage. And one whole dance consisted of a single tableau with Paul
standing and his partner, Toby Glanternik (a Juilliard classmate of ours),
sitting on the floor for an interminable length of time. As Calvin Tomkins
pointed out in his book *Off the Wall,* this could be seen as a choreographic
equivalent of Cage's silent piece $4'33''^2$ (which of course could be heard as
a musical equivalent of Rauschenberg's white paintings). The concert was
probably Paul's deepest foray into avant-garde territory, and even though it
was an experiment that he never repeated, it was an important event in his
choreographic career and in the annals of dance history. It got a mostly
negative reception, but it certainly put Paul on the map, making it clear
that he was going to loom large on the modern-dance horizon no matter
what his next direction might be.

It was four weeks before I could return to a full schedule of classes and
rehearsals; even then my ankle continued to bother me, and I was fearful
that it wouldn't hold up for the three performances scheduled for the end
of the year. For Merce, at least, everything concerning the first of these
performances at the Brooklyn Academy of Music turned out to be a
calamitous ordeal. Just when I began to function normally, about two and a
half weeks before the concert, Marianne was stricken with flu, a particularly virulent strain that kept her in bed for a week or more. No sooner had
she returned than Viola began to feel ill. Cynthia, the newest member of
the company, had to miss about a week of rehearsals because of a prior
commitment she felt obligated to fulfill—a paying television job with Pearl
Lang in Montreal. And then there was a disconcerting twenty-four hours
when it looked as if the Brooklyn program would be canceled altogether or
at least postponed until the following spring, because American Ballet
Theatre wanted the Academy's Opera House on the same evening we were
scheduled to perform in the Lecture Hall. (In the eighties, Harvey Lichtenstein—the director of BAM beginning in 1966—often filled its four theaters to capacity, but in 1957 it would have meant box-office disaster: there
simply wasn't a large enough audience.) Luckily for us, Ballet Theatre
withdrew its claim. That dilemma solved, there were still more to follow.

On the day of the concert we awoke to no recognizable dawn—only rain.
Sheets of it—a deluge, in fact. And Merce's roof, leaky with the slightest
drizzle, under this downpour did a remarkable imitation of a colander. In

the storage area, costumes, sets, clothing, even a Rauschenberg painting were soaked, but Merce had no time to cope with this disaster; more awaited him in Brooklyn. The women's costumes that Bob had redesigned for *Springweather* weren't finished. Because of their peculiar construction—a triangular half-skirt of silk chiffon attached to the back of the waist and down the seams of the tights—each of us had to stand very still while the sewing was done on us; a form of torture. We were cold and stiff and unbearably anxious as Merce's precious onstage rehearsal time ticked away. Even more serious was Viola's health. The flu had caught up with her; she could barely stand. Dancing seemed out of the question.

Pleased and excited as we were about having an orchestra play Earle's music for *Springweather and People,* this treat provided its own problems. In those years, at least, it was difficult to find serious, classically trained musicians who really wanted to play new music. Those devoted to it, like David Tudor, were a rare breed. Even when willing, if they were good enough to play it, they were bound to belong to the musicians' union, which meant there was never enough rehearsal time because union rules and regulations made it prohibitively expensive. Earle stood anxiously by while John coped with the problem of getting the music adequately performed in the limited time allotted.

On the stage—more trouble. The fire inspectors took one look at the original *Nocturnes* set, declared it unsafe, and banned its use, even though it was the same set we'd used on the same stage only ten months earlier. Was this concert jinxed? It seemed as though Merce was being besieged on every front. Happily, Bob relished a challenge. No backstage problems ever seemed to daunt or depress him. After a brief consultation, he and Jap disappeared, telling a tense and hollow-eyed Merce not to worry. They returned an hour or so later carrying carton-loads of artificial greenery,[3] all certifiably fire-resistant, and within minutes they'd dismantled the old set and created a new one. The stark column of white was replaced with a fantastic bower, a leafy green garden sanctuary as lushly romantic as the all-white one had been romantically pristine. Hearing Bob's wild, crazy cackle as he worked, I knew for sure that the alchemist had beaten the odds, had turned an ordinary substance into theatrical gold. Rauschenberg: the mischievous, merrymaking, ever-resourceful wizard! During that wearisome, bleak day in November, Bob's magic managed to cheer us up and pull us through, but not even Bob could save that night. The program itself probably went okay, but each of us onstage was affected to some degree by the stressful hours before and the agonizing uncertainty after the curtain went up. Viola was terribly ill; from moment to moment throughout the entire endless evening we never knew what to expect. I'll never forget Merce—his body rigid, nearly paralyzed with concern—peering through a rent in the rear drop cloth, watching Viola's every move onstage. Weak, dizzy, feverish, and wretched, she fought to stay in control. None of us was ever sure she would make her next entrance. It was distressing for everyone, but most of all for Merce. (And, of course, Viola.) The program over, he closed the door of his dressing room, refused to see visitors, locked himself in his bathroom, and threw up.

The post-performance party given by Bob, Jap, and Louis Stevenson for the company in Louis's Riverside Drive apartment was a subdued affair despite brightly colored streamers, a magnum of champagne, and delicious edibles. Viola couldn't come. Merce didn't come. Louis's wife, Fance, didn't come, either. She'd recently moved to Paris, giving Louis a private reason for being downcast, and the rest of us felt bad for him. No one did much celebrating. Only Earle felt like cheering: the musicians had played his music well, and the original version for orchestra had worked wonderfully with the dance. He'd waited three years to hear it. Had he known that it would never again be performed, his mood might have been closer to ours.

Long after the November rains had stopped, the gloom that had cast such a pall over our Brooklyn concert continued to darken Merce's spirits. First was the financial problem: due to the unusual expense of the orchestra, Merce had lost money. He had none to lose, of course, which meant he went still further into debt. On the other hand, at last, after months of inactivity, the company had five performances scheduled. But now Merce was dealt another blow: Viola's doctor insisted that she was much too ill and run-down to dance and that she would have to rest for several weeks at least, probably much longer. What irony! Even though there was a substantial repertory to draw from, Viola was in every group dance. And, of course, we had no understudies. To help the debt problem, every Thursday throughout the autumn of 1957 (both before and after the Brooklyn concert) Merce had made the tiring trek to Boston to teach two classes for the Boston Dance Circle. There he developed a strong following of mostly college dance students and dance teachers in the Boston area. It was the Dance Teachers Club of Boston that was to present the company at John Hancock Hall on December 14, only two weeks away. Luckily, our new company member, Cynthia Stone—a quick study and plucky—agreed to learn Viola's parts in four dances so that Merce could give the program as originally scheduled. Just as things began to appear possible, Marianne had a relapse—laid low once again by that virulent flu.

Nonetheless, the brief tour took place as planned. Marianne recovered sufficiently to make the Volkswagen trip to Boston, and Cynthia managed the repertory without a hitch. My parents were there, along with twenty-eight other Fitchburg-area residents (most of them students of my mother's), and afterward my father took Merce's whole company out to a late supper. Two nights later, we performed at Clark University in Worcester, Massachusetts, and once again my parents were there. They'd also made the trip to New York for both the January and the November Brooklyn performances. Their loving support was never withheld, no matter what private dismays they may have harbored about the work I was doing. Occasionally, in a spirit of deviltry, hoping to get my goat, my dad would perform wonderful takeoffs of Merce. He did them of Ted Shawn, too. Dad had a keen eye for mannerisms, and by imitating some tiny idiosyncratic gesture he would capture the very essence of a person. He also did hilarious renditions of whole sections of dances from the Denishawn repertory—he'd seen them often enough!—but his renderings were always affectionate, never mean-spirited.

My mother made a great effort to understand not only my involvement with Merce's work but the work itself. During the autumn of 1957 (and for several years after that), whenever Merce taught for the Boston Dance Circle she would attend, usually bringing one or more of her most advanced students with her. While they took his class, she watched and took notes. Often, after classes she and my father would take Merce to the Copley Plaza for dinner, then drive him to the airport. Whenever I went home to visit, my mother loved nothing better than to hear about life with Merce, my ballet classes, Earle's music, our friends, John's ideas, Zen Buddhism. Whatever was happening in my life was of interest to her, and we would talk for hours. She continually surprised me. Although fundamentally a conservative person devoting her life to teaching children and to keeping vestiges of the Denishawn repertory alive, she was fascinated by this alien world I was so caught up in, intrigued by what she saw and heard. She was forever asking me: "What do Merce's dances *mean*?" but like Margaret Lloyd, Boston's *Christian Science Monitor* dance critic, she found his work "provocative," agreeing with Lloyd that "One . . . can grow increasingly interested in [Merce's] experiments without in the least understanding them. One may be perplexed, but seldom bored, at his concerts. They are a challenging experience."[4]

We presented identical programs in Boston and Worcester: *Suite for Five, Labyrinthian Dances, Changeling, Picnic Polka/Banjo,* and *Septet.* Would these dances be considered perplexing, challenging, provocative in the 1980s and '90s? With the exception of *Changeling,* I think not. Already, New York critics were calling *Septet* "a minor masterpiece,"[5] "one of Mr. Cunningham's finest and most persuasive compositions,"[6] and "perhaps Mr. Cunningham's master work."[7] Of the three new works choreographed in 1957, only *Changeling* survived beyond the 1957–58 season.

Changeling was the last of the three extraordinary solos with piano music by Christian Wolff. Though less bizarre than *Lavish Escapade,* it was equally riveting, and, as in *Lavish Escapade* (but not *Untitled Solo*), Merce appeared in *Changeling* to be more "creature" than human being. Merce often said he was sure that he had been a changeling—that is, a child who had been secretly exchanged for another in infancy. Perhaps it was his way to explain his odd-man-out-ness within his rather orthodox Catholic family. "Changeling" can also mean "simpleton" or "idiot"; yet another meaning is "waverer" or "turncoat." Whatever he meant by the title and whatever the dance meant to him, words such as "desperation," "anguish," "torment" came to my mind when he performed it. Dressed in tattered, holey red woolens over a faded red leotard disintegrating with runs and rips, and wearing a red skullcap from which his ears protruded, he presented himself as aberrant, a deviant—grotesque and freakish. It's difficult to believe that these solos were composed wholly through chance processes, because in performance Merce made them painfully, brilliantly personal, acting/dancing with a raw passion that seared the very soul of the viewer. On the other hand, the material was so curious, incongruous, and original in its layered juxtapositions of arms, legs, head, and torso that it's equally difficult to imagine someone creating such movement from the basis of *any* recognizable dance vocabulary or his own resources. Not then, in the 1950s. And not now.

The company's only New York performance in all of 1958 took place shortly after we returned from the Massachusetts mini-tour. At a Sunday matinee on January 5, Merce's company shared a program with May O'Donnell and Company and dance satirist Iva Kitchell at the Dance Center of the YM-YWHA—better known as the 92nd Street Y. We performed *Labyrinthian Dances* and *Septet.* Cynthia danced especially beautifully at this performance, with more confidence and quality than before, and Merce's pleasure in her was so obvious that both Marianne and I experienced little pangs of jealousy as we watched them walk offstage together hand in hand after our final curtain calls. Cynthia was flushed and all aglow; Merce beamed down at her with unconcealed admiration. Viola was in the audience and came backstage to report to Marianne, Remy, and me how different the dances actually looked from what she had imagined them to look like when she performed them. It appeared that she was disappointed—whether with the work, the company's dancing, or both, she didn't say. There were mixed reactions from the critics as well. They again found *Labyrinthian Dances* "too loosely organized"[8] and "to lack centrality of purpose,"[9] but they were ecstatic over *Septet* and wrote that "the dancers gave a truly superb performance"[10] of it, and "performed with surpassing brilliance of action and mood."[11] *Septet* was nearly five years old. It always was one of the best-loved works in the repertory, but it had taken that long for the company (four of the six original cast were still dancing it) to bring it to its complete realization, to fully evoke the gentle wisps of wit and understated humor and the subtle irony and tenderness in the choreography. Surely one of the reasons it had taken so long was that we performed so seldom. The creeping, tortoise pace of the company's performance schedule was agonizing, and what lay ahead in 1958, as far as we knew, was a single out-of-town performance in February, another in March, and one more in July. That was it.

So, in mid-January, when Pat Neary, a friend in the New York City Ballet who studied regularly at the Met with Tudor and Craske, asked me if I'd like to go to the Orient for five months with the New York City Ballet, of course I was interested. Apparently she had given my name to the ballet mistress, because another City Ballet dancer saw my name on her list of possible recruits. Nothing came of it until I went to SAB one day to take Oboukhoff's class. He was sick, and Muriel Stuart taught in his place. After class, she took my hand, led me to the office, and told the secretaries that "Mr. B. simply *must* see this girl." And the very next day, Barbara Horgan, Balanchine's personal assistant, phoned to say that I should go to Madame Doubrovska's pointe class on the following Tuesday so that Mr. Balanchine could see me. I explained that I was still recovering from a badly sprained ankle and had not been on pointe since September 3 (the day of my ill-fated fall at Radio City Music Hall); she promised to tell Mr. Balanchine. Whether or not she did, I don't know, but I doubt it would have made any difference. Idiot that I was, I should have insisted on being seen in a regular technique class. My ankle was still stiff. I hadn't had a pair of pointe shoes on in five months, let alone taken class in them, and I'd never been to a pointe class at the school. Had I ever taken Doubrovska's professional pointe class, I would have known better than to go to this one. Long-legged, petite-headed, perfect-bodied girls—the new breed of New York City Ballet dancers, patterned after one of Mr. B.'s most recent favorites, Tanaquil LeClercq—filled the room. I was totally intimidated. Even the barre work was daunting, and I was too terrified even to attempt the steps across the floor when Balanchine might possibly have noticed me. No surprise: the "audition" didn't happen. I don't think he ever, not even once, looked at me, saw me, even knew which dancer he was supposed to be looking at. And I'd given up before I'd begun, without a fight. It was pathetic and humiliating. Not that I wanted desperately to be taken into the New York City Ballet or to dance Balanchine ballets, but I did desperately want a permanent situation where I would have the opportunity to grow as a dancer, and of course the allure of traveling to the Orient, or anywhere abroad, was very great. My sense of humiliation came from what I perceived quite accurately to be my own cowardice.

At the end of the month, I got a phone call inviting me to go to the Winter Garden Theatre to "work with" (not "audition for") Jerome Robbins, who was in the process of assembling a company to perform three of his ballets at the Festival of Two Worlds in Spoleto, Italy, and at the Brussels World's Fair and possibly in Paris. I'd sent him my photograph, résumé, and excerpts from reviews on a Monday afternoon and was called the very next morning while taking Miss Craske's class at the Met. I was one of ten "girls" and ten "boys" called to work from 2:30 to 6:30 on the Winter Garden stage, where only a month before I'd seen *West Side Story,* which had opened to wild acclaim the previous September. Robbins had us do jazz steps, supported adagio, and about a half-hour of pointe work. This time I gave it everything I could. Working with Robbins that afternoon felt more like a wonderful rehearsal than an audition. It was relaxed and fun, with lots of easy banter and camaraderie among the twenty dancers, many of whom had worked with Robbins before. My partner for most of the afternoon was the modern dancer Jack Moore. At one point, Robbins had another girl and me try out some steps from his *Afternoon of a Faun,* a ballet he'd made for Tanaquil LeClercq and Francisco Moncion in 1953. At the end of the afternoon, he asked everyone to sit on the floor while he talked about the tour and the living conditions in Spoleto, even going so far as to tell us we should bring our own alarm clocks—so for a minute or two I really thought I was among the chosen. But he ended by cautioning that nothing was definite yet, and that he'd let us know. Then he pulled me aside and said he couldn't really tell how I danced and asked if I'd come the next day from 1 to 4 p.m. to work some more.

Present at that session were two male dancers from *West Side Story* and a woman who'd danced on Broadway with Robbins in *High Button Shoes.* The woman, Sondra Lee (a tough, pugnacious, cute little blonde who kept popping her chewing gum maddeningly all afternoon), was more Broadway show dancer than anything else; her pointe work was practically nonexistent, but when Robbins questioned her about it her answer (audacious and rather rude, I thought) was something like, "Hey, Jerry! There's still months before the Spoleto performances, so, not to worry, plenty of time to work up whatever pointe technique I'll need!" Wow! Her self-confidence was overwhelming, making me feel even more shy and awkwardly self-conscious. While Sondra worked on some of Tanaquil LeClercq's steps from Robbins's *The Concert,* I learned the female part of *Afternoon of a Faun* with Jay Norman partnering me. As I did a *developpé à la second* on pointe, Robbins asked if I could raise my extended leg any higher. (My extended foot was only slightly above waist level.) Surprised, I replied, rather primly I fear, "Yes, but I'll have to lift my hip to do it." "Then lift your hip," he laughed. What a fool: intent upon "perfect placement" (my idea of the English school—Fonteyn, in particular), I was obsessed with being "correct" and morally opposed to "cheating" for effect; in my book, lifting the hip of the extended leg was cheating. What Robbins was looking for, I'm pretty sure, was amplitude, largesse, and the ability "to take the stage." (As was Merce, of course; that's why he'd encouraged me to go to Balanchine's school.) For obvious reasons, I was not nearly so relaxed at the second "private" work session as I had been at the first. Still insecure on pointe since spraining my ankle, I was sure Robbins would not cast me, but I felt that, whatever the outcome, it was thrilling to be working with him in such intimate circumstances. When the session was over, he smiled sweetly and said I'd be hearing from him. I never did. Some weeks later I learned that the number of dancers for his *Ballets: U.S.A.* company had been cut back, and my partner-for-an-afternoon, Jack Moore, and I were among the casualties. Sondra Lee was not. (Lesson: chutzpah pays off?) I think I was far more disappointed not to be going to Europe than I was not to be dancing Robbins's ballets. While I admired him, I rarely felt a strong inner identification with his movement or the kind of longing to dance it that I experienced when seeing Ashton and Tudor ballets.

The winter of 1958 was a curiously indecisive period, a time when I was open to whatever new possibilities presented themselves. Despite the fact that Merce now had a company manager (other than John) working on bookings and publicity, the company's future continued to look bleak. Since there was no other company I would rather have been a member of, it was never the cruel disappointment it might have been when nothing came of my tentative forays into new territory. I was sufficiently fatalistic to believe that what happened was meant to happen. So when a third opportunity arose and the decision this time was my own to make, not dependent upon someone else's judgment, I was in a quandary. A friend of Earle's, the jazz clarinetist Jimmy Giuffre, was going to take his group into the Bijou Theatre on Broadway in April for a limited engagement. Tired of playing in the nightclub ambience of indifference, smoke, and booze, tired of trying to be heard over the hubbub of clinking glasses, incessant talk, and shuffling waiters, Giuffre planned to present an evening of experimental/avant-garde jazz in concert, and he invited me to be a part of this venture, working as a member of his improvisational ensemble, which included Jim Hall, Bob Brookmeyer, and Ralph Pena. What a treat! What an honor! The hitch: there would be only two weeks of rehearsal before opening. Jimmy had seen Merce's company perform, but I don't think he realized that there was no improvisation whatever involved in Merce's work. The only improvisation I'd ever done was as a kid, when for hours at a time I'd improvise whole ballets, making up all the steps and dancing everyone's parts, usually to *Swan Lake* or some other familiar score.

Obviously I'd had no training in the kind of rhythmically complex improvisation Giuffre and his ensemble were engaged in. To be sure, I'd heard a great deal of jazz, due entirely to Earle, but I knew very little about the methods and constructs of jazz. Giuffre didn't want the jazz dance of Broadway or Hollywood, and I was equally convinced that it shouldn't be the modern dance of Cunningham or anyone else, but dancing that evolved from working closely with the musicians over a period of time. Certainly it was flattering to have been asked and it was very tempting to try, but I felt that it wouldn't work—not with only two weeks of rehearsal. But when I declined Giuffre's generous invitation, even though I believed I'd made the right decision, my refusal was vexing. I'd been offered a terrific challenge, and I hadn't had the guts to take it on; to risk failure. Annaliese Widman (who danced with Merce from 1950 to 1953 before his permanent company was formed) *was* willing to take the risk, and later on Jean Erdman did, too. To be frank, I don't think either of these collaborations was particularly successful. What Giuffre needed, I think, was a unique dancer accustomed to working alongside jazz musicians, someone who could have contributed a genuinely improvisational dance "voice" with weight equal to that of the other ensemble players. Camden Richman would have been perfect, but the Jazz Tap Percussion Ensemble with whom she worked wasn't conceived until more than twenty years later.

I never told Merce that I was auditioning for Ballet Theatre or Balanchine or Robbins. I doubt that I told him about the Jimmy Giuffre invitation, either, but since Remy, Marianne, Viola, and Cynthia all knew, it's unlikely that Merce didn't hear of it. Had I actually been invited to join another company I'm not sure to this day if I really would have been willing to leave Merce and John, but that year, while I considered the possibility, it helped to know that there was now someone (Cynthia Stone) who could step easily into my parts, and that made the idea of leaving a little less reprehensible. In the same week that I auditioned for Robbins, Merce began working with me on a solo which he said he planned to add to *Suite for Five*. This was about a month after he'd seen me perform *Galaxy*, as a solo, at Cooper Union. Perhaps my performance convinced him that I could handle solo assignments, or perhaps he realized just how desperate I was to have some challenging new material to work on. It's also conceivable that he'd heard of my possible defections and hoped this solo might discourage me from leaving. Whatever his reasons, he didn't reveal them, and I didn't inquire. As usual.

In the continuity of *Suite for Five*, my solo, "A Meander," followed Merce's opening solo. The title is descriptive to some degree. The dance begins in darkness, upstage right. The first movements are in place, but then the dance moves straight downstage, back and forth across stage-front before a final slow circuitous walk that ends upstage left. As the lights dim to blackness once again, a slow, twisting, reaching-offstage-into-the-distance movement, midstage left, is repeated three times, each time becoming progressively slower. There are no falls to the floor or jumps into the air. The solo is mostly a kind of "plastique," quite often with the quality of liquid slow motion; there are many held positions followed by sudden bursts of energy. It was these unpredictable changes of dynamics and the opportunity to play with the phrasing that I loved best. Although the overall rhythmic structure and tempi were Merce's, he wanted me to find my own phrasing within the sections. "Punctuation," "attack and decay" were only loosely indicated. Ballet choreography tends to be specific about dynamics since the steps are usually constructed on, around or against the musical pulse and the phrase. It was easy to identify those exquisitely musical dancers like Margot Fonteyn, Violette Verdy, Gelsey Kirkland, Anthony Dowell and Mikhail Baryshnikov who, although totally different one from another, unerringly revealed a breathtaking and unique artistry *through* the music of the ballet she or he danced. In most of Merce's choreography, the performer must function differently. As in ballet, what's given is line/shape, space/direction, pulse and tempo. But unlike what happens in ballet, there is no other impetus, no additional source of inspiration or energy, no aural stimulus like that provided by the music of Tchaikovsky, Chopin, or Stravinsky. There is only movement, learned and rehearsed in silence. In order for Cunningham dancers to be "musical" they must discover, *in the movement,* out of their own inner resources and innate musicality, what I call, for want of a better word, the "song." By "song" I mean the melody/rhythm/content—a single entity—of the dance. The "meaning," if you will. Again and again, I feel it is necessary to insist that there *is* meaning in every Cunningham dance, but the meaning cannot be translated into words; it must be experienced kinesthetically through the language of movement, just as music must be experienced through the language of sound. In "A Meander" I sought to discover the lyrical continuity (or what the brilliant Russian ballet coach Elena Tchernichova calls *cantilena*), not by counting out measures and phrases but by totally immersing myself in the movement, physically and emotionally; sensing it, feeling it acutely, discovering the weight and breadth and length of each movement, not in relation to anything other than my own body in time and space. A dancer, after all, is both instrument and musician and therefore capable of revealing "musical" artistry without accompaniment. For the fourteen years that "A Meander" was in the repertory, never once was I bored with it. The solo's meaning (for me) was discovered in the process of rehearsing and even more while performing it, and this meaning metamorphosed continuously right up through my very last performance of it in an Event on the stage of the Théâtre de la Ville in Paris in 1972.

The occasion of its first performance—in Pittsburgh, on May 21, 1958—was also the occasion of the only duet concert Merce and I ever danced in America. The program opened with *Suite for Two* (*Suite for Five* minus the trio and quintet), which was followed by Merce's solo *Collage I,* then the duet *Amores* (originally choreographed for himself and Tanaquil LeClercq in Paris in 1949), which Merce and I hadn't performed since the 1953–'54 Theatre de Lys season, and finally by a suite of duets and solos from *Springweather and People.* Naturally, I was elated. I loved these particular dances, and I was gratified by Merce's trust. It didn't matter at all that we were dancing on a dirty little stage with inadequate lighting equipment before a small audience in the middle of the day. If this was a kind of tryout, another one of Merce's "tests," it was one I was determined not to fail.

The company was in disarray. The winter-spring performing schedule consisted of twice driving all the way to North Carolina and back to give single performances—once in February at the North Carolina College at Durham, where we had to make crossovers by running out one stage door, racing around outside the building in the dark, and coming in another. It was a very poor "Negro" college (as African Americans were termed in

1958), but what it lacked in facilities it more than compensated for in enthusiasm. Then, for a March performance at the Women's College of the University of North Carolina, we made the long drive once again, and repeated the program we'd done in Boston and Worcester. Viola hadn't returned, so Cynthia was still dancing her parts. Bruce King, discouraged by the dearth of performances and the fact that Merce wasn't making new pieces on the company, left at the end of March. Shortly after that, Marianne decided she could wait no longer to start her family and told Merce that she would leave after our last scheduled concert, on July 1. Of the seven original members of the company begun at Black Mountain five years before, only Remy and I remained for certain. At the time, Viola's situation and intentions were unclear. Merce pondered aloud whether he should continue trying to maintain a company at all or give it up and develop a duet repertory for the two of us, which was undoubtedly more practical from an economic point of view, but not at all satisfying from a choreographic one. Then, out of the blue came an invitation that made the decision for him. To his astonishment, that citadel of modern dance—the Connecticut College American Dance Festival—invited him and his company to be in residence for six weeks.

In this mid-fifties period, while Merce's company was fumbling along in fits and starts, his close associates, the composers and painters, were having a slightly better time of it. John continued to arrange music concerts, and there was always a loyal following of friends in attendance, though few from New York's musical "establishment." (The *New York Times* always sent a reviewer, even though its dance critic, John Martin, continued to ignore Merce's concerts.) Opposition, however, was practically unanimous. The music was subjected to ridicule, sarcasm, and scorn. It was all "noise," not music. In Europe, a far livelier, better informed, and much larger audience for new music was developing. Since there was only sporadic work with Merce, and only so many concerts John could manage to arrange, David Tudor's trips abroad—with and without John—became more frequent.

Aware of the need to develop audiences for new music and impressed by the rationale behind Pierre Boulez's *Domaine Musicale* concerts in Paris, Earle began presenting concerts of works that had played a vital role in the evolution of modern music, as well as works by the avant-garde. When Boulez came to America in January 1957 as music director of Jean-Louis Barrault's theater company, we saw him quite often and hosted several parties in his honor. At about this time, rifts began to develop between Cage and two of the younger composers with whom he'd become closely associated. Cage and Feldman had a falling-out that lasted a year or two, and they never returned to their former closeness. Morty wanted recognition for himself—separate and equal—and refused to be pigeonholed as a mere member of "Cage and his school." Morty and Earle, not John, had pioneered indeterminacy, so it was understandable that they would come to resent him receiving all the credit—even all the blame! To compound the difficulties, Earle no longer felt the strong support from John he'd felt when he'd first arrived in New York. A truly generous man, John was happiest when *he* was the dispenser of generosity, and he admitted being envious of Earle's ability to find a publisher and to interest European conductors in performing his work.

Meanwhile, Bob and Jap, doing well with their window-display jobs for Bonwit Teller and Tiffany, wanted to share their good fortune with John. Joined by the entrepreneur Emile de Antonio, they organized a twenty-five-year retrospective concert of John's music at Town Hall on May 15, 1958, and contributed one thousand dollars each to cover the costs.

Through John's study of Zen, he came to believe that reality is completely indeterminate and undifferentiated, and that the natural world is one of infinite variety, flux, and change. Thus, having found a philosophical rationale for accepting indeterminacy in performance, he followed Feldman's and Brown's initiatives taken six or more years earlier and embraced the concept whole-hog in his *Concert for Piano and Orchestra,* which premiered at the Town Hall retrospective. In this composition, each player independently makes his own time-program from John's material, and everyone, including the conductor, is given both specific directives and specific freedoms. Standing on the podium, erect, regal, and elegantly dressed in a rented cutaway, Merce presided over this potential circus-of-chaos in the role of the conductor, performing a peculiar sort of port de bras and functioning as a kind of irregular, glorified stopwatch.

Concert for Piano and Orchestra presented John the aspiring Zen Buddhist at loggerheads with John the frustrated Methodist minister. He wanted to "let the sounds be themselves," but he was not happy letting people be themselves if they behaved irresponsibly, and musicians, faced with one of John's unconventional scores and the freedom to choose their own actions, all too often mistook freedom for license. They made fun of the music, and thereby fools of themselves. John wanted people to behave "nobly." He burned with evangelical zeal to convert them to the Zen view

of the world but was rendered powerless by the very philosophy he so ener-
getically espoused.

The piece lasted twenty-five minutes. Throughout there were jeers, catcalls, and vain attempts to stop the music altogether, and its end was
greeted with a chorus of boos, hisses, derogatory whistling, and laughter,
as well as wild applause and cheering from the loyalists. People likened
the event to the Paris premiere of Stravinsky's *Le Sacre du printemps* in
1913.

Rauschenberg and Johns had one-man shows of their own in 1958,
thanks to Leo Castelli—an elegant, cultured, charming European gentleman with an enduring passion for literature, architecture, and especially
painting and sculpture—who had opened his own gallery in his apartment
on East Seventy-seventh Street the year before. When he saw Bob's work
at the Jewish Museum in 1957, it convinced him that Bob "was the most
original young artist [he] had come across in a long time."[12] Two or three
days later he visited Bob's studio to select paintings for a show he was
planning and was surprised to meet Jasper there. Castelli had never heard
of Jasper Johns before seeing his *Green Target* encaustic painting at the
Jewish Museum. The painting had greatly intrigued him. Discovering that
Jasper was a close friend of Bob's with a studio in the same loft building,
Castelli immediately asked to see more paintings and gave Jasper his very
first one-man show in January 1958. The show was an immediate *succès
d'estime.* Most amazing of all, Jasper's paintings *sold*! Bob had a one-man
show (though not his first) at the Castelli Gallery the following March. In
Bob's case, it was more a *succès de scandale.* Nothing sold, and the critical
response was brutal. Almost overnight, Jasper went from being an
unknown to having his work purchased by museums and reproduced on
the cover of *Art News.* Such sudden, unexpected success at such an early
age, unheard-of by the previous generation of painters, didn't seem to
faze Jasper—outwardly, at least. He just kept on painting. Bob was truly
delighted by his friend's success. Also aroused by it. That playful, competitive streak of his, the always barely concealed smoldering fire, now
blazed. He kept painting, too, with a kind of ferocious ardor.

For Merce, John, David, Earle, Bob, Jasper, and the dance company,
1958, I think, marks the end of our beginnings. It also inevitably marked
our loss of innocence and saw the first tentative steps our strange, disjointed family was to take, more or less together, into the real world.

A six-week period with nothing to do but dance! Black Mountain all over again! At least that's what I hoped our summer residency at Connecticut College would be, never really considering how very different the two colleges were. Black Mountain—that freewheeling experiment in education, more process than institution—was a jumble of heterogeneous cottages and buildings hidden away in the backwoods of North Carolina, deliberately out of touch with society and culture, and it had existed for only a short period. During our brief summer session there, while it had been peopled with artists of many disciplines, the only dance company was ours. Connecticut College, on the other hand, was a well-established women's college in New England whose manicured campus and imposing buildings of cut granite exuded a sense of formal erudition and tradition-bound breeding. Its relatively close proximity to Boston and New York assured the visitor (if not its faculty and students) that the school was in touch with mainstream culture. Nothing of the sort at Black Mountain, where one felt isolated but totally free. At Black Mountain the subject of mealtime conversation depended upon with whom one sat. The possible topics seemed endless, not necessarily limited to the disciplines of the composers, musicians, painters, sculptors, poets, potters, architects, and theater people in residence.

Summer at Connecticut College, alas, was monolingual: the world reduced to one topic—*La Danse*—and even conversation on that subject limited to rather stultifying discussions of technique or worse: one's weight, one's diet, one's injuries or ills, until finally degenerating even further into gossip about personalities. When we arrived in the summer of 1958, it was populated, as it had been for the previous ten summers, with teachers of dance, students of dance, and choreographers; with composers who made music for dance, musicians who played for dance, aestheticians who discussed it, designers who costumed and lit it, plus the members of several dance companies in residence who just did it. Added to this single-focused gathering was a sizable administration and support staff devoted solely to the dance population's needs. Liken it to a greenhouse whose humid, steamy atmosphere bred little white flies of contention and tiny red spider mites of jealousy even while, more nobly, nurturing young plants and cultivating flower-show specimens. By the time Connecticut College School of the Dance and the American Dance festival, two separate entities, were in their eleventh seasons, the organizational gears were well synchronized. Scheduling had become a high art, hierarchies had been firmly established, and the juggling of artists' egos was a required administrative skill. If there had once been a sense of revolution or a spirit of unorthodox experimentation, it had certainly vanished before we arrived. We were told by Merce (who was with Martha Graham in 1940 and 1941) that the atmosphere of the original festival and School of the Dance, housed at Bennington College in Vermont from 1934 until 1942, was quite different. In those years, Bennington was more like Black Mountain, a young and venturesome college eager to explore new ideas in education. Thanks to its president, Robert Leigh, and to the efforts of two women— Martha Hill and Mary Josephine Shelly—both fervent modern-dance educators, modern dance began to come into its own as an independent art; an art to be reckoned with. In 1934, Miss Hill convinced Martha Graham, Doris Humphrey, Charles Weidman, and Hanya Holm, all at crucial periods in their careers, to teach and make new works at Bennington. She invited Louis Horst to teach composition. The students were mostly older women, dance instructors from physical-education departments in universities and colleges across the country, who came to study with Graham, Humphrey, Weidman, Holm, and Horst; they returned to their respective campuses as converts, ardent believers and proselytizers of the new "serious dance art." In the following years their students joined them in their pilgrimage to Bennington and later to Connecticut, and in this way, a new, young generation of bona fide modern dancers was born. With the passion of the totally committed, those first generations of physical-education instructors, even before they escaped from the calisthenics and competitive sweat of gymnasiums to the sanctity of performing-arts departments, spawned a dance revolution in America. They not only brought the idea of dance as an art into the colleges and attempted to teach it, they also brought professional modern-dance companies to the campuses to perform, thereby nurturing and supporting the discipline on two levels at once.

Martha Hill must be credited with the vision and, most importantly, the energy and determination to see it through, first at Bennington and, after the Second World War, at Connecticut. I'm embarrassed to admit that when I was a student at Juilliard under her administration I knew little of her history and did not appreciate just how remarkable a woman she was. Nor did I ever get the opportunity to know her better. But, as revealed earlier in these pages, neither did I know until 1998, when I read Naima Prevots's book, *Dance for Export: Cultural Diplomacy and the Cold War,* just how damaging Martha Hill had been to Merce and John's attempts to get government funding for several foreign tours. During the Cunningham company's first summer at Connecticut College, Miss Hill was on leave of absence as codirector of the school and didn't return the following year, having decided to give her full attention to the dance division at Juilliard, which she directed for thirty-three years—from its inception in 1952 until her retirement in 1985.

In 1958, Louis Horst was seventy-four, Graham was sixty-four, Humphrey was sixty-two, and Limón was fifty. This grand quartet held absolute dominion over Connecticut College Summer School of the Dance. Graham limited her presence to a star turn of only one week, teaching technique at the beginning of the six-week session and then disappearing. Her company was not in residence. After the first week, the Graham-technique classes were taught by the company member and rehearsal master David Wood. Doris Humphrey and Louis Horst, however, were full-time faculty, and Humphrey was also artistic director and choreographer for the Limón company. No one realized it then, but 1958 was to be Humphrey's last summer at the college. It was not a happy time for her. At the final faculty meeting, "she announced her intention not to return. . . . The School, she claimed, had become too much of a closed corporation; new people should be coming to teach in new ways. They were all getting in a rut."[1] And a few months later, she wrote, "I've been there too long."[2] Another reason for her departure was that she had become desperately ill, in addition to suffering great pain from arthritis. Yet another reason was Limón's growing need to feel independent of her, and the pain *that* caused may have been even more difficult to bear than her physical disabilities. Reading her autobiography many years later, I was shocked to learn of the hardships, stoicism, and sadness that had permeated her life. So much suffering. So little joy. I felt a certain amount of guilt, too, because I still blamed her for the way Merce and the rest of us were treated when we auditioned *Springweather and People* for her at Graham's studio in 1955 and were rejected. Most unforgivable, I thought, was that no one had had the courtesy to notify Merce. And I suspect that my own ego was still hurting from her rejection of me at Juilliard when I'd auditioned for "Desert Gods" from *Song of the West* and heard from a fellow student that she thought me, a Denishawn dancer, "too balletic." It's odd. Doris Humphrey, in her autobiography, relates that *she* had been told at an audition that was very important to her that she was "too balletic."[3] So often, it seems, dancers inflict on other dancers what was once inflicted on them: is it subconscious or conscious, I wonder, this need to make others go through disappointment or suffering similar to their own?

Humphrey was always a formidable presence, both at Juilliard and at Connecticut College. I was in awe of her and probably misread her absolutely forbidding, humorless, and imperious manner whenever our paths crossed. I was convinced that she disapproved of Merce, and, by extension, of those who worked with him. I was totally ignorant about her views and years later was chagrined to read these words, originally spoken by Humphrey to Juilliard students in 1956: "We must not tend to discount any kind of modern dance in which we are not personally concerned— 'Mine is the only kind!' This viewpoint is very narrow and destructive. We had better have more concern for the whole field, or we won't have any."[4]

During the first eleven summers at Connecticut, Humphrey's presence had far more impact than Graham's due to her three-part role as artistic director of the Limón company, choreographer of eight festival premieres, and teacher of Advanced Composition and Repertory. Graham taught technique for nine years, but rarely for the full six weeks; she choreographed only one festival premiere, and her company was in residence only once—in 1948.

Limón was Humphrey's heir and heir to the Humphrey-Weidman legacy, so it was reasonable that for twenty-one years he should make Connecticut College his summer home. Through him, Humphrey's influence lived on. Limón benefited tremendously from these six-week residencies with his company. Though brief, they still provided that badly needed constant that had eluded Merce—a place where he could choreograph, rehearse with his dancers, and perform new works, undisturbed by the hand-to-mouth exigencies of day-to-day existence in the city. Like Merce, unlike Graham, Limón had neither a permanent studio in New York nor a generous benefactress offering financial support. Graham didn't need Connecticut. Limón did. And he made good use of the opportunities offered him there, producing twenty-three premieres in twenty-one years, the most celebrated being *The Moor's Pavane*, in 1949. His was a situation to be envied, and it most definitely was.

When Merce and his company arrived on the scene for the eleventh summer season, we were very much outsiders. Limón was "King of the Hill." Through physical deportment alone—a distinctive regal bearing, epitomized by the peculiarly rigid way in which he held his head and spine as though an invisible hand were clasping him firmly by the back of his skull and pulling his head up and out of his body—Limón gave the impression that it was only through *his* generosity and largesse of spirit that the rest of us on campus were allowed to share his private domain. We weren't made to feel like trespassers, but I didn't feel that we were warmly welcomed, either. Without eye contact and with just the slightest of nods, José acknowledged our existence. In our four years there, I don't think I (or anyone else in our company except perhaps Merce, who shared a dressing room with him) ever exchanged more than twenty words with José. In retrospect, I'm fairly certain that the condescension I perceived (and probably misconstrued) was that of someone ill at ease, shy—perhaps even threatened by the presence of Merce, who in those years was near the peak of his physical powers.

Apparently, curious rumors about Merce and his working methods had preceded us to the campus. We were greeted politely but very cautiously. Social exchange among "The Biggies" (as we called Graham, Humphrey, Limón, Cunningham, etc.) never developed into anything more than a brief good morning; a vague nod of recognition (along with a self-conscious clearing of the throat) as they passed in and out of studios; and the rare, tentative smile, with a murmured "Hope everything's going well . . ." at the changing of the guard backstage at Palmer Auditorium when one company replaced another for an onstage rehearsal. It must have been a lonely and difficult time for Merce that first summer. He was an alien, under suspicion. John Cage would not be with us until performance week, and since Merce rarely discussed his work with his dancers, he had no one with whom to share his thoughts. The intellectual stimulation he'd so enjoyed at Black Mountain was completely absent. Egos, pride, insecurities, and petty jealousies seemed to isolate The Biggies on tiny islands of their own making. It struck me as foolish and unfortunate at the time but—who knows?—maybe by maintaining their distance they kept themselves pure: no cross-pollinations, no hybrid species. Perhaps that has historical significance: their idiosyncratic differences remained intact. Inevitable hybrids evolved aplenty without any assistance from them.

It was different for the dancers in their companies. Most of the "worker bees" (as we sometimes referred to ourselves) were less protective, defensive, aloof, or whatever it was that kept The Biggies in their separate corners. Of course we had far less at stake, and after the first week of prickly unease between Merce's dancers and members of the other companies, some of us began to reach across the aesthetic barriers to make friends. What released awkward tensions better than anything else was the fact that at least half the Limón company, and David Wood from the Graham company, often came to Merce's classes.

No, it definitely wasn't going to be like Black Mountain. I sensed that the moment we arrived. Quite apart from the differences in location, circumstance, and atmosphere, *we* were different: all that remained of Merce's original Black Mountain College company were Remy, Viola, and me. Cynthia had been with us only eight months. William Burdick was "jobbed in" at the end of our Connecticut residency to dance Bruce King's part in *Nocturnes.* Bill had helped out at very quick notice by learning Bruce's parts in *Septet* and *Picnic Polka/Banjo* for our last spring tour date, but he was employed by the Metropolitan Opera Ballet and needed that income to survive, so he never became a regular member of Merce's company. Brand new to the company was Marilyn Wood, who came to Merce via Alwin Nikolais's Henry Street Playhouse school. Marilyn was married, with twin infant daughters, and thus faced an even more difficult scheduling problem than the rest of us. For that reason I was amazed when Merce chose her; but Marilyn was incredibly organized and utterly determined to juggle her many commitments successfully without neglecting any of them. Our new family also included Valda Setterfield, a young Englishwoman, whom Merce had invited to apprentice with the company. Valda had studied at the Rambert School, but discovered she didn't fit the mold of the average Birtish ballet dancer, so on the recommendation of David Vaughan she'd come to New York and through him met Jimmy Waring and Merce. Merce, she said, knew what to do with her, so, finally, she knew what to do with herself.

My problem with all these changes was having to adjust to life without Marianne. Even before she'd gone I was unhappy, and unreasonably critical of Marilyn's first efforts to learn Marianne's roles—so much so that one day Marianne wrote me a note, a loving reprimand that chided me for expecting Marilyn to accomplish in a few weeks what she, Marianne, had taken seven years to achieve. I mended my ways—but nothing could help reconcile me to losing Marianne. And of course, I seemed oblivious to the fact that I wasn't making it any easier for her. Leaving had been a wrenching decision: "Lots of sadness and tears for Merce and nine years of growing an identity as an artist, a dancer, a part of a group, a not-dilettante, a professional."[5] Generous, outgoing, direct, warm, and compassionate, her sunny disposition, her genuine sweetness of personality, her unerring gift for being able to understand the other fellow's problems, her infectious sense of humor that spilled out in bell-toned giggles and hearty peals of laughter—all these qualities illuminated her dancing.

Maybe, I realize only now as I write, one reason I was so despondent over her leaving was that she'd become not only my friend but, unwittingly, my own wise and empathetic therapist. Marianne came to dancing late, and nothing was easy for her, but she had persevered and developed rapidly into a lovely performer. She knew that her legs would never stretch as beautifully as she wished them to, nor would her feet turn out and up in the perfect Cecchetti arabesque; even so, she went to ballet class and struggled to overcome these limitations. Merce tended to treat Marianne with a kind of playful good humor, answering her technical questions with jokes and hugs. This troubled her. She wanted him to take her more seriously. She worried that he still saw her as she was when she first started studying with him and would forever treat her as a lovable, bumbling beginner. It was a concern common to many of Merce's dancers over the years: that his first impression pigeonholed them, that no matter how much they might change or develop, Merce's view of them would remain the same. I do know that Marianne was very dear to Merce, and that no one ever filled that place in his affections he reserved for her alone. Her journal entry for June 23 noted that "Merce was restored to his most cheerful, natural self. He was very sweet. Said *Septet* and *Banjo* were mine and not to teach them, that they'd be dropped. (I really don't think so, but how sweet.) [*Banjo* was dropped, *Septet* was not.] And [that] Marilyn would do well but was not me. All the right things. How infinitely kind and loving he can be."

From the beginning, when Marianne befriended him in Paris and found him a studio where he could work, Merce knew he could count on her to be steadfast and reassuringly supportive. In *Galaxy* he cast her as Earth, perhaps realizing even before she did that she would not choose the performing life but would fulfill herself first as a wife, then as a mother, and finally through a career as therapist—a holistic approach to living. Marianne's last performance with us was at Ball State Teachers College in Muncie, Indiana, on July 1, less than a week before the start of the summer session at Connecticut College. Even before the bows were over there were tears in my eyes; in the dressing room, Marianne and I bawled like babies. And for once, Merce was able to share the hugs and sadness and show a little of his own feelings.

This was unique in the history of the company, at least until and including my own leave-taking in 1972. No one but Marianne managed to leave so openly, so totally free of ill will and discord. When one of Merce's dancers decided to quit, the information was rarely passed along to the rest of us. Sometimes the departure was a complete surprise, but usually (one realized after the fact) one had been forewarned by a certain kind of grumbling in the dressing room or by weeks of seeing the same glum, stony face in rehearsal. In almost every case, the leave-taking was prompted by undisclosed resentments or disenchantment on the dancer's and/or Merce's part. But the event was always clouded with ambiguity and the causes kept secret from those remaining. By July 1958 we'd lost Paul Taylor, Jo Anne Melsher, Anita Dencks, Karen Kanner, and Bruce King. Each defection was troubling. Nothing was ever explained. Reasons were never given. Inevitably rumors and gossip took over in the dressing room: "What happened?" "What do we do now?" "Who will replace him/her?" Our concern might seem out of proportion today, when companies' rosters change more regularly than the seasons, but then we were, truly, a family, bound together against the odds, and the smallest change seemed an ominous cloud, a threat to our existence. With Marianne it was all aboveboard— humane and rational and simple. Marilyn Wood was Marianne's find and, I suspect, as much Marianne's choice as Merce's to succeed her. Marilyn worked with us before Marianne departed, which contributed a sense of continuity and greatly eased the rehearsal problems. Even so, the group that Merce brought to Connecticut in the summer of '58 was unused to working together, and he had barely six weeks to mold us into a company.

We were assigned to Winthrop House, a large wooden dormitory built in 1916 that overlooked the Thames River, and my room, a single on the southeast corner of the third floor, was a delight. Leafy branches (complete with resident songbird) filled my southern window. The eastern window looked out to a distant view of boats plying a glistening river, and in the afternoon, the sun-bleached buildings on the opposite shore looked as I imagined Greece or maybe southern Italy might. The room was spartan: a single bare lightbulb overhead, an old wooden desk with stiff ladder-backed chair, a wooden bureau, and a thin mattress on a sagging metal-springed cot. The cot, after the first night, joined five others stacked in the corridor and my mattress, like five others, went onto the floor.

I loved the nun's-cell austerity: blank walls, bare floors. No personal belongings, no reminders of another life. It was like being born again, opening up the spaces in my mind and freeing me to concentrate totally on the task at hand. Only a reading lamp was required to make it perfect.

Our weekday schedule did not vary: up at seven, bed by eleven, with two morning technique classes and afternoon and evening rehearsals in between. On Saturdays and Sundays we had three to eight hours of rehearsal. With whatever remained of the day or evening we rested, took trips to beaches, and sought out local seafood restaurants. Once, we rode the Ferris wheel at Ocean Park, screaming with laughter like demented teenagers. John Cage showed up one weekend and provided a glorious picnic: porterhouse steak, corn cooked in the husk, wild-greens-and-tomato salad, wild mushrooms, ale, and ice cream—all devoured in a charming little state park where we swam in a pond and cooked over an open fire. "Such a <u>dear</u>, <u>sweet</u>, <u>thoughtful</u> <u>loving</u> fellow he is! It's such a joy to be with him," I wrote to my parents, underlining all the adjectives in effusive adoration. Several times during the summer, Earle journeyed up from his job at Capitol Records in New York City, arriving after Saturday's rehearsal to whisk me off to a beautiful beach in Watch Hill, Rhode Island, and a quiet dinner *à deux*—a brief, heavenly respite from community living. Actually, though, I truly loved both the life I was leading and where I was leading it: I loved being out of the city, wandering amid majestic trees, flowering shrubs, tiny wildflowers, and more songbirds than I'd ever seen or heard. Because I missed my own cat, Sam, I loved playing with affectionate little Willie, whom Viola and I befriended on our daily walks to and from rehearsal. And I loved the intense work schedule, the close camaraderie of the company and, most of all, being a *full-time dancer* involved in the making of new work.

Unfortunately our schedule didn't permit taking classes other than Merce's, or even observing them. But on the first day of the session I was able to watch Martha Graham teach an advanced class in her technique. Just as when she taught my class at Juilliard in 1952 and 1953, my impression was of a sorceress wielding magic powers over her subjects. That night, in Palmer Auditorium, Graham formally opened the 1958 summer-school session with a lecture called "Sources of Dance." I wrote in my journal:

Such an exhibit!! [I must have meant "exhibition."] She is truly an incredible personality—a wild sorceress—ever trying to enchant, mystify, shock, entrance, lure, capture and consume her audience. I think, more often than not, she succeeds! She talked about the sources of her dances: *Medea*,

Judith, Clytemnestra, etc. She gyrated, mouthed, wriggled, caressed herself and "carried on" in best show girl tradition. Merce said he was shocked and horrified. I think she managed to capture the rest of us in her "net," although we knew it probably was, in some very distressing way, phony and perhaps obscene.

Breakfast—my favorite meal at Connecticut—was a time for jolly cross-table conversations. It was also a time for rubbernecking, particularly when Martha was present, hiding—as was her custom—behind large, heavy-rimmed, opaque sunglasses. Her jet-black hair (surely it was dyed) was pulled back, piled high, and secured so tautly with some aboriginal bone that her parchmentlike skin looked nearly translucent, stretched as it was across those remarkable facial bones. A tiny, amazingly erect creature with the most peculiarly ugly yet somehow beautiful calloused and bunioned feet, sandal-clad, she sat demurely with her friend, former lover, mentor (and nearly everyone's beloved) Louis Horst, talking to him ever so sotto voce. (Was she perhaps flirting?) "Miss Hush" indeed![6] At another table, rather distant from the Graham/Horst tête-à-tête, was Doris Humphrey, her restrained, faded elegance diametrically the opposite of Graham's vivid, electric energy. Humphrey—her lovely auburn hair now mixed with gray, her face set firmly as though abjuring pain, her once-beautiful, slender body now strangely thickened yet regal still, even when she was forced to rely on a cane—often chose to sit alone, or else with Ruth Currier or José Limón and his wife, Pauline Lawrence. José loomed larger than life at breakfast time, king of the puppets, whose gallantry and courtesy at such an hour, in such a place, seemed antediluvian and incited us to giggle impolitely behind our napkins. Merce, clever fellow, escaped everyone's rude scrutiny by breaking his fast on an elaborate "health drink" alone in his rented house.

As for cross-table conversations: in the beginning, each clan pretty much stuck together, but it wasn't too long before the mutual reluctance to intrude on others at that early hour relaxed and verbal exchange sprang up, usually initiated by one-liners thrown out by Louis Horst and pianists Glen Mack, George McGeary, and Evelyn Lohoefer, and "our" Remy, who, as always wherever he went, endeared himself to nearly everyone. That summer, Remy was recuperating from mononucleosis, and a staphylococcus infection he had contracted in the hospital while trying to recover from the mono. Each morning, he made a theatrical event out of downing the twenty-one vitamin pills prescribed to him by Merce's physician, Dr. Lawton. The doctor, renowned as a great diagnostician, was responsible for the yeast, yogurt, wheat germ, fruit drinks, and myriad of vitamin pills that Merce had ingested faithfully every morning since the time in the early fifties when he suffered from malnutrition. Over the years, mostly by example, Merce indoctrinated quite a few of us. We credited the regimen with fewer colds, increased energy, greater stamina. But most of us popped our pills discreetly. Not Remy! He made it a grand spectacle: twenty-one pills placed with impressive ceremony into his mouth—one by one. Then, with a sovereign flourish, a colossal swig of wheat-germ oil! His eyes would roll heavenward as he downed the whole hideous concoction in a single great swallow, followed by much licking and smacking of lips. Onlookers were either amused or disgusted, and Remy's performance ended up as a constant source of jokes. Another silliness source was wordplay on the names of dances from Louis Horst's composition classes. Louis indulged in this himself. He had a wonderfully dry, laconic sense of humor and a great sense of timing. He especially loved to tease Viola, of whom he was very fond. They chatted together in German, and Louis complained loudly and grumpily that she was the only one of the Cunningham clan who hadn't studied with him—it wasn't true; only a few of us had. Viola had a delightful gift for storytelling, and that summer she wove a charming yarn, using as her cast of characters Pa Vane, Ma Zurka, Sara Bande, Alle Mande, Gal Liard, etc. Louis loved it and joined in with a few choice characters of his own.

With the exception of the still-recuperating Remy, the entire company took both of Merce's classes faithfully, in a huge, long gymnasium without mirrors, at the far end of the campus. When Merce demonstrated in the center front, those at the far ends and the back had difficulty seeing him. Since almost none of the students had ever taken Cunningham technique before, company members lined up across the front of the class so those behind could follow, and thus we held ourselves accountable for every second of both classes. I fear I tended to place too much emphasis on being careful and correct for the sake of those following (and undoubtedly, for my own self-esteem) rather than to expand my range by risking error and lack of clarity. This added unnecessary tension to an already strenuous day, but compared to Merce's, my day was a breeze.

His day began much earlier than ours. While we were socializing over breakfast, he'd already done his yoga and was giving himself a warm-up and preparing his classes before facing the rest of us in the studio at 8:30 a.m. His summer responsibilities included teaching two daily technique classes, choreographing and rehearsing two new dances, rehearsing two others from the repertory in preparation for the festival performances in August, rehearsing his own parts, and consulting with Rauschenberg about decor and costumes and with Feldman and Cage about music. Most people seemed surprised when he continued to teach both classes each day throughout the summer, and they were really impressed by his willingness to teach the beginning class at all, especially at such an ungodly hour of the morning. He was the only Biggy to do so, but at thirty-nine he was younger than Graham by twenty-five years and than Limón by eleven. Anyway, perhaps no one thought of Merce as a Biggy except us. It's unlikely that either Graham or Limón looked upon Merce as a peer, at least in 1958. Yet Merce's classes were well attended by many of the dancers in José's company.

In 1958, Merce was still formulating his own technique—continuously searching for ways to develop strength, speed, flexibility, and clarity and to discover the best continuity and overall structure for the class. He wanted to know what worked and what didn't, and we were his willing guinea pigs. Merce has always claimed to hate teaching, even going so far as to say that he felt it was degrading, but he never totally relinquished the teaching to others, and he continued to think of the technique class as an ongoing experiment. "It's trial and error most of the time," he has said. "You try something out . . . and finally you keep what works."[7] So Merce's technique, at least in the beginning, was wholly of his own devising. Since he taught almost all the classes for many years, the technique was little influenced by any of us who occasionally taught for him. (However, that began to change in the late sixties and especially after the move to Westbeth in 1971, when an assortment of teachers of widely differing backgrounds took over the bulk of teaching at the studio.) At Connecticut College in 1958, there was a genuine excitement in his classes, felt, I think, by everyone who took them, as well as by those who filled the spectators' gallery. Thunderous applause rained down on him after every class. If Merce felt "degraded," it certainly wasn't apparent.

For many people, teaching can be deeply rewarding, but love it or hate it, it always consumes one's energy and leaves one drained. That summer, Merce had no time to pause and recoup after teaching. Our free time was his only time to work alone on the new pieces and to rehearse the solo he would be dancing in the festival. He slept badly, sometimes not at all. Still, he was remarkably cheerful. My letters home reported: "A happy time, for the most part. . . . Merce has been so wonderful this summer. Gentle, pleasant and good-humored almost consistently . . . The new dances are exciting and challenging to work on . . . We're very, very busy and very, very ache-y. A new ache and pain each day, it seems. We just begin to think we're in good condition when we do some new thing in rehearsal and find a whole new set of muscles!"

Two or three times during the summer, Merce had to be away from campus. When this happened, I taught his two morning classes and the company rehearsed itself. On one of those occasions, he left us a typed note. It was addressed to "the Cunningham troupe" and read:

DEAR FRIENDS*** I WILL BE AWAY THIS AFTERNOON, AT LEAST THE EARLY PART OF IT, WILL YOU PRACTICE THE LANDSCAPE DANCE IF YOU CAN FIGURE OUT WHICH ONE THAT IS. IT'S THE ONE WHERE YOU DON'T GO ONE-TWO-THREE FALL.... WE WILL WORK THIS EVENING.... WHY NOT SUP CHEZ MOI. I SUGGEST A LARGE SALAD, COLD CUTS AND FRITOS, SOME WARM ALE. IF THIS IDEA YOU LIKE, OBTAIN FOOD, AND APPEAR AT MY HOUSE 5:30–5:45–5:50, I SHOULD BE BACK DEF BY THEN. IF THE IDEA IS NOT EXHILARATING SEE YOU THIS EVE. HAVE A GOOD TIME

"Landscape Dance"? That was the first we'd heard of it. Typically we had no idea what Merce was working on. We just guessed that he was making two separate dances, although he never actually told us he was. Among ourselves we called them "this one" and "the other one," but we were never quite sure which dance we were talking about at any particular time. My journal says it all:

The first weeks left us all with aching muscles, bruised hips and knees, and ground meat for feet. What an ordeal. Merce is at work on what seems to be *two* pieces: both technically difficult in different ways. One is in the tradition of *Springweather and People without* the "People." The other, we suspect, is the "funny dance" made up so far primarily of falls which at present are great crashings to the floor in a multitude of crazy ways. Merce has also made a strange little ballet duet for Cynthia and me—perhaps, it too is part of the funny dance—at present, I dislike it. The joke made is *not* funny, the rhythm of the steps arbitrary and, to me, mostly *un*rhythmic. Actually it is the connecting links that make for awkwardness. Or maybe it's me.

Merce wrote to Bob Rauschenberg describing the falling section: "Everybody is falling as though they didn't mean it, I've been working on this one, and the trouble is they do look as though they didn't mean it."[8] In the letter, written less than a week after our arrival, Merce described his tentative ideas for a dance he'd tentatively titled *Antic Meet,* but he told us nothing. To Bob, he reported that this new work with John's music was "barely begun" and that "it should be unbegun."[9] In fact there were a few false starts on Merce's part and much bewilderment on ours in the first rehearsals of *Antic Meet*. In several sections with complicated floor patterns and near-miss timings, we had difficulty understanding exactly what he wanted. The geometry of the spatial arrangements was baffling, and we kept finding ourselves in a muddle and then we'd bicker among ourselves trying to straighten it out. In the middle of one of these bollixed-up rehearsals, Merce, in total exasperation not only with us but with his own inability to clear up the confusion, sent us away. We were sure he was going to chuck the whole thing. At the next rehearsal, in a tone of quiet desperation, Merce drew careful diagrams on a blackboard and then meticulously counted out each person's part again and again. The fog lifted. The light dawned.

When completed, *Antic Meet* included most but not all of the ideas in the tentative outline that Merce had sent Bob. There were ten sections, which Merce described as "like a series of vaudeville scenes which overlap."[10] "Opener" (for company), "Room for Two" (a duet for Carolyn and Merce), "Mockgame" (company), "Sports and Diversions #1" (a ballet duet for Carolyn and Cynthia), "Sports and Diversions #2" (a tumbling duet for Merce and Remy), "Social" (company), "Bacchus and Cohorts" (for Merce and four women), "Sports and Diversions #3" (a solo for Viola), "A Single" (a solo for Merce), and "Exodus" (company). At the end of the letter to Bob, Merce confided, "this is all from dostoevsky"—information Bob must have found cryptic at best until "Let me tell you that the absurd is only too necessary on earth—Ivan Karamazov" appeared in the program as a subtitle to *Antic Meet,* giving not only the audience but us dancers a clue about what we were going to do—a clue that Merce, apparently, hadn't felt we needed.

One afternoon, as the company lay sprawled on the floor during a break in an *Antic Meet* rehearsal, Marilyn Wood looked up at Merce, who was seated on a chair scrawling undecipherable hieroglyphics on his notepad, and in all sweet innocence asked him, "Do you have something particular in mind in these dances?" In the awful stillness that followed, the same thought raced through all our minds: had she *really* asked? We didn't know whether to giggle or groan. As badly as we, too, might have wanted to know what he had in mind, we would never have presumed. The silence was excruciating. Merce sat motionless. After what seemed an interminable length of time (which was probably only a few seconds), Merce merely smiled benignly and said, "Yes." Not another word. Marilyn didn't know that the very last thing one could expect of Merce was that he would discuss his intentions. She was thoroughly perplexed both by Merce's uncommunicativeness and our flabbergasted response to her having asked that question in the first place.

We had to explain to her that Merce mistrusted words as descriptions of dances and was leery of putting literary ideas into our heads, fearing that we'd attempt to interpret them rather than allowing the choreography to speak for itself. It was not that he wanted us devoid of our own ideas about his dances, but that he hoped our ideas, whatever they were, would grow from the mute seed of movement. I respected this opinion, even if I sometimes felt it to be counterproductive: a tiny clue pointing us in a specific direction, like the Dostoevsky quote, *might* have enriched our perceptions of the choreography, but Merce chose to trust the truth of the steps. He was not the first person to believe that if the movement is executed fully, everything will be there—meaning, content, emotion. In his autobiography, Charlie Chaplin explained the extraordinarily moving performance of six-year-old Jackie Coogan in the movie *The Kid*. Coogan hadn't understood intellectually what he was supposed to portray, but through repetition of the physical business, he achieved the exact performance that Chaplin was looking for. Chaplin's simple explanation: "The mechanics induced the emotion."

Antic Meet has absurdity in abundance—in the movement non sequiturs, in the peculiar juxtapositions of bodies and rhythms, and in the props and costumes. Unlike so many of the dances for which Bob designed decor and costumes, *Antic Meet* was truly a collaboration. Merce gave Bob a scenario, with many ideas for props and costumes already specified, and Bob took off from there. It was Merce's idea to have a chair strapped to his back in our duet *Room for Two* ("like a large mosquito that won't go away . . . or like a leech, like chairs are"[11]) and Bob's that I should appear in a full-length starched white cotton-and-lace Victorian nightdress from behind a door—set in its own frame—that I wheeled onstage. Merce dreamed up the bizarre sweater with four sleeves and no opening for the head, an octopuslike garment in which he becomes hopelessly entangled in "Bacchus and Cohorts." The knitting of the sweater was a company project: Merce designed it, with some pertinent advice from Valda Setterfield, and those of us who knew how to knit (including Merce, who had recently taught himself the rudiments) contributed at least two or three triangles. But Valda did most of the knitting, and she sewed the dozens of triangles together into its curious shape. For this same dance, Bob dressed the four women in honest-to-god Second World War surplus silk parachutes, which weighed a ton and looked astonishingly like some exotic and fabulously expensive Balenciaga creation. We rushed about in them, feet and wrists flexed, stomping and triplet-ing and lamenting in an outrageous parody of some yet-to-be-choreographed Martha Graham epic. (Merce, of course, was Martha.) Although, in the outline he sent to Bob, Merce envisioned Viola "loaded down with bundles" in her solo (an endless series of small foot maneuvers that slowly moved her across the stage), Bob chose to put her under a large black umbrella with tiny white Christmas-tree lights attached to its underside. It also weighed a ton, due to the big batteries hidden there, and it was difficult for Viola to hold it out in front of her because of the top-heavy weight. But what a wonderful image! She looked like the silhouette of a lady in Seurat's painting *La Grande Jatte*. It was a surreal and magical bit of theater.

Bob made other wonderful contributions to *Antic Meet:* for the male duet, he used the macho-male symbolism of tattooed chests by painting imitation tattoos directly onto flesh-colored tank tops; for "Social" (Merce's ironic and rather nasty depiction of male-female relations in so-called polite society), he had us wear dark glasses with mirror-reflecting surfaces; and for "Mockgame" (the falling and leaping section) he had big hoops sewn into the hems of black tank tops, which altered the shape of the body in a curious and amusing way.

Merce has a gift for making non-narrative jokes with movement alone, and in *Antic Meet* such jokes are plentiful. His view of the petty rivalries in the ballet world show up in the "ballet duet," in which Cynthia pan-tomimes throwing stones at my head and I retaliate by throwing a bucket of water on her (both props, in this case, are imaginary); it's a bitchy little dance that I found a bitch to execute because the rhythms of the ballet steps were so peculiar. In "Room for Two," after a sedate sort of courtship, Merce—the madcap cavalier with a chair strapped to his back—had his way with ("raped" is probably too strong to describe the event) his prim and proper lady friend (me) and then brushed his palms in an emphatic "That'll take care of *you*" gesture as I *bourrée-ed* off the stage behind my rolling door. Macho-masculinity was spoofed in the tumbling duet, a goofy sort of acrobatic contest in which Remy was eventually "knocked out"; Merce, the victor, exited, then reappeared in a full-length fur coat (Bob's contribution, although Merce decided in which dance and when it would be used) and dragged Remy offstage. In one of Merce's most caustic com-ments on social mores—the curious section called "Social"—each dancer was a loner, slowly circumnavigating the stage space on three-quarter *relevé* while the arms performed a series of hypnotic swimminglike motions. The mirror-surfaced dark glasses cast a distinctly sinister pall over the proceedings. When individual paths crossed and contact was made, the outcome was inevitably hostile, and it was always the woman who was the culprit. For example: I rested my extended leg on Remy's shoulder (he was kneeling) while we both performed the slow port de bras, and then abruptly I gave him a rather malicious shove with my foot that knocked him sprawling onto the floor; later on, Marilyn and Remy would be doing a laborious tiptoe pas de deux, their four arms "swimming" in a careful counterpoint when suddenly she (domineering wife/aggressive female?) crooked one arm around his neck like a vise and led him (submissive husband/trapped male?) off the stage.

Antic Meet was full of such silly skirmishes and petty hostilities. But there was also a wonderfully sentimental Chaplinesque moment when Viola spurned Merce's offer of a pop-up bouquet (found in a magic shop by Bob), pulled from his sleeve like a rabbit from a hat. In response, Merce buried his face in the flowers and his whole body crumpled in utter dejection. Perhaps the highlight of the entire work was Merce's solo "A Single"—an exquisitely nonchalant soft-shoe number, a nostalgic homage to vaudevillians of an earlier epoch, which Merce performed with throwaway grace. For this number, Bob dressed Merce in all-white—shoes, socks, shirt, and workman's overalls. Its effect was Keatonesque and brilliant.

Although *Antic Meet* was zany and fun to do, I always dreaded the ballet duet, knowing full well that spoofing ballet, even ballet manners, was treacherous territory unless the steps were executed perfectly. And even though *Antic Meet* required great bursts of sustained energy in several sections, it was not nearly so difficult to perform as we'd first supposed. Looking back, I can't imagine why the group dances gave us so much trouble in the beginning. "Mockgame," with its dozens of falls, was agony, but only in the first week of rehearsals, when our muscles weren't used to repeating again and again and again (as one must do in rehearsal) so many kinds of falls at such a variety of speeds. My part included being the latecomer who rushes in long after the others have entered, and, in order to catch up and end the section in unison with everyone else, has to do every fall the others had already done at twice the speed. As *Antic Meet* rehearsals moved into high gear, things got a bit frantic: I got hit three times in one rehearsal—not out of malice, just poor timing—twice in the mouth which bled, swelled, and turned black and blue.

By this time, we had more than an inkling that *Antic Meet* was supposed to be "the funny piece," so naturally we couldn't help having certain expectations about audience response. But at the final dress rehearsal, which summer faculty, students, and company members were allowed to attend, there was not a laugh, not a chuckle, not even a stifled snicker. The Connecticut College summer dance community seemed totally nonplussed. The lack of reaction was thoroughly disheartening. Gloom replaced high spirits. As we left the theater that night, Merce sounded perplexed, a bit despondent. Softly, almost inaudibly, he murmured, "I guess I failed. I thought I'd made a funny dance." He had. What we didn't know was that applause, laughter, audible response of any kind was strictly forbidden at dress rehearsals. And on Thursday night, August 15, at the first performance, the audience let him know it. The students and faculty, who hadn't dared to laugh at dress rehearsal, let loose at the performance, and Merce's loyal fans who'd journeyed up from New York joined in.

It was *Summerspace*, the second new work that Merce choreographed for the festival, and not *Antic Meet*, that went unappreciated. As Merce said many years later in *The Dancer and the Dance*, his book of conversations with Jacqueline Lesschaeve, "When [*Summerspace*] was first done at the Summer School in Connecticut, nobody saw the dance, nobody heard the music. It simply passed. There it was going on, among those modern dances, its turn came and we performed it. Nobody saw it."[12] The public response was of little consequence to me. *Summerspace* was every bit the challenge I'd been hankering after, and it served as a turning point in my personal relationship to Merce's work as a whole, channeling my aspirations. During the previous spring, when he and I were rehearsing for the duet concert in Pittsburgh, he had begun to work on new and, for me at that time, extremely difficult material—mostly turns, my bête noire! He gave me slow turns, fast turns, jumping turns, turns ending in falls, and complex combinations of turns. He seemed to be throwing down the gauntlet, and I snatched it up as though somehow my honor depended upon it. With real zest, I zeroed in totally on Merce's work once more, to my tremendous relief, and my unfocused openness to auditioning wherever and whenever the opportunity presented itself vanished.

In addition to turns, the movement vocabulary for *Summerspace* included far more balletic leaps, jumps, leg extensions, and arabesques than any of his previous group dances, and yet the abrupt changes in direction and speed, the rhythmic permutations, the devouring of space using walks, runs, skips, and leaps, and the intermittent and surprising use of falls to the floor were not at all familiar to the ballet dancers who later came to perform *Summerspace*: New York City Ballet, 1966 and

1999–2000, Cullberg Baletten, Stockholm, 1967, Boston Ballet, 1974, or Théâtre du Silence, Paris, 1976. Nor were these ballet dancers attuned to the concept of "stillness." In Cunningham's dances, stillness is to movement as silence is to sound in Cage's music: integral. Stillness is not merely a gray area between the end of one movement and the beginning of the next; it is not a void with no meaning of its own. Nor is it taking a position or posing for effect. In Merce's work, stillness must be understood as a physical reality, distinct, absolute, vibrant with its own raison d'être. To be still and yet still to be dancing.

By the time Merce arrived at Connecticut College in July, he'd completed most of the time-consuming chance operations for *Summerspace*,[13] finished most of the paperwork, and had begun constructing and teaching the dance to the company. He devised and taught each of the six parts separately. We worked in a wonderful space—the enormous parlor of Knowlton House. It is an elegant room with a high ceiling, chandeliers, a beautifully polished wood floor and tall windows opening onto an expanse of green and vistas of lush and stately shade trees. Stripped of its furniture, the room, approximately one hundred feet long and fifty feet wide, gave us the glorious feeling of dancing in a vast Viennese ballroom, with limitless space. Space, as the title implies, was Merce's central choreographic concern in this dance.

In his preparatory exploration of movement for the dance, Merce sought steps and phrases that would carry the dancers *through* space, not just *into* it. There were twenty-one different spatial paths—horizontal, diagonal, or circular—that came from and went to one of the three entrance/exit places on each side of the stage. The movement was for the most part continuous. Much of it fast. ("Seems to be doing with people and velocities,"[14] he told Rauschenberg.) Merce hoped to make a dance that gave the illusion of existing offstage, as well as on, "like a passage of birds, stopping for moments on the ground and then going on."[15] And in *Summerspace*, every place onstage, as well as every person, was deemed of potentially equal interest. Thus the form and the structure of the dance could be perceived as making a political statement as well as an aesthetic one. *Summerspace* is, I believe, the first extreme example of Merce's challenge to the precepts of classical ballet, with its hierarchy of ballerinas, soloists, and corps de ballet whose rank was inevitably revealed by the place onstage each occupied. In the same way that people in Elizabethan times believed Earth to be the crown jewel in the center of the universe, the ballet world, rooted in the traditions and perspective of the Renaissance theater, believed center stage to be the regal territory of the ballerina, the Star. But in the universe as we've come to understand it, there is no center stage, but rather an ever-changing, multifaceted field of activity, and Merce's choreography reflects this contemporary scientific view of the world. In selecting the gamut of spatial possibilities for *Summerspace*, Merce actually avoided center stage except as an area any one of the dancers might pass through as he or she traversed the space. We were all soloists, each with a distinct path to follow. Our paths met, crossed, joined, separated, and continued on as we appeared and vanished and reappeared again from some other point, like meteors in the night sky following their destinies' trajectories.

Working on *Summerspace* in the Knowlton "ballroom" was exhilarating, but subsequently rehearsing it on the Palmer stage proved terrifying. Gone was the sense of flight, of freedom, of buoyancy in a boundless space. There were so many obstacles! We had to avoid crashing into real stage wings as we exited whirling or leaping at great speed, and just two steps offstage left we would career into a wall of rope pulleys and metal hoists. Underfoot (on *both* sides of the stage) were nests of electrical cords and plugs to cripple us. Even worse was the uneven, old, patched-linoleum stage floor, which held special terrors for us in the turning sections and caused deep, painful splits in the calluses of our bare feet. But apparently there were compensations. To my parents I wrote: "We're working on the stage several days a week now—this is a joy! Makes us feel as though we really are professional dancers. One begins to forget after working so long in a studio." But in the first performance of *Summerspace* we were suddenly confronted with the additional problems of dancing with unfamiliar music and unexpected theatrical lighting. (Of course these problems were not new to us.) Morton Feldman's music consisted of mostly quiet, suggestive sounds and was not difficult to assimilate, but we were still too inexperienced to be able to master the technical demands of new and difficult choreography while negotiating the perils of a terrible floor and sudden, disorienting changes of light. Under these circumstances, I'm certain that the first performance of *Summerspace* was not a stellar one. But we coped.

Several years after the first performance, Merce revealed that "the summer part of the title came after the dance was finished."[16] (Had he really not envisioned the complete quartet—*Springweather and People, Summerspace, Autumn Rune,* and *Winterbranch*—ahead of time?) Certainly the "summer" quality of the dance was created by Rauschenberg's shimmering pointillist costumes and drop cloth, and Nick Cernovich's through-the-branches-of-some-giant-shade-tree, dappled-late-afternoon-warm-and-hazy-sunlight lighting. Like *Antic Meet, Summerspace* was a true collaboration, although the information Merce proffered was far less specific, far less detailed. But he did give Bob something to go on. The same letter that described Merce's ideas about *Antic Meet* briefly mentions the other, still untitled dance: "I have the feeling it's like looking at a part of an enormous landscape and you can only see the action in this particular part of it. I hope it's dazzling rather than willy-nilly." Bob saw to it that his contribution was indeed dazzling. Borrowing a painting technique from the French impressionist painter George Seurat, who created land- and people-scapes through the application of small dots of pure, intense color, Bob painted both backdrop cloth and costumes (tights and leotards, again) in myriad dots from an enormous palette of different hues and tints. Jasper Johns said to me, years later, "Bob's original idea was flowers—can you imagine, flowers, for god's sake!"[17] The idea of the dots came from Jasper. Unlike Seurat's, Bob's colored dots were applied almost randomly, with no attempt made to organize them into realistic forms.[18] The result was a lush, romantic infusion of pointillism, impressionism, and 1950s abstract expressionism. Like Merce's dance, the painting had no center. Wherever the eye fell, each dot of separate color was its own center. The whole was an enormous landscape of the imagination, and Merce's idea of a continuous, ongoing action, only part of it visible to the audience, was reinforced by the way the dancers' costumes seemed to appear out of and disappear into the painted backcloth. Once costumed and lit, *Summerspace* became an action painting, a living canvas. But to have the concept truly successful, floorcloth and wings should have been painted like the backcloth.

Morton Feldman had been commissioned to write music for orchestra. Titled *Ixion*, it was one of Feldman's graph pieces that indicated only how many (not which) sounds were to be played within a certain time frame, with the added direction that they were to be played in the high registers of the instruments except for one brief section in which the lower registers were indicated. The dynamics could be freely chosen by the performer. The music was pointillistic as well. When asked how he could write a score for a dance he would not see until the performance, with no idea what the choreographer and the designer were doing—Morty's response was "Well, it's like this. Say you're getting married and I tell you the dress won't be made until the morning of the wedding. But I also tell you it's by Dior."[19] The problem was, Morty either didn't know how to or didn't want to transcribe his score for the orchestra, so it was John who had to do it at the last moment, while Morty sauntered off to tour the Connecticut College gardens. After Morty left, John muttered, "The Dior of Fourteenth Street!" and set to work on Morty's score.[20]

Whatever *Summerspace* was meant to be and whatever it actually was, it apparently failed to make any impression on the audience who saw it on the last day of the Eleventh American Dance Festival. We'd worked fiercely hard on that fifteen-minute dance; it had pushed us to the very edge of our technical ability. It wasn't easy for any of us, but we were all committed to conquering the difficulties and I do think we managed to give a competent rendering of the piece, if not a glowingly definitive one. (I suspect it was not until 1964, after the dance had been in the repertory for six years and performed many, many times, that the work was fully realized.) At its first performance it was sandwiched between Ruth Currier's *Quartet* and Pearl Lang's *Falls the Shadow*, with José Limón's *Serenata* completing the program. Those particular dances may have disappeared from memory, but at the time it was *Summerspace* that slipped by unnoticed. It was just as Merce said: "Nobody saw it."

In Louis Horst's review of the festival, he coolly dismissed the dance as not realizing "any of the high standards so patently evident in [Cunningham's] three works presented earlier in the week,"[21] and Doris Hering, writing for *Dance Magazine*, thought it "a little sparse in movement invention."[22]

Two critics, Margaret Lloyd in the *Christian Science Monitor* and Walter Sorell in the *Saturday Review of Literature*, remarked upon the chasm that yawned between the aesthetic orientation of the Humphrey/Limón/Graham views of choreography and the Cage/Cunningham one. Sorell commented that the Eleventh American Dance Festival "made clear the irreconcilable cleavage between the older approach to choreography and the new trend, between the pictorial presentation of a dramatic-realistic subject matter—may it be psychological, mythological or social—and the impersonalized, objective, rather than non-objective, conception."[24]

"Mr. Cunningham and his company slashed across the accepted state of things like creatures from another world,"[25] wrote Margaret Lloyd about our presence in the festival. And so we felt: alien, suspect, without proper passports and—because we spoke a different language by choice—misunderstood. Yet, "outsiders" or not, our commitment to and belief in Merce's work made us surprisingly strong, in fact very nearly defiant! We were the newcomers, and no one forgot it for an instant, yet we were something more than that. As Margaret Lloyd put it, Limón was "the festival's own shining knight" and Cunningham "the mysterious challenger."[26]

ive days after the *Summerspace* performance, I was aboard the *Île de France,* bound for Le Havre with John and Nick. I'd lost out on the New York City Ballet tour of the Orient and the Ballets USA tour of Europe, but by god, I wasn't going to miss the premiere of Earle's *Pentathis* at the Thirteenth Internationale Ferienkurse für Neue Musik in Darmstadt, Germany. As chance (and John) would dictate, I did end up dancing in Europe—with Merce on a mini-tour of our own. Earle would be crossing via Icelandic Airways. He needed the extra week's salary from Capitol Records, and he'd learned from experience that he didn't enjoy the social life on ocean liners. John used the mornings of our seven-day Atlantic crossing to proofread the galleys of a book he'd co-authored on Virgil Thomson's music. In the afternoons he worked on three lectures he was to give at Darmstadt.

Five days at sea and the ocean got rough, adding spice to the general delight. We drank stout and champagne, John's preventative therapy for seasickness, and hadn't one queasy moment, but swimming in the indoor pool became an impossibility and pliés in the cabin-class gym an unusually interesting challenge. On the morning of the worst day of the storm, I went to check up on John and Nick. "Come in!" John called gaily in answer to my knock, and as I opened the door, John, seated in his desk chair, came sliding pell-mell across the room at me accompanied by flying papers, tumbling flowers, rolling fruit, and water splashing from the basin. The ship groaned and sent John right back to his desk again. I slid to the floor amid the wreckage and we all laughed till tears spilled down our cheeks.

The boat train took us to Paris, from which John departed for an engagement in Brussels, placing Nick and me in the care of Bénédicte Pesle. Bénédicte had been present at the company's first New York season at the Theatre de Lys in 1953–54 and had become our unofficial publicist, sharing her enthusiasm for Merce's company with the Parisian art-world intelligentsia. She would play an increasingly important role in the company's life for the next fifty years. Her friendship extended to searching out inexpensive hotel rooms, decent rehearsal spaces, a good apothecary, great little restaurants. As Merce's popularity in France grew, so did Bénédicte's role. Eventually she founded Arts Services and became the company's official representative in Europe. But all this was yet to come. In 1958, she worked in La Hune, a bookstore on the Boulevard St. Germain des Prés a few doors away from the celebrated cafés Les Deux Magots and Café de Flore. If one lingered long enough at Les Deux Magots one *might*, with luck, see Jean-Paul Sartre and Simone de Beauvoir or the wonderful actor Roger Blin. One could not, on the other hand, *escape* seeing every American artist or would-be artist who came to town. Before leaving for Brussels, John asked Bénédicte to assist Nick and me in searching out suitable theaters for a dance performance. A hopeless venture. The only stages we could even consider were too small—even they were too expensive—and we had no luck in finding managers willing to produce Merce and me in concert. One evening, Nick and I went to the Théâtre Sarah Bernhardt to see Madeleine Renaud with the Jean-Louis Barrault company in *Madame Sans-Gêne*. We sighed, "Now *this* is a theater!" Fourteen years later, in that very theater, the Cunningham company played for a week, the week I danced my last performances with Merce.

Left to my own devices, I rushed around Paris at a snail's pace, starry-eyed, breathless, and nearly swooning with pleasure. Earle arrived two days after we did, but Paris was merely our *rendez-vous*. Our official destination was Darmstadt, where we were housed in the small picturebook village of Seeheim, a trolley-ride away from the Schloss Heiligenberg, where classes and lectures and many performances of the Thirteenth Internationale Ferienkurse für Neue Musik took place. "In Darmstadt between 1952 and 1958," according to Boulez, "the discipline of serialization was so severe that it was ridiculous." John's presence in 1958 literally brought an end to that. In ten days, with three lectures and one duo-piano concert presenting new music by Brown, Cage, Feldman, and Wolff, John had the place on its ear! He was not invited back, but Darmstadt was never the same again.

The duo-piano concert was greeted with derisive laughter, loud talking, and rude noises, and it ended with violent vocal opposition. Throughout, John and David maintained a Buddha-like serenity. The lectures, given in English by John, were "simulcast" by three composers who'd holed up with John in a classroom for two days and three nights to translate the musicological, philosophical, and literary sense of John's writing into German. All three lectures were theatrical events, but it was the second lecture, "Indeterminacy" (which John described as "intentionally pontifical in character"), that grabbed my attention. He cited Earle's *Indices*—the music for Merce's *Springweather and People*—as an example of the whole history of Western orchestral music, in which the instrumentalists are merely "workmen who simply do as they are bid," and he declared that "this situation of subservience of several to the directives of one . . . is intolerable."[1] John would never have contemplated applying this idea to the workings of a dance company, but I did, immediately. It would certainly have made him unhappy to know that he had planted in me, albeit unwittingly, a tiny seed of discontent. Furthermore, his notion that a pianist or other instrumentalist—a dancer!—is merely a slave to his material would indicate how little John seemed to comprehend the manifold challenges, revelations, and satisfactions inherent in rehearsing and performing.

Darmstadt's seriously serial-minded music scene was upended and *bouleversé*, much to the discombobulation of its older generation. British composer Richard Rodney Bennett, twenty-two at the time, said of Cage's impact: "He shook people awfully. Everyone started to think his way. His became *the* forthcoming style. Stockhausen went absolutely over-board. And almost everyone went along with Stockhausen."[2] Luciano Berio felt Cage, "with his simplicity, accomplished a great deal. He proved to be a strong catalyst."[3] Boulez, who wasn't present at all of the lectures but apparently heard about them in minute detail, reacted more critically: "In 1958, Cage came to Europe with a bag full of tricks, of theatrical gimmicks. It was because of the tricks that I was repelled; one cannot recite jokes forever. All his invention was in action, not in composition. Still his performance had its good side. It cleaned out the academics."[4]

At the Schloss, social interaction began at breakfast over coffee, continued throughout the day, extended into the evening at dinner, and renewed itself again after the concerts in the early hours of the morning over glasses of fragrant German white wine or huge mugs of dark beer. Between classes, everyone gathered on the terrace at tables set up around the fountain, the sounds of music-making emanating from the open windows—a lone student practicing flute or piano, or a string quartet or chamber ensemble rehearsing. Having just come from six weeks at Connecticut College's summer session, I found the contrast between the two places startling. Among the Biggies at Connecticut, the atmosphere could only be described as guarded and suspicious, with none of the animated give-and-take that invigorated the international group of contemporary composers at

Darmstadt, where the intellectual excitement was actually visible. In particular, John's presence at Darmstadt sparked crazy, improbable theories of composition that were bandied about amid hoots and howls of laughter to the general merriment of everyone. One couldn't help overhearing almost constant Cage-related babble: "So uninhibited!"—"So very American!"— "So charming!"—"So amusing."

John's popularity was certainly as much personal as professional, and he was quick to make hay for Merce while the sun was shining. When he received an invitation to perform, he always suggested the possibility of a dance concert. A few people expressed interest, and with only this to go on, John had me wire Merce to come to Europe. Although I couldn't tell John, because he was working so hard on our behalf, I was not all that eager to dance. I was deliciously content being the wife of the composer Earle Brown, sharing in his activities and interests and meeting his newly acquired friends. I found it nearly impossible to find the space or the inclination to do even the minimum daily barre. In any case, the forty-five-minute workout I usually managed was not nearly enough to keep me in performance shape.

For the first time in my life I was having a glorious time staying up late and partying. Some nights hordes of us would descend into the Keller, a dank yet poetically mysterious place in the vaulted cellar of a partially destroyed castle (victim of Second World War bombing) inside the city of Darmstadt. Tables, lit only by candles, ran along both sides of the room. Between the tables on the far end was a tiny dance floor. American popular music from the forties and early fifties roiled the smoky blue-black Gauloise- and Gitane-laden air. As many as thirty avant-garde composers and musicians, often with wives or lady friends, plus a few dozen students crowded into this underground nightclub. There was much brotherly embracing and back-patting among the men—natural expressions of affection rarely seen in America—as the composers indulged their mutual admiration for one another. Such an appetite for a good time! The Cedar bar painters sprang to mind, but while the Cedar bar was purely American, the Keller was distinctly international, and there *was* a difference. In Darmstadt, hierarchy and sense of protocol were in effect, especially among the Germans. One night, a strikingly beautiful young Swedish student-composer named Karl-Erik Welin asked me to dance with him. I was delighted to accept—he was a good dancer—but within thirty seconds, Karlheinz Stockhausen cut in and whirled me away, indignantly reproving the young man for overstepping his place. I suppose I'd broken protocol, too. Apparently the wife of a bona fide composer was expected to dance only with her husband's peers. It was my very first encounter with Karlheinz's arrogance. I should have been angry, but I was too amazed. Thinking and living by democratic principles did not come easily to Karlheinz, wonderfully likeable, charming, and personable fellow though he could be.

On September 11 in the Congress Hall in Darmstadt, with Bruno Maderna conducting the Chamber Ensemble of the *Domaine Musical,* Earle's *Pentathis* for nine solo instruments was performed on a program with music by Anton von Webern and Arnold Schoenberg. "Earle's piece was a success!" I reported to my parents. It was lucky that I'd attended most of the rehearsals, because at the actual performance I was so anxious I heard nothing but the thudding of my own heart. Why was I always far more nervous attending performances of Earle's music than I ever was before or during my own performances with Merce?

When we arrived in Cologne, John greeted me with what he expected to be the thrilling news that Merce and I were to dance on the stage of the Royal Opera House in Stockholm on October 5. Much to my own surprise and John's utter dismay, I was hopping mad. Earle and I had decided to spend the two weeks before Earle's *Indices* rehearsals in Brussels, realizing my long-cherished dream of touring Italy and the south of France. *That* prospect did thrill me. I suggested that Merce give a solo concert, but John said "they" (I never learned who "they" were) insisted on a duet program. "You can go to the south of France any time," said John sternly. "The chance to dance in the Royal Swedish Opera House may be offered only once in a lifetime!" I seethed with resentment at John for scheduling my life and quarreled with Earle, who said I should go to Stockholm. I wrote to my parents that I'd begun to hate dancing, and John. (What on earth was happening to me?) But, in the same letter, I told them: "It's happening." I was incapable of resisting John's drunken, tearful pleas to "go to and be happy about Stockholm."

John got royally drunk after the performance of his *Concert for Piano and Orchestra* in Cologne on September 19. It was an unmitigated disaster, a scene close to chaos, where John discovered just how stupid and childish the average orchestral musician can be when faced with the freedoms he offered them. The work was played twice: once for a live audience and again behind closed doors in an empty auditorium where it was recorded for radio transmission. The rude, demonstrative audience reaction encouraged the players' insulting conduct, yet without an audience their behavior was even more offensive. Later, at a party, John startled me by confessing in a tearful, sweet-tempered, champagne-laden state that in the middle of the performance he'd prayed: "Forgive them, Lord, they know not what they do." Earle had always said that John was a religious composer, but he certainly didn't mean it in quite *that* way. John actually admitted to identifying with Jesus Christ even while not *wanting* to do that. It was touchingly evident that his pain was very real and he was helpless to fight his feelings. And there I was, balking about going to Sweden, making him even more unhappy.

The next morning, Earle and I headed not south toward the Mediterranean as we had intended but north toward the Baltic as John had pleaded we should. We had two days together, driving lovely backcountry roads, stopping to explore the eleventh-century city of Celle and to stroll the beach in Travemunde, wistfully admiring its stunning resort hotels. Finally, at the end of a peninsula jutting into the Baltic Sea, we reached a tiny speck of a village called Grossenbrode, the town where we had reasoned I would meet up with John and David to take the boat train and continue on to Stockholm. Grossenbrode: eerily remote, misty, smelling strongly of the sea, mysteriously quiet except for the soft, incessant lapping of the water and the moaning of the wind. By the time we arrived there, the place was dark—a forbidding, godforsaken spot at the very edge of the world. In a lodging a few hundred yards from the docks, we dined and tried fitfully to sleep.

Early the next morning, as we walked through the mist to the pier, Grossenbrode still felt like the far reaches of the earth, with not a living soul in view. A solitary boat awaited at the end of the empty railroad track. Earle accompanied me on board with my luggage. I attempted a bravery I did not feel but then succumbed to a tearful good-bye. When he went ashore I rushed up on deck so that I could wave farewell. I saw a train chugging slowly into view. He signaled that all was well: it was from Germany. As the boat pulled away from shore, I stood alone on deck waving my scarf until Earle was a mere dot in the landscape. Weeks later he told me that as the boat disappeared into the mist he suddenly thought aloud, "My God, I may never see her again!" Standing on deck, my own thoughts mirrored his. I felt utterly abandoned. I set out to find the dining room, half-expecting to discover my compatriots already gorging on the breakfast smorgasbord, but the room was empty. Since I was hungry and had no idea when I might get another meal that day (I didn't), I heaped a tray and sat down to await my friends—but no familiar faces appeared. The rest of the trip, from Grossenbrode to Gedsen, I spent on deck. The mists cleared.

The sun burned bright—an auspicious omen, surely. Every fifteen minutes or so I checked the dining room, but there was no sign of John, David, or Nick. Nor in Gedsen, where I boarded a train for Copenhagen.

The sixteen-hour journey via two ferries and three trains required four changes as well as coping with three countries' languages, customs, and exchange rates. My final destination was a city about which I knew nothing. The farthest I had ever traveled alone was New York to Boston. I had no viable language skills, not so much as a Danish or Swedish/English dictionary or guidebook. My large suitcase was too heavy to carry any distance. No one was expecting me. No hotel reservation awaited me.

It was raining when the train pulled into Stockholm shortly after ten p.m. A taxi took me to the hotel where John would be staying. I handed the driver a piece of paper with the name and address. "Thank the sweet lord for the common bond of numbers and letters," I thought as he sped through the dark streets to the Hotel Ornskold. No porter. No doorman. The taxi vanished. I dragged my suitcase up a steep staircase and stood breathless at the desk. To each question I put to the night clerk the answer was no. No Cage. No Tudor. No, they weren't expected. No, they had no reservations. And the final, devastating no, there was no vacancy. I must have looked as aghast as I felt because the man took pity on me and proceeded to make five telephone calls to other hotels, but from the way he shook his head, more sadly after each call, each one of them must have said no, too. Desperate, I wrote out on a pad of paper the names CAGE and TUDOR and pointed to the reservation book. It was then that I realized he hadn't understood anything. He checked his book, smiled broadly, pointed to the calendar, and said, "Tomorrow, come back tomorrow." He gave me a slip of paper with "Hotelcentralen" written on it, and the address of the railroad station. Back down the stairs, out onto the street I went, lugging my suitcase. Still raining. Street empty. Fighting back tears, mad as hell—at John, at Earle—I let my anger and anxiety sweep away all self-composure. Eventually another taxi took me to the Hotel Central. No vacancy there, either. The clerk wagged his head sympathetically and said "Try across street." No luck. Again I was given directions to the railroad station.

This time I walked. It was getting on toward midnight. The suitcase handle cut painfully into my hand. The rain didn't let up. Suddenly a gang of Sweden's version of London teddy boys blocked the side-walk, leering at me. Slowly—laughing unpleasantly—they broke ranks and opened a path. I wanted to run but could barely stumble along with my accursed suitcase impeding every step. Inside the station—in debris-cluttered upheaval due to renovation—unsavory-looking young men, more dissolute than the teddy boys I'd encountered on the street, were loitering everywhere. Hotel-centralen was nowhere in sight. When asked where it was, the woman at the fruit stand obligingly wrote out directions. In Swedish. I debated with myself: "Sit here all night or take the first sleeper to Germany, find Earle, and go to the south of France?" Heading for the ticket office, I met an official-looking man in uniform and fairly shrieked at him: "DO YOU SPEAK ENGLISH?" "A little," he admitted kindly and directed me to the hotel service bureau I didn't know I'd been trying to find. The young woman behind the window regarded me seriously, making me blushingly flustered. After a phone call or two, and requesting sixty cents, she handed me a piece of paper with the address of yet another hotel. Once again I set out in a taxi, with the sinking feeling that I was on my way to a home for wayward girls.

I was deposited at the door of what looked to me, in my overwrought state, like a Third Avenue flophouse. A steady rain beat down on the pavement. The only light came from a closet-sized room at the end of the entrance hall, where a sullen night clerk fussed over my passport and repeatedly requested my visa (which Americans were not required to have). Finally he handed me a key to a room on the fourth floor. The lift was broken. Blisters smarting, I literally ran up the long, winding flights to escape strange laughing, moaning sounds that echoed in the long corridor and scared me silly. I was convinced I'd ended up in a whorehouse, and everything became a race to safety: hunting up and down the halls for the room number, getting the key to work in the lock in the absolute terrifying blackness, and once inside trying to discover how to lock the door behind me. I found myself in an anteroom with another door to unlock, then another search in near hysterics for a light. With the flick of a switch, sanity returned. I was in a clean, thoroughly respectable room. Not able to relax enough to sleep, and needing to tell someone about the day's adventures, I wrote—venting my spleen—first to Earle, "I told you so . . ." and then in my journal. Exhausted, I fell into a long, utterly peaceful sleep marred by one brief dream in which Miss Craske said sternly: "You should be taking class every day."

I'd found safe haven just before midnight at the Hotel Clara Larsen, 29, Birgir Jarlsgatan. Contrary to my wild imaginings, it was certainly no flophouse and in fact occupied the top four floors of a business building in a commendable neighborhood. It was more like a *pensione* than a hotel, and Miss Larsen herself presided there with Nordic dignity. Number 29. (If by chance the reader has noticed an overabundance of meticulously noted dates and numbers, it is because both Earle and I were irrational believers in numerology and held the number eleven in whatever form—2 + 9, 3 + 8, 33 ÷ 3, the letter "K," the month of November, the year 1956, etc.—to be especially lucky for him, and by extension, me. And there it was again, guarding me from harm.) Tickled to discover providence at work on my behalf, I decided to stay put, even if John's hotel did eventually come up with a room for me.

By morning I regarded my terrifying adventure as a wonderful lark and set off in high spirits to explore the "Venice of the North" on my own and to luxuriate in my newly acquired independence. By the time I spoke to John later that same day I was feeling positively liberated, and when he said, ever so sadly, ever so sheepishly, "Nothing looks very promising, *please* don't kill me!" I roared with laughter. When John had announced in Cologne that Merce and I were to dance at the opera on October 5, the performance was more an optimistic dream than a factual reality, and by the time John arrived in Stockholm negotiations had faltered badly. When he discovered this, he telephoned an acquaintance, Kristina Hasselgren-Sjöman, in last-ditch desperation. Three years earlier, Kristina had been touring the United States on a professional writing assignment and completely by chance attended a performance of the Cunningham company at the University of California, Los Angeles. Profoundly impressed, she'd tried ever since to arrange a performance in Sweden for the company. Upon receiving John's frantic phone call, she immediately sprang into action, enlisted the aid of Holger Rosenquist, one of Stockholm's foremost dance educators, and together they persuaded the management of the Royal Opera House to meet with John the following morning. Only minutes before Kristina, John, and I were to leave the hotel lobby for the meeting, Merce burst into the hotel with mounds of baggage, bearing gifts, laughing, and kissing everyone. He hadn't time even to catch his breath before they whisked him off to the opera house, where the management agreed to present us on October 5, to do all the publicity, and to pay us two hundred dollars.

That night we attended a performance of the Royal Swedish Ballet in the Kungl Teatern, an intimate, majestic jewel, resplendent in gold, marble, plush red velvet, crystal chandeliers, graceful arching staircases, immensely dignified statuary, and paintings of Sweden's monarchs—the most elegant, exquisitely beautiful opera house I'd ever seen. I was undone. The more John hopped up and down in delight, the worse I felt, literally sick with fright at the thought of dancing there. The next day we had our first rehearsal on the immense, cavernously deep, steeply raked stage. We were told it would probably be our *only* stage rehearsal before the performance ten days away. We'd never worked on such a severely raked stage before, nor on one so vast. We were allotted just three hours—from eleven to two. While Merce and I figured out the spacing and half-walked, half-danced through the duo repertoire and our individual solos, Nick worked feverishly to understand the lighting setup. Staring into the infinity of the flies, he stepped backward and suddenly disappeared from view. Only a slight thud and a single surprised "Oh!" alerted us to his predicament—he'd fallen into the prompter's box. Luckily he wasn't hurt, merely chagrined as he looked up at us from his hole in the floor and said feebly, "I'm sorry. I've never worked in an opera house before," exactly expressing what the rest of us were thinking to ourselves. I was so alarmed at the prospect of dancing a solo on that stage that I totally forgot I'd per-formed on the stage of the Metropolitan Opera House both as a super with Sadler's Wells and in the Met's corps de ballet. But those experiences didn't count for much now. How could Merce and I sustain an entire evening in the Swedish Royal Opera House? I'd been on vacation for over a month and, damn it, every muscle in my body knew it! Merce, of course, was in superb condition. While I'd been playing, with only halfhearted attempts at keeping in shape, he'd been (*as always*) doing his yoga, giving himself a daily class, experimenting with new movement, and dancing his heart and guts out, just, it would seem, for the sheer pleasure of it.

Every day, for the next ten days, we did our own warm-up, separately rehearsed our individual solos, and together ran through the old duets before finally settling down to work on the new one, *Nightwandering*, to three pieces for piano by the young Swedish composer Bo Nilsson, whom John, David, and I had gotten to know at Darmstadt. Merce began work on the dance in a foul temper. Perhaps he didn't like Bo's music, or perhaps he was angry to be pressured by John into making a new work on such short notice to music he hadn't heard and knew nothing about. Perhaps it was just the irregularity of the rehearsal hours—having to rehearse when-ever and wherever time and space could be found for us—that made him appear so frantic one day, so morose the next. The best space was the stu-dio in the opera house, which had a steeply raked floor approximating the rake of the opera-house stage; but we often had to make do with a room at the radio station where John and David were rehearsing for their upcoming concert. Merce finished the duet in six days, with John and Nick kibitzing and making suggestions, leaving three days for us to absorb the material and make some coherent kinesthetic sense of it. For whatever reasons, Merce was glum and moody most of the time, so it was not a pleasant expe-rience for either of us. I wrote at the time: "It's a strange dance. I don't think I like it very much. I was rather unhappy in the process of its mak-ing—but often it is this way. It makes few demands on technique—strange kind of sexy ? dance, I guess. Except, it's not really sexy just *awkward* and uncomfortable. Perhaps with more doing, it will come into its own." Merce's only public statement about *Nightwandering* (similar to the one about *Amores* in Paris) appeared ten years later in his book *Changes:* "If you have three days [in fact, he had nine] to make a duet (this happened in stockholm with carolyn brown), do you worry about ideas, or do you make a dance involving two people, a man and a woman, together?"[5]

Merce may not have *worried* about ideas, but I'm fairly certain that he had some. Years ago, in a *Dance Perspectives* article[6] about Merce, I sug-gested that *Nightwandering* may have been his tribute to Ingmar Bergman. I believe it was Merce's intention that the stark, remote quality and the dis-tilled dramatic intensity of the dance should capture something of the Nordic neuroses depicted in Bergman's films of those years. The dance began offstage as both dancers moved in close counterpoint to each other at an excruciatingly slow, deliberate pace across a seemingly Bergmanesque boundless landscape—from upstage right, along an interminable diagonal path, toward downstage left. The dance ended about twelve and a half min-utes later (after a good deal of more active dancing) with Merce dropping back onto his hands, knees at a right angle, feet flat on the floor, his torso parallel to the ground, to form a kind of bed upon which I sat. Then, gradu-ally, I lowered my torso into the curve of his, extended my legs parallel to the floor, let my arms fall limply downward and nestled my head against his shoulder. Slowly, hypnotically he would begin to rock—"into eternity." Even the curtain's descent seemed to take forever and a day.

Nightwandering's unyielding tension may have derived from its repeti-tive movements, whether long and sustained or rapid and abrupt. Nothing happened that was not repeated many times or else held for a long time, so that every gesture was necessarily imprinted on the viewer's retina. Merce made a dance about "a man and a woman"—yes—but not about just any man and any woman. To my thinking, he deliberately constructed an oddly awkward "Nordic" dance about a couple whose passion, though obsessive, was coolly understated, and whose tenderness, though restrained, was carefully articulated. He'd encumbered this dance with constraints some-one of Ingmar Bergman's temperament and psychological persuasion could instantly identify with. It was a difficult dance for me to fathom. I had to grow into it, to wear it a number of times in the same way that one must wear an unusual new dress before the weight and texture and cut of its fab-ric will conform to the body and one can recognize *oneself* in it, not some stranger. Merce didn't offer any suggestions, of course. Nothing new in that, but without anyone—Earle or Marianne or Remy—to engage in discussion regarding it, I felt uncomfortably bereft and unhappy throughout.

The curious thing about Merce's behavior during our ten days in Stockholm was that his moodiness, which was so evident in every rehearsal, vanished the instant we walked out of the studio. That was fortunate, since we were caught up in a whirlwind social life from which we couldn't escape even if we'd wanted to, beginning with a bona fide press conference (my first!) in Holger Rosenquist's studio, complete with photographers, four or five gentlemen from the press, some of Stockholm's most illustrious dance personalities, and sherry and cookies. The interview and picture-taking were conducted with extreme courtesy and quiet discretion, although I balked at being asked by one photographer to sit on the grand piano for a bit of cheesecake publicity. What made the press conference memorable was meeting Rolf de Maré, who, when only twenty-one years old, founded Les Ballets Suédois in Paris in 1920, and in 1924 produced the infamous Dadaist extravaganza *Relâche*, which boasted the collaborative efforts of Francis Picabia, Erik Satie, Jean Borling, and René Clair. Both John and Merce had often spoken of *Relâche* and had sent me off to the Guggenheim Museum to see René Clair's extraordinary film *Entr'acte*, in which John's heroes—Marcel Duchamp, Picabia, Man Ray, and Satie—made cameo appearances. Although Rolf de Maré's Ballet Suédois was even shorter-lived than Diaghilev's Ballets Russes, both men had created collaborative meeting grounds for avant-garde painters, composers, and writers, and, I believe, served as role models and inspiration for John.

Just to exacerbate our situation a little more, after September 30 David was unavailable to play for rehearsals. He and John were in the midst of a concert tour on the Continent. Their Stockholm engagement on September 29 was followed by one in Copenhagen two days later, and David had a solo concert in Warsaw on October 3, so he couldn't rehearse with us again until the very day of the performance.

Much has been said and written about the separation or coexistence of music and dance in Merce's work. The idea is sacrosanct, part of the Gospel According to St. John. But what is never said, and should be, is that in many of Merce's dances choreographed in the fifties and sixties—certainly those to Satie but even, for example, with Cage's music for *Suite for Five*—choreography and music were relatively fixed. The dancers did pay attention to the music in its temporal relationship to the movement, and they did rely on it for cues. But more than that, whether the score was determinate or indeterminate, the simultaneous action of the music and dance together had—on us as well as on the audience—a greater effect than the sum of their individual parts. And because we were *not,* after all, robots, neither mindless nor heartless, there was always a deeper, visceral involvement in response to the sound. How could we be human and it be otherwise? So for Merce and me, David's absence from our rehearsals was a serious deprivation. Fortunately, John stayed on in Stockholm a day longer than David to give moral support and suggestions to Merce as he was finishing *Nightwandering;* then he took the night train to join David in Copenhagen, and returned to Stockholm immediately after their program to play the music for our *Amores* and *Suite for Two* rehearsals.

To make costumes for *Nightwandering,* we bought some yardage of fine Swedish wool and made ourselves tunics. Nick "designed." Merce and I sewed. His was short, of a soft, dull avocado-green color. Mine was floor-length, slit at the sides to above the knees, of a soft, dull lavender-gray. We wore basic tights and leotards underneath. Nick suggested that I plait my hair and wind the braids around my head. The costumes' overall image was simple, plain, stark.

On October 3—two days before the performance—we were at last given dressing rooms in the opera house. I'd never seen such a dressing room, except in films. Arranged like a little sitting room, it had a rug on the floor and lounging chairs, a full-length wall mirror, a curtained French window opening onto the park, and a spacious makeup table, brilliantly lit. Suddenly, with a thrill, I knew we were truly going to dance in that glorious gilt theater, even if we still were not allowed to rehearse on its vast, magnificent stage! Mr. Rosenquist and Kristina Hasselgren-Sjöman came to watch our run-through in the raked studio that day, and afterward, Kristina, overly generous in her compliments, said to me: "I think you are the most beautiful dancer to dance on this opera stage!" I scribbled to my parents: "Did she mean 'beautiful dancer' or 'dancer who is beautiful'? I hope she meant the first." Whatever she meant, her words, though unbelievable, served as a needed boost to my flagging sense of self-esteem, especially the next day, when at last we got to rehearse onstage—the only full run-through we would have there before the performance. We worked from nine in the morning until noon. For me it was disastrous. I was completely unnerved, shaky, unable to hold a balance, to turn without hopping or falling off, incapable of extending my legs fully or stretching my feet. My feet? I couldn't even *feel* them. I was so tense in the middle of my *Galaxy* solo that turning my head sharply in a turn sent a searing fire-javelin of pain shooting up into my skull; for a second I blacked out and froze in terror, not even daring to breathe. Working in that glorious space should have been exhilarating, but I was too paralyzed with fear and far too preoccupied with my technical inadequacies to appreciate anything. I don't think Merce noticed how miserable I was. Put *him* on a stage and he's immediately plugged in, wired, lit up. All trace of moodiness vanishes. The stage is an oasis for him.

Luckily, I had no time to fret over that ghastly rehearsal. It had been strongly recommended that we not miss a visit to Drottningholm's exquisite tiny court theater on the grounds of King Gustavus III's magnificent seventeenth-century summer palace, less than an hour's drive from the center of Stockholm. It turned out to be an afternoon of perfect enchantment.

"I love John Cage!" said our guide, Birgit Berling, on the way to my hotel after we'd dropped off the others. "Oh, yes!" I responded, "So do I!" In fact, at that moment my heart was fairly bursting with gratitude. Dear John—our wonderful cockeyed optimist! Join him in his wildest, most implausible pipe dream, and chances are it will materialize. Just how soon I was made suddenly aware (having totally forgotten about my dispiriting rehearsal that morning) when Miss Berling said good night and wished me much success the next day. Alone in my hotel room, I readied my costumes and makeup, packed my recently purchased theater bag, went to bed early, and tried to sleep. Of course it was useless.

On performance day, we had no rehearsal time onstage and ran our program in the studio. David had returned from Warsaw and played for us. We all had an early dinner together in our favorite milk-bar restaurant before going back to our hotels to nap. It was twilight when I set out on foot for the opera house for the last time. I walked at a leisurely pace down Norrlandsgatan into the Kungstradgarden, looking hard at everything, pressing each singular sound and sight and smell into awareness to savor it then, in the moment, but also to cherish it, like some precious posy that one presses between the pages of a book. Sunday evening. The air was still, and damp. The fountains, emptied a day or two before, were quiet. Dull, lifeless leaves hung motionless and limp from the branches of trees, despite the slight, cool wind with its promise of rain. In the distance, hundreds of lights cast squiggly reflections in canal and river. Shimmering halos graced each streetlamp. To my surprise, I realized that my nervousness was gone. In its place was a pleasant, warm, excitement-tingling happiness.

Relinquishing the soothing autumnal twilight, I stepped into the brightly lit, bustling backstage of the Royal Opera to be greeted by the resounding music of Mozart's *The Magic Flute* just finishing its matinee performance. By the time Merce and I had made up and done a barre in our respective dressing rooms, the stage had been cleared for us to work.

We warmed up, tested all our difficult balances on the severe rake, once more spaced the dances in the vast area, which felt to me more like a football field than a stage. A few photographers milled about snapping their cameras at us while we worked.

"Half hour, please! Half hour until curtain!" My stomach flip-flopped with my heart. Back in our dressing rooms, we got into our *Suite* costumes, touched up our makeup. "Fifteen minutes, please!" Back onstage I ran huge circles—uphill, across, down, and around. I jumped in place, skipped in circles, and leaped down the precipitous diagonal from upstage left to downstage right, all the while forcing myself to breathe deeply— inhale/exhale (especially exhale)—to loosen up and get the adrenaline flowing. "Places, please." I walked quickly into the wings while Merce took his place onstage. The work lights faded. A moment of utter heart-stopping stillness, and then in the darkness the great ruby-velvet-and-gold embroidered curtain parted, swung up and away, revealing Merce, alone in a pool of light. It had begun.

Our program included four duets: *Suite for Two, Nightwandering, Amores,* and a duet version of *Springweather and People* devised especially for this occasion. There were four solos: three by Merce—*Collage, Changeling,* and *Untitled Solo,* and my part from *Galaxy* performed as a solo. Interspersed throughout the evening, David and John played four duo-piano pieces: Cage's *Variations* and *Winter Music,* Feldman's *Two Pieces for Pianos,* and Wolff's *Duo for Piano. Suite* was a difficult opener— for me, if not for Merce. My solo, *A Meander,* was full of balances and held positions and stillnesses that required precise control and extreme clarity without sacrificing fluidity and the appearance of serenity. Complete concentration and inner calm were the means of realizing those goals, but they were not easily achieved in a setting as awesome as Stockholm's Royal Opera House. Almost without exception, *Suite* was placed first on a program—a purely aesthetic decision on Merce's part. Chance means, to my knowledge, were never employed to determine the order of the dances, except perhaps in Events. In fact, Merce's ideas about programming, in the years I danced with him, were surprisingly conventional. He seemed to separate his dances into specific categories: light, heavy; funny, serious; lyric, dramatic; active, passive. Of course, decisions could not be made entirely on an aesthetic basis. Being a supremely practical man, Merce naturally had to consider the dancers' energy and stamina, his own in particular, because, until the late seventies, he usually danced in every piece in the repertory.

Merce's opening solo in *Suite* ended in a blackout. He exited in darkness and I entered, walked to my place three or four steps in from the wings, and took my opening position: feet in first position facing directly front, with my arms overhead in open fifth position, palms facing out. Alone in the darkness before the pool of light came up, I prayed that the calm and wonderful sense of happiness I'd felt walking through the park on the way to the theater would stay with me. But alas, Ego—fear of fail-ure—froze both body and spirit. The stage lights seemed to enclose me in a kind of prison; I couldn't see the audience (wasn't even sure there was one). Some of the wretched self-conscious nervousness I'd suffered during the terrible stage rehearsal the previous day returned. I was too intimi-dated to dance full-out, too shaky inside to dare to hold positions confi-dently, so tense that I compensated by being too careful, too precise, risking nothing (not even breathing!), and disappointing myself a lot. The *Suite* duet went much better, although some of the balances due to the rake were precarious for us both. When I went onstage to do my *Galaxy* solo to Earle's music, I was breathing more normally. "It's now or never!" I said to myself. "There's no sense in not enjoying this fantastic, once-in-a-lifetime experience!" And that change of mind changed my dancing. Doing *Galaxy* all alone on that immense, glorious stage was fully as exciting, as exhila-rating, as it should have been. And for the first time, taking bows, I was aware of the audience. "You can't imagine the thrill and the surprise to look out at the audience from that huge, magnificent stage and see people in every balcony, in boxes, in the orchestra—full house!"[7] We could hardly believe it. "Where did they all come from? Who are they?" Merce asked, in absolute amazement. Representatives of the king's court and of the Cultural Department of the American Embassy, we were told, and artists, musicians, dancers, composers, writers, as well as a fair mix of society in general. We were flabbergasted. We'd hoped for five hundred people at most and had expected to see persons scattered through the house among empty seats. At each bow we looked out into the packed house in wonder and disbelief.

The first half of the program ended with *Nightwandering*. It seemed to go very well until we discovered we'd rushed it, ending much too soon, which meant Merce had to rock me for what seemed like five full minutes until David finished the piano part and the curtain made its slow descent. Cradled in the curve of Merce's body I was so comfy and relaxed that I very nearly fell asleep, but Merce, who was supporting both our weights on his hands and feet in that awkward position lying back on all fours, was in real agony. By the time we danced *Amores* and finished the program with *Springweather* it was clear sailing, home free. "At last I felt as though I was *really* dancing," I wrote in my journal. "It felt good and right and warm . . . The audience was wonderful." In the final bows, Mr. Rosenquist presented me with a bouquet of red carnations, and it was over. Such an incredible evening—the most thrilling dance experience I'd had, and one that remains to this day among the most joyous, ecstatically happy memories of my dancing life with Merce and John.

It was three o'clock in the morning when Kristina's party celebration wound to a close and we got back to our hotels. Blissfully happy, deliciously exhausted, I lay on my bed at 29, Birgir Jarlsgatan, staring wide-eyed into the darkness, smiling. I couldn't stop smiling.

Bushed but jubilant, the five of us arrived in Brussels a day and a half later. For most of thirty hours of travel via an assortment of trains, boats, boat-trains, and sleeping cars, we pondered our surprising and delicious success at Stockholm's Kungl Teatern. It would have been easy to believe that the whole amazing experience had been a dream had we not incontrovertible evidence of its reality: reviews, with photographs, in four daily newspapers that we purchased just before boarding our train early the morning following our performance. What fun it was discovering them! It didn't matter that we didn't understand a single word of what was written. Even if they'd hated the evening (they didn't), the fact that four reviewers had actually come and cared enough to write about us was gratification enough.

Once in Brussels, with scarcely a second to catch our breath, we were propelled into the maelstrom of musical activities whirling in and around the Brussels World's Fair. John and David had two scheduled performances, and Earle, who'd been in Brussels since September 30, was immersed in rehearsals of his orchestral version of *Indices*, scheduled for its premiere on October 9. Nick, Merce, and I were tagging along simply as spectators, or so we thought. Late in the afternoon of the day we arrived from Sweden, Earle returned from his rehearsal ashen-faced. He and Bruno Maderna, who was conducting *Indices*, had sadly concluded that the musicians of the Orchestre de Chambre des Émissions Flamande de L'N.R. would not be able to play Earle's music, even with the two days of rehearsal remaining. The technical demands of the piece were too difficult and Earle's aesthetic too foreign to be assimilated in the time allotted. Earle accepted the harsh disappointment with a "grin and bear it" cynical good humor and a "*c'est la vie*" shrug that failed to hide his misery from me.

That same evening, we attended a Musique Électronique concert, one of many concerts presented over six days as a part of the Journées Internationales de Musique Experimentale. Nearly all our Darmstadt friends had come to participate and to visit the pavilion—designed by Le Corbusier for the Philips Corporation—where Varèse's *Poème électronique* was in continuous performance. When the Philips Corporation first heard the Varèse music, they were aghast and pleaded with him to write something "more pleasant." Reportedly Varèse replied: "Make concessions? In music? That is something that has never happened to me."[8] Edgard Varèse at the age of seventy-five could still knock the socks off composers twenty, thirty, forty years his junior, and young musicians on both sides of the Atlantic were eager to pay him homage. For them he personified the impassioned hero-artist of irreproachable integrity, the uncompromising rebel idealist, unswervable and prophetic in his belief in a new music beyond anything then imaginable. Paradoxically, Varèse was totally unsympathetic to the current Darmstadt School mania for total organization, saying, "When every note in a composition has to be or can be explained, according to a system, the result is no longer music. Composition according to system is the admission of impotence."[9] Although it sounds like Cage, it was Varèse who stated, "I want simply to project a sound, a musical thought, to initiate it, and then let it take its own course."[10] His plea for "the liberation of sound" predates Cage's by decades, but these two composers were not really in agreement. According to Cage, "letting sounds be themselves" meant the abdication of the composer's will. In Varèse's music the controlling force, Cage felt, was always the human imagination. "Rather than dealing with sounds as sounds," John said, "he dealt with them as Varèse."[11] What I've never been able to comprehend in John's philosophy is his reluctance, even refusal, to let *people* be *themselves*!

Poème électronique was a gut-level experience, not only aurally and visually but intellectually and spiritually. It was, in a word, awesome. Four hundred and twenty-five speakers were embedded in the wall of Le Corbusier's building. Each showing lasted only 480 seconds—exactly eight minutes. For each hearing, one was free to move around the many-leveled, soaring space of the pavilion and to be engulfed by the music from a different aural and visual vantage point of one's own choosing.

Compared with Varèse's "cataclysmic spacial encounter," the electronic music concerts presented in a conventional auditorium were, at best, anemic. At a highly animated champagne reception following one of them, someone (surely it was John!) suggested that Earle's *Indices* could be heard in its piano reduction version accompanied by the danced *Springweather and People* duet. The authorities were delighted with the idea, and Merce and I began to rehearse the dance with David Tudor the following evening. Within moments, one of the festival directors burst into the auditorium, wringing his hands in extreme agitation and crying, "*Le Pape est mort. Le Pape est mort. Je regrette, il est necessaire décommander le concert demain soir. Quel dommage! Le Pape est mort.*"

Catholic Belgium virtually shut down for a day of mourning. Thursday's concert was canceled, and all the music scheduled for that evening was added to Friday's program. All except *Indices*. It was decided that the arrangements for our dance, which required the removal of all the music stands, chairs, and instruments from the performance space and then their replacement, would take too long.

A friend of Stockhausen's named Hervé Thys, who directed the Apelac Electronic Music Studio in Brussels, had invited Earle and me to stay with him and his family in their large country estate in Rhode Saint Genèse, outside the city. Keenly aware of our disappointment over the cancellation of Earle's music, Hervé arranged to have the *Springweather* duet filmed for television. And so it came to pass that on Sunday afternoon, in the cramped and dusty marble-floored Studio Michiels (formerly the elegant drawing room of an old country estate situated in Boitsfort on the outskirts of Brussels), Merce and I found ourselves performing again. The situation could hardly have been more different from dancing on the vast opera-house stage in Stockholm exactly one week before. The spacial constrictions were excruciating. Preparation was limited to two quick run-throughs for the camera man and the ten-minute duet was filmed in one take. I felt as if we were dancing on a dime on a slow-motion conveyor belt moving in reverse through a musty closet. In less than an hour we were on our way back to Hervé's for tea, our work done, having been paid the equivalent of one hundred and four American dollars each. Not a very satisfying experience, but at least *making* money performing Merce's choreography, instead of *losing* it, was novel. We never saw the film, nor were we ever sure that anyone else did.

Sixteen days later, as part of Das Neue Werk music series in Hamburg, we had another unexpected booking. Many weeks earlier, David and John had been engaged to share a program with the North German Radio Symphony Orchestra, to be conducted by Robert Craft, but while we were still in Brussels John managed to convince the director of Das Neue Werk series that he shouldn't miss the opportunity of presenting Merce's work in conjunction with the duo-piano concert of American music. Although I'd no intention of remaining in Europe for the rest of October, I accepted the change of plan without argument. It seemed that chance was beginning to play as large a role in our lives as it did in the Cage/Cunningham aesthetic. My faith in John, once again restored, was now absolute. Whither he would lead I would follow. Happily. No questions asked.

Between the Brussels and Hamburg performances, Earle and I headed south on a night train, leaving behind Belgium's stubbornly overcast skies. We awoke in Italy and suddenly the heavens were endlessly blue, the sun blinding. We'd crossed the Alps into another world and were embraced by Bruno Maderna and the Berios in magnanimous, expansive, uniquely Italian warmth. Then it was off to the Donaueschingen Musiktage, to hear Boulez's *Poésies pour pouvoir* and another dose of avant-garde music. After traveling for more than two months, I found myself eager to go home—but there was still the performance on the twenty-eighth in Hamburg to get through and prior to that, two days of filming for television—not the slap-dash ten-minute quickie we'd experienced in Brussels, but a deadly-serious variety, the sort Germans are so very good at, with hours of rehearsals consisting of continuous stops and starts, space changes, lighting adjustments, camera angles revised, endless takes and retakes.

On the first day, we did a complete run-through of our solo and duet repertory so that the television producer could select the pieces he thought most suitable for filming. For much of the day I was able to sit on the side-lines and watch the filming of Merce's solo *Changeling*. At least fifteen men—directors, technicians, stagehands—rushed around plotting and scheming, shouting, continually requesting that Merce do the dance again. And again. And still again. I kept waiting for Merce to explode with exas-peration. But he fooled me. "It's just like a Mack Sennett comedy," he laughed. He was having the time of his life. The wild mayhem surging around him never disturbed his concentration. He danced—*each time*—like a devil possessed, full-out, never stinting, always giving a total perfor-mance whether it was the first or the fifteenth time through. While the dressers and makeup ladies hovered around him, fussed over him, mopped away his sweat, reapplied powder, wrapped him in shawls to make sure he kept warm between takes, Merce merely beamed. It was an aspect of his personality I'd never seen before.

The following day, it was my turn. As luck would have it, my period had arrived, in force. The curse of every healthy female dancer, particularly those who have to appear onstage in skintight leotards, body stockings, or unitards, is the specter of some ghastly bloody accident onstage or even in rehearsal. In Hamburg, the nightmare became an all-too-awful embarrass-ing reality. It was fortunate we had dressers and makeup women to take care of us; I desperately needed mine. In the morning we filmed the duet from *Suite*. My costume: yellow tights and a sleeveless tank-top leotard with the bra and leotard straps needing to be sewn together after I got into them. Between each take I'd dash to the dressing room, get the straps cut apart, dash to the ladies room, dash back to the dressing room to be sewn together again, and dash back onstage. Merce looked puzzled and eventually bemused at my endless succession of exits and entrances. He must have finally fathomed my dilemma, although no words were exchanged on the subject. The morning passed without mishap, but at the lunch break I started to hemorrhage and the duet from *Springweather and People,* which we filmed in the afternoon, had some fairly strenuous acrobatic partnering maneuvers, with a number of upside-down lifts. I wore rubber-lined underpants and prayed, but no one up there was listening; the pants leaked, my costume was stained. When I retreated to the dressing room, tears streaming down my cheeks, mortified, bloodied, my dresser opened her arms, pulled me to her bosom, embraced me tenderly, and murmured over and over again the same two words. She spoke no English; I, no German. But I'm sure she was saying, "Poor child! Poor child!" She repaired my tear-stained cheeks and smudged eyes and cleaned me and my costume as best she could. The torture continued. When finally it was over I knew that the last take would *have* to be the last, no matter what. Neither my costume nor I could have gone through that duet one more time. I longed for bath and bed, but after the filming, until nearly ten p.m., we had to do a full technical rehearsal—spacing and lighting—for the following day's live performance. The television director had agreed to help with the lighting, but halfway through the rehearsal, frustrated by the lack of equipment, he threw a royal tantrum, stalked out of the television studio, and did not return. We plodded on without him. By this time I was dressed in layers of black practice clothes and felt relatively safe from further embarrassing incident. As Merce has quipped over the years, *"Noir reste noir,"* referring to the unwashed practice clothes and grubby wardrobe endemic to long tours of one-night stands, but in this *particular* situation it had a very special significance for me.

The filming and the live performance took place in the same television studio, Studio X, of the Norddeutscher Rundfunk—a great open space with the audience seated above and on three sides of the stage floor. A backdrop had been especially constructed for the dance part of the concert, which was preceded by the Norddeutscher Rundfunk Symphony Orchestra playing Krenek, Schnabel, and Webern under Robert Craft's direction. Our half of the program consisted of *Suite for Two, Galaxy, Changeling,* and the duet from *Springweather and People,* with two musical interludes—Morton Feldman's *Piano Piece '56—For Cynthia* and

Intermission #6. On performance day we were back at the studio at four p.m. to rehearse with the television director, who'd managed to obtain the desired stage-lighting equipment. By intermission, well after nine p.m., when it was almost time for us to go on, Merce and I were exhausted. The performance was anticlimactic, a non-event. Neither terrible nor wonderful. We hadn't danced so close to an audience or in-the-round since Black Mountain, and I was disconcerted by it. I couldn't figure out where or how to focus, and seeing a man actually laughing during my *Suite* solo shook me up a bit. (Oh God, was the bleeding staining my costume again?)

Sweet, simple relief—that is the only emotion I could muster as Merce and I stood side by side, clutching flowers David and John had presented to us onstage at the final bow. Even Merce seemed grateful that it was over. Many of our new European acquaintances were waiting, in the Rundfunk Restaurant-Bar, for a final farewell. I was quite certain I sensed keen disappointment in what they'd just seen. John's Darmstadt lectures and the performances of his, Earle's, Morty's, and Christian's music had led them to expect something far more radical, even though they'd little experience of *any* dance. There was nothing in the work we presented in that duet concert that would shock, nothing *except* the fundamental concept that the dance and music coexist rather than be wed, and for the avant-garde music intelligentsia in Europe, this idea posed no problem.

It was nearly two o'clock in the morning when we said our farewells. We were going our separate ways: Merce to Copenhagen to see the Royal Danish Ballet before flying home; John to Milan to work at the RAI Radiodiffusione Italienne as a guest of directors Luciano Berio and Bruno Maderna; David upon his ever-mysterious errands before returning to America; and I, that very morning, embarking for New York from Bremerhaven on the Swedish-American ocean liner *Gripsholm*. How I looked forward to eight days at sea with nothing to do. The future was veiled in uncertainty, yet I hadn't the smallest desire to tug aside that veil in the hope of catching a glimpse of what might lie ahead. Instead, snuggled under blankets in my deck chair, I daydreamed in slow motion and minute detail back through each of the preceding days. All seventy of them.

n less than two years, the four of us would be back in Europe performing again. In the twenty months between, Merce struggled to maintain a company. It was no easier, despite the earnest efforts of his young new manager, Isabelle Fisher. Not even auspicious personal recognition for him—a second Guggenheim Fellowship and being named the first-ever dancer-in-residence at a university—did much to augment his company's bookings.

It was spring of 1958 when Merce received the invitation to be dancer-in-residence at the University of Illinois at Urbana-Champaign. Margaret Erlanger, head of the university's dance division, was among those rare and stalwart dance visionaries who, in the late fifties, *still* directed dance-as-an-art from within the physical education department. If the University of Illinois could have painters and composers in residence, she thought, why not choreographers? It was a historic first. To fill the post she chose the relatively unknown Merce Cunningham, whom she idolized. He took up residency in December. His responsibilities were flexible, and happily for him, didn't include teaching technique classes to hordes of nonprofessional college students. Instead, he was asked to participate in seminars on choreography, give lecture-demonstrations, mount his *Collage II,* using students and faculty members, and present his own company in two new ballets, collaborations set to newly commissioned scores by two of the university's faculty composers, Ben Johnston and Cho Wen-Chung. There was one problem. John Cage had not been invited, and the conditions of the invitation clearly excluded him. Merce was faced with a dilemma. Since first encouraging Merce to break away from Martha Graham in the mid-forties, John had been Merce's faithful mentor, undying enthusiast, hard-working booking agent and publicist, as well as his most intimate friend. When Merce told me about the Illinois invitation and his quandary over accepting it, he finished by saying something like, "I feel like a pig, but I'm going anyway." His sense of guilt was obvious, but so was the allure of work for his company and a modicum of independence. So, after our summer adventures together (brought about solely through John's efforts), John remained in Europe for four months, accepting an invitation to work in Milan, where he composed *Fontana Mix*. While doing so he also gave solo performances of his *Amores*, *Water Walk*, and *Sounds of Venice* on television and appeared as a mushroom expert on an Italian television quiz show called *Lascia o raddoppia*—and won six thousand dollars by answering all the questions correctly in five appearances. To his amazement, he became a recognizable and greatly loved celebrity; in cafés, restaurants, vegetable markets, and streets of whatever Italian village or city he visited, people greeted the sunny mycologist with undisguised delight. He said they made him feel like a movie star!

Life was not so glamorous for Merce. During his four-month residency at the University of Illinois he commuted between Urbana and New York, staying in New York for a week to ten days to work with us on the new dances, then flying back to the university to fulfill his duties there. In his absence, the responsibility of teaching his classes fell to me. In a letter postmarked December 6, 1958, Merce wrote: "first week gone, i hope more interesting for you than me. this is educational flummox. i should get back late evening of the 18th, and will teach on friday if you are in fit about it. maybe you are enjoying it?"

In a way I was. The most enjoyable part of teaching, I discovered, was making up new combinations. The actual teaching turned out to be sort of fun, but I always dreaded it beforehand and allowed my apprehension to ruin most of the day. Luckily, I was able to hold the dread in abeyance each morning when I studied at the Met with Miss Craske or Mr. Tudor. Their classes continued to nurture and inspire, and to provide a reliable technical home base, but in those days I hadn't the confidence to apply their teaching methods to my own. That came later. To Margaret Craske, in particular, I owe a great debt for the clarity and wisdom of her instruction and for the love and respect she expressed for dancing. My debt to Antony Tudor is more ambiguous. When he died in the spring of 1987 I was totally unprepared to feel such pain and extreme sense of loss. How much I loved that wicked, wonderful, witch-of-a-man! As a teacher, Tudor probed deeply and inevitably found the acute nerve-end of each dancer's being. He demanded raw, undisguised truth in movement, and although Martha Graham has assured us for generations that the body cannot lie, in fact it can. Tudor always spotted the lie and refused to accept it. Merce spotted it, too, but it was not his way to grapple openly with his dancers' psyches, and especially not his students' psyches. Nevertheless, year after year—under some self-inflicted moral imperative—Merce gave much time, thought, and effort to what was, for him, the physically painful, intellectually aggravating, spiritually discouraging process of teaching.

Margaret Erlanger, the dance students, and the university's administration viewed Merce's residency as a success. Merce viewed it as a disaster. The first and continuing problem was the music. Working closely with John and John's colleagues for so many years had in no way prepared Merce for working with two unknown composers whose compositional methods and aesthetic orientations were vastly different and far more conventional. His choreography reflected this by relating more conventionally to the music than was his normal practice.

Ben Johnston's *Gambit for Dancers and Orchestra* was a quasi-jazz score, sort of "Third Stream" à la Gunther Schuller. The music by Chou Wen-Chung, *From the Poems of White Stone,* was for orchestra and a chorus of seventeen. The poems by Chiang Kuei (c. 1155–c. 1221 A.D.) were sung in Chinese, but one reviewer commented that "the inflection was strictly *Italiante.*"[1] Both compositions, entirely different one from the other, were light-years apart from the music we'd grown accustomed to hearing. It was not an unwelcome change for the dancers. The fun was dancing to a live orchestra. The problem was that the student orchestra, unused to playing for dance, struggled in vain to keep their eyes on their scores and the conductor, preferring to watch the activity onstage.

Music problems were never completely solved, although they improved when John arrived a few days before the first performance to lend Merce support and to offer some much-needed (and -sought) choreographic and musical advice. Merce had been floundering, altering the choreography from rehearsal to rehearsal (an uncommon occurrence with him). He appeared unclear about the directions he was taking. In those days he still lacked confidence in his own judgment and seemed to rely on John's input, so there was a communal sigh of relief when John appeared.

By that time, most of the dancers, including Merce, were injured, always a real possibility when working on new material. I was the first to succumb. Just about one week before we had to leave for Illinois, my left ankle and calf muscle, still weak from the 1957 Radio City Music Hall injury, began to trouble me. I'd worked long and hard on the Ben Johnston dance, especially on the duet material and an offbeat solo that was tricky and intriguing and unlike anything Merce had given me before. I practiced it for hours by myself during his long absences. The injury wasn't actually crippling, merely bothersome, but I considered the discomfort suffered worthwhile since Merce actually expressed approval of my efforts, an occurrence extremely rare in my twenty years of working with him. Even rarer was receiving the compliment in written form: "By the way, I never told you, but hearing the music yesterday made me think of it, you've done marvelously with the *Gambit* solo. It looked wonderful."

We were in Urbana from March 7 to 16, days so filled with activity that I never wrote to my parents at all and kept no written record except a note to Earle, hastily written the day before the first performance:

> it's all getting wild, exciting, exhausting
> the pieces are still being choreographed or re-choreographed
> John is a *lamb.*
> it's *great* to rehearse with orchestra—even though it's pretty *awful.*
> They don't watch the score . . . need blinders so they don't watch the
> dances . . . or danc*ers.*
> Merce has bad knee, bad foot, bad wrist—my foot *all* but kills
> *me* . . . being dramatic *of course,* by your standards
> went swimming 3 × Merce uses whirl pool
> *He's a lamb, too. And how they LOVE him*!
> costumes 'til all hours—
> ale, now that John is here.
> floor is utterly hideous—treacherous—terrifying and ghastly. Merce has
> *fallen* several times, I *re*-turned my ankle in some abysmal hole—Judy
> fell, etc., etc.
> wish you could see piece, been "sold out" for weeks they say

"Costumes 'til all hours." Actually, Rauschenberg had designed and dyed the costumes in New York and mailed everything to Merce in Urbana. But the skirts and wreaths for the Chou piece had to be constructed, fitted, and sewn. Bob never saw the dances (in rehearsal or performance), but Merce must have conveyed enough information about them for Bob to create two entirely different sets of costumes: For the jazzy *Gambit* he dyed tights and leotards brilliant colors, somehow harlequinesque, and for the Chinese-influenced *From the Poems of White Stone* he dressed the four women in floor-length skirts (hung from the hips) made of multilayered panels of gray silk, lined in shades of blues and grays, with wreaths of flowers in the hair. The men wore billowing gray silk shirts and gray tights. Merce appeared to be truly delighted with Bob's work, although he greeted the wreaths with one raised eyebrow and a wry smile. He knew we loved them and especially loved dancing in long skirts. For his part, Bob loved finding new ways to foil the ubiquitous uniform of leotard and tights.

While we were rehearsing in Urbana, Bob, in New York, was working on the first of his five *Trophy* combine paintings.[2] *Trophy I* (*for Merce Cunningham*) is the only one of the five that bears the identifiable image of its title: a photograph (by Bob) of Merce appears in the upper right quarter of the 66-by-41-by-2-inch combine. Merce is in a long, low arabesque, his standing leg in *plié* (a signature move in Cunningham's oeuvre). Below the photograph on the right are two rectangular pieces of old rough wooden board, and on the left is a beat-up metal sign bearing the words CAUTION WATCH YOUR STEP. Between the sign and the wood is a narrow, rectangular, gaping hole. In Urbana, Merce failed to heed Bob's prescient warning. On the morning prior to the first performance he slipped and twisted his ankle in a gaping hole on the stage, and this time the injury was serious. "It sent shivers," Bob said when told of the accident. In the *Champaign-Urbana Courier,* this news item appeared:

SPRAINED ANKLE, DANCES ANYWAY
Merce Cunningham danced a full program Saturday and again Sunday night with an anesthetized ankle which had been sprained Saturday morning. It was unnoticeable to his audience, which watched the famed modern dancer perform, apparently in considerable pain.[3]

No one should have been allowed to dance on that treacherous floor, and Merce, justifiably, might have sued the university for his own quite serious injuries as well as for the minor injuries sustained by most of the dancers in his company. The company flew back to New York, leaving Merce to sit out the rest of his residency in the whirlpool. His last letter from Urbana, postmarked March 18, was dour and funny. Excerpts:

...ALL LOOK AT ME WITH SOLICITATIONS FOR MY FOOT. THE "EXCLUSIVE" IN THE PAPER TOUCHED EVERYONE'S HEARTS
ONE FINE OLD LADY AT ANNA'S [Sokolow] CONCERT LOOKED AT ME AND SAID THE PROGRAM WAS BEAUTIFUL, AND THEN HER FACE BECAME A MASS OF PAINFUL FURROWS AS SHE LOOKED DOWN AT MY FOOT AND SAID, IS IT IN TERRIBLE AGONY?
I GO EVERY DAY TO SIT WITH THE FOOTBALL PLAYERS IN THE WHIRLPOOLS AND THEN MEDITATE WITH THE SOUND WAVES.
BOB SENT ALL THE SLIPS, AND THE BUDGET IS BUSTED BUT "IT'S ALL RIGHT" SAYS MARGARET "I'M JUST GOING TO GIVE IT TO THEM, AND THEY CAN JUST TAKE CARE OF IT."
EVERYONE SAID YOU WERE ALL SO BEAUTIFUL, PETER FARRELL SAID YOU LOOKED LIKE SISTERS AND HOW HAD I MAN-

AGED THAT, HARRY PARTCH WANTED TO KNOW WHERE THERE
WERE MEDIEVAL COSTUMES IN A CHINESE PRODUCTION, AND I
SAID IT WAS CHINESE MEDIEVAL, THE IDIOT.
    MARGARET SAYS "IT'S ALL BEEN MORE THAN MY FONDEST
DREAMS" AND SWEEPS OFF TO A MEETING OF THE GRADUATE
COMMITTEE . . .

A week later, the residency completed, Merce returned to New York and
a regular repertory rehearsal schedule was resumed. The many weeks of
work for just two performances soon vanished from memory, along with the
two new dances, which were never mentioned again. What could not van-
ish or be banished was the harm Merce's body had suffered from dancing
while injured. Over the years this abuse continued; its effects were cumulative and Merce paid dearly for it. He has never been easy on himself, but
such "self-sacrifice" for one's art and one's public (and, to be practical, the
company's bank account) is a prime example of the masochism dancers
are famous for: "The Show Must Go On" syndrome, The Gospel according
to Saints Thespis and Terpsichore. I never subscribed to this belief, but in
a company as small as ours it hardly mattered. Merce could be almost as
demanding of his dancers as he was of himself. Only three times in twenty
years did I fail to perform as scheduled. In that same twenty years, and no
doubt the twenty after, he never missed a performance.
    Merce flew home from Illinois on March 25 and scheduled a rehearsal
for the same day. We had less than three weeks to prepare for three repertory performances in Washington, D.C., and Chicago. Marianne Preger-
Simon, now exultantly pregnant and radiantly beautiful, returned to
rehearsals in order to coach Marilyn, and Merce managed to "borrow" Dan
Wagoner, who was dancing in both the Graham and Taylor companies at
the time, to dance *Septet* and *Nocturnes*. Unfortunately, Dan was only
moonlighting and could not be persuaded to stay on with us.
    Washington, D.C.! It sounds like the big time, but our concert was in the
Roosevelt High School Auditorium on the outskirts of downtown Washington. Even so, the *Washington Post* sent critic Jean Beatty, who reported
that the performance "had the astringency of a bite out of a lemon."[4] In
Chicago we danced in a real theater, the Goodman Memorial, were lavishly
wined and dined yet again in that fabulous apartment on the twenty-sixth
floor of Mies van der Rohe's Glass House. We stayed in a huge metropolitan hotel and awoke the following morning to four newspaper reviews,
three of them agreeing that the dancing had been superb.
    New to the company was Judith Dunn, who had joined us for rehearsals

in New York in the late fall of 1958. Unbeknownst to us, another of those mysterious and sudden changes of company personnel had occurred at the end of the Connecticut College summer session: we'd lost Cynthia and gained Judy. Judith Goldsmith Zimmer first caught Merce's eye in a master class at Brandeis University. She studied regularly with him when he taught for the Boston Dance Circle, and she continued her studies at Connecticut College during our first summer there. Robert Dunn, the pianist who had played for the Dance Circle classes, also came to Connecticut, highly recommended by Merce, to play for Cunningham and Graham technique classes, as well as for our *Nocturnes* rehearsals. One day between classes, without warning or fanfare, Judith Goldsmith Zimmer and Robert Dunn, without missing a step or a note, dashed to New London, got married, and dashed back again as Mr. and Mrs. Robert Dunn. The following autumn they moved to New York.

Judy's presence changed the chemistry of the company. An indefatigable worker who came to dance late in her life, she was endowed with an intense intellectual curiosity and a strong appetite for large, expansive, weighted movement. Of all the women who have ever danced with Merce, she alone came close to Merce's own way of moving. But instinct and a natural kinesthetic empathy are only part of the explanation. It had to do with being grounded, connected viscerally to the earth, as opposed to classical ballet's ideal of ethereal weightlessness, being poised for flight or airborne. At one time Merce possessed both gifts. Remembering his electric performance in *Letter to the World* when Martha Graham summoned him onstage with "Dear March, come in!" the *Chicago Daily Tribune* critic Seymour Raven in his 1959 review captioned "Dancer Shuns Random Flight" admitted disappointment that Merce no longer took to the air.[5] By necessity, the emphasis in Merce's dancing had shifted, and Judy's dancing paralleled his. My qualities as a dancer served as a foil to Merce's. So did Viola's, though they were totally different from mine. But with Merce and Judy there was, in my opinion, a kinship no other dancer in his company has ever shared. That kinship was the special gift of rootedness, a gift few female dancers have.

For nearly five years—"the golden years," some of us now call them—Judy, Marilyn, Viola, and I formed the nucleus of Merce's company. (Actually it was Merce who was the nucleus around whom the rest of us orbited.) A new energy and determination and belief rallied our spirits and strengthened morale. The four of us worked well together, although our temperaments were distinctly dissimilar. Many people thought we looked like sisters, but neither facially nor in physical proportion did we actually resemble one another. If we appeared to, I think it was the result of a shared intensity and rhythmic accord honed in hour upon hour of rehearsals where only the snap, clap, slap of Merce's hands beating time and the sound of our own breathing kept us moving as one.

In *Rune,* choreographed at Connecticut College in the summer of 1959, Merce devised extremely difficult unison passages for us. The rhythms were crucial. Sections of short, jagged quick allegro were juxtaposed with long phrases of lentissimo. Sometimes three women danced in unison while a fourth danced a solo or a duet with one of the men, then rejoined the unison group at some exact moment—in endless and endlessly tricky permutations. We worked without music, which was usual, and without mirror, which was not, learning the dance together by breathing as one, sensing one another's phrasing, accents, and dynamics. One had to have eyes in the back of one's head, so to speak, and to develop an acute sense of time. In the beginning, it was maddeningly difficult. Four distinctly different dancers, whose natural affinity for particular movement qualities and phrasing could scarcely have been more diverse, had to be melded into one complementary unit. We had to allow the movement to shape us, not the other way around. This way of working demanded both generosity of spirit and willingness to compromise. As corny as it sounds, by giving up the self we discovered togetherness without the support of music to sustain the rhythm and phrasing.

The structure of *Rune,* like that of *Dime-a-Dance* and *Galaxy,* was not intended to be fixed in a final form. Conceived specifically as an indeterminate work with five five-minute parts whose order was variable and interchangeable from performance to performance, the dance had no set beginning, middle, or end. But Merce never explored the range of possibilities inherent in his original conception and, as I recall, he changed the order only twice in all the years I performed *Rune,* always giving as his reason the difficulties of touring: "It was not possible to do that kind of changing because it takes too many rehearsals and since the dancers, including myself, were often tired, we simply couldn't do it."[6] Was this the real reason? I wonder. Of course the numbers of permutations are mind-boggling, but since there are only five blocks of movement and no transition sections, it would not have been so very difficult to switch the order, even from performance to performance; in fact, only the endings and beginnings of the five parts would require extra rehearsing. It was not our bodies that would have been taxed, just our brains. Years later, we managed far more complicated section switching in *Story, Canfield,* and *Scramble,* and in "Events." I think Merce really *liked* the first order he came up with for *Rune,* and through repetition it simply came to feel right. Chance and Indeterminacy offered tantalizing possibilities, but in the case of *Rune,* Choice and Aesthetic Discrimination won out, by default.

In any case, *Rune*'s interest did not lie solely in its structure. Merce had originally intended to title the dance *Autumn Rune;* it followed sequentially after *Springweather and People* (1955) and *Summerspace* (1958). In 1947, he'd choreographed a four-part ballet called *The Seasons* for Ballet Society, which was performed at the Ziegfeld Theatre by himself, Tanaquil LeClercq, and six other dancers; in 1949, Ballet Society having evolved into New York City Ballet, *The Seasons* was performed again, this time at the City Center. Speaking of that ballet, Merce said: "If time and the seasons are inseparable, it seems to me that time and dancing are hardly less so."[7] Searching for a definition of "rune," one discovers such words and phrases as "mystical," "obscure," "a poem or canto," "any of the characters of the runic alphabet," "a magic incantation," "having secret or magical meaning." Certainly the dance felt like a ritual, a ritual of extremes that swung from turbulent, wind-tossed anarchy to silent, near-motionless meditation. I remember a fast, rhythmically intricate solo entrance I had. I always revved myself up for it by visualizing being shot out of a cannon. The dance needed that kind of energy as well as the ability to float in somber stillness. But when I saw a revival of *Rune* some years after I'd left the company, the dance was unrecognizable to me. The whole work was homogenized into a thin, bland ersatz mayonnaise. The rhythms were gone, along with the jagged edges, the explosive energy, the eerie somnambulant quiet. In vain I looked for some expression of the white-heat passion and the cool meditative containment—the wild swings of physical and emotional states of being—that *Rune* had always induced in me. Could this have been the same *Rune* about which Bob Rauschenberg said, after seeing a complete stage rehearsal at Connecticut College's Palmer Auditorium in 1959, "You-all dance like a bunch of minks in heat!" And then he ran out and bought bits of tatty mink to trim the necklines of our brown-toned leotards. The mink on the women's costumes lasted only through the dress rehearsal, when the fur flew. Literally. Sneezing and sputtering, Merce nixed it for good. Jasper Johns had beautifully dyed the tights and leotards, melding chestnut and ginger, cocoa and walnut browns, and Nick Cernovich, in one of his most astonishing lighting designs, bathed the stage in glowing, undulating bronze and gold. The dance was greeted enthusiastically by the college community. Even bravos and cheers, although *Antic Meet* garnered more curtain calls (nine, according to my mother). Years later, reading her 1959 diary, I discovered that she'd been completely won over by *Rune.*

The new piece is *terrific*! The dancing, the groupings—even the odd music of Christian Wolff's. It seemed to fit the work perfectly. The costumes were tan and brown leotards and tights and though they don't sound like anything, were really quite stunning. . . . The whole group was exciting and Merce's solo—no music at all except the rhythm of his *deep* breathing—was *thrilling*! It was really excitingly beautiful. I'd love to see it again and again. The audience loved it too.

The critics welcomed *Rune* with varying degrees of interest but were unanimous in their praise of the dancing and their dislike of Christian Wolff's music. Only Doris Hering, among all the reviewers, seemed to grasp the essential nature of the work.

Rune transcends. It has a stillness and an agitation, a flow and violence that seem to emanate from some secret, non-revealing source. It is the very essence of drama without one stroke of dramatic action. And as in Oriental dance, its rhythmic structure is subjective, rather than metric. The most exciting moment of the entire dance was a heroic statement for Mr. Cunningham. With scooping reaches and sure extensions and quick sorties into the air, it synthesized his "playful animal" style of a decade ago with a new, more noble dimension. Our only regret was that the *pointilliste* score of Christian Wolff so sparsely sustained the pulse and breadth of the solo.[8]

If a performer can judge accurately from within, *Rune* felt like a masterpiece. Big. Important. A major statement. And yes, noble. Not only Merce's dancing, but the whole work. But the making, teaching, and rehearsing of *Rune* were arduous tasks, and throughout the process Merce seemed to have no awareness of the importance of the dance he was creating. In fact, throughout that second summer at Connecticut College he was depressed. One afternoon, arriving early at a rehearsal, I found him alone, standing at a window, staring into the distance. He was gloom incarnate. I hesitated to disturb him. "Are you okay?" I ventured. Caught off-guard he responded, "If this is success," and he made a sweeping gesture which seemed to include his place in the dance world as well as the Connecticut College Summer School and the American Dance Festival, "then success *is* dust."

Eclipsing all was Merce's fierce need to perform, a need that was not being satisfied. At forty he could feel the crucial years of his peak physical energy and ability slipping away. Six years and twenty-two dances after the birth of his own company at Black Mountain, Merce could still only hope for the odd performance, scheduled helter-skelter throughout any given

year. In 1959 we gave a total of nine performances, three of those on programs shared with other companies. At Connecticut in 1959, José Limón's
company gave two full programs and one-half of a third, and members of his
company appeared with their own companies in another two concerts. In
one guise or another, Limón company members danced ten of the eighteen
works in the Twelfth American Dance Festival. The Cunningham company
danced only two, *Antic Meet* and *Rune,* on separate programs. In 1958, we'd
danced four. Merce's time onstage had thus been cut in half. Little wonder
he was despondent, bitter about this inequity, and bitter, too, about not
being invited to teach a choreographic workshop or a repertory class where
his ideas could be discussed. In the four years he taught at Connecticut he
was never given this opportunity. At least John Cage was invited to lecture
that second summer and Merce was given one opportunity to air his views
(as well as to perform alone, unencumbered by his company). The lecture-
demonstration was called simply "Talk by a Dancer." I reported to Earle:
"[It] was *very moving* as John predicted. Merce danced magnificently but I
really began to wonder why he bothers with a company. His movement
looks best on him just as Graham's *was* best on her."

One of our class accompanists in 1959 was Frederick Rzewski, a college
friend of Christian Wolff's. Although a brilliant pianist-composer, he was
hopeless as a dance accompanist, as well as being unbelievably arrogant,
overbearing, and intolerant as only a precocious Harvard-trained twenty-
one-year-old can be, but he was also very poor and desperately needed the
job. Scornful of the art he was paid to serve, he would caustically observe
that dancers are stupid because they require rhythmic accompaniment.
Scornful, that is, *until* Merce's lecture-demonstration, when Fred was visibly humbled by the simple eloquence of Merce's words and the virtuosity
of his dancing. Immediately afterward, he turned to me shamefacedly and
muttered, "I feel like a fool." From that moment his attitude toward us
changed radically. Merce, the dancer, could have that kind of effect on
people. He could permanently change their lives.

But nothing changed for Merce. Only days after that performance, I
wrote Earle in rather turgid prose that "Merce is deeply darkly densely
depressed," and I admitted to going th°rough "a pretty ugly few days
myself—hating it all." And to my parents, "I must confess I'm counting
the weeks—a thing I haven't done in *YEARS!*" Merce's moods could be
contagious, but for reasons mostly unrelated to him I, too, was depressed
that summer. In May, my father, at age fifty-seven, learned he had cancer.
Throughout that spring and summer he was undergoing radiation treat-

ments, suffering terribly from side effects, and the solid ground, the sure safe haven my parents had always been for me, was badly shaken.

A sleepy-eyed, soft-spoken work-scholarship student named David Gordon had become part of our social family because he was Valda Setterfield's special chum. He was twenty-three. They had been dancing together in James Waring's company and seemed inseparable. Valda was once again an apprentice with our company, so David joined her at Connecticut and took classes with Merce and Louis Horst. With Louis, he managed to get into a peck of trouble. I'd known David only from seeing him at Greenwich Village parties and concerts—a large, shy, mute bear, standing just outside any circle of conversation taking it all in from under hooded eyelids. I was never sure if he was actually listening or in a trance. I'd also seen him dance a few times in Jimmy Waring's pieces, where he projected a strong stage presence despite a very limited technique. One day David stopped me on the street and began to talk. Nonstop, the words spilled from his mouth in an avalanche of ideas, impressions, reflections, questions. Within seconds I realized this was no sleepy, sloe-eyed, stage-struck kid but an astonishingly articulate, intelligent, and very curious adult. Yet, for years after this encounter, David claimed to be nonverbal, tongue-tied, too reticent to express his ideas and feelings. It got to be something of a joke.

Back in New York after a frustrating summer of too much rehearsal and too little performing, we were faced with more of the same. In fact we hardly rehearsed because there was so much work to do getting settled in the new studio at 61 West Fourteenth Street, on the top floor of the Living Theatre's new headquarters. In October we danced *Suite for Five* on a concert shared with Alwin Nikolais and Anna Sokolow at Douglass College in New Jersey. Our last performance in 1959 was a full program on the minuscule Harkaway Theater stage at Bennett College in Millbrook, where the linoleum gleamed with layer upon layer of non-skid wax that was impossible to turn or slide on in bare feet and, simultaneously, too slippery to stand on in ballet slippers.

So much for 1959—barely seven full performances. Not nearly enough for someone who's said dancing gives you "nothing but that single fleeting moment when you feel alive."[9] Dancing and performing were synonymous for Merce, in those years at least. To feel alive, he had to dance. Unlike the fulfillment that intense rehearsal gave me, rehearsal for Merce was insufficient, incomplete. He needed the sharper flame of a public's gaze to kindle his soul.

Nineteen fifty-nine, for Rauschenberg and Johns, *was* a stellar year: prolific, successful, exciting. Bob sold his first painting to a museum (the Albright-Knox in Buffalo), had a one-man exhibition of his drawings in Rome, and had his work included in ten group shows in cities on both sides of the Atlantic. He began a series of drawings based on the thirty-four cantos of Dante Alighieri's *Inferno* from *The Divine Comedy* and, after numerous modifications over a five-year period, finally completed what is often considered his best-known work,[1] *Monogram,* a freestanding combine painting displaying a stuffed angora goat with a rubber tire around its middle. It was presented in a group show at the Leo Castelli Gallery that April and was eventually purchased by the Moderna Museet in Stockholm. In 1959 Jasper had his first foreign solo exhibitions—in Paris and Milan—and his work was included in group shows in America and Europe. In this same year, a radical change in the imagery and content of Jasper's work took place when he began a new series of paintings using stencils of color names. Color became both subject and object for him. These new works were sensuous explosions of hues that, on first viewing, disguised or hid the intellectual intent of the painter—the investigation of color per se. The interplay of the intentionally mislabeled stenciled names of colors juxtaposed with the vivid visual sensation of other colors (applied to the canvas with brushwork associated with abstract expressionism) created a curious conflict for eye and mind.

Who were these two guys, anyway? Four years earlier they were virtually unknown. The art world was still capable of feeling outrage in 1959, and Bob and Jap (thirty-four and twenty-nine years old, respectively) seemed to have emerged from nowhere, bursting onto the scene and completely upsetting the status quo. How dare each of them have a room all his own at the Museum of Modern Art's *Sixteen Americans* exhibition? The private opening of that show on Monday, December 14 (two days before the official opening), was by far the most exciting event of the year, if not for them, certainly for their friends. We were all there—amazed, beaming with delight, basking in their reflected glory. Our social life seemed to accelerate in direct measure to their success. There were more dinners out in uptown restaurants—a favorite was Billy's, where the theater and movie crowd (including Arthur Miller and Marilyn Monroe) often went. Another favorite was Japanese—Jasper had developed a fondness for sushi when in the army in Sendai, Japan. Thanks to Bob and Jap's insistence on sharing the fruits of their success, life became a bit more glamorous. In any case, most of us weren't quite so poor as we had once been. Merce had the Guggenheim money—for as long as he could make it last. John had returned home from Italy with his six thousand dollars of Italian quiz-show booty, and he began to teach courses at the New School for Social Research: Mushroom Identification, The Music of Virgil Thomson, and Experimental Composition. Earle worked regularly for Capitol Records, earning sufficient money to support us both; my occasional modeling and teaching jobs paid for my ballet classes and dance clothes. Remy kept turning out award-winning children's books and book-jacket art, and Nick now ran Orientalia, the Eastern-cultures bookstore on Twelfth Street.

While both Bob and Jap were shaking up the uptown art world, an underground avant-garde, bearing the distinct imprint of John Cage's influence, was materializing downtown. Students from his earlier New School classes (1956–58) included filmmakers, poets, musicians, painters, and sculptors (among them Allan Kaprow, Jackson Mac Low, George Brecht, Al Hansen, and Dick Higgins, along with George Segal, Larry Poons, and Jim Dine, who sometimes audited the classes) who were exploring mixed-media three-dimensional environments, some with live action. In the fall of 1959 Kaprow presented his *18 Happenings in Six Parts* at the Reuben Gallery, and the word "happening" was appropriated to define a new art form. Kaprow himself credits Cage's influence and cites the Black Mountain event in 1952 as the prototype of the happening. John was more disappointed than displeased with Kaprow's *18 Happenings*, finding it too pedantic, with its many rules for the performers and endless directions for the audience. There was little pleasure to be had on any level and a nagging resentment at being told when to stay seated, when to move about freely, when not to applaud, when one could and could not leave the building. It was a bit like being in a kindergarten for half-wits. Not even the presence of Bob and Jap, painting on opposite sides of a piece of fabric, could lighten the gloom. The cumulative effect was drier than sawdust in the mouth, and stultifying. A hundred times more engaging and totally without intellectual pretension was Red Grooms's *The*

Burning Building, presented at the Delancey Street Museum (not a museum really, just Red's loft). Edwin Denby, who always knew about the most far-out goings-on in town, insisted we not miss this zany production. It lasted about ten astonishing minutes—a kind of Dada-for-kids, with its slapdash sets and cartoonlike vignettes clumsily acted by non-actors. Although it was unlike their own work in every respect, John and Merce loved it, just as Edwin had predicted they would.

At about this time, another art form—the underground or independent cinema—was beginning to excite much interest, and another zany production, a film called *Pull My Daisy,* was being discussed in all the downtown bars and bistros. Known today as "the key beat film of its generation,"[2] *Pull My Daisy* is a wacky, plotless romp featuring Jack Kerouac, Allen Ginsberg, Gregory Corso, Peter Orlovsky, Larry Rivers, David Amram, Richard Bellamy, Alice Neel, and one professional actress, Delphine Seyrig (far better known for her work in Alain Resnais's *Last Year at Marienbad* two years later)—all friends of the two directors, Alfred Leslie (a painter) and Robert Frank (a photographer), whose loft on Third Avenue was a couple of doors down from Earle's and mine. To celebrate the film's first screenings, Walter Gutman, the man who had helped fund the film and was known to most of us only as "The Angel of Wall Street," threw one of the gaudiest parties of the season—the Grand Ball of the Quarter Moon—at a Puerto Rican social club in the East Village called Club La Bamba.

This was the scene on the eve of the sixties. Making the scene was not a part of my life, since I was addicted to nine hours of sleep and going to ballet class every morning except Sundays; nor was it a part of Merce's, whose life was even more prescribed than mine. In those years John and Bob seemed to love parties, Jap and Viola only to tolerate them. Earle liked them if there was music worth listening to and the bourbon was good, and Merce, David Tudor, Remy, and Nick seemed to enjoy them when the food was interesting or plentiful. For whatever reasons, no one wanted to miss the Wall Street Angel's raucous and joyous Grand Ball of the Quarter Moon—a fitting end to the decade and surely a precursor of the disco scene.

Bob and Jap, keenly aware of the importance of having Merce's new dances seen in New York, employed their personal good fortune in ways more significant than treating their friends to a few glamorous dinners on the town. In 1958, as Impresarios, Inc., with Emile de Antonio, they'd organized and funded the John Cage retrospective at Town Hall. Their next project was to present Merce and company on Broadway at the Alvin Theater for a single performance (all they could afford), with John conducting an orchestra of fourteen first-class musicians. The Alvin didn't work out, but the plan, relocated downtown to the Phoenix Theatre on Second Avenue, did. In February of 1960, I signed my third union contract (the Theatre de Lys season in 1953–54 being the first, Radio City Music Hall the second). My employer this time was listed as Emile de Antonio. The compensation for a single performance was $27.25. No rehearsal pay. Why was it so awesome, the pressure so great, whenever we performed in New York? My heart skipped a beat or two when I merely signed the contract.

A brief tour to Illinois and Missouri preceded the February 16 Phoenix performance, and it gave us a chance to work through our anxieties out of town. We danced the same dances in exactly the same order in each of three cities within seven days and discovered through repetition that we did have the stamina to get through the program—the most arduous of any we'd yet tackled. Knowing this in our heads as well as in our bodies provided a modicum of comfort as we returned to New York to face the Big One. On tour, Merce's original order for the program made supreme physical sense; it also conformed to conventional notions about programming, placing the weightier, more dramatic work in the middle and the funny work at the end.

Summerspace
Intermission
Rune
Intermission
Changeling (Merce's solo)
Five-minute pause
Antic Meet

But then, a simple switch in the order of the dances played total havoc with our energy. John wanted Merce to end the New York City program with *Rune,* the newest and most mature choreography of the four works. Merce very reluctantly agreed, and the pacing we had so carefully established on tour was shot to hell. With *Antic Meet* always coming at the end of the program we were accustomed to giving it every last ounce of throwaway energy we had; so at the Phoenix, even though we knew that *Rune* was still ahead of us, our reflexes took over and we threw ourselves into the crazy shenanigans of *Antic Meet* with the same abandon as always. Without a lot of experience it's very tough to yank the body back together after that kind of no-holds-barred exertion. *Rune* required rigidly defined rhythmic timings and changes of tempi, close-knit unison phrasing, pulled-up legs, "placed" bodies, and highly focused concentration. Before we'd danced a step, most of us were already exhausted, our energy dispersed, and we were unable to muster the control necessary to give *Rune* the kind of dynamic performance we'd managed at its premiere at the American Dance Festival the previous summer.

It was a traumatic performance for other reasons. After the eleven-day tour, six of them spent in the close quarters of our Volkswagen bus, everyone had or was getting a cold. In Viola's case the cold developed into bronchial pneumonia. By February 16 she was acutely ill. At the end of her umbrella solo in *Antic Meet* her legs were cramping so badly she barely made it into the wings. Merce, entering from the opposite side for his soft-shoe number, couldn't help seeing her, on the floor in the wings, unable to walk, tears streaming down her face. Afterward he said that as he went through the motions of his solo his mind was racing: What happened? Will she be able to continue? What will we do if she can't? At the intermission he picked her up in his arms and carried her upstairs to the women's dressing room. The cramps finally subsided and she assured him she could continue. God knows how she got through *Rune,* but she did.

It wasn't a good night for me, either. I was self-observing and self-critical, unbearably tense, unable to feel my extremities or lose myself in the movement. In Carbondale, Illinois, during an afternoon rehearsal, I'd had an attack similar to Viola's—a deep muscle cramp in the calf of the same leg that had been giving me trouble since I'd sprained my ankle at Radio City Music Hall. I was unable to put weight on it without excruciating pain and was paralyzed with fright just thinking about the evening performance. Luckily, the university had a fine sports-medicine facility that treated professional athletes as well as their own students; one of their therapists worked out the cramp with ultrasound, deep heat, and massage. Miraculous! Elated, overcome with gratitude, I said to him, "I wish I could take you with me! Wouldn't you like to join a dance company?" He thought I was propositioning him. Blushing, he replied ever so primly, "Oh, I couldn't do that, I'm married." That night in Carbondale, I sailed through *Summerspace* determined to be relaxed, to stay cool. It felt as if I was just marking it, but the dancers said it was the best performance of *Summerspace* I'd ever given. I wasn't able to recapture the same ease at the Phoenix, alas, but my uptight dilemma there may have had other origins.

Nine days before the concert, I had gotten myself into hot water with Bob and Jap by overreacting to the flyers and newspaper advertisements sent out by Impresarios, Inc. I was incensed by the omission of credits for choreography and musical direction. Although the composers' and dancers' names were listed, Merce's was not even included among the dancers, nor was David Tudor credited as pianist. Even more distressing to me, Robert Rauschenberg was named artistic director. Outraged, I sent Bob the following letter:

> What a shock to read that flyer. I can't explain to you how disturbed I am by the credit line "Artistic Director: Robert Rauschenberg" (and equally disturbed by the omission of the credit lines "Musical Director: John Cage" and "Choreography: Merce Cunningham." The function of an artistic director is the over-all coordination of the component parts of a theatre project—in this case: choreography, music, costumes, decor, lighting (the artistic director of the N.Y.C. Ballet is George Balanchine, of Ballet Theatre, Antony Tudor; perhaps the greatest in all dance history was Diaghilev). If there is an artistic director of the Merce Cunningham Dance Company *other* than Merce Cunningham, that director is unquestionably John Cage. I have worked with Merce and John for eight years. In all that time, John has devoted himself to the Cunningham Company in organizing, fathering, loving and caring for each part of the aesthetic whole as well as for the people involved. John Cage has such power of personality, such strength in his optimism and love for people that each day my admiration and love for him are renewed and increased . . . It is his interest and enthusiasm for your work which brought you to the company to do costumes and sets. To indicate by that credit line that you play the role of artistic director of the M.C. Co. is truly a gross misrepresentation, and I believe, deeply wrong. I am so grateful to you, Jap and De for making this concert happen for all of us. Because I am afraid I will not tell you, and because I feel so strongly that injustice has been done [I must write this letter]. I know that John will be very unhappy if he learns of this letter because he is all for positive action, for "happy endings" as Merce says. There is no reason for an unhappy ending but I am so unhappy about this that I must tell you.

Jasper's response was brief: "Troublemaker," he said to me, without emotion of any kind. I seem to have blocked out Bob's response; I don't even recall if he responded at all. But it became clear to me that neither the omissions nor Bob's assuming the title of artistic director for advertising purposes was either deliberate or insidious—just a slapdash last-minute-before-deadline mix of carelessness and ignorance. When I'd expressed my concern to John, before writing to Bob, he said it was of no consequence and I should forget about it. But I didn't, and upon later reflection I supposed Jasper was right. I shouldn't have meddled. The situation troubled me and for weeks I was ill at ease with Bob and Jap, Merce and John.

No gala party followed the Phoenix performance, just an awful sense of anticlimax. The company members dispersed at the stage door with muted good-byes. The very next evening, I found myself with Merce and John and Merce's parents (who'd totally surprised Merce by flying in from Seattle for the Phoenix performance) at the Majestic Theater watching Robert Preston and Barbara Cook in *The Music Man,* the biggest hit of the 1957–58 season, the show that had stolen all the awards away from the more contemporary and innovative *West Side Story* of Jerome Robbins, Leonard Bernstein, and Stephen Sondheim. No doubt Merce's parents had selected the evening's entertainment. What an abrupt and disorienting contrast in entertainments for them, but nothing compared to what I experienced. After weeks of tunnel-visioned commitment to the Cage/Cunningham aesthetic, dropping in on Meredith Willson's River City, Iowa, in 1912 America, with all its simple, homespun charm, was like waking up on the other side of the world. No wonder middle-American audiences in Carbondale and Macomb, Illinois, were having trouble with Morton Feldman's *Ixion* (for *Summerspace*) and Cage's *Concert for Piano and Orchestra* (for *Antic Meet*) if what they really loved was "Seventy-six Trombones."

Middle America was definitely *not* our audience in New York City. *Time* magazine covered the Phoenix concert, beginning its writeup by quoting a member of the audience: " 'This,' said the young man, 'is the avant-garde of all the arts in one hall.' He was standing in the lobby of Manhattan's off-Broadway Theater, surrounded by an intermission crowd of beards, ponytails and beatniks."[3] Emily Genauer, art critic for the *New York Herald Tribune,* also commented on our audience: "Normally the house at a modern dance performance is largely filled with other dancers and choreographers. Musicians turn up occasionally; artists and museum people rarely. But the Phoenix last Tuesday was jammed with New York's avant-garde painters, sculptors, art dealers, museum directors, all of whom, I had thought, would flock to the gala opening, the same night, of David Smith's exhibitions."[4] And *Newsweek* reported: "As the performance ended at the Phoenix, there were shouts of 'Bravo,' many curtain calls, and much applause. 'This is so advanced,' said a young girl thoughtfully, 'that it hasn't even happened yet.' "[5]

The company had no more work until the summer, but Merce's one-night stand at the Phoenix certainly didn't lack for press coverage.

Reviews and articles appeared in at least seven publications, including the two national weekly magazines, *Time* and *Newsweek; The Village Voice, Dance Magazine, Dance Observer, Dance News,* and both the daily and Sunday editions of the *New York Herald Tribune.* Conspicuously absent once again was a John Martin *New York Times* review, yet he had been there sitting in the fourth row on the aisle. One can't help wondering how he rationalized his unshakable resolve never to write about Merce's work and how he explained this peculiar boycott to his bosses at the *Times,* when both *Newsweek* and *Time* magazines deemed the Phoenix concert newsworthy and the *Times*'s rival newspaper, the *Herald Tribune,* devoted considerable space to it in three separate articles. Walter Terry, summing up his impressions in his Sunday column, called the Phoenix program "an absorbing, disturbing and fascinating event" and called Merce "a difficult artist perhaps, but a genuine one."[6]

On Monday, March 7, about three weeks after the Phoenix concert, John Cage's *Theatre Piece* was given its world premiere at the Circle in the Square Theatre. *Theatre Piece* is an indeterminate work that evolved from *Water Walk,* one of the solo pieces John made for and performed on television when he was appearing as a mushroom expert on the Italian quiz show *Lascia o raddoppia. Water Walk* involved the use of a large number of properties and a single track tape. *Theatre Piece,* as we performed it at Circle in the Square in 1960, had no tape, but it had a veritable junkyard of props and foolishness. "A 3-Ring Circus of Lunacy"[7] headlined the *New York Herald Tribune*'s review. There were eight of us performing: David Tudor, piano; Don Butterfield, tuba; Frank Rehak, trombone; Arline Carmen, contralto; Nicola Cernovich and Richard Nelson, lighting designers; Merce and me. Each of us had been given a part, each different from the others, that consisted of unbound pages with a curious assortment of randomly placed brackets of different lengths marked with large numbers (under which were sometimes small numbers and/or x's)—daunting in their indecipherability. Included with each part was a full page of directions and explanations meant to remedy the incomprehensibility, plus a page of clear plastic on which five different rulers had been marked out. Reading the directions was only slightly less baffling than looking at one's part, and even after a half-dozen readings one or two paragraphs remained opaque, at best. Unable to comprehend the instructions any better nearly three decades later, I queried John about them. He admitted that they were "ambiguous." I would guess that of the eight performers only three of us actually sat down with our parts, and with rulers and cards measured and shuffled, asked the four questions allowed, and honestly tried to realize the piece as John had intended. Our only rehearsal served principally to demonstrate the colossal proportions of our many misunderstandings. If the end result was chaos, it was perhaps not the chaos John had envisioned.

In order to discover what to do, and when and in what order to do it, we were required to choose twenty nouns and/or verbs, write each on a separate card numbered one through twenty, and then apply this gamut to the large numbers written over the brackets of our individual parts. The brackets referred to the time within which an action could be made, and time lengths were determined by using one of the five rulers provided (or any other of our choosing). Arline Carmen and I did our homework as best we could and in performance followed our scores in relation to John's time schedule. David Tudor, who by this time was adept at creating his own parts from far more complicated and even more obscure graphic scores than that for *Theatre Piece*, did the same. As for the others, well . . . I'm not so sure. Once again John had offered "freedoms" to the performers and in return had gotten "license."

"The audience, far from puzzled or outraged, was nearly hysterical,"[8] and their response to our tomfoolery seemed to encourage the performers to chuck their scores and play it for laughs. Not everyone found it amusing, as composer-critic Eric Salzman, in his caustic and witheringly nasty review for the *New York Times*, made abundantly clear: "Oh, it was just jolly, this *gesamtkunstwerk* of Mr. Cage was. One couldn't begin to describe all the fun that went on. It was as big as all life itself; and just about anything that happens in life might have happened last night (well, almost anything). Only trouble is real life is bigger and better (or smaller and worse) and it isn't easy to play God and make life all over again in a poor little 'Theater Piece.' "[9]

An "anarchistic situation" was how John described his *Theatre Piece* to a *Time* magazine interviewer.[10] Although John professed to believe in the abolition of government and governmental restraint as the indispensable condition of political, social, and artistic liberty, the byproducts of anarchy made him extremely uncomfortable. He was deeply offended by and opposed to violence, blanched at the mere thought of physical pain, and was unbelievably tenderhearted and sentimental. Furthermore, he remained extraordinarily naive and idealistic in his expectation that, given freedom, man will behave nobly. Doomed to disappointment when performers did not perform his works in the spirit in which they were composed—i.e., seriously—John time and time again found himself caught in a philosophical quandary of his own making. I suppose it had to do with intent, with attitude. When John gargled onstage with a microphone attached to his throat he was not clowning, although I confess I often thought he was sermonizing rather than music-making—that is, he was giving a lecture-demonstration: "Wake up to the very life we're living, which is so excellent once one gets one's mind and one's desires out of its way and lets it act of its own accord."[11] Cage's indeterminate works need performers who are true believers or, at the very least, supremely well disciplined. With the exception of David Tudor, they rarely had them while John was alive.

Writing to my parents the day after the world premiere of *Theatre Piece*, I gave the following report, primarily of my own activities, since I was too preoccupied following my own score to see much of what the other seven participants were doing.[12]

We did the *Theatre Piece* last night. I enclose a really nasty review. It was fun to do although I didn't want to do it right up until the last moment. It took such a *long* time to make my part. There was no room to dance. I did a few "steps" here and there but mostly it was a big crazy romp. . . . Earle said Merce was marvelous—a real clown. He said I was pretty good but felt I should have clowned more. I played it fairly straight . . . The stage was filled with *stuff*! Piano, drums, tubas, [a] huge bucket of water, phonograph, a huge table covered with props, a swing (for me), a small table of props. Such litter and junk you can't imagine. John "conducted"—clock style. I did all kinds of crazy things: opened a magnum of champagne and poured a glass and gave it to a man in the audience (who was scared to take it for a minute); played a Basie jazz record and "improvised" jazz; put a clothes line of leotard, tights, toe shoes, leg warmers into the piano and played my piece *Isis* (the only piece I still remembered from childhood piano lessons) with great *bravura;* opened an umbrella filled with confetti over the trombone player; waltzed around giving away tiny *real* yellow roses; jumped rope with musical jump rope; read lines from Dostoevsky; put the huge bell of the tuba on my head and turned around slowly (that got huge applause! it was the tuba player's idea, and what a good one!) wore a wild mask (of Remy's) and played flute; put on a huge red button which said SAM on it [our cat's name]; sat on a swing and "swang" (haha) and then cut it down, etc., etc., etc. I did some *grand battements*, a *glissade* or two, some waltzing, some falls, an improvised jazz dance, some *frappé* and *battement degagé*, some turns, a lot of running and skipping about. That's about the extent of my dancing. Merce did a lovely noisy tap dance and walked on his toes in wooden shoes, and did some cartwheels—and that's about all the dancing he did! ["David Tudor especially recalls Cunningham slapping a dead fish on the open strings (of the piano) as a very memorable event."[13]] A lovely blonde singer dressed in a deep turquoise satin dress sang. David ran in and out and under and thru the piano, made tea, put on phonograph records, etc. The tuba player played guitar, several tubas, changed from dress suit to informal clothes, drank Jack Daniels whiskey, etc.

Do you have the picture, yet? Wait—meanwhile Nick and two or three "helpers" ran around painting people (putting material on them and painting them) and lighting matches, burning things . . . *Unfortunately.* He was in the piece to produce wild lighting and then he gave that up and joined the activities on stage. So there were no lighting effects at all. John was very disappointed with what Nick did. Everyone else did his own part and Nick had people to help him do his. John didn't like *that* either. Although poor John is committed by his philosophy to accept everything. Poor man.

After the performance John told me he especially liked my little jazz improvisation and asked me why I hadn't done more of it. "It only came up once, for only that length of time," I replied, mildly astonished that he seemed to be suggesting that I could or should have ignored my part (which I had diligently labored over to make it precisely according to his directions, or at least as precisely as my comprehension of them would allow). Six months later and a bit tipsy from champagne, John told me he would never ask Merce or me or Nick (or any of the musicians who had taken part in the premiere) to do the *Theatre Piece* again because, he said, we had all done it "improperly." All but David Tudor, that is; only he and David do it "right." I knew I had tried to do it "properly" (and what a time-consuming, tedious job it had been—not the performing of it, which turned out to be sort of fun, but the hours of worker-bee drudgery paperwork prior to the performance), so I was surprised that if John truly felt that way he still continued to make pieces "indeterminate with respect to their performance," abdicating all aesthetic judgment and control, if, in the end, he was unable to accept the consequences. "Right?" "Wrong?" This from the man who wrote: "There is no need to cautiously proceed in dualistic terms of success and failure or the beautiful and the ugly or good and evil but rather to walk on 'not wondering' to quote Meister Eckhart, 'am I right or doing something wrong.' "[14]

David Tudor could do no wrong; John's admiration for the man seemed limitless. And it was well warranted. John owed David a great deal in those years. David was almost the only person besides John himself who performed John's piano music. By 1960, David had come into his own, acclaimed (well-nigh revered) abroad for his performances of *the* most avant-garde music being written (much of it expressly for him). He had a power shared by no other living musician, because he was usually the first person to see the scores of the very newest piano pieces being created both in Europe and America, and he, alone, could see the *whole* picture of avant-garde music *as it was evolving.* For an avant-garde composer to find out what other composers were doing, he had to talk to David Tudor and attend his concerts.

A six-page article about David, written by Harold Schonberg, chief music critic of the *New York Times,* appeared in the June 1960 issue of *Harper's* magazine. In it Schonberg called David "the world's outstanding piano specialist in music so arcane and rarefied that it leaves all other contemporary manifestations far behind," and described him as "the unsurpassed keyboard executant of new music . . . in constant demand on two continents."[15] It was true, and yet David continued to be available to play for the Cunningham Dance Company for over forty years until a stroke curtailed all his activities shortly before his death in 1996. Despite the many options open to him, David remained absolute in his loyalty to Merce. A remarkable tribute.

Nineteen sixty. The beginning of a new decade. John's *Theatre Piece* was only one of dozens of mixed-media events—"Happenings," "environments," "installations"—that shot up in full bloom in a half-dozen downtown lofts and galleries. Like tough, gaudy wildflowers pushing their way through cracks in city concrete, they burst forth in shocking profusion, startling everyone who saw them. It was a race to keep up. We ran from the Reuben Gallery to the Judson Memorial Church, to the Living Theatre, to Pratt Institute. For me, the truly brilliant stars of the Happening circuit were Claes Oldenburg and Robert Whitman—both artists whose sense of visual theater was electrifying. Little of their Happenings could be traced to Cage's influence. Indeterminacy and rules of chance played no part in their schemata. Eastern philosophies did not govern their thinking. Oldenburg's world was manifestly human—robust, vigorous, cluttered; sometimes riotously funny, sometimes macabre or touchingly pathetic; often absurd, always surprising. The visual element was predominant: one's eyes were assaulted with objects, things, junk in comic disarray. In Whitman's work the visual element also predominated, but the world he conjured up was one of mystery and magic, exquisitely precise and technically astonishing. He created erotic, scatological, philosophical visions that were spellbinding for their pristine beauty and disturbing implications. Bob Rauschenberg was enthralled by the hands-on, untidy, and unpredictable aspects of theatrical enterprises; in the early stage of the Happening phenomenon he managed to straddle the downtown and uptown art scenes, participating in both but not quite belonging to either. Jasper Johns kept a cool distance and was rarely tempted to dabble in such goings-on.

With the publication of Robert Lebel's study of Marcel Duchamp in the fall of 1959, followed by the publication of Duchamp's *Green Box* in book form in 1960, a legendary figure reemerged as a potent influence on young American artists. Duchamp had long been a hero for John Cage, who had met him years earlier when John and his wife, Xenia, first arrived in New York in 1942 and were staying temporarily with Peggy Guggenheim and Max Ernst. Bob and Jasper didn't meet Duchamp until 1959, *after* critics began to label them "neo-Dadaists" and *before* they knew very much about Dada or Surrealism.

When Earle and I arrived in New York, Earle already knew of Duchamp from books and esoteric periodicals, and I, from an art history course taken at Wheaton College. In the spring of 1953 we saw Duchamp's work firsthand for the first time at the Sidney Janus Gallery in the International Dada Exhibition, a wonderfully eclectic show that had been assembled, catalogued, and installed under Duchamp's direction. The installation reminded me of a fun-house labyrinth. The catalogue—if one can so name a single large piece of tissue paper crushed into a wad, with copies to be found heaped in a wastebasket at the entrance of the show—was, according to Duchamp, "a Dada gesture to cancel the seriousness of exhibition catalogs."[16] In order to read the thing, one had to open it ever so gingerly, and ever so gently smooth out the millions of wrinkles. It was an instant collector's item. One day, while Earle was in Europe, I made the unforgivable mistake of wallpapering the hall with a number of art-gallery announcements, including the Duchamp collector's item. It nearly destroyed our marriage!

If one insists upon putting one's heroes on pedestals, it's probably best never to meet them. Legends, in the flesh, are all too often disillusioning. Yet, if this is the rule, Marcel was its exception. Meeting Duchamp actually enhanced his aura. Here was an artist whose reputation had attained mythical proportions and whose real-life presence did nothing to dispel that impression. Duchamp and his wife, Teeny, were the guests of honor at a small dinner party given by Jules (a lawyer) and Betty (a sculptor) Isaacs to which Virgil Thomson, John, Merce, Earle, and I were invited. It was just two nights before the performance of John's *Theatre Piece*, which they all attended. Arriving at about 7:30, we found Duchamp sitting in a corner of the small living room by a window overlooking University Place; there he remained—serene, utterly at ease, seldom speaking although in no way aloof—until nearly three o'clock in the morning. His participation in the evening's social intercourse took the form of a twinkle in his eye and a barely perceptible hint of a smile, and yet his presence charged the room. Virgil Thomson did all the talking and monopolized all the attention— albeit with wit and much brilliance. But for those of us who kept hoping to hear Duchamp's views on any of the subjects upon which Virgil held forth so loquaciously, it was a frustrating evening. We discovered at subsequent social gatherings that Duchamp usually seemed content to let others do the talking. In his own apartment on Tenth Street the buzz and chatter of his guests' conversation would swirl and eddy around him, but even there, on his own stage, he maintained the role of observer, ever tolerant; slightly, but only slightly, amused. He once expressed the notion that "words are absolutely a pest as far as getting anywhere. You cannot express anything through words, because language is an imperfect form of communication."[17] All of us have experienced this feeling—vexation at the inadequacy of language—but forced by social necessities, we all give in to it; we play the game, we chatter away. Duchamp didn't.

Merce is a loving sweet-natured sweetie pie these days," I wrote to Earle at the beginning of our third summer at Connecticut College. Was it the weather? For the first three weeks, New London's normally humid, sweltering clime had put on a terrific imitation of sunny, clear, dry Colorado. Or was it that he'd been successful in negotiating more visibility for the company in the festival; or that his classes were being received with overwhelming enthusiasm? Or could it have been Jeannette Schlottman, in her second year as director of the summer school and festival? Previously Merce had been an outsider, but with Jeannette—a lovely, gracious woman—he connected; they could talk, she could empathize. She'd won everyone's affection and respect by fairly and generously administering to the genuine needs and temperamental whims of her exotic menagerie of choreographers, teachers, dancers, musicians, and students.

I was on cloud nine: happy to be out of the city; delighted to be living once again in a spacious, light-filled room looking out on the River Thames; pleased to be hired as a bona fide member of the faculty; thrilled anticipating returning to Europe to perform with Merce, John, and David immediately following the festival; and elated to be working on two solos, newly choreographed for me by Merce especially for the European tour. All these wonders, plus Merce's good spirits, set my spirits soaring.

Even teaching was enjoyable. The awful pre-class panic dissipated, partly because the classes were only an hour, and over with so early in the morning that there was no time to worry about them, and partly because I'd had more practice teaching for Merce in New York and Boston, as well as completing a three-week stint, giving two classes a day, while Merce taught at the University of Colorado. Appreciative students helped. So did the studio space in Crozier-Williams, a huge new facility that boasted several vast gymnasiums, a swimming pool, a cafeteria, and two real dance studios. East Studio, where I usually taught, was enormous, with wall-to-

wall mirrors and a wide expanse of windows—which opened!—letting in
fresh air and looking out on evergreens reaching to the sky.

A record-breaking student enrollment in 1960 required the making of
three levels of classes in Cunningham, Graham, and Limón techniques.
Except for the advanced level, Merce's classes were immense—around
seventy in the beginning level, sixty in the intermediate. Merce taught all
three levels on a rotating schedule. I taught either the intermediate or
beginning class, only rarely the advanced, and Viola assisted for the first
time that summer. Merce's students were volubly ecstatic, and so were the
members of his company, prompting me to write Earle: "Merce is teaching
like crazy—wild-great-glorious-inspired-maybe divine. And difficult.
People give him standing ovations after class and splutter deliriously:
'genius,' etc."

With one exception, the company personnel was the same as it had been
the previous summer: Remy Charlip, Judith Dunn, Viola Farber, Marilyn
Wood, and I were the regulars; Valda Setterfield joined us again as an
apprentice. New was Jack Moore, the first winner of the newly established
Doris Humphrey Fellowship in Choreography that summer and the partner
with whom I'd auditioned for Robbins's *Ballets USA*.

This year, Merce was given the opportunity to present four works from
his repertory—he chose *Nightwandering, Septet, Suite for Five,* and
Rune—plus a new work, *Crises*, commissioned by the festival.[1] The company was to appear on four of the five festival programs, the fifth being
devoted entirely to an evening by the Limón company. In the beginning
Merce took rehearsals at an unusually leisurely pace. *Septet* and *Suite*, old
friends by now, fell quickly into shape. *Rune* was not quite so tractable
because Merce completely changed the order of its five parts, but after the
first few disorienting rehearsals we had little problem coping with the new
continuity. Still, the dance, in no matter what order we did it, always
needed hours and hours of painstaking rehearsal. I confess *Rune* never felt
quite right in any order other than the first one. The dance lost its inner,
emotional structure, the one *I'd* invested in it. I've always suspected that
Merce felt this, too.

The greatest luxury for me in the first two weeks was having time to
work alone, and with Merce, on the new solos. On Thursday, July 14, a
rainstorm equal to a Colorado cloudburst deluged the campus. Power out-
ages everywhere. No afternoon rehearsal. Rain fell continuously all day.
After dinner, Merce and I met in our usual rehearsal studio in Holms, the
little music building off campus. We were alone, and except for the glimmering of just one candle, in the dark. Neither one of us could quite see

the other, but the solo I rehearsed with him that rainy night came eerily alive for the first time—in the stillness, in the darkness, by the light of that single candle.

The easy pace, the frequent outings to the beach, the rosy ambience— we knew they couldn't last forever, and by the end of the third week my letters made it clear that the pressure was on:

Wednesday, July 27
     He's having trouble with the new work. Not very far along yet . . . I think Merce hates that Nancarrow music. At least it is giving him a difficult time. Viola and I think he's making a witches' dance. It is all quite sinister, wild and strange. Once Viola said to Merce she'd like to be a witch in a dance. So who knows? Maybe he is granting a wish (witch).

Monday night, August 1
     Merce is in decline at last. I suspected his marvelous disposition couldn't last forever. He seems very, very sad, despondent, lonely—utterly miserable in fact. He is so alone—with no one to talk to. Pearl Lang has her husband; José, his wife. Etc. Merce has no one—no friends and although I try to be helpful, something, someone more is needed.

It was common practice for Merce to call us for rehearsals separately or in twos or threes when he began work on a new dance. With few exceptions he used the full company in every dance he made, but at least three weeks went by without Remy's participation. Then, quite by chance, Remy caught a glimpse of Merce's program copy for the festival lying on Jeannette's desk. It was thus that he learned that he would not be in *Crises*. He was hurt, naturally, to be excluded. And angry because Merce had not told him, face-to-face. Accustomed to Merce's secrecy, especially while he was in the throes of making a new dance, we rarely asked questions about work-in-progress. We all believed Merce had every right to make a dance with any combination of dancers he might choose and was under no obligation to use all of us in every dance, but all of us thought it was unfeeling to let Remy discover that *Crises* was a dance for Merce and the four women by reading the program copy!

Remy deserved far better. Other male dancers had come and gone, rarely staying for more than a year or two, often just pinch-hitting for a single tour or a Connecticut College summer season, but Remy remained the stalwart, loyal to Merce unequivocally, willing to work on the company's behalf unconditionally. He designed costumes, props, flyers, programs; he wrote publicity releases, addressed flyers, ran errands, and I've little doubt he would have stolen the moon for Merce had Merce merely hinted he'd like to have it. No company member served him with such devotion. Every woman in the company adored Remy. Fun and funny, affectionate and caring, Remy was there whenever any one of us suffered the blues or the blahs, to massage the aches, reinforce self-worth, and make laughter out of tears. He was my dearest and closest friend in the company. Viola, Judy, Marilyn, and Valda, at one time or another, might all have said the same. In the bleakest moments he could turn on the sunshine and make one feel like a princess. His unhappiness couldn't help distressing us all. It was the one dark cloud in an otherwise cloudless, sky-blue summer.

Was *Crises* really Viola's witches' dance? Would Merce make a witches' dance? Not likely, and yet . . . Absurd as it now seems, we never dared to ask him. But then, we didn't need to ask. We'd decided it for ourselves. Years afterward, in print, Merce called *Crises* "an adventure in togetherness."[2] More and more, as he continued to choreograph using chance procedures, he set himself movement problems that could be solved by listing a gamut of possibilities and tossing coins to determine what, when, where, how many, how fast, etc. In *Crises,* the problem to be solved was "togetherness" in a very literal sense. Specifically, the dance was concerned with various means of physical contact between dancers: holding and being held, as well as having contact by what Merce called "outside means"—in this case, being attached to another dancer by means of elastic bands around a wrist, an arm, a waist, or a leg. In his words, "Where these contacts came in the continuity, or where they were broken was left to chance in the composition and not to personal psychological or physical pressure."[3] And yet the dance was fraught with erotic tension from the moment the curtain opened.

At stage right, Viola faced the audience, balancing on one leg as she rippled her arms, torso, and extended leg in curiously arhythmic and spasmodic undulations. Upstage left, Merce faced her in parallel position, with his hands at the side of his head, fingers forming horns of sorts, as he twitched, jerked, and writhed. What was this image? Pan? Faunus? Was Viola the tantalizing temptress, the alluring nymph? I'll state once again, as I intend to do throughout this book, that the meaning of and in Merce's dances was never merely the steps, and that even if he and John Cage intended them to be (and I am convinced Merce did not), it's impossible for human bodies placed together in time and space not to reek with secret and not-so-secret meaning, be it spiritual, psychological, sociological, physical, chemical, emotional—whatever. Yes, it's there for each member of the audience to discover for him/herself, and yes, of course, the meaning *is* in the dancing, but dancing can never be merely the sum and substance of mechanically executed steps. The interconnectedness of mind/body/ spirit belies this.

In Merce's notes for *Crises,* he tells us that the gamut of movements for each dancer was individualized to a great degree, and in particular that "one of the special characteristics of this dance was due to Viola Farber [whose] body so often had the look of one part being in balance and the rest extremely off." Merce described it as "Now and again like two persons, another just ahead or behind the first. This coupled with an acute rhythmic sense."[4] Viola's qualities as a dancer were extraordinary, and inimitable. I know this from my own very unsatisfactory attempt to dance her opening *Crises* duet with Merce on a tour when she was ill, a slightly schizophrenic experience for me since I had to dance my own part as well. I could do her steps but not her *part;* the aura and ambience she created were missing, and the steps as translated through my body read entirely differently. The movement was made for her body, her idiosyncratic way of moving. This was true to some extent of all our parts in *Crises.*

For me, *Crises* was a kind of breakthrough. When Merce demonstrated my entrance, which followed that brilliant and erotic duet for Viola and himself, he showed it to me so quickly that my impression of it was only of his tremendous vitality, speed, and wildness. I think he purposely blurred the actual steps, forcing me into a way of moving beyond my experience at that time. My usual inclination had always been to want to know precisely what Merce wanted me to do, but on this particular occasion, I didn't want to know the steps—I wanted desperately to be the wildness.[5] "The dance is full of violence," Merce wrote in his notes. "How this came about . . . I don't remember, except if you have to bend and turn, attached or not to someone, and they are turning differently from you and at a greater or lesser speed, some kind of violence might occur."[6] But I think the sense of violence emanated directly from him—in the frenzied manner in which he demonstrated the movement material he'd created for each one of us, in the ferocious way he attacked the strange chance couplings, even without the intimidating elastic bands! His fervor was passed on to us tangibly, as if by blood transfusion. We four women, from the very beginning of the teaching process, absorbed *his* passion into *our* steps. We were convinced that *Crises* was unlike anything he had done for us before and that its vocabulary was just a wee bit closer to the wonderfully eccentric stuff he often gave himself to do in his solos, which I, at least, had always secretly coveted.

The wildness extended even to the way we wore our hair. Our customary hairstyle for performance was a modern-dance version of the classic ballet style—with our long hair pulled tightly up and back from the face, wound into a bun, secured with a net, and hairpinned to the backs of our heads. From the beginning Merce had indicated his preference for this modified rendition of one of Martha Graham's famous hairdos, chosen more, I think, for practical reasons than aesthetic ones, although he did want to get away from the free-flowing tresses and ponytail stereotypes associated with interpretative dance, and that curious brand of early modern dance found in the colleges in the fifties. He'd opted for a confined, sleek, impersonal hairstyle, and with rare exceptions (*Banjo, Collage II*) that is how we had always worn it. Actually, I wore mine in this manner from morning till night until one day shortly before the previous Christmas, when I inadvertently caught a glimpse of a prim-looking, proper lady's-maid-of-a-girl reflected in a subway-car window and realized to my dismay that it was me. After a similar reflection of that dismal-looking creature appeared in a Woolworth's window some days later, I went sneaking off to Antoine's, a fancy beauty salon that a ballet dancer at the Met had told me about. How daring I felt—like Audrey Hepburn in *Roman Holiday*! And scared, too: scared that chopping off my hair to shoulder length would meet with Merce's disapproval, verbally unexpressed, of course. And I was a bit superstitious, too. Maybe, just maybe, chopping off my nearly waist-length dancer's hair would actually make me less of a dancer. But feeling my hair bob and bounce and blow in the wind as I walked down Fifth Avenue was absolutely exhilarating. I was a new person—liberated, walking on air. Remy said I looked like the 1940s. David Gordon greeted me with, "Well, if it isn't Suzy Parker!" Being likened to the top model of the day was delicious . . . I'd done in that prim little lady's maid! (Thus did I deceive myself.)

I was the only one with short hair that summer (1960), but all the women in *Crises* wore their hair loose, held away from the face by an elastic ribbon tied around the head. Curious what a difference it made—my hair moving naturally in response to the way my body moved. I felt unshackled, reckless—the way Merce danced when he demonstrated the steps in *Crises*. Why was it that a dance that we felt, indeed *knew*, to be dramatically different from Merce's previous company works, and that stirred in us powerful emotional responses as we danced it, was *not* perceived as such by the dance critics?

Were we deluding ourselves? Jill Johnston, in one of her very first dance reviews for *The Village Voice*, described *Crises* somewhat as we felt it: "Probably the most personal dance for his group [M.C.] has yet made. The contacts, especially those between Mr. Cunningham and each girl, are direct involvements—they seem bruising, frustrated contacts—but many things 'happen,' in the lift of an arm, an expression, a sudden fall, an excruciating stillness, which implies much more than a simple defined emotion."[7]

The general audience response was outright laughter plus much ill-suppressed giggling. We were unnerved. Was the laughter derisive or did people really think the dance was funny? Or was it laughter born of discomfort? One shocked woman, apparently caught up in the drama of the dance, was overheard to murmur to her companion during Viola's and Merce's opening duet, "If I were that girl's mother I would have her taken off that stage and never let her dance again!" Our fans and friends found nothing laughable about *Crises*—on the contrary, they considered the dance "disquieting," even "nightmarish." In her *Dance News* review of the first performance, P. W. Manchester observed: "*Crises* aroused a good deal of laughter but may not have been meant to be funny—the penalty which must be paid for working in so highly individual . . . a style."[8]

Conlon Nancarrow's raucous music—player pianos jangling as though a hundred barroom doors had been thrown open to the wind, to paraphrase Doris Hering's review in *Dance Magazine*[9]—blasting forth from the auditorium's loudspeakers pinned the audience to their seats even before the house lights dimmed and the curtain opened. Backstage, unaware of the ear-shattering levels of the clangorous overture, we were watching Nick Cernovich, our lighting designer—who seemed to us to have gone mad—run obsessively back and forth, back and forth across the stage, puffing furiously on a cigarette: inhaling, exhaling, blowing the smoke upward into the flies. It wasn't madness, just dear Nick, passionately at work, creating atmosphere. With no budget for smoke machines or dry ice, Nick was forced to improvise, and when the curtain opened, eerie, swirling smoke-filled shafts of light spilled into the darkness, isolating Merce and Viola in separate worlds. According to Doris Hering: "*Crises* may someday achieve the undercurrent of tragic humor characteristic of Mr. Cunningham's finest work. At the present time . . . Mr. Cunningham has not been able to fully assimilate the wild score by Conlon Nancarrow."[10] But it wasn't Merce who hadn't assimilated the score. It was his dancers. Merce knew the music well, had listened long and carefully, but since we had not rehearsed with it, the first performance was as aurally amazing to us as to our audience, and far more disconcerting.

So *Crises*, like almost every Cunningham premiere in those days, opened amid controversy rather than consensus. To be sure, partisanship fueled some of that controversy. Where did you stand? With José and Doris? With Martha? With Merce? Somehow one was expected to choose, defend, and proselytize. Even Emily Genauer picked up the vibes, becoming "aware for the first time," she wrote in her Sunday art column, "that the battle of the isms among painters is a small quarrel compared with the bitter factualism raging in the dance world."[11] Then she proceeded to toss fat on the fire by disgorging the old divisive clichés about humanism (Limón, Koner) versus abstraction (Cunningham), ignoring or ignorant of Merce's repeated assertions that dance cannot be abstract. As for partisanship, Merce's fans were as guilty of it as were Graham's and Limón's; Ms. Genauer pointed this out:

> Many painters—mostly avant-garde—were in the audience. (Larry Rivers told me he chartered a plane to fly him over from the artists' colony at East Hampton for the Sunday matinee; the flight took ten minutes.) The interesting thing is that they seem to have come as partisans rather than as dance enthusiasts. For any work choreographed and danced by Merce Cunningham (always costumed, according to the program, by abstract-expressionist painter Robert Rauschenberg . . .) they applauded wildly, leaving the auditorium immediately thereafter.[12]

I don't know if Larry Rivers actually flew from East Hampton, but he was there with his gorgeous, flaming-redheaded lady friend Maxine Groffsky, and so were Bob and Jap and dozens of other New Yorkers. If it's true they applauded wildly and vacated the auditorium immediately after our performance, Merce and I might well have beaten them to the door. There was no time to talk things over, digest, or assess. We had forty-eight hours to return to New York, unpack, do laundry, pack again, and fly to Europe aboard an Icelandic Airlines flight, destination Luxembourg, our six weeks in New London all but forgotten.

The August 28 Sunday *New York Times* dance column, Dance Travels, under the headline "Limón on Tour of South America: Ballet Theatre's Russian Dates," concluded with the following: "Not all the foreign tours are government sponsored. Quite on their own (since it is a very small ensemble) Merce Cunningham and Carolyn Brown, with John Cage and David Tudor as their musicians, departed on Tuesday for Europe, where they are to make a number of appearances . . ."

The air is dead, hot, fetid. Overhead vents don't work. Our narrow seats back directly over the propellers, hard against a bulkhead, with no window, and won't recline. Scrunched into them, Merce, John, and I laugh, wipe the sweat as it drips, try to read. We put cotton in our ears and try to sleep. The noise, heat, and constriction of limbs are close to unbearable, the continuous rattling of the plane unnerving. "Never again by plane," I say to them, not knowing it was to be quite the contrary—that never again would I enjoy the civilized pleasures of leisurely transatlantic crossings stretched out on a wooden deck chair, snuggled under a pure wool blanket, breathing sea air, sipping hot bouillon and black velvets for six dreamy, restful days while my internal clock calmly adjusted to time zones' gradual change between continents.

Icelandic Airlines was no picnic under the best of circumstances, but *this* flight was indisputably horrific. After four and a half sweltering hours of cramped misery, we land in Gander, Nova Scotia. Says John as we deplane, "This will be one of the happiest moments of my life!" We stretch our limbs and suck in the cold air like the drowning gasping for breath. Back on the plane again, lights out, we try in earnest to sleep, sweat dripping, backs protesting. My watch and I keep silent vigil. Suddenly, two and a half hours from Iceland, the lights snap on. "Oil leak," the pilot announces. "We are returning to Gander." This time ambulances and fire trucks await us on the runway. For fifteen intolerable minutes we remain seated while firemen douse the plane, the first time I really understand the meaning of claustrophobia. As we disembark in Gander for the second time, John says, "Another one of the happiest moments of my life." Our plane is grounded for repairs a minimum of twelve hours, perhaps as long as twenty-four. There are not enough beds for all eighty-seven passengers. So, families first, women second. I elect to stay with Merce and John. At five a.m., with blankets and pillows from the plane, we arrange a little house of three couches and settle down to sleep. Alas! Muzak everywhere, even in the restrooms. John is *not* "beyond likes and dislikes" when it comes to Muzak. He loathes it. Zen be damned! He asks to have it turned off and is informed that an engineer is required for that. At eight a.m., there's room for us at the inn, two shabby primitive barracks called the Jupiter and Saturn Hotels, not far from the terminal at the end of a dirt road. A rusty yellow school bus belching dark clouds of smelly fumes ferries us the short distance.

Airborne again, *four-thirty the following morning!* Five and a half hours, Gander to Reykjavik, in the same lousy cramped windowless seats. For the Reykjavik/Amsterdam leg of the trip we manage to commandeer reclining seats, but a change of planes in Amsterdam finds us on a barebones rattletrap. Must be a converted troop plane. Arrive in Luxembourg at ten o'clock at night. No hotel reservations. Already more than a day overdue at our final destination. Head directly to the railroad station. John learns of a train to Venice at 2:14 a.m. Bar-hop for the next three hours, moving to the next when the one we're in closes. First-class compartments to Basel! Able to stretch out fully. Sleep divinely. Change trains for the next leg, Basel to Milan. Simply cannot afford porters. Shove mounds of baggage, personal and professional, out the window, lug it up and down stairs platform to platform, haul up and through other windows. From Basel to Como I sit mesmerized, face pressed against windowpane, eyes and soul feasting on Switzerland's verdant mountain-lake-valley wonderland. At almost any point ready to jump train and stay forever. Arrive Milan two p.m. John dashes to local music publisher to buy back rights to *Fontana Mix*, sold to them for thirty thousand lire in 1958–59. Milan to Venice on the *Rapido*. Three hours. At eight o'clock in the evening—three days and three hours after embarking from New York— David Tudor and Frank Amey come rushing along the platform to greet us, and escort us through the station, out to the Grand Canal and into a waiting gondola.

The next day I wrote to my parents: "I'm sorry I ever used words like 'incredible' or 'fabulous' because suddenly there aren't any words to describe the last eighteen hours." The sleek, gold-trimmed gondola awaiting us was Peggy Guggenheim's—one of only seven private gondolas in Venice in 1960. Peggy had sent it to fetch us, as John and Merce were to be her houseguests. Snaking its way through inky waters glinting with reflected light, our gondola passed along large canals and small, through ten centuries of Venetian architecture. Above us a handful of stars, a tiny thumbnail moon, hung in a blue-black sky. I held my breath. Fairy tale? No, it was real, and I had four weeks and two days to let that fact sink in.

Although we'd had only snatches of sleep over the past ninety-five hours, the night was young and our hosts had other ideas. At Peggy Guggenheim's Palazzo Venier dei Leoni on the Grand Canal, a maid ushered us into rooms to bathe and change for a party being given by a Count Balbino Balbe at a nearby palazzo. I've no reason to doubt that Balbe was, as we were told, "a true Venetian count"; or that his elegant, chandeliered home was a true Venetian palazzo, but his guests struck me as vulgar, grade-B Hollywood versions of international café society. Right there and then, my love-hate relationship with Venice was born. By the time we arrived, Count Balbe's party was winding down. After obligatory greetings and ogling the vistas of the Grand Canal from the palazzo balconies, David and I left to gather up my belongings from Peggy Guggenheim's and transfer them to the Ameys' flat. My hosts then led me off to a simple late supper under an arbor of greenery at Montine's, an inexpensive and popular garden restaurant inhabited by dozens of cats. It was past midnight before (at last!) I crawled into bed, and near midday before I awoke to find a pretty child peering in at me through the curtained doorway of my tiny makeshift bedroom.

Lowell Amey was eight years old, a pale, blond waif of a girl, fluent in Italian and English, altogether too streetwise and savvy for her years. Pointing out the hospital island on one of our excursions together, she informed me matter-of-factly, her voice devoid of emotion, that she'd twice been stricken with diphtheria and that if she was again taken there she would die. Upon my awaking in Venice that first morning Lowell became my guide, my friend, and, whenever she was permitted, my constant companion. Without her I would have seen much less of Venice and been far, far lonelier than I was.

Lowell's parents, Frank and Nicola, were American expatriates who, after Frank was badly injured in a car accident, had moved to this metropolis where automobiles are banned. Frank composed music and was a concert pianist. Nikky, who had wanted to be a singer, now was learning to paint. They lived with their three children—Christopher (eleven), Bryan (ten), and Lowell—as well as a redheaded Venetian manservant named Ennio, plus any number of guests, in a sprawling flat on parts of two floors of the Palazzo Contarini-Corfu, a splendid edifice that fronts on the Grand Canal. The Ameys', however, had no views of the water and except for the *grand salone,* most of the rooms overlooked the inner courtyard and were dark and dank. Still, on first viewing, the flat was impressive, a little like a museum. Upon closer inspection I realized it was more like a stage set. With a consummate eye for period, Frank had scoured the city's flea markets and demolition sites and decorated the two-storey-high rooms with tapestries, ancient friezes and statuary, antique furniture and paintings, heavy damask draperies, Persian carpets. Mostly the stuff was chipped, battered, faded, threadbare, and torn. But with pins and tacks and a window dresser's flair he'd arranged an authentic look of former glory. But he warned: "Don't look too closely, and choose your chair with care!"

The children claimed me as their own. My room was a tiny cubbyhole, partitioned off by means of screens and curtains, at the far end of the *grand salone.* With no door to shut I had no privacy; and with no walls to shield me, I had no peace, since the *grand salone* was in constant use for music rehearsals, theatrical rehearsals, piano practice (David's, John's, and Frank's), and music discussions. In less sober moments it was the venue for social gatherings and children's rambunctious fun and games.

At Peggy Guggenheim's, life was vastly different. Peggy had no use for children or noise. Not, at least, at this time of her life. Her vine-covered, one-storey, white stone palazzo, begun in 1748 but never completed, boasted the widest frontage of any palace on the Grand Canal, superb views, and at the back, under a canopy of magnificent ancient acacia, cedar, elm, and magnolia trees, one of the largest gardens in Venice. The palazzo had a flat roof, ideal for sunbathing, which Merce was quick to take advantage of. Inside, the rooms were spacious, airy, and light-filled (on the canal side) with decor strictly in keeping with Peggy's extraordinary collection of twentieth-century painting and sculpture. Only in the large dining room, where Picasso, Léger, Braque, and Duchamp graced the walls, was there Venetian furniture, dating from the fifteenth century. Meals were elegant affairs, punctually served. Maids, gondoliers, boat captain, private secretary, seamstress, and cook kept the place in smooth running order. Peggy's home did double duty as a museum, open to the public on Monday, Wednesday, and Friday afternoons. During museum hours, while the household staff served as custodians and curators, Peggy secluded herself on the roof. At sixty-two she was still an avid nude sunbather, which Merce discovered inadvertently, much to his dismay.

In addition to supervising her museum, Peggy regularly presided over an informal "salon for intellectuals." She suffered fools not at all and was extremely blunt in her assessment of people. At first she quite terrified me. From June to October, while Venice was hosting its renowned international art, film, and music festivals, she was caught up in the frenzy of the city's sociocultural life—endless performances, receptions, luncheons, teas, cocktail parties, and dinners—to most of which she, as one of Venice's most famous residents, was inevitably invited, if she was not actually giving them herself. However, what none of us knew until much later was that a segment of the old aristocratic Venetian society ostracized Peggy because of her aggressively unconventional behavior and notorious sexual escapades. Merce and John were, of course, included in all her social activities; David and I seldom were. I remember on one early evening I'd taken the *vaporetto* from San Marco to the Accademia stop and the boat passed directly in front of Peggy's palazzo. There in her living room, John, Merce, and Peggy, drinks in hand, were talking with Marcel and Teeny Duchamp and the Chilean-born painter Matta and his wife. I knew there was no reason I should have been included in this meeting of old friends, and yet . . . how abandoned I felt, like a second-class citizen. Even if David had been inclined to care about such matters, he was far too busy practicing and rehearsing to have time for socializing. But in the beginning, for days at a time, except for the daily workout with Merce and catching an occasional glimpse of John rehearsing at the Ameys', I saw very little of my friends. Lonesome and dispirited, adrift amid decaying splendors, I would find myself holding Lowell Amey's dry, rough little hand as she tugged me aboard a *vaporetto* headed for the Lido. It was not my idea of how best to experience Venice, and I longed for Earle to join me in what must be the most romantic city in the world. But it was not to be.

After finally giving notice that he was quitting his job as mixer with Capitol Records to compose full-time, Earle had a new job offer as director of a Time Records Contemporary Sound Series, with complete freedom to select the repertoire and the artists, dropped in his lap. He was in New York working like a demon. There wasn't much money involved, but it was an opportunity to record the music he passionately believed in. Immediately, he began work on a recording of Cage's early percussion music. Later he would go to Europe to line up European composers and performers for future recordings. Every one of my letters to Earle pleaded with him to come to Venice. John, very sensitive to my predicament, also wrote Earle: "[Carolyn] requires rescue of some type. I am putting my mind to it, but it wd be more successful if you were with us." John did put his mind to it and came to my rescue as often as he could. Gradually the tone of my letters revealed a happier me.

John, Merce, and I had arrived in Venice on the last Friday in August with absolutely no guarantee that we would be performing there. Once again we were operating on a hope and a prayer. The following Monday afternoon, a little posse of self-proclaimed American cultural ambassadors—John, Merce, David, Frank and Nikky Amey, and I—descended upon the administration offices of Teatro La Fenice, expecting to have to convince the authorities that they did indeed want us to participate in the Twenty-third International Festival of Contemporary Music. To our amazement and delight, there was no need to convince anyone. A contract was quickly drawn up for a *spettacolo di danza*. Fee: $600. Place: Teatro La Fenice! Before the management had time to change their minds, we signed the document and waltzed out of the offices. As we left the building we stopped to take a peek at the stage. Though not so enormous as the Royal Opera House in Stockholm, the Venice stage was still huge and extremely deep, with a terrifically steep rake, even steeper than Stockholm's. It was pretty scary, actually. The floor, we were quick to notice, like the one in Sweden, was terrible. Standing there, stage center, staring out into the empty house of Teatro La Fenice is an experience guaranteed to weaken the knees of the most veteran theater pro. Was there a more perfect or more perfectly beautiful gem of a theater anywhere in this world? Surprisingly, the auditorium was small. Only seventeen rows of plush rose velvet seats, and only twenty-six seats in the widest row of the orchestra. Behind it, a five-tiered horseshoe of balconies, exquisitely carved and gilded, ascended straight up into an azure blue dome, lit by a single crystal chandelier. Ringing each tier, golden candelabra softly illuminated heavenly hues—pure white, pale blue, tender rose, lustrous gold.

Obtaining a performance date at Teatro La Fenice was one thing; rehearsing was another. Luckily, Nikky Amey knew the director of the art school of the Galleria dell'Accademia and was able to arrange for Merce and me to work in a basement classroom. We had to push aside easels and canvases and contend with four support columns, but the studio was large and blessed with a wood floor. Merce worked halfheartedly, without passion or even interest, I thought. Over the twenty-year period that I was able to observe him, rarely did I see this apparent lack of appetite for dancing. It was obvious he was exhausted. He kept putting off starting a new duet that was to be a part of John's *Music Walk* and the finale of our Venice program. Occasionally he'd look at my solos, to check direction, spacing, and timing. Once or twice he made a suggestion or two about changing dynamics within the small, subtle movements of the dance called *Waka*, and near the end of the second week he choreographed a more difficult but far better ending for the other solo and changed its title. He'd originally called it *Huntress* or *Diana—Goddess of the Hunt*—titles liked by neither John nor Earle (whose music from *Folio* was to accompany it). The new title, *Hands Birds*—two words that comprise an entire poem[1] by M. C. Richards—

freed me from implied imagery I'd been uncomfortable with. *Hands Birds* was far more evocative, mysterious, and poetic, and opened doors rather than closed them.

Waka, with music by Toshi Ichiyanagi, was excruciatingly slow, almost hypnotic. It was a dance for the torso and arms, with almost no movement through space. Gravity—of spirit and body—a sense of quietude, introspection, and rapt concentration were needed to pull it off. Merce, concerned that I didn't have sufficient "weight" in my arm gestures, asked Bob Rauschenberg to design hand weights as part of my costume. Shortly before leaving for Venice I received small round, gray, sculpt-metal weights with this message: "Dear Carol Sorry these took so long. They have the same soft geometry as the skirt. I think the metal gray is right too. Elastic can be attached to as many of the brass rings as needed. Flat side is for the palm. Wt. is aprox. 20 oz. Good luck & Love Bob."

Working with weights introduced a completely new consciousness of how I moved my arms and added that sense of gravity that was essential to *Waka*'s full realization. My costume—borrowed from *The Poems of White Stone*—was gray tights and leotard, with floor-length panels of overlapping gray silk, lined with shades of blue, attached at the hips.

Although Merce's original idea for *Hands Birds* was apparently based on Diana ("A woodland goddess, perhaps a tree spirit . . . the mistress of forest creatures and the hunt . . ."[2]), in teaching it Merce never mentioned Diana or hunting or any other imagery. The dance was fast and expansive, required high energy and a sharp attack; it covered space, went into the air. It was difficult, challenging, exhausting, and fun. Eventually I loved working on it by myself.

Upstairs in the Galleria dell'Accademia, both Merce and I were much more inclined to wander leisurely through its galleries looking at Titians, Tintorettos, and Tiepolos than we were to work in the damp, windowless basement studio plié-ing for an audience of dreary student canvases. Eventually Nikky managed to secure permission for us to rehearse regularly in the *sala di ballo* on the top floor of Teatro La Fenice. What a glorious change! Sunlight streamed through a row of windows that opened onto a long, narrow terrace ideal for sunbathing and drying laundry; in that climate a godsend. From the terrace one had a very different perspective of Venice. Not a canal in view. Instead, one looked out on a sea of red-tile rooftops, all a jumble of crazy, marvelous angles, punctured here and there with church spires and a leaning bell tower. Instead of easels and brushes and the smell of turpentine, this studio was filled with wooden crates, racks of costumes, and the smell of sweat. Pushing the stuff back against

one wall, we discovered barres and mirrors. We were home! Our only disappointment was the floor. Wood, yes, but unlike some of the rehearsal studios in Stockholm's Royal Opera House, this one wasn't raked, and we
desperately wanted to practice the many balance adjustments Teatro La
Fenice's stage would require. How much more incentive I felt in this
proper dance studio: I practiced longer, concentrated better, and discovered that I really enjoyed working by myself. Merce usually left before I
did: Guggenheim palazzo houseguests were expected to appear promptly
for a prelunch cocktail hour followed by a lengthy luncheon.

With my time less structured, I could take advantage of the *sala di ballo*
to rehearse alone, to sunbathe on the roof-terrace, and, curiously, to luxuriate in my aloneness—at those moments never feeling lonely at all. And,
once I knew a bit of the language, could cope with the lire, and learned
how to get around the city—via *traghetti* (ferries), bridges, the fascinating
little *calli* (alleys) and tiny *campielli* (squares)—I was rarely lonely. I suppose Peggy Guggenheim was right when she stated, "To live in Venice or
even to visit it means that you fall in love with the city itself. There is nothing left over in your heart for anyone else."[3] Still, my heart ached to share
the mysterious, exotic beauty with a beloved. It didn't help that Madame
Guggenheim completely ignored me. I automatically had two strikes
against me: not famous, not a man. Paradoxically, it was the dreadful parties to which I *was* invited that made me miserable: *La Dolce Vita*, Venetian style. Fellini, it turns out, was a realist, not a fantasist. God, what
utterly meretricious performances by the titled rich and the gigolos, syco-
phants, and fortune hunters who sucked up to them! Overly painted, over-
dressed dowagers (contessas, marchese, duchesses—perhaps half of them
owing their elevated rank to Mussolini) surrounded themselves with sim-
pering, mincing, decadently handsome young men who fawned and
preened like silly lapdogs. On fine warm days, that same bogus society
partied in private cabanas on the beach in front of the fin de siècle Excel-
sior Hotel on the Lido—the dowagers lounging about in teeny bikinis, sipping negronis, their slack and wrinkled flesh held in check by chokers of
jewels around necks, wrists, ankles, fingers, and ears while the mincing
pretty-boys displayed their oiled, tanned bodies less to the titled rich than
to one another. After witnessing one such party, I wrote outraged letters to
Earle and my parents vilifying decadent Venice and ended the letters wail-
ing "I want to go home!"

In retrospect I now realize that the bad times were few, the wonderful,
many. For the first two weeks, Merce and I worked only in the mornings;
our afternoons and evenings were free. The two of us spent an afternoon

browsing through the pavilions at the XXX Esposizione Biennale Internazionale d'Arte; with David I saw several films presented by the XXI Mostra Internazionale d'Arte Cinematografica at the Lido; and with John I went gambling. Observing John in a gambling casino is a little like watching a clown at a wake. The atmosphere of the ultramodern casino on the Lido was deadly serious, the atmosphere oppressive and charged with tension. Winning or losing, the elegantly costumed patrons who crowded around the gambling tables never revealed a trace of enjoyment or disappointment. Their faces were death masks of utter inscrutability, while John's fairly beamed with pleasure—whether losing or winning. After all, what could possibly be more fun than a game of chance? When John won really big, he'd laugh like a kid and look around the table, fully expecting his fellow gamblers and even the croupier to be as delighted as he. The icy stares and cold shoulders fazed him not at all. He just kept grinning and winning. With only one token to play I watched and waited. I'd told John I was going to play number three, my number, but at the crucial moment of no return I placed the token on Earle's number, eleven, the magical number that so often appeared fortuitously in our lives. Three won. I lost more than fifty dollars. Peggy remarked later that love and gambling don't mix. It took a second trip to the casino, this time with Merce and John, to discover I did *not* enjoy gambling. This time, after losing twenty dollars, I felt horribly guilty and cross for two days. Merce lost, too, about thirty dollars, money he could ill afford to throw away. Meanwhile John won every time he played, but his exuberance was somewhat quashed by our losses. He was determined to go on playing until he recovered them, but we dragged him away before his luck could change. I never went again, but, happy as a bird dog in hunting season, John continued his trips to the casino and went on winning.

Another Cage-inspired outing involved us in a day-long mushrooming expedition.

One afternoon, John called to ask if I'd like to go to the cemetery island of San Michele with Peggy Guggenheim, who was going there to visit the grave of a former lover. No doubt it was John's and/or Merce's idea to include me: they remembered I'd expressed a desire to make a pilgrimage to San Michele to visit Diaghilev's grave. My answer was yes, if John or Merce would be going, too; no, if not. I'd been in Venice for more than a week, and this was my first invitation from Peggy. She still intimidated me dreadfully. John said he'd be happy to accompany me and told me to meet them at Peggy's palazzo, where I joined Peggy, Merce, John, David, and Barbara and Nick Bentley, a British couple in Venice to discuss publishing Peggy's latest book, *Confessions of an Art Addict.* They were all in the garden, seated around a stone dining table in a curious rotunda made of stone columns and a kind of canopy covered in vines, still finishing lunch. Embarrassed to discover I was the only one of our group not invited to this luncheon, I apologized for arriving early. Peggy asked me to join them for coffee, which made me feel all the more the poor relative. But the adventure that followed proved well worth the discomfort of its inauspicious beginning. By the time we left Peggy's there wasn't time to go all the way by gondola as she had intended, but what a sublime ride we did have down the Grand Canal, past all the magnificent palazzi, under the Rialto Bridge, and through the winding, narrow rios as far as the Fondamenta Nuove where we caught the bus-boat to the island.

Upon arrival at San Michele we parted company: Peggy, alone, to her lover's grave; the Bentleys in search of a poet friend's, and John and I to look for Diaghilev's. We found it in a Greek cemetery behind a locked gate. John obtained the key so I could put flowers—four carnations and a fern, which Peggy had kindly extracted from her bouquet—on his grave. My small token of respect was added to those already there: marigolds, planted in front of the tombstone; several bunches of flowers, long dead; a bouquet of dusty plastic ones; and a wreath of artificial daisies with a note attached. We could not resist reading this note. Protected from the elements by cellophane, written in French, dated August 1959, it was signed "Nikitina," and said, as I recall: "My admiration, respect and affection have grown rather than diminished in the thirty years since your death." In Paris in 1928, Alice Nikitina had created the role of Terpsichore (one of three muses—the others were danced by Doubrovska and Tchernicheva) in the Balanchine/Stravinsky *Apollon musagète* and remained with the company until Diaghilev's death in Venice on August 19, 1929. When she made her pilgrimage to Diaghilev's grave to leave this wreath of flowers, the Russian ballerina would have been fifty. Standing where she must have stood only one year before, I felt a tiny, vicarious unspoken welcome into the presence of ballet's preeminent impresario. Four symmetrically planted trees curved in asymmetrical grace over Diaghilev's tombstone, forming a protective bower. Through the branches, the waters of the lagoon glinted and sparkled. A lovely spot. Serene and private, and strangely moving. I was very happy to have come. Looking at John, I thought he—for reasons of his own—felt the same.

Floating just offshore, Peggy's gondoliers patiently awaited us. Awaiting us, too, was what Peggy called *"il capolavoro di giorno"*—"the master-piece of the day"—the magic sunset.

During that sunset gondola ride, Peggy began to take some interest in me, or let's just say she no longer ignored me, and when she learned that I'd spent time with her former husband, surrealist painter Max Ernst, in Sedona, Arizona, and, more important, played with his dog, Kachina, who was the great-great-great-grandmother of her many and much beloved Lhasa Apso Tibetan terriers, she took me into her palazzo and introduced me to her precious "children"—the current ménage of three furry friends—and bade John show me her painting and sculpture collection, as well as the extravagant array of earrings (which included originals by Tanguy, Calder, etc., and ancient art exotica from India and Tibet) that decorated her bedroom walls. This hospitality signaled some sort of breakthrough—a thaw, if not a meltdown—and I began to feel more at ease with her.

The next afternoon was Peggy's regatta party. Unlike the other Venice parties I had attended, Peggy's was peopled with painters, actors, film folk, writers, diplomats, and only a few of Venice's *La Dolce Vita* crowd. However, the very nicest party of all was the small one in honor of John's forty-eighth birthday, in the candlelit Renaissance setting of the Ameys' tapestry-walled *grand salone,* where we presented John with drawings, tiny presents, a big bottle of Campari (his most recent booze of choice), and a heavenly rum cake decorated with mushrooms of marzipan, and where we toasted his health with much champagne.

On September 12, John and David left for Germany to give duo-piano concerts. With less than two weeks before our *spettacolo di danza* at La Fenice, Merce and I settled down to serious work, often two sessions a day. His choreographic contribution to John's *Music Walk* was scarcely begun and still he seemed reluctant to work on it. The movement material he eventually did come up with was desultory, square, dry, bare-bones class-room stuff: some *tendus, grand battements,* a turn in *arabesque,* a *ronde de jambe* turn, a running, leaping, skipping phrase, a little ballroom-style waltzing—nothing of interest rhythmically, dynamically, or spatially that I could determine. In rehearsal, it felt sketchy, aimless, and rather silly. When John saw it six days before the performance he said almost nothing, but I was sure he was disappointed. So was I. John's score, written in 1958, is for one or more pianists at a single piano, but it also includes use of radio and/or recordings as a part of the gamut of possibilities. It is an inde-terminate piece involving sound and action, with a good bit of walking about the stage to reach various sound sources. In realizing their parts of the score, both John and David had come up with some zany, unconventional means of producing sound in, on, and under the piano, but there was nothing unconventional about the movement that Merce had produced for us. With one exception, all the actions the two of us performed were determined by him. The exception: I dreamed up an entrance for myself that involved a long climb up into the highest reaches of the flies, a crawl on all fours along the catwalk and, with the help of a stagehand (astonished by my bravery), a precarious clamber into an armchair that had been rigged for my deliciously terrifying descent to the stage floor "miles" below, where the grand piano looked no bigger than a kidney bean!

Each day when Merce and I climbed the many flights of stairs up to the *sala di ballo* to rehearse we'd pass the glorious stage—still unavailable to us—and sigh. The Fenice was even busier than before; daily orchestra rehearsals and some evening performance kept the stage littered with platforms, podiums, pianos, and percussion instruments. In mid-September there was a changing of the (avant) garde: the art and film folk mostly left town, music people moved in, and the Twenty-third International Festival of Contemporary Music replaced both cinema and fine art as the preeminent cultural event in Venice. Suddenly the Ameys' flat was overrun with musicians. Inevitably, along with rehearsals, our schedule now included more socializing and a series of contemporary music concerts, arranged by Frank Amey, that took place at the Accademia.

A change of weather accompanied the change of art forms—for about four days: rain, Rain, RAIN. Walking home from the Fenice to dress for the first of Frank's concerts, Merce and I got caught in a downpour. As always, we parted at the Accademia Bridge and went off to our respective lodgings. It was pointless to run, since I couldn't have gotten any wetter if I'd fallen into the Grand Canal. My thin dress was soaked through and plastered to my body, rainwater streamed down my face and neck in steady rivulets from sodden, dripping hair. Carefree, deliciously happy, once again in love with Venice, I just strolled along, suddenly in no hurry at all even though I was late. Then: an appreciative wolf whistle, followed by a familiar voice shouting "Hey! You!" It stopped me in my tracks. I whirled around to see Earle standing at the far end of the *calle,* laughing. I ran . . . we hugged and laughed and hugged and both talked at once and hugged some more. He wasn't expected for another two or three days, but there he was, appearing out of nowhere, surprising me as he so often did. Arriving minutes earlier, he'd found the Ameys' flat, discovered I was at the Fenice rehearsing, and set out to look for me. Question was, where were we to stay? Mine was only a narrow, single bed, and the Ameys' flat was already overbooked. But there was no time to think about that. Earle had come early expressly to hear the three *Manifestazioni di music d'oggi* that Frank had arranged, and the first one was about to begin at the Accademia di Belle Arti. A quick change into dry clothes and we were there.

An exhibition of avant-garde music scores decorated the walls of the concert hall, and among them was Earle's "December 1952" from *Folio,* the first score of its kind, but certainly not the last. In fact, eight years after Earle's first and numerous subsequent explorations in graphic and "time notation," graphic notation had become fashionably *au courant* among the most far-out young European composers. The most amusing score at the Accademia was a composition by Frank Amey, written on a roll of toilet paper and draped elegantly over easels all around the room. To my un-Tudored ears, although I was not alone in this, most of these European copycat scores offered more in the way of visual delight than aural pleasure.

At the end of the second concert devoted to John's music, Merce and I were called out of the room and informed that we were to go to the Fenice, to the office of Mario La Broca, the director of the International Festival of Contemporary Music. Instant alarm! Earle and Ronny Valpreda (who acted as translator) went with us. It was Wednesday evening. Our concert was scheduled for the following Saturday. Making our way across the city, we kept speculating upon the purpose of this curt summons, fearing but not willing to believe the worst. The worst it was. "No concert at the Fenice," we were told. An acting company from Genoa was to open at the Fenice four nights after our performance with a complicated production requiring elaborate sets and a revolving stage, and they claimed they needed the exclusive use of the stage to start building immediately. In place of the Fenice we were offered a stage on the island of San Giorgio. Grim with rage, Merce agreed to look at the stage but refused to accept the substitute until he had seen it. An underling had been assigned to accompany us to San Giorgio via *vaporetto* (public transportation), but by the time Merce had finished speaking, an official much higher up the festival's administrative ladder was told to take us via private motor launch. In twenty minutes we met at Harry's Bar. By this time our entourage had increased to seven and now included John, David, and the composer Mauricio Kagel. The first place we were shown had no real stage—just a lecture platform at the end of a long, narrow lecture hall. "No. Impossible. Too small," said Merce. Next they took us to a huge, handsome room, its walls covered with tapestries. It had no stage at all, but they said they would build us a platform. "Impossible," said Merce, and the official agreed with him. The motor launch deposited us back at Harry's Bar. "Come to La Broca's office at ten tomorrow morning," the official said, "and we will discuss the difficulties." Peggy joined the seven of us in a restaurant across from her palazzo to discuss the debacle. We had a valid contract that specifically stated La Fenice as the location of our September 24 *spettacolo di danza.* Peggy advised getting a lawyer and suing.

The first stage rehearsal for Merce and me was scheduled for that evening; he decided we should go to the theater as planned. But it was closed, locked up for the night, and when Merce finally located the watchman he refused to admit us. Poor fellow! All Merce's pent-up anger and frustration, in tight control until that moment, exploded in senseless, if understandable, fury as he took out his wrath on the wrong person. The watchman spoke no English and our Italian was totally inadequate to the occasion. Apparently the man had not been informed about our rehearsal, but eventually Merce's violent raging intimidated him and he allowed us to go to the stage. It was hopeless. The Genoa theater company had already moved in; the stage was littered with their sets. Realizing there was nothing to be done, Merce calmed down. Leaving the theater we met John, who'd come to lead us to the Grand Hotel to talk with Virgil Thomson about our dilemma. Virgil was a friend of La Broca's; John hoped Virgil might be willing to exert some influence on our behalf. But Virgil wasn't there. It was suggested that the breach of contract be reported to a Communist journalist in order to create a huge scandal, but John said he'd prefer to make a capitalistic scandal than a communistic one, and he set off to find Virgil, who was attending a concert at the Palazzo Ducale. The rest of us stumbled home to bed. But, with nothing resolved, sleep was hard to come by. At ten the next morning, Merce (still angry) and I (still anxious) dutifully arrived at La Broca's office to discover John already there. Without Virgil or lawyers, without angry words or threats of causing a scandal, John had prevailed; a compromise had been agreed upon. Our *spettacolo di danza* was on again at Teatro La Fenice—*but,* with NO rehearsal time onstage until six p.m. on the day of the performance. We sighed and went upstairs to work as usual.

At least Earle and I weren't homeless. After the first of John's concerts, the night of Earle's unexpected arrival in Venice, Peggy had invited us to have supper at her home. Afterward she kindly offered to call *pensiones* and hotels to find a room for us. After a few minutes on the phone, she reported that the few rooms available were far too expensive; on the other hand, we were welcome to stay with her, provided we (and more importantly, John and Merce) were willing to forgo meals there, since her staff would be busy with the museum on Wednesday and Friday and simultaneously preparing for a big party on Thursday evening that Peggy was giving in honor of (guess who?) John and David, Merce and Carolyn. John and Merce expressed delight at having us move in. We were hesitant, not wishing to inconvenience anyone, but overjoyed to accept. Little Lowell, on the other hand, was heartbroken, and her tears tugged at my heartstrings. Her newfound pal, her very own playmate (she had none her own age), was forsaking her.

Earle's first and my twenty-sixth night in Venice was spent in a big canopy bed between pink sheets in a pink bedroom with a window opening directly onto the twenty-four-hour operatic spectacle of the Grand Canal, its magical sounds and scenic splendor. Wherever we turned, we saw distorted reflections of ourselves in the smoke-gray antique Venetian mirror over the desk and the dressing and bedside tables. Our bathroom was easily three times as large as the screened-off cubicle I'd been living in at the Ameys' for the previous three and a half weeks, and it was done up in black marble with separate cubbyholes for toilet, bidet, and sunken bathtub. The next morning, moments after I'd pushed the bell at our bedside, there was a knock on our door and a cheery voice called, *"Buon giorno! Colazione?"* Breakfast in bed in a palazzo overlooking the Grand Canal? I suppose one can get used to anything. No matter what Peggy eventually came to think of me, I'm fairly certain that without Earle I would never have been invited to stay in her palazzo. It was no secret that she was partial to men, be they straight or gay, and she tolerated only the most illustrious women.

Despite all her entertaining, Peggy had a reputation for being stingy—not to mention ruthless and arbitrary—in dealing with people. Paradoxically, she could also be wonderfully kind and generous. Precisely what sort of test one had to pass before this side of her character revealed itself remains a mystery, but by the time Earle appeared in Venice her manner toward me had grown increasingly cordial, beginning with that afternoon expedition to the cemetery. She began to send me out in her gondola or her motorboat with Merce or John or both, claiming, "It needs exercise!" I can't believe a more romantic luxury exists than savoring Venice lazily afloat in a private gondola! Or one more thrilling than Guido calling "Hold your hats!" as he revved up the motor of Peggy's speedboat and headed out to the broad Giudecca Canal for a prolonged spin—magical Venice blurring into an impressionistic watercolor, gauzily unreal. Zipping through the water at high speed, giddy with exhilaration, wind and spray in my face, hot sun beating down, I would wonder naively, "Is this what it feels like being a movie star or a millionaire, or both?" Peggy certainly knew the feeling intimately, and the generous part of her nature wanted us to share it.

Among many kindnesses to me was her help in solving my costume problems. I needed a white top to wear in *Music Walk*. Nikky Amey, Merce, and I spent an entire afternoon searching for one with no luck at all. The only dance shop in town had nothing suitable; however, the lady who ran it happened to be wearing the *perfect* top, and told us she'd bought it at Rizzardi's. At that elegant, rather snooty establishment a courteous gentleman offered to make up a white one for me, but when we went back the next day, the salesladies were frightfully uppity and said their dressmakers were far too busy with large, important orders (and obviously important clients) to be bothered with my paltry one. Hearing this, Peggy immediately offered me a white Rizzardi top of her own as well as the services of her laundress to alter it and to do any other sewing I needed done.

My *Hands Birds* costume (leotards and tights plus a kind of half-skirt of nylon chiffon like the one Rauschenberg designed for *Springweather and People*) was designed and dyed emerald-green by Bob in New York before we left, but the skirt needed to be sewn to the leotard and tights with me in them. Obviously I couldn't do it myself, but Peggy's laundress took one look at the strange flimsy fabrics and literally trembled with fright. A resident of the palazzo *before* Peggy—she'd come with the property—she was very old and spoke not a word of English. She'd lived in the recesses of the basement for so long that I doubted she could see; surely she'd never seen a leotard before. Taking pity on her, Peggy sent a maid into the city to summon a seamstress.

Put on *Hands Birds* green tights and leotard so that the seamstress could sew the nylon tail directly to the costume on me. The sight of me in this getup—leaning over a chair—put the maids into hilarious giggles. Everyone admiring my slimness. I suppose this costume was pretty shocking to everyone. Very little dance goes on in Venice. And not many people have TV. There is TV in the bars, though. Peggy thought my figure "remarkable." Apparently people not used to dancers' bodies are utterly *amazed* to see all that muscular thinness. . . . The seamstress fitted Peggy's white top to me. Then she left. Julianna, one of the maids, was in the garden. She and the seamstress went into hysterical gales of laughter together. I was watching them from the window as I dressed. The costume certainly had delighted everyone! Except me—bending over for half an hour while it was being sewn.

That letter downplayed my true emotions. In fact, I felt like a damn fool with Peggy, her daughter Pegeen, John, Merce, and most of Peggy's household staff standing around gawking at me, commenting on my body as though I wasn't present in it. With my rear end in the air I felt miserably self-conscious, and thanks to the tittering and giggling, just plain humiliated. "A beautiful snake," "a Hindu swan," is what Peggy said I looked like, even before the costume fitting. I wasn't sure how to respond to those observations. Best to ignore them, I figured, and concentrate on her conversation, which was unlike any other I'd ever encountered. With her acerbic wit and candid comments, she was never uninteresting. By this time I was regularly included when Peggy, John, Merce, and friends dined in restaurants (everyone went Dutch on these occasions), and now and again she invited me to lunch or dinner at her palazzo, but it wasn't until Earle arrived that I finally felt like a full-fledged member of the grown-up world again.

The 1960 Venice Music Biennale was Darmstadt-Donaueschingen revisited, Venetian style. Composers, conductors, music critics, historians, and publishers crowded into cafés and *ristoranti* to exchange gossip, discuss, eat, and drink music along with the *vino, cannelloni, fegato alla Veneziana e espresso.* Igor Stravinsky, Robert Craft, and Virgil Thomson were in town, as well as many of the people we'd met at the European music festivals in 1958. Peggy's cocktail party given for John, Merce, David, and me on Thursday, September 22, proved mind-numbing. Excerpts from my journal:

> David never showed up and Peggy was extremely "put out" by this rudeness. I hate cocktail parties. This one was certainly typical: millions of people crammed together in one room, balancing glasses, making polite and idle conversation. The usual consulate people were there, and the rich, and the elegant, and a few artists . . . Stravinsky was invited, but did not attend. . . . I was hustled about from important personage to important personage by Peggy or Merce or John. "You're so decorative," says John. I must say that brings my back up. It finally ended. Peggy went off to bed. Merce drank too much. And kept saying that was all he wanted to do. John was utterly wrung out, exhausted, pooped, used up, etc. so he went to bed too. . . . Earle and I went off to join the musician crowd at Montine's restaurant. Young, animated lively people, with things to talk about, with laughter in their natures—it was like breathing fresh air. Four languages were being spoken. Italian, English, French, German. After a while, we didn't know

who was speaking what [language]. . . . [Nam June] Paik (a Korean fellow)—no matter what language he spoke was hilarious.

SPETTACOLO DI DANZA TEATRO LA FENICE
SABATO 24 SETTEMBRE ORE 21:15

Plastered up all over town, these *affissi* confirmed the fact. It was happening at last. It was lived so completely in the moment, I doubt I could remember very much about that extraordinary performance were it not for my journal. My description of the event—all I could remember of it—was written the following morning and I quote from it directly:

The bells are ringing for Mass. I don't know the time. Earle is asleep beside me. There are three bouquets—all received *on stage* at the Fenice last night at the finale. WOW! What an evening!!!!

At five o'clock, Guido took Merce, John and me to the theatre in the motor boat. Picture: exit from PG Palazzo on Grand Canal to motor boat, with costumes held aloft and arriving at the theatre by motor boat, wind in hair . . . one has to know Venice to appreciate the incredible luxury and romanticism of such a trip. I doubt I will ever again be delivered to a theatre such as the Fenice, probably the world's most beautiful, by chauffeur-driven motor launch, from a palazzo on the Grand Canal. It *did* happen. It was real.

We arrived at the theatre to discover the men still clearing the huge sets from the stage. We found dressing rooms—unpacked and spread out the costumes in order of appearance, arranged makeup. I went down on stage at about 6:20. The men were sweeping and rolling up set cloths. A newspaper reporter interviewed us. I warmed up, a little. Tried to practice between and around the men to get the feel of the size (HUGE) and the rake (VERY STEEP). The workmen rigged up my chair for descending from the rafters. [My own contribution to *Music Walk.*] One man experimented in it and went up. Then I went up to the "cat walk"—miles above the stage in the "flies." Two men put me in the chair. I looked down just twice. The piano looked like an ink spot below me on the stage. But it was lovely going down. Sandwiches and milk arrived at seven. Woman still washing the floor. Then the lighting rehearsal began.

Suddenly it was 8:45—and we still hadn't rehearsed. Merce had to sit out front to work with the lighting man—I ran around the stage showing what the light hit and didn't hit. John told me to go make up. Program scheduled to begin at 9:15. Merce still working the lights. At 9:30 we were told we should begin in 5 or 10 minutes. So we began. We weren't particularly warmed up anymore. We were very nervous in a way because we had NEVER rehearsed anything on stage. *Music Walk* was *never* rehearsed with John and David or really even finished!!!! So—on with the show! "Professionalism" and all that. The *Suite* [*Suite for Two*] was very shaky. But the audience was quiet. Then, John and David played John's *Winter Music*. We dancers were changing—I imagine the audience started acting up during the music. When Merce started *Untitled Solo* they were giggling. They were fairly quiet during my solo to Earle's music [*Hands Birds*] but from there on—in the solos, they hooted, whistled, hollered and talked. People who liked it shouted back. *VERY EXCITING!* In my 2nd solo, *Waka*, which is 7 minutes of *slow, slow*, almost nothing movement—I hold still for long times—how they whistled—but I was angry and determined—and danced *better* then. And I *made* the audience be quiet. John said I got a thunderous applause for that dance. I didn't hear it. *Nightwandering* went well. They were quiet for that. Another music piece [Variations]—humorous one. Then *Music Walk*. What fun! I descend in a chair. The piano is on a moving stage [trap-door] and goes up and down with John on it. Merce and I eat a sandwich, do a waltz together. I do ballet steps. It was all fun. The audience had fun, too. But the piece was really a riot because it started before I was ready to descend and the cues were crazy and Merce and I did our whole part in about 5 minutes. The piece is 10 minutes. So we ad-libbed the end! John came on stage in the beginning looking around, wondering where we all were!! David and John went up and down into the pit and onto the stage. We had quite a number of curtains—and *three* bouquets of flowers presented to me on stage!! One from Peggy Guggenheim—2 doz. red roses, one from Pegeen Helion (Peggy's daughter)—6 pale lavender gladioli and a small hand bouquet of sweet smelling white, pink and lavender flowers from Nikky Amey and family. People came back to congratulate us. Some to say how good of us to go *on* with the program, in the face of all the whistling, etc. (Whistling in Europe is derisive.) In fact, a high-ranking member of the *Biennale* administration came back at intermission to apologize for the uproar. And Merce remembers hearing a voice [it turned out to be that of British composer, Sir Arthur Bliss, no less!] in the corridor outside his dressing room exclaiming: "John Cage! I'm so happy to meet you. I've been looking forward to hearing your music. I do hope you are going to continue! Just a few malcontents, don't you know!" A few malcontents? The entire audience was in a complete uproar! Thoroughly amused, Merce said that it had never occurred to him or to John *not* to continue!

We packed, dressed, met Peggy, Pegeen, Earle (Earle sat with Peggy and Pegeen in a box), the Ameys, etc. etc. in a café outside the Fenice. Then we went to a little restaurant to have *pasta fagioli* (Venetian speciality— spaghetti and bean soup—which is awful!). The only thing the restaurant had *hot*. On our way home we passed another street café filled with students playing instruments. They saw John and called to him to play a piece. John and M. Kagel, Heinz Klaus Metzger, Frank Amey and I, and I think some-one else (probably David Tudor) did the La Monte Young chair music— pushing, pulling and sliding chairs around over the cobblestone square. The students cheered. They asked us for dancing—but we said we were too tired. A young man student rushed after me to kiss my hand. All very charming.

We walked home—over the Accademia Bridge across the Grand Canal for the last time—and walked the narrow cobblestone streets, hearing our own footsteps echo in the stillness. Gondolas tied up for the night in the small canals. Cats lurking about. Such a beautiful, beautiful city. We went home to Peggy's (Peggy had gone home earlier) leaving the Ameys and guests at the Bridge. . . . John, Merce, Earle and I had a nightcap in the liv-ing room in order to talk about the program. It was certainly exciting—and the audience was clearly divided—People bravo-ed themselves hoarse and boo-ed themselves hoarse. Some people had *come with* whistles—prepared to cause a small riot. The theatre was quite full—they brought extra chairs in at the last moment, and opened up an extra tier of boxes. It was the best attended event in the whole [music] *Biennale* Festival up to that date.

That ends my report. Here are excerpts from *Time* magazine's: In his 48 years, self-styled Non-Expressionist Composer John Cage . . . has reduced more than one audience to near lunacy. Last week U.S. composer Cage and the Contemporary Music Festival linked forces in a concert at Venice's famed old La Fenice Theater. The explosion could be heard across the Grand Canal."

What follows is a paragraph of description, rife with outrageous inaccu-racies and distortions, of what John and David did. Only one sentence is devoted to the dancing: "Presently Dancer Merce Cunningham started undulating in symbolic suggestion of an embryo wriggling toward man-hood." No other mention is made of the choreography or even that the evening's "entertainment" was billed as a dance performance. But it *was* true, as *Time* reported, that by the end of the evening traditionalists versus modernists were screaming at one another: "Go to San Remo" (a jazz and popular music venue) is what *I* heard hollered by a Cage fan in response to some angry classical music lover's shouts of outrage. It was reported that when Igor Stravinsky (another disgruntled nay-sayer who left the concert early) was asked if the pandemonium equaled that of the Paris premiere of his *Sacre du printemps* in 1913, he replied proudly: 'There has never been a scandal like mine.' "[4]

A mellow Virgil Thomson described the event somewhat differently: "The music of Cage and his group, surely the 'farthest out' among all the music heard [at the festival], did not fail to incite a spontaneous audience participation in its own thumps, bangs, whacks and whistles. Indeed, throughout that evening, a good-humored time seemed to be had by all; and everybody, absolutely everybody loved the dancing."[5]

On Sunday, September 25, our last day in Venice, Earle's train for Paris left earlier than ours to Munich. Peggy, kindly, asked Guido to take Earle and me to the station so that we could be alone to say our teary good-byes. Then, a last *fast* run on the big Giudecca Canal, the nose of the boat high, the spray whizzing past, before Guido dropped me off at the Accademia Bridge for a farewell visit with the Ameys. Little Lowell hugged and kissed me, crying, nearly hysterical, because we were leaving. Peggy's boat, piled high with luggage, took Merce, John, David, and me the long way—the full length of the Grand Canal—to the station. It had been one month and two days since our arrival. Again, an inky sky, a thumbnail moon. Stars. Lights reflecting on the water. Gondolas gliding slowly up and down the canal with colored lanterns. Muffled voices and water sounds . . . and music . . . and singing . . . and . . . What a finale!

BALLET RIOT AT HEBBEL THEATER
IT WAS CRAZY BUT STILL ART

Just Like Vaudeville   DADA DANCES

SENSE AND NONSENSE

THE BEST THING WAS   *WAS THIS*
THE INTERMISSION   *REALLY*
                                              THE END OF ART?

How to Go Too Far   **Tumult at the Dance-Duo**
                                           Cunningham & Brown

Dance of the Future From America

Oct. 1, 1960. "We were a great wild roaring event in Berlin. Reviews and/or pictures in eleven [actually sixteen] newspapers." This is the message I dashed off to my parents on a picture-postcard of the Brandenburg Gate. In 1960, only the gate (destroyed in 1945, rebuilt in 1956) divided war-ravaged Berlin, east from west. Nikita Khrushchev's infamous wall was built some eleven months later to halt the hordes of East Germans escaping to the west. We discovered we needed only a pass, obtained at the gate, to walk from the Allied Sector into the Soviet. Fifteen years after the Second World War, East Berlin still lay mostly in ruins—a ghost city of bleak, lifeless streets, dull gray, eerily quiet and somber, as if that half of the divided city were in perpetual mourning. West Berlin still had ruins but, by contrast, it was a city resurrected. An astonishing amount of reconstruction had been achieved, and the city appeared brashly colorful and manic with activity as if in perpetual celebration. Bolstered by an avalanche of American dollars, British pounds, and Uncle Sam's determination to advertise democratic-capitalist values, the shops and restaurants overflowed with an embarrassment of Western goodies, flaunted, gleefully, in the Soviets' faces. Small wonder they built the wall! And Art with a capital "A" was subsidized to a degree unheard-of back in the USA. For seventeen days the Berlin Festival ran a marathon of opera, symphony, theater, jazz, new music, ballet, and modern dance in twenty-one locations, from the State Opera House to the Sports Palace, and included performances by Herbert von Karajan conducting the Berlin Philharmonic; Leonard Bernstein conducting the New York Philharmonic; London's Royal Philharmonic; Schoenberg's *Moses und Aron* at the Opera; the *Comédie Française;* the Berlin Opera Ballet; the Ballet of Two Worlds, etc. Our modest music-and-dance quartet presented three performances at the Hebbel Theater within a few blocks of the eastern sector and prompted one reviewer to write that the most unusual event, not only of the last week but of the whole festival, was probably the dance concert by Merce Cunningham and Carolyn Brown.[1]

The experience was no less unusual for us. Venice vacation over, the glories and terrors of La Fenice behind us, we were looking forward to some professional work: seven performances within eight days in three German cities. Berlin, Munich, and Cologne. With no stage manager, lighting designer, or even a written light plot to carry along from theater to theater, Merce and John repeatedly faced the arduous ordeal of explaining the technical requirements for our program to German stage crews who are—if I may risk a generalization—maddeningly meticulous, exasperatingly slow-moving, and all too often rather arrogant. Arriving in Berlin on September 26, we were met at the airport by a representative of the festival and taken immediately by cab to the Hebbel Theater to have a look at the stage and to work out any technical problems. But the Dublin Festival Company was opening in *The Playboy of the Western World* that evening and they were still having such a difficult time with the ancient lighting equipment that we were allowed only a peek at the stage and told to come back the following afternoon. By then the Dublin company, with one more performance to go, was in a state of mild hysteria over the lighting—a warning to us!

Next morning, the day of our first performance, Merce was at the theater at nine. When I arrived at 10:30, it was obvious that it would be hours before we got any rehearsal time. It was a nightmare. Each one of Merce's lighting directives had to be translated, misunderstood, questioned, discussed, evaluated, and argued over as it was passed down a mystifyingly hierarchical chain of command—some fifteen men in all. John was nearly out of his mind trying to be go-between and pacifier. I futzed about on the sidelines unpacking and ironing costumes, only to discover later that we'd been assigned a wardrobe lady. I gave myself a class and, as inconspicuously as I could manage, tiptoed around, over and/or through workmen, equipment, wire, and cables in order to get some sense of the stage space. The day dragged on. No run-through. No rehearsal of any sort. A photographer arrived expecting to take pictures of our "dress rehearsal." What a joke! He insisted on shooting something. Leaps and jumps, preferably. Merce was infuriated, his rage just barely contained, but since it was John who had made the arrangements for the photographer to be there (we needed publicity, after all), he agreed to pose for a few shots. It was the only semblance of dancing Merce got to do before the actual performance. When I left the theater at 5:45 p.m., he and John were still struggling with light cues. When finally they tore themselves away at six to get some pre-performance nourishment, a booking agent from Frankfurt trailed them to the restaurant to discuss future engagements while they tried to eat.

We were back in the theater by seven. Unlike what had happened in Venice, and typically German, the curtain rose at eight sharp. Standing in the wings as Merce began his opening solo "At Random" in *Suite for Two,* I felt numb, spiritless, and hollow. God knows how Merce was feeling. To my amazement, the performance went well. At last my solo in *Suite* (as always, my first appearance onstage in our duet programs) had become like a friend with whom I was happily familiar. During the dances the audience was quiet and extraordinarily attentive, and we were warmly applauded. There's little doubt that it was John's *Winter Music* for two pianos and especially *Music Walk with Dancers* that were responsible for the sensationalist headlines. *Un succès de scandale. Music Walk* was chaotic, improvisatory—full of gaffes as in, but different from, those perpetrated in Venice. We'd never rehearsed it, of course. One critic described it thus:

It starts with Cage stepping to the footlights and roaring loudly at the audience, whereupon of course a many-voiced echo answers him furiously. Two phonographs play classical music and kitsch simultaneously. The dancers stalk the stage, without meeting one another. A few bars of waltz—they crouch, swinging their legs on the edge of the stage. Cage works continuously at his piano with great concentration as he sinks slowly into [below] the stage floor and then reappears just as calmly. Tudor also returns to the stage. He's lying down under the piano, and gets up only to produce some snarling sounds from a pipe. The stage revolves and the dancers continue to walk through their parts, until the curtain suddenly falls and puts an end to this pointless nonsense. The audience, much to its own surprise, is amused and entertained, and now has time to think about the sense behind the nonsense, a mirror image of this absurd, mechanistic world.[2]

The audience went berserk during *Music Walk:* hooting, stamping, whistling, booing, sending signals both pro and con. Some of the shouts and verbal exchanges among members of the audience were quoted in the newspapers: "You're crazy, baby!" "Ouch! You're off key!" "Get a hammer!" "Philistines, shut up!" "Oh, she's one of the intelligentsia!" "Wrong notes!" "This can only be the end of all art!"

It was a free-for-all, but clearly the audience was having fun. They laughed, with delight rather than derision, or so we were told. One newspaper reported that at the end of the performance a large part of the audience had dissolved into tears . . . of laughter. We went about our business utterly straight-faced. The press had a field day: "Seriousness and silliness, art and trash of the most refined sort." "Festival? More like carnival." "It was ghastly!" "Like Dada gatherings of the twenties." "The dance is independent of the music—why do they do this to us?"

We'd never had so many curtain calls. After the fifth or sixth one we realized that at least half the audience applauded just long enough to get the curtain up again and then their vociferous boos and catcalls overwhelmed the cheers. Some people adored us. It was a new experience to have such an audience response from total strangers. People crowded backstage. The opening-night audience included Mary Wigman and teachers from her school; some young dance students, wide-eyed, eager and touchingly warm and generous in their appreciation; Nora Kaye and Herbert Ross and members of their Ballets of Two Worlds, which, they told us, had fared badly in Berlin: poor reviews and no audience. Nora, who may have remembered me from Antony Tudor's ballet classes at the Met, whispered in my ear as she left, "I wish you were with *us!*" Backstage, Mary Wigman kissed me and murmured complimentary words, but just what she said I couldn't hear, so flustered and honored was I to be meeting Germany's most famous, indeed legendary, modern dancer.

I was even more honored to find myself seated on her left at an after-performance supper party given in our honor at the Ritz, a small, ultra-elegant restaurant, reputedly the best in all Berlin. Miss Wigman presided over a table laid with silver and crystal, and she held us all spellbound with stories about her past life and harrowing tales about her suffering during the war. At that time I had no idea she'd once been an admirer of Adolf Hitler, even collaborating with the Nazis in order to keep her company, her school, and her career from extinction.[3] What *was* strikingly clear was that she remained fiercely, proudly German. Her acidly scathing condemnation of the Allied firebombings of Dresden, which destroyed great architectural and cultural treasures as well as civilian dwellings, left us cringing with discomfort and feeling guilty for *our* governments's crimes against her people. Her government's crimes were not discussed. At seventy-three, still animated by some unquenchable fires burning deep in her being, her razor-sharp intellect dauntingly intact, Mary Wigman held court. We listened. She talked. But of the dance she'd just witnessed not a word was spoken. Not a word, that is, until Dorothy Floyd, the American woman who'd arranged the dinner party, asked her to make a toast. Here is my journal's notation concerning that event:

> [Wigman] said she disliked toasts, and then she went on to say, "I hope no one will misunderstand . . ." [Pause] and she raised her glass and said, "To true artists." Emphasis on the word *true*. (Of course, this is *my* own personal subjective interpretation of the event.) Wigman then looked briefly at Merce on her right, then turned to her left and looked at me for what seemed to me a very long time, and looked around the table as we all raised our glasses. One could interpret this or misinterpret this in many ways—the first possibility that none of us were true artists, but that we should drink to them, and on down the list of other possibilities. It was a rather strange, potent (and a little embarrassing) and very *still* moment.

She'd still said nothing about our program, and that, of course, said much. We met with her again the next morning at her school, which was housed in a large, converted family residence in Dahlen, a lovely suburb of Berlin. We were invited to observe her dance class already in progress. A tall, stoop-shouldered man with white hair was playing an upright piano. As we entered the room the music stopped, the students applauded us, Mary Wigman greeted me with a kiss, and a sweet-faced young student, who'd been very appreciative backstage the night before, rushed out of the room, returning seconds later with red and yellow carnations for me. The entire one-and-a-half-hour class was built on one basic movement idea: a kind of bouncing action on the ball of the foot, on three-quarter point, repeated two or three or more times depending on the rhythm, and then changing to the other foot, all the while moving forward. The rhythm varied, arms and torso movements were added. The body bounced and jiggled, or the torso leaned from side to side. By the end of the class my calf muscles ached just watching them. The students worked like Trojans, but the kind of vitality and inspirational quality I associate with most dance classes was missing. Most interesting, by far, was seeing the dancers improvise on the original theme.

For every waking minute of our five days and nights in Berlin we were on the run, cramming in as much activity as would fit. We made the obligatory bus tour of East Berlin and environs: a bleak world, terrible to behold. The buildings scarred and mutilated. Weeds growing over Hitler's burial mound and choking the rubbled ruins of former ministries, embassies, churches, and dwellings. What few people we saw, more ghosts than human, moved listlessly along the gray, cheerless streets. At first, without thinking, I'd made the mistake of romanticizing the ruins of West Berlin, where ivy and flowering vines crept over the remains of our hotel and the stark, bombed-out shells of buildings formed wonderful jagged sculpture against the sky. But seen for what it really was—the gaping wounds from the horrors of war—there was nothing romantic about it.

On the morning before we opened, we were required to attend a press conference with uninteresting questions put forward by a congregation of bored-looking journalists from around the world. John had a way of enlivening his listeners with the eclectic gallimaufry of his philosophical concepts and his humor, and his charm rarely failed to beguile an audience. Merce spoke, as always, in practical, no-nonsense terms about the realities of being a dancer. I'd begun to question the Gospel According to Saint John, but I held my tongue; not a problem, of course, since no one asked me a single question. After all, I was only there to be, in John's word, "decorative."

Whether it was the press conference or our brief television performance at five p.m. the day after we opened, by our second performance we had good houses and standing ovations, and one newspaper even accused us of having an organized hired claque in the audience. Critics and the audience took our program very seriously indeed, the majority agreeing with Horst Koegler, then Germany's foremost dance critic, who wrote: "The very stimulating protests of the Berlin audience were not once aimed at the dancers but only at the nature of their musical accompaniment."[4] It was a peculiarly awkward time. Merce, in a blue funk, seemed as morose and unenthusiastic as he'd been in Venice. In a letter to Earle I related some of the difficulties:

> I had such a STRANGE conversation with John one night in Berlin, at a champagne mid-night reception for us and the Basel Ballet. Merce was drinking *great quantities* of champagne and getting quite looped. John said that Merce was making a fool of himself. That he wasn't working or doing his yoga. That he wasn't dancing well. And that the reason for all this was that *Music Walk*, which Merce refuses to consider his own piece and will not really enter into, is the most successful with public and press. And this annoys Merce.
>
> But the *really* amusing part of all this is the reviews in Berlin unanimously agree the dancers are great, the dancing interesting, it's just that awful music that ruins everything. The fact that John even said "success with press" interests me. I said, "Who the hell cares what the press says?" (I'd had a lot of champagne too. And of course John had, too.) And he said, "You and I don't care, but Merce does!" Wow! Who is fooling whom????

John's analysis of Merce's dour mood seemed simplistic to me. Merce's contribution to *Music Walk with Dancers* was certainly minimal; he'd scarcely bothered to deal with it at all. A value judgment on his part, I thought. I think he deemed *Music Walk* a silly romp, one of John's philosophical statements about life-and-art dressed in outrageous theatrical form, and he just wasn't interested. Furthermore, Merce and I were on this tour due to John's and David's efforts and reputations, not Merce's own, and except for the Berlin Festival, our engagements had all been booked through avant-garde music circles, not dance entrepreneurs. So, despite John's intentions—for in truth he always had Merce's interests at heart—Merce may have felt uncomfortable in these circumstances, and resentful at having been coerced into "collaborating" on *Music Walk*.

My "who the hell cares what the press says?" was born out of the many years when we persevered under a barrage of negative criticism, but it would be hypocritical to say we didn't care about reviews—of course we did!—although Merce always claimed he never read them. But if John was right in his assertion that Merce did care about the critics' appraisals, then the Berlin reviews may well have upset him, though not for the reasons John stated. Undoubtedly, *Music Walk with Dancers* was the most written about, but I think it much more likely that the following negative comments about *Music Walk* would have troubled Merce:

For the sake of the dancers, the public held out. . . . we dislike seeing two such serious artists as Cunningham and Brown lending themselves as foils for such pranks.[5]

The laughter turned against the dancers as well only in the end, when they joined with the musicians in *Music Walk with Dancers* in ridiculing their own art, otherwise taken so seriously.[6]

For the longest time the spectators did not know whether this [concert] was or was not meant to be taken seriously. . . . But the last piece offered a solution. . . . It was an hilarious Dada-act, and people who left during intermission missed the whole point of the performance. . . . Because it was so provocative, the evening at the Hebbel Theater was one of the high points of the festival.[7]

But there may have been still another problem, which I became aware of only when I read the translations of these reviews for the first time decades later while working on this book. Because Merce's dancing was unique, neither classically balletic nor German-expressionist modern, its feral brilliance was foreign to European sensibility. My dancing, by contrast, was close enough to the classical ballet tradition for Europeans to identify with what they already knew. Horst Koegler discussed the program and our dancing in three separate articles:

Watching the dance-duo Merce Cunningham and Carolyn Brown, you repeatedly asked yourself how far ahead of their time they had already moved, how many new possibilities in theatre dance they might reveal that would be brought to fruition only by future generations.

The physical control of the dancers is tremendous; if finally one admires Carolyn Brown even more than Cunningham himself, it is because in the accomplishment of his choreographic structures she shows once again a classical awareness, that he himself has not yet achieved with such absolute sovereignty. If modern dance is going to look in a few decades the way it was shown to us in Berlin by Carolyn Brown, we may look forward to some extraordinary times. What was completely unexpected in these dances was precisely that they were of an incredible beauty.[8]

Obviously I can't report on the quality of Merce's Berlin performances, but John was right in saying that Merce was not working with his usual passionate dedication. Yet if Merce did know the content of these reviews, it would explain something of his subsequent behavior on that tour and afterward. Earle, in Paris, received a postcard from Merce: "Your piece is beautiful. Carol's the belle of Berlin!" That was the first I'd heard of it.

Then he came down with a terrible cold. Only three hours of sleep separated packing up after our last Berlin performance and boarding a seven a.m. plane to Munich. Without the pressure of a performance that night, Merce was able to set the lighting in a relatively easy three hours. I washed costumes. Munich audiences weren't particularly responsive, and *Music Walk* was not so funny, either. Without the Fenice's or Hebbel Theater's mechanical apparatus—ascending and descending stage floors, trapdoors, and a revolving stage adding zany gimmickry—the proceedings seemed tame indeed. One of the three Munich reviews ridiculed the concert and suggested that the performers might be in need of psychiatric care. The other two, to varying degrees, attempted to consider our program—both music and dance—fairly seriously, and again my classical training was viewed as a plus. Merce's moodiness continued. When the four of us walked from theater to restaurant to *pensione,* Merce chose to walk by himself, morose and out of step with the rest of us. Silently I wondered what I might have done to upset him. John fretted aloud and was saddened.

What a precipitously downhill slide from Venice's glorious La Fenice to the Friedrich-Wilhelm Gymnasium in Cologne! At least Merce had no hassles with the lighting, because there were no lights to hassle with. The stage floor—linoleum-covered cement—was brutal; the stage decor— "legs" and back curtains mismatched in three ugly colors—hideous. *Music Walk with Dancers* lost all the technical stunts, including my descending chair, because there were no flies for me to fly from.

And so, on a dingy little high school auditorium stage, we presented our last full performance of the tour. In compensation for the dreary venue, we had a wonderfully lively, responsive audience of young composers, painters, musicians, and writers. Earle was in the audience, along with many of our Darmstadt friends. Their fervor helped us to ignore the cramped space, the terrible floor, the dismal *mise en scène.* In each theater our program was the same, beginning with *Suite for Two* followed by Cage's *Winter Music* for two pianos. Next came five solos: Merce's trilogy—*Untitled Solo, Lavish Escapade,* and *Changeling*—all with Christian Wolff's music, the only times these three solos were performed on the same program. In between were my *Hands Birds* and *Waka,* which provided Merce time to change costumes between his solos. After intermission, *Nightwandering,* our 1958 Stockholm duet, opened the second part of the program, followed by Cage's *Variations* for two pianos. We closed every program with *Music Walk with Dancers*. There were no bows until the end of the concert. After *Music Walk* . . . Merce and I would enter from opposite sides of the stage, meet at center stage, and bow together. Then I would step forward and bow, he would step forward and bow, and then John and David would join us.

The last performance of the tour! I was determined not to waste it. On the linoleum-floored high school stage, the ballet shoes we'd been forced to wear on the ancient splintery wooden floors in previous theaters proved treacherously slippery, so it was back to bare feet and the reassuring feeling of being in touch with the ground, rooted, secure at last. It was completely liberating. In Venice, Earle had been so enthralled listening to John and David play *December '52* from *Folio* for the first time that he did not see me dance *Hands Birds* at all. In Cologne, his second exposure to the piece, I was hell-bent on forcing him to *see the dance* and see *me* dance it! I knew it was a tough assignment, because he'd be all ears, not eyes, once again. My resolve made me dance *Hands Birds* better than I'd ever done before. I felt as though I were flying, yet in control, and full of joy and a surprising self-confidence. And Earle saw it! In his words, it knocked him out. The applause was deafening, but I had no time to appreciate it because I had to change into my *Waka* costume. John came backstage in a dither to say that we really should take individual bows, that the audience was clamoring for them, but the rule held. At the finale, when it came time for me to step forward to bow alone, Merce took my hand and did not let go. All our bows were taken together. Whatever personal tribute I might have received from that wildly enthusiastic audience was denied me, and I was never given the opportunity to perform those solos again. Why did Merce do this? What was going on in his mind? Unanswered questions, and I was not at all sure I wanted to know the answers.

Compared with the next night's event—twenty-eight-year-old Nam June Paik's hilarious, terrifying, bizarre concert—our program was tame. With hammer and saw and much demented high-pitched screaming, Paik assaulted two upright pianos, destroying them before our eyes. Was this frenzied, grinning little man who crawled in and out of the pianos as he tore the strings from their housing and pursued their savage destruction unstrung himself? Abandoning the wreckage, Paik came at the audience armed with scissors, eliciting an audible communal gasp, but only John Cage need have worried. It was John's necktie Paik was after, nothing more. He grabbed it with one hand and with the other cut it off just inches below John's throat. The destruction of John's favorite handwoven necktie, a gift, was bad enough, but the symbolism of the act was truly shocking. Earle wrote about the event in an article, *Planned Panichood:*

> I got pretty nervous too. And so would you, what with not knowing if Paik, me, a friend, an enemy, or a piano is eventually if not NOW going out that three story window into the Rhine, or if the scissors will stop at (with) the necktie, or if bejeezes the day of *rechnung* is upon us all.[9]

Paik later told Earle: "I do homage John Cage. He great Zen master." Once again John's message seemed to have gone awry, and losing his necktie was only the first indignity he suffered that night. Paik proceeded to lather John's head with shampoo, and this time he included David Tudor in his unwelcome attentions. Neither man was amused. (This "composition" was a follow-up of an earlier work composed after meeting John at Darmstadt in 1958, in which Paik also destroyed two pianos.) Eventually, Paik stuffed a dead mouse between his teeth and rushed pell-mell out of the studio. The audience, stunned, sat in edgy silence for several minutes awaiting the next onslaught. After several more minutes, a telephone rang. Paik, on the other end of the line: "The performance is finished."

On October 11, in Brussels, John, David, Merce, and I wrapped up the tour with television performances of *Suite for Two* and *Music Walk with Dancers*, but about that day I remember absolutely nothing. I do recall the evening, in an expensive café on the historic Grand Place celebrating the end of the tour with a bottle of pink champagne, an elegant dinner, and divvying up of the tour's profits. Breaking even would have been more than satisfactory. Reaping a profit was cause for celebration! My share was $220, plus an extra $100 for the T.V. Pretty terrific, I thought. And this after all travel, hotel, and food bills had been paid, explained Merce, who'd kept the books. And so it was farewell to John, who was returning to the States to take up residency as a Fellow at the Center for Advanced Studies at Wesleyan University. The rest of us planned to stay on awhile in Europe to see what the future might bring.

I'd been approached to work in television by an American dancer/choreographer named Bill Milie, who'd studied with Miss Craske and Mr. Tudor and was currently dancing with the Bremen-based American Festival Ballet. Bill, along with a director from Bavaria Television Studio, sent a letter proposing that I appear "as Guest Star in a danced version of Jean Anouilh's *Antigone.* I sincerely hope that you will be pleased with the idea of doing *Antigone.* I feel it's a perfect role for you." I still yearned to dance a dramatic role . . . ideally, of course, in a Tudor ballet. But *Antigone* was not to be. The television studio was completely booked until February, and I couldn't afford to linger that long in Europe. Moreover, not knowing Merce's plans for the company, I was unwilling to commit myself to Bavaria Television in February.

Merce, David, and I went our separate ways. In Cologne, Earle had purchased a 1951 black Mercedes Benz for $130, and between recording sessions for Time Records' Contemporary Sound Series, talks with publishers, and trips to hear performances of Boulez, Stockhausen, et al., the two of us were able to travel a bit for fun. It was heaven. To be alone with Earle. To be NOT dancing, NOT performing, NOT taking class. Heaven to indulge in pastries drenched in *Schlagsahne* (whipped cream) and to get giggly-tipsy on just a swallow or two of new wine. Heaven being a spectator.

On November 2, we set out for London in the Mercedes. I played secretary to Earle's role as Artist and Repertoire Director for the Time Records series in order to justify my presence there. Earle never liked London; his city of choice was Paris, always. But I knew London well—Marjorie Allingham's London, that is—from reading every one of Allingham's mysteries. A week may not be time to know a city intimately, but it's time enough to fall in love with it. And fall I did—an affair too soon over, but always renewed on each subsequent visit. My money ran out (I'd found the wonderful secondhand bookstores, where I began in earnest to collect dance books) and I was experiencing twinges of conscience about not taking class. I flew home in early November. Earle stayed on in Europe for five more weeks.

The ugliness of New York City overwhelmed me. After three months in Europe I returned to a frigid loft buried in soot and grime, its ceiling a crumbling mess from innumerable leaks, the dining table buried beneath stacks of mail. Merce phoned that very afternoon. In a letter to Earle, I commented: "I guess he wanted to know if I'd gone commercial."

After Merce's initial phone call, I heard nothing from him. Five weeks had passed since I'd danced a step and twenty weeks since I'd been to a ballet class. I felt rottenly out of shape. Tudor patted my derrière (all that *Schlagsahne* and goofing off had settled down there) and remarked upon its enlargement with his inimitable wry sarcasm. On November 28, 1960, the Living Theatre gave a cocktail party to celebrate their one-thousandth performance. Remy Charlip and I met at their quarters beneath Merce's studio on Sixth Avenue and Fourteenth Street, expecting to see him there, but no Merce, so we went upstairs to say hello only to discover an advanced class in progress, with Merce teaching it and Judy, Marilyn, and Viola all in class. No one had told Remy or me that Merce had resumed teaching. We were stunned. He saw us there watching. Afterward, between his class and Viola's, he might have come over to speak with us, but instead, clearly avoiding us, he immediately started teaching Viola's class. Ignored, we left. That night I had a terrible dream that I fought with him, screaming, "I quit!"

I kept wishing I'd stayed in Europe. Earle's letters describing his adventures were tantalizing. What was I doing living alone in a freezing cold loft on Third Avenue's wino-infested skid row with the Atlantic Ocean separating me from my husband? Each morning I lay rigid with cold, having shivered through the night under every blanket we possessed, wondering, "What do I really want?" But I had no answer. Just that same nagging question repeating in my head like a mantra, but unlike a mantra it was deeply disturbing.

I went faithfully to the Met to study with Craske and Tudor, but stubbornly refused to go to Merce's classes until he called. Wanting to be wanted. It never occurred to me that he might be waiting for me to call him, to prove my loyalty to him. Another week went by. And then he did phone to invite me to accompany him to the Cherry Lane Theatre to see some one-act plays directed by Nick Cernovich. The ice was broken, and an unspoken truce was declared. Of course, little between us had ever been spoken. Genuine communication with Merce continued to be rare. And dear John, Merce's go-between, his voice, so to speak, was at Wesleyan University, where he was deconstructing the Advanced Studies Department by giving parties for all the faculty where they played hide-and-seek and "giant steps." As some wit suggested at the time, John was humanizing the Humanities Department. The *Hartford Courant,* under the headline "Cage Cages Audience with Cagey Audiometrics," reported: "The freshmen, with the honesty that goes with youth, didn't hide their confusion over Monday's lecture. 'I guess this is pretty advanced stuff,' said one, 'and I'm sure he's making a real contribution to music. But there's only one problem. It doesn't sound good.' "[1]

In the January issue of *Musical America* I discovered that "Susan Pimsleur, director of Musical Artists, is presenting this year Merce Cunningham and Carolyn Brown, John Cage and David Tudor. In addition to their engagements here, they go to Mexico in the spring." Merce, mum as always, had never even mentioned the possibility. But the "engagements" did not materialize. Our quartet touring days had ended forever. When we resumed rehearsals immediately after Christmas it was with full company and, although I regretted never again having the opportunity to dance *Waka* and *Hands Birds,* I was relieved.

We settled into a fairly regular schedule, juggling various ballet classes, jobs, and family obligations as we always had in the past. No one was paid. On tour we still functioned more as family than as a professional dance company. Merce paid hotel and food bills and gave the dancers a twenty-five-dollar honorarium for each performance. I earned an additional fifteen dollars each week by teaching a Saturday-morning technique class at Merce's studio when we were in town. (My total dance income for four months was $445.) Earle's work with Time Records continued, but with minimal recompense and no regular salary. What little savings he had managed to accumulate working as a mixer for Capitol Records were fast disappearing. So when I was offered a bona fide professional dance job by Alek Zybine one evening in early January I was again faced with that old dilemma—shouldn't I be earning my own bread and butter as a dancer?

The problem was that Alek wanted me to dance the *Nutcracker* pas de deux and Sugar Plum Fairy variation, *Spectre de la rose,* and a Spanish duet with him on a chamber concert program with Hungarian dancers Nora Kovach and Istvan Rabovsky a week from that Saturday, and then tour, winding up in Australia for two months in the summer. I didn't know any of the dances, had never in my life performed a classical pas de deux on pointe, in tutu, onstage! The pas de deux in Tudor's neoclassical ballet at Juilliard and his pas de deux class were the closest I'd come. By contrast, Kovach, Rabovsky, and Zybine were classical soloists who had worked in major ballet companies. I was flattered but flabbergasted. The mere thought of attempting that repertory with only five days of rehearsal was unimaginable, and yet I cursed myself for lacking the guts to try it. Was I lazy or a hopeless coward? Earle implied that I was both, but I knew my limitations and was greatly relieved to learn that several ballet dancers with years of performing experience also turned Alek down on the grounds that it was too short notice. Much as I wanted to earn my own living as a dancer, performing the showpiece ballet pas de deux was not the way I wanted to do it. And no matter how uncomfortable I'd felt with Merce on the last European tour, I was not willing to abandon his work.

In February, March, and April, Merce Cunningham and Dance Company gave ten performances in nine states, everywhere dancing the same repertory—*Suite for Five, Crises,* and *Antic Meet.* No new choreography was in the works, a major disappointment for all of us, but rehearsing and performing the same dances over and over again was an opportunity we'd rarely had and badly needed in order to grow both as a company and as individual performers. As it turned out, there were some unexpected challenges for Judith, Valda, and me due to a leg injury suffered by Viola, who was forced to miss the first five of our ten engagements. Judy took her part in *Suite for Five,* and Valda, until then an understudy, danced the other pieces. Viola's duet with Merce in *Crises* and her umbrella solo in *Antic Meet* were assigned to me. Doing Viola's opening part in *Crises* and then going right into my own part nearly killed me, but it was a very good endurance test.

I think Merce was even more relieved than I to be touring with the full company, and his self-confidence seemed fully restored knowing that the company had been engaged on the basis of *his* reputation as dancer and choreographer rather than by avant-garde musical festivals based on John's and David's reputations. John and David were with us, of course, to play piano for *Suite* and *Antic Meet.* John, on leave from Wesleyan, also resumed his duties as chief chauffeur, cheerleader, guru, and gamesman. Once again, nine people tucked themselves into the Volkswagen Microbus, sometimes spending as many as eighteen out of twenty-four hours together. Singing, snoozing, reading, knitting, arguing, laughing, telling stories, playing games, munching, and sipping, we whiled away the hours and miles between New York City and De Kalb, Illinois, De Kalb and Lynchburg, Virginia . . . etc. We totaled six days and one full night on the road plus six hours in the air just to give four performances. Ridiculously long journeys. One performance we gave having had *no* sleep at all, dancing in Lynchburg, Virginia, on Tuesday night, then, after a party, driving all night to Richmond, Virginia, to catch a plane to Atlanta and another to Macon, where we performed Wednesday night after rehearsing in the afternoon. It was impractical. Exhausting. Wonderful.

We had a new lighting designer: Richard Nelson—early twenties, tall, thin, quiet, gentle, thoughtful, and extremely kind. We women gathered Rick under our collective wing like mother hens with a newborn chick. His arrival coincided with Nick Cernovich's disappearance, typical of so many comings and goings in the company. Nick was at first unaware that he'd been replaced. According to him, Merce eventually told him that John had decided he wanted to work with Rauschenberg. This was typical—passing the buck to John, who was always willing to take the heat for him—but it was only partly true. Unbeknownst to Nick, he'd provoked Merce's wrath during a lighting rehearsal of *Rune* at Connecticut College the previous summer. Amber gel was problem one. Sometime during his years with Martha Graham, Merce had acquired her profound aversion to amber light and, like Martha, he would not knowingly tolerate its use. Nick, inspired by Rauschenberg's *Rune* costumes, which had been tie-dyed in October/November hues by Jasper Johns, turned the stage to autumn gold. The lighting, from all reports, was glorious, but from the stage Merce saw only the offending amber gels. Problem two: Merce could not endure tech rehearsals; he considered them a waste of his and his dancers' precious energy. Nick made the unforgivable mistake of spending too much time setting cues while instructing us to walk here and there, go off, come on, face upstage, downstage, stand still, move fast . . . although Merce did as he was bid, he was smoldering. We, onstage, knew it. Nick, out front, did not. When Nick unwittingly said, "Will *my* dancers please move to . . . ," the last bridge burned beneath his feet. Merce left the stage, too furious to speak. Nor did he, ever. Instead of discussing the situation with Nick, he found it easier to get another lighting designer. Irrelevant was the fact that the lighting Nick had conjured up for *Rune* was thought by many to have been extraordinary and extraordinarily beautiful.

Rick's fifth performance with the company was his Armageddon, if one can so name a battle against sloth, ineptitude, and hopelessly antiquated equipment. Many hours before our Volkswagen pulled up to the stage door of the Play and Players Theatre in Philadelphia, Rick had arrived at this dismal excuse for a theater, having taken the train from New York City before dawn with the expectation that he would get the technical work finished by the time we showed up. But when we walked in, Rick's wan face, apologetic smile, and glazed-over eyes revealed the truth. He never lost patience with the lone, decrepit, doddering old geezer of a stagehand, nor did he give up trying to provide the best possible lighting under the wretched conditions, but he understood Merce's priorities and we got our rehearsal as scheduled. What a crucial difference his presence would have made on our 1960 European tour!

March engagements took us west to Ohio and south to North Carolina; in April we went north to upstate New York and Vermont and east to Connecticut, as usual spending far more time in the Volkswagen bus than on the stage. About future company activities Merce continued to be vague, even evasive. Twice, in February, I screwed up my courage and asked him if he planned to return to Connecticut College in the summer. He shrugged and—a bit peevishly, I thought—said he really didn't know. Zybine's offer was still open at that point. If the company had no summer work, I knew I'd have to get some sort of job. Only four days after I had asked Merce for a second time, I received a letter from Jeanette Schlottman requesting that I look over the galley proofs for the Connecticut College 1961 Summer School Bulletin. With no little amazement I discovered not only Merce's name listed as faculty but mine as well! I wrote Merce the following letter within hours of receiving Jeanette's:

Merce dear,

What can we all do to develop an adult relationship of mutual trust and respect between you and your company (collectively and singly)? For eight years, more or less, you have had the love and devotion and loyalty of three of your present company, and yet we have failed to earn your trust and confidence. You continue to treat us as though we were dull-witted children, with whom you are playing some complicated game of secrets, and only you know the rules.

This morning, I received a letter from Jeanette with a galley proof of the Conn. 1961 prospectus, with a list of faculty, including both our names. And yet, only Saturday you said you weren't sure whether or not we were going to Conn. You were still waiting for a letter from Jeanette. It must take a week or two to set up a galley. You have not discussed, in any direct or factual way, my position, salary, etc., nor have you received from me a direct answer whether I will go. You have told your company that they are free to make other plans for the summer, giving them no indication that you were still very much involved in the possibility of going.

The members of your company arrange their whole lives in order to work with you. What further indication do you need to know that they are devoted? Is this devotion not worthy of your confidence? Must we learn that you have won a Guggenheim [Fellowship] by reading the *N.Y. Times*? Must Remy learn that he is not in *Crises* by seeing a program proof in Jeanette's office? Must the company learn that you and I are going to Europe by reading the yellow pages in *Dance Magazine*? Is it not courtesy to show me the pictures which I spent several hours posing for *before* the final selections are made? We love you. We love your work. And, we love one another. But your actions or sometimes your in-actions seem to indicate a lack of love for us. We deserve your respect. We have earned it. When Remy spoke up at the meeting last summer, we should all have backed him up—but I was a coward. I could not defend him, and I could not attack you. I ran away. I can't run away any more. If we organize our lives in order to dance your works, surely you should respect us enough to inform us of your plans, to include us in discussions about your plans. We are not a huge ballet company; we are not working under union rules, with union pay. We don't sign contracts. The hurt, the injury mounts up.

Again,—if you are displeased or dissatisfied with the way one of us is dancing—why not express this dissatisfaction DIRECTLY to the particular person? We all want to dance your pieces as you want them danced. We care very much what *you* think—and yet, it seems that if you do express any displeasure, it is to some *other* one of us, instead of directly to the person involved.

If I go to Conn. this summer, I would like to have special "billing," *there,* and in all future dance programs given elsewhere. A week ago, I would not have *considered* asking this; because I am an idealist of the most romantic, if not corny, variety, believing worth and merit will eventually be recognized. (Obviously, the recognition I value most is yours. And I was willing to wait for it.) But, I begin to realize that in order to receive respect, one must respect oneself, and if formal recognition of my growth as a dancer is not given me, then I must ask for it.

Merce, dear, we are adults, not children. If I have devoted eight years to dance with you, rather than do opera ballet, or TV, or musical comedy, or the *Nutcracker* Pas de Deux,—I didn't do it *for you.* It was *not* a sacrifice. I did it for me. Because I love your dances; because I can feel honest and vital doing them; because I can do something I can believe in. I thank you for that. Please, please accept our love and devotion. It should be a source of *joy* to you—not the awful burden it seems to be. Carol

These thoughts had been stewing in my head and had been discussed many times with Earle and my mother, so they spilled out onto the page easily. Merce telephoned me. He was friendly, his attitude positive. He'd taken the letter extremely well. Even admitted his own failings as a communicator. I was surprised and greatly relieved. Our conversation was one of the few serious heart-to-heart discussions about company affairs that we'd ever had. I no longer remember his explanations about Connecticut College, but he did tell me that he and John had only recently discussed my development as a dancer and had concluded that some recognition of it should be made in the billing. And it was. We didn't discuss it again. Things returned to normal. The company was officially informed that we would be in residence for the fourth summer at Connecticut College. The intermittent touring continued through April.

Performing in America in those years always meant compromise, adjustment, making-do. And yet we worked hard, danced as well as we could, and had fun. In Ye Olde Wishing Well Lodge, in Saratoga, Muzak blaring, John composed, but did not perform, a variation on La Monte Young's *Composition 1960 # 2* (5/5/60) in which a fire is built and burned in front of an audience. John's version:

Loudspeaker playing Muzak.
Light fire under loudspeaker.
Listen.

Also that day John decided that since people were not convinced that what he wrote was actually music, he would call his work "U-sik?"— pronounced with a slight Japanese accent. John could always make us laugh.

The last of the season's ten performances was at Wesleyan. Because the stage was minuscule, we couldn't use it. Trying to dance *Crises* or *Antic Meet* on it would have been as absurd as trying to pack a live octopus into an orange crate, so we turned the auditorium into a stage, placed the two grand pianos at far ends of the rectangular room, split the audience in half, and placed the dancing area in between. We changed our front throughout the program, facing first one way, then another within a single dance— foreshadowing more complicated spacing challenges in the years ahead. We were nearly seasick while rehearsing, but in performance we joined in the spirit of the new adventure and had a very good time.

Much to his and everyone else's amazement, Merce was given a *Dance*

Magazine Award, along with Maria Tallchief and Igor Moiseyev. Among previous awardees were Martha Graham, Doris Humphrey, José Limón, Agnes de Mille, Jerome Robbins, and George Balanchine (who declined the honor the preceding year on the ground that he did not approve of awards in general).[2]

The awards ceremony took place at the New York Athletic Club. The key speaker was the assistant secretary of state for educational and cultural affairs, which was quite ironic since the President's Special International Program for Cultural Presentations had been sending American dance companies abroad since 1954 but had consistently refused to sponsor Merce. *Dance Magazine* noted this, saying that Cunningham's "forays into Europe had been without government fanfare or help of any kind."[3] Editor Lydia Joel, in her preliminary remarks, referred to our Venice performance and stated that Merce had "created an enormous *scandale.*"[4] Fortunately, Merce's citation, read by publisher Rudolf Orthwine, presented a broader view: "Dance innovator whose visual concepts and performing language have influenced a generation of choreographers and have given European audiences a stimulating image of contemporary American dance."[5] In his acceptance speech, Merce remarked: "As for what was said about my shocking the European audience, I have only one thing say about that. I think when Miss Carolyn Brown and Mr. John Cage and Mr. David Tudor and I gave our program in the Fenice Theatre in Venice—*we* were shocked."[6]

The winter-spring touring had seemed to buoy Merce's spirits, despite the awful stages and the endless hours cooped up like a flock of chickens in the VW bus. Receiving the *Dance Magazine* Award lifted them still further. Our personal relationship was again amicable. Merce invited me to dance performances and social occasions, such as a *Dance News* reception for P. W. Manchester, which was crowded with dancers and dance critics who were suddenly ever so nice to us. All except John Martin, of course, who managed a smile but otherwise ignored us.

The day after the *Dance Magazine* Award ceremony, Merce and I saw an electrifying performance by Lupe Serrano and Erik Bruhn in the *Don Quixote* pas de deux, which commanded eighteen curtain calls and deserved even more. It was fever-pitch brilliant, technically impeccable dancing. I'd spent most of that day with Merce—teaching at his studio in the morning, going with him and Earle in the afternoon to a cocktail party in the New York digs of my Venice host Frank Amey, dining in a Japanese restaurant with Merce, John, Toshi Ichiyanagi, his wife Yoko Ono, Frank, and Earle. Merce and I attended the ballet, and afterward returned to his studio where John, Earle, and Toshi were madly copying a new carillon piece of John's so that David Tudor could take it with him to Europe the next day. My reason for describing this day in such detail is merely to explain why, after spending close to twelve congenial hours with Merce, sharing a variety of experiences and having had—I thought—a truly splendid time together, I was so completely unprepared for what happened the following afternoon at his studio, where his dancers gathered for what was a rare event in those years: a company meeting.

Merce's purpose in calling that meeting, it turned out, was to announce to the company that I had asked for billing. Excerpts from a letter written to my parents four days later tell the story:

It seems I created "a scene" in my request for billing. Merce said he realized this changed the Company situation completely but there it is and "we just have to deal with it." . . . He said if anyone had questions they would have to ask me. Imagine! So Remy said, "I want billing, too." Merce then said, a bit sarcastically, "You do?" More conversation resulted in Merce telling Remy he should ask Carol to explain her position. I said I would explain nothing, that this was a matter concerning Merce—as *director* of his Company (Hah!) and me. Merce got a bit salty, saying, "wait a minute, you said any billing other than the one I read would be unrealistic." I agreed. But I said not one word more. Judy said that the billing should be up to Merce, not to the Company and *he* should do it, not ask them.

Merce's performance seemed to me to be cowardly—really contemptible. . . . Oiy! I walked out and away as fast as I could. I decided then and there to quit the whole mess. But, after talking it over with Earle at length, who has been after me like you have, to ask for billing, I decided to swallow my hurt and disillusionment and face the situation for what it is.

Billing will make my life more difficult and complicated with Merce and with the Co. I'm not sorry I asked for it, only very sorry I *had* to ask for it. What I'm really interested in is dancing well. If this new situation separates me from the Co.—fine, I'll accept it. I really do think billing is ridiculous— a good dancer is a good dancer no matter what her billing—and what I had hoped for was recognition from Merce. *Asking* for recognition makes the eventual receipt of it worthless. Well, he *really* made it worthless by intimating that I was blackmailing him for it—I was naive enough to think he would say to the Company that I deserved it.

Never had I walked from 61 West Fourteenth Street to 40 Third Avenue so quickly. Propelled by anger, fighting tears, burning with humiliation and disappointment, I burst into the loft and headed straight for the type-writer to write my letter of resignation.

Earle watched. Waited. Listened to my story. Read the letter. Then quietly advised me not to send it right away. "Give yourself time to think it over," he cautioned. Luckily, we were due at Louise and Edgard Varèse's for cocktails with Robert Craft. The following evening at Town Hall, Craft was to conduct an all-Varèse concert, including *Equatorial* (1933–34), Varèse's first composition with electronic instruments, and Earle was going to "play" one of the oscillators. Varèse was now seventy-seven years old, virtually ignored by the American musical establishment, so he was understandably excited and happy about this concert. Sharing Varèse's pleasure that evening was a tonic and a most welcome change of atmosphere. It gave me time to simmer down, even to forget for a while how painfully betrayed I felt. That particular evening I appreciated how fortunate I was, thanks to Earle, to have another life outside the company.

My options lay themselves out clearly the next day. In three hours I earned seventy-five dollars modeling for photographer Saul Leiter and *Harper's Bazaar.* I could earn more in a month modeling than I could in a year dancing with Merce. But is that what I wanted? No other modern-dance company interested me in the slightest, and beginning a ballet career at my age was not realistic. Oh, probably I could have gotten into a ballet company, but dancing on pointe still felt alien to me, a limitation I doubt I could have entirely overcome. Full expressivity in pointe shoes demands that they be a completely natural extension of the legs and feet. It's the small, connecting steps that expose the truth. I always felt fettered, never free, with my feet imprisoned in those pretty, box-toed satin slippers.

At six o'clock that evening, I went to Merce's studio to take his advanced class. The whole company was present for the first time in months. A different vibration, discernible yet undefinable, charged the space. My letter of resignation was filed away, to be taken out and read upon occasion for the purpose of reflecting on fate, choice, chance, and circumstance. Working with John and Merce was not a career. It was a way of life—the life I wanted—although I sensed there would be rough times ahead. My hero worship and blind trust were going to need tempering. A colder, clearer eye would be needed if I was to survive.

I suspect I was not the only person in Merce's company who came within a hairsbreadth of resigning that year. Viola left for Europe to vacation with her sister and brother-in-law shortly after that painfully memorable meeting, and while she was away Merce began work on a new dance for three women and himself. This time it was made clear from the beginning that Remy was left out, but not so clear which of the four women would be. Merce's words were ambivalent and evasive. The steps he choreographed, however, were not. The dance was made on Judy, Marilyn, and me. When Merce first told us about it, he said he *should* use Viola but he didn't know how to reach her in Europe. Later he told Judy he felt he had to go by seniority, which meant Judy would lose out. Even so, he had Judy fitted for a costume and the choreography he set fit her to perfection. It was impossible to imagine Viola dancing that part. Poor Judy was on a roller coaster of highs and lows, passionately involved in the dance and terrified it would be taken away from her. Why, we asked each other again and again, was Merce seemingly so incapable of casting his dances as he wished, informing the members of his company, and then assuming responsibility for his decisions? Not one of us questioned his absolute right to cast his dances however he liked, no matter how unhappy it might make us. Seniority was not really the question. Had it been, Remy, the elder statesman of the company since Marianne left, should have been in every dance.

In some misguided way, Merce no doubt agonized over the situation, too. Obviously he hated his role as director, but the pretense of operating in a kind of quasi-democratic mode and shunting accountability onto us was little more than moral cowardice. Viola returned to a fait accompli, yet Merce still presented her with the problem. He may have felt somehow exonerated by seeming to let her make the final decision, but what options did she have? The rest of us, Judy most of all, felt absolutely terrible. The cruelty may have been unintentional, but it was a diabolical game and caused considerable unhappiness.

The new dance, *Suite de danses,* set to a jazz score by a thirty-one-year-old Canadian composer named Serge Garant, had been commissioned by Pierre Mercure for Canadian Broadcasting Corporation in Montreal and was to be broadcast live as a part of a half-hour program called *Sérénade éstivale* on June 12. *Suite de danses* vanished even more quickly than the vapors of our plane as we flew home at weekend's end. Merce never resurrected the dance or even recycled the movement. Jasper Johns's "TV-blue"-dyed costumes went into storage and stayed there. But for Judy and me at least, *Suite de danses* had provided a thrilling occasion to dance in close proximity to a jazz ensemble and full orchestra—a deliriously intoxicating, joyful, one-time fling that we would never forget. Dance and Music can do much, much more than merely "coexist," but perhaps one has to dance to know empirically just how *much* more. John Cage could not dance. Nor, I suspect, would he have approved of the wild cascade of endorphins released if he could, because somewhere beneath his Zen-Buddhist nonattachment, the Methodist minister he once intended to be was always lurking.

Within hours of our return to New York, I received a phone call from a distraught Remy. In our absence he had received a letter from Merce stating that he was no longer needed in the company, a bolt from the blue for which Remy was completely unprepared despite the rancor that had festered between them for months. After phoning me, Remy went to the studio to confront Merce, to ask him, face-to-face, why? It went, according to Remy, something like this:

M.C.: You're more interested in your other projects—the Paper Bag Players, your children's books, book jackets, designing costumes, et cetera.

R.C.: My first priority has always been dancing with you. I have never let my other work interfere with your rehearsals, tours, performances or with doing costumes and publicity for your company.

M.C.: But you haven't been dancing very well.

R.C.: I'm dancing better than ever, Merce. Too bad you can't see it.

M.C.: . . . something of a "ham."

R.C.: Can there be only one ham in the company?

M.C.: And you stopped wearing your toupee.

R.C.: [Aghast] But *you* never asked me to wear it in the first place! I only heard rumors that you wanted me to wear one. You've never *ever* mentioned the topic to me before this moment!

Then Remy listed a number of grievances he'd been harboring about Merce's treatment of him, to which Merce replied, "Martha treated her people much worse than that!" "Since when," asked Remy, "do we hold up Martha Graham as a model of propriety?"

In spite of the acrimony of their exchange, the outcome was this: Remy could go to Connecticut College with the company if he wished. Merce could promise nothing after that, and if Remy did choose to go, Merce said he feared they would have a very difficult time getting along but he was willing to try. We *all* loved Remy. We could not imagine life without him, yet given Merce's negative feelings it seemed pointless to us for Remy to subject himself to still further misery. Devastated, Remy stubbornly determined to stick it out.

No doubt about it, in 1961, the Cunningham Dance Company was a wounded body, and I, for one, was very wary of further hurt.

The summer of '61 was unlike any other we'd spent at Connecticut College. Performances in Boston and Montreal broke up our six-week residency, so the single-focus concentration we'd experienced in previous summers was gone; it felt as though we had only one foot on campus while the other was out testing new ground. Once again the company was housed cozily in North Cottage, but this year, John was in residence, too, sharing Merce's first-floor faculty suite in the opposite wing. From my light and airy room on the second floor with its east- and south-facing windows, I could sit at my desk and observe John below at his, laboring in northern-exposure gloom, intensely immobile from seven in the morning until midnight. I called him Stone Buddha Pregnant Beaver—that is, immovable yet slaving ceaselessly at his task, which was to compose a new work for orchestra.

Commissioned by the Montreal Festivals Society, the music would have its premiere in a matter of weeks, and although he'd hired Toshi Ichiyanagi to help him, John still didn't know how he'd finish in time. Titled *Atlas Eclipticalis,* it involved chance operations and included placing transparent templates on an astronomical atlas and transcribing the positions of the stars. With less than a month before the premiere, John, in desperation, employed dancers in the company to toss pennies for him in order to speed up his laborious chance operations. I've forgotten the pay scale (a penny a toss?) but I still have the check for $2.50 with which he paid me on July 30. Like all but one of the dancers who tossed pennies to help him, I never cashed it. John complained we'd screwed up his checkbook. Apparently deadline pressure affected more than his checkbook, because he reported to me that he was not writing very well: "The harp part stinks," and "There'll be lots of rehearsal problems."

Soon after Toshi moved in to assist John, Bob Rauschenberg joined our community in North Cottage. He'd come to design not only costumes and decor for the new dance but also the lighting. Rick Nelson had been engaged only on a performance-to-performance basis, and he had taken a job working full time at Bucks County Playhouse. Bob didn't know a leico from a shin-buster, had never run a light board, focused a special, cut a gel, hooked up cables, or written a light plot. Truth be told, about theatrical lighting Rauschenberg was completely in the dark, but he was so disgruntled with the way other people had lit his costumes and sets that he was determined to learn. His initiation took place in Montreal, ironically under the tutelage of Nick Cernovich, whose lighting he'd so disliked. Nick was in Montreal to light the James Waring Dance Company. Having neither hands-on skills nor technical knowledge, and being totally unversed in backstage lingo, Bob was at a complete loss when trying to convey his wishes to the electricians. With extraordinary magnanimity, given the awkward circumstance of his dismissal, Nick stepped in to translate Bob's intentions into theatrical reality. Thus, under difficult circumstances began Bob's tenure as the Merce Cunningham and Dance Company lighting designer. It was a monumental change. For at least four years, Bob's active presence would have a profound effect on the look of the work and on the morale and social life of the company.

In the dancers' wing there were changes, too. Three new company members—Shareen Blair, Steve Paxton, and Valda Setterfield—joined Remy, Judy, Viola, Marilyn, and me. Work on the new dance soon revealed that Merce was choreographing for all nine dancers, Remy included, which we read as a good sign, although still hanging over Remy's and by extension all our heads was Merce's assertion that he could promise Remy nothing after the summer.

From the college's point of view, our residency was predicated on teaching technique classes, not on the creation of new work. The Cunningham classes had become wildly popular. More than eighty students squeezed into Crozier-Williams's East Studio for my first elementary class. The class was so unwieldy that it had to be divided into two sections, and so Viola's "assistant" status had to be quickly changed to that of "faculty." As far as Merce was concerned, our teaching was merely the means by which he kept his company together, a penance to be endured. But who would ever have guessed this from those classes he taught at Connecticut College? Carefully planned, brilliantly paced, devastatingly difficult, exhausting and inspiring, they inevitably ended with thunderous applause from a starry-eyed student body. How he gave that much energy to teaching two classes every morning, when what consumed him was making a new, forty-five-minute work for nine dancers every afternoon and evening, is hard to comprehend. By contrast, his dancers, even those of us who had to teach, had it easy. Merce was well into his warm-up by the time I greeted the morning. Sitting on the stoop that led down to North Cottage's basement kitchen, I luxuriated in birdsongs and dew-drenched earth smells, ate a soft-boiled egg drowned in wheat germ, sipped my yucky health drink, and awaited the morning-shattering lion's roar that erupted faithfully from Remy's window as he performed his yoga in the nude. For some, that ear-splitting roar served as a reliable alarm clock. It never failed to make me laugh aloud and sent me off to teach my class with a smile on my face.

Work on the new dance, *Aeon*, began immediately. My journal entry for the first rehearsal reports: "So far the new work is 'groupy.' Six girls and two boys dashing around like crazy, in phrases of 6, 8, 10, 12, etc., all quite fast-footed. We worked hard—things went happily and well." My notes divide the dance into nine parts, each part having from two to seven sections with a total of thirty-five discrete sections comprising solos, duets, trios, quartets, on up to sections employing the full company. In the beginning we rehearsed them in no particular order while Merce played around with various sequences in order to discover how the sections could connect. I don't believe that chance played any role in this procedure. In the end he settled on one order, no matter which of three versions—long, short, or touring—we performed. The short version deleted one section but had the full cast of nine dancers; the touring version deleted several sections and had a cast of six—four women, two men.

The program note for *Aeon* reads: "This is a dance of actions, a celebration of unfixity, in which the seasons pass, atmospheres dissolve, people come together and part. Its meaning is the instant in the eye and ear, and its continuity is change." But this did not appear until *Aeon*'s second performance, on August 17 at Connecticut College. At the premiere in Montreal on August 5, the dance was not completely finished and the order of the sections differed from the final version. Of course the dancers had been told nothing. We devised our own program notes among ourselves and, as often happened in Merce's dances, in order to facilitate rehearsing the many sections, we would give them names. Usually it was the dancers who played the name game, but Merce often contributed to it as well. A sampling from *Aeon:* Sweetie's Waltz (named after Bob Rauschenberg's rather perverse pet kinkajou); Moonflower Trios; Queer Turns; Flying Sixes; Horse Tango; the Coney Island; Flashbulb Relay; the Horror Phrase (a unison section that was close-to-impossible to do in unison and caused endless squabbles among us all); Firehose Bounce; Folk Quartet; Gentleman Caller.

Let loose on *Aeon*, Rauschenberg's theatrical imagination took wing.

Although constrained, as usual, by Merce's insistence that the body be visible, Bob managed to circumvent the rule while still complying with it. Tights and leotards (tank tops for the men), dyed in blues and blue-grays, served as the basic costume. Then he proceeded to transform stage space and dancers with dazzling invention. Literally dazzling, if not blinding! All nine dancers were onstage when the curtain opened. From wing to wing, a scrim stretched across the back. Before a step was taken or a muscle moved, three separate explosions of flash powder stunned the ear and blinded the eye while affixing the dancers' silhouettes on the retina. The dance had begun. Much later, in the Flashbulb Relay section, tiny flashbulbs attached to wrists, arms, and legs were ignited at random, turning the stage into a field of fireflies. At times, Bob had the women don flowing floor-length scarves ("sleeves," we called them) that were gathered on elastic, slipped over our shoulders, and fell in two full panels on either side of the body. In another section, the men mutated into ungainly birds in Bob's outrageous cowboy chaps covered in feathers. An idiotic section— let's just say it *felt* idiotic to do—involved the hoisting of a very heavy length of grimy gray firehose as we formed a complicated little knot of bodies while bouncing up and down and changing directions according to some maddening mathematical scheme of Merce's. Crossovers behind the scrim, lit so as to be always visible, became a mysterious part of the dance: "Seasons pass, atmospheres dissolve . . ." A curious Rube Goldberg-like contraption constructed by Bob flew through the air, spewing foggy clouds (or, when malfunctioning, trickles) of dry ice across the stage. While it moved, suspended, the dancers lay still where they had fallen, in the darkness below. The object's presence seemed ominous, even threatening. We called it "the Aeon Machine." The "Coney Island" section should have been fun. And dazzling in its own way. It got its name from the front somersault I attempted to perform with a length of rainbow-colored scarf attached to my waist. Three men stood close behind one another, stage left, facing into a stage-right wing. Out of that wing I came running in a kind of Olympic vault start, scarf trailing. I leapt and landed sitting on Man #1's shoulder, fell face forward over Man #2's back, flipped my legs over and down onto Man #3's back as he caught me under my armpits and carried me offstage. At most, a seven-second bit. The scarf, when well behaved, was supposed to arc over the three of us in a momentarily glorious rainbow. It rarely worked; whether it did or didn't, my body screamed in protest. I was no gymnast, and the necessary speed meant I couldn't control the final impact of the somersault; even so, I loved doing it. It felt daring, and I was always rewarded with Bob's expressed delight when the scarf made its arching rainbow.

One piece of Bob's *Aeon* costumes, however, I still associate with the tension and the mostly unspoken, unpleasant relations I experienced with Merce that summer. My interpretation of events: I was being punished for rocking the boat with my request for billing. As *Aeon*'s structure evolved, it seemed to confirm Merce's newly arrived-at democratic casting philosophy. He choreographed something special for each of the regulars: a duet for Marilyn and Merce, a duet for Judy and Merce, a trio for Merce, Remy, and Steve, a quartet for Merce, Carolyn, Judy, and Viola, a long solo for Viola, a brief solo for Carolyn, and several solos for Merce. As I recall, my solo was the last special to be made, and I had begun to assume that I would not have one. Viola's was extraordinary—like a long sob of anguish and inner torment, and she performed it with a sinuous, gutsy passion. One day, after she'd done a run-through of it onstage in Palmer Auditorium, Merce turned to me and said, "Now I suppose I have to make something for you." If, by this remark, Merce intended to humble and humiliate me, he of course succeeded. What I perceived intellectually as mean-spirited, spiteful, even cruel was emotionally even worse: a hard slap across my face. But my tears were shed in private.

The movement he'd given Viola was weighted, earthbound, full of peculiar curves and angles and unusual rhythms. As she performed it, it was intensely human, full of angst. In contrast, the movement he gave to me covered space, felt airy, birdlike, balletic (which was okay, though I was hankering to try some gutsy stuff for a change). But it wasn't the steps that disturbed me, it was the rope that Merce himself tied around my feet and then had me tie around my own neck while I sat astride Steve Paxton's shoulders. The rope was a Rauschenberg construct; that is, an art object in and of itself: thick, old, dirty. From it dangled a tin can, an old sneaker, and a baseball cap much worse for wear. Were Bob and Merce in cahoots on this? I imagined they were. Wasn't the symbolism too explicit to misconstrue? Obviously I couldn't dance with rope and its dangling detritus around my neck without literally choking while simultaneously flagellating myself to death, so Merce had to choreograph its transfer from neck to waist before I could begin the solo. The psychological implications seemed to me at the time utterly transparent and despicable. I couldn't have felt much worse if I'd had acid dripped into an open wound. Later, hurt feelings subsiding, a more objective me was not unaware that the rope business superimposed a strong dramatic character onto the dance. I did my best to focus on that dimension and to ignore the personal stuff.

Merce inflicted one other wound that summer, which, again, I perceived to be quite intentional, one more means of putting me in my place, so to speak. Midway through the summer session, he dispatched Valda to inform me that he and I would not be performing our duet *Nightwandering* at the festival as originally scheduled. It wasn't the cancellation that so upset me, it was being told about it by an intermediary. That Merce had neither the backbone to tell me himself, nor sufficient respect for me to explain his reasons, was, in my *Antigone* eyes, another demonstration of moral cowardice. I did not suffer this wound in silence. Far more angry than hurt, I immediately marched myself to Creon's rooms to tell him so.

Merce hated confrontation. Over the years, those who have had the guts to confront him rarely benefited, and I knew this all too well from recent experience, but I could not allow my own moral cowardice to win out. Taken aback by my sudden, uninvited appearance at his door, his only response was a slightly sarcastic, "I'm sorry if your feelings have been hurt," but he made it sound like the opposite was true and seemed to miss the real reason for my rage. I returned to my room even angrier and more frustrated than when I'd left it. To Earle I wrote: "Our 'leader' has just displayed another show of moral cowardice. My hands shake, my heart pounds and I'm angry, disgusted, depressed. If it weren't so theatrical, I'd like to pack up, and drive away—quietly and for good. But it's too dramatic, too easy—and too silly. I don't know the whole story—as usual. . . ." Of course I never did know, and the topic was never again discussed.

Was I making mountains out of molehills? Dredging up those old memories, reliving them through my letters and journals, has proven to be acutely painful and disturbing all over again. Only the anger is missing. Whether real or merely perceived, those events that began in Europe during the 1960 summer tour and continued intermittently into the following summer inevitably colored my professional relationship with Merce. Without genuine trust there's bound to be edginess, the disquieting need for self-protection. My attempts to build the necessary trust—his in me, mine in him—had apparently failed, thus tainting the wellspring of our rapport. Poor Merce. All he wanted was to dance. Even *making* dances scored a very distant second place in those years. And when it came to coping with personnel and the personal problems of his dancers, his social skills were hopelessly inadequate. We all knew it, so why did we continue to want him to be different, to be what he was not?

Dancing, thank god, has a way of dispelling anger, easing pain, and charging the spirit, at least in the very best circumstances, providing one allows it to happen. Pesky ego evaporates in what Merce has called "the synthesis of the physical and spiritual energies."[1] There's no competition, not even with oneself. Neither past nor future is relevant. Everything exists in the immediate present, *in the dancing*, when mind, body, and spirit function as one. And that's what happened in Montreal.

La Semaine Internationale de Musique Actuelle, under the direction of Pierre Mercure, opened the monthlong Montreal Music and Drama Festival. It was an ambitious and largely successful attempt to replicate the festivals of new music renowned in Europe, except it went further by including showings of experimental film and dance. Choreographers were asked to team up with a contemporary composer of their own choosing, which resulted in collaborations between James Waring and Richard Maxfield, Françoise Riopelle and Pierre Mercure, Cunningham and Cage.

But Cage's intention was always that his music should have a life beyond Cunningham's dance, and so it has. In Montreal, the work's world premiere was heard on the festival's opening concert without the dance. *Atlas Eclipticalis* is a work with eighty-six instrumental parts, which may be played in whole or in part for any duration, in any ensemble, chamber or orchestra, with or without *Winter Music* (for piano[s]), and with or without an electronic version made possible by the use of contact microphones and associated amplifiers and loudspeakers operated by an assistant to the conductor. On this occasion, John conducted a chamber orchestra of seventeen musicians, David Tudor played *Winter Music*, and Toshi Ichiyanagi was in charge of electronics. Thirty-one years passed before the first performance of the complete composition with eighty-six instrumentalists. It took place in Carnegie Hall on October 29, 1992, with Petr Kotik conducting and David Tudor playing *Winter Music*. Intended as a celebration of Cage's eightieth birthday, it was instead a deeply moving memorial tribute. John had died just three weeks and three days before his eightieth birthday, on August 12.

Atlas Eclipticalis proposes a far more flexible situation than Cunningham's choreography permitted. Except for its length (the inclusion or exclusion of a section or two) and the number of dancers on stage, *Aeon* was always recognizably, consistently the same. Once again, ideologically, John had led the way and Merce had gone along—but just barely. However, in whatever form *Atlas Eclipticalis* and *Aeon* might appear, John's basic idea was that whatever the audience saw and/or heard was the whole—not an excerpt, not a reduction, not a variation of the whole, but the thing complete in itself—a full and physical realization of the philosophical stance in which John stood firmly rooted. We were the flesh-and-blood, muscle-and-sinew embodiment of John's ideas, without the knowledge of them.

Of course, none of this was in our minds when, at 10:30 on the third night of the festival, we finally got onstage. The curtain had been held for twenty minutes, we dancers knew not why. Unbeknownst to us, Bob had disappeared, no one knew where. Merce and John were outraged, thinking he must be in a bar drinking, when, in fact, he'd gone out into the house to see for himself how his lighting looked. It was a naive lack of communication that resulted in a rather serious waste of time. Until that moment, Bob's sense of theater time was nil. After the performance, John lit into him on its paramount importance, and his angry lecture was apparently something Bob would not forget. His next three paintings—the Time paintings—all incorporated clocks.

There could have been a further ghastly goof-up. Our new lighting designer almost didn't make it to Montreal. With no company manager, communications were scanty at best in those years, and for some reason Rauschenberg was out of the loop—completely oblivious to everything except the objects and costumes he was making. On the day of our departure via bus from New London to Logan Airport in Boston to catch an early evening flight to Montreal, Bob, who was still working feverishly on his Rube Goldberg contraption, was there to see us off. "Why isn't Bob with us?" Merce asked, peering out the window at a smiling, waving Bob. No one spoke the answer, which was, obviously, "Because no one told him he should be!" John, David, and Toshi were already in Montreal for the opening of the festival, and everyone else in the Cunningham company was on that bus. Bob, finding himself abandoned, realized he'd have to fend for himself, but to his dismay no commercial flight would get him to Montreal in time for our early-morning rehearsal. Nothing if not resourceful, Bob chartered a plane and pilot to transport himself, Rube Goldberg machine and all, to Montreal. Doubly lucky for Bob, Nick was there willing to offer a helping hand. Amazingly, everything went wonderfully well, and Earle, rarely given to rapturous enthusiasm, declared *Aeon* to be "one of Merce's *great* works."

In Montreal, Toshi Ichiyanagi had operated the electronics. In New London, twelve days later, this task was performed by Richard Maxfield, who badly misgauged the acoustics of Palmer Auditorium and set levels intolerably high. The distortion created by the contact microphones was nearly unbearable. Sitting in the audience that night, my father, who had recently undergone radiation treatments for cancer in the ear canal and throat, was reduced to tears by the excruciating pain caused by the sound and had to leave. He was not alone. Many people suffered profound discomfort and some felt compelled to escape the cacophony as my father did. After the performance even Cage-Cunningham "friends" deplored the loudness. It's unlikely that John, conducting in the pit, could have experienced the full brunt of it because the loudspeakers were behind him. Still, under the barrage of objection, John defended the cacophony by likening it to the screech of the subway, jackhammers drilling through pavement, the roar of a jet plane taking off. It was, he declared, part of contemporary life, and everyone should not only get used to it, but enjoy it! It was at such moments that John was his most maddening. Terrified of pain, faint at the sight of blood, wincing in the face of dancers' sprains and aching muscles, John stubbornly defended this intolerable assault on the hearing of his audiences, even though caused by miscalculation on the part of an assistant. Chance working its diabolical worst! One of the post-performance party guests was Yvonne Rainer, then a New York City student of Merce's who'd come to Connecticut to see *Aeon*. With guileless naiveté she questioned John: shouldn't art be a search for the beautiful? To which John replied that art's function is not to search for the beautiful but to discover the new.

Until this performance, loudness per se had never been one of the complaints about the music that coexisted with Merce's dances. Of course, it wasn't just the level but also the character of the sound that engendered the outrage. Perhaps, had Buckminster Fuller or someone equally revered by John confronted him with the facts concerning hearing loss caused by high-decibel noise—that it is slow, permanent, and absolutely incurable—John might have been persuaded to abandon its use, but certainly carping dance critics never persuaded him.

Would that he had involved himself in the many experiments that have demonstrated that music works directly on the body itself to produce emotional effects—influencing blood flow to the brain, stimulating metabolic glands, increasing or decreasing muscular energy, accelerating breathing or decreasing its regularity, affecting blood pressure.[2] "At an unexpected or unwanted noise," says the famed ear surgeon Dr. Samuel Rosen of Columbia College of Physicians and Surgeons, "the pupils dilate, skin pales, mucous membranes dry; there are intestinal spasms and the adrenals explode secretions. The biological organism is disturbed."[3] It is so strange to me that John never revealed the slightest curiosity about the physiological *effects* of sound on the human body/mind. His mind was as open to all manner of noise as his spirit was closed to the pleasures of great music from Beethoven to bebop.

So, while John's music made enormous demands for attention to itself, appreciation of Merce's choreographic efforts often suffered. Wrote Louis Horst (who must have snorted and sniffed a great deal in his seat on the aisle): "The stage action may have had its large share of somewhat dull aridity, but it also had sections of plastic beauty of design and movement, especially Merce Cunningham's solo passages that attained the high places of dance with fine dramatic expressiveness. But the insensitive hullabaloo in the pit, amplified umpteen millions of degrees, made it completely impossible to appreciate these beauties with the intent absorbing attention they deserved."[4]

It amazes me to this day to read reviews of dances I knew intimately, not from seeing them but from working on them in rehearsal for weeks, then dancing them again and again onstage. What I understood kinesthetically, what I felt while dancing them, what I imagined them to look like, so rarely squared with any critic's view. How is it possible that what my body/mind *knew* was there in Merce's work could have gone unseen, unexperienced, unfelt, unacknowledged by the witnesses on the aisle? How much this can be blamed on the music, I can't say. But one dance critic, Jill Johnston— not blinded by the sound—did see, and her wonderfully perceptive review in *The Village Voice* certainly made up for the deprecating censure of the others.

It is not easy to see. Outside the theatre, living as we do, most of us see very little with our eyes wide open. . . . it is rare to see more than a general outline. Or to see more and still *enter*. That is the crucial transition, from seeing to entering. Not only crucial but mysterious, so I won't say any more except to note that I think most people who go to dance concerts don't see very well, not even dancers, sometimes dancers especially, and most often critics, who must attend special classes in becoming blind.

Mr. Cunningham presented a new dance, *Aeon*, almost 50 minutes long, to a score by John Cage and with decor by Robert Rauschenberg. *Aeon* is a dance of great scale. It moves through so much, in range of quality, physical force, the human condition—that the whole thing is staggering to think of in retrospect. Human events: the activity of dancers on a proscenium stage. Other human events: the ways people communicate with each other, or speak for themselves. Exterior events: explosions, clouds, lights, a machine, sounds. And always the dancing, the superb dancing. The stillness too, which is never a mere choreographic stop, but an act of undaunted containment, of simple yet magnificent composure, of not-being which is the essence of being. A complete act, not a choreographic or dramatic transition.

Cunningham's own range in this dance is fantastic. Not only those typical sudden shifts from motion to stillness, but the subtle gradations of energy (I have a vivid recollection of an "incident" originating as a vibration in the thighs, transferred to the stomach, traveling upward to the arms and shoulders and exploding like a geyser at the top); not to mention all the complicated coordinations, and wordless drama that every movement event secretes.

Cunningham is a great dancer, and you know it not by his technical range and command alone; you feel it in the whole man, the whole man is in it every time. You may see a procession of selves and the man never makes a move not true to himself.[5]

After our Montreal high we were raring to go, but sadly, our Connecticut College summer came to an abrupt end with a single performance of *Crises* on the second night of the festival. In his fourth year there, it would seem that Merce had made no headway at all in establishing his rightful place as a choreographer. Indeed, he'd lost ground. For Remy, whose last performance was in *Aeon* on August 17, the summer of '61 was the bitter, painful dénouement of his eleven-year commitment to Merce. It was unthinkable to me that Remy would be with us no longer.

New York in late August. Hot, grimy, depressing. My least-favorite time of year in that manic-depressive city. Eager as I was to cut loose from six weeks of community living and the unpleasant vibrations emanating from Merce—wrongly or rightly perceived—I was not overjoyed facing months of living alone in our Third Avenue loft with no compelling reason to be there. While I unpacked, Earle packed. In two days he'd be off to Europe again for performances of his own music and to produce recordings for Time Records's Contemporary Sound Series. I couldn't bear the thought of being left behind. It meant I would miss the September 9 premiere of *Available Forms*, his bold, innovative work for chamber ensemble that had been commissioned by the city of Darmstadt. Considering our tenuous financial situation, I knew I shouldn't even think about Europe, but the past rather rocky year had left some raw wounds that needed time to heal. Earle maintained absolute neutrality. "Consult the *I Ching*," he suggested. I opened "The Book of Chinese Wisdom" randomly, and there it was—the very message I sought: "It furthers one to cross the great waters." Without asking Merce's permission—brazen? cowardly? probably both—I gave myself a six-week furlough. I knew only that I had to attend the first performance of Earle's new work, and once in Europe there was no urgent reason to return. What better cure than traveling in France,

Germany, Switzerland, and Italy with Earle, as I'd always dreamed of doing?

At Darmstadt's sixteenth annual Internationale Ferienkurse fur Neue Musik, Earle Brown was about to make some revolutionary history. His *Available Forms* was the first strictly open-form work for orchestra ever written. "Being placed on a program at the contemporary music festivals at Darmstadt or Donaueschingen became the modern equivalent of being commanded to perform at Versailles by the Sun King,"[6] wrote the *New York Times* music critic Donal Henahan, not without sarcasm, but those composers so honored by Darmstadt (as well as those who were not) would probably have agreed. Although Tudor and Cage had performed some of Earle's earlier open-form piano pieces on previous trips to Europe, no orchestra anywhere in the world had experienced this kind of indeterminate composition.

An important distinction needs to be made between Earle Brown's open-form works such as *Twentyfive Pages,* which John pronounced "epoch making;" and Cage's indeterminate works begun some years later. Cage was attempting a kind of hierarchy-less, democratic situation in which sounds should be allowed to be themselves, unsullied by ego, taste, desire, memory, history. John's deepest concerns were as philosophical and sociological as they were musical. He wanted to change the world— not just music, but the very nature of human beings.

Earle's concerns were *musical.* He was little concerned with how to improve the world, and he wholeheartedly affirmed conventional, historical artistic process. His inspiration for open form had come from the visual arts—above all the mobiles of Alexander Calder and the action painting of Jackson Pollock. For a single mobile, Calder carefully designed and constructed perhaps a dozen different metal objects, but then he put them into space, allowing them to float in ever-changing relationship to one another. Looking at Calder mobiles made Earle aware that within a single work of art the relationships of one part to another and between himself and the work could constantly shift—one work of art, yet an endlessly modifiable one. As for Pollock, Earle wanted his music to sound the way Pollock's paintings looked. They reminded him of polyphony: their lines, textures, densities, and details were the kinds of things he heard in his head, and he wanted to hear them with orchestral textures and colors, so he wrote *Available Forms.* It consists of twenty-seven composed sound events grouped on six unbound pages whose order is chosen by the conductor in performance. Sequence, the juxtaposition of two or more events, the timing, speed (accelerando and ritard), the dynamics, the attack and decay, the silences between events, all are determined *spontaneously* by the conductor in performance and indicated to the orchestra through hand signals.

Earle returned from early rehearsals alarmed and distraught. Conductor Bruno Maderna had devised complicated hand signals that were too difficult for the musicians to assimilate and act upon. On the spot, I thought up and made a simple conductor's aid out of cardboard, with big black numbers to indicate the page and a sliding indicator arrow. Everyone seemed to like this solution; Bruno used it for the first performance and it became the prototype for all subsequent performances—a part of the published manuscript.

Even before the first rehearsal, *Available Forms* had become *the* sizzler topic at Darmstadt that summer, just as Cage's very presence and presentations had been in 1958. It was performed on the festival's final program with music by Stravinsky, Schoenberg, Webern, and Boulez.

Bruno had been scared out of his wits. At the beginning of the piece, when his left hand went up to signal, it was trembling. Afterward, beaming with pride and pleasure, he exclaimed, "I did it! I did it!" meaning he'd created the form spontaneously, in performance, and had not preplanned the final form ahead of time. I wrote in my journal:

> Earle's piece was fabulous! Bruno conducted it with such intensity! The musicians were very alive, really *THERE*, and concentrated. It was received with thunderous applause, cheers, some boos, foot stomping (which is *good* in Europe). Earle took many bows on stage—he was really happy and embarrassed. The applause continued and eventually Bruno played it again. Of course, it's different every time. The audience loved this. Earle's piece was just before intermission. Backstage, everyone came back (Boulez, Stockhausen among the many people) to congratulate Earle and Bruno. It really was THE event of the whole two weeks at Darmstadt and everyone said so. I nearly cried. My heart beat so loudly and so fast. I was very moved. It sounds corny but it really was *an important event.* And many people knew it.

And then it was off to Switzerland, the Côte d'Azur, the Italian Riviera, and the happiest vacation I'd ever had with Earle. On September 29, in Luxembourg, I boarded an Icelandic plane, alone, haunted by an irrational fear that I'd be killed, that I'd never see Earle again.

Clad only in a devastatingly sexy nightie, Ruth Kligman greeted me upon my return to 40 Third Avenue around 2:30 in the afternoon the following day. Ruth was attempting to be an artist, but her reputation as lover to Jackson Pollock, Bill de Kooning, and others of the Illustrious Brethren was probably as close to it as she'd ever come. She was subletting the loft below ours while David Budd was in Europe, and she always made me feel I was living a nun's life. Just as I'd be dragging myself up the two flights of stairs to my loft after a day of classes, rehearsals, and teaching, having nothing planned except an evening of painting my loft, down she'd come, setting out for a night on the town, flashily garbed and heavily made up. "Poor Carolyn!" she'd say, "What a dreary life you lead. Don't you ever go to parties? Have any fun?" Unlike Ruth's idea of fun, hanging out at the Cedar bar with the smoking, boozing painting crowd was never mine, and I rarely went to the sorts of parties she frequented. I never did get the hang of the sixties. During the weeks Earle was in Europe, my primary entertainment was to read all the books about Diaghilev and his company I'd bought the previous year in secondhand bookstores in London. I wrote to Earle: "It's only Monday morning and I feel a burden of months of Cunningham blues! Remy has been officially 'fired.' By phone. Dear God, the whole thing depresses me."

Some other changes had occurred while I was away. One could no longer say "Bob and Jap," because quite suddenly (for me, at least) it was "Bob and Steve [Paxton]." And Bob had officially become our lighting designer and planned to tour with us. He'd moved out of his 128 Front Street loft above Jasper's and into a vast space on the fifth floor at 809 Broadway between Eleventh and Twelfth streets, a move that mirrored his greatly improved financial situation and the respect he was garnering at last in the art world. In 1961 he had one-man exhibitions in Paris and Milan and at the Leo Castelli Gallery in New York. Two works were shown in the Museum of Modern Art's exhibition "Art of Assemblage"—*Canyon*

(1959), the combine painting with a large stuffed eagle poised in simulated flight and a feather pillow hanging below it, which William Seitz, who organized the show for MoMA, considered the most beautiful and successful work by Rauschenberg up to this time,[1] and *Talisman* (1958), another combine painting. Both were fabulous, but neither thrilled me quite as much as Jasper's *Map* (1961) of the United States, which could be seen at Castelli's at the same time. About a year after that Castelli show, Jasper asked me to have a strip of photos taken in one of those photo-machine booths. Apparently he'd intended to use it in his next *Map* (1962). He didn't. However, if one looks *very* closely at the west coast of that *Map*, one can just barely make out the words MACHINE PHOTO: CAROLYN BROWN. He told me, with considerable disdain in his voice, that I was probably the only person who could go into one of those booths and come out with Avedon pictures. That might be considered a compliment from anyone else, but from Jasper, I'm quite sure it was not. He asked me to take the photos again. I didn't. So much for being immortalized by one of the great painters of the twentieth century.

Meanwhile John Cage had become "Vice-Chairman of the Eastern Division of Edible Fungi of the People to People Society"! Its official newspaper: *The Toadstool Pickers News.* So hilarious did he find this that he related it to everyone he met, each time roaring with laughter until tears ran down his cheeks. But what truly thrilled him was the publication of his book *Silence.* This was no laughing matter. In the copy he presented to us he wrote: "for Carolyn and Earle with love—and excitement over music and dance as for ten years now we have been making them. John Cage Nov. 1961." He was convinced that *Silence* would be a best-seller and, although it never hit the best-seller lists, over time he's been proven correct. John continued to work diligently on *Atlas Eclipticalis,* and just as diligently on convincing Leonard Bernstein to conduct it.

Two days after returning from Europe, I began teaching at Merce's studio again, traveled to Boston to teach for the Dance Circle, and resumed ballet classes with Miss Craske and Mr. Tudor. Their classes were a joy, a place to work unencumbered by the anxieties, jealousies, and disappointments endemic to a dance company. In any case, Merce's company class and rehearsals did not resume until the last week in October. I was unable to muster any enthusiasm about dancing with him that fall. The first rehearsals were spent teaching Remy's parts to Steve Paxton. Boy, did we resent that! It wasn't Steve's presence we resented, it was just that we felt Remy's absence so deeply. On Thursday nights, whenever I wasn't in Boston teaching, I would audit Bob Dunn's weekly composition workshop held at Merce's studio. Bob Dunn had taken John's classes at the New School, and I was curious to see how John's ideas would be realized by dancers other than Merce, and to hear those ideas explained by someone other than John. Among the participants were Simone Forti, David Gordon, Alex and Deborah Hay, Steve Paxton, Yvonne Rainer, and Trisha Brown, whose work was the most courageously adventuresome in the classes I observed.

New on my agenda was a weekly class with Yogi Vithaldas. Years earlier, Merce had taught himself yoga from Vithaldas's book *The Yoga System of Health and Relief from Tension,* and he'd practiced it faithfully every day. Since then Vithaldas had become something of a celebrity, but he charged according to one's ability to pay, and I think he really enjoyed teaching our little group: Remy, Judy and Bob Dunn, ballet dancer Sylvia Kim, and me. After his class we'd chant "om," and he would lecture us upon the evils of materialism as we sat on the plush wall-to-wall carpeting of his Upper East Side high-rise, with its spectacular views of the city through floor-to-ceiling glass. Then he'd teach us how to cook Indian food, which we ate sitting cross-legged around a sheet spread on his living-room floor. Well fed and thoroughly chastened about the materialistic life, we'd return to our own digs, some without heat or hot water, in considerably less glamorous parts of town. Obviously, our purpose in studying yoga was not to shed the shackles of materialism; mine was to learn how to breathe properly while performing. Merce's breath control always amazed me; no matter how difficult the dance or how great his exertion he never panted, never appeared to be out of breath. I hoped studying with Vithaldas would provide some insight into how he accomplished this.

Aeon was the single new work choreographed in 1961 (excepting the *Suite de danses*). In 1962, Merce did no choreography at all. But 1961, '62, and '63 were great touring years, in fact the end of the golden years, which is how many of us described the period between November 1956, when John and Merce borrowed money to buy their first Volkswagen Microbus, and June 1964, when the company set off on a six-month world tour. For as long as we had the VW bus, it was the bus that defined us as a company. It held only nine people and a small amount of luggage, thus "Merce Cunningham and Dance Company" comprised six dancers, two musicians and one lighting designer/stage manager. We traveled with minimal or no sets, mostly tights and leotards for costumes, and few props. Personal luggage was limited to one small suitcase each. At least one-third of the rear luggage space was devoted to food. John served as company manager, bus driver, philosopher-in-residence, master chef, and chief minister in charge of entertainment;

Merce as business manager, accountant, and co–bus driver. Nick and Remy took on food shopping and preparation. I occasionally spelled John or Merce at the wheel, as did Steve Paxton and Bob Rauschenberg when they joined our traveling circus. Everyone pitched in with loading and unloading, cleanup and K.P. duty, and yes, firewood gathering.

Eating was easily our number-one entertainment. "America's Best-Fed Dance Company!" That, according to Remy, was how we should continue to bill ourselves. We'd have lavish cookouts in local, state, and national parks, at various times of day or night, in many sorts of weather. John would gather wild mushrooms if there were any to be found; even in winter he'd find wild greens for salad. We'd broil steaks and chickens over open fires, steam vegetables wrapped in foil. If cooking out wasn't feasible, John would search out some out-of-the-ordinary restaurant, often driving miles off-course to find it, in the hope of discovering a regional delicacy like morels, fiddlehead ferns, or crisp-fried fresh-caught catfish. Maybe he'd find a truck stop famous for twenty kinds of pie, or a word-of-mouth local greasy spoon that served fabulous spaghetti.

Every non-performing day included Happy Hour. It was a ritual seriously observed. Punctually at five o'clock John would relinquish the wheel, usually to Merce, and have his first drink of the day. Nick and Remy would bring out raw vegetables, exotic dips, stone-ground wheat crackers. David Tudor pulled out his flask of homemade homeopathic brew, which was probably 100 percent alcohol. Whatever John was drinking that year—bourbon, beer, or wine—he stuck with it religiously for months or years at a time, but when a doctor or some well-meaning friend convinced him that some other form of alcohol was healthier, or at least less harmful for whatever ailed him, he'd switch loyalties on the spot. Over the years he went full circle at least twice. John was compulsively precise about both work and play. He held tenaciously to a nine-to-five work schedule and just as tenaciously to a five-to-seven Happy Hour. His ideas about wardrobe were equally prescribed. When Earle and I first met John, he wore sober black suits, business shirts, black shoes, and black stockings. Only his ties were a bit peculiar—short dark knit oddities that looked as though they'd been chewed off by a chipmunk. This was his uniform; except for the tie, conventional and circumspect. It was a shock for most people to learn that this conventionally clothed person was John Cage, the notorious avant-garde composer. Quite unexpectedly, after many years John switched uniforms from black to blue: from stark business suits to blue jeans, blue work shirt, denim work jacket, and woodsman's boots. He let his crew cut grow out and grew a full beard. The switch coincided with his Thoreau period, which began around the time of the Vietnam War.

Not everyone enjoyed the touring as much as John and I did. It wasn't always all fun or galvanizing intellectually. Exasperation could and did set in after long days of driving, especially if one of John's whimsical detours had led to a frustrating dead end, or when it was just too cold to cook out but we were doing it anyway as we stood around, numb and dumb, while John and Nick did all the work. At those moments we'd have given anything for the shortest distance between two points, Howard Johnson's being one of them.

But that time together shaped and molded the particular group of nine known as "Merce Cunningham and Dance Company," circa 1956–1964, even though the personnel changed somewhat from year to year. The sense of community was genuine; sharing work, exchanging ideas, being around at the beginnings of things made the dancers feel we were participants in the process rather than employees hired to do a job. John's newest enthusiasm for some artist, writer, philosopher, social thinker, mushroom, wild green, or wild idea spilled over into the bus, embroiling us in lively conversation for hours at a time. We were privy to John's and David's discussions about the new music coming from Europe. Books were passed around—including Merce's favorite mystery stories, John's most recent esoteric discoveries, David's theosophy tracts, plus the reading interests of the rest of us. We played games the way John went about doing everything—seriously. We played all kinds—guess-who games, word games, cards, chess, Scrabble. We played for fun, yes, but earnestly, accepting through his example, the Cagean spirit of purposeless play pursued with seriousness. (One can learn a lot about the people with whom one plays games.) John was a fanatic about winning at Scrabble. He played mostly with Marilyn, who was *very* good at it, and he went into momentary *despair* when he lost—which was most of the time.

If Merce was in a particularly cheery mood he'd tell outrageously naughty stories about working with Martha Graham, Louis Horst, and Erick Hawkins, or lovely sentimental ones about his tap-dancing teacher, Mrs. Barrett, whom he remembered with great fondness. Merce, in the VW-bus milieu, was forced to be a social being, and sometimes he appeared to enjoy it. With the end of the VW-bus touring came the end of any real social intercourse between Merce and his dancers. Big-bus touring relieved him of the close quarters forced on everyone in the VW. In the big buses, Merce could separate himself from the rest of us, drop out rather than join in. Surely those hours in the VW bus created us as a company as much as Merce's choreography did. They probably even influenced the choreography, because Merce came to know us in ways quite different from the ways he knew us in the studio.

For many years we seemed to be operating *in* the world, not in a world apart. There was a richness and variety of experience. Vital to this was meeting interesting people from a wide spectrum of disciplines, not only those in the arts. John had friends from coast to coast and was always making new ones. And if there was a really fine museum, or notable architecture, or maybe just a good movie around, John would find time to get us there. Slow scenic routes were chosen instead of mind-numbing thruways. "Have you seen Niagara Falls?" John would ask, and since most of us had not, he'd take us there. Our existence then was governed by process, not product. The means and the end justified each other. Despite the fact that getting there (traveling) seemed to take precedence over being there (performing), and what and where we ate appeared to be far more important than any single performance that we drove two, three, or more days to present, our focus nevertheless was single: art-and-life. No separation. John's credo—accepting the multiplicity of things—was actively lived in the VW days. Later on, Merce's credo—weeding out everything not absolutely essential to putting on a performance—became the company doctrine. Perhaps this was inevitable as the company became larger, unionized, weighted down with the psychological and financial freight of full-time administrators, office staff, wardrobe and stage crew, as well as more dancers, more musicians, tons of electronic paraphernalia, more-elaborate sets, specialized lighting equipment, and video and film apparatus.

But the more was not the merrier. Not for me, anyway. Nor, I think, for John. And although Merce talked about the multiplicity of events in everyone's life, he was never quite able to embrace the idea in his own. Going from the small bus to the big bus was symbolic of the company's shifting priorities, and to accomplish this shift a quasi-professional, and eventually a fully professional, management took over our lives, bringing about a dramatic change in John's role in the company. His many active contributions to the dancers' well-being were curtailed; his influence shunted behind the scenes. Officially he acted only as musical advisor and, occasionally, as one of many composers. He was no longer needed even in the orchestra pit. In the seventies and eighties he complained of feeling obsolete, of being patronized and treated like an eccentric, slightly dotty mascot. Obviously under these circumstances anything faintly resembling friendship—at least the Aristotelian definition of friendship between equals—was impossible. Nor did it help to have the age span between Merce and his dancers widen year by year. As older dancers left, the ten to fifteen years or so that had once separated Merce from his dancers began to stretch to twenty, then twenty-five, thirty, until in 1994 when Merce turned seventy-five there were fifty years or more between Merce and the youngest member of his company. Predictably, as the age difference expanded, communication of the sort that went on in the VW Microbus in the fifties and early sixties dwindled to nothing. In my last years, the company became self-contained, self-nurturing, and insular, moving from place to place as though under a Bucky Fuller dome. Even the air we breathed seemed to have been recycled.

Inevitably, the choreography had to change. Whether it got better or worse is not at all the question. It was simply different—plainly, clearly different, even though the aesthetic base remained virtually the same. My hypothesis is that the company environment altered from life as an *organism* to life as an *organization*. The changes, beginning in the late sixties and early seventies, were partly caused by Merce's desire to use a larger palette, to choreograph for more dancers and for dancers more highly skilled technically. But they were also caused by the complex exigencies—political and economical—of the dance boom. Economic feasibility meant five to eight performances a week. Getting there now had to be as direct and fast as possible. Being there was almost tunnel-visioned in its singularity of purpose: dancing. And by this time the dancing had become totally consuming, utterly exhausting, rarely leaving either time or energy for anything else. It was a schedule that unbalanced life in the opposite direction from the first VW touring days. But there was a brief period of several years in the early sixties when living and art seemed in near-perfect proportion, when the company way of life was more resilient, more richly textured, encompassing a sense of wholeness, of give-and-take, and of receptivity to the stimuli outside itself.

The 1961–62 winter season had us all over the map: from Springvale, Maine, to Vancouver, British Columbia. The longest tour was to the West Coast. Many of our performance dates were in universities and colleges, the usual sponsors of modern dance. But we also played big cities—Boston, Denver, Detroit, Pittsburgh—and a few small ones, under the auspices of local arts groups. Rain, warm weather, and floods resulted in disaster areas declared in three states, requiring a three-hundred-mile detour on our trip from Denver to Cheney. Towns we were heading toward were being evacuated. En route in flood country, John, peering out of the window from the backseat, asked innocently: "What river is this?" Merce, grimly, from the driver's seat, replied: "You mean the one we're in?" The detours sent us into Nevada and gambling territory. John and Bob were in seventh heaven. In a greasy-spoon gambling bar, Bob stood clutching a tumbler of bourbon in one hand and a one-armed bandit in the other: "I could live forever in a joint like this if someone would just send money."

We often played to half a house that produced barely enough applause to get the curtain down. But sometimes a wonderful surprise was in store: a real stage, a professional crew; every seat taken (even standing room only!); response terrific for every dance, roars with delight during *Antic Meet.* We never knew what to expect as we traveled from town to town, theater to theater: sour and unresponsive audiences one night and cheering, ecstatic ones the next and, in between, magnificent scenery to marvel at and camaraderie to enjoy.

Rauschenberg's move to 809 Broadway and his daily presence on our tours began to change the social dynamics within the company. In the early fifties, John's apartment overlooking the East River was the hub of social activity. There John was a sort of firefly, drawing others to him with his erratic bursts of energy and enthusiasm and flashing high spirits. Later, even before John moved to Stony Point, Merce's loft on Sixteenth Street became the principal gathering place for much of the company's communal social life, although it was John who encouraged the familial congeniality, not Merce. Merce's need for privacy, his predilection for secrecy, made it impossible for him to embrace an open community, but John's delight in the role of guru and his pleasure in sharing his ever-expanding enthusiasms with us all rather compelled Merce to open his doors upon occasion. It's doubtful that Rauschenberg, more gadfly than firefly, ever wished to be thought of as a guru, but he most certainly relished community, loved having people around while he worked, and thrived in an atmosphere of a playfully combative, even aggressive exchange of ideas. At 809 Broadway, Bob held open house for dancers, often allowing them to use his loft space for their own rehearsals, and he welcomed young unknown artists from the States and abroad, as well as a few starry-eyed scientists who wanted to be part of the art scene. Bob would cook chili and steak for anyone who happened to be around. Bourbon and vodka, beer for the dancers, were in endless supply, but thanks to Steve's influence and to touring with the company, Bob drank far less, and appeared healthier and more physically fit than at any time since. Bob once claimed that those years were the happiest of his life. Although his good spirits and overwhelming largesse were made of very different cloth from John's, they were equally irresistible, despite a rather daunting (to me anyway) competitive streak that seemed to color the way he perceived the whole world and everyone in it.

A surprising aspect of his personality surfaced in Los Angeles, where he had a one-man exhibit during the period when the company was performing in six California cities. Bob's show at the Dwan Gallery in Westwood opened on Sunday, March 4, the same day that both Jean Tinguely and Niki de Saint Phalle also had openings on the strip in Hollywood. Leo Castelli flew to L.A. for the occasion. To celebrate his opening California-style, Bob threw a lavish lobster-and-steak champagne brunch for us all at Virginia Dwan's beach house in Malibu, where he was staying. John had a rehearsal and didn't attend. Nor did Merce, who was in a terrible mood after a student broke a leg in the class Merce had been teaching the previous day. Their absence from his party was clearly a disappointment to Bob. While we cavorted in the heated pool and the numbing, exhilarating Pacific Ocean and feasted on all the goodies Bob had provided, he ate nothing and began to drink heavily. By the time we left for L.A. he appeared nervous, even miserable. When we started the rounds of the galleries, Bob begged us not to leave him, confessing that he truly was frightened, that he hated the way Leo kept pushing him around to hobnob with local art critics, collectors, and moneyed L.A. society. I think it may be this gut-wrenching distaste for the *business* of art, of selling not only the work but himself, that made Bob get so royally, monumentally drunk at all his openings. In the 1950s and '60s it wasn't always obvious, but as the years passed his inebriated state was, even for total strangers, impossible to ignore.

Bob's misery that day was shared, for very different reasons, by Niki de Saint Phalle. Niki's exhibit was actually a Happening—or perhaps it should now be described as a precursor to performance art. Behind the Renaissance Club, one of the jazz spots on Sunset Boulevard, Niki had built a fantastic structure out of dozens of commonplace objects such as headless Maidenform-bra busts, an umbrella, mannequin heads, a baby seat, a child's scooter, a vacuum cleaner, cans of spray paint, artificial flowers, and Coke bottles. She'd then painted everything flat white. Dressed in a tight, white, space-lady bodysuit with black boots, shotgun in hand, she strode from place to place, mounted ladders and tables, took careful aim, and fired. No dancer could help admiring her. Beautiful woman. Beautiful body. Exquisite movement control. Eloquent back poised to shoot. A stunning sight to behold. And what a fabulously good shot! Jean Tinguely, serving as Niki's stagehand, carried and supported the ladders and tables from which she fired. As her meticulously placed shots found their mark in the cans of paint, a glorious array of *Vogue* decorator colors—blues, greens, and purples together with brilliant reds, yellows and oranges—splattered over, trickled down, sprayed across, stained and misted the formerly stark white three-dimensional wall of objects. The grand finale was a final shot into a tear-gas bomb! What street theater! Curiously feminine despite the violence of means, and strangely, hauntingly beautiful, too. About two hundred people gathered to witness the event—an assortment of Beats and hippies, beards and ponytails, the just-happened-to-be-there folk, and of course buyers and sellers and curators of art, although there was nothing to buy or sell or curate. Niki had no time to savor the result because Tinguely's exhibit of Rube Goldberg-esque mechanical constructions opened immediately afterward just down the street. It was too crowded even for Tinguely, so we all escaped to a café, where Niki called Bob into a back room, burst into tears, and sobbed uncontrollably. She'd intended her work to have only the life of the moment—no afterlife. Like a dance performance. Nothing to hang on a wall, nothing to sell, nothing even to view a second time. But walking away from the work without one glance at the results, as dancers inevitably must do after every performance, was apparently intolerable to her. Later she did go back and took away four parts of it, but she told Bob she felt like a whore for doing it. Of course she was not the only scavenger. The next day we all went back for souvenirs, including Bob.

The marathon art day climaxed with Bob's show at Virginia Dwan's gallery, where he was assailed by more crowds, more liquor, and more fear. It ended at a wild dancing party on a pier in Santa Monica.

Three days later, we gave our last West Coast performance of that tour. And Bob? He was back to sweeping the stage floor, hauling costume trunks, setting lights, and calling the show—totally sober and completely happy.

Repertory for 1961–62 touring was limited to *Aeon, Antic Meet, Crises, Suite for Five,* and, very rarely, *Changeling* and *Nightwandering*. If the program was *Aeon, Crises,* and *Antic Meet,* Viola was an equally featured female dancer, which made my new billing ridiculous. And since there was no way for audience or critics to identify one dancer from another, the situation made me uneasy and probably overly sensitive. Although I got a mention in the *Palo Alto Times*—"Carolyn Brown moves with an uncanny style that distinguishes her"[2]—I was sure it was meant for Viola. The *San Francisco Chronicle*'s Alfred Frankenstein did know us, and although I should have been reassured by his writing that I was "one of those people like Cunningham himself, who cannot as much as cross a stage without just naturally making an event,"[3] I was plagued by self-doubt about my dancing. Even worse, I felt abandoned by Merce. There was no feedback, no direction, no criticism. I wrote: "It's very difficult to keep dancing without guidance and so difficult to know what actually happens between stage and audience, what one should work on, work for. It is very lonely, and I really don't know who to turn to for advice. I would certainly love to know Merce's real thoughts and feelings—but I guess I never will."

Compounding those problems was my trepidation about performing anywhere near New York City, and it was years before this anxiety was overcome. Although we danced all over the map in 1961–62, no amount of performing quelled my apprehension. Clearly, my ego was getting in the way of my dancing:

> If I danced badly Friday, it was nothing compared to last night. I was tight, tense, forced, off balance, rigid and needless to say—MISERABLE. My oh my what a problem I have dancing in this damn city, or anywhere near it. I *hated* dancing. Hated myself. Ached all over. After *Aeon*, I sobbed. What a miserable mess I made of it. The whole evening was traumatic. Remy came—and came backstage, and into our dressing room. I was there alone. He burst into tears. Said Merce wouldn't speak to him.

> Talked to Remy on phone last night for about three hours, until 2 a.m. He *hated* Merce's concert. Thought we all looked cold and mean. Thought our potentials as dancers and people were unused. He's very prejudiced by his own experience and by this Reichian analysis he's undergoing but none-the-less it made me feel "better" somehow. I really don't feel fulfilled as a dancer—and I'm just "chicken" to stay clinging to it any longer. I've known this since Europe *1960* tour and there's no point in kidding myself. It's no good. My body knows it. My intellect knows it. And my soul knows it. So the time must be close at hand.

Luckily, it wasn't. On April 14, in Princeton, New Jersey, Merce and company presented the last performance of the 1961–62 season. John had the flu and was feeling terrible. Merce had a bad cold and had injured his knee. Marilyn hurt her back in performance. Judy didn't dance at all, so ill with near-pneumonia that she'd had to miss the last two performances. It was obviously time for a rest. Perversely, I had finally pulled myself together: "Danced moderately to fair . . . nothing spectacular. David Vaughan says my dancing is terribly romantic, and he loves it. I said you mean I'm not a cold fish? He said, if I ever was, I certainly am not now . . ." That was some consolation. Between December 3 and April 15, Merce Cunningham and Dance Company were on the road for fifty-five days and gave twenty-three performances. A record, to date. But with nothing scheduled for three weeks and Merce's summer plans for the company still unknown, my mind was riveted on Earle and on his *Available Forms II*, which he'd just finished composing in Paris and was to premiere at La Biennale di Venezia on April 19, five days away. I wrote to him:

> The last performance at Princeton, last night. Got back to NYC at about 3:30 a.m. I didn't go to bed until after 4:30 . . . just kept pacing around, realizing the touring was done, I was free, I could go . . . I CAN'T STAND IT! I don't know what to do . . . I think I MUST go to Venice. . . . I MUST I MUST I MUST . . . but how???? I rock back and forth holding onto my mouth, wondering what to do, hoping there'll be a sign from somewhere, or someone which will tell me what to do. I want so to hear it, to see you conduct . . . it makes me ache with sadness and frustration. [It would be] Just like my dreams in my sophomore year in college . . . me, sitting in a box, watching you conduct, in some gorgeous proper for-real-type theatre . . . ooh what will I do? Beset with bewilderment and anxiety.

At eleven o'clock in the morning two days later, I suddenly decided I had to go, and at 5:45 that afternoon I was seated on an Alitalia flight bound for Milan. In the hours between I'd phoned Bob Rauschenberg, woken him up, and asked to borrow seven hundred dollars. He was a bit taken aback by the amount, but said he'd get on it right away. I started packing in earnest. Bob called back to say everything was okay. At 1:30 p.m. Bob and Steve arrived in their white jeep. A windy, warm, heavenly day seemed to bestow its blessings; intoxicated by my madness, the three of us laughed like idiots all the way to Seventy-seventh Street, where Leo Castelli provided the check. It was crazy, especially since Earle might not be all that pleased to see me. Our finances were shakier than ever, and this was a reckless indulgence on my part. As the plane landed in Milan the next morning, pelting rain dashed against the window and instantly I had second thoughts. Tears welled up and spilled over as I pressed my nose against the rain-spattered glass. Was Earle going to be furious? Depression and worry replaced the giddiness and elation I'd felt the day before. Another plane took me to Venice. No rain there, just overcast gray skies. At the Piazzale Roma I took the *vaporetto* to the Giglie stop, near La Fenice. Venice's ravishing beauty astonished all over again, but this time it also felt reassuringly familiar, welcoming me home.

It was two in the afternoon. Neither Earle nor Bruno Maderna was at the opera house. I asked to speak with Mario La Broca, the director of the XXV Festival Internazionale di Musica Contemporanea, and was told that he was out to lunch and would not be back until four. Suddenly aware of how hungry I was, I trudged off, luggage in tow, to Angelo's—a favorite restaurant near Piazza San Marco, and, to my overwhelming embarrassment, stumbled upon a party for Peggy Guggenheim given by her artist friends to celebrate her having been made an honorary citizen of Venice that very day! Not wanting Peggy to feel compelled to invite me to join the party or to stay with her (as though she would ever feel compelled to do anything she didn't want to do!), nor wanting to admit that Earle wasn't expecting me or that I had no idea where I might be staying, I ducked behind a newspaper, praying to be ignored. But the painter Vedova seemed to recognize me at the same moment that I recognized him. Later, in an agony of discomfort, I realized that they were whispering about me. It seemed hours before they all left and I was free to eat my lunch. But Vedova had lingered, and was wandering around the foyer ostensibly looking at the paintings. There was no escape. "Mr. Vedova?" I queried, feigning slow and surprised recognition. "Signora Brown?" he replied, equally playing his role. Since he spoke English even more haltingly than I spoke Italian and neither of us could understand the other's language when it was spoken to us, it took the help of a bilingual waiter to explain my circumstances. Gallantly he kissed my hand and I trudged back to La Fenice alone.

"So you came." Three words, wryly spoken—that's all Earle had to say when first he laid eyes on me backstage at La Fenice. My heart sank. Was he annoyed or pleased? In fact he was both. His financial situation was dire. Before leaving Paris, he'd sent me a frantic SOS to wire him two hundred dollars. When he arrived in Rome, where the first rehearsals took place, he'd gotten down to a dollar and seventy-five cents and had been subsisting on fifty-five-cent meals of pasta with meat sauce and one-quarter of a liter of wine each day until the money arrived. Although the new composition had been commissioned by the Rome Radio Orchestra, Earle had yet to receive a penny. Expenses, though promised, had yet to be provided. Earle's only conducting experience was with his own jazz band in high school. He'd never owned a tuxedo, much less white tie and tails, and was forced to explain that he could not possibly afford to purchase them. That was embarrassment enough! My sudden presence on the scene appeared to contradict his avowed predicament. How could he plead poverty if his wife had just flown in from New York?

Within the hour of my talk with Vedova, Peggy knew all. She loved gossip and intrigue and always had her spies provide her with the very latest. But what a generous lady she could be when she so chose. Much to our surprise, she chose to play hostess to Earle and me for much of the ten days we spent in Venice: insisting I sit with her at La Fenice for Earle's premiere; throwing a grand bash at her palazzo in Earle's honor on Easter Sunday; inviting us to dine out as well as to lunch *chez elle.* We were truly touched by her attention and kindness.

Available Forms II was on a program with music by Anton von Webern, Arnold Schoenberg, and Zoltan Kodaly. I was faint with anxiety. Although Peggy had insisted I sit with her, I would have much preferred to sit alone, so certain was I that everyone around me could not only hear but feel my violently pounding heart. The very walls of the Fenice seemed to reverberate with my heartbeat! Although wearing tie and tails borrowed from an Italian musician much bigger than he, Earle managed to pass inspection on first viewing. The trousers had been gathered to the front at the waist with the extra folds vaguely hidden by a cummerbund. From the back they looked okay. But the jacket was another story: when Earle raised both arms overhead, the jacket—as stiff and hard as a board—went with them and his head all but disappeared into the collar. It would have made a great scene in a Danny Kaye movie. Peggy muttered under her breath, "Good god, where did the poor boy get that suit!" But despite this ludicrous detail, *Available Forms II,* in a twenty-five-minute version, went well, was well received, and subsequently had numerous performances with other European orchestras.

We were in Venice for ten days. I returned to New York on May 7, the day Merce's studio reopened, and was greeted with unpleasant news: the Living Theatre owed ten thousand dollars in back rent. Merce feared he would lose his studio. Added to that bombshell came the announcement that the company might not have a summer residency at Connecticut College. Merce had balked at the performance schedule presented to him by the festival committee. At a hastily assembled company meeting, we all voted no to going unless Merce's terms were met. Nineteen sixty-two was the festival's fifteenth anniversary season, and instead of grouping the public performances in the last week, the powers that be had decided to scatter them throughout the season. The final weekend was to be shared by the companies of Martha Graham and José Limón, each giving one matinee and two evening programs. Merce's request that his company be given equal time with Graham and Limón on that weekend had been refused. Merce's company was never again to be in residence at Connecticut College. Jill Johnston, in *The Village Voice,* commented on Merce's absence from the festival:

The exclusion of Cunningham this summer, despite the anniversary, despite the facts that Limón is a charter member of the whole affair and that Graham is almost a national monument, is a sad reminder of how impossible it is at any moment in a history of anything for certain (controlling) groups of people to see where a thing is going, to put their fingers on the heartbeat of a movement . . . maybe New London should stick to a museum policy only. In this category they can hardly miss. And Limón and Graham easily command the field where statues are in question. They both have attitudes about themselves and about dancing that have more to do with the glory of Greece and grandeur of Rome than they do with life in America at the present moment.[4]

A discouraging time for all of us: there were no performances until late October, and Merce did not choose to choreograph a new work or even to hold rehearsals until mid-September. Viola and I had some employment teaching at Merce's studio through July. My one diversion that spring–early summer—auditing Bob Dunn's composition classes—culminated in the now-historic "A Concert of Dance" at the Judson Church on Friday, July 6, which marked the birth of Judson Dance Theater. The concert was free. The church was mobbed, people were even turned away. At the risk of alienating everyone involved, I have to say that the concert seemed to me more like a college dance recital than the cutting-edge avant-garde stuff it has so widely been touted to have been. I thought it offered very few genuinely innovative or arresting moments, with three exceptions: David Gordon's two uniquely personal solos, *Helen's Dance* and *Mannequin;* Yvonne Rainer's most un-ordinary *Ordinary Dance* (a solo in which she talked nonstop quite matter-of-factly while throwing herself around in high energy movement that seemed to be totally unrelated to the rather moving tale she was telling); and Steve Paxton's stolid, egalitarian/pedestrian works *Proxy* and *Transit.*

Merce's Summer Course ended on August 4. To save money, I went to Massachusetts to stay with my family until early September. My only income—a total of $225—came from teaching for the Boston Dance Circle: two classes, once a week, for three weeks. Time Records had suspended funding the Contemporary Sound Series, and thus Earle was unemployed and thoroughly depressed about it. True, he had a commission from Tanglewood to compose a work for chamber orchestra (*Novara*) to be premiered on August 24, and his *Available Forms I* had been published by Associated Music Publishers. In 1962 alone, it had been performed in Charleroi and Liège, Belgium; in Hamburg, Palermo, Helsinki, and at a repeat performance in Darmstadt, but Earle still could not begin to make a living as a composer. I still owed Rauschenberg seven hundred dollars—but however reckless my decision may have been, I never regretted going to Venice to see Earle conduct the first performance of *Available Forms II.* I did, finally, manage to pay off the loan.

It's doubtful that Merce realized just how perilous was the nature of our poverty and, foolishly, I could not bring myself to tell him it was the reason for my absence. I disappeared from town, taking with me our newborn kittens, all suffering from distemper, whom I attempted, mostly in vain, to nurse back to health. It was a sad summer, made sadder still by letters I received from Judy Dunn who wrote several times to keep me abreast of the news. She related that after the studio closed for the summer and without telling anyone else in the company, Merce had begun to work with her and William Davis, a tall, handsome man who'd recently started taking classes at the studio and whom Merce was obviously grooming for the company. Merce was reviving *Summerspace:* "Making changes in it he says and today he made a new ending—It's hardly anything to worry about not being here for," wrote Judy. The new ending just happened to eliminate a solo section for me. To further fuel my paranoia, Merce had told Judy he wanted her to learn my part in *Nightwandering,* the duet he'd made for himself and me in Stockholm in 1958. What this bit of information really meant was unclear because, to my knowledge, she never learned it, but the rumor alone was wounding, sowing more seeds of self-doubt and insecurity. Who knew? Perhaps that was the intention. I stewed away August in misery.

I suppose it was lucky that Earle and I got into an automobile accident shortly after my return to New York in September. Ironically, we were on our way to Bridgehampton to try to sell our car. Earle bruised an arm, I suffered minor whiplash, and we both had headaches, aching backs, shoulders, and necks. The car's damages were serious enough to warrant one thousand dollars in repair reimbursement. We didn't make the repairs and used the insurance money along with a "Long Bow Ranch Grant" from Earle's uncle Carl to feed and house us into the new year.

Less than two weeks after our automobile accident, everyone in the block between Ninth and Tenth Streets on the west side of Third Avenue received eviction notices. The many three-storey buildings where so many artists resided were to be torn down and replaced with one mammoth high-rise. I went into a kind of numb coma of despair . . . I was teaching in Boston, teaching at Merce's studio, attending ballet class at the Met, and taking Merce's classes; the company was in rehearsal and going out on short tours—to Pennsylvania, Maryland, upstate New York, and Virginia. And Earle was about to leave for Europe again. When and how would we ever be able to find another place to live that we could afford?

or the next nineteen months we were on a roller coaster, hopes mounting high only to plummet within hours. When my mother expressed concern about Earle's and my welfare, I wrote back: "I think we live a wonderful life, exciting, rich, varied. I really don't mind at all scraping pennies." Eventually even our impoverished financial situation took a slight turn for the better: Earle's publisher, B. Schott Sohne, agreed to pay him a $500-per-year advance, and Broadcast Music Incorporated offered him a $750-per-year "retainer fee." Even better was the fact that he began to receive fees for conducting his own music.

Fortune blessed us in other ways. A month before Earle left for Europe, we found an apartment in the West Village. A gem: a small, fifth-floor walk-up, with heat, hot water, full bathroom, working fireplace, and windows facing north, east, and west; even a glimpse of the top of the Empire State Building could be had from a bedroom window—all this only a few blocks from Merce's studio on Fourteenth Street and Sixth Avenue. It was in a rear building with a garden separating it from the larger main building. My heart leapt when the agent took us and two other couples through the tree-shaded garden. The second I saw the apartment itself I knew: "We'll take it," I said, with only a cursory glance around the place. Jaws fell open: Earle's with amazement and the other couples' with dismay. The real estate agent nodded with approval and commented dryly, "That lady knows when she's seen a good thing." I knew we couldn't wait: that very afternoon I had to leave on tour. The fact that the rent was twice the price of our Third Avenue loft—a whopping ninety-nine dollars—did worry me, but after all the dismal places we'd seen for even more money, I knew we'd be crazy not to snap it up. Earle had to agree. He couldn't run off to Europe leaving me with no place to live, and this apartment seemed to him a perfect safe haven for his wife, whom he was so often leaving alone.

The on-again/off-again dream of a Broadway season was the big carrot dangling just inches before the company's nose for much of the 1962–63 year. My journal chronicled the pendulum-swings:

[9/21/1962] It looks *very* much like we will have a Broadway Season in late March or early April.

[1/16/63] Broadway Season going ahead . . . John has been working like crazy on the money angle.

[1/30/63] A staff meeting about Broadway today. Looks more and more like it will go through.

[2/25/63] The Broadway season postponed due to the newspaper strike . . . If the strike isn't settled soon, the season will be postponed until fall.

[3/8/63] Newspaper strike is settled. *Dance Magazine* has a fantastic picture of Merce on the cover, with the caption "Merce Cunningham Comes to Broadway" . . . the magazine says we're to have a two-week season starting mid-April . . . The real hang-up seems to be finding a theatre that Merce will accept.

[3/14/63] Bob Dunn just called to say that Merce called him this afternoon to say that the Broadway Season is suspended. No theatre. No time after April because John and David go to Europe. So that is the end of that glorious dream.

[6/14/63] Things happen and "unhappen" so fast, I can't remember whether I told you we *were* going to have a Broadway Season or that we weren't. Every day there is a new rumor, new gossip. Today, it seems, we *are* going have a season—at the Winter Garden for one week, the first week in October.

[7/21/63] Broadway Season is again in *great* doubt. Can't get the Winter Garden and the sure theatre is the Broadhurst, which Merce doesn't really want. In fact, Merce doesn't even want to *have* a season. Bob [Rauschenberg] is angry about it. Says Bob: let's not have the season unless everyone involved is delighted to do it!

The Broadway roller-coaster ride ended abruptly with a very formal letter, dated August 8, 1963, and sent to everyone in the company, from Merce's new business manager, Lewis Lloyd: "I'm writing you to say that the Broadway season has been cancelled." For more than a year, enormous amounts of energy and time had been invested by many people to make "Merce Cunningham Comes to Broadway" a reality. Jasper Johns, whose continuing support of Merce's work over the years almost rivaled Cage's, was instrumental in setting up the Foundation for Contemporary Performance Arts, a nonprofit foundation, created by artists for artists. Producing Merce Cunningham and Dance Company on Broadway was to be the foundation's first project. The initial endowment was launched at the Allan Stone Gallery, at Madison and Eighty-sixth Street—a gala opening with the sale of works donated by more than seventy painters and sculptors, including Joseph Cornell, Willem de Kooning, Niki de Saint Phalle, Marcel Duchamp, Jasper Johns, Roy Lichtenstein, Richard Lippold, Robert Motherwell, Barnett Newman, Isamu Noguchi, Robert Rauschenberg, Larry Rivers, James Rosenquist, Mark Rothko, George Segal, Jean Tinguely, Mark Tobey, Jack Tworkov, and Andy Warhol—many of whom were regular members of Merce's audience whenever the company performed in the New York area.

Merce's quandary regarding a Broadway engagement may have appeared capricious to those working so hard to make it happen, but he did have a valid reason: the loss of two of his four women dancers midway through the Broadway negotiations. Suddenly the entire repertory had to be taught to two new dancers in time to meet the company's summer performances, the hoped-for two-week season on Broadway, and a two-month tour in October and November. By this time, Judy, Marilyn, Viola, and I had been working together for nearly six years, and five of the seven group dances in the current repertory had been made on us. In late fall of 1962, Marilyn Wood announced that she was pregnant and would be leaving at the end of the spring season. Then, in May of '63, Judy shocked everyone by quitting. Whatever her reasons—no doubt there were many—the one that apparently precipitated her seemingly out-of-the-blue resignation was discovering that Merce had bypassed her when recasting Marilyn's part in *Nocturnes;* he'd given it to Shareen Blair. Although Shareen, along with Steve Paxton and Valda Setterfield, had danced with the company at Connecticut College in the summer of 1961, her status was still that of an apprentice. Now she was to become a bona fide member of the company, with her very first new role one of the three women in *Nocturnes.* Considering how much Merce admired Judy's dancing, this was as surprising to the rest of us as it was to her. No explanation was given, but rumor had it that Merce felt that Rauschenberg's all-white costumes would be unbecoming on Judy's derrière and thighs.

Judy's resignation was met with enormous regret. It was terrible timing, not only for the company but for her: she was just coming into her own in realizing her extraordinary gifts as a performer. Merce had clearly intended to give her more and more special things to do. Judy was justly angry and understandably disillusioned, but perhaps a bit impatient. How often she used to say to me, "Nothing ever changes in this company!" From her perspective, perhaps, but from mine it seemed as though there'd been nothing but change: Paul Taylor, Jo Anne Melsher, Anita Dencks, Bruce King, Marianne Preger, Cynthia Stone, Bill Burdick, Dan Wagoner, Remy Charlip—all departed. In the social fabric of the company, Marianne and Remy were irreplaceable, and Remy's absence, in particular, changed the dynamics of the company forever, at least for me. But what Judy meant, I fear, was: "Nothing ever changes—Carolyn and/or Viola always get the juicy parts." Over the years, just as a dancer (female, in most cases) is on the verge of bursting into full bloom and recapturing Merce's serious attention, she quits. In the first months the newest dancer will inevitably engage Merce's attention almost exclusively. This is a heady, exciting time for both dancer and choreographer. For Merce, it's like having a new, unknown instrument added to his small orchestra. He's intrigued. But once he becomes used to working with that instrument, he moves on to exploring other new possibilities, solving new problems; and yes, perhaps appearing to take for granted the most recent addition to his company. In most cases, I prefer to think, he's giving the dancer a chance to develop, waiting for her to grow, always hoping she will surprise him. But until she reveals new shades, tones, and rhythmic acuity to renew Merce's interest, she must learn to dance for herself and to live with Merce's seeming indifference. This is a really difficult and crucial period in a dancer's development. Much more than patience is required. In Merce's company, self-motivation is an absolute necessity; without it, growth and true maturity are unlikely and there will be no breakthrough for the dancer in the choreographic material Merce chooses to give her.

Between September '62 and April '64, the company gave forty-seven performances in twenty-three states. Our presenters continued to be, for the most part, colleges and universities, but there were other sponsors as well: the Walker Art Center, "which has run up quite a record of sniffing out the new and progressive in the performing arts,"[1] brought the company to Minneapolis in '63 and '64, and thanks to the Walker's director, Martin Friedman, this was the beginning of a productive relationship that lasted for decades.

Repertory through May 1963 included *Aeon, Antic Meet, Crises, Rune, Septet, Suite for Five,* and *Summerspace,* plus Merce's solo *Collage* and our duet, *Nightwandering.* No new works were created for nearly two years. We had little expectation of wildly enthusiastic reviews as we drove up and down and back and forth across the country, so we were fairly astonished when, after Judy and Marilyn's last performance with the company at the State University of New York in Albany, we received ecstatic reviews from two local newspapers. There wasn't a negative word—not even about the music. In fact, the music garnered praise in both reviews as well. We'd never received quite such rapturous, unequivocal approval before, and after *Aeon*'s dour reception by the New York critics we were totally unprepared for it. This was the company Merce had intended to present on Broadway, but it was not to be. With Judy's and Marilyn's departures he now had to start over, to attempt once again to build a company that would "breathe together." Little wonder that his courage failed him when the final decision to go ahead with booking a Broadway theater approached a deadline.

Merce was incredibly fortunate in finding a replacement for Judy. Barbara Dilley Lloyd was both a beautiful woman and a lovely dancer. Like Shareen's, her early training had been in classical ballet, but while Shareen was cool to the point of seeming indifferent about dancing, Barbara was ever willing to fling herself into whatever she did with passion and abandon, always appearing to be totally comfortable with risk and the possibility of failure. Merce loved this quality. I had much to learn from it. Both Shareen and Barbara were bright, articulate college graduates— Shareen from Barnard, Barbara from Mount Holyoke. Both had performed in other companies before joining Merce. Barbara was married to Lewis Lloyd, the theatrical producer and the current business manager of the Cunningham company, and only recently they had had their first child, Benjamin. Merce's very bad mood, brought on by Judy's departure, evaporated after only a few rehearsals with Barbara. It was obvious to everyone that he was *very* pleased with his newest dancer, and there was a communal sigh of relief.

Ten days later, though, he was again depressed about Broadway. There was far too much work just teaching all the repertory to new people—forget about fine-tuning it. Nevertheless, he started work on two new dances, both of them unlike any others in the repertory. He had decided, finally, to explore fully the use of "indeterminacy" in his work, thereby giving the dancers an opportunity to make spontaneous choices *in performance.* Pioneered by Morty Feldman and Earle Brown, and later adopted by John Cage, the use of indeterminacy had by this time become an accepted practice among the avant-garde composers in Cage's circle, but with the exception of *Galaxy* in 1956, with its very limited options, Merce had been reluctant to incorporate the idea in his own work. "Too dangerous," he always said.

Perhaps the Judson dance scene changed his mind. It's well known that Merce's work had a strong influence on many of the Judson choreographers, but I believe, for a brief period, their work wielded some influence on Merce. Some of the Feldman/Brown/Cage ideas—avoided by Merce in his own work—had been transmitted through Bob Dunn's composition course to the young choreographers who evolved into Judson Dance Theater. The result was some very far-out choreographic efforts, very different from and, to some viewers, much farther out than the work Merce had been producing in the previous ten years. In any case, Merce's next two group works, *Story* and *Field Dances,* and *Paired,* a duet for Viola and himself, proved to be his most extended explorations involving indeterminacy. After that he beat a hasty, though not total, retreat. Embracing indeterminacy meant relinquishing his control of structure, time, and timing, and I'm convinced it drove him crazy.

An uninterrupted work period in which to rebuild company morale, rehearse the repertory, and develop new choreography was sorely needed, and a three-week summer residency at the University of California, Los Angeles, in July 1963, provided just that. Heaven-sent—for us, if not for Merce, who had to teach daily technique classes to university students and direct a choreography workshop, in addition to working with the company. Certainly it was close to idyllic for the rest of us, starting with the leisurely three-thousand-mile trip across the country. Merce flew to California well ahead of us. With John at the wheel of the minibus, we left New York on Monday, July 1, and didn't show up in L.A. until a full, fabulous week later. Fourth of July in Kansas at 105 degrees! (Well, that wasn't fun.) Only motels with swimming pools. Picnics and cookouts by lakes and streams. From Denver, Colorado, we drove over Wolf Creek Pass and Kanosha Pass to Durango and its hilariously funky, derelict hotel. Through the northern part of the Navajo reservation to Moencopi Village, where Hopi Indians were performing their Kachina dances. Intoxicated by the glorious country and discovering that none of us had been to the north rim of the Grand Canyon, John decided on a detour. Five miles from the north entrance to Grand Canyon National Park, on Highway 87, we came across Kaibab Lodge in the heart of Kaibab National Forest and the breathtaking sight of wild horses galloping across lush meadows. A wildly enthusiastic John phoned Merce in L.A. "Forget L.A.," John told him; "Come join us! We'll establish the company here at Kaibab Lodge. We're not leaving!" Just imagine Merce's response to that! However guilty we may have felt (not much, to tell the truth), it didn't spoil our visit to the Grand Canyon by moonlight or again, under a blazing sun, at midday. And at three o'clock

Sunday afternoon, when we should have been pulling into L.A., we were still gazing in rapture out across the north rim of the Grand Canyon. Driving all night, with a stop in Utah's Zion National Park for a cookout, and another stop in Las Vegas at three in the morning to play the one-armed bandits, we finally showed up, not having slept at all, Monday noon—at least a day late—at Malibu Beach, where a house had been rented for us next door to Dean Martin's.

Merce had certainly mellowed in the ten years since the company's beginnings at Black Mountain: he called no rehearsal that day! Even more amazing, he was in excellent humor and didn't seem put out by our tardy arrival. The dancers' work schedule was a breeze: class didn't meet until eleven a.m., we rehearsed at two p.m., nights were free; on the weekends there was no class, and rehearsals began after lunch. Viola and I were hired to teach a few classes in the second and third weeks, but the workload was light, the extra income welcome. We spent our leisure time beach-bumming on the very un-pacific Pacific, which has its risks if one takes to the water: Bob and I nearly drowned. Both of us are strong swimmers and we'd swum out to a float some distance offshore and sunned ourselves there (for too long), and when we tried to swim back against the tide and a ferocious undertow we were literally swimming in place. The breakers were gargantuan, and more than once we both got pummeled and thrown topsy-turvy to the ocean floor, sucked back and thrown up with a wave as we fought landward. Steve Paxton, realizing the situation, came dashing down to help us. He saved Bob; they both saved me. It was only then that I understood why so many Malibu residents had swimming pools and never went near the ocean.

The living situation was perfect. John had an enormous master bedroom overlooking the ocean. David Tudor, Bill Davis, Steve Paxton, and Bob Rauschenberg had bedrooms on the ground floor; the four women shared a four-room apartment over the garage. Our house boasted fireplace, flagstone terrace, green lawn, screened-in summerhouse—miles of beach and the pounding Pacific—luxury we never dreamed we might enjoy in smoggy, hot L.A. We cooked our own wonderful meals, partied with lively, interesting guests and hosts, swam and sunned, endlessly talked work and art and nonsense. Bob worked on the costumes for the new dances, tie-dyeing tights and leotards on the kitchen stove, dashing around neighborhood thrift shops in search of a crazy assortment of garments for *Story*, involving everyone in his decisions. This was Art-*and*-Life, Cage style, at its best. Merce did not share this familial existence, yet it was he who had found the beach house for us, and he was delighted with our pleasure in it.

Since his own work schedule permitted little leisure, he chose to live in town, near the university, but each evening he would join us for dinner at Malibu Beach. Music critic Peter Yates, writing for *Art and Architecture,* described the company as he found us that summer: "Visiting them at the Malibu Beach home where they stayed, I found them as cheerful, unpretentious, non-egotistic a group of artists as I have ever encountered. Cage as cook turned out a splendid simple dinner. Rauschenberg, helped by the dancers, was building a sand castle, reinforcing it with seaweed against the heavy tide. There were no cripples, no complainers, no apologies, no explanations. Let me find out for myself what I might think they were doing."[2]

We had two new, very different kinds of dances—*Story* and *Field Dances*—to engage us. *Field Dances,* the most open, unstructured work Merce has ever made, is described in his *Changes: Notes on Choreography:*

> The original directions indicate "to be done anywhere." the original premise is a dance for x number of people. as the name suggests, a "field" of activity. [the dancers] have a number, about 7, I think, of things or small events they can do together, and each dancer has one, two or three short dances he can deal with as he chooses. they can leave and enter at any point. the movements given them are purposely simple. an aisle, a street, a field, a theatre, a basketball court. The movements had been given to the dancers. The dancers are free to find the movement and speed within their own range, to do it as often as they want and to complete it or not.[3]

When Merce chose the title for his first indeterminate work, he was not unaware of what was going on in the sciences at this time, particularly physicists' explorations in "relativistic quantum field theory." The dance more closely reflects the repulsion and attraction, the moving apart and coming together found in the electromagnetic field—energy shifting back and forth through space and time—than any literal representation of a football field, hay field, or field of daisies. John Cage philosophy: We're not going in a single line. We're in a field of activity.

At its premiere in Los Angeles on July 17, *Field Dances* was performed by Merce, Viola, Shareen, and myself. My two "short dances" were different from those given to the other dancers in that there was even less specific choreographic material; mostly my part consisted of Merce's verbal instructions; he made no attempt to demonstrate anything. The first dance required that I keep a steady rhythm going in the feet ("1-and-2-and" for the equivalent of seven counts of eight, repeated four times—a total of 224 counts!) while the actions of head, torso, and arms were to be determined by me in performance—that is to say, spontaneously, different every time. Space and time were also free. The other dance was open-ended: a central phrase for the arms (described, not shown) performed in place, whose phrasing, length, speed, and direction could vary, was to be followed by movement for the legs and torso of my own invention but always arising out of the momentum of the given material. This section was far more difficult to realize spontaneously than the "running dance." The communally shared "small events" that allowed playing off and with the other dancers could be amusing, but the dance as a whole was severely limited and didn't wear well. In the beginning the freedoms allowed us were novel and stimulating and the results surprising. Although the simplicity of the choreography and the rules for performing it certainly challenged one's ingenuity, after dozens of performances its secrets were revealed, as were our limited imaginations, and it became difficult to stay interested in the extremely restricted vocabulary. The real challenge for us lay in discovering how not to repeat ourselves and how to avoid our predilection for favorite moves. (Spontaneity doesn't come easily.) Rauschenberg's costumes for the women were lovely pastel tie-dyed tights and leotards with floor-length trains of gauzy tie-dyed nylon attached to the backs of our scoop-necked leotards. The trains added a simple yet elegant feminine touch that we loved. A London critic, in 1964, called them remarkable, "like nightdresses for butterflies . . . The colours all had a soft brightness and were some of the most beautiful and elegant I have seen for a long time."[4] The music, Cage's *Variations IV,* involved noises made outside the concert hall—transistor radios, records, tapes, doors opening and shutting—performed by John, who ran in and out of the theater while David sat in a control booth manipulating dials. Peter Yates's description:

> Flat voices of announcers describing athletic events, news broadcasts, never quite clear enough to be understood, came through the hall loudspeakers and through open windows. In the hallway outside the auditorium Cage wheeled a cart, loaded with a portable speaker, producing a variety of noises, to the bafflement of some persons in the audience who asked him to be quiet. Outside a balcony door, several times angrily shut by members of the audience, Tudor periodically stirred up a similar confusion.[5]

Story, a far more complicated work than *Field Dances,* had eighteen sections—solos, duets, trios, group passages—with specific and detailed choreographic material. From performance to performance the number of sections danced may change, as well as the order and the time of each section. Although never the same from one performance to another, *Story* offered the dancers only one opportunity for actual improvisation. The freedoms Merce did allow us related to entrances and exits, space, direction, tempo, continuity of material within sections, and in some cases, phrasing—but except for the section dubbed "Space," the movement itself was all of Merce's devising. Toshi Ichiyanagi's score, titled *Sapporo* (after his Japanese home island), is also indeterminate: it calls for a conductor and up to fifteen musicians who may play any one of sixteen parts, choosing any kind of sound-making objects capable of meeting the requirements of the written score. (Earlier, when Toshi had been an accompanist for Merce's technique classes, he'd been married to Yoko Ono, a Sarah Lawrence classmate of Judith Dunn's. He was exceedingly shy, very pale, had a sweet disposition, and appeared to be malnourished. We worried about him. Why didn't his wife take better care of him? But Yoko refused to play wife, cook, and bottle-washer, and was utterly scandalized to discover that the rest of us "liberated artist women" did indeed cook for our husbands. Yoko fancied herself an avant-garde artist, but her work seemed to me derivative, opportunistic, and trivial. She once looked me in the eye and said matter-of-factly, "I always get what I want." No doubt!)

Once *Story* had joined the repertory, rehearsals of it were devoted to the precise execution of the basic choreographic material in each section, "in order to return it to its original quantity in case the dancers had begun to shorten or lengthen it in performance," as Merce explained decades later. "In performance, shape of arms, tilt of head, exact position of leg may be changed due to the exigencies of immediate choice and the particulars of each venue."[6] Given freedom to play with the material, we dancers still had a responsibility to execute the details of Merce's original. Lack of clarity, carelessness, and attempts at humor or cuteness could reduce the work to banal mush. It was a danger Merce was all too aware of, and I don't think anything irritated him more than our mental laziness or what he perceived as a laissez-faire attitude toward the realization of *Story* onstage.

Unlike *Field Dances*, whose continuity and length of events were never established beforehand, each performance of *Story* had a determined order with allotted times. The permutations were nearly endless but not disclosed to the dancers until thirty minutes before curtain, when the score for the night's performance would be posted in the wings on each side of the stage. That was when we would behold what Rauschenberg had concocted for that evening's decor—different for each theater and usually for each performance. Next, we'd discover what new treasures he might have added to the grab-bag of accessory costumes. Absolutely in his element, Bob presented us with an endlessly inventive, deliciously unexpected succession of surprises. To add more spice to the indeterminate mix, we could select anything from the outlandish array of thrift-shop garments and other oddities, including football shoulder pads that he stored on or off the stage in a gigantic tattered U.S. Navy duffel, and we could change costumes as often as the spirit moved us.

After the L.A. residency, Viola and Merce flew to San Francisco for a teaching gig at the University of California, Berkeley, while the rest of us stayed on at the beach house until it was time to join them. On July 30, John drove the rest of us to Hot Springs Lodge in Big Sur, and there, on the following evening, we presented *Event-minus 1*. That's my name for it. It actually anticipated the now historical June 24, 1964, *Event #1* in Vienna by eleven months. John's idea was to give a performance for Big Sur's local residents—artists, writers, potters, poets, sandalmakers, beatniks, and wealthy art patrons. Great fun! We performed in the dining and living rooms of the lodge—with the audience and performers in both rooms. John composed a structure for the hour-long event. He read stories from *Silence;* the rest of us, along with Bill's friend Albert Reid (who would later join the company) and Bob Rauschenberg, did bits and pieces—together or separately—of Happening material, excerpts from Merce's dances, a dance of Bill's, an improvisation by Steve and Barbara. John paid each of us $3.75.

In Berkeley, we performed on a lecture platform in the university's miserably inadequate Wheeler Auditorium. It was almost impossible to believe that on that same ill-proportioned platform only a year and a half earlier we'd actually gotten through *Crises* and *Aeon* without killing ourselves. This time a totally different program included the two new works plus *Septet* and Merce's *Untitled Solo. Story* seemed to work well even in that unfortunate setting and it was precisely this kind of venue that Merce had in mind when he made *Field Dances* and *Story*—dances that could be flexible and accommodate even the worst of performance spaces.

We had only nine days before a Lincoln Center performance in New York City, with an eight-day drive ahead of us. Merce, Shareen, Barbara, and Viola all opted to fly home. I didn't dare spend the money, but the thought of all those days without class and rehearsal, just sitting for sixteen hours a day in the VW bus before facing my bête noire, the New York audience, rightly terrified me. Merce was worried, too, and at the last minute offered to pay for my flight, but by that time I couldn't get a reservation. I traveled in the VW until Omaha, where I caught a flight the rest of the way. Driving east for five days with John, Bob, Steve, Bill, and Albert, how could I help enjoying myself? Reno—I won $7.50. Searching for mushrooms in the Rocky Mountain National Forest and cooking them with a juicy steak over a fire in the dark. Flat tire beside a meadow of sad-eyed, lowing cattle. Running out of gas on the freeway in the hot Nebraska sun. Discussing dance, religion, aesthetics. I knew even then that despite my anxieties about New York, this life with John was every bit as important to me as the performing life with Merce.

Next stop: "August Fanfare," Philharmonic Hall, Lincoln Center. For this concert it was necessary for the company to rejoin the union, the American Guild of Musical Artists. According to the contract, compensation for the single August 13 performance was to be $27.25 apiece. AGMA deducted $8 dues plus a $2 "reinstatement fee." After subtracting $3.73 for miscellaneous taxes, "my fee for performing in America's greatest cultural center came to a total of $13.52 for an evening-long program," I wrote to the union; "Can you explain to me what benefit *I* get from belonging to your union, which is supposed to BENEFIT artists, not make paupers of them?" Without the union's interference, Merce would have paid us a flat $25. This was not the last time that we'd fret over AGMA's role in our lives.

The *New York Times* principal dance critic was at Jacob's Pillow reviewing "Stars and Soloists of the Opera of Paris." It figured. Jill Johnston's lengthy article in *The Village Voice* compared José Limón and Cunningham—their very different Philharmonic Hall audiences and their choreographic and philosophical approaches to dance. It's worth reading and pertinent, even decades later. Some excerpts:

> The dance world is embarrassingly backward. Cunningham should pack Philharmonic Hall for a week at least. He has no peer in the dance as a consummate artist. Moreover, he continues to be abreast, if not in advance, of all recent developments. . . . Cunningham belongs to that great shift of focus—from representation to the concentration on materials—which is so central to the revolution in art in this century. . . . The curious thing about this kind of dancing is that emotion is created by motion rather than the reverse, which is the traditional view of modern dance. But since there is no specified emotion, I believe that what you feel in the movement is the impact of a total action. Each movement means only itself and it moves you by its pure existence, by being so much itself. It is Cunningham's magic as a performer to make every action a unique and complete experience. The gesture is the performer; the performer is the gesture.[7]

As so often happened when I was fully engaged in performing, I recall nothing specific about that concert or the following one at Connecticut College on Friday, August 16, which generated column after column of Cage castigations (good god, was there really nothing on the stage to write about?) by Hughes and Terry, despite the fact that neither of them had attended the Lincoln Center performance. Ironically, the reviewers who had been to Philharmonic Hall made no mention of intolerable sound levels, yet Allen Hughes responded to audience complaints sent to Lincoln Center by writing:

FAR OUT DANCE MUSIC RAISES PROTESTS

Something must be wrong somewhere when decisions about watching dancing depends on the ability to tolerate the music that goes with it . . . the attention the public can give to looking is only what it has left after attending to the crashing assaults on its eardrums.[8]

Certainly the problem was serious. I sympathized with Merce's audience in 1963, much more so after I became a member of it, and for years I've worn protective earplugs when attending Cunningham concerts. What is the solution to the dichotomous puzzle—sensitive John/cruel Cage? Cage's indeterminate scores for live-electronic media can be performed quietly as well as deafeningly. Nothing in the scores, as far as I know, requires extremes of volume. If they are realized by the performers in decibel levels that are painful and harmful to the human ear, that's their choice and the chance Cage took. He gave the performers freedoms and refused to interfere with the results—a moral decision on his part. My view: producing sounds that are known to be painful and probably harmful is to engage in hostile and aggressive acts of intentional violence. So let's place most of the blame where it belongs: on the Live-Electronics Jockeys who call themselves musicians. It should be remembered that in the last decades of Cage's life, the music he composed and realized himself gave no physically injurious offense; by then he had already abandoned regular participation in the Cunningham company's live-electronics music pit, and I am absolutely convinced that despite his avowals of "beyond likes and dislikes," he often hated what emanated from there as much as I did.

Attending art openings, at the invitation of our newly acclaimed artist friends, became high points in our social lives in the sixties. Richard Lippold's dazzling, airy *Orpheus and Apollo* flew high above a throng of well-wishers gathered for the sculpture's dedication ceremony in the Grand Promenade of Philharmonic Hall at Lincoln Center on December 19, 1962, and Richard spoke with his customary elegance, self-deprecating humor, humanity, and warmth. Some forty years later, that exquisite sculpture still floats serenely above the heads of thousands of concertgoers.

Rauschenberg's star kept rising on both sides of the Atlantic, and he went at a madcap pace keeping up. He dashed off to Paris for his opening at the Sonnabend Gallery and returned the next day to be present at the opening of his one-man exhibition at Dartmouth. A show of his black-and-white silkscreen paintings opened at the Castelli Gallery in October and, most important, a major retrospective of his work was presented at the Jewish Museum in New York—he was thirty-seven—and another one the following year at the Whitechapel Gallery in London. Meanwhile, he continued to tour with the Cunningham company as lighting designer and stage manager. He wanted to do everything and be everywhere. And he wanted his friends to join him. He managed to convince Steve Paxton and me to take the midnight sleeper to Dartmouth—after a continuous thirteen days of rehearsal with Merce—to see his show. At four a.m., in the dark and blistering 18-degrees-below-zero cold, he was there to meet our train, stamping his feet in the crunchy snow and grinning with delight. Later that same day he drove us to Wheaton College. We didn't arrive until 2:30 a.m., prior to two performances and a two-week tour with Merce. We were exhausted. Bob was unfazed: exhaustion wasn't even in his vocabulary. Why was it in ours? In the midst of a Cunningham tour of the South, Bob flew back to New York for his Castelli Gallery opening, rejoining the company in time to sweep the stage and set the lights for the next night's dance performance.

The opening of the Jewish Museum show on March 30—a black-tie affair, aswarm with uptown collectors and dealers and downtown artists and friends—was *the* art and social event of the season, at least from the perspective of Bob's chums. Painters and sculptors (a few of whom probably never thought they'd have to take Rauschenberg seriously) were there, no doubt green with envy, and eager to pose with him in front of his thirty-three-foot black-and-white silkscreen painting, *Barge*. Twenty-seven artists and one choreographer solemnly stare out from this remarkable photograph. Among them—Claes Oldenburg, Richard Lippold, Barnett Newman, Perle Fine, Alfred Jensen, Andy Warhol, Marisol, James Rosenquist, George Segal, Alfred Leslie, Frederick Kiesler, Lee Bontecou, Isamu Noguchi, Allan Kaprow, and Merce Cunningham.

> A Glamour Exclusive: This extraordinary photograph . . . cuts across all party lines in the New York art world. All generations, media, and techniques represented. Said a beard in black tie: "With a machine gun you could knock off two squads of the best avant-garde artists in America."[1]

Conspicuously absent from this lineup were Bill de Kooning, Franz Kline, Philip Guston, and most noticeably, Jasper Johns. When Rauschenberg moved into 809 Broadway with Steve Paxton, Jasper stayed on at Front Street during the winters until 1963, but he spent most of the spring, summer, and fall of each year in a house on Edisto Island, South Carolina, which he'd bought in '61. At about this time, art critics noted a decisive change in Jasper's paintings. If Rauschenberg's and Johns's personal relationship had terminated, their art still was linked and often shown together in group exhibitions. Both were now incredibly successful. At thirty-two, Jasper was hailed as "probably the most influential younger painter in the world."[2] In the late summer of '63, he moved to a penthouse at 106th Street and Riverside Drive that Earle and I, through a friend of cellist Charlotte Moorman, had seen. It was huge, with a wraparound terrace and fabulous views, and learning that it was about to become vacant, we'd shown it to Rauschenberg, but Bob said he couldn't imagine bringing his friends to such a posh place, it would be too embarrassing. He told Leo Castelli about it, but Leo, having just recently moved to a place in the Village with his new wife, suggested Jasper, who loved the views and had no problem with the posh location, despite the fact that there was no studio space in which to work. He painted in the unfurnished living room and stored his books in the gigantic freezer.

Bob's apartment at 809 Broadway exacted an irresistible, magnetic pull on the downtown art and dance community. Pied Piper Bob's "Let's make stuff! It's fun!" ideology revved up the creative engines of everyone beating a path to his door. His wildly gregarious, democratic spirit encouraged everyone to unleash their imaginations and participate. There was no barrier he wasn't willing to crash through, no boundary he refused to step over, no artistic discipline he was afraid to tackle. Choreography was next on his list! He asked me to dance in the piece he was making for "Pop Festival," a six-week event organized by Alice Denney for the Washington [D.C.] Gallery of Modern Art. This was my second dance venture that spring outside the Cunningham company. Saying yes instead of no, a first tiny step of independence, was exhilarating.

In early January 1963, I'd received a phone call from Martha Hill at Juilliard: Grant Strate, from the Canadian National Ballet, was to choreograph a work based on Greek legend, and Antony Tudor had suggested me for the part of Electra. Would I be interested? It wasn't Tudor choreography, but it would be a chance to dance an acting role. After meeting with Miss Hill, Tudor, and Strate, and listening to the Alberto Ginastera *String Quartet No. 2*, I tentatively agreed, dependent upon Merce's elusive on-again/off-again Broadway season, and began to rehearse Strate's *The House of Atreus*. Chase Robinson from the Limón company played Agamemnon. Maggie Black was the Leader of the Chorus (the only person in pointe shoes). Among the dancers in the chorus was Jennifer Muller. March 8, in a letter to Earle:

> I've been rehearsing *The House of Atreus* almost every day since I've been back [from tour]. Tonight was the first complete run through. WOW—what an emotional number! I was absolutely exhausted by the end of it: cloak waving, hysterics, passion, fiendish glee, blood and thunder. I play Electra out to murder Mom and her lover, with brother's help. Really exciting! I find it really fun to do . . . like being let out of a strait-jacket . . . into the world of schmaltz and passion . . . yeah!

Merce attended the first performance—the one I felt I didn't dance well, of course—but he spoke not a word to me about it. Tudor offered little by way of comment, but wishful thinking had me hoping that Hugh Laing's gracious comments might have been a reflection of Tudor's own opinion. Miss Craske didn't think much of the choreography, asking, "Why do young choreographers tackle such pretentious subject matter?" but Agnes de Mille was said to have "adored" the ballet. Whatever the merits of the choreography, I loved dancing it and reveled in performing with live classical music. The second performance went well. The ballet received good reviews. Unsure of my own abilities as dancer-actress, I especially treasured Allen Hughes's comment: "This performance was distinguished by the presence of Carolyn Brown in the part of Electra. It seemed too bad that she was not given the part of the child Electra as well as that of the mature character, for with her acting ability, she could surely have made the character believable from start to finish."[3]

A little more than a month later, my sandal-footed balletic turn consigned to oblivion, I was "ass-scutching" along the floor of the *America on Wheels Skating Rink* in Washington, D.C., clad in black pointe shoes and a gray sweatsuit, my costumes for Rauschenberg's first dance work, *Pelican.* The program included dances by Trisha Brown, William Davis, Judith Dunn, David Gordon, Steve Paxton, Yvonne Rainer, and Albert Reid—the Judson Dance Theater bunch. Two more disparate experiences would be hard to imagine.

Performing *Pelican* presented a new set of unaccustomed challenges. In the first place, Bob had to learn how to roller-skate and I had to learn to trust his new skill in the adagio and lift sections. It was an endeavor not without risks, especially considering Merce's busy touring schedule, which I couldn't jeopardize by being injured. Only Bob's piece, of all the dances presented on this program by Judson choreographers, took advantage of the unusual venue. *Pelican* is a trio for two men on roller skates and a woman in pointe shoes. The men, Rauschenberg and the Swedish artist Per Olaf Ultvedt, entered the rink each kneeling on an axle between a set of bicycle wheels. Parachutes—stretched open with struts—were strapped to their backs. Like giant magical insects on the prowl, they propelled themselves along by "walking" hand over hand. When finally they stood and began to skate, the wind filled their silk parachutes and the insects were transformed into mammoth mystical birds, twirling and swooping through space. By comparison, I was grounded, unable to sail or fly, and the directions Bob gave me were mostly simplistic: "Stand. Hop. Mark time. Developpé," or peculiar, as in "ass-scutch"—the name Bob gave to one of the moves he choreographed for me. But turning and leaping the length of that vast roller rink were elating, and the supported adagio work proved sufficiently precarious to make for real excitement. We had only four rehearsals. The first was at 809 Broadway, but even that huge loft was too small, so Bob rented a skating rink in Brooklyn where we worked for one full day and two mornings before flying off to Washington for the performance. Every bit of that work—costumes, props, movement, and the soundtrack (a collage of radio, record, movie and television sources)—was conceived by Bob. Result? A work ungainly and lyrical, awkward and poetic, innovative and romantic. I was back in New York rehearsing with Merce the next afternoon, unscathed. Unlike Strate's *The House of Atreus,* Rauschenberg's *Pelican* had a future life. We performed it again at "The First New York Theatre Rally" in 1965 and the following year at the Rollerdrome, in Culver City, outside Los Angeles. Its final live performance took place once again in Washington, D.C., at the original roller-skating rink, in 1966. Filmed in New York in 1965, *Pelican* would live on for decades as a part of Bob's oeuvre in documentaries and retrospective exhibitions.

In September 1963, Cage realized a long-held dream to present the first-ever performance of Erik Satie's *Vexations,* a curious piece requiring a brief motif to be played 840 times. The world premiere took nineteen hours, beginning at six in the evening of September 9 with Viola Farber at the piano and ending at 12:40 a.m. on September 11—Viola again at the piano, this time with a rose in her hair. In between were ten other pianists, including Cage himself. It was a sensational press affair—UP, AP, radio people with microphones, phone calls from London—all in an uproar, and of course treating it as a joke. John never considered Satie's work a joke, but oh how he delighted in the publicity!

By default, due to the cancellation of Merce's Broadway season, Earle and Morty were the first to receive grants from the Foundation for the Contemporary Performance Arts, which commissioned new compositions and presented a concert of four works by each composer at Town Hall on October 11, 1963. Unfortunately for Earle, his half of the program came after intermission. After hearing only one of Earle's pieces, the music critics from the *Times* and *Herald Tribune* left to meet their papers' deadlines. What imbecilic editors would require their critics, reviewing a *one-performance-only* concert of contemporary music never before heard, to leave early in order to meet an early-edition deadline? For Earle there was small comfort in the *Herald Tribune*'s acknowledgment that "It was perfectly true that [Brown and Feldman] have been, to a great extent, prophets unhonored in their own land and perhaps their big two-man show last night at Town Hall was only a measure of their just due,"[4] or that prior to the concert, the *Tribune* called Earle "a genuine pioneer and a brilliant spokesman for the truly new."

Three months later, Leonard Bernstein and the New York Philharmonic presented *The Avant-Garde,* a series of five programs of contemporary music, the last of which included compositions by Cage, Feldman, and Brown. Bernstein tackled Earle's two-conductor work *Available Forms II* as a *competition*—his orchestra jousting with Earle's in an "anything you can do I can do better" (flashier, louder, faster, whatever) contest—instead of approaching the work as a collaborative effort in adventurous music-making. Although most of the critics gave Earle's *Available Forms II* short shrift, Alan Rich wrote: "Finally (it was now 10:55, and the hall was about one-third full), came a genuine piece of music, Earle Brown's *Available Forms.* This is an extremely complex work . . . Dense, fascinating, intensely colored and full of creative fire, chance or not, Mr. Brown's creation made musical sense. It made a spectacular ending to a series that, with all its ups and downs, its false starts and faulty premises, has enlivened the musical season no end."[5]

Earle left for Europe a month later. We didn't see each other until mid-June.

In the fall and winter of 1963–64, the company toured fourteen states, performing a repertory of twelve dances—crazy, impractical jaunts that had us dancing on every sort of stage imaginable, but it's the non-dance experiences I best remember. From my journal:

> The sighting of a doctor's office with one door for whites, one for blacks in Little Rock, Arkansas.
>
> Two architectural visits in Arizona, arranged by John, to Frank Lloyd Wright's *Taliesen West* and to Paolo Soleri's *Cosanti.* Lunch at *Cosanti* with the fascinating visionary "urban prophet," his wife, two daughters and three apprentices. Soleri showed us huge drawings of his imaginary cities and treated us to an exposition of "arcology," his revolutionary philosophy of combining architecture with ecology.
>
> Another Cage gift—a two day mid-tour "vacation" at Tal-Wi-Wi Lodge in Alpine, Arizona. At breakfast: fourteen horses galloping up the meadow in the snow, bucking, rearing, high-stepping, prancing, frisky and playful, nuzzling and chasing one another in exuberant spirits. Exhilarating improvisation.
>
> The impression that John seemed close to a nervous breakdown, or a very serious shake-up in his life. Why was he so depressed?
>
> David, too, in a very strange way; avoiding the group and disappearing

into his room. Was his suggestion to Viola that they start a dance company of their own with music by Debussy *only* in jest? Or frustration?

Two days in Lafayette, Louisiana with Bob Rauschenberg's family—eating wild duck, crab gumbo and pecan pie. Bob's sister's breakfast: Coca-Cola and cookies.

A John-inspired detour to Gethsemani Trappist Monastery near Bardstown, Kentucky: in a balcony, behind latticed screen, observing monks at their devotions, hearing heavenly chanting.

Most vividly, searingly—Friday, November 22nd: the Pennsylvania Turnpike, returning to New York. Sighting flags at half-mast. John stopped the Volkswagen bus at a gas station. We learned the chilling news—John F. Kennedy slain in Dallas, Texas.

In the winter of 1964, Merce made three new works: *Open Session,* a solo for himself; *Paired,* a duet for Viola Farber and himself; and *Winterbranch* for six dancers, including himself (which completed the quartet of dances named after the seasons begun in 1955). The new dances were premiered at the Wadsworth Atheneum in Hartford in March in a mini-season of three performances, preceded by a lecture-demonstration. *Open Session* was both premiered and retired with just that one performance. As well it should have been. I wrote to Earle:

A new solo . . . *à la* Judson. He sits in a chair . . . drinks a can of beer while sitting in the chair, wipes his hands on paper towels and drops them in a waste-barrel, which he then removes from the stage. In between these mundane events he dances like a possessed demon or mad-man with many of his usual solo movements. Bob, Steve, Viola, Bill Davis and I were *really* appalled! Bill saw it from the front and said Merce doesn't understand what the Judson kids are doing, that Merce's approach is superficial. Yvonne [Rainer] thought Merce shouldn't do those things, that he should do what *he* does. . . . John, of course, thought Merce was magnificent! And, that he was in fact *teaching* the Judson kids how it should be done!

Open Session appeared improvisational. *Paired,* although *appearing* improvisational, was actually an indeterminate work with nine choreographed events, their sequence determined in performance by the dancers themselves. Each event was color-coded. Nine pots of paint in the wings. One or the other dancer selected a color—for example, green—and then ran onstage and slapped or smeared it across his/her partner's costume—a sort of diaper made of rubber baby sheeting over flesh-colored tights and leotards—thus signaling the green section, and so on until all nine colors were used. Action painting in the most literal sense! Merce admitted to having "a streak of violence" in him,[6] and it was certainly evident in this wildly out-of-control, violent dance that evoked a curiously hostile battle of the sexes. Unintentionally, Viola once kicked him in the forehead; another time Merce dropped her on her head, and at still another they cracked heads.[7] At the end, Merce would shout "Let's go!" and the two dancers—Viola now panting for breath, their frantic, passionate energy nearly spent—dashed back and forth across the stage in a frenzied leaping phrase.

Violence of a different sort—the clandestine sort that lurks in darkness, inscrutable, furtive, and menacing—permeates *Winterbranch.* Cold fury smothering raging fire. It felt like the movement embodiment of the soundless "Scream" by Edvard Munch. But soundless, *Winterbranch* most emphatically was *not.* La Monte Young's electronic soundscape, *2 sounds,* provided that scream, first high-pitched, then low-pitched—the second even more earsplittingly torturous than the first. Merce, of course, didn't choreograph a dance about violence, or anything else other than the act of falling: slow falls, fast falls, arching falls, leaping falls, turning falls, serpentine twisting falls, supported falls, all connected by pedestrian walking, dragging, rolling, crawling, performed by six dancers in navy-blue sweatsuits and grubby white slip-on sneakers, thick black smudges under the eyes—the kind football players use to cut the glare. Although the costumes are officially credited to Rauschenberg, he claims only the black smudges. Sweatsuits and sneakers were Merce's decision. Merce was also unusually specific about the lighting. He wanted the darkness of a roadway at night, with headlights picking up objects, animals, road signs at random changing, distorting, obfuscating what is seen, different for each viewer and different every time.

The dance begins in silence and total darkness, with a just barely perceptible "thing" wriggling its way across the floor from upstage left to upstage right. "The chance play of lights obscures it, stretches it into a long dark shadow, accents the sharp staccato changes of its shape."[8] A mysterious tension is created and continues to build. Much of the action that follows is executed in excruciating slow motion. One-third of the way into the dance, the viewer—now accustomed to the silence—is suddenly assaulted by the first of La Monte Young's screeching, nearly intolerable sounds. The tension now, for both dancers *and* viewers, is palpable. Some-

times it's virtually impossible to see what is happening onstage; Rauschenberg used handheld lights to sear the space, etch the outline of a dancer,
or throw ominous shadows into the darkness. First rehearsals of *Winterbranch* wreaked havoc on our bodies. "Merce dropped me on my hip in
rehearsal today and it hurts like crazy. I hope it's just a bruise and not
something more serious. He's *so frantic* he just dashes into things with violence and no sense."[9] Although sometimes terrifying—it felt dangerous
and *was* dangerous—the dance was thrilling to perform. For me, *Winterbranch* remains one of Merce's greatest, most original works.

The Hartford performances were sold out a week in advance. Dozens of
loyal Cunningham fans made the trek from New York. Curator Sam
Wagstaff, who had invited the company, was ecstatic with the success of
the weekend; so was his boss. For me, however, it proved to be a mortify-
ing ordeal. In Providence the evening before, my bruised hip was so
painful that I didn't dance *Story* and had to leave out much of my part in
Antic Meet, the first time in eleven years that I'd ever missed any part of a
performance. The whole weekend in Hartford was traumatic. Most distressing of all: the news that my father was back in the hospital, seriously
ill again. By the third performance I was a wreck. Compensating for one
injury can cause another, and almost immediately in *Aeon,* the first piece
on the program, my left calf muscle cramped unbearably and I was
reduced to hobbling through the rest of the forty-five minute dance. *Winterbranch,* I faked. Most humiliating of all was having to omit parts of *Nocturnes* and feign my way through the rest. Paradoxically, I had begged
Merce to let me have an understudy for at least one dance in the repertory,
and *Nocturnes* was it, but Merce would not allow Sandra Neels to perform
it in Hartford. I had been in such good condition before Merce dropped me
on my hip! I was so looking forward to the rare opportunity of performing
nine of Merce's dances in three consecutive programs and the chance to
explore the uniquely different qualities of each work. Lurching about in
abject frustration, I blamed Merce, but surely it was the mind/body connection as much as my bruised hip that destroyed that weekend for me. My
resentment toward Merce, my anger, even paranoia—*maybe he'd dropped
me on purpose*—had poisoned my own body.

Merce created one more new work that spring, a seven-and-a-half-
minute trio for himself, Viola, and me called *Cross Currents.* Before the trio
rehearsals began, the sounds of some big-band forties jazz wafted through
the locked doors of the studio when Merce was there working alone. It was
not unusual for him to work alone with all sorts of conventional music, but
it was exceedingly unusual for the company to actually rehearse, much

less to perform, to any of this music. Curious! John disliked jazz. Would we actually get to perform the piece to jazz? But, no, much to our disappointment (even, Merce's, I'd wager) John nixed it; the jazz was replaced with a tape of a Cage-arranged collage of Conlon Nancarrow's *Rhythmic Studies for Player Piano* and the lighthearted fun of the piece deflated like a leaky balloon. I think it must have been Merce who was unhappy with the Nancarrow, because mid–world tour it was replaced with a version of Cage's *Variation IV.* (Not a particularly jolly substitute, either.) Sadly, I don't think we ever recaptured the original playfulness and three-part rhythmic intricacy we'd experienced in rehearsals.

After the Harford performances, I spent two weeks with my parents trying to provide some cheer for them before returning for the intense rehearsal period prior to a six-month world tour. From the end of March until we left in June, I commuted to Massachusetts as often as I could to help my mother with her annual recital and to visit with my father.

Through John Cage's connections with the Sarabhai family and the Sogetsu Art Center, the Cunningham company received invitations to perform in India and Japan. With these two offers as incentives, John wanted to arrange a full-fledged foreign tour, and he asked David Vaughan (the secretary at the studio at the time) if he would take on the assignment. During the winter of 1963–64, David wrote letters to everyone and anyone who might help us to get an engagement. A world tour seemed another one of John's extravagant fantasies, a nebulous, if glorious, dream like the continually promised, ever-postponed, never-to-be-realized Broadway season. Twenty thousand dollars of the funds raised for that season by the Foundation for the Contemporary Performance Arts, plus a generous $10,000 contribution from the JDR 3rd Fund for travel expenses in the Far East (another $10,000 was given later in the tour), as well as some private contributions to the newly established Cunningham Dance Foundation, gave the company a cash basis of around $40,000. It was hardly sufficient to travel around the world with eighteen people for six months, and I don't think anyone thought it would happen. Not even when we were instructed to get valid passports, and to start getting typhoid, typhus, paratyphoid, cholera, and tetanus shots, plus a polio booster and a smallpox vaccination.

"We had no business not knowing what we didn't know."
—LEWIS L. LLOYD, ADMINISTRATOR, MERCE CUNNINGHAM AND DANCE COMPANY, 1964

At five o'clock on the evening of Wednesday, June 3, 1964, eighteen people, most limp with exhaustion from a myriad of last-minute preparations, gathered in New York's East Side Air Terminal: Ten dancers: Merce Cunningham, Carolyn Brown, Viola Farber, Barbara Lloyd, Sandra Neels, Shareen Blair, Deborah Hay, Steve Paxton, Bill Davis, Albert Reid. Two musicians: John Cage and David Tudor. Two stage technicians: Robert Rauschenberg and Alex Hay. Two administrators: Lewis Lloyd and David Vaughan. And along for the ride, the Lloyds' baby son, Benjamin, and his English nanny, Mrs. Gray. There were fifty-one pieces of luggage weighing over one ton; we were twelve hundred pounds overweight.

At Kennedy International, we bumped into Paul Taylor and his company, who were also on their way to Europe, via Icelandic Airlines. My condolences! This time the Cunningham company was traveling Air France, with VIP treatment adding a touch of glamour to our departure—drinks served in a special lounge, publicity photos just before boarding the 707 jetliner to Paris—just as though we were some internationally famous ballet troupe. Less glamorous were huge gaps in our performance schedule, not nearly enough cash to tide us over during these idle periods, and being blacklisted by AGMA for not meeting their salary stipulations.

Had we heeded the union's warnings and not gone, the company would have missed the most consequential six months in its history. Despite the lower-than-AGMA wages, most of us managed to save a little money each week. My weekly salary was $125, $19.07 of it withheld and deposited in my New York savings account; what remained paid for hotel, food, and sundry expenses. No per diem in those days. That, of course, was part of the reason AGMA blacklisted the company. Viola also received $125. Merce, John, David, Bob, and his assistant, Alex, were paid more. I believe the other dancers received slightly less. No one starved or went without a bed. No one, I'm quite sure, wishes he or she hadn't gone. The experience—wonderful and terrible, glorious and gloomy, enlightening and depressing, hilarious and disheartening—all of it, I would have been happy to pay for.

At Orly, a beautiful blue-and-white bus, light and airy, awaited us and served as our home-on-the-road for most of the next two months, a bus so large that each person could have both an aisle and window seat to him/herself. Our driver, a delightfully eccentric Venetian named Bill, who had driven the Jean-Louis Barrault company all over the world, quickly assumed additional roles as our guide and protector. He flirted outrageously with the women, joked madly with the men, had strong opinions about everything (hated Cage's music for *Aeon,* liked Boulez and Mozart), drove like a demon, leaning on the horn while swearing and shouting at everyone on the road, and made sure we were not cheated, overcharged, or taken advantage of in any way. He spoke barely a word of English but French like a native. How we adored him!

After an eight-hour trip, we arrived in Strasbourg around nine in the evening and moved into a small, inexpensive hotel near the railroad station and overlooking prostitute row. From midnight till dawn chattering voices, laughter, cruising automobiles, and the tattoo of the hookers' high-heeled shoes on the cobblestones resounded and echoed into the night, making sleep nearly impossible. I shed tears of frustration: a cold coming on, feeling skinnier and older by the minute; most of all, depressed. David Vaughan had just informed me that Viola would be dancing her duet with Merce in Paris but that I would not. Standing by the window at three in the morning, I stared disconsolately into the predawn sky, dispirited and lonely. Not exactly a stellar beginning.

Our first performance took place on a dusty, splintery wooden floor in the *Théâtre de la Comédie,* a nice, smallish opera house with three balconies and stage dimensions adequate even for *Aeon.* Arriving at the theater on our first rehearsal day, Viola and I discovered stars above our names on the door of our shared dressing room. "*Étoiles*" we were! David Vaughan, dear man, with his endearing Old World theatrical sensibilities, was giving a little lift to our morale. It was not an easy program—*Aeon, Crises,* and *Nocturnes*—that Merce chose to present in this picturesque

Alsatian city on the French-German-Swiss border, a city where one would expect to find an affluent bourgeois audience with very prescribed ideas about dance. In his journal, Merce confessed to feeling some apprehension about what the evening would bring.[1] The curtain opened to a full house, composed predominantly of young people, who responded enthusiastically after each piece and, to our surprise and delight, greeted our final bow with a tremendous outpouring of applause, ending with rhythmic clapping in the manner of an enthusiastic American audience cheering the Royal Ballet. Backstage, we celebrated our successful beginning with sparkling honey wine provided by David Vaughan. We celebrated again the next morning when we read the strongly positive reviews by different critics in both the French and German editions of *Dernières Nouvelles*. What a boost!

Next stop, Paris. But not the Left Bank Paris I knew and loved. The company was booked into the Hôtel Comprador on the Right Bank, just below Montmartre, near the Boulevard Poissonière. Rooms were luck-of-the-draw, and Viola and I were not among the lucky ones who got large airy chambers with baths on a high floor with tiny balconies and big views. We were assigned a double room scarcely bigger than a closet on a smelly air-shaft with garbage on the ground below, so we set out to find another hotel. Just around the corner, the Hôtel Central on Cité Bergère provided us with single rooms with views of sky and rooftops, although no private bath, which cost twenty francs (four dollars) per night (double the rate of the first hotel)—but no matter. Part of my sleeping problem in Strasbourg was that Viola smoked—lighting up first thing in the morning and last thing before lights out. Walking into my *own* room, shutting the door, and finding myself completely alone was bliss. Viola was equally happy with the arrangement.

Malheureusement, the week in Paris was hell, with stresses none of us could possibly have imagined. Our administrators, Lewis and David, still very new at their jobs, inevitably goofed up a bit with occasional miscommunications over place and time of bus departures, rehearsal schedules, meal and hotel arrangements, or the little nitty-gritty details that individually are unimportant but added up can irritate and finally anger even the most sanguine. One point of contention for many of us was being ordered about like so many unruly children. Viola and I soon let Lew and David know that we were having none of it.

At the rehearsal in the Ballets Modernes de Paris Studios off the Boulevard Clichy, prior to a lecture-demonstration planned for the evening, we learned that some French filmmakers would be there to commence shooting a documentary of the company's sojourn in Paris. It was bad enough taking class in front of an audience, but being filmed for posterity added an entirely different level of anxiety to the ordeal. If we were nervous, Merce was more so. He threw new material at us, even new beginning exercises, and was so rattled himself that he couldn't repeat what he had demonstrated. Steve finally broke the ice by asking a question, and I followed suit; the tension eased and we even managed to smile a bit. After the torturous class, dancing *Suite* and *Field Dances* was pure joy, at least for me, but Merce seemed to have a miserable time performing—off-balance and technically insecure in a way I'd never before seen him. Martha Graham's Paris debut in 1950 had been disastrous, the season canceled after only two performances, the French audience reportedly bored, silent, and hostile. Was Merce foreseeing a similar fate in store for us?

Next day, with a free morning to luxuriate in by myself, I took a bus to the Left Bank to wander the Sixth Arrondissement, the Paris I knew so well and loved best of all. Earle had written that I must not miss the Max Ernst exhibit at the Iolas Gallery on St-Germain-des-Prés because a surprise awaited. I understood immediately. Dead center as one entered the gallery was *Capricorn,* a huge bronze sculpture that we'd first seen in a plaster version at Max Ernst's ranch in Sedona, Arizona, fourteen years earlier. I'd had the audacity then to sit on it, and Earle captured the moment on film. We were on our honeymoon, and had had the good fortune to dine with the Ernsts on several occasions. Like hundreds of women before and after me, I fell under the spell of Ernst's austere beauty and elegance, and of course, his transporting blue eyes.

An omelet in a small outdoor café on the Seine, a stroll across the Pont Royal to the Louvre. A perfect morning. Before a not-so-perfect afternoon. No one, Merce least of all, was pleased about the previous evening's event. At this rehearsal everyone was a bit wary. From my journal:

> Merce was in a terrible mood. We warmed up in TOTAL silence and then did a "run through" of *Rune*. The most difficult dance in the repertoire. Considering the various states and degrees of ill-health and fatigue, it did not go too badly. But at the end of the piece, Merce said darkly, in his threatening voice, that it was a terrible mess, and he didn't think we'd perform it. Well, his threat fell absolutely flat. No one (except Sandy) believed him in the first place, nor gave a damn in the second. And everyone knew perfectly well that if *Rune* was NOT in good performance shape, it was NO one's fault except Merce's. He has never rehearsed that dance properly since Judy and Marilyn left. *Rune* makes me extremely nervous. It is terri-

bly difficult to do—certainly the most difficult dance Merce has ever made. The unison parts are a terrible strain on everyone—trying to keep the rhythm and phrasing together, and still execute the steps correctly—with no help from music, and only our muscular memory to go by. The film people were very awed by the seriousness and quiet. So awed that a girl taking still photos didn't dare to snap the shutter of her camera for fear the *noise* would disturb us! How about that for irony!?! The film people whispered to one another and tiptoed around, *so* respectfully!

Their documentary would reveal that particular afternoon's rehearsal in all its joyless reality—Merce, grim, counting aloud while savagely clapping his hands and snapping his fingers to mark the rhythms, more drill sergeant than dance master, and we dancers, equally grim, desperately attempting to do what was required of us. In the film, the anxiety we were all experiencing looks to me like anger. The camera didn't lie: an element of hostility was definitely lurking there, too.[2]

The next evening, from 8:00 until 11:30, we rehearsed in the Théâtre de l'Est Parisien in the Twentieth Arrondissement, a working-class neighborhood some distance from our hotel. As the bus pulled up to the front entrance and we caught sight of a huge poster with a *Rune* photo, blown up, and two windows full of pictures of the company, we couldn't help feeling a surge of excitement. After the previous two demoralizing days, a bit of enthusiasm was badly needed prior to our brief three-night "Paris season." Pre-performance publicity articles by John Ashbery in the *New York Herald Tribune* and by Nora Ephron in the *New York Times* International Edition as well as articles in the French press had heralded the event, and we wanted desperately to live up to expectations.

TEP was a *maison de la culture,* one of many theaters that André Malraux developed throughout France when he served as minister of culture after the Second World War. Malraux argued that "art—and not any social or moral system—is humanity's only permanent expression of the will to triumph over fate." The concept of will triumphing over fate would be severely tested by the Cunningham company in the next six months, starting right there at the TEP. The modern theater's only nod to traditional elegance was red plush seats, but it had a huge stage, only slightly raked, and dressing rooms with windows opening onto a courtyard where Rauschenberg was able to construct his for-these-performances-only *Story, Aeon,* and *Winterbranch* sets.

Again the film crew hovered, catching every move, missing nothing. Once again rehearsal was fraught with tension, tempers barely kept in check. The unusually hot weather didn't help. Despite the presence of Fance Frank (Stevenson) acting as translator, Bob was having difficulties getting the lighting he wanted. Unexpectedly, midstep, we'd be plunged into total darkness or suddenly blinded by the strongest, most searing illumination I'd ever experienced. Being hit by one of these light beams felt like being struck a physical blow. Other problems: the dancers new to *Rune* didn't know how to adjust to the larger stage, so the spacing was off. We never got through the whole of *Aeon*. Bone-weary and apprehensive, we crawled into bed that night fearing the worst for the next day.

A perilous opening night: stiflingly hot weather caused the power to fail during *Aeon,* the first dance on the program. The entire lighting circuit blew out, leaving Merce to dance his *Aeon* solo in total blackness. He came offstage livid, having assumed the goof was Bob's, because whatever Bob had accomplished with the lighting the previous night had somehow been botched and he'd had to start all over again at the morning's rehearsal. Middance, the curtain fell and rose again. A miscue on Bob's part? Who knew? *Nocturnes* was always iffy because John's piano playing was so erratic, and for me, during the sections when I wore the veil, terrifying because I was literally blinded by the lights.

The next two performances presented different difficulties. "Turista" had begun insidiously invading our ranks. Few were immune. We'd scarcely begun this ambitious world tour and already most of us were exhausted and ill with anxiety. With bruised ego and low spirits, I began to wonder if Merce was deliberately trying to punish me by his decision not to program *Suite for Five,* in which I have a solo and a duet with him, or our duet *Nightwandering,* or even the tiny solo sections he'd made for me in *Story,* at any of the three Paris performances. Although I didn't begrudge Viola getting to dance their duet and her special bits, I did feel unfairly treated. My misery was, in fact, absurd: I had duets with Merce in *Crises, Septet,* and *Antic Meet;* a brief solo in *Aeon,* and marvelous sections in two of my favorite dances, *Summerspace* and *Winterbranch.* I had no real cause for complaint, but I was obviously becoming a bit paranoid about Merce's attitude toward me. After the *Rune* performance, which went fairly well, I collapsed in tears in my dressing room: "I felt like a robot, like a machine performing arduous tasks—with no breath, no air, no freedom and I *hated* that feeling of anti-humanism."[3] Later that night, sitting in a restaurant, pinned against a wall on a banquette at a long table filled with company members and friends, I was engulfed by nausea and fatigue and suddenly, with no warning, tears rolled down my face and a huge lump swelled in my throat. I slipped down under the table, crawled to the other side on hands and knees, then made a mad dash for my hotel. Within seconds Fance appeared at my side, and ten minutes later she and her friend Francine came to my hotel room with hot tea, an ice-cream sundae, some kind of tranquilizing pill, and a hot water bottle. How much I appreciated and needed their maternal kindness! Sick, exhausted, and pretty damned miserable, I cried myself to sleep.

I was not the only teary one. The sound levels set for *Aeon* had reduced Barbara Lloyd to tears and made some of us physically ill. *Antic Meet* presented the same problem at the matinee. Before the performance, I discussed the situation with John and David, explaining that when the loudspeakers were directed onto the stage, the loudness is actively painful and can literally knock us off balance. David responded, unhelpfully, "You don't understand our problems." To which I replied, "And you don't understand ours." John's advice to Barbara had been to stuff cotton in her ears (which can also disturb one's balance!), and that infuriated her husband, Lew. After some discussion, I felt that the dancers' message had gotten across.

By the Sunday matinee, Shareen was so ill that she was confined to her bed. Sandra replaced her in *Summerspace* and *Antic Meet,* which meant extra rehearsals of those dances and no rehearsal of Viola and Merce's duet, *Paired.* With good reason, Viola was unhappy. With or without rehearsal, the performance of *Paired* ended with a historic event—at least for Merce's company. I was in my dressing room when I heard Steve holler, "Come here quickly, you've never seen anything like this before in your life!" Midstage, taking their bows, Viola and Merce were being pelted with eggs and tomatoes and boos. No one claimed to know the perpetrators or what their demonstration signified. Did it have political, anti-American implications, or was it just a merry Dadaist prank in the spirit of the slapdash painting of the costumes and the indeterminacy of the choreography? Unfortunately, no one bothered to find out. The ever-present film crew quickly ejected the disruptors from the theater. Later, Merce claimed to think the experience "*marvelous!*" Viola, however, did not: "It was meant to be insulting and that was what it felt like." They both took the onslaught with unflinching grace, bowing as though eggs and tomatoes were not flying through the air in their direction. No new colors were added to their paint-smeared costumes: the assailants had lousy aim.

Whatever we felt about the performances, most in the audience, which included British stage director Peter Brook, and Michael White, who would be our London producer, responded with cheers and bravos, and the reviews were, for the most part, genuinely enthusiastic.

By the final performance, I'd recovered from my blues and panic, delighted in dancing, and lived in the "now" of it with no ego-bruised thoughts to mar the joy. Afterward, a gallant, utterly charming gentleman by the name of Mark Rudkin, son of the Pepperidge Farm bread family, whom Earle and I had met some years before, came backstage and swept me off my feet, saying he wanted to take me on a tour of Paris, caress me, take care of me, and feed me. And he did just that: first, we joined the company in a neighborhood café for champagne on the house, and then Mark, with two other American gentlemen (mutual acquaintances—a painter and a dancer) whisked me off to 7 rue Monsieur where he had a handsome apartment on the top floor with a huge window looking out on rooftops and a garden of massive, ancient trees. More champagne! Then dinner in a very quiet, small, elegant restaurant where Mark took total charge, ordering steak *au poivre, haricots verts,* salad, raspberries with *crème fraîche,* and a lovely bottle of wine. Louis Jourdan could not have done better.

Shareen, meanwhile, lay ill in bed all day, totally forgotten by everyone; no one had sent for a doctor, brought her medicine, or even so much as given her a cup of tea. Right next door was Mrs. Gray, baby Benjamin Lloyd's nanny, but no one had thought to tell her to look after Shareen. I'm sure that day of utter misery was the deciding factor in Shareen's decision to quit the company in London and marry the man who had been relentlessly pursuing her for months. The company had to bus to Bourges for its next performance without her. By then, turista had leveled Sandra, too, but although she'd fainted in the john, she insisted she was well enough to travel.

At the Théâtre de la Comédie de Bourges, another Malraux *Maison de la Culture,* the three-quarters-full house was clearly baffled. The quality of the dancing was appreciated but not the choreography and, with the exception of Satie's piano score, certainly not the music, which one critic called "biologically insupportable." From start to finish the Bourges trip was a disaster: Viola and I, late for the scheduled bus departure, couldn't locate the bus; David Vaughan was in a snit; John was fussing, frowning and scolding, and so irritated with us that he refused to allow Alex Hay to get off the bus to smoke a cigar—thus Alex was furious with John. As were Viola and I. Turista leveled me. Hit John, too. Rehearsal was a nightmare. However, the film crew, all their inhibitions gone and feeling very jolly, were all over the place, even on the stage, walking around the dancers. Merce, understandably in an awful mood, endured it in hostile silence. Cast changes: Barbara replacing Shareen in *Septet* for the first time; Sandra replacing Shareen in *Crises* for the first time. In the evening's performance, I barely got through *Septet,* then desperately rushed to the loo, weak, dizzy, hideously queasy. I didn't see how I could get through *Crises,* with its upside-down, twirling, rather violent pas de deux moves. Viola rushed away to explain my predicament to Merce. "Shit!" he exclaimed. "Precisely," she responded. But he saw no humor in it at the time. A little later, I was asked whether it could help if Merce did his solo first. "It might," I moaned from my perch in the john. And so he did, and it did, and I was able to get through *Crises* by holding my breath and clenching every bodily orifice. In *Crises,* Sandra fell while attached by elastic band to Barbara, and she later dissolved in a sea of tears, moaning that Merce would surely fire her. Surely Merce was ready to fire the lot of us and call off the whole tour! Fortunately, *Story* could be done without both me and Shareen. On the bus ride back to Paris, the film crew were uproariously drunk and totally out of control. To their delight and amusement, the bus got stuck for what seemed like hours in a narrow street, wedged between two corners as it tried to make a turn. Beer bottles rolled in the aisle; one crew member threatened to pee into his beer bottle when the bus driver refused to stop to let him relieve himself on the side of the road. Most of us hunkered down in our seats, ignored them, and tried to sleep.

There was no time for anyone to recover health, sleep, or good humor, for early the following morning (mercifully leaving the film crew behind), we were on a plane to Italy. Destination: Venice. Instantly that enthralling city of wondrous beauty worked its magic, elevating the spirits of the sick, disgruntled, and unhappy among us. The company's single performance at La Fenice, booked months in advance, coincided with the XXXII Esposizione Biennale Internazionale d'Arte Venezia,[4] and the painting and sculpture prizes were to be announced the day following our performance. Naturally all eyes were focused on Robert Rauschenberg, America's thirty-eight-year-old enfant terrible, one of eight artists chosen by Alan Solomon, the United States commissioner for the Venice Biennale, to represent the USA. Despite political machinations and critical brouhaha,[5] the International Grand Prize in Painting went to an American for the first time ever, and it was Bob! (Alexander Calder had won for sculpture in 1952.) The press clamored for Rauschenberg interviews, Rauschenberg photo opportunities. Young Italian painters, passionately in his favor, hoisted Bob on their shoulders and ran him around Piazza San Marco, singing and cheering. Merce and John were left on the sidelines, their healthy egos chafing. How, despite their sincere admiration for Bob's work, could they not help feeling some resentment and envy? And so it was, I believe, that in this city, at this time, seeds of discontent were sown between John, Merce, and Bob, through no real fault of anyone. Great success so often carries with it risk of disrupted friendships.

For Merce and me, returning to La Fenice conjured memories—still vividly intact—of our monthlong stay in 1960 that culminated in the thrilling duet performance before a divided audience, which probably had booed and cheered each other far more than it had booed and cheered us. The pleasure of dancing in that most glorious of theaters was again (but only slightly) diminished by the treachery of the vast stage, with its rough and splintery floor full of holes and uneven ridges and the steep rake that terrorized us when we tried to negotiate turns, circular paths, leaps upstage, tricky partnering. But for some reason, I wasn't frightened: I enjoyed the challenge, was overjoyed just being there. Merce grew cheerier than he'd been since we'd left New York, although he lectured us rather sharply about the use of the *Story* costumes ("they are to be used as *cover*, not as design or decoration . . . if design or decoration had been desired, a great deal of time would have gone into selecting the costumes!"). Later on, I was amused to see Merce rummaging through the *Story* costumes offstage. When he saw me, he pretended to be doing something else. Once the curtain went up, as far as the dancers were concerned, the actual *dancing* went wonderfully well.

But the event itself was contentious, even before the curtain rose. Backstage, tension mounting, we were warming up, getting cold, warming up again and yet again, not knowing what was causing the delay. Part of the problem was that much of the audience arrived late, having attended the American Consulate cocktail party honoring the American painters and sculptors being exhibited in the Biennale (Rauschenberg and Jasper Johns, Morris Louis and Kenneth Noland, Claes Oldenburg, Jim Dine, Frank Stella, and John Chamberlain). Calvin Tomkins described the lobby scene: "The ticket crush in the lobby was appalling. Everyone in Venice, it appeared, not only wanted to get in but expected to get in, had influential friends who had *seen to it* that they would get in. What with the confusion and the shouting outside, the start of the performance was held up by nearly an hour, and the audience, impatient and keyed up, generated a volatile electricity of its own.[6]

When the curtain finally did go up, it wasn't long before someone in the gallery shouted *"Merde"* and made loud, derogatory noises that threw the entire gallery into a tizzy; people shouted at one another, other people attempted to hush up the shouters. Chaos reigned. A reporter from the London *Financial Times*, having lost his ticket but certain he remembered its number, was finally allowed to take his seat. When someone else claimed the very seat, a terrific row ensued, and when the guy in the gallery shouted *"Merde,"* the police, believing that the reporter was causing the commotion, lifted him under the arms, dragged him from his seat, and threw him downstairs, kicking and fighting![7]

Rauschenberg's contributions to the evening added to his already considerable reputation among the European arts community, while the sour-grapes contingent considered his presence with the company an unfair political ploy to tip the balance in Bob's favor. The *Summerspace* pointillist drop cloth looked magnificent. *Story* was fantastic. Bob went wild: Trapdoors opened, stage levels rose and lowered, light bars flew in and out, the "legs" disappeared into the flies, and stagehands moved about in the background, changing props, pushing brooms. The work, thus presented, took on a completely different dimension, not just visually but dramatically as well. We dancers were as amazed and dazzled by the spectacle as the audience was.

Thus for reasons quite different from those that affected our 1960 duet concert, we again had a split audience. The anti-Bob crowd booed and hissed and the pro-Bob crowd (a good number of Americans among them) cheered and stamped. How much of it was actually for the dancing is difficult to know; Tomkins reported that "the Cunningham dancers surpassed themselves . . . the dancing never faltered. When Rauschenberg came out on stage with the dancers for one of their many curtain calls, the cheering and the booing reached a new pitch, becoming positively warlike."

The morning following our single performance, Lew Lloyd went to the box office to pick up our money but was told there was none because the opera-house expenses had exceeded ticket income. It was not at all the arrangement understood by Lew. On the empty stage of the Fenice, Lew met with Alan Solomon, Leo Castelli, John, and Bob. Lew was profoundly angry. "John, what are we to do? I have a payroll to meet. How am I to pay the dancers? They must have money to eat, to pay hotel rooms, and their rent back home!" John, in his usual optimistic, genial way, attempted to soothe Lew with "Don't worry, it'll be all right." Alan promised to look into the situation. Leo offered assurances. "You don't understand!" Lew cried, "I have a payroll to meet every single week!" Several such exchanges produced no immediate solution. In utter frustration, Lew sent a bottle of Coke flying across the stage, where it exploded against the back wall. Shattered glass. Shocked silence. Coca-Cola dribbled slowly down the wall. No one moved. Then Bob went over to Lew and quietly offered to lend the company the funds. This tale of financial woe was ongoing, and meeting the payroll was a perpetual dice game for Lew from Day One, worthy of a book unto itself.

Throughout most of the tour we dancers went about our work (and play) oblivious to the company's unremittingly perilous finances. I had no idea that throughout the European part of the tour David Vaughan was continually writing and telephoning presenters in the hope that the many gaps in the itinerary could be filled. How to cover the weekly payroll was Lew Lloyd's unrelenting, agonizing worry for the entire six months. The negotiations for the Venice performance had been ambiguous at best, but the understanding on Lew's part was that the company would be paid a flat fee of $3,000. Bob's Biennale prize money, ironically, turned out to be two million lire ($3,200).

The company had the grand luxury of spending three completely free days in Venice—three days to revel in the city as well as to visit the Biennale grounds and the United States consulate, where most of Rauschenberg's and Johns's paintings hung in regal splendor. Following the formal award ceremony in the *giardini pubblici,* Leo Castelli threw a huge celebration party for Bob at Ristorante Lotizia, inviting the entire company to the festivities.

Especially memorable for me was lunching with Nigel Gosling and Maude Lloyd. Gosling was the London arts columnist for the *Observer Weekend Review,* and he and his lovely wife, Maude Lloyd, were together "Alexander Bland," the dance critic for the same publication. But more importantly for me, Maude Lloyd was the original Caroline in Antony Tudor's *Lilac Garden,* and she had wonderful tales to relate about working with Tudor. A week later, we read the Alexander Bland review of our Venice performance: "Nothing has hit London yet anything like as far out as the Merce Cunningham dance company . . . Cunningham (who is himself a beautiful dancer) has invented a wealth of fascinating new movement, and his whole approach is so original and odd that dance-audiences will find enough in the entertainment to dine out on for a month."[8]

Earle had arrived in time for the Fenice performance and remained in Venice until the company left by bus on June 22. I waved a tearful farewell to him as our big bus pulled away down the highway. He was headed west, in his thirdhand Porsche, to Lingueglietta, where he could live, rent free, in Luciano Berio's country place; we were headed north, to Austria. Earle and I weren't exactly estranged, but our lives had taken us on such separate, separating paths, and throughout the European part of the world tour I was feeling the loneliness of our growing distance each time we had a day or two together and then were parted again. So, as with every other Venice visit I've ever made, this one was tinged with sadness.

In Vienna, we were scheduled to perform in the Museum of the Twentieth Century, but it had no theater. In order to present our work in this unconventional space, Merce and John created a special format, reminiscent of Cage's 1952 Black Mountain Happening. This format would serve Merce well over the next forty-plus years, allowing the company to perform in almost any situation, from New York's Grand Central Terminal to Ghirardelli Square in San Francisco to the Piazza San Marco in Venice to North Cotteloe Beach in Perth, Australia. For want of a better title, he called the performance in Vienna Museum Event #1. In November 2004, forty years later, Event #725 took place in the Turbine Hall at the Tate Modern in London. Usually about ninety minutes in length, performed without intermission, with or without a set, costumed from the repertory but not necessarily in the costumes designed for the particular dances (in later years, Events had costumes especially designed for them), and with music arbitrarily selected from the repertory, Events comprised parts of dances (or even whole ones) that could be juxtaposed in new sequences, or overlapped with other dances. Depending upon the size of the space, two or more works could also be danced simultaneously in separate areas. Event #1 began at 6:30 in the evening, with the dancers warming up in full view of the audience as it entered, and ended at 9:30 p.m. It was accompanied for the entire three hours by Cage's *Atlas Eclipticalis,* performed by John, David, and four members of the Vienna ensemble Die Reihe. Rauschenberg was once again in his element, reveling in the freedom to improvise. The glass walls of the museum allowed him to use the soft early evening June light—fading into dusk, then darkness—as his palette, only adding electric light as night consumed day. Then he utilized the glass walls to bounce and reflect the lights in unusual ways. Random automobile headlights from the street added another source of unexpected illumination. Instead of live stagehands, as in the Fenice performance, a serendipitous parade of passersby sauntered across the background outside the museum, and later on Rauschenberg, the "Pop-Clown,"[9] himself became a part of the decor, "traversing the hall as an original umbrella-shaking scarecrow, [and a second time] adorned with broken, picturesque everyday objects."[10] As one reviewer noted, it was "a unique captivating evening. No theater in the world could have been more appropriate for this display than the cool, objective space of the Museum of the Twentieth Century."[11] There was much bewilderment, but the dancing got raves. Astonishingly, that single Event performance garnered twelve reviews! This was heady stuff for a dance company largely ignored by New York critics in its own hometown for the last ten years.

But we were in Germany from June 25 through July 12, with only two performances scheduled. David Vaughan's attempts to arrange more bookings hadn't succeeded. In Mannheim, we performed in Mies van der Rohe's Nationaltheater. Great architecture it may have been, but the stage floor—with protruding nails, loose tacks, broken staples, and splinters—threatened to tear our bare feet to shreds. The stagehands offered no assistance until after we'd spent a good part of our rehearsal time on our hands and knees trying to rid the stage of the debris; only then did they produce a vacuum cleaner.

For sixteen days we lived in a clean but dreary little hotel in Cologne, busing out to the *Stadion* each morning to have class and rehearsal, spending our afternoons and evenings as we wished. I saw my first Buster Keaton film there in Cologne, a performance of Tchaikovsky's opera *Pique Dame*, and two evenings of ballet; I had dinners with the Stockhausens, with Khris and Hans Helms, with Todd Bolender; I spent a whole day cruising the Rhine. Earle arrived and stayed for four days, and we moved to Stapelhäuschen, my favorite little skinny hotel overlooking the Rhine.

While marking time in Cologne, Merce, John, and Bob met Kurt Jooss, who then invited the company to perform at his Folkwang Hochschule, a former monastery, in Essen. We considered the invitation a great honor, but after the performance we felt neither honored nor particularly welcomed. The audience went totally berserk. Primarily made up of faculty and students from the Jooss school and students of Joseph Beuys from the Düsseldorf Art Academy, this audience reacted ferociously. The stage—in a former chapel—was, in Merce's words, little more than "a shelf," and the dances we presented—*Suite for Five, Winterbranch, Untitled Solo,* and *Story*—were chosen as the easiest to accommodate the cramped space, but they still felt compressed. The audience erupted in an alarmingly violent demonstration when we took our final bows. We were told that the Jooss group was "anti" and the Düsseldorf students "pro." Those bravoing also demonstrated their approval, it was said, by thumping their chairs up and down on the floor. I viewed the chair-thumping as menacing, certainly not as a sign of approval. One man stood on his chair and twirled his index finger by his forehead to indicate he believed us to be insane. Another man, apparently crazed beyond control, raced down to the edge of the stage with his chair and pounded it at our feet until it broke. The man seemed unbalanced, his actions terrifying. Very soon Merce realized that the thunderous applause was only to bring us back onstage so that the audience could continue to boo and hiss and stomp, and that the situation might become dangerous. Abruptly, without so much as a word to us, Merce—now very angry—left the stage and disappeared. The rest of us followed. The applause continued. Merce refused to return. The work had evoked real hostility from this public, evidence, perhaps, that it was striking deeper than merely calling into doubt a shared aesthetic of what is and is not a dance.

Our last scheduled gig on July 12 came about through an invitation from Todd Bolender, formerly with the New York City Ballet and now director for the Cologne State Ballet, to open Cologne's first Ballet Festival. We were *un succès fou,* as well as *un succès de scandale.* A lively, very vocal audience again greeted us with boos and bravos, but their response was nothing like the bizarre, psychopathic behavior we had witnessed at the Jooss school. We were told that there had been that kind of audience response in Cologne only once before, for Luigi Nono's opera *Intolleranza.* *Winterbranch* garnered the most negative vocal response. In Germany, interestingly, no one thought to liken *Winterbranch* to the Holocaust, although this happened regularly in other European countries. Reviews appeared in nine German newspapers.

Much was made of Rauschenberg. Rarely did a review fail to mention his Venice Biennale Prize, or his growing European reputation as the bad boy of American art, which only heightened the unease that Merce and John were experiencing. At times Bob would engage in aggressive, belligerent shouting arguments about politics and art with Alex, Steve, and Lew. This was the competitive, antagonistic, verbally combative Rauschenberg I've always sought to avoid. Why, in the light of his enormous recent successes, did he feel compelled to engage in such confrontational behavior? Perhaps it was simply a matter of temperament. Alex and Steve relished the battle, while Bill Davis and Albert Reid were visibly appalled. Most of us chose to absent ourselves from the fray.

On the road again. Tired of filling my journal with reports of rehearsals, performances, company morale, audience responses, reviews, I indulged in page after rapturous page describing the charms of rural France. In even the tiniest village, the blue, white, and red French flag waved from every building on Bastille Day. Who would not feel national pride living in such a beautiful land?

Paris Match had arranged an interview with Bob at the famous three-star restaurant Oustau de la Baumanière, on July 16, the day of our single performance in the village of Les Baux, and Bob, with characteristic generosity, invited nine members of the company to join him there for a magnificent lunch and a swim in the pool. Our customary performance-day schedule would ordinarily have made such an outing unthinkable, but the suffocating midday heat in the outdoors was unbearable, so we rehearsed the night before under the moon and stars, working into the wee hours, and didn't get to bed until three in the morning.

The theater was a makeshift platform slammed into the side of spectacular rocky cliffs below the ruins of a medieval castle. The stage floor, the worst yet, consisted of masonite rectangles, badly warped, nails protruding. Dressing rooms were nonexistent, the backstage conditions best described as medieval primitive. No running water. No plumbing facilities of any kind. Our changing rooms were grottoes with earth and rock rubble underfoot, sky overhead. Buckets of water were provided for washing. Privacy was impossible. Who cared? The surroundings were surreally magnificent. The program: *Crises, Septet,* and *Story.* Somehow a grand piano was trucked up especially for *Septet.* Both *Septet* and *Crises* must have looked dwarfed by the soaring rocks and limitless sky. *Winterbranch* might have been a better choice in such a spectacular site. But from all reports, *Story,* this wonderfully flexible, chameleon dance, took on what Merce characterized as an "ominous quality," and Bob played the dramatic possibilities to the hilt. Three automobiles were used as a backdrop set, high above and behind the performance platform, and at one point in the proceedings the vehicles drove slowly forward, turning their headlights on and off, illuminating the dancers from the rear and momentarily blinding the audience. "There were cries of indignation, sarcastic laughter, and some noisy departures, but on the whole, applause and shouts of enthusiasm drowned out sounds of disapproval."[12]

There followed a two-day drive to Paris, where we met up with Remy—alone and a bit lonely, in Paris for the first time, having just arrived from New York. Viola, David Vaughan, and I joined him for dinner, and then Remy and I walked magical nocturnal Paris from the Left Bank across the Seine, past the Louvre, through the Tuileries, past place Vendôme and the Opéra, and ending at our lovely Hotel Queen Mary at about two a.m. I still missed my closest friend from the company and couldn't resist regaling him with tales of our tour. Laughingly he commented, "It's great seeing you, but why do we always end up talking about Merce?"

Next day: bus from Paris to Calais, boat to Dover, an all-night bus trip to Totnes in Devon, and within a half-mile of our final destination—after twenty-nine hours of travel without sleep—our bus ran out of gas. But oh, what a destination! Dartington Hall—surrounded by four thousand exquisite acres of woodland, pasture, formal and informal gardens, its original manor dating back to 833—provided us with a brief and much-needed interlude of bucolic tranquility. The joy of the place radiates from its total respect for art and agriculture, forestry and pig farms, vegetable and flower gardens, weaving and sculpture, pottery and painting, theater and music. *Art-and-Life.* No separation. My perpetual love affair with English gardens and England's rolling farmland was born there. Gazing from my bedroom window, which was set two feet deep in the ancient fifteenth-century stone manor house where I was fortunate to be housed in a quiet single room, I could swear I felt my ancestors rising in the morning mist from the graveyard outside, from the very roots of one of England's oldest and most magnificent trees growing there. I felt I'd come home. Later, I discovered that indeed, some of my mother's ancestors had been inhabitants of this part of England.

Dartington residents saw eight dances in three performances in their minuscule Barn Theatre, whose stage limitations had somewhat squelched Bob's enthusiasm. Instead of walking into the theater to find one of his dazzlingly unique *Story* sets, we discovered a crate of empty milk bottles, an enormous bundle of tattered cardboard cartons, and two ironing boards placed upstage. Bob had decided to catch up on his laundry, and in both performances of *Story,* he and Alex proceeded to iron their shirts, a blatant upstaging of dancers and dancing. Merce seemed not at all amused. The barn was packed, and from the enthusiastic reception, it seemed the restricted stage space in no way diminished the audience's pleasure. Nor mine. It was a familiar feeling, dancing in that barn. My delight in Dartington was all-inclusive: eyes, heart, and mind devoured the serenity and beauty of the place and the wisdom of its philosophy as eagerly as I devoured Devonshire's scones and clotted cream. How much we would need Dartington's gift of rest and respite we never guessed at the time.

ondon. The Imperial Hotel, Russell Square. The original, magnificently Victorian relic—not the modern slab of a building that now bears its name. My room, #602—no more than a narrow cell but blessed with the luxury of a gigantic tub—would be my home for the astonishing month to come. Scheduled to give seven performances in six days, we would present a repertory of fifteen works. Merce would dance in all fifteen; Viola and I in thirteen; challenging for all three of us, but especially for Merce. Every two days would see a complete change of program. The theater? A musty, decrepit, warren's nest of a place called the Sadler's Wells, former home to the not yet Royal Ballet, where a young girl named Peggy Hookham was transformed into a princess, one destined to be the royal queen of ballet whom the world would come to worship as Margot Fonteyn. Not for one minute did I forget this. Warming up on the splintered floor in the ballet room at the top of the old theater where she must have taken class, getting lost in the bewildering maze of corridors she once knew so well, dancing on *her* stage—I felt Fonteyn's aura everywhere, daunting, inspiring.

In the beginning I was nervous, but nothing like as nervous as Merce. "He's convinced the audience will hate the work—and of course they probably will! This is *ballet* territory at its *strongest!*"[1] Again, as in Paris, the specter of Martha Graham's miserable experiences on her 1950 European tour and her disastrous 1954 London season haunted him. Like Graham in 1950, he had no understudies for his parts, and he, too, felt that the burden of the company's success or failure was his alone. Although never incapacitated as Graham was in 1950, Merce was ill, and looked it, much of the time in London. He was pale, thinner, and more gaunt than I'd ever seen him. His energy and resilience were taxed to their limits, yet night after night after night he performed with a fierce passion, satisfying a hunger that surely had never been fulfilled so completely before.

Opening day. Everyone was cheerful. Even Merce appeared to be in good spirits, undeterred by the hordes of photographers and journalists milling about the theater before our regular rehearsal. A one-hour photo call sharpened the edge of our excitement; my nervousness eased into pleasant anticipation rather than escalating into sick fright. Opening night was suddenly upon us. Curtain went up fifteen minutes late. We were informed they'd had to hold until the ambassador arrived; which ambassador, no one knew.

Our London season opened with *Suite for Five, Crises, Untitled Solo,* and *Story.* Despite a few technical glitches, all went well; I actually found performing a pleasure. The spirit was right. The audience seemed to love *Story,* although we knew it was a mess. The final bows were chaotic. Merce had never taken time to set its bows, and this time it was obvious, but he seemed furious not with himself but with us. Barbara Lloyd's decision to adorn herself with every rag in the costume duffel and turn herself into a rotund bag lady produced laughter on both sides of the footlights, although the rest of us, having been relegated to just tights and leotards, felt quite naked without the crazy assortment of garments to choose from. Unfortunately, we'd grown dependent upon them to add spice and variety to the choreography. Alex Hay, carrying a stuffed bird, joined the dancers onstage as a living part of the decor and managed to convulse the audience. Merce, once again, was not amused. In his journal, he complained of "clowning."[2] Furthering his displeasure, and the spectators' amusement, were some rather rude, jokey sounds emanating from the small orchestra playing Toshi Ichiyanagi's music which only added to the clowning effect, even though lovely "Oriental sounds" were produced as well. *Story* was the fun hit of the evening.

In a departure from traditional Cunningham company protocol, each of the women received two bouquets onstage, one from Michael White, our producer, and the other from the Baroness Nancy Oakes de Tritton, a long-time Merce friend and benefactress. Backstage, in the dressing rooms where many well-wishers gathered to compliment us all, champagne elevated the giddy exhilaration at the outset of our London season at The Wells. Although critical opinion was still needed to confirm it, opening night—ending with a glamorous post-performance party—felt like a success.

At the stage door, taxis awaited to drive us to Canonbury House, an eighteenth-century Georgian home in Islington, the gorgeous dwelling of Francis Mason, Deputy Cultural Attaché of the United States Embassy, his wife, Pat, and her father, an elderly English gentleman who played the perfect host.[3] At the elegant supper party, I felt faint with embarrassment, so many people came to my table with lovely compliments. Anya Linden, my favorite among the junior ballerinas of the Sadler's Wells when I supered in 1955 and now Lady Sainsbury, and her husband joined our table. "If only we [at the Royal Ballet] had such control," she said. I laughed incredulously and protested that they did, and she said, "No, they couldn't go up and down to the floor or move in strange balances as you did." Lord Sainsbury thought the Royal Ballet should have more ballets like Merce's.[4] Maude Lloyd joined us and offered warm and generous words about the evening and my dancing. Tears welled in my eyes. No words of praise could be more meaningful to me, more gratefully received than those from dancers. Marie Rambert was also at the party and was reported to have truly liked Merce's work; she'd been heard "rhapsodizing about it,"[5] much to the amazement of those who knew her. Apparently she was not one to say she liked something when she didn't.

Our single week at the Sadler's Wells, beginning on July 27, 1964, changed the course of the company's history forever. No performances, either before or after that London season, were as crucial to the company's future as those, when as many as seven newspapers reviewed a single performance. The *Guardian* reported, " 'Word of mouth,' that mysterious grape vine which stirs multitudes no public relations man can galvanise, had got the world, and his wife, and a few other types to Sadler's Wells in tumult last night where Merce Cunningham and his Dance Company, fresh from triumphs and riots on the Continent, were making the first of a week's appearances at this theatre. They will be the 'talk of the town.' "[6] The *Daily Mail* predicted that "one of the most violently discussed topics around London in the next week will be the work of the American Merce Cunningham and his Dance Company."[7] Rereading the dozens of lengthy, thoughtful, detailed, and varied responses to the choreography, music, and decor impressed me even more decades later than when I first read them in 1964. Then, it was having the work we all cared about so passionately considered seriously, and of course, it was also the thrill of receiving personal recognition for our dancing. But decades later, what one admires is the vividness of the writing, the extensive dance knowledge, the intensity of involvement, and the willingness of many to engage in open-minded philosophical analysis of the Cage/Cunningham aesthetic—comparing the theory with what was actually seen onstage. For example, Andrew Porter, writing for the *Financial Times*, could admit that "at the least, the dances set you thinking about the relationship between music and movement—and questioning basic assumptions. Intuition (plus, I hope, an experienced eye) tells me that Cunningham is O.K. And more than O.K.—a genuinely creative mind."[8]

Clive Barnes went further: "Cunningham's work asks marvelous questions, such as why *must* dance and music be combined? or why must choreography be fluent? He is a great innovator and a born humorist, and knows a great deal about the trap-door of social insecurity and the fears of western society."[9] "Merce Cunningham, John Cage and Robert Rauschenberg . . . have been taking us square limeys round the gun embattlements and barbed wire entanglements of ballet's new frontier."[10]

Indeed, what was so exciting and surprising to us was the willingness to examine the Cage/Cunningham/Rauschenberg aesthetic on its own terms, not castigating it for what it wasn't but openly trying to see it for what it was. As one humorously put it, " 'The controversial' music-rejecting, improvising Merce Cunningham dancers drove ballet critics to the limits of broad-mindedness."[11] "A much needed shot in the backside," conceded Richard Buckle. The *Times* declared that "[Cunningham] stimulates by rejecting the most solemn precepts about the art of dancing and is still producing something to enjoy."[12] John Percival, who reportedly came to every performance, seemed to capture something of the Zen spirit of the work in writing that "Cunningham . . . brought into dancing the ordinariness, the vexations, the adventures and the sudden glories of life—something to remember with gratitude and pleasure."[13] And, "His ballets are providing plenty of food for thought, and this is something anyone should welcome."[14]

It would appear that the critics surprised even themselves and were equally surprised by our enthusiastic audiences. "How refreshing to find audiences so open-minded," commented Percival. The articles by those who saw the company many times were lively, imaginative responses to all aspects of the work. Significantly, those reviews did not go unnoticed across the ocean in the United States. At that time, Clive Barnes was dance critic for London's *Times, Daily Express, Dance and Dancers,* and *Spectator.* His long special to the *New York Times* amusingly expressed the traditional critical mind-set that our presence seemed to alter:

Mr. Cunningham is having a popular success with music students, art students and the general public. For years [London] was the home of ultra-conservatism in dance, and our minds were always as open as clams.[15]

The London reviews ran the gamut from ecstatic to sheer hatred. Most important among them were Alexander Bland's in *The Observer.* In one, he wrote, "We are not so far here from the world of Petipa and Balanchine, and the total effect has the aloof conviction of the best classical dance." And the opening paragraphs of his extensive review of our week at Sadler's Wells proved prophetic as well as, I believe, a brilliant summing-up of the company's strengths. Bland acknowledged "the cloud of theory in which the company moves," but dismissed it with "What counts is the soup not the recipe."[16]

> Merce Cunningham and his company have burst on the British scene like a bomb, for a simple reason. At a blow, ballet has been brought right up in line with the front-rank experimenters in the other arts—something which has hardly happened since the days of Diaghilev. Here is heart-warming proof that it is an art with a future, opening up ranges of possibilities which stretch out of sight; it ought to be celebrated with champagne in every dancing academy in the land.
>
> Diaghilev would have loved Cunningham. Besides admiring him as an artist he would have respected the seriousness and discipline of his company, the spare wit and style of Rauschenberg's costumes and lighting, the consistent invention of the choreography and the provocative strangeness of John Cage's musical accompaniment. Above all, his acute artistic antennae would have tingled at the sense that Cunningham was talking in the voice of today.[17]

Bland's preview and after-review in the *Observer* had a profound effect on the success the company would enjoy in London. Surely his views influenced other critics and were responsible in part for our noteworthy audiences.

But Oleg Kerensky expressed outrage and disdain. Writing for the *Daily Mail,* he vented in fury: "This joke has gone on long enough. The idea that Merce Cunningham's limited range of ugly and elementary movements combined with ear-splitting, non-musical music deserves to be taken seriously was not very funny in the first place. But London has fallen for the idea as no other city has ever done."[18]

To everyone's amazement, London had indeed "fallen" for us, to such an extent that our London producer, the handsome young impresario Michael White, decided to risk producing the company for another two and a half weeks. With absolutely no bookings until September 8, the company was facing financial disaster. Michael's offer was manna from heaven! We closed at the Wells on Saturday, August 1, after a matinee and evening performance—utterly "whacked," as the British might say—and we opened

at the Phoenix Theatre on Charing Cross Road in the West End the following Wednesday, August 5. Despite killing fatigue, the entire London fairy-
tale month could not help but be a pinch-me-am-I-dreaming experience.
Living a full professional dancer's life (and the bone-weary exhaustion that
goes with it) was intensified by the social whirl that caught us up in a
round of late-night suppers at our favorite Soho restaurant, Bianchi's;
lovely small suppers in the homes of new friends and old; many glamorous
parties; and even a midnight wedding celebration. We never got to bed
before two a.m. Our attempts to experience something of London itself
were limited: brief visits to the British Museum, a Sunday off in Regents
Park, the first act only (alas—all we had time for) of Peter Brook's *Marat/
Sade*—a shattering experience.

The surprising and continuous newspaper coverage kept interest alive.
We never played to sold-out houses in either theater, but the audiences did
grow steadily. At Sadler's Wells we enjoyed the exceedingly rare luxury of
a small and very good orchestra playing the music for *Summerspace, Rune,
Story,* and *Aeon.* The opening-night program was repeated, and then two
days later, we danced *Rune, Septet, Nightwandering,* and *Antic Meet.*
Backstage after a performance, Merce received "an astonishing note,"[19]
proclaiming *Rune* one of the most brilliant dances the writer had ever
seen. The author of this note turned out to be Robin Howard, who, after
seeing the Martha Graham Company in 1954, decided to pledge his considerable personal fortune to her and began by funding her 1963 London
season. This very large, very tall (six foot six) bearded man, who moved
about on hand crutches and prostheses, eventually would become a pivotal
force in Britain's modern-dance world, creating the Graham-based London
School of Contemporary Dance and its affiliated company. At a party given
in our honor by the Western Theatre Ballet, this amazing man, who had
lost both legs below the thighs in World War II, thanked me for my "consistently brilliant dancing" and with charming gallantry and self-deprecating
humor said he would get down on his knees to me, if he thought he could
get up again. I suspect Robin had used this line innumerable times and
would use it many more.

After *Rune,* dancing *Septet* was like swimming nude in the moonlight;
and oh what joy to have music that helped! The very responsive audience
seemed to like *Nightwandering* and had a good time with *Antic Meet,*
which, in Richard Buckle's words, "went down like iced Coke in a heat
wave. It is hard to make dancing really funny but this ballet was."[20]

The third program, *Aeon, Changeling, Cross Currents,* and *Nocturnes,*
we performed just once at the Wells. While some complained that *Aeon*

was aeons too long, and that they couldn't get beyond the cacophony of its music, the *Times* thought it showed Cunningham at his "eccentric best," "humorous, quirky and once in a while naughtily shocking."[21] The accompaniment for *Cross Currents* was now a tape of collaged Conlon Nancarrow music, arranged by John and David. I raged in my journal: "*I HATE IT!* It's aggressive, ugly, loud, humorless and just does not go with the dance at all. Merce originally made the dance with a jazz score, and it had been such *fun* to do. Remy thought the score awful too. We both told John, and he was hurt of course, but said he'd fix it."

Ninette de Valois appeared backstage after the third program to tell Merce how much she liked *Aeon.* He didn't recognize her. Then she came to the dressing room Viola, Shareen, and I shared. She remarked upon our "wonderful control," expressed concern for Viola's bandaged ankle (an inflamed Achilles tendon dating back to Paris), and then reminisced a bit about the old days at the Wells. We were speechless!

We closed the week with *Summerspace, Winterbranch, Paired,* and, at the Saturday matinee, *Nocturnes,* and in the evening, *Story.* It was a relatively easy double-performance day for me. I wasn't in *Paired,* and I had arranged for Sandra to understudy my part in *Nocturnes,* providing me with a cover for at least one work in the repertory should I be injured or ill. This matinee seemed the perfect opportunity to give her a chance to perform it. Merce thought this very generous of me. It was, as it turned out, rather selfish. I don't think Merce ever could imagine giving up a role, no matter how ill or exhausted he might be. He had eight works to perform that Saturday—none of them easy—yet how patient and gentle he was in rehearsing *Nocturnes* with both Sandra and Barbara (replacing Shareen). Unfortunately, I realized only in retrospect that while I got a rest, I had only added to Merce's burdens. The London season was both heaven and hell for him: heaven, in that it fed his insatiable hunger to perform, and hell in that the nonperforming demands and stresses multiplied as the days went on. By week's end he was clearly unwell, far beyond overwhelming fatigue.

I believe that *Winterbranch* is one of Merce's greatest works, and for me, dancing it with Merce was always one of the greatest performance experiences—wildly unpredictable, charged with a kind of volcanic energy that created itself out of the movement and stillness, darkness and light, silence and sound. The first *Winterbranch* at the Sadler's Wells was electrifying. Every *Winterbranch* was an adventure, a drama that created itself in the moment, but this one felt singularly impassioned and profound. I want to quote at least part of Clive Barnes's long description of that particular *Winterbranch,* because it evokes some of the mystery and dramatic intensity the work can generate, and brilliantly illustrates Duchamp's hypothesis that it is the viewer who completes the work:

> The beginning is science fiction. The *thing* emerges out of primeval ooze and slithers painfully across the plain—but now this moving shape is caught in a searchlight and what we thought was a monster is a man . . . the whole theatre is silent except for the breathing of the shape crossing the stage.
>
> *Winterbranch* is an exercise in fear and intimidation. The dancers wear track suits in black, and black bars of grime are slashed across their cheeks. Bodies roll over in unloving, unfunny judo—a group piles up, buddy-buddies afraid of the dark, afraid of the crunch. The mood of the ballet is like a dark stain on blotting paper. At times you want to shout out to the people on stage that it's all right, it's only a game, damn it. But you hardly like to and you take refuge in suppressed, embarrassed laughter. At last the silence comes to a climax and you have the noise of La Monte Young's music to hide away from, so you can think yourself down from the pain threshold of the music. It takes the mind off the creeping sickness on stage and suddenly—like a flatulent, red-nosed comic on dead cue—an object, half-familiar, wholly terrifying—trundles across, and this is hysterically funny . . . Myth and technology combine to make a joke of a nameless terror, and make it with domestic objects put to undomestic use.[22]

One had to marvel at Bob's relentless inventiveness in the creation of the monsters for *Winterbranch,* although the *thing* Clive referred to here was actually Merce encased in a knit garment from head to toe. What we called the "monster" changed from performance to performance, and in this case was the "wholly terrifying" and "hysterically funny" *object* that trundled across the stage. Every performance of *Winterbranch* and *Story* presented Bob with the opportunity to create—wholly from scratch— whatever his endlessly fertile imagination might conjure up, and each night we looked forward to a surprise, a delightful gift from him to us, which, simply by its presence, could alter the character of the dance. For the last performance of *Story* at the Wells, Bob hung a mix of white clothes on a laundry line stretched across the width of the upstage. During the dance, Bob and Alex dipped the clothes in big vats of colored dye, then rehung them on the line—red, white, and blue (was this Bob's "hip-hip-hooray-USA"?)—where they dripped onto plastic sheets. Merce may have considered this artists-upstaging-dancers once again, but what a terrific idea![23]

Merce could be as unpredictable onstage as the *Story* set. In a most peculiar mood during that performance of *Story*, he came on near the end of "Space"—a section that gives the dancers some very limited freedoms for improvisation—and, before picking me up to carry me off in the "Exit" section, sharply slapped my hand. "What was *that* for?" I wondered. "Was he registering general aggravation, disapproval of what I'd chosen to do, or was it just in fun?" No explanation given. None sought. And later, when it was time for his solo and Shareen was still onstage, unaware that by then she should have been off, Merce marched out, picked her up, carried her into the wings and, to quote her, said rather angrily "What do I have to do to get you offstage?"

Story, as aptly described by Alexander Bland, "is a series of goings on, in movement and decor . . . It neither begins nor ends but is fascinatingly there."[24] Bland rightly perceived the Cage/Rauschenberg affinity with the now-ness of Oriental (Zen) thinking, the *act* of creation—fresh and unrepeatable—as opposed to the thing created, but therein lay Merce's dilemma. Chance procedures in the choreographic process result in as fixed a form as any other way of making a dance. But, indeterminacy *in the performance* is unfixed, and unpredictable. *Story*, with its rearrangeable sections, flexible spacing and timing, and improvisational options, drove Merce to distraction when anyone exceeded or stretched the time beyond what he believed worked.

The week at Sadler's Wells required daily, near-endless rehearsals. Not only did all fifteen dances have to be rehearsed in the space, and the new trio, *Cross Currents*, readied for its premiere, but we were also in the throes of replacing Shareen with Barbara or Sandra. For *Aeon* and *Story*—which required the full company—Merce enlisted the services of Alex Hay's wife, Deborah, who had originally come along "just for the ride" and to help out with costumes but luckily happened to be a dancer who had studied with Merce. All this demanded still more rehearsals—a stressful situation for the newcomers and tedious for the rest of us but an unavoidable part of our workload. For Shareen, London was the end of the tour. Merce's lack of concern for her in Paris when she was so ill, indeed the entire company's lack of consideration, had finally tipped the scales. On Thursday, August 6, the company was invited to a post-performance supper party at Annabel's—the very "in" sixties discotheque in Berkeley Square—to celebrate her marriage to Richard Brukenfeld. Richard's sister, Baby Jane Holzer (of Andy Warhol film fame), was no doubt responsible for the unusual assortment of famous and would-be famous guests, including the Rolling Stones, with whom we Cage/Cunningham avant-gardists rather "gawkwardly" mingled. It all felt a bit surreal.

Once we'd moved to the Phoenix, the really hard lessons commenced. How to sustain the exhilaration, overcome the weariness of body and spirit, accept the inevitability of a poor performance, and still, despite having disappointed oneself, take on the next performance, and the next, and the one after that, freshly, with total commitment and enthusiasm? This was what it meant to be a professional. And in this, Merce excelled. For the rest of us, with no guidance or input from him, it was hard going. After a particularly demanding performance, whether it had gone well or badly, I would sometimes sit in the dressing room, sobbing out of sheer exhaustion and pent-up tension. A journal entry from August 8, 1964, reads: "Some nights, I really felt that I was dancing badly—without good technique, without spirit, without joy. It was *awful*. But there were several good nights too. I guess one can't expect more than this. It's a *very* different thing—dancing night after night. It takes a kind of strength & energy & point-of-view that has not been required before."

By the last day, I'd begun to learn important lessons about how a dancer manages to perform night after night, attempting, always, to dance her absolute best but humbly accepting the lows with the highs, bad nights with the good, and acknowledging those frustratingly mediocre in-betweens. Merce was an inspirational role model throughout the monthlong London season. Though often moody, irascible, and cantankerous offstage, while onstage Merce, the dancer, prevailed: always totally present, fully committed, unstinting in energy, ablaze with passion as though his very life depended upon it.

One couldn't help being impressed by our audiences. The simple fact that members of the Royal Ballet, which I so revered, not only came to see Merce's work, often more than once, but took the time to come backstage to express their interest and appreciation was especially meaningful, at least to me.

SHE CAME! Last night! Margot Fonteyn actually came! She sat in the dress circle. David Vaughan came back stage after it was all over to tell me: "I'm glad you danced so beautifully tonight because Margot was in the audience!" Thank God he didn't tell me before or during! It's very strange. For the last few performances I didn't feel that I was dancing well. No heart in it. Very tired in spirit as well as body. Last night I gave myself a lecture— "Go out there and *do it*, fully and well and enjoy it!" And I did!

Next morning, Merce rang my hotel room. His dear friend Nancy Oakes de Tritton had just called to tell him that Fonteyn had phoned her to explain why she hadn't come backstage. It was at this time that Fonteyn's husband, Tito Arias, lay in critical condition outside London in Stoke Mandeville Hospital after an assassination attempt in Panama on June 8 and his subsequent relapse into a coma after being transported to England a month later. No longer in a coma, although paralyzed, he had at last begun a slow recovery, and Fonteyn was able to make brief trips away from his bedside. But immediately after our performance, she had rushed back to the hospital to be near him. She told Nancy Oakes that she would try to come again. How remarkable that she had made the effort to come at all!

The following week Frederick Ashton appeared backstage to see Merce after attending a performance that included *Winterbranch*, which he loved,[25] and *Nocturnes*, which, according to David Vaughan, he had particularly enjoyed. " 'It was poetic,' " he told Cunningham, " 'and I like dances to be poetic.' "[26] Seven months later, in March 1965, Ashton created *Monotones*, costumed all in white, also set to music by Satie. Julie Kavanagh, in her biography of Ashton, suggests that an "obvious modern influence is Merce Cunningham . . . who alerted Ashton to new ways of relating shapes against space."[27] Merce, in his published journal, quotes Ashton as saying, "I'm glad to see you keep sex in the right places."[28]

Rudolf Nureyev's attendance will be remembered for his sleeping through *Winterbranch*! So much for outraged complaints about La Monte Young's intolerable, earsplitting sounds that ostensibly drove audiences out of the theater. Years later Nureyev told me that he'd fallen asleep in the dance's opening silence and darkness, overcome with fatigue, having just gotten off a plane from Lebanon at the end of a grueling tour.

One evening during the Phoenix weeks, Maude Lloyd and Marie Rambert appeared together at my dressing-room door. Among the lovely, kind, and appreciative words, I best remember Maude Lloyd saying, "I'd like to see you in *Swan Lake*," and Marie Rambert responding, "Oh, I'd like to see you in *Firebird*." Dame Marie also came to watch company class and was said to be wildly enthusiastic.

Our audiences were a continual astonishment. London theater directors Peter Brook, Lindsay Anderson, William Gaskill, George Devine, and

Peter Gill came and came often; actors, too—among them Irene Worth and Harold Lang. And who was that exceedingly intense, attractive man who appeared at my dressing-room door after a performance to invite me to sup with him? "My god, Carolyn, that was *Robert Shaw,* the actor! You turned down Robert Shaw?" Sheepishly, I admitted I'd declined the offer of this intimidatingly handsome man. His dark intensity scared me to death! Also among the theater-lovers was a young American named James Klosty, who'd been told by a friend, "If you ever get a chance to see Merce Cunningham, *go!*" In London to attend theater and visit an aunt, he got his chance. Instantly smitten, he came back four or five times. At a matinee performance of *King Lear,* after having seen the company for the first time the night before, he suddenly asked himself, "Why am I not enjoying this? I want to be at the Cunningham performance!" and at the intermission he jumped from his seat and made a dash to the Phoenix. This was the beginning of a love affair that would last for decades and radically alter his life. More of that later.

And who were all the others? British poets and composers; musician friends from Cologne; Bénédicte Pesle, Remy Charlip, Ileana and Michael Sonnabend from Paris; Richard Lippold showed up, as did Valda Setterfield, who offered me invaluable constructive criticism; Jasper Johns and Lois Long flew in from New York; Leo Castelli appeared suddenly, word having reached him that Bob was making a painting onstage each night during the four *Story* performances at the Phoenix. Leo lavishly entertained Bob and many of us dancers at lunches and after-performance suppers, then whisked the paintings back to the safety of his gallery.[29] For the first time, I had a real sampling of Leo's legendary charm with the opposite sex. On the Sunday after our last London performance, he arrived at my hotel to take me on a tour of Saint Paul's Cathedral and Westminster Abbey before joining Bob and Steve at the Connaught for lunch. Never had I had a more elegant, gallant, and totally delightful escort.

Rauschenberg had his own coterie of English fans.

There is the handsome look of all the dances on stage, thanks largely to the astonishingly imaginative lighting of Robert Rauschenberg. . . . There are two important differences from ordinary stage lighting. First, it differs from night to night instead of being firmly set for all time at the rehearsals. Secondly, it is more like the lighting of nature (sunrise, lightning, moon and shadow) than artificial light in the way it catches the dancers suddenly, indirectly and by surprise.[30]

The music had its usual share of detractors, scoffers, the irritated, and the angry, but it also had some interested, open-minded supporters. Even the ushers who, at the beginning of the season, complained that the music would drive them up the wall, at the end volunteered that not only did they like the music (and mostly John Cage's) but they had never had a show in the house they would miss so much.[31] Marie Rambert, sprightly, voluble, generous, was heard to say, "and I didn't mind the music at all!"[32]

The recognition the company received could not help but be deeply affecting to us all. With rare exception, the dancers and the dancing got kudos all around. While humility precludes relating many of the generous words said to and written about me personally, the fact is that they had a tremendous impact upon me. It was here, in London in 1964, that I finally came to believe that, yes, I really am a dancer, doing what I should be doing. I'd been plagued by self-doubt my entire performing life, and the London reviews provided something to think back upon in darker hours. For this reason I include a sampling:

This Is London: "One must emphasize yet again how important a part is played by the superb techniques of the individual dancers and in particular of Merce Cunningham himself. Not a single slipshod movement, not one falsely placed arm mars the perfections of each succeeding pattern. There is a purity of line and form that would do credit to any of the world's great classical ballet companies, and yet there is also a freedom, indeed a positive liberation in the whole idea of what dancing should mean. Even the skeptical must be won over by the authoritative ease of Mr. Cunningham's own expertise and let it be noted that he is as formidable a mime as he is a dancer. Among the company, exquisite Carolyn Brown has the sinuous flexibility of the true prima ballerina assoluta, while Viola Farber, Shareen Blair, Sandra Neels, Barbara Lloyd, Steve Paxton and William Davis share the distinctions that must be awarded to dancers of outstanding accomplishment."[33]

Daily Express: "American Cunningham, looking like a choreographic Buster Keaton, is a delight in comedy. And in the gazelle-like Carolyn Brown the company boasts one of the world's loveliest dancers."[34]

Dance and Dancers: "By this time I found myself growing more and more aware of the remarkable standard of Cunningham's dancers. Apart from Cunningham himself, in Carolyn Brown and Viola Farber were two of the most brilliant modern dancers to visit London, while Shareen Blair,

Sandra Neels and particularly Steve Paxton were not very far behind. Lithe and vital, these dancers all possessed the most remarkable poise and balance. . . . The contrast between Farber and Brown (the exquisite, faultless, flame-like Brown) was one of the season's delights. If Cunningham had not got them in his company he would have to have invented them."[35]

The New Daily: "These performers are really rather impressive. Cunningham himself, tall and lithe; the entirely absorbed Viola Farber with an ungainly grace all her own; Carolyn Brown as remotely and passionately beautiful as Artemis, with Steve Paxton, a Yankee Apollo; and Barbara Lloyd brimming with dedicated eagerness. What is even more impressive, though, is the way these and their less prominent colleagues subject themselves entirely to the dance as a whole. As individuals they are excellent; as a team even better."[36]

Unaccustomed to receiving accolades from the American press, we found these glowing reviews heady, dizzying, delightful stuff. For John, they were affirmation of his own profound belief in Merce's work and the strength of the company. Financially, the company broke even, with a tiny surplus, but as Lew Lloyd said, "Not too good economically, invaluable in every other way." Yet despite the joy we all felt about our London triumph, we were only eleven weeks into the twenty-five-week tour, and Merce was unwell. Fortunately, there was a full week respite before we were due in Stockholm. Francis Mason gave us a farewell party at Canonbury House, and then we went our separate ways—some directly to Stockholm, others remaining in London. Viola and I flew off to Paris for a week, she to stay with Bénédicte Pesle, I to join Earle at 18 bis Blvd. de la Bastille in the eighth-floor apartment of Diego Masson, on loan to Earle for the month of August.

How odd, after a month in the vortex of a tornado, to suddenly spend a totally relaxing week with barely a thought given to dancing, although the Paris film folk showed Viola and me rushes of their film. We were amazed at how in unison we actually were! In fact, we decided we were much better than we had thought we'd be as a company. Alas, most of what we saw never made it into the final film, and unforgivably, what landed on the cutting-room floor ended up in the trash. Hours and hours of footage, documenting the entire repertory of the '64 tour, lost forever!

A slow unraveling of company morale began in Stockholm. Fault can't be assigned to anyone in particular, but a series of events conspired to undo the trust between Merce/John and Bob, disturbing the close-knit sense of family we all prized. Our presence in Stockholm coincided with an exhibition of works by Rauschenberg, Claes Oldenburg, Jean Tinguely, Niki de Saint Phalle, Per Ultvedt, and Oyvind Fahlstrom at the Moderna Museet, arranged by its director, Pontus Hulten, a great admirer of Bob's work. We were to be part of Five New York Evenings, a museum-sponsored series with two performances by the Cunningham company, a duo-piano concert by Cage and Tudor, and two other dance/Happening concerts—one by Yvonne Rainer and Bob Morris, the other by Bob Rauschenberg, Alex and Deborah Hay, and Oyvind Fahlstrom—all to take place in a mammoth gallery space, an area three times as wide as the Metropolitan Opera House stage. After Merce's personal triumph and his company's phenomenal success in London, this situation was anticlimactic at best. There's little doubt that Merce's invitation to participate in the Five New York Evenings owed much to Rauschenberg's presence in the company.

Stockholm was fantastically expensive. We were there sixteen days. With only two paid performances, both company and personal budgets were severely drained. The company's original budget was, in Lew Lloyd's words, "a document of pure fantasy" and he was writing desperate letters to the CPA and others in New York, where they were juggling finances, and Jasper Johns was considering the possibility of another show of donated paintings to rescue the company. Meanwhile, David Vaughan never stopped writing madly to possible venues in Europe and Asia. There were other worries. Although his health was never openly discussed, Merce did not seem well. Thirty-one years later, in his published 1964 *Story* journal, Merce cursorily mentions "that terrible illness and those formidable injections."[1] Only then did I learn that he had been suffering some serious malady. Unmistakable, however, was his moodiness and what I read as repressed anger. Several members of the company had agreed to appear in Bob's evening. Merce was not happy about it, and one could scarcely blame him. Lew Lloyd was furious, especially with his wife, who allowed herself to be dragged around by the ankle in one of the Happening pieces. To risk serious injury, possibly jeopardizing the rest of the tour, seemed to most of us unwise at the very least. In what appeared to be some sort of retaliation, Merce began to choreograph a new work, without Steve, Barbara, or Debby, who were rehearsing with Bob. For those of us who had elected not to be in Bob's Happening evening, this seemed a futile and foolish endeavor. Basic class we needed, new work we did not—we were much too spent to assimilate anything new after a month of continuous performing, and Merce was far too tired and ill to attempt a new work, but he did anyway, in an atmosphere that was extremely unpleasant. He was surly. Viola and I smoldered in barely suppressed resentment. Nothing ever came of this work, and it was annoying to be used just to vent Merce's wrath, especially since the three dancers left out cared not at all. In the process Merce managed to anger Viola, prompting her to lash out, "If you can't choreograph for me after ten years, why do you try?"[2] Wow! Had she forgotten *Nocturnes, Crises, Aeon,* and *Paired*? Clearly, things were on the brink of incivility. John, too, lost his cool, not to mention his Zen non-attachment. Merce's withdrawal into a sullen, unapproachable state made John utterly miserable, desperate to remedy the situation, and his passionate protectiveness of Merce caused him to lash out at Bob: "There's room for only one star in this company!" The problem was not really stars, but egos. Bruised ones. Meanwhile, Bob, enthralled by his own project, seemed oblivious to the tensions mounting daily.

Museum Event #2 was a daunting, nonstop, intermissionless two-and-a-half-hour marathon. The music was again Cage's *Atlas Eclipticalis*, performed by David Tudor and five Swedish musicians. One of them, Karl-Erik Welin, was the handsome fellow I'd danced with (until Stockhausen cut in and sent him packing) at the Keller in Darmstadt in 1958. Unfortunately, *Event #2* lacked the magic and wit Rauschenberg had provided in Vienna. Immense space was the challenge for both choreographer and dancers. It went well, but what an ordeal! (For the audience, too, it seems, because for *Event #3*, the museum requested that Merce schedule an intermission.) Still, in the vast gallery, liberated from the constrictions of a proscenium stage—wings, light booms, blinding theatrical lighting—

we had the freedom to really cover space. Indeed, our job was to devour space and still keep the rhythms and relative spacial relationships accurate. For me, anyway, it was a joyful and exhilarating evening, and the overflow audiences, seated on three sides of the room, sitting on the floor, and even standing against the walls, were enthusiastic.

Post-performance, many of the Swedish dance people Merce and I had come to know six years earlier were there to greet us. Scheduled for the following night at the opera house was Antony Tudor's ballet *Echoing of Trumpets*. Its leading lady, three months pregnant, had had a miscarriage and been rushed to hospital, and her understudy was not prepared to step in. Brian MacDonald, the director of the Swedish Royal Ballet, wanted to know if Merce and I would be willing to do our duet *Nightwandering* in its place. We agreed. The information went immediately to the press, and the program was printed with the change.

But it was not to be. In his journal, Merce seemed to have forgotten the reason: "Why I chose *Winterbranch* I don't know, probably knew there would be little or no rehearsal time."[3] He was right about no rehearsal time. But in my journal, I provided a different answer. Bob, upon hearing about us doing *Nightwandering* at the opera, expressed annoyance to me. Next day he and John suggested doing *Winterbranch* instead. It seemed a wise idea: if only Merce and I performed at the Royal Opera House, the other dancers might resent it.

After marathon *Event #2* and getting to bed at 2:30 in the morning, we faced ten tedious hours filming for Swedish TV. Between 8:30 a.m. and ending shortly before 6:30 p.m., three dances—*Antic Meet, Crises,* and *Nightwandering*—were filmed. "That killing TV day," Merce called it. We warmed up and waited. Spaced and waited. Rehearsed for lighting and waited. Performed a segment and waited. Repeat, ad infinitum. Sheer torture on the muscles! During the lunch break, Merce disappeared. Again, only by reading his journal did I learn that he had rushed off for another of those "formidable injections." As he and I taxied to the opera house after filming *Nightwandering,* he wondered aloud, "Was it all worth it?" To his surprise, I told him I loved our life—all of it; that the pleasures far outweighed the hardships. Some months later he was to remind me of this.

We were at the opera house at seven o'clock. As expected—no time to rehearse. Merce told us what wings to enter and exit from, where to begin a phrase, and that was it; into makeup and costumes and onto the stage. The wings were *jammed* with dancers and stagehands trying to watch us. We could barely make entrances and exits. The audience certainly didn't like it. One man yelled (in Swedish), "When are you going to get that shit off the stage?" Someone told Merce, "There hasn't been a booing in the opera house in a hundred years," but according to the review in *Dagens Nyheter,* not everyone was offended: "The conventional audience, who had come to applaud the usual ballet fare, reacted violently. Whistles and protests were heard, hands were held on ears and several left during the performance. At curtain fall, a sigh of relief from the dissatisfied immediately was drowned in bravos and applause from the grateful. Stockholm has not seen such a controversial dance performance and lively audience response for years."[4]

Five days later we presented *Event #3,* accompanied by Cage's *Variation IV,* played by the same group of musicians. Afterward, Holger Rosenquist presented Merce with a medal from the Society for the Advancement of Dancing in Sweden. "Only other recipients have been the Queen of Sweden and the late Rolf de Maré, impresario of Ballet Suédois during the 1920s."[5]

Elgin Tie, Bob's totally outrageous, utterly surprising, gut-bustingly funny contribution to the Happening evening, was the hit of the show. My god, what a fabulous, crazily inventive artist! A giant steadfast cow led by a stalwart farmer lumbers slowly across the length of gallery, stagehands following to sweep up cow flaps as they fall. Bob descends, barefoot, from the ceiling, crawling laboriously down a stout rope, and disappears into a giant barrel strategically placed on a flatbed cart beneath him. A lengthy pause. He emerges soaking wet. Hauling himself out with the help of the rope, he drops into a large pair of boots on the cart, ties the laces, and then solemnly proceeds to put on a tie. A stagehand appears and picks up the handle of the cart and drags cart—with barrel and the now booted and dripping Bob—after the cow. As the cart starts to roll, Bob leans forward, stiff as a board, all of a piece, at a precipitous, gravity-defying angle. Why doesn't he topple over? Because his hefty boots are nailed to the flatbed. Even so, the balance is not easy. At a snail's pace Bob, wearing the impassive poker face and dignity of Buster Keaton, is moved majestically out of the gallery to hoots and hollers, whistles and guffaws. Tumultuous applause! A brilliant performance!

Contrary to John's peevish, anxious, and anxiety-ridden statement, it seemed there did have to be room for more than one star in our company. And if John, before his passionate outburst, had thought about what he'd always professed, he would have said that everyone is a star and there's room for everyone. But when the subject was Merce, John's abiding love usually blinded him. Merce summarized the Stockholm leg of the tour: "Two weeks of searing the body; warmth from people, both audiences, and singly, and maladjustments with a dance company."[6]

At 6:30 in the evening on September 15, we boarded the M/S *Ilmatar* for an overnight cruise to Turku, Finland, where a last-minute engagement had been arranged. The fee was only five hundred dollars, but we were given first-class accommodations provided for by the director of the Abo Svenska Teater, Miss Sara Strengell. For most of the journey we were in sight of land. Distant lights from villages along the shore twinkled just on the horizon, stars glittered overhead, and a strange gold moon rode low in the sky. The sea was calm; it wasn't cold. Such a lovely, leisurely way to travel! Miss Strengell, a gracious, handsome woman, met us at the dock early the next morning. Our performance was that evening.

The Abo Svenska, a lovely theater built in 1839, had a nice stage—small only in comparison with the vast reaches of Stockholm's museum gallery. I wrote, "We were pretty exhausted. My knee was *extremely* painful in full plié. We warmed up but Merce didn't get ready to rehearse for some time. He doesn't seem well. I really just walked through pieces—knee injuries are too dangerous & tricky and can't be forced. Apparently Merce hurt his ribs one day working by himself."

I was feeling very depressed about my unwilling body, and about dancing in general. After the first two dances, I was even more depressed. Now it was my turn to wonder, why *do* it? Why dance? It's such hard work and demands such energy and dedication. The audience bravoed after *Suite*. After *Nocturnes*, which I did enjoy dancing (perhaps it was dancing to music that made it such a pleasure), the audience was again wonderfully appreciative, and suddenly I felt ashamed of my lack of resolve to do my best, no matter my aching body and depressed state of mind. Sara Strengell, appearing genuinely moved, presented flowers to Merce onstage and gave a little speech of thanks. To John—quite stealing his heart—she presented a basket of chanterelles. The audience kept applauding, and when the curtain opened again on John giving Sara a big kiss they were still more delighted. The Turku sojourn ended with a quiet candlelit supper party in Miss Strengell's elegant antique-furnished riverside apartment. We walked back to the hotel. Merce seemed to be in pain or else ill. He didn't talk about it and was quite withdrawn. Again and again, beginning in London, my journal and letters comment on Merce's health. For at least two months he had appeared ill. Only John might have known the cause.

Our next port of call, Helsinki, as Merce recalled in his journal, "gave us three days of trauma." I'm not sure what he meant by this, but it reflects the severe toll the tour was taking on him. We'd no sooner arrived by bus from Turku the following morning than he had to appear at a press conference, which he dreaded, and then rehearse for four hours. Next day, the day of the live televised performance with audience, we spent entirely in the theater. Certainly that was a day of trauma! The TV people busied themselves setting up equipment while we found whatever space we could in which to warm up, and then, in the company's usual fashion, we proceeded to run the dances without music, costumes, or lighting. No one had bothered to tell Heiki Seppala, the young TV director, who eventually asked Bob if we'd be ready to start rehearsal soon. Suddenly, Bill Davis shouted "Look out!" Viola emitted a kind of soft moaned scream, and crouched down with her arms over her head, saying something like "Not my head!" A metal gel frame had fallen from above. I described the scene:

> There was blood everywhere. Everyone was terribly frightened. They put her on the *Antic Meet* fur coat—Sandy and I rushed up three flights of stairs [to our dressing rooms] for towels and I got her coat to cover her. An ambulance was called. All work on stage stopped. There was blood all over Vi's head and arm. A pool of blood in the fur coat. Merce crouched over her, stroking her. I held her left arm. She didn't pass out; in fact, she laughed a little. Both Sandy and I were, for a short moment, in tears. When the stretcher & men arrived, I was crouched beside Viola and they picked *me* up, and I cried, "NO, not me!" but they were just getting me out of the way FAST. That made everyone laugh. Viola laughed too, saying she didn't really need a stretcher. . . . What *miserable* luck that girl has![7]

Bill Davis had run upstairs after it happened. He was terribly shaken by the accident and felt responsible, sure that if he hadn't shouted a warning, the gel frame would have fallen directly in front of Viola, not on her head. But there was simply no way to predict who might have walked under at that precise moment. David and Lew went with Viola to the hospital. Knowing the show must go on, Merce, ever practical, resumed rehearsal. With Sandra dancing Viola's part, we rehearsed *Septet* and figured out the rest of the program without Viola, a needless precaution. She was back for the performance and determined to do everything. Although she had lost a great deal of blood, she had suffered only a glancing blow resulting in a superficial head wound. It did give her a massive headache and require a number of stitches. Still, had the sharp corner of the gel frame gone straight into her skull, it might have killed her.

Because of this near disaster, neither the director nor the TV crew ever got a proper rehearsal for their live broadcast that evening. Heiki Seppala took it in stride, made no fuss or demands, and without having a clue about entrances, exits, or spacing managed to do the job quite well—the film is good enough that it continues to be used for archival purposes in reconstructing these dances. The theater had a marvelous revolving stage, and Merce took advantage of it to design a very different version of *Story,* creating a completely new set of challenges for us: moving as the stage moved, balancing with no place to fix one's focus, changing directions while our directions were already *being* changed, traveling one way while being carried another. Turns, jumps, and leaps were scary. All this Viola handled like a trouper, though her head ached and the wound throbbed.

Then she had two days to recover and Merce had two days to rest. Some of us enjoyed a very Finnish custom—a real sauna party—and I joined John, Bob, Steve, and David Tudor on a wonderful mushroom walk. These kinds of outings, which profoundly enriched being in Merce's company, happened because of John and his holistic embrace of the life around us.

Helsinki to Stockholm to Copenhagen to East Berlin to Prague, all in one interminable day of flying. Once we were "behind the iron curtain," the next eleven days were mostly grim and dispiriting. My journal entry for September 21, 1964, written in Prague:

> What a terrible disappointment! We're in an ugly, dreary hotel. Dirty, with no hot water or even heat. [The elevator didn't work, either.] My room looks out on an air shaft. It was raining when we went out to dinner—to a "club," also very dreary & ugly, with non-descript food and very expensive. The city, what we've seen of it, is ugly. The whole atmosphere is so *DEPRESSING*! One really wonders how the human spirit can survive. We will dance in a Congress Hall—3000 seats on a flat floor. People won't be able to see anything.

In Russia, early in 1964, Nikita Khrushchev had been ousted, and the new regime—under Kosygin and Brezhnev—had immediately taken a much harder line with the middle-European Communist countries that the Soviet Union controlled. This was reflected in the faces of the people one saw on the street and in the wary, guarded way people dealt with us. Petr

Kotik and his mother, Madame Pavla Kotikova, had seen our Venice performance in June; Petr had played for our Vienna *Event #1*, and it was through Madame Kotikova's efforts that the Czech authorities were persuaded to present the company in Prague and Ostrava and to have Petr's ensemble, Musica Viva Pragensis, perform with us. Lew Lloyd has suggested that the reason the Czech government was willing to sponsor us was that the United States government had refused, and John in his many press conferences early in the tour "went out of his way to be critical of his own government's cultural exchange program."[8]

For reasons never explained, the Czech agency's advertisements and the posters around town omitted the names of both Cage and Rauschenberg, probably the only two names known to the Communist regime. Did John and Bob represent the dangerously decadent and revolutionary artistic pollution of the West? Of course it was a foolish precaution; word of mouth proved far more effective than state advertisements. Artists from miles around Prague came to see the performance and speak with John, Merce, and Bob. We were the first American dance company to perform in Czechoslovakia since the war. People were curious, hungry for something new, and they filled the Congress Hall of Science and Culture to capacity. Advertised as "American Ballet in the Style of *West Side Story*," our program must have been baffling to the huge audience, which nonetheless responded warmly to what little they could actually see. We performed on a raised wooden platform, far too unstable to risk dancing *Aeon*. *Story*, always amenable to the most difficult performance spaces, was substituted, much to the dancers' relief. Aggravating problems with the petty bureaucrat-functionaries directing the crews in the Congress Hall—every one of Bob's requests was met with "No, not possible"—finally drove Merce to declare that unless the carpet was removed from the platform floor, the potted plants and artificial flowers taken away, the piano moved so that David could see the stage, THERE WOULD BE NO PERFORMANCE! It worked. Merce is not one to stage tantrums, but this time it was the only way to get anything accomplished. After the performance we were invited to a private club (supposedly with no Communist spying eyes and ears allowed) where we met with many artists who pelted us with questions about the work, our lives, the outside world.

On the third day, the sun came out, and with it a fresh view of Prague and the realization that it was, after all, a very beautiful city. All it took was to cross Smetana's River Moldau over the Charles Bridge into the historic old town, explore its streets and byways, its churches, and be taken to a really nice restaurant high on a hill near the castle. That evening, after a cocktail party in the company's honor at the American Embassy, David Vaughan, the Lloyds, and I had a taste of true Czech culture, Smetana's 1868 three-act opera *Dalibor* in the stunning Baroque National Theatre. My gloom lifted. For a day.

Next morning no bus arrived to take us to the airport: due to a mix-up, our sponsors had neglected to order one. Our translator came to the rescue. The two-engine prop plane was held for us. When finally we did arrive, all the other passengers were made to stand aside while we boarded. This special treatment was embarrassing, even more so upon arrival in Ostrava after a ghastly bumpy, rocky, shaky flight through pea-soup-thick clouds. Upon disembarking, the other passengers were made to wait outside the airport bus while we got on and our mounds of luggage after us, cluttering the aisles. Was this standard Communist protocol for "artists," we wondered, or special treatment for Americans?

Ostrava, the "Pittsburgh of Czechoslovakia," may have been a coal-mining town, but it had a handsome old theater (sadly in need of repair) just across the street from a good hotel that had private baths with hot water, an elevator that worked, and a decent restaurant—everything to make weary dancers happy. But Ostrava was a bleak place for those living there. There was no electricity in the stores in the daytime—in any case, there was next-to-nothing to buy, not even magazines. Our dresser in the theater marveled at the quality of our Kleenex and our makeup.

In the Ostrava program, we women suddenly had become Slavs: we were *Brownova, Farberova, Hayova, Lloydova and Neelsova*. What fun! The performance that night was unmemorable except for an architectural feature of the stage that Bob and Merce put to imaginative use. A scenery-loading ramp at center stage led down to doors opening onto the street behind the theater. *Story* began as the curtain rose on an empty stage, stripped to the walls; in Rauschenbergian eerie semidarkness, Merce enters from the street and moves slowly up the ramp through the gloom. "It felt like Kafka, appropriately enough, a long uphill push through the dark."[9] Merce's description was equally appropriate for what it felt like to be on the wrong side of the Iron Curtain. Onstage, at curtain call, each of us was presented with a bouquet of flowers and a tiny miniature coal-miner's lamp—to light one's way in the dispiriting, dismal Soviet darkness? That, too, seemed appropriate.

Next stop, Warsaw—and chaos and anxiety from the moment we arrived at the station. Lew had reserved three first-class compartments, but when the train pulled in, we were on the wrong end of the platform. Scrambling into the only first-class car we could find, we discovered it was almost full.

A conductor told us our seats were seven cars back and would be ready in about fifteen minutes. Just before the train pulled out of the station, we tossed the mounds of luggage through the windows to whoever would catch it. At the next station, Lew and David Tudor jumped out and ran along the platform. Sure enough, there were three locked compartments at the rear of the train. By this time we had split up in search of any seat available. Lew described his ordeal:

> We got back in the train, fought our way forward to the others and then tried to get everyone back to our real seats. When we hit the frontier we were [still] nicely spread out throughout the train; some of us had passports [with them], some did not. I had *all* our train tickets and the group visa from Czech. and I was in between the group in front and the group in the rear, and the various guards, Polish and Czech, refused to let me move one way or the other. After about 45 min. of running around it was straightened out and we went on. At the first station in Poland, Katowice, all the able bodied men from the co. leapt out on the platform from our coach in the rear and, grabbing a baggage truck on the way, ran forward to our luggage which we had not tried to move. We piled it on the truck, after the usual exchange of shouts with various uniformed guards, and pushed it back to our coach and through the windows again.[10]

We checked into a wretched prisonlike hotel around midnight. Our performance, part of the ten-day VIII Festival International de Musique Contemporaine Automne de Varsovie, was scheduled for Sunday, September 27, the last day of the festival, at the odd hour of twelve noon, in the Theatre Dramatyczny of the Palace of Culture and Science. The first thing built by the Russians after they took over these rubbled remains of a city, this was a massive Soviet skyscaper with what looked like rather bizarre Byzantine or Moorish decoration. It housed theaters, restaurants, and meeting halls and cast a forbiddingly authoritarian shadow over the entire city.

On the morning of September 26, my birthday, I sat in the bathtub—a public one—looking down into the tepid water and thinking, *I won't live very long.* Melodramatic nonsense! But in a visceral way, I can still feel the power of that morbid conviction as I write, dozens of years later. Warsaw's old town had been reconstructed from paintings, and no hint of the horrors that had defiled the original site were in view. But close by, in a large, barren treeless park overlooking the river, stood a naked wall, the only remains of a three-storey building near the Jewish ghetto where Jews had fought to their deaths, where they had leapt from burning buildings set fire to or bombed by the Nazis. Until 9/11, 2001, when America's sense of safety was irreparably destroyed, it was impossible for me to even begin to comprehend that misery, suffering, and horror in Warsaw.

Bob was determined to cheer me up. That night he invited everyone to celebrate my birthday at the Crocodile, an atmospheric, Gothic-arched, cellar restaurant in the reconstructed old town. Joining us was a young scientist from Kraków who had been attached to our group as official helper-translator. Rumor had it that he was really a Communist Party member assigned to spy on us. The birthday party was a rather wild affair: many ice-cold vodka shots downed in one swallow apiece, platters of food, and still more vodka. We danced to a much-too-loud orchestra playing mostly American pop music. Bob got very drunk, dancing up a storm in a down-and-dirty, sexy twist style with Debby, providing much amusement for the Poles at neighboring tables but not, I surmised, to the amusement of Steve, who left early. Or to Merce and John, who left soon after Steve. Gradually our group dispersed, leaving Bob alone with a huge bill to pay and not nearly enough Polish zlotys to cover it. Fortunately, David Tudor, sitting apart with some musician friends, came to his rescue.

The Cunningham company and the Pittsburgh Symphony, under the direction of William Steinberg, were the only American groups to perform in the 1964 Warsaw Autumn Festival. Our concert was sold out well in advance. Richard, the official translator, told Merce that we were well received by the official Warsaw press and that the critic in the official Communist paper wrote that Merce's art was *"for* the people" and therefore *for* all Poland.[11] By government decree, it would seem. Actually the reviews of our performances in Czechoslovakia and Poland were uncomprehending, and mixed, at best.

In Poznan, no one from the opera house met us; the local government canceled a post-performance party for us and provided us with no assistance whatsoever. Instead, people from the American Consul for Cultural Affairs arrived with cars and a truck for the theater luggage, arranged for our stay in a modern, functioning hotel, and gave us a splendid party after our sold-out performance at the Panstwowa Opera House. *Aeon* and *Winterbranch* were not easy for an audience. I don't think they knew *what* to make of us. I don't think the Americans (from the consulate) knew what to make of us either!

At the party, we were informed that plainclothesmen had observed us at the railroad station upon arrival, in the lobby of the hotel, and, at that very moment, were across the street outside the consulate. We were further warned that, very possibly, our hotel rooms were bugged and probably had been in Warsaw as well. We were so entertained by this idea—as David Vaughan mused, "Who on earth would want to listen to dancers' conversations?"—that we plotted to have an elaborate, convoluted, quasi-scientific discussion in Bob's hotel room about the secret powers of the Rauschenbergian *Aeon* machine, hoping that we would utterly confound and confuse our eavesdroppers. In fact, it was really the Polish party guests at the American consul's home who were being carefully watched. The Polish ballet dancers, whom we met at the party, were aware of this, but when we left, they risked walking along the street with us. For them, it was not at all amusing to be constantly under surveillance, and knowing this was sobering for us.

We had nearly two full days to be tourists in Poznan, one of the oldest cities in Poland and one whose fine historical buildings managed to escape much of the Nazi destruction. Merce spent his free day visiting ballet schools, talking to dancers and young students, answering questions with the ever-present Richard feebly attempting to translate a vocabulary with which he had no familiarity. At the end of the day, he told Merce "how grateful he was to us for letting him stay." Merce's unspoken response: "As if we had anything to do with it."[12]

Our presence in Poznan had been a complete surprise to the American Embassy. Lew Lloyd was peppered with questions: "How on earth did you get here? Who invited you? Why were we never informed? How do you propose to get out of Poland? By train? Through East Germany? Impossible. They'll never permit it!" But PAGART, the arts organization that had arranged for our performances in Warsaw and Poznan, assured Lew they'd get us out.

Lew was meticulous in his instructions: "*No* Polish money may be taken out of Poland. On the train you will need: a/ your passport b/ your green exit card from Poland c/ the white slip from hotel d/ receipts for any money-changing in Poland e/ your railroad control card f/ your railroad ticket from Helmstadt to Koln. I have the group transit visa for East Germany. I will have German Marks for you on the train when we reach Germany. You will be paid the balance of this weeks pay in W. German DM on arrival in Cologne."

The train ride that would eventually transport us out from under the menacing Soviet gloom began in Poznan with yet another frantic departure—bags flung through windows and another mix-up in seating arrangements—but once under way, we traveled in comfort and relative calm. Crossing into East Germany, everything changed. There was no sleep to be had. Our documents, singly and as a group, were checked again and again by uniformed guards; it was unnerving to never quite know who they were or whether we would be detained for some arbitrary irregularity.

But it was not us that was detained, it was all of our theater luggage! In East Berlin, at midnight, we changed trains. As we pulled out of the station heading toward West Germany, Merce spotted our freight piled up on the platform. In Warsaw, the American Embassy had warned Lew not to travel in East Germany, since in case of trouble there was absolutely no way of getting in to help us.[13] Panic ensued, followed by much running up and down through the cars, searching for someone to complain to. Only Viola could speak German. The freight would follow, she was told, on a later train. This information was not reassuring. The question was not only when, but if.

A performance was scheduled in Krefeld exactly thirty-six hours after our arrival in Cologne. For most of that day, Lew or David, with Viola speaking in German, phoned Cologne from Krefeld, and each time the response was the same. "No luggage. The next train is due at . . ." And the call would be put through again. Finally, John decided to consult the *I Ching*. He came up with the hexagram "waiting," but "be of good cheer," "eat and be hearty," "it will work out in its own time." So heeding the oracle (in our company we welcomed any excuse for a wonderful meal), we splurged on a grand dinner, and when the station was called again, at ten o'clock, the answer this time was, "Yes, your luggage just arrived on the last train!"

Next day the recovered theater luggage was trucked from Cologne to Krefeld, showing up in time for the performance. Bob had an exhibit of his work at the modern museum in Krefeld, so it wasn't surprising that the program copy for our performance at the *Stadttheater* read: "Rauschenberg Cage Cunningham in Krefeld" instead of the customary "Merce Cunningham and Dance Company." Next stop, Brussels, where we taped *Crises* in a television studio with a concrete floor and a demanding director who insisted we rehearse the piece full-out three times before he would actually tape it. This infuriated Merce, but from the director's point of view, surely it made sense.

The European segment of our peripatetic six-month adventure ended with a whirlwind of three one-night stands—traveling, rehearsing, and performing on the same day: Le Palais des Beaux-Arts in Brussels, Théâtre Royal Néerlandais d'Anvers in Antwerp, and De Kurzaal te Scheveningen in Holland. The headline in *Beaux Arts,* the journal published by Le Palais des Beaux Arts, hailed Cunningham, Cage, and

Rauschenberg as *"Les trois noms les plus insolent de l'art actuel,"* saying they were "Insolent because they're not afraid to break the taboos of art, because they're indifferent to the audience's reaction, because their manifestations have often provoked scandal though this was not their aim; because, unswervingly faithful to their ideas, they represent one of the most curious and symptomatic tendencies of our times."[14]

Mary Sisler, mother of Hartford Atheneum curator Sam Wagstaff, was in Brussels and gave us an elegant post-performance supper party. Driving off with Merce and John in her Rolls-Royce, she let the rest of us find our way by more plebeian means of transportation. "Crazy woman with a warmth that comes and goes like the sound of passing automobiles"[15] was how Merce described her. Crazy, perhaps, but in her way she had come to the financial aid of the company by agreeing to purchase the exquisite small wire Richard Lippold sculptures that had hung in John's beloved Monroe Street apartment. John, in turn, gave the ten thousand dollars to the company. With such incremental and often very personal interventions, the company miraculously managed to survive.

Although we again had our own private bus, this time the driver assigned to take us from Germany to Belgium and Holland "distinguished himself by having no idea at all where we were going, nor did he recognize the names of the cities."[16] On his own, he was unable to get out of Cologne, much less find his way anywhere else. Lew had to sit next to him with maps and direct him with shouts of *links* and *rechts* and *gerade aus.* In his journal, Lew described his attempt to locate our hotel in Antwerp, which played out like a scene from a Marx Brothers film:

To avoid the usual charade of trying to find the hotel by intuition in a strange city, David Vaughan and I decided to employ a maneuver that our Italian driver had taught us in Vienna. He hailed a cab, told him the name of the hotel, followed the cab, paid the cabby at the hotel. . . . [so] we hailed a cab. David Vaughan got in and told the cabbie where he wanted to go. The cabbie tore off down the street, with the bus in pursuit. The cab ran a red light, which we didn't make, and disappeared. We proceed *gerade aus* as we do in times of crisis and suddenly the cab comes careening at us from the opposite direction with the driver and David waving frantically and telling us nothing. They then disappeared to the rear. The bus goes on and this time the cab never reappears. Finally we're near the railroad station and I get out in the rain and run from kiosk to kiosk trying to get a detailed street map. Which I got, and I was able to locate the hotel on it. So we find the hotel except that David and the cab aren't there and don't show up for some time. When they do arrive David explained that the cabbie, after passing us in the wrong direction, then wheels around and follows the *wrong* bus into oblivion.[17]

The Antwerp theater provided us with a severely raked stage and the worst floor we'd encountered to date. Equally disturbing was discovering on the title page of the program the pronouncement: "This program is presented under the auspices of the Consul-General of the United States." The fact that the State Department had refused all assistance to the company made this especially infuriating to John, whose personal pleas over many months had consistently been rejected. The producer would not remedy the error. To solve the wretched floor problem, a floor cloth was stretched over the holes, uneven boards, metal cleats, and nails, and Merce changed the program, omitting *Rune* (the floor considered too treacherous), replacing it with *Suite for Five.* By this time most of us, in varying states of the flu, were suffering deep, penetrating exhaustion, aching muscles, and flagging spirits. A virus had struck the company, starting with David Vaughan in Poland. Albert and I succumbed on the train from Poznan; Barbara, Lew, and Bob in Brussels; Viola in The Hague; and in Paris it caught up with Steve. Even so, aching and miserable, waiting for the four o'clock rehearsal to begin, I still could savor the romance of theater life:

> *Theatre Neerlandais d'Anvers* dates 1830. Gorgeous! Four tiers of gold trimmed, deep dusty red seats and painted ceiling. It's raining very very very hard and we can hear it on stage. I'm lying way upstage looking out at the house. Sandra is lying downstage writing postcards. David T. and John are setting levels for the *Crises* tape. The rain is splashing thunderously, louder than the music! It's a lovely moment in the theatre—the lights sparkling dimly in the house, the stage bathed in spotlights, the towering curved blue cyclorama a beautiful evening blue.

Our last European performance took place in the Kurzaal of the magnificent sprawling seaside hotel, the Kurhaus in Scheveningen, adjacent to The Hague. The delicious luxury of the hotel offered some compensation for the miserable performance conditions—a minuscule, poorly equipped concert hall, the worst "stage" situation we'd yet encountered (every other one seemed to vie for the distinction), coupled with insurmountable communication problems. An artist acquaintance, Bob Lens, had fought valiantly to bring the company there, and he'd requested a specific program. Merce felt bound to honor this, but he complained mightily in his journal:

> (Painters have such odd ideas about space.) We danced *Summerspace* out by the pianos placed on the sides of the stage in front in full view of the public, with all of us nonplussed as to how to exit, hide behind them, or battle the edge of the drop to get off? *Winterbranch* was one lump on top of another. I got a monstrous bolt of wood in my foot during *Changeling* . . . The hall was ornately beautiful, the audience (most from Amsterdam) was puzzled, and we were upset to play under such poor conditions, particularly *Summerspace.*[18]

Not a stellar ending to the European leg of the tour. The company broke up into small groups and eventually we all made our weary way to Paris, where we had four days to recoup and regroup. Earle was now staying in an unheated, sixth-floor walk-up apartment, which was not only frigid but relentlessly damp. Most mornings I simply hunkered down under the covers and read. Washing eight sets of costumes and practice clothes and drying them in front of the tiny oven took the entire four days, but the apartment was rent-free, on loan from one of the film folk.

Earle hadn't been at the station to meet me. On his way in pelting rain he'd had an accident—crashing into the rear of a car, and then getting hit from behind. A three-car tie-up. Later that same day, again in the rain, a motorcyclist injured his leg when crashing into Earle's beloved old Porsche, and Earle had to take him to the hospital. This bit of bad luck, on top of Earle's dire financial situation, depressed us both. We came to the sad decision that we had no choice but to sell the black Rauschenberg painting we'd purchased in September 1953. Earle reluctantly spoke with Bob about the possibility of selling it to Ileana Sonnabend for a thousand dollars,[19] but no decision was arrived at, and on Tuesday, October 13, at 2:45 p.m., the company was aboard Air India, with no little trepidation and excitement, heading east into exotic lands.

Nothing prepared me for the onslaught to the senses that is India: sounds, smells, colors; its roiling sea of humanity; the nobility and degradation of poverty impugning Victorian British decorum and the riches of the Raj; the sacred cows nonchalantly perambulating alleyways while prostitutes languished in cages. How to assimilate the deluge of images, the rush of emotions, the staggering strangeness?

India had frightened me, even before I went there. I was afraid of my own cowardice when faced with devastating poverty, disease, and the plight of the untouchables. What I did not expect was to feel deep, profound gratitude for each precious moment. John said he was glad he had lived his life in such a way that made it possible for him to be in India. I felt the same—overwhelmed with awe, wonder, and respect, emotions so strong they were almost beyond endurance. It was like a sudden blow between the eyes repeated again and again; there was no real comprehension, no time to analyze or digest. M. C. Richards once said that she wished that I would come back from one of our tours "scathed." Little could she have imagined the extent to which her wish would come true. India sears the soul.

We flew into Bombay airport at 6:30 in the morning. The sky was a smoldering beige-pink. Gita Sarabhai, handsome in Punjabi dress, was there to greet us and to get us through the maze of passport control and customs regulations. Outside on the street—in the still-early morning— steaming, sticky heat seemed to suck the vitality out of one's bones and dizzy the brain. As garlands of flowers were placed around our necks, a small woman appeared with her children, put down a dirty, ragged cloth, and placed her naked baby on it. Her other children sat, too, and stared at us, and we—disconcerted—stared back at them. Driving into the city— past huts of straw, mud, paper, cloth, metal scraps, and wooden bits, all run together helter-skelter for blocks in a wasteland of mud—we could scarcely take in the scene before us: people urinating and defecating in full view; untended children in only shirts or nothing; men, in filthy rags, scratching at their balls; young girls, brass pots on their heads, silver jewelry in their noses, barefoot, in brilliantly colored saris, spitting streams of blood-red betel juice, and women—more beautiful than any in the world, I think—walking through the chaos with long elegant strides, great burdens carried as if weightless on their heads.

The street outside our hotel baked in blinding white sun. On the sidewalk a tiny beggar child smiled up at me, sparkling black eyes set in a radiantly beautiful face, framed by shiny short black curls. Inside, with crows cawing madly and fluttering around the eaves of the small balcony of my air-conditioned room, I fell into the cool dark bliss of deep sleep—only to be rudely awakened by the phone jangling in my ear: "There's a reporter here to interview you." (And one each for Merce, John, and Viola.) "NO!" I protested groggily, feeling hideously ill with fatigue after more than twenty-four hours with no sleep. A few minutes later David Vaughan was knocking at my door, insisting that I "get up and talk to this lady." Disruption of rest time is what consistently happened to Merce in almost every city we played in. Until that morning I had never fully comprehended what he had to endure.

With only eight performances in twenty days—two in each of four cities: Bombay, Ahmedabad, Chandigarh, and New Delhi—we had time to enjoy the extraordinary hospitality of our hosts, the Sarabhai family, and the privilege of seeing an India that most tourists do not. At that time, Bombay was the most culturally Westernized of the four cities, and the least responsive to our work. We were presented there by the Bombay Madrigal Singers' Organization, whose patron-in-chief was the British conductor Sir Adrian Boult; one suspects that their true artistic sympathies lay somewhere in the early nineteenth century. Certainly the lively sensibility that greeted us with such excitement in London just two months earlier was decades away from infecting the British-influenced culture in Bombay. (Although at a dinner party that first evening, given by wealthy Indian friends of the Sarabhais', the background music was the Beatles— whose very first recording had been cut only in January!) Our sold-out audiences were unresponsive, and members of the Sarabhai family, seeing the company for the first time, appeared bewildered, a bit unhappy, and strangely quiet after our performances. But two very enthusiastic women came backstage to tell us how much they had enjoyed the program, and to explain that we had the wrong audience—mostly made up of dowager women, all Indians who knew only conventional Western culture and/or their own.

John was crushed by the lambasting given the music. The *Times of India* advised its readers: "Do go and hear this very advanced art—so advanced that it appears to have caught up with the chaos of the primeval slime."[1] In its second review it commented: "To the uninitiated it was not so much a performance on a prepared piano as a peevish assault on an unprepared piano."[2] Poor John—naively believing that because he so ardently admired India and its arts, India would respond in kind. From my journal:

> *Suite,* first on the program. Felt what dancing, at its best and mine, should be at last—again. The *spirit,* the love of dance, the warmth between dancer and audience—the really *spiritual* nature of dancing. Why do I let petty feelings mar this possibility? I get filled with resentment toward Merce, even hatred and despair about the dances themselves. And yet, doing my solo in *Suite,* I rediscovered the thing about dancing which makes it worthwhile, which makes it more than theatre, or work, or art, or pleasure. But it is so difficult to keep, to even remember. I felt both wonderful excitement and shame for allowing myself to be buried in pettiness.

Sadly, after the next performance that bit of wisdom was forgotten: "*Crises* duet went badly again and I just sobbed when I got off stage. Merce is just IMPOSSIBLE to dance with. And he just won't rehearse the parts that aren't going well. Filled with despair and misery again."

My self-involvement precluded all empathy with Merce, who no doubt was struggling with his own demons and insecurities. I was unwilling to excuse him despite knowing he wasn't well. The heat, so different from anything most of us had experienced before, made us strangely queasy, dizzy, nauseated. The unfamiliar food caused problems, too. Having barely recovered from the last bout of illness, we were about to be clobbered by a more exotic malaise.

Each day, I passed the curly-haired beggar child outside our hotel. Love at first sight! Could I adopt her? No, I was told, she was not an orphan and most probably was the sole provider for her family who, it turned out, was camped just around the corner. On our last day in Bombay, I gave her all the rupee change I had. Suddenly she began to dance and sing. Here was a Bharata Natyam artist in miniature with ravishingly subtle, exquisite skill, yet she could not have been more than six years old. What would become of her? Could she be a *devadasi,* a sacred temple dancer, or would she end up in one of the cages on Prostitute Row?

An unforgettable ride to the train station, sky dark, like dried blood, cab driver leaning on the horn as he wended his tortuous way through masses of humanity, conveyances of every imaginable sort. . . . Finally settled in the train with enormous relief. Relief to be *still*, in a fairly usual situation. . . . Relief to see our own pale, familiar faces because one couldn't bear the almost physical pain of looking at everything so unknown. The night porter made up the beds and we quickly got into them and turned off the lights.

Our night train, the *Gujurat Mail*, pulled into Ahmedabad early the next morning. On the platform to greet us were other members of the Sarabhai family, whose guests we would be for five extraordinary days. Sorted into several cars, we made our way out of the teeming city into the countryside. Waiting at the gate of a walled-in compound was a band of musicians from the local jail, dressed in white, with red-and-gold epaulets and fezzed turbans, who serenaded us with bagpipes, drums, and other instruments. When all the automobiles had assembled, our caravan proceeded into the Sarabhai compound with the band bringing up the rear, still playing. The frenetic hurly-burly of Bombay quickly receded as we inhaled the tranquil oasis of "the Retreat"—a tropical paradise of trees, flowers, shrubs, lily ponds, and pavilions of intricate Moghul-inspired decoration with peacocks strutting under luxuriant foliage among Indian and Greek statues. Set amid the vast acreage was the main house, a four-storey structure with terraces and balconies, large enough to accommodate fifty houseguests, with a complete apartment for each of Ambalal Sarabhai's seven children. (As they came of age, however, they all had chosen to build houses of their own, several of them within the compound.)

Intimately tied to Ambalal Sarabhai, great calico merchant and patron of the arts, his wife, Saraladevi, and his saintly sister Anasuya is the life story of Mahatma Gandhi (high on my list of heroes).[3] Gandhi received moral and financial support from Ambalal, was often a guest at the Retreat, and when ill was cared for by Saraladevi and Anasuya, both of whom wore *khadi* (Indian homespun cotton cloth) in support of Gandhi's fight for independence from Great Britain. We dancers had only glimpses of Ambalal and Saraladevi. It was five of their seven children—Gautam, Mani (daughter-in-law), Geera, Gita, and Bharati—whom we came to know, however briefly. The youngest son, Vikram, a nuclear physicist, had married Mrinalini, a classical Indian dancer who had her own dance company. Their daughter Mallika would grow up to lead that company and to star in Peter Brook's *Mahabharata*. Mrinalini had a school and theater near the Retreat where we rehearsed and performed. It was an extraordinary privilege, if only for five days, to live among these remarkable people, all of whom were vitally engaged in a wide spectrum of activities—art, science, politics, business, and philanthropy—and whose work was profoundly beneficial to others.

Our company was split up and housed with different members of the family. The two Davids and I were in Mani's very modern Le Corbusier house, to which the jail band was invited to tea by the swimming pool, where a private concert was played just for us and for Mani's household servants. Then, with scarcely time to catch our breath, we climbed into the back of a truck and were driven off to a picnic at Mani's brother's farm, past vultures lurking in treetops, water buffalo submerged in muddy ponds—only their heads were visible—camels loping in ungainly grace along dusty roads. On horseback, men in swirling turbans and ruffled, embroidered shirts aided by their women, regal as queens on foot, herded the sacred cows.

That night we were the guests of Ambalal's eldest living son, Gautam, his wife, Kamalini, and their two daughters, Mana and Shauna. Before dinner, we sat on mats on a lawn where male cowherd dancers performed for us. Musicians sat in the center; the dancers danced around them, swooping down and out, adding turns, moving faster and faster. This was followed by a hypnotic stick dance, similar to the Stick Nautch my mother had learned from Denishawn, but theirs was an exciting men's version with drops to the heels, turns, and jumps. As twilight faded to dusk, the performers—now illuminated only by candlelight—cast giant shadows into the gloom. The evening ended with a puppet show on the riverbank, high above the water where we sprawled about on mats and cushions. The puppets, squeaking and chattering like monkeys or birds, performed fantastic contortions—fights, horseback rides, somersaults. How this was accomplished without hopelessly entangling the strings was miraculous. Several such magical evenings were to follow.

Day Two was altogether different and probably the worst day of the entire tour in terms of company morale. Morning class was scheduled at Mrinalini Sarabhai's home/studio, quite a distance from the Retreat. Before the class began, Merce announced that we were to give a lecture-demonstration that evening. News to us! He then muttered something to the effect that he didn't know what he was going to do, but we'd do some sort of class and maybe a few of the dances. Barbara Lloyd told Merce she did not want to do a class in front of an audience. Totally surprised, Merce asked why. She explained that she did not feel she was in any condition to perform a technique class for an audience. I agreed with her. In the brief moment of silence, an unmistakable, unspoken antagonism permeated the studio. Merce then asked the others. Viola agreed with Barbara. With the exception of Steve, who said he enjoyed performing class for an audience, the others said they didn't care.

Throughout one's performing life there is a certain imbalance going on all the time between the dancer in performance and the dancer in the classroom. Ideally, of course, there shouldn't be. While weeks of performing the same repertory over and over again on tour can definitely improve performance skills and one's sense of security onstage, as well as the technique required for particular dances, one's overall classroom technique often suffers. And, of course, the reverse is true: with a diet of only technique classes, performance suffers. Classes on tour had to be simple, basic warm-up sessions; there wasn't time or energy for more. But, at home in the studio, Merce usually used class to explore new movement and complex rhythms in order to extend our range; often he would demonstrate the material differently each time. Which version to choose? Even more difficult was when he chose material from a dance in the current repertory but changed the rhythm or the arms or the direction. This often proved more confusing than dealing with completely new material. Not having had a real class in months, some of us felt vulnerable and naked. Performance mentality *is* radically different from classroom mentality and, I would wager, uses different parts of the brain. *All* parts of our brains were exhausted! Nearing the end of the fifth month on tour, we were chronically tired—mentally, physically, and emotionally on the edge.

Making matters worse that morning, some of the Sarabhais came to watch the morning class, along with some of Mrinalini's students and company members. The floor was stone. When Merce gave jumps, I left class, went outside, and did a ballet barre where, quite suddenly, India blotted out the smoldering discontent with the sounds of women doing laundry in the river, slapping clothes on the rocks, the sounds echoing in the river valley; curious birdcalls; water buffalo, up to their ears, cooling off; the riverbanks strewn with drying laundry—Bible times come to life.

Rehearsal in the asymmetrical outdoor theater was brief. Another stone floor. Late-morning sun scorching hot. For each dance, Merce inquired of his visibly unhappy, sullen dancers if they would be willing to do it. I said to Merce, the less we work on the stone floor in the midday sun, the better. We marked the pieces quickly, for spacing only, and departed, most with ruffled tempers.

That evening, Mrinalini made a brief introductory speech; Merce followed with a few words, then called us onstage, and introduced us. My account: "The class began. It was fine for a while. Merce did nothing new or alarming. The combinations were taken from the morning class. Barbara stopped and moved off to the side. Then he gave a complicated phrase, with elaborate arm gestures, which he didn't do the same twice, and I left and walked off to the side. By the end of 'class' Steve, Albert and Sandra were still dancing. Perhaps Debby."

For the four of us who quit the class without Merce's permission, this mutiny felt momentous in importance; we'd taken a stand and acted on it. For Merce, too, I think our rebellion was important, and troubling. Between the class and the performance of excerpts from a few dances, Merce spoke again while we sat on the curving wall, stage right. At one point Bill turned to me and asked, "Where did he get all that nonsense?" Day by day Bill had become more and more disillusioned, unhappy not only with the company but with the dichotomy between the expressed aesthetic—the propaganda, so to speak—and the reality of the working relationships, the so-called collaborations, and Merce's own working methods. The disillusionment had begun in Hartford the past spring when Merce, in Bill's words, "spouted a bunch of bull" and performed his Judson-esque solo, which had horrified both of us. Inevitably, the stresses of this tour had now exaggerated all the negative emotions all of us experienced at one time or another. I wrote, "After the applause, Merce didn't call us out [to take a bow], as I remember, but Mrinalini did. The whole experience is muddled in my mind . . . no doubt because I want to forget the whole miserable affair. It was mutiny during that class when one by one we left. I don't think the audience knew; but he did. It was a very bad evening in terms of company relationships. We were bitter; and the last shreds of respect were going."

Despite the hostile atmosphere during the lecture-demonstration part of the evening, as I began to perform my solo from *Suite for Five* the fractious I/Me dissolved. "Instantaneous uncluttered awareness" is how this experience has been described by Zen Buddhism. In the distance, behind the low, curved wall, the Sabarmati River flowed through the countryside; a funeral pyre burned at the river's edge, and voices, in song or mourning, floated up across the valley. A siren wailed, other strange, unidentifiable sounds, barely audible, lingered in the night air. Across the river, lights from a distant village flickered, and above, moon and stars gleamed under a vaulted sky. There was no "I" separate from all this, but rather I was one with it. For me this was the quintessential performance of that solo. The dance took on a sacramental quality, imbued with joy and a reverence for the mystery and magic of each single moment, and the potent realization that dance can truly be—in Merce's words—"a spiritual exercise in physical form."

Unfortunately, this experience—although its power is unforgettable to this day—failed to be transformative. The superficial discontents and unhappinesses and resentments accrued over twenty-two weeks of touring could not be so easily banished. Meanwhile, India continued to inflict its wonders, horrors, and beauties, for which we were always unprepared.

The following day was free. Merce taught class but, still chafing from the previous day's unpleasantness, few of us attended. At five in the morning, Bob, Steve, Lew, Barbara, Debby, and Alex all went camel-riding. Merce disapproved because of the possible risks; but, as usual, refused to express his concerns. Wary of muscle soreness or injury, Viola, Sandra, and I chose not to go, as did Albert and Bill, but we were certainly made aware of the thrilling adventure we had missed.

Viola, Bob, Steve, and I rehashed the miserable "mutiny evening." I was very emotional; tears kept welling up in my eyes. I confessed to feeling disillusioned, both with Merce and with dancing. Viola admitted to feeling the same way. Bob, at this point, could not agree; whatever the difficulties, he loved the work and the people he worked with. But later, when John and Bob spoke at the Sarabhais' Design Institute in Ahmedabad, there was a peculiar resonance in their exchanges. John gave a prepared lecture; Bob simply asked people to question him. He adhered to the party line regarding the independence of dance, music, light, and decor, never suggesting that this was not always the case.

> He is very loyal to Merce, and did not express how impossible Merce often is in their working relationship. It wasn't one of Bob's most lucid times. There was a very strange atmosphere of animosity between them, I felt. Sarcastic jest on Bob's part. John, without humor, terribly serious and slightly on the defensive when he *thinks* (often groundlessly) that someone is attacking him.

That evening, in the same outdoor theater where we had performed the lecture-demonstration the night before, Mrinalini Sarabhai's Darpana Company performed Bharata Natyam and Kathakali dances for us. We sat on mats and pillows on the grass in the moonlight. It was deliciously, surprisingly cool. The Indians all remarked that winter was in the air. Earlier in the day, I had gone to watch the dancers being made up. For Kathakali dancers, this takes hours of preparation. Each dancer lies on the floor while a makeup artist, surrounded by pots and brushes, creates a living mask. The face is painted vividly, with the coloring determined by the character the dancer will play, be it virtuous, heroic, or diabolical, and it is said that gradually the dancer assumes the personality of the character he will dance as the makeup is applied.

Our Ahmedabad performances were in the Mangaldas town hall, where seats in the gallery could be had for just one rupee; Mrinalini wanted to make it possible for anyone who was interested to attend. Plumbing, as Westerners know it, was nonexistent. Water for washing was provided in large jugs. Toilets were simply holes in the concrete floor. In the car on the way to morning rehearsal with John and the two Davids, the four of us discussed the sad state of company morale and what could be done about it. John was distraught, and when he was distraught on Merce's behalf, he was apt to lash out.

A curious discussion took place at Bharati Sarabhai's home, where some of us had lunch after rehearsal that same day. Bharati (married to and separated from an Englishman, the only one of Ambalal's seven children who had not married an Indian) peppered Merce with questions related to the stated Cage/Cunningham philosophy and use of chance procedures. If, in the music, any sound is music, any sound can follow any other—be it ugly or beautiful to the human ear—why is it that all the dancers in his company are tall and beautiful? Why not choose the dancers by chance too? Merce laughed, and said he'd always wanted to have a company of midgets. This of course, begged the question. Choice, not chance, was involved in the selection of dancers, as well as the composers and designers invited to collaborate with Merce. What were the criteria for these choices? Surely likes and dislikes played a crucial role. Surely it was not by using chance procedures that Bob Rauschenberg had been invited to design costumes, sets, and lighting? Both Merce and John seemed somewhat taken aback and uncomfortable under this intensive scrutiny and barrage of questions. Privately, Bharati questioned me about my relationship to Viola. Were we *really* friends, considering how different we were from one another? She said she thought Merce and I were asexual in the way we danced, but that Viola was very womanly, very sexy. Indian dance, though religious, is very sexy, she said. Did I think Merce's choreography was asexual because he is homosexual? I agreed that sexy, in its literal meaning, was not a word I would use to describe Merce's dancing or his work. But certainly both could be described as "sensuous." There were more questions than I was unable or not prepared to answer.

When we returned to the theater in the evening, the sky was a smoldering blaze of color—violent rust-orange, pink, peach—mingling with the smoke of a thousand fires, fueled by dried cow dung. Brown-tinged colors, brown-tinged smells. The pungent, exotic odor hovered on the edge of my brain cells—in my mind, not my nostrils. As we approached the stage door, I saw Bob outside, staring at the sky. From his body language, I read: "forlorn, depressed, disillusioned." What had happened? Apparently John had indeed lashed out. After the morning rehearsal, he'd accused Bob of alienating the dancers' loyalties and affections and destroying company morale. This was bitter stuff for Bob to swallow. He'd saved the company from financial disaster more than once, had in fact bolstered company morale when it languished, and I knew, even if John did not, that he was deeply loyal to Merce. After that confrontation, Bob asked Lew to repay the thousand dollars that he had recently loaned the company. A deep wound had been inflicted, and it would have tragic consequences. Lew Lloyd reported the altercation:

> While we were in Ahmedabad, company morale was very low. The reasons for this are very complex, as complex as the 15 personalities involved. John made an attempt to pull things together by talking to various members of the company. However, in his dealings with Bob, John, as he says, rather put his foot into it. The upshot of this unfortunate event is that it is clear that Bob is not interested in contributing to the company's bank account beyond that obligation which he has already assumed, that is Alex's salary and expenses.[4]

Whether in empathy with Bob, or due to the onset of illness, I now felt deeply depressed. Getting through *Aeon, Cross Currents,* and *Nocturnes* was like wading through mud; like being on a conveyor belt moving backward in slow motion. A strange sickness engulfed me: I felt I was losing my mind. No will, no strength. Fever. Vague aches and pains. Headache. On the second evening, and for the first time, I missed a performance. I succumbed totally. The nightmarish dizzy sense of the conveyor belt moving slowly backward continued for a day or two. Never before had I felt like that. In the morning, I was not to be roused from my bed. The company danced *Summerspace* (omitting my parts), *Collage III, Paired,* and *Story.* As Merce succinctly put it: "Worked, too!"

I was not the first to be leveled by this exotic malady. It began with Lew and Alex and worked its way through the company indiscriminately, sparing some, downing others. Viola was laid low in Chandigarh and missed a performance there. We flew from Ahmedabad to Delhi, had a day to rest before setting out for Chandigarh in a chartered bus, supposedly arranged for us by the Tagore Theatre in Chandigarh. No charter bus arrived. The next ten hours, indeed the next three days, proved to be a comedy of errors—hilarious only in retrospect. Confusion, miscommunication, mistreatment, shouting, and hysteria ruled. Eventually the local bus was persuaded to come to our hotel to pick up theater luggage and company members, then swing back around to the bus depot to pick up local passengers. What a trip! For five and a half hours the bus bounced up and down and back and forth as much as it labored cautiously forward over the miserable roads. The promised air-conditioning was merely a few small rotary fans. We sweated and sweltered as we were jostled and jerked about. But who would have missed it? Glued to the windows, we took in every astonishing inch of landscape, villages, and people.

When finally we arrived in Chandigarh, those of us who were recovering from, getting, or suffering from the flu were desperate for bed. No such luck. The hotel—actually a Government Rest House—had assigned four of us to each room. That announcement was greeted with unqualified hostility. Since the hotel did not have enough rooms to accommodate us, we went on to another, which turned out to be a hostel. "Where are your bedrolls?" they inquired. The third, the Mount View, was a real hotel, though very simple, with large rooms, private baths, and a view of the Himalayas. Not even tiny newts, dashing up and down the walls and across the ceiling, could deter us from falling gratefully into bed at last.

There was no fee paid for our two performances in Chandigarh. The city was on our itinerary because the Sarabhais thought John would wish to see Le Corbusier's city, designed in 1950 to be the new capital for the Punjab. The sponsors agreed to pay for travel and accommodations, but of course the promised charter bus had not materialized and the company ended up paying for the hotel. Had Lew and David known what they would face, I doubt we would have made the trip. Fourteen years after Corbusier designed it, the city was still incomplete. The handsome theater, named in honor of the philosopher, poet, and Nobel laureate Rabindranath Tagore, was also unfinished. Backstage there were no functioning electric outlets yet, so the ironing was done by a ten-year-old boy whose iron was heated on a charcoal brazier tended by a still smaller, younger boy. We expected the *Nocturnes* veils to be burned to a crisp, but never again would they be ironed so beautifully.

Both performances sold out, but the people who attended had no idea what or whom they would be seeing. The posters simply read: "American

Ballet with Artistes from the United States of America." But what wonderful audiences! Totally un-Westernized, they responded to the dances with uninhibited gusto—whether laughing and applauding with childlike glee in the middle of dances when we jumped and leaped, or gasping in shock whenever a man lifted or even touched a woman. At moments they became suddenly silent, whether in awe or bewilderment we never knew. Such spontaneous, freely expressed responses were refreshing and a source of delight for us—well worth the minor inconveniences and discomforts experienced by the dancers, but perhaps not for Lew, who took his responsibilities for Merce's and the company's welfare very seriously.

The company was asked to give a third performance. Incredulous, Lew asked, "Without a fee?" No fee, he was told, but the company could collect the proceeds from ticket sales. "All the proceeds?" Lew inquired. Well, except for the rent, publicity costs, staff charges, programs, and other things. Lew requested a written contract. They were amused. Write it down? Oh, no, nothing in writing. The negotiations went on for most of one day. Finally Lew told the man from the Cultural Affairs Department that without a written agreement, without a guarantee, the company could not risk it.[5] As we were boarding our (this time) chartered return bus, Gurnam Singh Tir, who worked for the Tagore Theatre, apologized to John for all the confusion and bad feeling that had surrounded the performances in Chandigarh, saying finally: "If we'd known how good you were, we wouldn't have treated you so badly."[6]

Four days in New Delhi. The company received considerable attention from the press, with four newspapers reviewing the performances. The *Times of India* began its review with the delectable "The Merce Cunningham Dance Company danced for a Delhi audience at the Fine Arts Theatre on Thursday night and unless forcibly prevented will do so again on Friday night."[7] Four reviewers—even that one—considered the work seriously, and all were appreciative of the dancing and the dancers, and of Rauschenberg's contribution: "If you go to see the Merce Cunningham Dance Company, you have to be prepared to throw overboard most of your antiquated notions of what dance is. Let me add at once that it is fascinating, fantastic, and much of it downright beautiful—especially the movements of the bodies, superbly trained."[8] Once again John's music (and he was blamed for all of it, whether it was his or not) was sharply criticized, even denigrated.

These two performances seemed incidental, so inconsequential to the experience of India itself that I had given up writing about them in my journal. We were now hell-bent on being full-time tourists, at least those of us feeling well enough. It was Merce's turn to be ill. Although he missed no performances (has he ever?), he was too ill to attend the party given for the company by Ambassador and Mrs. Chester Bowles at Roosevelt House, the stunning contemporary embassy designed by Durell-Stone in 1954 and built around an atrium water garden with fountains and islands of plantings. We enjoyed the irony of this invitation. The United States government had consistently denied financial aid to the company, yet several times on the tour we were fêted by an American ambassador or cultural attaché without prompting from the State Department.

In New Delhi, John met the poet Octavio Paz, who was the Mexican ambassador to India, and Paz and his Indian wife, Marie-José, hosted a party for us in their home. This was the beginning of a much-valued friendship; Paz was one of those people like Buckminster Fuller, Norman O. Brown, Marcel Duchamp, and numerous others, who fed John's voraciously eclectic philosophical appetite.

One more month to go! Breakfast in Delhi, lunch in Calcutta, dinner in Bangkok, and, as if by magic, we found ourselves in a very different world.

David Vaughan informed us, in a typed announcement, of our next engagement:

> About Bangkok. Our visit there is becoming a very important event and our performance is now advertised as a **Royal Command Performance**. On arrival at the airport we will be met by TV, Radio, and Press. This will be a red carpet affair and they have politely suggested that we dress "in accordance with the importance of the occasion," meaning I suppose that gentlemen should get off the plane wearing ties and the ladies should not wear pants. As if you do. . . . But I think everyone might wear a smile. We will be decorated with leis and there no doubt will be interviews. Tiresome as it may be, after a long plane trip, the company is requested to submit to these formalities with at least their customary grace. dv

A certain amount of sarcasm can be detected. David was fully aware that the morale of the company had not improved much in the days since the Ahmedabad mutiny.

A Royal Command Performance for the king and queen of Thailand! Immediately we envisioned a classical Siamese theater—a king and queen resplendent in the royal box while a Siamese orchestra played an exotic national anthem . . . visions quickly dashed. The theater for our Command Performance was on the campus of Thammasat University and resembled an American high school auditorium. His and Her Royal Majesties sat not in a jewel-encrusted royal box, but simply in the balcony. The king had chosen this venue because it had air-conditioning. Elaborate protocol had to be followed to the letter: the audience must be seated by 8:30 p.m. and remain seated until the king and queen leave (if displeased, Their Royal Majesties might choose to leave at any moment); the performance must begin exactly five minutes after the king and queen arrive, when the Thai national anthem would be played—alas, a rather militaristic sounding, ghastly taped rendition screeching forth from an excruciatingly terrible public-address system.

When we arrived at the theater, Bob discovered that the light board, cables, lamps—everything!—had been taken down and returned to a rental agency, thanks to a communication snafu. To an inquiry about the company's lighting requirements, David Vaughan's response—"only ordinary lighting"—had been misunderstood to mean literally *ordinary lighting*, i.e., no theatrical lighting. Several panicky phone calls and much haste righted the error, and we were ready to perform upon command. We opened with *Story*. By dividing the stage horizontally with a scrim, Bob managed to create a quasi-dramatic, mysterious setting for the dance. On one side he installed a huge ladder; on the other, off to one side, an enormous metal rack, with bicycles, a long metal funnel, and lights. Against the back wall, he piled up miscellaneous junk. The dancing took place in front of and behind the scrim. There were to be no curtain calls until the end of the program; this was Merce's decision, because he wasn't quite sure how they should be done. The length of the intermissions was at the discretion of the king. We had to begin whenever His Majesty gave the command. *Septet, Untitled Solo,* and *Antic Meet* completed the program. The applause, from the disappointingly small audience, was not spirited. "Modern Ballet Did Not Invoke Responsive Chords" headlined the single English-language newspaper review, which began: "The Merce Cunningham Dance Company was honored . . . by the presence of Their Majesties the King and Queen, but the audience was less than enthusiastic and no doubt went away puzzled."[1]

But Their Majesties, if not enthusiastic, were most decidedly interested. All during *Antic Meet,* a highly agitated court functionary, standing in the wings backstage, would ask David Vaughan "Is it over, is it over?" after each segment of the dance, and no sooner did the curtain close than the scratchy national anthem blared forth again. Out in the auditorium, to Lew's utter astonishment, the entire audience—as one body—stood, turned its back on the stage to pay obeisance to the royal couple, quite decisively circumventing a full-company curtain call. Merce was immediately informed that the company was to be presented to the king and queen. Had they disliked the evening's entertainment, we were told, this honor would not have been bestowed. Given not a minute to change or even to wipe the perspiration from our faces, we were hustled out of the theater by guards, promenaded single file outside and around to the front of the building, through the exiting crowds who could not suppress their giggles at the sight of us wearing nothing but black tights and leotards. Who could blame them? How utterly ridiculous we felt! Three times we were lined up in the foyer at the foot of two merging staircases by several agitated attendants. First we were to face right, then rearranged to face left. Finally we were arranged in a phalanx: Merce at the point, Bob, Viola, myself, and John behind him, and rest of the company behind us.

If regal glamour was what we'd hoped for, it was provided in full measure by the exquisite, bejeweled Queen Sirikit, in a Pierre Balmain gown, her husband, King Bhumibol Adulyadej, at her side as they descended the staircase—she, bathing us all in her radiant smile; he, solemn and dignified as, I suppose, a king must be. Merce was introduced to them both, and he then introduced each one of us to them. A ludicrous scene: barefoot modern dancers in sweaty leotards curtseying or bowing, one by one, before resplendently attired royalty standing well above us on the landing. The king, born in Cambridge, Massachusetts, in 1927, educated in the West and a student of *le jazz hot,* was said to be a passionate musician, as well as an able poet and painter. In 1946, at the age of nineteen, he had succeeded to the throne after his cousin was murdered in his bed. Small wonder he looked so solemn! It was difficult to believe that this bespectacled young man was actually the grandson of that flamboyant king in *Anna and the King of Siam.* We were told that American music, especially jazz, was a serious interest for this king. With what seemed to be genuine curiosity, he asked Merce many questions and commented that the music was very new to his ears. Afterward, the court chamberlain rushed up to Merce to inquire, "What did he say to you? What did he say? Well, whatever he said, he meant it. Sometimes they only nod and leave."[2]

The queen presented each of the women dancers with a bouquet of orchids in tiny silver wicker baskets. While the king talked with Merce, Queen Sirikit stepped down two steps to converse with John, Viola, and me. She told us that she had seen much ballet, but had never seen modern dance and thought our work to be "an expression of today's modern world." She spoke of our "beautiful poses and postures," but confessed she did not understand most of the music. The royal couple were then escorted to their waiting limousine by guards who dropped to their knees before them, unsheathing their swords and raising them in salute. It was all a bit like a delightful Gilbert and Sullivan operetta and made us want to giggle.

We devoted our one free day in Bangkok to sightseeing. Some rushed to purchase Thai silks and have dresses or jackets made; unbelievably, they were delivered to our hotel by evening. The workmanship was impeccable.

And then, with only the tiniest taste of Thailand, it was time to hop another plane and prepare ourselves for one more change of cultures and customs.

The city of Tokyo—big, ugly, jazzy, chaotic, materialistic—appeared to be an unsavory mix of 1950s Times Square, Fourteenth Street, and Canal Street, with a touch of Detroit and L.A.'s Sunset Boulevard thrown in, all bubbling in a contemporary Japanese cultural stew. Even the guidebook said Tokyo was probably the ugliest city in the world. We arrived to a great hullabaloo, cameras clicking, flowers given to Merce and me. Toshi Ichiyanagi, Toshiro Mayuzumi, and many other Japanese composers were there to greet us—plus artists and theater people. Being domiciled at International House, a modest, quiet, inexpensive hostelry with a tranquil classical Japanese garden on the grounds, provided respite from the frantic pace of the city and the disheartening dissolution of company morale.

The Sogetsu Art Center and the daily newspaper *Yomiuri* cosponsored our performances in Tokyo. John's desire to attempt a world tour was, in fact, sparked by the art center's invitation to the company sometime in 1963. Its director was the filmmaker Hiroshi Teshigahara, whose film *Woman in the Dunes* had sent shock waves through the world of cinema that very year, and we were honored with a special showing of this strange, disturbing, powerfully moving film. Hiroshi's father, Sofu Teshigahara, was the founder of the Sogetsu School of Ikebana and the leading figure in the movement that had transformed traditional flower arrangement into a highly expressive art form. The center engaged the Cunningham company for four performances and sponsored a music event with Cage and Tudor (who were both already well known and respected in Tokyo) as well as an evening called "Twenty Questions for Bob Rauschenberg." It also helped arrange engagements for the company in Kobe and Osaka. The posters, brochures, mailers, and programs they designed for the company were the most beautiful provided us on this tour. We were in Japan for almost a month, but luckily for us burned-out dancers, though not for the company's financial well-being, the performance schedule included only six performances, plus an open dress rehearsal at one o'clock on the day after we arrived.

The open rehearsal was a de facto unpaid full performance—in costume, makeup, and lighting—for about five hundred invited guests and fifty members of the press. This was a carefully organized publicity event, followed by a reception. There must have been fifty cameras clicking away throughout the performance. We had to suppress our amusement as crescendos of clicking cameras caught particularly pose-y moments.

Our first performance in Tokyo included *Aeon, Changeling, Cross Currents,* and *Story,* and was well received.

Cunningham is not to be missed. You will surely not be bored; you will be troubled perhaps, puzzled certainly, and entertained endlessly at his very fascinating performances. My one fear is that local imitators, will, like the recently departed Yoko Ono, mistake the seemingly haphazard but actually very controlled and technically demanding art for an invitation to bore us with longeurs, while they stand about the stage and wonder what to do next. Believe me, Merce Cunningham knows full well from one minute to the next what he is doing.[3]

Merce was not pleased with the first Tokyo performance of *Story,* complaining in his journal: "It was one of the performances of the piece that irritated me greatly. None of the dancers seemed at attention (after six months, what do you expect?) other than personal, and there was little instant connection between us. In fact, so little I angrily said: This is the last time I will ever present this piece. (It almost was.)"[4]

Although Viola, Merce, and I had some interesting and varied material in *Story,* the other dancers were restricted to a small, repetitive, pedestrian movement vocabulary that offered few technical or improvisatory challenges. While Bob could create an entirely different set every night, the dancers' creativity was limited to selecting the garments they would wear and to varying the time and space in some of their phrases. The possibilities were easily exhausted, and by the end of the tour, several of the dancers found *Story* tiresome. In fact, they *hated* it. Barbara Lloyd, out of boredom or just exploring a new possibility, "stripped to the buff" while Merce, Viola, and I did a trio section. Merce mentions the fact in his journal, but without judgment. Was he miffed? There was nothing sensational or exhibitionist about the way she did it. She simply faced upstage, disrobed and dressed again in a mundane, matter-of-fact way—rather in the spirit of a sixties Happening. Of course it did capture one's attention. The one person who *was* miffed was Barbara's husband. I recalled,

Barbara had arranged an elaborate Birthday Party for Lew in a Chinese restaurant. Everyone there. Lew never arrived. Barbara phoned hotel, returned to say Lew wasn't coming. SILENCE at the table. Then, people tried to make small talk. Barbara was very quiet, fighting back tears. Eventually she stood up, with saki cup in her hand and proposed a toast: "I would like to propose a toast to a man—[pause] who does not like to have his wife undress on stage, even though he did not see it." This was said very, very slowly and quietly with *great* dignity and style. Wow! What a beautiful performance. Really—I had tremendous admiration for [her in] that moment.

Merce scheduled class and rehearsal daily. Throughout the tour he honorably maintained this discipline. But as pressures and exhaustion intensified, he neither *really* taught nor *really* rehearsed us, so it often seemed a waste of our energy and his. The demands on him were inhuman (if self-inflicted), yet he never missed a performance, and there were nearly seventy of them. As usual, his problem was his inability to communicate authentically with his dancers, to say what was really on his mind.

At one rehearsal, on a non-performance day in Tokyo, Merce asked each of us to do our individual slow phrases in *Story* (the phrase might take a minute, give or take a few seconds), and to do them as slowly as we could. Oh, man! Was *that* ever asking for trouble! Give Steve Paxton such a challenge and he will meet it in spades. We took turns while Merce sat with his stopwatch, notebook, and pen, merely noting the time. Time was all that seemed to matter to him. Of course not one of us attempted to follow Merce's direction literally, until it was Steve's turn. As usual, Merce said nothing. No comment, no correction. After fifteen minutes or so, the rest of us began drifting out of the studio, into the hallway. It had become increasingly awkward and embarrassing. One half hour later, Steve—with excruciatingly *slow* deliberation (he was terrific)—was still moving while Merce sat, stoically, studying his notebook. He did not stop Steve, he just stopped watching him. Neither man would capitulate, or acknowledge the ludicrousness of the situation. If we hadn't been squirming with discomfort, we would have been howling with laughter. Years later, Steve explained that he'd been ill and was glad Merce hadn't asked us to do the phrase as fast as possible, because it still would have taken him a half hour.

As Cage discovered time and time again with his own compositions, there are dangers in giving performers freedoms. But despite musicians who interpreted "freedom" as "license" and chose to make fun of the music or fools of themselves, John continued to make music that was indeterminate with respect to its performance. His commitment to this idea was philosophical and unwaveringly optimistic, as was his hope that performers would respect the work and act nobly. Merce came to indeterminacy reluctantly, and he never truly believed in its practicality for dance. I suspect he did not trust the dancers, and more importantly, giving up control of the structure, of time and space, was against his nature.

Immediately following the second Tokyo performance, which had a completely different program, we dashed from the theater to catch a 10 p.m. plane to Osaka. A bus took us from there to a lovely hotel in Kobe, where we performed still another program the following evening. Between Kobe and our engagement in Osaka, we had a whirlwind three days of sightseeing and an introduction to historical Japan. In Nara, the first capital of Japan (A.D. 710–748), Hiroshi Teshigahara arranged for us all to attend a special performance of Bugaku in the white-pebbled garden courtyard of Kasuga Taisha, the largest Shinto shrine in Nara. That evening we made a pilgrimage to a monastery up in the hills above Nara to witness a ritual Buddhist ceremony, which began with a dirgelike procession of robed monks chanting (the best part), followed by a staggering two and a half hours of inscrutable droning. We sat on hard, backless wooden benches in the open-air temple; it was dark, miserably cold, and damp. No amount of innate curiosity could quell our overwhelming desire to be released from this torture and to climb into warm beds. Nor did any amount of droning or incense or fitfully flickering candlelight awaken even a nanosecond of spiritual illumination. "What strange things man does in the name of religion," I wrote to my parents. "Surely Buddha NEVER had this sort of ritual in mind!"

Unenlightened, shivering, and tired, we trudged down to the train station. After two and a half hours via train and taxi we finally arrived, dead on our feet, at the Mt. Hiei Hotel, high in the mountains overlooking Kyoto and a vast lake. When morning dawned, we looked out on a roiling sea of mist and clouds. The sky seemed to change every fifteen minutes, the landscape to shift with the sky. *This* and the Zen gardens in Kyoto were, for me, the true spiritual essence of Japan, together with the theater arts of Kabuki, Bunraku, Bugaku, and Noh.

Sightseeing had to be disrupted for our own performance in Osaka. In both Kobe and Osaka we performed on vast stages, the widest of any on the tour. By some miracle, not credited to us dancers apparently, Merce was delighted with the *Story* performance. He wrote: "Marvelous! Why? Due to music? The Japanese musicians are marvelous. Their attention in everything is noticeable (as is that of the Japanese public . . .) but particularly with Toshi's *Sapporo*, the quality is first-rate, and to my ear magical. The Osaka experience was what I had in mind in making *Story*, the whole a grave field, on which all the elements, clowning, serious, inert and trivial, can happen."[5]

The most dramatic, extravagant social occasion of our stay was the evening on which Sofu Teshigahara invited us to one of the finest geisha houses in Tokyo; an evening which, to quote Lew Lloyd, "the feminists in the company found a hideous experience and which the men enjoyed immensely."[6] We were seated around the outside of a huge U in a very large rectangular room. Merce and John sat with Sofu and Hiroshi and other dignitaries at the head of the table. At the open end of the U, one of the greatest traditional (and quite ancient) geishas of the day performed for us. That part was fascinating. We were the only women guests at this gathering: the Japanese men, and there were many of them, had come without their wives. A half-dozen or more modern geishas served us, subserviently scuttling about on their knees, bowing each and every time they presented us with anything. Of course it was an ancient ritual, interesting in a historical context, but to take part in it was unsettling. The most deeply affected was Barbara, who broke into tears and fled the room, sobbing. She did not return. However, on the evening that the company was invited to Sofu's home for dinner and the gentlemen were invited to view his collection of Japanese erotica, Barbara joined the men—perhaps to take a stand or make a statement about the equality of the sexes? Viola and I avoided the evening altogether.

Japanese society, Japanese cultural mores (in my admittedly superficial understanding of them), evoked none of the overwhelming awe I'd felt in India. Quite the opposite. The excessive politeness, the exaggerated formality, the bowing and scraping, the forced smiles, the subservient geishas, the rigid social rituals dripping (in my view) with hypocrisy, and the thin societal veneer—all were anathema to me. What was really going on behind those masks of intense civility? By the end of our visit I fully realized that I understood nothing. The culture remained utterly impenetrable. Of course, I probably understood very little of Indian culture, either, but while impenetrable Japan repelled, tumultuous India enthralled.

Whatever antipathy I felt toward Japanese social life, it certainly did not extend to its arts. Kabuki and the Bunraku puppet theater were compelling theater experiences. Twice, I went with Merce and David Vaughan to see the Kabuki in Tokyo. The first time, with a break for dinner, we were in the theater from 4:30 in the afternoon well into the evening and were completely captivated. The second time was the afternoon of a performance day. Only once before had we done this, when we attended the first act of Peter Brook's *Marat/Sade* in London. But we could not miss the opportunity to see Utaemon, considered the greatest Kabuki *onnagata* (female impersonator) of his or perhaps any generation, playing a demented, vengeful former court lady reduced to living in a hut by the seashore with huge crabs, said to be the angry spirits of defeated warriors. With those images in our minds, we dashed off to Sankei Hall to give our final performance of the world tour and, for all we knew, the final performance of Merce Cunningham and Dance Company.

In our last two performances, we did eight of the dances from the repertory. We opened the first with the killer *Rune,* and, unbelievably, it went well, according to Merce's journal: "Despite the imminent collapse with the approaching end of the immense journey, and even the grand fatigue . . . the dance rose well, almost spendidly, having a good deal of its original lean sharpness and elegance. It was a great personal pleasure to me that we managed such a feat at this point in time and relations."[7]

The following morning, Thursday, November 26, the company met formally for the last time. My journal account: "Merce thanked us all—said he realized it had been very difficult, but thought we had managed very well, and that on the whole we had danced very well, some of us brilliantly. Then he said he didn't plan to start work again until February and he'd like to know our plans by December 15. When Lew Lloyd asked if he should tell the Company the spring plans, Merce said 'No.' "

Merce, in his journal, revealed his own discomfort in that meeting:

> I wished to find some way to convey to them that I thought they had been superb and remarkable. Despite the monstrous difficulties and our disastrous relationship (or my impression of that) on this long tour (there were almost seventy performances and I managed them all) they had been a brilliant company . . . but how to tell them, as whatever I said seemed only to aggravate the scene further. So I spoke little, prepared for all of them to say they wouldn't be continuing to dance with me. It is not unusual after such long and exhausting tours for personnel to leave, but it is when it happens to you.[8]

Immediately after the meeting, Debby and Alex told Merce they were leaving; Merce never considered them true members of the company, so this was not a wounding blow. To his surprise, the only other person to resign that day was Bill Davis. Most of what happened next, and in what order, I was not privy to. My journal entries make no mention of our final performance. What more was there to record? Instead, I focused on the disintegration of the company and Bob's extracurricular activities in Tokyo, which were still further irritants to Cage/Cunningham/Rauschenberg relations.

The evening billed as "Twenty Questions for Robert Rauschenberg" turned out to be the turning point for Bob in his relations with Merce and John. It consisted of Bob making a combine painting on a gold-leaf screen given to him by Sofu Teshigahara for this purpose. Drink in hand, Bob worked nonstop from 6:30 p.m. until 10:30 p.m. Alex, Debby, and Steve assisted him. Questions were asked. Bob worked. And drank. For four hours. No verbal answers were given.

Merce and John arrived late. Viola left early. After five minutes, Merce left, then returned in about an hour. No one knew why. Shortly upon his return, both he and John left. David Vaughan, Barbara, and Lew left early. Bill and Al didn't go. Only David Tudor from the company went backstage. The deepest hurt was learning that Merce and John had arrived late and had left early. After the event Bob got very drunk and wrote Merce and John a letter:

> dear john and merce
>   i am not going to work with the company anymore.
>   it was so nice of you to share last nite with me in such a friendly way.
>   thanks bob[9]

Here was another instance when Merce's secretive behavior was not explained (to most of us) until the publication of his 1964 journal in *Dance Ink* some thirty years later:

> We arrived at Sogetsu Hall after RR's program had begun. As I arrived, Viola was leaving on her way to the International House for dinner and then the airport for the plane to San Francisco. I said goodbye to her; she said she wanted to talk with me—"This wasn't the time"—and she left. I went into the auditorium . . . I sat for about five minutes dwelling on VF and then got up and left, to taxi back to International House, rushed to find her at dinner before taking the airport bus. It was a sad talk, the end, but I could not have her, after this six-month odyssey, leave in a bus for a plane to San Francisco without anyone to say thank-you and good-bye. She left and I returned to Sogetsu . . . my head thick with VF; when John suggested leaving, I docilely agreed (it was impolite), and we left the hall.[10]

I did not attend Bob's evening because I went to still another Kabuki performance—an unusual one by a woman Kabuki artist—which was spellbinding. It was so good that I couldn't bear to leave. I had often witnessed Bob painting in his own studio—a joyful experience—but seeing Kabuki in its own ambience, an opportunity I might never have again, was how I rationalized what I feared Bob might read as a betrayal of my loyalty to him. In any case, Bob was so very unhappy about having to do the lecture, and so nervous about the prospect of it, I didn't *want* to go. Bob understood. He took me to see the finished painting the next day and told me that he'd written Merce a sarcastic letter, quitting. He was distraught. We both were. The combine painting, entitled *Gold Standard,* which today would probably finance the cost of twenty or more 1964 world tours, resides at the Sogetsu Art Museum.

Both Merce (politely) and John (impolitely) responded to Bob's resignation note. In a touching follow-up letter, Bob responded to Merce's letter, apologizing for his rudeness, expressing his gratitude and desire to be Merce's friend and fan, and ending with "I hope to look you in the eye with good conscience & love, if I haven't screwed that possibility up. thank you for this great tour."[11]

The closely woven fabric of aesthetic belief, mutual respect, and family loyalty that had held the company together throughout the exhilaration and the exhaustion, the ups and downs of this remarkable six-month odyssey, finally unraveled completely in Japan. Each of us experienced this unhappy denouement differently. As Lew Lloyd put it, "The reasons were very complex, as complex as the fifteen personalities involved."

On our first day in Tokyo, John spoke privately with David Tudor and me, expressing his agonized concerns about the company. I reported some of this in a letter to Earle:

[John] is drunkenly happy to be in Japan but he's terribly upset about his life, the state of the company, his own relationship with Merce which he says he fears is irreparably damaged, with my unhappiness with the state of the company, his friendship with Bob which he thinks he ruined, his mother with whom he thinks he must now live (she broke 4 bones in her shoulder when she fell down after being attacked by a dog), *ad infinitum* of gloom. Poor guy is really in a very, very bad state. In India, he kept talking about moving there. Now in Japan, he's talking about moving here.

Plunging John even further into misery, David Tudor told him that the rotten state of the company had been brought about by John's constant meddling, his defending Merce at all costs while trying to make everyone happy and everything right.

But perhaps the most desolate and depressed of all of us was Merce himself, although he gave no inkling of this to his dancers. My letters to Earle were full of melodrama, but the pain was genuine: "God knows the future of us all—I sometimes wake up in the middle of the night—filled with emptiness and despair—my life has led to where? no husband [conversations with Earle in Venice in June seemed to indicate that the future of our marriage was also in doubt]—no place to work with devotion and love and respect. what to do? where to go?"

I had no intention of making any decision until brain and body were completely rested. Disappointment, despair, and anger had annihilated any rational thought. The only decision I did make was to swear I would not dance again until I really missed it, until I really *wanted* to dance, and if I didn't miss it, then my answer would be self-evident.

Sadly for us all, our extraordinary and courageous adventure came to its exhausted end—less in Japan than in disillusionment—with a few broken hearts, mine among them. Yet what had been achieved was monumental. Merce Cunningham and Dance Company would not only survive, it would prevail. Neither Merce nor John was a quitter. Faced with adversity and change, Merce proved perpetually resilient. Fully forty years later he would still be breaking new ground, traveling the world with his company, but never again—wisely—for six months at a time.

A despondent and weary band headed homeward—singly, in pairs, or in small groups. Merce, admittedly miserable, went alone to Hawaii for three days, where he wrote two letters to John: the first saying he saw no reason to continue with so much unpleasantness and animosity around; the second saying he would come back and start again with whoever and whatever there was.[1] Classic Cunningham behavior: when all seemed lost, Merce would threaten to throw in the towel, sending everyone—especially John—into a tailspin, but, on second consideration, if a choice was available, he would not give up, no matter how discouraged. After spending barely a half-day in Centralia to say hello to his mother, he whisked his badly beaten body and unsteady mind to New York with every intention of somehow carrying on.[2]

In a hotel near the airport, my parents awaited my New York arrival. Next day they whisked my not-nearly-so-badly-beaten body but equally unsteady mind to Massachusetts, where I remained for six weeks, a week of rest for each month of touring. Until my internal clock adjusted, I slept the days away and prowled about the house in the middle of the night pondering what I should do; what, in the end, truly mattered to me. With my mother, I discussed the anger and disappointment that had so crushed the company at tour's end. With infinite wisdom, she exposed my criticisms and hostility to some much-needed light and air. "You all wanted too much from Merce," she admonished. "How could he possibly fulfill your expectations with all the responsibilities he had thrust upon him?" It was clear where her sympathy lay; she allied herself with Merce and delivered a wake-up call to me.

In early December, I received a phone call from a very concerned Jasper Johns. He had returned only the day before from London, having attended the opening of his one-man exhibition at the Whitechapel Gallery, and already he'd heard about the company's calamitous state of affairs from John: at least six members had quit, and there was unsubstantiated news that Viola intended to leave and that I might, too. Jasper asked to hear my version of what had gone so terribly wrong between Bob, John, and Merce. I told him that I believed the problem could be directly traced to the Venice Biennale and the beginnings of Rauschenberg's international fame. From an interview Cage gave years later, I learned that John was in agreement with this view, but for slightly different reasons. He, too, placed the first seeds of discord in Venice when Bob won the *Grand Prix*. John's distress originated with a remark of Bob's—"The Merce Cunningham Dance Company is my biggest canvas"—that was quoted in a newspaper. If accurately reported, Bob's choice of words was indeed unfortunate, but I do think John chose to misinterpret that statement when he said, "I didn't think it was proper for Bob to say that. In all my connection with Merce, I have given him the stage and I have stayed in the curtains. Bob didn't do that."[3]

John famously mixed metaphors, often to hilarious effect. "I have given Merce the stage . . . I have stayed in the curtains," conjures up an amusing picture but I suspect what John meant to say was "stayed in the wings." I wonder if he heard himself say "I *have given*." Who was this lordly "I"? No more or less lordly than Rauschenberg, I'm thinking. In any case, I believe John deceived himself: he got *his* attention from the orchestra pit—aurally—so one might contend that for many years the Merce Cunningham Dance Company was actually *his* biggest canvas as well, although he might not have wanted to admit it.

My version of events in Venice differed slightly from John's: I believe that a perfectly understandable poisonous drop of green envy had begun eating its insidious way into fragile egos, both John's and Merce's. Inevitably, after winning the *Grand Prix,* Bob became a magnet for the paparazzi, and in the rush to hear Bob's latest bon mot, interviewers all but ignored Merce and John. Combine this with the overwhelming stress Merce faced daily for six months, his inability to communicate with anyone, even John, plus the pressures on John and Lew to keep the company financially afloat, and one has a sure recipe for disaster. The fact that Bob had more than once rescued the company from bankruptcy with his own funds further complicated their relationship. ("Neither a borrower nor a lender be . . .") The damage was done and appeared irrevocable, but the dissolution of the company was unacceptable to Jasper. Immediately he set out to find a remedy.

Eventually, after letters to and from Earle and talks with my mother, I wrote to Merce and mailed a copy to John. I wanted to enter into a dialog with them in order to understand their thoughts and feelings, as well as my own. John was the first to answer with three typewritten pages [excerpt below]:

> Thank you for sending letter . . . Your having the time to rest and ponder is quite different from Merce's and my situation. *[Upon reading the rest of this paragraph I blushed with shame.]* The moment I arrived I fell into my mother's problems (2 days) (nearly did me in) and late the second night was advised by Lew that the bank account was $1800 overdrawn and I'd have to cover it by the next afternoon at 3. By that time it was $2200 overdrawn. But I managed with the money that was supposed to be for a car to settle matters. The Williams are still of no heart to help. I still have the problem . . . of raising money in order to pay the final payroll taxes. Add these problems (mother, money raising) to the fact that I have to write an article abt. Modern Japanese music (finished, Thank the Lord!), try to resurrect the mushroom society from what Lois thought was ruins (succeeded, Thank the Lord No. 2!), write two new lectures promised for California (not started yet) and deal with Merce's problems to help him. I forget what day he arrived, but the electricity in the studio had been somehow cut off. It took a whole day—both of us nearly frozen stiff—to get it fixed. Merce's knee is still not up to par. And the studio is in bad shape. The ceiling nothing but peeling paint, the floor covered with soot, no hot water, the dismal stairway. It's difficult.[4]

While I rested and ruminated in the warm embrace of loving parents, dear John, as usual, was desperately trying to put the world in order. My three-page typewritten letter—an attempt to present my view of what had gone wrong, why it had, and where to place the blame—had only added to his problems. Although it was cheeky of me, both John and Merce seriously considered and responded to each point I had made, whether they agreed or disagreed. Merce wrote three times—first with a brief typewritten note: "Thank you for your letter. Perhaps that is odd to say considering its contents, but you have spent much time and thought with concern about what we have been about, and I am grateful to you for it. I am unable to answer you immediately, partly due to my wish to think about it, and also due to a sudden attack of chills and fever, pysosomatic [*sic*], which has put me out."[5]

About a week later he sent a two-page typewritten letter; two days after that, I received a handwritten letter with dates of upcoming projects and performances. In their separate ways, John and Merce disagreed with both my question ("Isn't it wasteful?" which referred to my utter dismay at the disintegration of the company after such a "triumphant world tour") and my answer ("This particular ending is ignoble and pathetic—it is wasteful and stupid and sad"). John didn't think the question was a proper one because we'd done the tour and now there were other things to do; Merce replied, "I disagree quite completely with you that it was wasteful. We had six months of successful performances around the world. What is wasteful?"

They missed the gist of what I was attempting to say. I meant simply that we'd developed into a fine, strong professional dance company and that personality problems and lack of communication had brought about its dissolution. Of course the tour itself was not wasteful, but it seemed to me that by its end we had squandered something very precious—the flowering of an extensive repertory, devotion to the work and to one another. Now, if Merce wished to continue, he might have to start over again with a mostly new company.

My six-week rest in Massachusetts was not untroubled; my father's cancer had returned and my mother was worn with worry. On Christmas Day, I caught a glimpse of my father—present yet removed—taking in the family scene around the Christmas tree, as though seeing us from a great distance for the last time. An anguished presentiment warned me that this would be his last Christmas with us, and by the look in his eyes I believed this was his presentiment as well. Still, he was in good spirits, cheerful, much like his usual self and going to work every day. It was time for me to go to work, too, at whatever it was going to be. I'd managed to save more than eight hundred dollars on the tour, I'd be able to collect unemployment insurance, and with a teaching job lined up at the Boston Dance Circle starting in March, I felt I'd be financially fine for a while.

What a joy it was to be back in Miss Craske's classes at the Met, and to be fully engaged in Merce's classes, which were rigorous and challenging. Yes, I *did* want to dance again! Hallelujah! I don't know when exactly I made the decision; I do remember that I decided to make a professional commitment to dancing that would no longer be predicated on the pleasures of the company as family. Those I'd felt closest to in the twelve preceding years were, with the exception of John, now gone. Within another four months, Viola Farber would leave as well.

On the last day of January, Jasper attempted a reconciliation between Bob, Merce, and John. The meeting was not a success. I heard only Bob's version, which I relayed to Earle: "It was really awful. John accusing him of all manner of things . . . and telling him that he, John, *let* Bob take over the leadership of the company, and that the reason the company was so attracted to Bob, was because he was a glamorous figure and a monetary success! How about that for insulting both Bob and us! Anyway, Bob has really had it with John. He says he doesn't think John is a very nice person."

Decades later, Jasper told me that their meeting was indeed awful, and he wondered how people who had been such close good friends for so long could have come to such a sorry ending. I, too, met with John and Merce to discuss the situation. This time John accused Bob of alienating our affections by buying them through his generosity. My response was that Bob couldn't be blamed for his success or for wanting to share it with those he loved. "In any case," I said, "you and Merce had abdicated your leadership roles and Bob just stepped in to fill the vacuum. What you're saying is demeaning to Bob, but it's truly insulting to us dancers." Merce turned to John and said wryly, "I told you you'd put your foot in your mouth!" Alas, there was to be no reconciliation, and an era of brilliant, freewheeling collaboration came, in this saddest of ways, to an end. Bob was devastated and bitter; John, chastened and miserable; Merce, silent and guarded. Not until 1977 would Bob design for the company again, and not until after John's death, in 1992, would Bob and Merce really renew their collaborative friendship.

At first, I felt uncomfortable with Merce, but any awkwardness wore off once rehearsals began. By February 3, we were rehearsing every day, including weekends. The company now consisted of Merce, Viola, Barbara, Sandra, Albert, and myself. The only new member was Gus Solomons jr., but in many respects it felt like a totally different company because all Steve Paxton's and Bill Davis's parts had to be taught to Albert and Gus, significantly altering the dynamics among the dancers. From mid-February through mid-April of 1965, the company hopscotched about the country to give eleven performances, dancing a repertory of eight dances. In addition, two performances of *Winterbranch* and *Summerspace* were given at the the New York State Theatre in mixed-bill programs with other modern-dance companies.

There was no new choreography until the summer, after Viola left. Her last performance was on April 14 at the Music Hall in Houston, Texas, where we performed, on its vast, glorious stage, a program that the *Houston Post* described "as a three-stage escalator to hell," and the music as "bitter and devastating mechanical maelstrom."[6] With Viola's departure, Merce dropped *Crises, Paired,* and *Cross Currents* from the repertory.

With Viola's departure from the company, an unspoken tension went with her. Often ill or injured and thus, not surprisingly, the moodiest among us, she could cause considerable anxiety in the company. Several times at the last minute Merce had to replace her, which meant juggling roles and extra rehearsals. Although highly intelligent, Viola had a prickly, volatile nature, with mood swings ranging from sunny radiance to deepest gloom. One day she could be ebullient, bright, fun, and funny; the next day, a spoiler, casting a pall over everything. One never knew what to expect. Before Viola arrived at rehearsal one day, Marianne said to me, "I will no longer allow her mood to ruin mine," but as Miss Craske once commented, Viola had a lot of stored-up anger she needed to vent. As peers (sharing special billing beginning in 1963), we were inevitably compared, even though our dancing and stage personalities were completely different. Were we friends? Yes, although not close ones. I do think Viola resented me, whereas I experienced a troubling insecurity in relation to her. I knew perfectly well what it was: because Bob and Jasper so clearly adored both her and her dancing, I always felt they thought she was the *really interesting* dancer while I was merely the *conventional balletic* one. Without question, her dancing *was* unique and idiosyncratic. And irreplaceable.

The Cunningham company was one of five modern-dance companies in the Hunter Playhouse Inaugural Dance Series; the others were those of José Limón, Alvin Ailey, Paul Taylor, and Pearl Lang. Our single performance on February 12 was sold out; a second was added, and when that one quickly sold out as well, we were booked for a third. Compliments lavished on the company by Walter Terry and Allen Hughes for these Hunter performances left us ill-prepared for their indignation just one month later after we danced *Winterbranch* at the New York State Theatre. How radically different were their responses from those of most critics elsewhere in the world! At the State Theatre, *Winterbranch* shared a program with Sophie Maslow's *The Village I Knew* (1951), Anna Sokolow's *Ballade* (1964), and Doris Humphrey's *Passacaglia and Fugue in C Minor* (1938). *Winterbranch*, unleashed among these civilized examples of modern dance, horrified much of the audience as thoroughly as if an army of aliens had been catapulted into their midst. I recounted:

> State Theatre programs were an absolute gas! That is, I had a glorious time!!! God, what intoxication it is to perform in a theatre like that. The space is so marvelously HUGE, it makes me giddy with delight. . . . The reception for *Winterbranch* was wild! The audience carried on throughout the whole piece, laughing, hissing, booing, coughing, shushing others, etc. Really extraordinary! When it was over, and we took curtain calls, I felt like some member of a tiny minority group that the whole world hated and was

booing ... we ran on stage—the six of us—as though electrified with strength, defiance, courage, and belief in what we were doing ... and the people shrieked, booed and hissed. And other people cheered and bravoed. Valda said there was more energy in the way we took our bows, than the dancers in the other pieces displayed all evening! Over 2,500 people stirred up to fever pitch, and apparently talked of nothing else all evening. Gus Solomons came off stage saying, "God, this is exciting." Honestly, it was an experience of a life time! A stranger came up to Viola, Al Reid and me in the subway, and asked us to tell Merce that he thought him courageous and brilliant.

When our little band of six—sweatsuit-clad, dirty-sneaker-footed, black-cheekbone-smudged—charged onto the stage to take our bows, total pandemonium did indeed break loose: boos, catcalls, and roars of derision. But neither Terry nor Hughes reported the equally vociferous opposing response: roars of bravos and cheers. Walter Terry: "Merce the Merciless," "Brash, boisterous guest," "had an audience howling in protest," "pitiful puerility," "childish, self-indulgent prank," "perilously close to sadism," "irresponsible," "outraged and tortured the majority of those present." Allen Hughes dispensed with *Winterbranch* as "a stale and bad joke that does disservice to Mr. Cunningham, his company and dance itself,"[7] and in a Sunday column commented on "the victimized spectators" as "unwitting participants in an action over which they had no control."[8]

At my typewriter I banged out rebuttals to both Terry and Hughes, defending Merce's work, chastising them for not having more insight and sensitivity, and quoting critics from abroad. Terry referred to it in a later article; Hughes responded, rather defensively I thought, with a letter laying out rules and regulations for what is and is not acceptable in the theater. When did any art remain for long stifled by "rules and regulations"? Had both these men forgotten Balanchine's *Opus 34*, first performed in 1954 at City Center, an extraordinary two-part work, unique in Balanchine's oeuvre? In the second section, for which Balanchine offered key words—*threat, danger, fear, catastrophe*[9] (all might equally be applied to *Winterbranch*)—Jean Rosenthal used far more aggressive lighting than anything in *Winterbranch,* focusing large klieg lights directly into the auditorium from the rear of the stage floor, totally blinding the audience. The Schoenberg music had been played twice for the two distinctly separate versions of the ballet. To quote *The Dance Encyclopedia,* "The use of the same music for two entirely unrelated, complete works, reduces to absurdity the idea that music and dance actually have any relation one to the other."[10] Sound familiar?

There's an ironic twist to this: the lighting for *Winterbranch* at the State Theatre was devised by chance procedures, something Rauschenberg never did. And Bob never blinded our audiences. He did shine lights into the auditorium, panning the ceiling, the walls, and across the audience itself—following Merce's suggestion that the lights should be like automobile headlights on a road at night, randomly illuminating the landscape, animals, buildings—but Bob's lighting was never perceived as aggressive or hostile. Since he chose to do something different for each performance, often using handheld instruments, even flashlights, there was no lighting plot to hand over to Tom Skelton, who was the director of lighting for the State Theatre performances. John attempted to solve the problem by telling Skelton to collect a number of random lighting options and arrive at an order using chance procedures. When John witnessed the results his suggestion had brought about, he was aghast. The lighting was modified for the second performance. With *Summerspace*, Merce was once again in the two critics' good graces, but neither could resist delivering further scolding.

March 18. A letter arrived in the mailbox with fabulous news: Earle had won a Guggenheim Fellowship! On his *eleventh* try! Meanwhile, John was facing serious money problems. In February, his mother suffered a stroke and was paralyzed on her right side. He told me that he had just begun to feel creative after recovering from the ordeal of the world tour, but after his mother was stricken, all his time and energy were spent worrying about her and raising or earning money. The nursing home he found cost forty-two dollars a day. That's all he could think or talk about other than a Jaguar sports car that Jasper had given him, which made him ecstatically happy.

In January, Steve Paxton and Alan Solomon (curator of the previous year's American art exhibit at the Venice Biennale) had begun organizing a ten-day theater rally and invited dancers and artists to create work for it. "Would you like to make something?" asked Steve. I responded with a hesitant yes, determined to stretch myself. In Rauschenberg's words, "If you're an artist it's very important to be willing and able to make a fool of yourself at any moment."[11] Question: was I an artist? Instantly I was overcome with massive self-doubt. A postcard to Earle cried out for help. His answer provided the needed kick in the pants: "Don't clutch up with all that *WHY* shit . . . commit yourself to yourself (taste, style, and all) and just make a dance . . . not important if it is classical ballet or an 'avant-gardy' thingamagig . . . just important that you have given yourself to it as completely and responsively as you can... *at that moment*... It is always *totally* honest (and an obligation) *to try!*"[12]

I opted for making a tender man/woman duet for Steve Paxton and Barbara Lloyd, choreographically neither particularly balletic nor "avant-gardy." The music was Earle's *Times Five.* Any avant-garde element in the dance (called *Balloon*) was due to a giant thirty-foot weather balloon that descended majestically (I thought) from the flies and served as a screen for contemporary newsreels (President Johnson, Lee Harvey Oswald, Nikita Khrushchev among the images) projected from the downstage corners of the performance space. I had purchased three balloons from an army/navy surplus store. They were incredibly fragile; it took four days to fully inflate one with air from a vacuum cleaner. The first broke, with ensuing panic on my part, so Jennifer Tipton, the lighting designer for the program, had one partially inflated should there be another disaster. I bought three more as spares just in case. Dancing in the huge television studio in front of the larger-than-life images, occasionally casting their own tiny reflections on the giant balloon, Barbara and Steve appeared small, vulnerable, and touchingly human.

Most of the Judson gang and Happening artists said not one word to me about the work; worse, Jill Johnston managed to insult me and dancers in general by deciding that a mere dancer couldn't have conceived such an idea, and she assumed the set (balloon/film) was Rauschenberg's creation. But Jonas Mekas, in *The Village Voice,* called it a "striking use of cinema,"[13] and Grace Glueck in the *New York Times* wrote that "a highlight of the program was the opening number, 'Balloon,' and reported hearing a spectator describe Barbara and Steve as "the Lee Remick and Paul Newman of the avant garde."[14]

The money to finance the First New York Theatre Rally came from Rauschenberg. What a difference between the fortunes of us dancers and those of our artist friends, Bob and Jap. A *New York Times* article headline asked: "Are contemporary art prices on the rise?" The answer was a resounding yes, and Rauschenberg topped the list of contemporary artists. In 1961 the price of a new painting by Bob was $4,500; in 1964, $75,000. While still on the world tour, Bob had wired Tony Holder in New York, instructing him to destroy all the silkscreens Bob had used in producing his paintings since 1963 as well as any unfinished work lying around the studio.[15] "You have to keep moving," he said. Totally beguiled by theater-as-community, he'd begun looking for a building to serve as a kind of experimental arts center for himself and his artist friends. But that dream was still in the future. This first rally included seven evenings in three different venues: Judson Church, Al Roon's Health Club in Hotel Riverside Plaza, and the former CBS television studio at Eighty-first and Broadway. At the third dance evening in the CBS studio, Rauschenberg and I performed his *Pelican,* with Alex Hay skating in place of Per Olaf Ultvedt. For the literal-minded among the audience, the so-called Dance Concerts might more properly have been described as a series of mini-Happenings, with only a few works conventionally classifiable as "dance."

In March I'd received a phone call from Ray Johnson—the enigmatic, eccentric, lovable Ray Johnson—who wondered if I still had a tiny piece of the very large geometric oil painting he had been working on when first we met him in 1952, which he had subsequently cut into bits and mailed out to his "New York Correspondence School" friends. He'd agreed to have a show of his work at the Willard Gallery and wanted to put the painting back together. Since the beginning of our acquaintance, I'd kept a Ray file; I found the fragment. He seemed *very* nervous when he asked if he could have it back. I said, *of course.* He started acting as though I'd said no, telling me he'd given us so many things. I kept saying, "Ray, you can HAVE it! We're delighted that you're having a show." His answer: "Yes, I'm being very good." The exhibit opened on Tuesday, April 6, with many friends gathered to celebrate the occasion. Ray appeared in a baby-blue suede golf jacket, blue corduroy trousers, a blue shirt, a blue tie and blue canvas shoes (he'd dyed them himself). Richard and Louise Lippold hosted a party afterward at a Czech restaurant. Ray seemed to enjoy it all, in spite of himself.

But another Ray Johnson tale—curiously ominous in retrospect—involves a request, a year or two later, for the return of a painting I'd had since the Third Avenue loft days. This one, called *Bird Sitting on a Bottle Looking at the Moon,* was much harder to part with, but again, it had been a gift, so part with it I did. In August 1993, about sixteen months before Ray committed suicide by leaping off the Sag Harbor Cove Bridge and was last seen alive backstroking into the distance, an oval scrap of paper torn from the front of an envelope arrived in my mail. On it, roughly drawn in pencil, was the image of a bottle, a full moon above, and, to the right, these words below: "BIRD IN A Bottle Looking at the MOON 8.28.93." And indeed, he'd drawn a bird *in* the bottle and it appeared to be drowning. Some months later he phoned me simply to chat, as he did sporadically over the years after he moved out of New York City to Locust Valley. It was the last time we spoke. He was found floating on his back, with his arms laid across his chest, his face as peaceful as a Buddha's.

In May, Nancy LaSalle gave a party in her huge duplex apartment overlooking Central Park to which every ballet dancer in the Western world seemed to have been invited, with the curious exception of current members of Ballet Theatre. Three modern dancers were present: Merce, Paul Taylor, and me, although Paul insisted that Beatrice Lillie made it four. After supper, every imaginable form of liquor flowed. A marvelous orchestra played nonstop and the dancing—mostly the frug, watusi, monkey, swim—was eye-popping. Although the Brits were fabulous, best of all was Arthur Mitchell, moving with subtle, sinuous rhythms, utterly free and gloriously beautiful. Merce, in rare form, got happily tipsy and although he hadn't a clue how to dance those sixties dances any more than I did, danced with me, saying "It's easy!" as he shook and pranced about, absolutely delighted with everything.

Most meaningful for me was having the opportunity to converse with Fonteyn and Ashton. When I thanked Fonteyn for her beautiful performance of *Giselle* the night before, she responded, "Was it really all right? You know, when it goes well, it's as though it's not really me who has anything to do with it." Having been swept away by Ashton's *The Dream*, I told him so, which seemed to please him; later, when I expressed my concern about the performance demands put on Fonteyn, he replied, "I don't want to disillusion you, but she gets paid by the performance." Then Ashton added, "So does *he*, of course," meaning Nureyev.

When Merce and I finished dancing, Nureyev and some young man were sitting on the back of a couch talking. The couch was empty, so we sat on it and Merce talked to me about how no one at the party really understood what he did, people didn't understand about how difficult the music had made his life, but that he was stubborn. Suddenly he tapped Nureyev on the sleeve, and said, "Hello, you don't know who I am . . ." but Nureyev said, "Yes, I know you." A curious three-way lengthy conversation ensued. Merce was certainly a bit drunk, and admitted later that he purposely baited Nureyev, "to see what was in his head." Nureyev appeared displeased to learn that Merce had never seen him dance, except briefly in a pas de deux on television. Merce said he refused to stand in line for tickets. (If that was a hint, Nureyev ignored it.) When Merce extolled the virtues of Erik Bruhn's dancing, Nureyev's jaw tightened and his cheek twitched. His good-bye was very formal and sweet to me, but Merce had clearly irritated him. When Merce finally agreed to leave, it took another half hour because he spent fifteen minutes learning the watusi from Arthur Mitchell, then was waylaid by dozens of people as we moved to the door.

During Merce's June course I taught five classes a week. There had been no discussion about a summer rehearsal schedule, but one day after class, Merce began working on a new dance with Sandra and Barbara. I was feeling strangely bereft. Viola had definitely left the company, although Merce preferred to tell people she was on a leave of absence for the summer. I was the last of Merce's original Black Mountain group. "Wouldn't it be best to leave, too," I wondered, "so that Merce can have a fresh start with new people?" Lack of communication between Merce and his company persisted. It was only through Lew Lloyd that we discovered that Peter Saul, a Craske student and good friend of Viola's and mine, had been invited to join the company.

June, July, and August were anguished months for my family. I was traveling to Massachusetts as often as I could. My father was now desperately ill, in and out of the hospital, undergoing horrific treatments and blood transfusions. It was heartbreaking to see him so gaunt and weak. When Merce learned of this, he was very gentle and kind and I realized (once again!) that he hadn't meant to be indifferent before, he'd just been concerned with his own problems. After a knee X ray, he had been told he had to rest for a very long time, which of course he didn't do. One day he apologized for not rehearsing with me on something new, saying he didn't know what John was planning for the new dance.

That Merce didn't know how to proceed was not surprising, considering the nature of John's new piece, which he had been invited to compose for the New York Philharmonic French-American Festival in July. *Variations V* was to be the final work on a program that would include *Hyperprism* by Varèse, Boulez's *Improvisations sur Mallarmé, No. 2*, and Carter's *String Quartet No. 2*. John had posed this question: is there some means by which dancers' movements can activate sound? With David Tudor and others researching the question, he found some answers from Robert Moog, who created the Moog synthesizer, and Bill Klüver, a creative electrical engineer doing research at Bell Laboratories in New Jersey. The final concept with which Merce had to deal involved twelve four-foot-tall antennae placed around the stage. In order to trigger the sound, the dancers had to weave in, out, and around them, the interaction operating much like a theremin. Klüver's contribution consisted of "seeing eye" light-beam devices that responded to the shadows made when dancers crossed in front of them, thus activating sounds from radios, tape machines, etc. The big question, of course, was, would their devices work? The simple answer to that question turned out to be NO! After the expenditure of six thousand dollars on equipment and labor, hours and hours of setting up equipment, laying wires, plugging circuits, switching this and readjusting that, nothing functioned as intended. At our final stage rehearsal, the dancers were forced to wait for more than two hours while the jumbled chaotic mess onstage was cleared. I wrote at the time: "Lew Lloyd had to pay $1000 extra over-time to the stage hands. He is absolutely FURIOUS with John and David's ineptness. He said they should have figured out all the wiring on paper *before* coming into the hall . . . but no, they were doing it there—like high-school physics kids."

Non-dance activities by the dancers contributed another layer of sound: Merce disassembled a potted plastic plant that had a cartridge microphone attached to it; later on I reassembled the plant. As if tying on a bonnet, Barbara donned a small pillow with cartridge microphone inside, then stood on her head; Gus lifted her off the floor and swung her gently back and forth. Merce and Peter sat on metal chairs and shuffled about in them; they, too, were wired for sound, as was the bicycle that Merce rode at the end. All these sounds could be manipulated electronically by four musicians seated behind a low platform at the back of the stage under a twenty-foot-high white canvas that stretched across the entire back wall of Philharmonic Hall. The canvas served as a screen for films provided by Stan VanDerBeek, which incorporated distorted TV images by Nam June Paik. When the musicians stood, they became part of the film from the waist up. Add choreography to this mix and you've got something like a three-ring circus, all rings vying for the attention of the audience. Unlike most of the electronic music gadgetry, the visual components of *Variations V* worked beautifully and, indeed, stole the show. The huge multiple images on the screen dwarfed us. We felt superfluous at best and, with only two run-throughs onstage with the rods and wires, exceedingly cautious about negotiating the very new and often difficult choreography.

The dance ended with Merce onstage alone, riding a bicycle through the maze of antennae. When making his final exit at a rather fast pace, he was to grab a beam in the doorway and swing back and forth as the bike sailed off into the wings to be caught by Albert Reid. Blackout. However, at a rehearsal a few days before the performance the blackout occurred *before* Merce caught the beam. He reached for it, hollered as he sprawled midair in an arched position before landing flat on his back. People rushed across the stage to him. He just lay there. A terrifying moment. Eventually, he recovered his breath and asked the men dancers to help him stand. Despite extreme pain, a swollen hand, and a badly bruised hip and back, he performed marvelously and was in great spirits. But he didn't go to the post-performance party—too stiff to move, he said, and he could barely get into or out of the taxi that took him home. Next day, on the phone, he seemed very happy with the event, even though he hurt awfully.

Allen Hughes wrote in the *New York Times,* "It strikes me that Mr. Cage and Mr. Cunningham may have given us a fascinating, if extremely primitive glimpse into an extraordinary theater of the future."[16] *Variations V* entered the Cunningham repertory with the gadgetry ignored or overcome. What worked, worked. What didn't, didn't matter. The choreography offered interest on its own terms. If *Variations V* was "a primitive glimpse into an extraordinary theater of the future," that future lay far ahead. Merce's next work, *How to Pass, Kick, Fall and Run,* seemed sublimely simple in comparison: eight dancers wearing black tights, white ankle socks, and sweaters of their own choosing, plus one or two people sitting at a table downstage with stopwatches reading stories from John Cage's *Silence. How to . . . ,* as it was dubbed for brevity's sake, traveled well: it worked on any size stage or gymnasium; in or out of doors. It was a joyous, happy dance that remained in the repertory until I left the company seven years later. After thirty years, it went back into the repertory again.

My mother called to ask me to come home. I flew to Boston and remained there for a week, spending most of my time sitting quietly in the hospital room with my father, who was now so weak it was too much effort for him to open his eyes. Hearing a doctor briskly walking by—all confidence and virility—my father said, "How wonderful to be able to walk like that." Life, in the face of death, seemed almost vulgar. I felt ashamed of my strength and my healthy body sitting in that room, all my strength utterly useless to help him. On August 12, I had to return to New York on a seven a.m. bus to collect unemployment, rehearse, and teach a class. A telephone call from my mother at 4:30 the next morning once again summoned me home.

Friday the 13th was the anniversary of the day my parents first met, at a Black Cat Halloween Party. The seven a.m. bus didn't arrive in Fitchburg until noon. My brother, Parker, met the bus. His tears told me I was too late. Our beloved father had died at 5:55 a.m. Less than a week later I was back in New York to rehearse for a performance. Mourning postponed. Pain and anguish borne. I spent the next five weeks with my family.

Rehearsals resumed at the end of September and went into high gear in order to ready a repertory of ten dances for a weeklong season at the Harper Theater in Chicago in November. Viola did not return. Merce asked Valda Setterfield to join the company on a permanent basis. From the very beginning Valda had a riveting stage presence and an immaculate sense of rhythm. Unlike most of us, she had a unique way of communicating with Merce and seemed comfortable discussing whatever was on her mind. From my journal: "Merce is at work on a new dance and the whole company is very excited and happy about it . . . It's wild, fast for the most part—with intricate space, and in-and-out continuity—I love it."

This was *How to Pass, Kick, Fall and Run.* As its title implies, it has the high-energy leaps and jumps, runs and falls one sees in sports activities but without any literal reference to a particular sport. It was "dance-y," with interesting groupings, changes in dynamics, rhythmic variety. Chance procedures were used to chart entrances and exits, paths in space, speed, levels, numbers of dancers—the usual gamut of possibilities Merce tended to employ for group dances, but the phrasing, the inner rhythms, were not dictated. Much of the time, we could discover these for ourselves. What felt so different from previous dances constructed with chance procedures was the sense of liberation, which allowed exuberance, joyfulness, and pure fun. Even tenderness!

In one brief section, I circled Merce doing a series of quick low *developpé*—front, side, and back—until I faced him. Then the phrase slowed down incrementally as he joined me doing the same movements, except that when I extended my leg back in low arabesque, arching my back away from him, he extended his to fourth front, curving his torso toward me, and vice versa. All the while, our opposing arms curved front, side, back, as if to stroke and embrace our partner. Sensuality, tenderness—that's what I felt when Merce and I performed it. But when coaching the technically superb 2002 company in *How to . . .* , I couldn't understand why the movement itself did not tell the couples this. The moment looked wooden, unfelt, mechanical. So, contrary to protocol, i.e., refusing to talk about such things, I risked spelling out what I believed was taking place: "Whatever your attitude may be in real life toward the person who is your dancing partner, at this moment you are *in love* with him or her, and if this doesn't 'read,' then this section simply doesn't work." Merce chuckled. Nodding in agreement, he let me get away with it. But I did not mean the dancers should emote, or act out a narrative; I meant they had to be *alive in* the movement. Merce, of course, was right: spelling it out doesn't work, either; the dancers' own imaginations have to fill the void between just doing the steps and meaning, never forgetting Miss Craske's cautionary "My dear, the meaning is in the movement!"

How to . . . premiered at the Harper Theater on Wednesday, November 24. We performed it four times, and at each of these performances John read his stories at a table downstage right, while David Tudor, in the pit, electronically manipulated a recording of John's lecture on *Indeterminacy.* After the second performance I complained to Earle: "David has started to get 'clever' with the electronic devices. I was very disappointed. The dance is so extraordinary, I think, on its own. It doesn't need ANY music or sound accompaniment."

Each story had to be read in exactly one minute—a very short story at a snail's pace, and a very long one rushed through breathlessly. The "score" specified eleven stories and eleven minutes of silence; however, sound and silence did not necessarily alternate, which resulted in endlessly variable permutations when two live performers read. The readers, without conferring with each other, chose their own stories, their sequence, and the sound/silence ratio, or they could arrive at these decisions through chance procedures.

The company did not work together again until January. During the month of December we went separate ways. Merce began teaching *Summerspace* to New York City Ballet dancers. John had received a thousand-dollar Koussevitsky commission to write an orchestral piece and now had time to write it. David Tudor had a residency at the University of California, Davis. My own life took some surprising turns:

In October I'd received an invitation from Pierre Mercure to be the featured dancer in *Toi* (Loving), an experimental one-hour opera for television by Canadian composer Murray Schafer, to be produced and directed by Mercure, with choreography by Françoise Riopelle, and videotaped by the Canadian Broadcasting Corporation in Montreal the last two weeks in December. Earlier that year Pierre had produced a CBC television concert of Earle's *Available Forms I*, conducted by Bruno Maderna, with Françoise Riopelle's *Le Groupe danse moderne de Montréal* and back-screen projections of still and motion pictures; they hoped to utilize skills developed during this experience in the Schafer project. Although I never saw the *Available Forms I* program, I was intrigued. Lew Lloyd, acting as my agent, negotiated a fee of a thousand dollars (what a pleasant surprise that was).

This has to be written in big bold brash hand because I'm too excited and nervous for proper penmanship. . . . Lucia Chase just called me to do a supporting role in *Pillar of Fire* for the Ballet Theatre season this Jan.–Feb. Rehearsals start now—and of course I'm on my way to Montreal in less than two weeks. My TV contract is signed. Other problem—we tour the first three weeks of Feb. so it looks IMPOSSIBLE. DAMN. DAMN. DAMN. . . . the role offered me was Lucia Chase's own role of the older sister which doesn't appeal to me madly—but it would mean working with Tudor at last!

Lew recommended that I try to juggle it all, since *Pillar of Fire* would have two casts and only four performances. Perhaps I could be flown back from wherever I was touring with Merce for the two performances with Ballet Theatre. I met Tudor at 10:30 on the following Sunday morning at the National Bohemian Hall on East Seventy-third Street for a first rehearsal. Bonnie Mathis, a young Juilliard student who danced with José Limón, was also there to learn the role.

I worked with Tudor for a couple of hours. It was really great fun working with him—his whole approach is Stanislavskian—but in the process I realized quite strongly that at this point in my dancing life, I should be doing Hagar (the Nora Kaye part), not the Elder Sister, a very non-dancing role. . . . Since it was Sallie Wilson's idea to have me (not originally Tudor's—they were trying to think of "strong stage presences") I feel less badly about my decision. . . . When I told Merce that I had decided not to do *Pillar*, . . . he smiled and said, "I didn't think you should do that part. If you'd been given Hagar, it would have been very good to do." . . . that made me feel very much better about my decision. . . . So, one more "courtship" between Tudor and Brown comes to naught. How strange our relationship has been over the years.

esson no. 1: ALWAYS ask to read the script before signing a contract.

- "Ishtar leans back in a lurid pose: *'Lave-moi dans le lait.'* "
- "The fatal splendor of my hips. Massive weapons of allurement."
- "Thine thighs swing with robust musicianship."

Had I read *Toi*, had I seen sketches of the costumes (feathers, sequins, mesh tights—a sort of poor man's version of the Latin Quarter's version of Zizi Jeanmaire—*ooh la la!*) I would have demanded $100,000 just to be assured that I wouldn't get the job. In describing the project, Pierre Mercure explained that I was to represent the feminine counterpart of the main couple. I was to have "multiple presences"—Modestié (as the name implies), Ishtar (provocative), Vanité (fierce, arrogant and vain)—would then be interpreted almost simultaneously by an actress, three singers, and me. As the project developed I was impressed and gratified to see that both Pierre and Françoise avoided literal interpretations of the libretto and used poetic imagery, abstraction, understatement, and complicated superimpositions to disguise (ameliorate) the excesses of the script.

An extraordinary piece of scenery involving a labyrinth of ramps, stairs, and platforms really made me work to stay alive, but running madly up the ramp and around corners was so dangerous and challenging, I actually found it fun. In one episode, on a confining eight-foot circular platform high off the floor and ringed in darkness, the dancing Ishtar had to strike dizzy-making poses with isolated shoulder beats, head changes, undulations; in another, there were runs, slow turns and balances, extensions, falls, and very fast turns and balances, all on a six-foot-high ramp. Scary as hell! That really focused my attention. Improvising like crazy, getting angrier by the second, suddenly I found myself enjoying it, quite pleased to discover that I could do what was asked.

I had one long solo, racing around the whole enormous studio, down corridors, behind plastic walls, tunneling between panels of aluminum, darting between mirrored posts—all rather Cocteau-esque. All this was performed in three different costumes, representing the multiple presences of the feminine; in the final edit, Pierre jump-cut from one to another, so throughout the filming, I had to evoke the different moods of Modesty, Vanity, and Ishtar through the movement and the eyes.

I learned something invaluable working on that project: even when I thought I'd put out enormous energy, danced big and full-out, what appeared on the monitor always appeared to me small, lackluster, shrunken. On the last day, most of which was spent filming my long solo, I managed to perform the third section in one take. I felt I'd really done it, had become one with the music, riding it and hitting things absolutely right on, but even this, seen on the monitor, wasn't as full as it felt while performing it. For dance on television to register at all, it has to be bigger than life, physically pushed to one's very limits; even then it can never equate with a living, breathing body on a stage.

The final four days of filming made every moment of the frustrating three previous weeks of rehearsal worthwhile. Intensity and involvement ratcheted up to fever pitch. The process was what I loved—being in the moment, on high alert every second the cameras rolled. Equally rewarding was observing Pierre in the control room at work—nerve-racking work—where he had to follow five monitors recording four cameras while following the score and directing the cameramen and the engineers. That's where the *real* work was, and the really creative fun.

How did *Toi* ultimately turn out? I don't know. Never saw it. Perhaps it was awful. Perhaps it was wonderful.

One month later, on January 29, Pierre Mercure was killed in an automobile accident on the Paris-Lyon highway. The vibrant, adventurous composer/director/producer was thirty-eight years old.

arly in 1965, Tom Wolfe began a series of newspaper articles on "The Scene." Wolfe's articles—so cool, so hip, so knowing—were a veritable orgy of name-dropping that propelled our world, the New York art scene, into the limelight. I wrote to Earle, "Twelve years ago we arrived in this beautiful, wild city filled with awe for the "giants," the celebrities of the art world—art, dance, music—and now [our world is] it! . . . We've been a part of a great thrust of activity important to our time. You have created some of the activity and I have given life to some of it. And that makes me so proud and happy and curiously elated. No matter what miseries were suffered in the doing."

This was continued in a different vein nine months later: "Earle—I sense everywhere we go dynamic changes in America—in the way people hear and see and respond. This is the place 'it' is happening—and it is *your climate* for thought and creation. Europe is beautiful, but it is so steeped in old-world charm and thought and culture. The stimulation is here—I'm sure of it—and the changes are enormous. . . . America *is* waking up, at last."

My enthusiasm was perhaps a little premature: in January and February 1966, on a Cunningham company tour of the Midwest and West, we performed for mostly indifferent or hostile audiences and garnered a wealth of lousy reviews. Even the dancers' technique and execution were declared "of very poor standard" by a Vancouver critic.[1] *That* was a first, and perhaps an *only.*

In September of 1965, Clive Barnes left London to become the dance critic of the *New York Times.* At about the same time, *Life* magazine published a feature article devoted to modern dance in America, which included a kind of "Modern Dance 101" by Barnes in which he described Merce as "the only established modern dance choreographer who has really come to terms with modern dance's own avant-garde."[2] Barnes's reviews, in his first years at *The Times* were fresh winds blowing away dusty cobwebs, and the Cunningham company benefited enormously.

> This great classic member [Cunningham] of the avant-garde, with his untamed musician, John Cage, and his group of splendidly trained and svelte dancers, was making his solitary appearance in New York this season and it was a disgrace. . . . Not the cerebral jokes, esthetic pranks, shafts of beauty and arrows of fear provided by Mr. Cunningham and his co-conspirators. These merely offer one of the most exciting and valid dance experiences of our time. What is disgraceful is that the City of New York can provide Mr. Cunningham with only a one-night stand in Brooklyn. How long is modern dance going to be treated as some poor relation theatrically? On the London West End stage, Mr. Cunningham was able to play a month's season. Is New York really less interested in American modern dance than is London?[3]

On September 29, 1965, The National Foundation on the Arts and the Humanities Act was signed into law by President Lyndon B. Johnson. At the signing ceremony, President Johnson declared, "Art is a nation's most precious heritage, for it is in our works of art that we reveal to ourselves, and to others, the inner vision which guides us a nation. And where there is no vision, the people perish."[4] In February 1966, the National Council on the Arts awarded grants to choreographers. José Limón received $23,000; Anna Sokolow, $10,000; Antony Tudor, $10,000; Alvin Ailey, Merce Cunningham, Alwin Nikolais, and Paul Taylor $5,000 each. But what took everyone's breath away was the $181,000 awarded to the Martha Graham Dance Company—more than double the combined sum of all the other grants to choreographers and dance companies. In the same year, the Cunningham company was again refused federal subsidy for its two European tours.

In March 1966, Merce rehearsed the New York City Ballet in *Summerspace*. The only intended change in the choreography was having the women wear pointe shoes, but this change was not insignificant. Running in pointe shoes is very different from running barefoot—unless, of course, you're Galina Ulanova!—and they subtly changed the quality and dynamics of the dance. Softly rolling up and down through the foot into sustained balances while maintaining an even rhythm proved fiendishly difficult. Other complications arose soon after rehearsals started. Mimi Paul, chosen by Merce to dance my part (which involved sudden falls to the floor), decided it might be injurious to her classical technique. Having difficulty finding a suitable replacement, Merce asked me if I would be willing to do it. On pointe? I was game to attempt it, and kept practicing it in toe shoes just in case, but it really didn't make sense for the New York City Ballet not to have at least one ballerina who could and would do it. "He's going to try Melissa Hayden, I think, and a couple of other girls next week. If none of them work, then he'll probably insist that I do it."[5] In the end, the only principal dancer in the cast was Anthony Blum, who danced Merce's role; a very young Kay Mazzo was chosen for mine. Viola's part was taken by Patricia Neary; Sara Leland, Carol Sumner, and Deni Lamont completed the cast of six.

Ten days before the performance I saw the first stage rehearsal and was horrified not only at what *was* happening but also by what was *not*. Whenever possible, the dancers had translated the movement into "steps" they were familiar with, adding a lot of ballet-gesture mannerisms with none of the directness, simplicity, lyricism, poetry, line, and rhythm of Merce's choreography. Bob Rauschenberg, Jasper Johns, John Cage, Bénédicte Pesle, and Judith Blinken (our new booking agent) were at this rehearsal. Everyone felt the way I did. Not knowing what to say to Merce, I said nothing until the next day, when I asked if I could spend a few hours coaching the young woman in my part. He seemed delighted. Kay Mazzo—small, dark, beautiful, and terribly shy—didn't jump well and was afraid to fall; her rhythms were unclear and movements stiff and disjointed. I worked with her and the other women several times.

> On Tuesday I worked with Kay Mazzo again. It was her day off but she chose to work with me for a few hours. Already it looks better. She really had worked on everything I told her. She manages most of the technique quite easily except jumping and falling. But the QUALITY is another thing. Too rigid, too cutesey-pie Balanchine.

At the final dress rehearsal on the afternoon of the performance, Jasper stood in for Bob Rauschenberg who was off to Los Angeles for performances of his own. The new Rauschenberg drop cloth was "absolutely glorious," but Jasper and Merce made changes in the lighting, taking out the deep red. The costumes, far cruder than the hand-sprayed Rauschenberg originals, had been silkscreened. After rehearsal, Jasper touched up three costumes by hand-spraying to give them a more vertical instead of horizontal look, and he toned down the Day-Glo pink of Tony Blum's costume.

What hoopla greeted the production! The *New York Times, Herald Tribune, Journal American, Post, Daily News, World Telegram,* and *Sun* all sent their critics. We had performed *Summerspace* in the same theater on the same stage one year earlier, with barely a nod. Clive Barnes and Walter Terry expressed opposing views. Barnes wrote a rapturous, highly poetic, two-column accolade that began: "A shimmer of light, a flash of dance, an instant of looking back on some experience of summer, of shaking, hazy heat, and eyeballs pressed red against the sun, of cool shade, and cooler lemonade, of dappled leaves, of innocent and fugitive summer love—all that is a tiny and optional part (for everyone must find his own sensory impressions . . .) of Merce Cunningham's *Summerspace,* which incredibly and triumphantly turned up at the New York State Theatre at Lincoln Center last night."[6]

As a description of the dance, I'd say he had it perfectly. But Terry, looking at the *dancing,* saw something else: the loss of lyricism.

> Mr. Cunningham, in his modern dance creation, devised a lyric dance. The lyricism flowed through the dancers' bodies, through torsos uninhibited by traditional rules of deportment. Even when there was a pause, it was a matter of arrested motion—the pulse was still there. With ballet dancers, *Summerspace* became a matter of steps, and pauses turned into inaction, into stoppings. Lyricism disappeared. . . . Mr. Cunningham's own dancers . . . communicated a sense of alertness, of responsiveness to stillness as well as to sound. The expectancy of summer was in their dancing.[7]

The performance was the best it had gone, and Tony Blum somehow managed, for the first time, to get through the whole of Merce's part. Anyone who has attempted it knows how fiendishly difficult it is. Merce, sitting in the wings, described Tony coming offstage after each section, collapsing on the floor at his feet, and panting like an overheated Saint Bernard during the dog days of August. "How did you ever get through this?" Tony asked between labored breaths. He was then about thirty. At that time, Merce, forty-seven, was still performing *Summerspace.* Never once, in the eight years he'd performed it, did I ever see him out of breath. In fairness to Anthony Blum, it was the first leading role he'd been assigned since being elevated to Principal Dancer status.

Elegant in a tuxedo, Merce took several bows with the dancers on stage and then, joined by the conductor, Robert Irving, in front of the curtain. A few boos and hisses—for the music, the choreography?—were somehow reassuring. In the lobby at intermission, present and former Cunningham dancers gathered for a postmortem. Several were in tears. Some were angry. Some, simply appalled. (All of us were in agreement with Terry's review when it appeared the next day. Still, we were relieved that *Summerspace* hadn't bombed.) After the show, I found Merce backstage, huddled in a chair, limp from nervous tension and hunger (he'd had no dinner), but like the rest of us grateful that it seemed to have gone over well.

Eight days after City Ballet's premiere of *Summerspace*, we gave our only full New York performance of the season. With the exception of Clive Barnes's review noted earlier, it was scarcely remarked upon.

The Foundation for the Contemporary Performance Arts, Inc., with two very different events, again raised money to support experimental dance, music, and theater. As before, artists were asked to donate works, and drawings by more than two hundred artists were shown in three galleries— Castelli, Tibor de Nagy, and Kornblee. Its other event was a series of five lectures by Norman O. Brown, Peter Yates, Buckminster Fuller, Merce Cunningham, and Marshall McLuhan at the Poetry Center of the 92nd Street YM-YWHA, spaced over a series of weeks from March to May. My journal account:

> Merce's lecture . . . was very beautiful. Very moving. He danced beauti- fully. Spoke beautifully. His voice "live" was low, friendly, warm. His voice on tape was clear, direct, objective. The contrast was integral to the whole—what he said, what he did. He spoke plain facts, some poetics, some stories—all about dancing, dances or dancers. Billy Klüver thought it the best lecture so far [because] Merce talked about what he really knows. I asked him, "Didn't Fuller?" And Billy said "No!"[8]

Jetting across the country in April, leaving the disciplined work ethic of the Cunningham company and the New York City Ballet behind, I plunged into the maelstrom of New York's downtown artists' "scene," transported to Los Angeles, where partying seemed to replace rehearsing. Among other events, Bob's *Pelican* was being sponsored by the Los Angeles County Museum of Art. Arriving at ten in the evening, I was immediately whisked off to a party at the home of an exceedingly wealthy collector. Rauschen- berg and Claes Oldenburg were the guests of honor for a "Question and Answer" event. By the time I arrived, Bob was in disgrace and host and hostess incensed. Bob's dog, Leica, had defecated *and* urinated on the wall-to-wall white wool carpet. Adding insult to injury, Bob, joined by sev- eral others, jumped into the swimming pool in his underpants in a drunken caper and then proceeded to drip all over the carpet in search of another drink. He was refused, and asked to leave. Harsh words were spoken about rudeness and drunkenness, and "Just because you're an artist you have no right to . . ." sorts of accusations.

At the roller rink next day everything felt rushed, hectic, disorganized, and out of control. Each of the participants had his or her own piece to stage and rehearse, with little time to do it. Bob, Alex, and I managed only one run-through. We hadn't performed or even rehearsed *Pelican* in a year. No wonder the performance went badly. Bob sweated and strained. Alex fell down. Both men were exhausted and out of shape.

I flew back to New York the next day and performed with Merce at BAM, and less than a week later I was in the air again, on my way to Washington, D.C., for the Now Festival and yet another performance of *Pelican*. Even more New York artists participated in this five-day event, including, among others, Robert Whitman, John Cage and David Tudor, Yvonne Rainer, and the Andy Warhol–influenced band the Velvet Underground. Three years earlier, about two hundred people saw the concert when *Pelican* was first performed. This time, more than eight hundred attended. *Pelican* had been fairly well rehearsed three years earlier and we'd gotten through it without mishap; this time it got no run-through or rehearsal of any kind, it did not go well, and—most worrisome—I injured my shoulder in performance. That did it! The undisciplined ad hoc nature of these engagements was too risky for me. I loved many of the people involved, but not the cavalier work ethic or the hard-drinking, partying stuff they seemed to thrive on, and so my flirtation with the far-out, swinging sixties abruptly ended.

An unusual request came my way. *Ballet Review* asked me to write an article about Marshall McLuhan and the arts.[9] Could my brain still function in an intellectual discipline? I was curious to find out. Then Margy Jenkins, a student at the Cunningham Studio, asked me to teach a Cecchetti pointe class (!) for Twyla Tharp, Sara Rudner, Theresa Dickinson, Marjorie Tupling, and herself, most of whom were also students at the Cunningham Studio. A few of them had had some ballet training, but none was proficient on pointe, and it was unlikely that they ever would be or (perhaps with the exception of Twyla) wanted to be. I'd followed Twyla since *Tank Dive*, her very first solo concert in Room 1604 in the Hunter College Art Department in April 1965. During her "Eight Jelly Rolls" period I became an honest-to-god fan, especially of Sara Rudner, one of America's greatest dancers, who performed with Twyla for nine years and appeared for another ten or more as a guest artist. The extent of Sara's personal contribution to that work has never been sufficiently honored or even recognized.

Twice a week for eight weeks in May and June 1966, at Dance Players Studios, these women donned their toe shoes and dutifully did their *relevés* and *échappés,* but I suspect that neither their hearts nor their minds were truly engaged. Twyla had written about herself: "I was obviously unsuited for ballet." In her case, perhaps, it was too soon to determine that, since anyone who knows her even slightly is aware of her ferocious intellect and determination, yet even tough Twyla could reveal a tender, emotional side. After her son, Jesse, was born, she was very close to tears as she told me of her fear that she could not be a good mother, continue the work she so desperately wanted to do, and support her company honorably. Observing feisty, brainy, tomboy Twyla in 1966 going through the motions of Cecchetti's elegant fifth port de bras with ever so serious intent was a touching and yet somehow ridiculous sight. The organic beauty of these movements and their precise but delicate shifts of weight, head, torso, arms, fingertips, and *épaulement* were utterly foreign to this brash, sassy-assed American kid, who did not approach the movement rhythmically from the inside out, but attacked it from its positional surface. In Cecchetti's deceptively simple, subtle port de bras, rhythm should radiate out from the core of the body. Shape and position are the end result. In all good dancing, the rhythm is integral to the movement. Twyla understood this deeply and viscerally in her own choreography for modern dancers. But having recently seen her blockbuster Broadway success *Movin' Out,* I must admit that much of her ballet choreography still strikes me as superficial, never going beyond a basic ballet/jazz/nightclub vocabulary. John Selye, however, was worth every penny of the one hundred bucks for an orchestra seat.

Earle arrived back in New York City on June 22 via the *Rotterdam,* one month before the company took off for Europe and a four-week tour. Requests made to the U.S. State Department for financial assistance were once again refused. Despite the miraculous success of the 1964 world tour, John and Merce were still anathema to those wielding the power behind the State Department's funding policies. Clive Barnes devoted an entire column to the dilemma.

For five or six years, the Cunningham Company has been sought by various European interests—theatres and festivals. Unfortunately it was impossible to take up the invitations because funds were just not available. This year the company also received a number of foreign invitations, among them a festival at Sitges, Spain, another in the south of France, a film-date in Hamburg and the very prestigious Berlin Festival. The story has a happy ending, or fairly happy ending. The great Spanish painter Joan Miró, who had seen the Cunningham group in Paris, was so interested in getting the company to Spain that he donated one of his paintings to pay for the company's fare to Europe and back. . . . Lucky old State Department—being subsidized by European painters.[10]

Jean-Paul Riopelle,[11] the Canadian painter, who was then residing in France, also came to our rescue by donating a painting to be sold on the company's behalf for the French leg of the tour. The Hamburg film project was funded by Norddeutscher-Rundfunk. The Berlin Festival had to be refused.

In late July, the Cunningham Company left for Spain and an idyllic four days on the coast of the Mediterranean at the Terramar Palace Hotel, which rose like a gigantic wedding cake at the end of a long white crescent beach, a short jitney ride away from the outdoor Prado Theatre in the ancient town of Sitges, where our single performance did not begin until one hour before midnight. Usual for Spain, unusual for us. The company's ranks had grown and now included eight dancers—Merce, myself, Barbara Lloyd, Sandra Neels, Valda Setterfield, Albert Reid, Peter Saul, and Gus Solomons Jr.; three musicians—John Cage, David Tudor, and Gordon Mumma (an addition to the musicians' roster); lighting designers/stage managers—Beverly Emmons and Rick Nelson sharing those roles; and Lew Lloyd, Company Manager. On this tour, the entourage also included my mother and one of her dance students to keep her company while I was working; Lew and Barbara's son, Benjamin; Valda and David Gordon's son, Ain; Rick Nelson's son, Mark; and Gordon Mumma's wife, Jackie. Quite a handful for Lew Lloyd, with no assistance, to keep track of, arrange transportation and housing for, and keep relatively happy. (David Vaughan was not with us that summer; he had taken a summer acting job that he couldn't bear to pass up.)

The leisurely pace we'd enjoyed in Spain was gone even before we crossed the border into France. Chaos took over as we left Sitges. The theater luggage, sent the day before, was supposed to be waiting for us at the Spanish-French border in the customs shed, but wasn't. Had it been hijacked? Would the costumes, practice clothes, makeup, lighting gels, music tapes, and electronic equipment arrive in St. Paul de Vence in time for the Monday-evening performance? Lew Lloyd stayed behind to trace the missing luggage while the company proceeded to Nice, where we dis-

covered that the hotel situation in St. Paul de Vence—our ultimate destination—was in disarray because a German film crew from Hamburg, having made no reservations of their own but claiming to be part of the
Cunningham company, had taken the hotel rooms reserved for us.

Lew called from Spain the next morning: still no theater luggage! John
was in despair. At Fondation Maeght, where we were to perform, the company gathered to discuss what to do. For Merce, cancellation was not a
consideration. Plans went ahead to give the performance, advertised as a
"*Soirée de Gala*," in whatever way could be managed. John, David, and
Gordon worked in feverish haste to construct a working electronic system,
borrowing equipment from Fondation Maeght, renting equipment from
filmmaker Henri Clouzot (luckily in the area), and running back and forth
from basement control room to upstairs gallery connecting wires. Merce
and Beverly Emmons set off for Antibes, Peter Saul acting as translator, to
buy or borrow costumes for that evening's performance.

At one end of the Giacometti sculpture garden, a platform—especially
constructed for our performances—was cantilevered out over the hillside
to a drop of fifty feet. In the distance—through the Plexiglas cyclorama—
the Mediterranean Sea, Nice, Antibes, and Cannes were barely distinguishable in the haze. A searing midday sun blistered the newly painted
surface of the makeshift stage. Pitch oozed from the raw pine board, which
was splintering from days baking in the sun and nights of heavy dew. The
Fondation Maeght has neither rehearsal studio nor dressing rooms, so,
while others dashed frantically around, the dancers sat still, guarding their
energy. As in India, it was impossible to dance midday on the Côte d'Azur.
We couldn't attempt it, in fact, before six o'clock in the evening.

The musicians labored on without pause. The problems were endless:
language difficulties, museum protocol, differences of opinion, unskilled
stagehands. Just hooking up the electrical current took three exasperating
hours. Miles away, in the customs shed at the Spanish-French border, Lew
Lloyd was attempting to retrieve the theater luggage, which had actually
arrived as scheduled two days earlier and had been in the shed all along.
At five o'clock Merce returned with sweat suits borrowed from the Cannes
police department, tights and leotards borrowed from Rosella Hightower's
ballet company, and various items purchased in the sporting goods stores
of Antibes.

A phone message brought news that Lew would arrive in Nice at 7:30 by
chartered plane! With next to no Spanish, he had been struggling with
recalcitrant customs officers and the inexorable ticking of the clock. By
Monday noon he was through customs, but had missed the train that would

have gotten the stuff to St. Paul de Vence by performance time, so he hailed two taxis, loaded as many boxes as would fit, and set off for the hour-and-a-half run to the Perpignan Airport via hairpin-turn roads along the coast. A Corsican plane was supposed to be waiting. No plane. Lew commandeered another. Exchange of money took place—in the form of exorbitant tips or, you might say, bribes. Lew recounted:

> In I get to the cockpit, next to the dapper pilot, and we not too steadily go. Once up the pilot takes out a large loose-leaf binder entitled "Operational and Directional Manual," several maps, props them on his knees and begins poring through them. The trip continued this way with the plane weaving slightly to the left while the pilot went over the maps and peered out the side windows. We did reach Nice by 7:20 pm though, and after bouncing three times (the pilot had the grace to say *merde* at this) we were home free, so to speak.[12]

The offices at the foundation served as our dressing rooms but were not available until seven. To save time, we did a spacing rehearsal in our street clothes. The musicians went on working. At 7 p.m., slabs of French bread, paté, ham and cheese, pots of yogurt, fresh fruit, and bottles of Évian were delivered to us. At 8:30, the theater luggage arrived. After the cheers died down, it was back to serious business. We warmed up in the storage room in the midst of Calder mobiles and stabiles, and racks of paintings by Léger, Miró, and Kandinsky. At 9:30, curtain time, we were ready and raring to go, but for reasons beyond our comprehension we did not begin until quarter to eleven. The performance ended with *How to Pass, Kick, Fall and Run* under a soft, steady rain which got heavier as the dance progressed. Two stage lights burst, shattering glass onto a corner of the stage. Soon the black floor paint began splattering into blobs and streaks of gray and black like a giant Pollock. It never occurred to us to stop. It was beautiful dancing in the rain. We loved it. Those in the audience who remained in their seats apparently did, too. Those who didn't, moved into galleries to watch. In the audience was a galaxy of art-world luminaries—Miró, Max Ernst, Dorothea Tanning, Jean-Paul Riopelle, José Luis Sert, and many others. Musician-composer friends Fred Rzewski, Cornelius Cardew, and Giuseppe Englert were there, too, along with some of French society's elegantly coiffed, luxuriously furred ladies and their escorts. Among them was a certain baroness who wanted to look at the wife of Earle Brown. Before the performance, I was told, she stood outside my office–dressing room surveying me through the open door as I was applying my makeup. I was unaware of her presence. Later that evening she was among the large group of artist and composer friends at the post-performance dinner. We were not introduced.

With no performances for the next three days, we bused into Cannes to rehearse at Rosella Hightower's studio. Merce was in the throes of completing *Place,* which he'd been choreographing off and on since January. Beverly Emmons had been asked to do the design for *Place;* she was thrilled, but also understandably nervous, so when Lew Lloyd rented a car and sent her (all of twenty-one years old) and some young guy, just out of the Peace Corps, whom she didn't know ("I was lucky not to have been raped!" she told me years later[13]), to the Spanish-French border to retrieve the rest of the theater luggage, she was not happy. They were gone two precious workdays. Merce was furious. Why hadn't Lew gone himself? Beverly had first met with Merce shortly after the company returned from the world tour. In a kind of preliminary interview at the Fourteenth Street studio, he'd had two things to say about lighting his dances: the light had to have life—had to move—and it should not telegraph to the audience where the dancers were going or what they were going to do.

As was his wont, Merce gave Beverly precious little information about "the new piece," except its title. But he did say that "if something big happens here, then something small should happen over there." And with only that to go on, she came up with two small "glowing globes" with Bucky Fuller–like geodesic shades, which could be drawn along the floor casting an unusually sharp edge of light made possible with an unusually tiny filament lamp, thus by contrast allowing the "something big" to be lit separately. Merce did express one desire: "Is it possible," he wanted to know, "to have smoke come out of my pockets, envelop me, and then cause me to disappear?" Nonplussed, she suggested, instead, that he climb into a huge plastic bag and crawl offstage as the lights fade. At Fondation Maeght, with the curious clear plastic cyclorama, there could be no set, but she did design the women's costumes—tunics constructed from twentieth-century industrial-weight see-through vinyl, in pastel shades of pink, green, blue, and yellow, worn over flesh-colored tights and leotards. Years later she explained this concept as "the natural under the modern." By chance, *Place* acquired a set in Paris in the fall. In the alleyway outside the Théâtre des Champs-Élysées, Beverly found some discarded wooden crate slats, and with those and sheets of newspaper hung randomly across the back of the stage, she created intimations of a rather desolate, junk-strewn cityscape. For reasons she can't quite explain, she envisioned the dance as urban and contemporary.[14]

What little we dancers knew about "the new dance" consisted of small, discrete sections, their order changing from rehearsal to rehearsal. Without any sense of the final continuity, we totally misjudged the nature of the piece. One section seemed like a jolly folk dance; it was such fun we would smile broadly at one another as we rehearsed it. Smiles were soon wiped from our faces. In another, the women became human wheelbarrows, wheeled about by the men at a precarious speed—hilarious when Merce first set it. In context, there was nothing funny about it.

The dance began with Merce's entrance into the deep gloom of Beverly's lit stage and Gordon Mumma's menacing music, "Mesa," a closely interdependent collaboration written for bandoneon, played by David Tudor, and electronic equipment, played by Gordon. We had never seen Merce's solos until that moment. Moving cautiously, as though exploring unknown and perhaps treacherous terrain, he suddenly exploded into action. In a fraction of a second all thoughts of fun and games were erased from our minds as we were propelled into an intense drama—anxiety-ridden and darkly tragic—which we didn't begin to comprehend but viscerally and instantly absorbed.

Place is a masterwork, and Merce is the master of it. Once he enters the stage space he never leaves it. He struts, flails, falls, joins me for a long, mostly tender yet passionate duet; he whirls through space, jumps, stands stock-still, crashes to the floor. When the company dances, he crouches, watching warily while slowly dragging "glowing globes" across the floor. The lanterns cast ominous shadows into the darkness. Even in the slowest sections of the dance an intense energy electrifies . . . us, if not the onlooker. Merce must have trusted us to follow his wild leap into an undefined dramatic mystery. We did—aghast, and deeply thrilled. At one point in *Place,* we formed a circle facing one another and, in unison, began a very fast complex rhythmic phrase—a kind of primitive incantation, pounding it out with our feet; repeating it over and over again. Most astonishing of all was the ending, when Merce crawled into the plastic bag and began to thrash and kick his way across the floor. Kenneth King, several years later, described the frenzied finale: "One of the most magical moments I've ever witnessed in Cunningham's work is the solo finale in *Place* . . . the lights were already beginning to fade and this happened very rapidly—as he rolled on the floor upstage toward the darkness and the void, the sack just up to his chest, his eyes beady and urgent . . . Surely this is a moment Samuel Beckett would have cherished—archly existential, also profoundly and magically mysterious."[15]

To insist that this dance isn't *about anything,* to insist that it is only about the movement, seems an insult to the emotional intelligence of the viewer. Merce may say whatever he likes about his highly dramatic dances, but clearly they were keenly *felt* by him—dramatically, emotionally, psychologically. Some critics connected *Place* with the ethos of *Winterbranch:* darkness, foreboding, terror, devastation, alienation, doom. *Place* is perhaps the first of his group works in which Merce casts himself as "the outsider," if not completely alienated from the world and the people in it, at least distinctly separate from it and them. Although I have no idea what *Place* may have meant to him personally, it was certainly powerfully evocative for me.

Place's premiere was on the last of our three repertory performances at Fondation Maeght. The final performance there was an *Event #4* that took place all over the museum—in the galleries, in the sculpture court, and on the makeshift stage. Then, with the exception of one rehearsal in Paris, we had an eight-day hiatus before filming *Variations V.* A two-day bus trip through the glorious French countryside took us to Oise, France, where, thanks to Bénédicte Pesle, the company had the extraordinary good fortune to spend four days at Pontpoint, the country château of her uncle Jean de Menil. As I relived my twenty-year Cunningham adventure while writing this book, I was continually struck by how much Bénédicte Pesle contributed to the company's success and well-being—not only in the bookings she arranged, the advice proffered, and the funds she raised, but also with her steadfast devotion and selfless care of Merce and his dancers. The company owes her boundless gratitude.

In Hamburg, we put in four long, hard, exhausting days on a cement floor, filming *Variations V* under the direction of Arne Arnbom. The cement floor took its toll—minor sprains, aches and pains—but luckily caused no major injuries. The resulting film is interesting, sometimes beautiful, with layered images from Stan VanDerBeek's movies, Nam June Paik's distortions, montage effects, overlapping dance images, and elaborate electronic devices; it provides a very different experience from seeing it in a theater. Watching myself in the early takes was, as it had been in Canada, a disappointing revelation: "I really did not like the dancer I saw myself to be in that kinescope today. Too light, brittle—not enough weight in movement. The speed was good, some of the quality wasn't bad—but generally *not* good. Not the camera. Me. Hope I can make it better by Friday."[16]

The company was off until the end of September. After Hamburg, I flew alone to London, checked into the Imperial Hotel, and rushed off to buy theater tickets for a superb Zeffirelli-directed *Much Ado About Nothing,*

Royal Hunt of the Sun (with Christopher Plummer), *Ubu Roi, A Flea in Her Ear,* a smashing, bawdy production of *Love for Love* at the Old Vic (with Laurence Olivier outrageously over-the-top), and a rather dreary Festival Ballet performance of *Swan Lake.*

One morning I received a surprise phone call from Marie Rambert, who invited me to tea. I bused out to the Mercury Theatre, excited to be visiting the scene of Tudor's first ballets, where "history fairly falls off the walls!" Madame Rambert asked me to stay on in London for a few days, at least until Merce arrived. She had asked him to create a work for her company and wanted to discuss it with him personally. Merce was in France, and I phoned him. He arrived the next day. If he agreed to make a ballet for Rambert, then I would stay on in London to teach classes and assist him. We had several pleasant meetings at the Mercury and watched her company in rehearsal, but nothing definite was determined, so I returned to New York, to class at the Met, to teaching at the studio, and to a husband I hadn't seen much of in months and whom I would leave again in six weeks. Was it abysmal naiveté or head-in-the-sand stupidity that led me to believe Earle's life in Europe, in the many many months we were apart, was as celibate as mine? Not even learning of the curious baroness who wanted to have "a look" at me in St. Paul de Vence had raised a red flag.

At the end of the June summer course, the Cunningham Studio had moved from Fourteenth Street, where the rent was $100 a month, to far more spacious quarters at 498 Third Avenue between Thirty-third and Thirty-fourth streets. Rent: $450 a month! We had the top three floors: the office, dressing rooms, and a small studio on one; the large studio (with a very high ceiling) and a hidden kitchenette on the next, and on the top floor a tiny living space, lacking all creature comforts, where Merce could sleep.

Two young dancers joined the company as apprentices in the early fall: Yseult Riopelle (the daughter of Canadian choreographer Françoise Riopelle and artist Jean-Paul Riopelle) and Niklas Ek (the son of the Ingmar Bergman actor Anders Ek and Swedish choreographer Birgit Cullberg). Miss Cullberg was in New York that autumn and suggested that I go to Sweden to work with her company for six months as a guest artist. I explained that it would be impossible for me to leave Merce for such a long period. Some weeks later, I received a letter from her, inviting me to share the "ballerina" role with Melissa Hayden, each of us to spend three months in Stockholm in the winter of '67: "I think I could bring out new sides of your talent. You should do one of Melissa's parts as dramatic role

(Fedra) and also other parts. It is not a classical ballerina-part that you should do. Melissa is not going to dance on point."[17]

Another missed opportunity. Although the Cunningham company had only a few scheduled performances for the three-month period I was invited to work with Miss Cullberg, there was no way I could accept.

In mid-October, the Cunningham company set off on tour again: first to Chicago and Urbana, Illinois, and then, without a break, directly from Urbana to Stockholm, and on to Paris, Lisbon, Coimbra, and Oporto in Portugal, and finally to London. We were away for seven weeks. Thirty-five hours after removing our makeup in Urbana we landed in Stockholm at ten in the morning, and with only one hour of sleep in our hotel beds—never had I felt so jet-lagged, groggy, physically ill—we rehearsed and performed. When the curtain went up in Stockholm's Stadsteatern we were amazed to discover that we felt just fine; more than that, we all danced really well. The audience and the dance critics agreed. *Nightwandering*, on the last of the three performances, received cheers and bravos. And then it was off to Paris and four performances at the Théâtre des Champs-Élysées.

On tour, David Vaughan was shouldering full administrative responsibility. In his frequent letters to Lew, he made clear that it was a tough assignment: "I really miss you. I keep having this terrible fear that there is one terribly important thing I have forgotten. Of course, everyone keeps telling me how I should be doing my job, especially Carol and Gus. I think I am going to start giving *them* notes and see how they like it. How do you do this job and not get paranoid?"[18]

Le Théâtre des Champs-Élysées—scene of the notorious Nijinsky/ Stravinsky *Le Sacre du printemps* premiere in 1913, the year the theater first opened its doors with Ballets Russes de Serge Diaghilev! In a reverential reverie, I lay on the raked stage of this legendary theater, gazed up into the flies and out into the house, and stroked the white wooden floorboards that once bore the footprints of Nijinsky and Karsavina. Pavlova, too, had danced on this stage. Were their evanescent ghosts still here, hovering about us?

In our own way, Merce Cunningham and Dance Company made history, too, but not before a turbulent day in the theater. After a noon rehearsal, a televised promotional bit of *Place* in costume, and a photo call with forty photographers jockeying for prime positions, Merce categorically refused to do a full *"répétition générale"* as is customary in Europe. This and his reluctance to have photographers of any sort present during our rehearsal caused quite a fracas with a very unpleasant Jean Robin, *Directeur Général du Festival International de Danse de Paris,* who threatened to break our contract and not pay the company. Luckily, John Cage appeared in the nick of time to smooth ruffled feathers. At a party after the second performance, Robin, cordial once again, admitted to being astonished by our success. David Vaughan wrote Lew Lloyd:

> The opening night was fantastic—tout Paris, of course. As the *France-Soir* said (in a banner headline across the top of the front page), it was "mini-skirts versus tuxedos." There were of course the regulation boos, rather surprisingly mostly from the upper reaches of the house. Eddie Constantine, the actor, whose wife is a dancer, was in the front row and shouted out "Why don't you keep quiet the first time you come to the Ballet?" It was a superb performance. *Place* especially. Merce said he could feel the whole attitude of the audience changing.[19]

Backstage, Maxine Groffsky told us that Paris society was out in full, not knowing whether to dig it or not. People booed, whistled, cheered, bravoed. By the final curtain, she said, they began to be very nervous that we were, in fact, *the in thing.* So "in," even New York society columnist Suzy Knickerbocker, writing in the *World Journal Tribune,* joined in the clamor: "The ultimate woman at the Merce Cunningham ballet in Paris was Mme. Helen Rochas in Saint Laurent's black velvet redingote edged with mink and picked up with diamonds and rubies. She really was far prettier than the little chits in their gold and silver miniskirts. Max Ernst was there with his wife in a long red dress and turquoise jewelry designed by Max himself."[20]

In 1950, when Earle and I first met Max Ernst and Dorothea Tanning in Arizona, there was no thought of me becoming a professional dancer, so how could I have imagined myself at a post-performance party at Maxim's, hosted by Michel Guy, seated with Max and Dorothea, Matta, George Auric, John Cage, and Merce Cunningham? When Dorothea—rather untactfully I thought—hollered across the table, "What's with you and Earle, are you still married?" I could only answer, "sort of," because it was impossible for me to say or even think no.

Maxine Groffsky arranged a very different sort of *très chic,* swinging party at 21 Place des Vosges, in the apartment of film actress Delphine Seyrig—she of *Last Year at Marienbad.* There I was deluged with more questions about Earle and me. My journal entry:

Betsy Iolas, Marguerita Russo, Joan Mitchell—all being terribly compli-
mentary and then from Marguerita: "Where is Earle? He disappeared from
Paris for over a year and never even sent a card. He's usually so friendly.
What happened to him? Why did he disappear without a word?" From
Betsy Iolas—"I love Earle. Where is he? How is he? What is he doing?"
From Joan: "What's with you and Earle? Is it all right? What's happening?"
etc., etc., etc. A lump the size of a grapefruit in my throat—tears spilling
out of my eyes—Thank God the countess [baroness] didn't show up as well.

Four sold-out performances at the Théâtre des Champs-Élysées, ecstatic audiences, glamorous parties, enthusiastic friends, a sense that I'd
danced my best, all were dimmed by these intrusive questions and
replaced by a feeling of profound loss: Earle conducting in Argentina, Carolyn dancing in Paris—never together, never sharing in each other's work,
neither its joys nor its disappointments. Had I faced the truth, I would
have had to admit to myself that our marriage had ended in Venice in 1964.

Klaus Wildenhahn arrived from Germany with a copy of his completed
Cage documentary. This beautiful, moving film captures the workings of
the company, and reveals John as the exceptional human being, "divine
idiot," and quirky genius I've always believed him to be. Writing to Lew,
David Vaughan confessed: "I cried a lot . . . there's a bit where Carol talks
about her life with the company that makes me cry even as I think about
it."[21] I cried, too, and cried even more when I looked at it again thirty-plus
years later. In the film, I tell Klaus that I've had a wonderful life, and yes,
of course I regret not having children and a more normal existence, but
that I love my life, am fully aware of how extraordinarily fortunate I've
been, and do realize that one can't have everything.

Thank god I had little time to linger over what might have been. With
five performances in four theaters and hours of travel in between, the
entire Portugal leg of the tour was grueling work, especially for Beverly
and the musicians. In Lisbon we danced in a movie house showing films
from three to six in the afternoon, and again at 9:30 at night. We were
sandwiched in between! Then we traveled by train to Coimbra and Oporto
to play in icy-cold theaters where fuses blew every few minutes and the
plumbing was as primitive as in Ahmedabad.

Our last two performances were back in Lisbon—unbelievably, in two
different movie theaters—where once again we were the "filling" between
movies. Our hosts, the Gulbenkian Foundation, provided generous assistance: they paid for first-class train tickets and arranged for good hotels,

and they seemed to feel well rewarded by our presence. David wrote to Lew: "They should be. Our opening night was terrific, lots of young kids came back afterwards hardly able to contain themselves, especially over WB [*Winterbranch*]. (John and I have discovered a mutual antipathy to La Monte's music and have taken to going out for a glass or two of port.)"[22]

Winterbranch caused a sensation. People stamped their feet in disapproval. Those approving banged the seats of their chairs with cries of "Bravo!" A really explosive response. Before the second Lisbon performance some teenage girls came backstage screaming with excitement, behaving more like Beatles groupies than modern-dance fans. They'd seen the first performance, knew all our names, and were heartbroken to discover that the last two Lisbon performances were sold out. So despondent were they that Gordon Mumma—a perpetual pushover when it came to pretty girls—put them in the pit with the musicians and even let one of them help run one of the projectors for *Variations V.* On our last night in Lisbon, a few of the young members of the audience and some older ones simply would not go home. We took many, many curtain calls.

The tour as originally planned was to have ended in Lisbon, but Michael White (our 1964 London impresario) had made inquiries when the company was in Stockholm about the possibility of us doing a London season in a very large theater, the Saville in London's West End, following the Portugal engagements. The financial risk was great. Back in New York, Lew Lloyd and Judith Blinken (the Cunningham company's exclusive representative) were in total disagreement about London. Lew said yes. Judith said no. Merce was ambivalent. Several members of the company wanted to go home and resented extending the tour. The Rambert Company and the Royal Ballet would be performing during our second week, adding still more financial risk. Other problems: after Paris, we lost Rick Nelson as stage manager—he had a theater job in Philadelphia he couldn't afford to turn down—and Gordon Mumma was unable to stay for the full London run. After much consultation, on the day we arrived in Paris John made the final decision. David wrote to Lew: "MC groaned when I told him today that London was set, but I am sure that when he's dancing for ten [actually eleven] nights in the same theatre to an audience that really knows what's what he will love it as he did before and dance like a god."[23]

In London, Merce was complaining of feeling unwell, his malady probably brought on by fears that this time "they" wouldn't like him, and that we wouldn't be able to repeat our astonishing 1964 success. Opening night at the Saville, compared to opening nights in Paris and Lisbon, seemed to confirm his fears. The ruckus we caused on those earlier occasions had ill prepared us for that quiet London audience or for the poor reviews, which overwhelmed the really good ones. However, ignored we were not! The reviewers were there in force; some resorted to caustic humor, others to outrage or outright dismissal. One was vicious, in an inexcusably personal way, about Merce's own dancing. One enraged theatergoer threw a potted plant through the Saville's glass-fronted case containing a Cunningham company poster and photographs, the choice of weapon mirroring the plastic plant that Merce dismantled and I reassembled in *Variations V.* The *Evening Standard* reported that the police were investigating.[24] Not unexpectedly, the sound for *Place* and *Variations V* was reviled, but it was not just the music that was hostilely received; the choreography got some negative criticism as well. A rude slap in the face for all of us, but for Michael White, who had gone out on a financial limb to present the company, it looked like disaster. He needn't have worried. Audiences grew, despite, or perhaps because of, the reviews by the same ballet critics who hadn't liked us in 1964.

> The season started slowly—the Saville is a very big theatre—and the initial press reception was cool. But the season built, and at the end there were cheering audiences. As when the company was here two years ago, the audience was made up of painters, musicians, artists and intellectuals and, most important, students in these fields. The ballet world was conspicuously absent.[25]

As in 1964, our champions were Alexander Bland (in *The Observer*), John Percival (in the *Times*), and Peter Williams (in *Dance and Dancers*), minus Clive Barnes who had already immigrated to New York. On the Monday of our second week, this review appeared in the *International Times*, written by a critic unknown to us.

> The Merce Cunningham Company performances are the most significant and brilliantly performed presentation of avant-garde to be seen in London or anywhere. They have everything—the highest standards of both conceptualism and dancing to be seen in the world today, cheap seats (from 7/6), a good theatre in central London (the Saville) and experimental music by John Cage and Gordon Mumma. Anyone who has given up ballet as a lost cause should have a good look at this company and have his ideas changed. . . . People under forty exist.[26]

That night a marvelous audience, full of animated young people, cheered the first of seven performances in our second week at the Saville with shouts of "Bravo" and cries of "Yes!" After the disappointing audiences of the first four days, this was truly heartening. At last we felt like celebrating, and that night we had the opportunity at an extravagantly grand post-performance party given by the American ambassador, David Bruce, and his wife, Evangeline, at their residence in Regent's Park, which once belonged to Barbara Hutton. A number of United States congressmen and Washington VIPs were present—one escorted me in to supper—and to my surprise they had actually been to our performance.

In addition to David Gordon, who surprised Valda by showing up on opening night, Frank Stella, Suzi Gablik, Claes Oldenburg, M. C. Richards, and Charles Olson all showed up, as did Jasper, who hosted a company party at Bianchi's, our favorite Soho restaurant, after our final matinee and evening. By this time, our bone-weary bodies and fatigued brains needed to go home, and home we went, but with just two days' rest before rehearsals began for three sold-out New York performances at Hunter College at the end of the week.

A pleasant surprise—all the New York reviews were positive. Barnes continued to write substantial, thoughtful articles about Merce's work, encouraging recalcitrant naysayers to open the lenses of their shuttered eyes, to take another look: "Mr. Cunningham is a serious artist who is rarely taken seriously enough—except, sadly, by Europe."[27]

A paradox, a paradox, a most ingenious paradox!" The reason given by the State Department for refusing to fund our 1966 European tour was that the government *advisors* [my italics] did not feel that "there was much interest in Cunningham's kind of thing in Europe."[28]

The company returned home in debt to the tune of fifteen thousand dollars, often despite often playing to sold-out houses, cheering (if battling) audiences, excellent notices, and the not insignificant fact that Merce had won the gold star for choreography at the Paris International Dance Festival. David Vaughan went to Paris to accept the award on Merce's behalf. When he arrived, he was prevented from receiving it and informed that someone from the American Embassy would accept it. The gold star would then be sent to Washington, and from there it would be sent to Merce, which indeed it was. The package arrived in the mail, forty cents postage due.

Technological innovation will shape the art of the future. Earle Brown, John Cage, David Tudor, and Edgard Varèse all said this; they all believed it. "Technology does not lead us back into history but advances us into the unknown. . . . From now on, the magic of the theater will take on unbelievable new dimensions."[1] So said Bob Rauschenberg. With the naiveté and exuberance of an amateur, he set to work to realize it. In the fall of 1966, he and Billy Klüver gathered a group of forty friends—Bob's artist friends (10), Billy's scientist friends from Bell Laboratories (30)—to work together on specific projects, fusing performance art, dance, music, painting, film, television, and advanced technology into a theatrical experience. These first, rather primitive, experimental collaborations took place at the Twenty-fifth Street 69th Regiment Armory, home of the landmark Armory show of 1913, where Duchamp's *Nude Descending a Staircase* caused such a sensation. I wrote to Earle: "Armory show began badly. Audience kept out of the hall one hour before entering Steve's [Paxton] tunnels of plastic which were really very beautiful. Then, at 10:15, after all the people had come through, they announced an intermission. The audience was irritated already and the evening never really got off the ground."

In the first few evenings of the *Nine Evenings: Theatre and Engineering,* three-quarters of the technical apparatus didn't work. At the start of David Tudor's piece, out of twenty circuits, only three were working. As Clive Barnes wrote, "If this is a sample of American scientific achievement, the Russians will surely get to the moon first." David and John Cage claimed that their pieces worked very well the second time.

To bring the audience closer to the action, musician John Cage hatched a plan. He sowed stooges among the spectators, cued to leave their seats when the performance began. One by one, they trickled into the arena to disport among his illuminated machines. Soon most of the audience followed suit. "It was a way of getting them involved, participating," said Cage.[2]

As the week progressed, the technical aspects improved somewhat, but stress took its toll on everyone: Bob was rendered completely voiceless with a serious case of laryngitis; Yvonne Rainer was rushed to the hospital after her first performance with gangrene in her intestines and came very close to dying; Billy Klüver hovered near a nervous breakdown. The armory event was $50,000 in debt; rumor had the total cost at $150,000. The critical response—"incredible amateurism," "feeble," "dull," "offensive pretentiousness," "paralyzing boredom," "vilely done"—must have been disheartening for those participants who believed they'd created something "beautiful," "marvelous," "exhilarating." One of the chief sponsors of *Nine Evenings,* Mrs. Albert Last, had this to say: "I believe in experimentation. Had it been successful it would have been a failure."[3] "We are only scratching the surface," said L. J. Robinson, the systems-coordinator of the project. "There are uncharted worlds yet to be discovered—technological worlds that could totally change the face of theater as we know it."[4] Clive Barnes had it right: "This depressing spectacle is very probably a ramshackle sign post into a genuine artistic future."[5]

Undaunted, Billy Klüver founded Experiments in Art and Technology, better known as EAT, and devoted his life to helping artists connect with appropriate scientists to work in whatever direction their imaginations would lead them. "EAT would be a success," Billy said, "when it is no longer needed, when artists and engineers felt it perfectly natural to know one another and reach across the divide for help and inspiration."[6] The passage of time has proved him correct, one example being NASA's recent invitation to Laurie Anderson to be an "artist in residence."

Despite Merce's professed openness to technology, his own experience with *Variations V* and witnessing the frustrations and failures of *Nine Evenings* dampened his interest in exploring further collaborations. The technological aspects of *Variations V* never worked as originally planned and consumed too much money and stage time. Although Merce would work with film, beginning in the seventies, and in the nineties seize on the computer program "Life Forms" as a way to triumph over his growing physical limitations, it was not until 1999, with his brilliant, groundbreaking, and very moving *Biped,* that Merce was willing to fully try again. In collaboration with Shelley Eshkar and Paul Kaiser (a true collaboration

Setting off on the 1964 world tour.
Front, left to right: Shareen Blair, David Tudor, Alex Hay, Bob Rauschenberg,
Mrs. Gray (Benjie's English nanny), Bill Davis, Deborah Hay, Barbara Lloyd,
Steve Paxton, Lew Lloyd, Merce.
On the steps from the top: (steward), me, David Vaughan, Viola Farber,
John, Sandra Neels, Albert Reid

Rome, 1969. *Left to right:* Jim Klosty, me, my mother,
Rick Nelson, Meg Harper

ABOVE: Jim, the photographer, on tour with the company
BELOW: "Tall Tale" with John, backstage at BAM

The touring life: exhaustion.
A B O V E : Merce. A quick snooze on Staten Island
B E L O W : One-night stands in Holland: Charlie Atlas, Gordon Mumma,
Mimi Johnson, and me

Between rehearsal and performance at The Walker in Minneapolis.
Left to right: Valda Setterfield, Merce, Jean Rigg, Charlie Atlas, and me

TOP LEFT: With Rick Nelson
ABOVE LEFT: Marianne Preger-Simon with John
ABOVE RIGHT: 1964 world tour administrators Lew Lloyd and David Vaughan
BELOW: Bénédicte Pésle with Merce in Venice, 1972

South American Tour, 1968. The company. *Seated, left to right:* Susanna Hayman-Chaffey, Meg Harper, Valda Setterfield, Gordon Mumma, Barbara Lloyd, Merce, me, Beverly Emmons, Jasper Johns. *Standing:* Sandra Neels, Mel Wong, Jeff Slayton, and John. Missing are Chase Robinson, David Tudor, and Lew Lloyd.

ABOVE: The 1969 *Dance Magazine* Award
ceremony at the Plaza Hotel. *Left to right:* Agnes
de Mille, Frederick Ashton, me, Ted Shawn
RIGHT: With Antony Tudor at my rehearsal of
West Country at Juilliard
BELOW: Curtain call, New York City Center,
1970. *What are two modern dancers doing with
this group? Front, left to right:* me, Lucia Chase,
Eleanor d'Antuono, Agnes de Mille, Margot
Fonteyn, Carla Fracci, Melissa Hayden. Merce
is behind, to the right of Lucia Chase.

this time), he explored the possibilities of the new animation technology of motion capture.

In *Variations V, How to Pass, Kick, Fall and Run,* and *Place,* the company had managed without a resident designer. How to replace the irreplaceable Bob Rauschenberg? Jasper Johns had helped Bob with almost all his Cunningham sets and costumes and was the logical choice, but he had already made it clear that he did not want to tour with the company, nor to assume all the costume, decor, and lighting assignments as Bob had done. However, he cared deeply about how these elements affected Merce's choreography. After considerable persuasion on John's part, he agreed to become the company's artistic advisor, and in that role to suggest other artists to work with Merce. In a conversation with David Vaughan, he explained: "When I thought of the people who might be available to do the work that I was being invited to do, I decided that I might do it in ways that would offend me less when I went to see the performance. It was a poor way to make a decision, an arrogant way, but that was my feeling."[7] There were no new works until the spring of 1967, when Merce began choreographing *Scramble.* Jasper invited Frank Stella to design the set and costumes. Frank's designs required nothing technological beyond rolling wheels.

In January, Merce and John joined "an unorthodox group of artists"— Robert Creeley, poet; Billy Klüver, electronic engineer; Leonard Lye, sculptor; Jack Tworkov, painter, and Stanley VanDerBeek, filmmaker— and were dispatched by the New York State Council on the Arts to enliven seven upstate campuses in a program called Contemporary Voices in the Arts. Their assignment was to speak with students, demonstrate techniques, and above all to interact as pioneers in their respective fields.[8] Not interested in the usual seminar format, they decided to give a series of Happenings in which each would "do his own thing." The tour culminated with *TV Dinner—Homage to E.A.T. (Food for Thought)* at the 92nd Street Y on February 25. It was an unmitigated disaster. New York City was presented with a most unorthodox, not to say maddening, performance, where once again technology failed and enraged the audience. On the back of my program, I wrote a blow-by-blow description of the unfolding events. An excerpt:

A Dada situation—movies on ceiling, on walls right & left—curtain opens on stage filled with the "contemporary voices" in the flesh—milling about in silhouette before sitting down to an elaborately set dining table, gold chairs, with red velvet, artists dressed quite formally in black, serving staff of several people. Contact mikes attached everywhere. Very huge Tworkov hanging overhead, suspended above the table. Stage lights changing, sometimes quite beautiful. People at table having conversation but the mikes aren't working properly so can't hear them. Two TV cameras on stage. Closed circuit TV cast on walls and ceiling. Cameras pick up flambé cooking, faces talking or chewing, the food or the wine on the table. "Tower Suite" serving dinner. How rude can you get? And *arrogant!*—to sit and eat a five course dinner [described in detail in the program: Scottish Smoked Salmon served with lightly buttered pumpernickel, Twin Tournedos au poivre, Château Latour Pauillac 1960 . . . etc.]

The original idea for this event was credited to Jack Tworkov (there couldn't be a sweeter man), who came to the conclusion that the best part of their upstate touring had been when they'd had dinner together, happily conversing. David Vaughan, who had functioned as their tour manager, was asked to join the others onstage, as the representative for Theater. As John explained: "We're widening our sense of syntax. We feel expanded by the relationship—and furthermore we're enjoying each other's company."[9] But "Reality Theater" in 1967 was no more convincing or authentic than "Reality TV" in 2005. When the mikes finally did start to work, I scribbled: "BORING—at cross purposes conversation. It was better before." People walked out in droves. Not even Merce rising and dancing for his supper saved the situation.

That winter, as my personal life shattered, I struggled with depression and terrible asthma attacks that kept me fighting to breathe. Any sense of serenity I might have possessed had evaporated. I spent sleepless nights. I lost weight. Foolishly, I didn't talk to anyone, not even to my mother, about the cause of my misery. Reading her journal years later, I discovered how worried she'd been about me. I could tell her only that Earle needed to be in Europe for his work, which was true, but certainly not the whole truth.

Earle took a small studio in Newark, New Jersey, to store some of his belongings and left again for France on January 29. On February 7, the premiere of his *Modules I & II* for orchestra and two conductors (Earle and Eleazar de Carvalho) was performed at the Théâtre des Champs-Élysées by the French National Orchestra and received ecstatic reviews: "constantly beautiful," "silky, shimmering . . . this dynamism of color is very extraordinary," "a character of pure beauty," "captivating, strange, and wildly applauded." Three weeks later, at the Théâtre de l'Atelier, his *Calder Piece* had its first performance, with Calder attending, and was equally successful: ". . . a ballet and a game. One is surprised that it is also music which develops and progresses . . . a triumph."[10] "A spectacle for the eyes as well as for the ears, and of the most poetic kind."[11]

On a perfect day in late May 1963, I had accompanied Earle on an expedition to meet with Alexander Calder at his New England farmhouse on Painters Hill Road in Roxbury, Connecticut. With no little trepidation, Earle was about to propose an audacious idea to this man whose work he so revered and had been so profoundly influential on his own. We were greeted by Calder's handsome wife, Louisa, who was the grandniece of William and Henry James, and "Sandy," as everyone was instructed to call him, a delightfully gruff, sturdy teddy bear of a man with an unruly shock of white hair. Across the pasture in the valley below was Arthur Miller's property, where the playwright lived with his third wife, Marilyn Monroe. After lunch and a tour of the vast, sunny studio, mind-boggling in its monumental chaotic clutter—mobiles hanging from above, stabiles stalking the corners, canvases stacked against the walls, metal, coils of wire, mysterious tools everywhere—I joined Louisa in their kitchen, where every utensil, gadget, pot, and pan seemed to be a handmade Calder artifact.

The time for Earle to make his proposition had arrived: would Calder consider collaborating on a mobile/stabile that could serve as conductor for a musical composition? The answer was affirmative. Would Calder object to having the mobile elements struck with drumsticks or other percussion implements? Sandy roared with laughter: "They can kick the thing if they want to!" Four years later, Earle reported that at its premiere in Paris, "*Calder Piece* went very well . . . musicians love to play it and I like it and it is funny (four guys chasing and banging on the mobile) and beautiful. It was a great success . . . Calder was unexpectedly there and seemed to like it but thought we should have hit it with hammers . . . thought we didn't because we didn't like the sound of it and said he'd have to make us one in brass, which would sound better."[12]

That winter and spring, Earle traveled the length and breadth of Europe—to France, Germany, Greece, Spain, Italy, Belgium, England, and Sweden—conducting his own music, teaching, lecturing, and again trying to make recordings of contemporary music, as well as holing up in borrowed apartments to write music and articles. France overflowed with disaffected American artists. Although he had many friends there and loved European life, his letters were nonetheless filled with bitter complaints about his lack of work and visibility in America.

Although Earle and I continued to write each other, my letters were constrained, self-conscious. I'd suddenly become aware that while I had always poured out almost every thought and feeling in my letters to him, that intimacy had been mostly one-sided. More than once in 1967 I wrote him that I was not enjoying performing and was feeling that it must all stop soon.

Sometime in the fall of 1966, Jim Klosty was driving uptown on Third Avenue when a car, attempting to back into a parking place in front of the Cunningham Studio, slammed into his Sunbeam sports car, purchased abroad the same year he'd seen his first Cunningham performance. Jim, very annoyed at the incompetence of the driver, got out of his car and was confronted with a grinning, embarrassed, appropriately apologetic John Cage. The identity of "the culprit" so delighted Jim that instead of asking John for his insurance information, he asked him if he would sign the dent. Cage said he would be happy to. And that's how I met Jim Klosty. In mid-January 1967, with a can of paint and paintbrush in hand, Jim appeared at Brandeis University (his alma mater) in Waltham, Massachusetts, where the company gave two performances on January 14 and 15. John signed the dented door. At the post-performance green-room reception, a man with a rich, resonant actor's voice introduced himself to me as someone who had fallen in love with the company in London in 1964. What I remembered later about the meeting was the voice, and the intelligent questions asked. Some years later, Jim sold the Sunbeam but kept the door.

The company had some out-of-state performances in the South and Midwest during the winter and spring of '67, plus an unexpected last-minute engagement at the Brooklyn Academy of Music to replace the Canadian Ballet, who had canceled a performance. In Rock Hill, South Carolina, our rented cars were vandalized. Tires slashed. One window smashed to bits. Random destruction or racial prejudice? Gus Solomons jr., an MIT graduate from a middle-class Boston family, had never been to the South. Traveling there for the first time as the lone black man in an otherwise all-white company had to be fraught with anxiety and pain, but he never spoke of it to us. He'd never seen "Whites Only" restrooms, segregated restaurants; never really experienced blatant racial discrimination, although when he had joined us in Chicago the previous year, the hotel management was less than cordial until Lew arrived to help check him in.

Nineteen sixty-seven in the United States was a time of profound unrest. An unpopular war in Vietnam, now two years old, brought hundreds of thousands into the streets of New York City to protest. College campuses were in turmoil. In the summer of 1967, known as "the hot summer," race riots erupted in major cities all across the United States. While we were performing at the Ravinia Festival in July, the worst race riot in our country's history was going on in Detroit. Forty-three people were left dead, more than two thousand injured, some five thousand arrested; looting, fires, and property damage in the millions ravaged the city. Martin Luther King proposed a merger between the antiwar movement and the civil-rights movement, calling the United States government the "greatest purveyor of violence in the world."[13] A year later King was assassinated and there was rioting in the nation's capital. Two months later Robert Kennedy was killed. More deaths and mayhem; our country was floundering in a moral quagmire. In contrast to these very real problems in the world, mine were insignificant. Dancing seemed a frivolous and unnecessary activity. John's response to the affairs of the world was to write *Diary: How to Improve the World (You Will Only Make It Worse)*. Merce simply went on dancing, making dances, doing what he knew how to do. Once, when asked by a student if she should make dance her career, he responded, "If you have a choice and can do anything else, run in the opposite direction as fast as you can."

In April, with the promise of spring in the air, I began taking ballet classes with Richard Thomas, in addition to studying with Miss Craske. I hoped that a change—any change—would snap me out of my malaise, my lack of interest in dance and dancing. With Yseult Riopelle, I took off for Canada to visit Expo 67 in Montreal and view Buckminster Fuller's magnificent dome and the Jasper Johns *Map (Based on Fuller's Dymaxion Air Ocean World)*.

In May, Merce began concentrated work on new choreography. The German documentary film team from Hamburg arrived and all but moved into the studio, their eagle-eyed cameras and eavesdropping microphones zeroing in on every facet of our working lives. Further adding to our self-consciousness was the presence of Calvin Tomkins, the author of *The Bride and the Bachelors*, a collection of profiles of Marcel Duchamp, Jean Tinguely, John Cage, and Bob Rauschenberg published in 1965. Eventually, the book would be republished with the addition of the profile of Merce he was writing at the time. Sitting unobtrusively on the sidelines, Calvin's presence could be forgotten, but there was no forgetting the film crew. Merce tolerated their invasion, but it made him as uneasy and self-conscious as it did the rest of us. Rehearsals were fraught with tension. The dance wasn't going well; he showed the material quickly, changing it from day to day, leaving us unsure of exactly what the rhythms were, or the phrasing, or even the steps. The film captures it all, along with the disagreements among the dancers, the exasperations, frustrations, and tears.

On the third of June, Mr. and Mrs. Jean de Menil and Philip Johnson co-hosted a benefit party at Philip Johnson's famous glass house in New Canaan, Connecticut. This was a society occasion covered gleefully by *Vogue, Harper's Bazaar,* and *Women's Wear Daily,* with photos of some of the four hundred "beautiful people" and a politician or two, including Senator Jacob Javits, strolling around Mr. Johnson's estate with glasses in their hands. "The clothes are fabulous," gushed *Women's Wear Daily,* but then, in its snide way, criticized two ladies (naming names) "who should know better" for overdressing in glitter and velvet.

It was no picnic for the dancers. Billed as *Event #5,* the hour-long program included bits and pieces of *Scramble,* the work-in-progress, plus sections of dances from the repertory. A platform had been built at the lower edge of a meadow, against a stone wall. The audience congregated on the sloping meadow above it. Large colored weather balloons surrounded the performing area. As our performance began, the sun was setting into the trees behind us. A beautiful event, everyone said. Calvin Tomkins described a moment near the end, during a section from *Scramble:* "One of several big helium weather balloons that had been tethered behind the stage cut loose from its moorings; it rose swiftly above the trees and into a violet sky, where it cut across the white vapor trail of a passing jet—an effect that seemed perfectly in keeping with the atmosphere of the dance."[14]

John's score, especially composed for this evening, was orchestrated for viola, tam-tam (a gong), radio, and three automobiles. An array of contact microphones were hooked up to just about everything including the automobiles' windshield wipers, doors, and engines. I described it for Earle:

It was one hour of sheer torture. I'm *not* exaggerating. A loud speaker had been placed in a tree, directed toward the left side of the stage and the volume was deafening. It made me nauseous, and actually HURT my ears. I kept trying to turn my head to get out of direct range but couldn't. Albert Reid said he did that, too—to no avail. Merce was bothered too. And Sandra and Gus. The others weren't on stage as much as we were and could escape it for long periods. Of course the sounds were ugly, relentless. . . . Sheer cacophony! Ironically no one meant that the loudspeaker should be aimed at the stage. Just last minute inefficiency. . . . No one thought to test its range in relation to the dancers. . . . hours and hours of rehearsal all shot to hell by the stupid, careless, thoughtless, amateurish last minute proceedings of the "musicians." Merce was FURIOUS! He said he would never work with that kind of sound situation again. . . . It is irresponsible of John, Gordon and David not to know about the medium they work with. If we knew as little about our bodies as they seem to know about the physical and psychological effects of sound we'd be considered RANK AMATEURS. They play at "music-making" like thoughtless children.

The event over, we jumped into a waiting station wagon at the platform's edge and were driven off to safety. Once in the car, our pent-up fury erupted like a hornet's nest run over by a lawn mower. I'd rarely seen Merce so demonstrably angry and distraught. Supper baskets with bottles of Beaujolais were provided in Philip Johnson's kitchen for those of us who did not wish to mingle with the hundreds of guests or join the dancing to the frantic sounds of the Velvet Underground. That music, taking over from the cacophony of Cage's "world premiere," soon outraged the neighbors, who called in the police. At midnight, when our bus pulled away and headed back to New York, my ears were still throbbing, but the benefit did what it set out to do: it wiped out the Cunningham Foundation's debts. Not only were we no longer in the red, we were actually just a little in the black.

On Sunday, July 23, at the Ravinia Festival on Chicago's North Shore, Earle's *Available Forms I* was performed by the Chicago Symphony Orchestra, conducted by Luciano Berio. I was there; Earle was not. Two days later, in the same outdoor pavilion, *Scramble* had its first performance. The entourage accompanying us to Chicago included Calvin Tomkins and French photographer, Hervé Gloaguen. Shortly before the performance began, Frank Stella arrived backstage in his usual T-shirt, a cigar stuck between the gaping hole where his two front teeth should have been (he hated wearing his false teeth), needing two dollars for his cab fare from O'Hare. "I wasn't going to come," he explained, "but then I decided I'd hate myself too much if I didn't, so I just dropped what I was doing and went out to La Guardia."[15]

Frank had watched one rehearsal of *Scramble* before designing the set. Toshi Ichiyanagi, who wrote the music, had also attended one early rehearsal. *Scramble* has at least fifteen interchangeable sections. The music, *Activities for Orchestra,* also has sections, like the dance, that can be scrambled in performance. And Frank's set—composed of varying lengths of canvas banners in the six primary and secondary colors, each banner stretched between aluminum rods of various heights on wheeled bases—can be arranged in dozens of configurations and changed from section to section, or even within sections.

In his preliminary notes for *Scramble,* Merce wrote: "To make a dance without flavor." Well, the choreography as a whole may have been "without flavor," as apparently he intended, but the individual sections certainly had quite distinctive "flavors"—discovered in the doing of them. Merce had a solo with pugilistic boxing moves; in another he covered his face with both hands, opened them and bellowed. No flavor? A women's trio had phlegmatic, isolated moves of head, rib cage, and hips, lazy crossing and opening moves of the knee and foot, broken by sudden sharply attacked *pliés relevés* into second, into attitude, before falling back into the slow indolent moves. The duet for Sandra and Gus, both of whom possess extraordinarily long legs, was like an erotic mating dance of praying mantises. No flavor? The men's trio for Merce, Albert, and Gus was described by Tomkins as "athletic . . . somewhat violent at times."[16] Water and Air— swimming and flying, undulating fish and darting bird—that's how my solo and much of my part's choreography evolved for me. Working on it was a challenge and a joy: playing with liquid, rippling port de bras, unlike anything Merce had given me before; discovering the phrasing—the quick accents, speed changes, subtle syncopations; and learning to stretch out a long *plié arabesque* or *attitude relevé* to their limits, then with all speed propelling myself through space and into the air. All this seemed bursting with flavor! But Merce stuck to his original premise. Standing in the wings, waiting to go on after a lengthy hiatus during which we hadn't performed *Scramble* for some months, I murmured to Merce, "It's been so long, I've lost the quality of this dance." His quick response: "There is no quality to lose." Well, I beg to differ.

Less than two weeks after the *Scramble* premiere at the Ravinia Festival we were performing it again at the American Dance Festival in New London, Connecticut. On the outdoor pavilion stage in Ravinia, the audience was a remote, distant sea of bodies, but in the smaller, very intimate Palmer Auditorium at Connecticut College, the audience was both visible and audible. During our "goofy duet" (Doris Hering in *Dance Magazine*), or "manic *pas de deux*" (Don McDonagh in the *New York Times*), the audience laughed. It had never occurred to me that the duet could be perceived as funny. Of course, I'd never really known what Merce was doing. After seeing it on film, I understood how the audience might react in that way, but at the time I wasn't prepared. I felt laughed "at" and humiliated. Not until we'd gotten through *Winterbranch* and *How to . . .* did tears fall. That same evening after the performance, Theresa Dickinson sent me a letter: "Conn. College may find the unfamiliar laughable but I for one find it both exciting and moving. I think that Merce must love you very much to give you the *most* different, most impossible things to do."[17]

Merce, love me very much? I hardly thought so. But, in fact, I think those tears of hurt and humiliation allowed me to vent a much deeper, far greater unhappiness. I recently found, folded small and tucked into the Connecticut program, a morbid note to myself about loneliness and loss—father, husband, my dear friend Remy, and in their place no one. The sadness was very real. Reading the note for the first time many decades after placing it between the pages of the program in 1967, I could viscerally revisit the despair I felt writing it.

Fortunately a complete change was in the offing and with it an opportunity to spend time with non-dance folk—conductors, theater and museum directors—all with wide interests and enthusiasms. Merce and I had a two-week residency teaching master classes in technique and choreography sponsored by the Walker Art Center, and the two of us presented a lecture-demonstration at the Tyrone Guthrie Theater. But the real joy of this mid-August engagement was having stimulating conversations with the lively artists working in the Minneapolis area, attending performances at the Guthrie, and best of all, getting to spend time with Sage and John Cowles, and Martin and Mickey Friedman. Sage—dancer, filmmaker, choreographer, and wonderful fun to be with—had known Merce since their years studying at the American School. She became a Cunningham Foundation Board member, eventually its co-chair, and remains to this day a loyal and fervent supporter, along with her husband John—a newspaper man deeply engaged in world affairs—whose family owned the *Minneapolis Tribune* and *Harper's Magazine*. Martin Friedman, a fire-brand enthusiast bursting with energy, was the director of the Walker, and his wife, Mickey, was a wonderful design artist. Their daughter Lise took my class and would one day join the Cunningham company. Those two weeks—including the teaching—turned out to be extraordinarily rewarding, and many of our students said they planned to come to New York to study with us.

Merce actually gave himself a brief vacation at Jasper's place in Nags Head, North Carolina. Then, claiming to dread the very thought of it, he flew off to Stockholm to work with Birgit Cullberg's company on *Summerspace*. Niklas Ek, Birgit's son, who had briefly apprenticed with us, was to dance Merce's part. I spent the next month in Massachusetts with my family, determined to rest and gain weight after seeing photographs taken in Chicago in which I looked appallingly like a concentration camp victim. With time on my hands, I began working on a new article for *Ballet Review* and began thinking about choreography for a dance commissioned by the Manhattan Festival Ballet. From a letter to Earle:

Ideas come from god knows where. They surprise the hell out of me! Movement, of course, is derivative of all I've ever studied: primarily Cunningham, Tudor, Craske with my Denishawn background lurking around. But
the other ideas (theatre ideas I guess you'd call them) they're crazy and
nothing I've seen before. That's why I'm making it. I want to see these things
for real on stage. It's probably my imagination that the ideas are new—they
aren't, I'm sure. But I'm excited about whatever it is I'm doing. Piggy me—
I'm doing costumes, decor and choreography. I understand Merce's reluctance to turn over HIS work to a designer.

After my McLuhan article was published, late in 1966, the *Ballet
Review* editor, Arlene Croce, suggested I write another one. This one, "On
Chance," would require much research and I looked forward to doing it.
Talking with all the lively people in Minneapolis had whetted my appetite
to delve into the history and philosophical raison d'être of the ideas that
John and Merce were working with. It was a productive, heady month. I
finished the article at the end of October and gave it to Merce to read. His
only comment: "So serious!"

The Manhattan Festival Ballet dancers learned quickly, and except for
one pesky section I kept struggling with, the choreography came easily. In
mid-November it had to be put on hold for a week of one-night stands touring with Merce and company ending with a single performance at the
Brooklyn Academy of Music. At the University of Illinois, we danced in
the vast new Assembly Hall, but compared to John's riotous *Musicircus* in
the stock pavilion the following evening, our performance was a tame
affair. *Musicircus* offered a mélange of activities including compositions by
twenty-five composers with nearly twice that number of musicians to perform them; a jazz band; a few dancers; and some films and projections.
There was no overall score, no directions other than to perform whatever
one wished. Creative anarchy! His comment: "You will hear all the music
at once; you won't be able to hear a thing; you'll be able to hear everything."

The performers were spread out on platforms in the middle of the pavilion from one end to the other and the audience was free to roam around
them at will. This went on for four hours. John—a beatific grin on his
face—wandered around the pavilion in rapture. To everyone he met he'd
gush, "Isn't it marvelous!"—inaudibly of course, since the multifarious
sound explosions made conversation impossible. The "musicircus" was
the crowning achievement of his stint as composer-in-residence at the
University of Illinois that year. The front page of the *Daily Illini* read:

"Musicircus Rocks Stock Pavillion" and continued, "c r e s c e n d o e s of screeches, thunderclaps of sound and flashes of multi-colored light . . . It was a night not so much for blowing your mind as it was for blowing an eardrum . . . It could have been conceivable to have seen Hannibal riding elephants through the large doors and not out of the context of the unexpected and the random. It was a Happening in which the ridiculous was made commonplace for a few hours."[18]

The *Daily Illini* also stated that "The participants were treated to performances by the French mime, Claude Kipnis, and lead dancer in the Cunningham dance troupe, Carolyn Brown, who individually performed routines from a platform as apparently the mood moved them."[19] We did? Can I really have completely forgotten something so totally bizarre? A postcard to my mother mentions the "Musicircus" only briefly: "Wild affair—exciting, noisy, fun. We did some impromptu dancing."

Our 1967 season came to a close at the Brooklyn Academy on December 2, with performances of *Scramble, Place,* and *How to . . . ,* our current *Cav & Pag,* i.e., the "ham and eggs" of touring opera companies. *Place* won the real kudos. Deborah Jowitt: "One of the best dances I've ever seen."[20] Clive Barnes: "It is Mr. Cunningham's finest and most powerful work to date."[21] Alan M. Kriegsman, reviewing that concert for the *Washington Post,* seemed to understand something about Merce's work that few others did, or at least articulated:

> The motions of Cunningham's dances are not the goal-directed movements of individual personalities seeking specific ends. But the motions themselves are rich in expressive implication. The dancers project fear, for example, not simulating the movement of fearful people, but by showing us motions that somehow articulate the very feeling of fear. There is also, of course, the emotionally charged presence of Cunningham the dancer, and in particular, his incomparably histrionic face. Enigmatic, cunning, wry, elemental, witty, it hovers like an omen over all his work.[22]

Gone were the three-day drives for a single performance. Gone, too, and sorely missed—at least by John and me—were the roadside picnics, frivolous detours, insane Scrabble-playing, tootling along the highway on the lookout for mushrooms, and most of all, the back seat Zen-philosophy seminars à la Cage. But management was doing its job and doing it well. In 1968 the company had thirty weeks of employment! With the exception of the world tour, we'd never had so much work, and yet the financial condition of the company hovered, as ever, on the brink of disaster. Still, it could be claimed that we were a bona fide professional dance company. For the first time ever, we dancers were given a full year's AGMA contract—from September 1968 through August 1969, although we didn't actually sign the contract until January 1969. It took nearly a year of negotiations between Lew Lloyd and AGMA, with input from the dancers, to create a totally new contractual concept that would reflect the special needs and problems of modern-dance companies.

The company left New York City in early February of '68 and did not return until early April. Upstate New York touring—to Ithaca, Hamilton, Rochester, Oneonta, Geneseo, Brockport, Fredonia—is not fun, especially in winter. The weather is guaranteed to be terrible, travel hazardous and, with few exceptions in those years, the accommodations poor, the food worse, the theaters dismal, and audiences unreliable. Fortunately, the first four weeks of this tour were taken up with a residency sponsored by the State University of New York at Buffalo and Buffalo State University College, giving Merce the luxury of having his company available to him twenty-four hours a day, with concentrated time to choreograph two major works whose premieres would take place at our residency's end.

Two new company members had to be taught the post-1964 repertory. Peter Saul had left, plagued with back injuries. Jeff Slayton, an Adelphi University student of Viola's and previously a soloist with the Richmond (Virginia) Ballet Company, was engaged to replace him. Tall, rangy, fearless, Jeff would propel himself into whatever he was given to do with utter abandon. His risk-taking was inspiring and instructive—indeed, shaming. Yseult Riopelle had also left. The rigor and discipline of the Cunningham work ethic was daunting to her. Not yet twenty, intimidated by her powerful artist parents and step-parents, Yseult confessed to feeling insecure and paralyzed with fear in Merce's presence. She booked passage on the *Queen Elizabeth* and sailed to France within the month. This saddened me: I was fond of Yseult and had come to feel responsible for her well-being when Joan Mitchell, on behalf of Yseult's father, Jean-Paul, brought her to New York and put her into my hands. But, alas, no one can ignite the passion to dance if the sparks aren't there to begin with.

Meg Harper, a magna cum laude graduate of the University of Illinois, replaced her. Meg needed no one to ignite her passion to dance. At Illinois, she was introduced to Cage/Cunningham ideas by Joan Skinner, one of the Graham-trained dancers who danced with Merce in some of his first choreographic efforts. Meg began listening to Cage music and read his book *Silence.* A pivotal, life-changing moment for her came when she saw the company perform in the fall of 1965 at the Harper Theatre in Chicago. "Well, I never slept that night," she told me. "Basically, I fell in love."[1] In the fall of 1966, she began studying at the studio; in the summer of 1967, she took Merce's repertory class and learned *Rune.* On December 7, 1967—a day she will never forget—Merce invited her to join the company.

The two new dances, nameless to us at the time of their making, were utterly different from each other. *Rainforest* is unique in its structure. There are five slightly overlapping sections, but each of the six dancers appeared with one or two others or alone, then exited and was not seen again (with the exception of Merce who was onstage at the beginning and at the end). It's "a character dance," Merce told an interviewer.[2] I would describe it as "a creature dance" set in an otherworldly jungle, inhabited by untamed solitary beings who meet in strange, sensual, inexplicable, mysterious, sometimes hostile encounters and part, much as animals might do in the wild.

To decipher what Merce is thinking about when choreographing a new piece, it can be helpful to know what he's reading. Colin Turnbull's *The Forest People,* about following pygmies through tangled underbrush, was apparently one inspiration. The rain forests of the Pacific Northwest that Merce knew as a boy provided the title. In the opening duet, two creatures (Merce and Barbara Lloyd) seemed to be awakening in primordial ooze— reaching, stretching, slithering around and across each other in a sinuous, sensuous, slow-motion reverie. More than thirty years later, Merce and

Jeannie Steele, who had inherited Barbara's role for a revival, watched a video of the first performance. "That Barbara," he said admiringly, "she knew how to crawl across a man's lap!" Merce had made the part for her feminine body, her soft, deliciously voluptuous way of moving, and her beautiful, angelic face.

Rainforest language—that is, the movement "spoken"—is idiosyncratic: cupped hands, like little paws, stretching, exploring and retreating; a woman's body rolled slowly across the floor, pushed along by gentle nudges of a man's head or by two men standing above her, solemnly gesturing with outstretched arms; wild head-flings, hair flying; arms flailing; hands clenched into fists assaulting the air; contorted twists of torso; isolated pelvic thrusts by two men, like male apes marking their territory, asserting dominance.

From its gentle, quiet opening, *Rainforest* slowly accelerates, takes on intensity and speed, and ends in a whirlwind fury with Merce's final solo. After the first rehearsal of our duet section, Albert said to me, privately, "We'll never be able to make *that* beautiful!" As Merce developed our duet material and my solo that followed, my character emerged: spitfire, hellcat—feral and dangerous. I ate it up! Never in my life had I moved so fast as I did in the first performance of *Rainforest*. I was consumed by a fiery urgency that propelled me through space and time. When I got off the stage, Gus Solomons said, "You left out . . ." Oh my god! I'd left out my most favorite part, and that was the performance recorded for posterity by the filmmaker Richard Leacock! It's been said, by whom I don't remember, that *Rainforest* set modern dance back thirty years. Or, as Jill Johnston wrote, "Take away the pillows and what you have left is a 'modern dance.' "[3]

Two dozen or so helium-filled shiny silver Mylar pillows floated around and above the dancers or skimmed along the floor. Untethered, they had a life of their own, and became active partners in the choreography as we moved around and through them. An arm slicing through the air, a kick, merely a body passing by could set them dancing with us through the stage space. When Jasper told Andy Warhol that Merce would like him to design *Rainforest,* Andy's reply, according to Jasper, was "Oh, just take a lot of those pillows," and when asked about costumes, said, "Oh, they shouldn't wear any clothes."[4] Merce had seen the Andy Warhol installation called *Silver Clouds* at the Castelli Gallery, and was immediately struck by their potential as decor, but Warhol's idea for the costumes—that we should dance naked—was deemed . . . impractical. Jasper took over the costume assignment. The closest he could reasonably come to total nudity was flesh-colored tights and leotards. Merce asked Jasper to roughen them up a bit, "as if the skin were torn."[5] Jasper recalls Merce showing him some ragged, torn practice clothes and saying "I think something like this might be all right."[6] Jasper's solution: cut and rip each costume, exposing flesh on a leg, an arm, the chest or back. Where the fabric was ripped, he tied a small knot in the loose end. Each of us had a unique, "original Jasper Johns," in our book more highly prized than any original Dior could have been.

Walkaround Time is a 180-degree turnaround from *Rainforest.* Spare, austere, inscrutable, forty-nine minutes long, it has two parts separated by an entr'acte—an intermission not for the audience but for the performers—during which the dancers don sweat clothes or robes, loll about the stage, talk with one another or with the musicians in the pit, stretch, rehearse difficult steps. Cunningham calls *Walkaround Time* his homage to Marcel Duchamp, but this idea began to evolve only after a suggestion made by Jasper one evening at Teeny and Marcel Duchamp's apartment on Tenth Street in New York. At the time, John was studying chess with Marcel. After dinner, while John and Teeny were playing with Marcel sitting quietly looking on (John's chess skills were no match for Marcel's), Jasper asked Merce if he would be interested in having a set based on Duchamp's *The Large Glass.* Although doubtful that Marcel would agree, Merce immediately responded, "Oh, yes!" Jasper crossed the room and spoke privately with Duchamp, who was horrified. "But who will do the work?" he wanted to know, indicating by his tone of voice that he certainly wouldn't. When Jasper assured him that he, Jasper, would do it, Duchamp agreed.[7]

As Jasper envisioned the set, there was an enormous amount of work required. Seven lightweight metal box frames of varying sizes had to be constructed. Silkscreens of the images from *The Large Glass* had to be made, then transferred onto heavyweight transparent vinyl and painted in the appropriate colors. (The front panels of each box had only a line drawing; the back panels were in color.) The boxes were then sheathed in the plastic, sealed, and inflated so that they could stand alone. Two of the larger ones were suspended from the flies. The others could be placed anywhere on the stage and moved during the dance. A cardboard replica of the set was constructed for us to use in rehearsal. Duchamp saw the set before it was taken to Buffalo, and according to Jasper, he seemed pleased, but he did have one request. At some point during the performance he wanted the seven boxes assembled in an approximation of his painting. Merce chose to do this at the end. After seeing the New York premiere of *Walkaround Time* at the Brooklyn Academy of Music later that year, Clive Barnes wrote, "A strong case could be made for its being the finest decor American dance has ever known . . . a thing of almost miraculous beauty."[8]

Jasper, Marcel, and Teeny came to Buffalo in time for the afternoon dress rehearsal on the day of the premiere. When it was time to set the bows, Jasper declined Merce's invitation to join the company onstage. Marcel accepted. Jasper related what happened after the performance: "When the time came for him to go up, I offered to help him, which help he shrugged off, saying, 'Aren't you coming?' And I said 'No,' and he turned and he said 'I'm just as frightened as you are.' "[9] My guess is Duchamp wasn't frightened at all. Even at eighty, his physical presence was impressive—he was elegant and slender, he dressed impeccably, and he had no trouble climbing the stairs to the stage, where he stood between Merce and me, coolly accepting applause with the aplomb of someone born to the theater.

Early in Duchamp's painting life he said: "I was interested in ideas— I wanted to put painting once again at the service of the mind."[10] What was Merce's own thinking at the time of choreographing *Walkaround Time*? Reams have been written about *The Large Glass* (the shorthand title for *The Bride Stripped Bare by Her Bachelors, Even*) and Merce clearly did his homework. *Walkaround Time* is referential, enigmatic, and witty. Years later, he confided, "I put in lots of things about Duchamp and his work. I never tell anybody because this confuses people."[11] If one wants to engage in deciphering the puzzles encrypted in the dance, it demands effort on the part of the viewer, just as Duchamp's enigmatic painting does. Ten years after *Walkaround Time*'s premiere in Buffalo, the film critic and archivist John Mueller made that effort, having studied the Charles Atlas film of the dance, but to my knowledge no other dance critic made even a passing attempt at discovering correspondences between *The Large Glass* and the dance, although the work was in the repertory for five years.[12] As Mueller said, "*Walkaround Time* is so filled with quiet happenings and exquisite surprises that no one could conceivably get a full appreciation in a single viewing." Mueller excerpts:

Walkaround Time has a structure similar to that of *Relâche:* two parts separated by an "intermission" for the performers, but not for the audience. *The Large Glass* is also in two parts. In the seven minute "intermission" of *Walkaround Time* . . . the dancers lounge on stage . . . to suggest the "readymades"—to display the dancers in the ordinary everyday movement that, properly framed, can be seen to take on a beauty of its own. . . . other choreographic references to Duchamp relate to the Dada-inspired ballet *Relâche* which Duchamp helped with and in which he appeared. Cunningham's solo [jogging in place while stripping from one costume to another] may also relate to the story that Duchamp himself fleetingly appeared on stage in *Relâche* in the nude. . . . In *The Large Glass* the "bride" is kept serenely separate from her attending suitors, the "bachelors." . . . And of course, the entire choreographic aesthetic of *Walkaround Time*, at once austere, whimsical, transparent and meticulous, is like that of *The Large Glass* and is likely to appeal to someone with Duchamp's sensibilities. . . . *Walkaround Time* is, simply and purely a masterwork.[13]

While Barnes considered the dance a major work and "quite exceptionally beautiful,"[14] and Patrick O'Connor called it "a great work,"[15] most critics disagreed. Among the naysayers, Arlene Croce dismissed it with "It doesn't work"[16] and Walter Terry with "[It] was certainly a bore."[17] With the exception of Barnes and O'Connor, almost all of them complained of its length. Why, given its Duchampian set and the title of David Behrman's music, ". . . *for nearly an hour* . . . ," which was itself an allusion to another Duchamp glass painting, much smaller than *The Large Glass*, titled *To be Looked at (From the Other Side of the Glass) with One Eye, Close to, for Nearly an Hour*, did none of them think to do any referential sleuthing? Perhaps this is the unfortunate result of their believing the Cage/Cunningham dogma. Or, conversely, perhaps the problem was in not truly comprehending what John Cage had been saying all those years. To quote Duchamp again, "The work of art is always based on the two poles of the onlooker and the maker, and the spark that comes from that bipolar action gives birth to something—like electricity.[18] Of course, the dance can be appreciated in isolation without any knowledge of Duchamp's *The Bride Stripped Bare by Her Bachelors, Even,* or his *Nude Descending a Staircase,* or of his readymades, or the films in which he appeared. But how much more could have been savored with a bit of imaginative detective work, since references to all of the above can be found in *Walkaround Time*.

Walkaround's title is computer jargon and refers to the "walkaround time"—oh so long ago, before high-speed computers blanketed the world—when computer programmers walked about while waiting for their giant room-sized computers to complete their work. But there is a more important aspect of time that Merce was attempting to realize in *Walkaround Time:* "Marcel always gave one the sense of a human being who is ever calm, a person with an extraordinary sense of calmness, as though days could go by, and minutes go by. And I wanted to see if I could get that—the sense of time."[19]

When we were learning the dance, Merce, true to form, revealed nothing. I knew *The Large Glass* from photographs in books. Only years later did I see the nine-foot-high, five-and-a-half-foot-wide original in the Philadelphia Museum of Art, and it wasn't until after performing *Walk-around Time* in the 1968 winter season and wondering about the meaning of Duchamp's iconography painted on Jasper's plastic boxes that I decided to do some research on my own. A prized possession in Earle's and my library was Robert Lebel's book *Marcel Duchamp*, published by Grove Press in 1959. I'd looked in it but never really read it. I wanted to know what role, if any, my part in the dance played in the scheme of things. Merce, in two separate interviews after I left the company, stated that *"Walkaround Time* was made with Carolyn Brown very much in mind . . . The solo she danced . . . was central to the first half of the work"[20] and "I also wanted to put in a kind of continuing thing for Carolyn . . . particularly in the second half. I suppose I was thinking of Duchamp's interests."[21]

What I learned then has been clarified most recently by Calvin Tomkins's writings on Duchamp. The subject matter of this curious paint-ing is the once-in-a-lifetime irreversible change from virginity to bride-hood. *The Bride Stripped Bare by Her Bachelors, Even* is, according to Duchamp, a mechanical apparatus "whose sole function is to make love." "The Bride has a life center, the Bachelors have not."[22] "The Bride above—bachelors below." In the Bachelor section, the principal forms are precise and geometrical with circles, rectangles, cones, funnels. Floating across the top of the glass like a large cloud is the "cinematic blossoming" of the Bride, representing the bride at the moment of her own blossoming, which is also the moment of her being stripped bare.[23] Time was also an integral element in Duchamp's thinking about *The Large Glass,* which he described as *retard en verre* or "delay in glass"—delay in this case refer-ring to the Bride and the Bachelors waiting to consummate their sexual desire, which never happens. Taken literally, this information was not use-ful to me: it would be difficult to find anything overtly sexual or even erotic in *Walkaround Time.* But the concept of being stripped bare was a useful image and an accurate description of how I viewed my solo. Entering from stage right, I walk to center stage, directly under the box bearing "the large cloud/cinematic blossoming of the Bride" icon suspended above me, and with deliberation step onto three-quarter pointe in fourth position facing diagonally downstage left, and hold—absolutely *still. Retard.* Delay. The bride element itself, suspended above me to my right, is the only elongated vertical component in *The Large Glass,* and the iconography of my posi-tion, my movements in stillness, are quite reminiscent of it. *"Still"* is the operative word. Slowly, really really slowly, the right foot tentatively lifts off the floor with little pulsing *developpés* ending in a full *developpé* to fourth front, then held there hip level, balanced and absolutely *still*. This happens in both halves of *Walkaround Time*. Doing this phrase, I felt utterly naked and exposed, as though standing in the center of a tightrope one hundred feet off the ground with no clothes on. Out of this balanced stillness, I had to find the resources to immediately move fast and big, to take to the air, to cover space, and then return once again to absolute stillness and repose. Merce has said that in my solo he tried to convey the sense of the "stopping and moving at the same time" that characterizes Duchamp's *Nude*.[24] John Cage once told me that what he most liked about my dancing was the appearance of serenity. Merce often said, "It is the stillness within the dancer which allows the dance to live." Serenity and stillness, inner calm and outward clarity—these, I discovered, were the demands I needed to meet in *Walkaround Time*. And the reverse—"clarity within, quiet without . . . the tranquillity of pure contemplation,"[25] a quote from the I Ching in Cage's book *Silence*—applied as well.

A warning! Lest the painting be taken too seriously, Calvin Tomkins tells us that "Duchamp intended *The Large Glass* to be a 'hilarious' picture: those who approach it with too reverent an air will miss much, for it is rich with comic spirit."[26] There is nothing "hilarious" about *Walkaround Time,* since it avoids the curious, convoluted, ironic, and erotic male/female relationship that is the subject matter of the painting, but there are witty allusions to Duchamp's oeuvre, and one—to *Nude Descending a Staircase*—went nearly unseen behind the largest box. While jogging in place at a steady pace, Merce stripped off one set of tights and shirt, and then donned another—all without losing a single beat. Several times this required him to hop on one foot many times while removing the leg of his tights or putting one on, but never did he interrupt his constant rhythm. An astonishing feat demanding hours of practice! Anyone who has ever tried to remove a pair of tights or, even worse, pull a pair of tights onto a sweaty body, let alone run in place at an even pace at the same time, will appreciate the tour de force this represents.

During the world tour and the four years following, significant changes in my life—some wonderful and some painfully difficult—forced me to become more self-reliant, self-confident, willing and able to take risks, and kindled my desire to be more active creatively. Choreographing *Balloon* had been a positive experience. I was eager to try again. *Car Lot,* my dance for the Manhattan Festival Ballet, opened on January 1, 1968. Earle, Merce, John, Jasper, David Vaughan, Remy Charlip, and Jim Klosty were there. (Jim had begun to photograph the company during the summer of 1967, and slowly he'd become a fixture around the studio and the theaters where we performed. Merce hated having photographers lurking about, but somehow Jim managed to be so inconspicuous as to be invisible. Early in 1968, he also became a very important part of my life.) The ballet was given ten New York performances and received mostly good or at least encouraging press. Its biggest fan was Patrick O'Connor, dance critic for the *New Jersey Journal,* who called it "an absolute, unqualified knockout."[27] To my astonishment, *Car Lot* won the 1967–1968 Jersey Journal Theatre Award for best ballet. And, wow! What astonishing company I was in! Tom Stoppard's play *Rosencrantz and Guildenstern Are Dead* won best play (I'd seen it in January). Zoe Caldwell won best actress, Albert Finney best actor.

However, since my overwhelming admiration for Stoppard's work developed years later, my greatest thrill was in having Antony Tudor come to see *Car Lot.* I hadn't seen Tudor in many, many months. When the Metropolitan Ballet School moved to the new Met in Lincoln Center, "older dancers" were told they were not permitted to attend classes there. But in February, on a three-day escape from Buffalo (Merce was in California that weekend), I decided to try. "Of course you can take Mr. Tudor's class," Marcella Corvino, the school secretary, responded to my request. "He never meant that you or his other professional students weren't allowed." After class, Tudor commented sardonically, "I hear you're stealing the bread out of our mouths," and then, "I'm coming to see it." He came that very night! Tudor had never seen the Manhattan Festival Ballet before, so I felt especially honored. Afterward, he told me he liked my ballet "uncommonly much" and said, "Do more." To Earle, I wrote, "Tudor's class, his coming to see the work, his words to me afterwards were all so exhilarating and meant so much to me." Merce, by way of contrast, never spoke to me about *Car Lot,* or, for that matter, about *Balloon.*

After my two articles for *Ballet Review* were published, I received a call from Selma-Jean Cohen, editor of *Dance Perspectives,* asking me to write a piece for its forthcoming issue on Merce, to be based on my contribution to a radio broadcast called "A Panegyric for Merce Cunningham." The radio program included essays or stories about Merce by Clive Barnes, John Cage, Arlene Croce, Edwin Denby, and Jill Johnston, and was produced by Martin Last and broadcast by WBAI-FM New York on May 5, 1968. The essay, a considerably expanded version of my ten-minute radio talk, appeared in "Time to Walk in Space," the *Dance Perspectives* issue devoted to Merce, published in the summer of 1968. On the cover is a darkly dramatic photograph of Merce taken by James Klosty.

There had been many partner changes within the company. Barbara and Lew Lloyd divorced, and Lew married Theresa Dickinson. Sandra Neels, who'd dated both Jim Klosty and Niklas Ek, married Jim Baird, the company's new production manager. Gordon Mumma's wife, Jackie, died, and sometime later Gordon and Barbara became a couple. I'd lived for years as an observer of other people's romances, entanglements, and breakups, never expecting to be other than Mrs. Earle Brown for the rest of my life, so the lovely romantic love affair that "just happened" took me totally and wondrously by surprise. Allowing myself to fall in love with Jim Klosty, a man much younger than myself, was a risk—a foolhardy one perhaps, but with the risk came joy and a new lease on life.

At long last, in May 1968, Merce Cunningham and Dance Company had its "First Major New York" season in the opera house at the Brooklyn Academy of Music—the word "major" employed because our self-produced, unreviewed week of performances at the Theatre de Lys had been the first. It had taken fourteen years since then, and four years since our season in London and Clive Barnes's constant carping in the *Times*, for this to happen. Even Chicago had managed to present the company in a "major season" before New York.

Merce wanted to present as much of the current repertory as possible, but three days before our departure for Chicago in late winter he had gotten some very bad news. My journal entry: "Things are in a ghastly mess. Gus is out for good . . . and so we're faced with a week season in Chicago and the Brooklyn season without him. Obviously it is a disaster, and I don't even know at this writing what poor Merce is planning to do. He's pretty sick at heart, I know that."

For the many weeks on tour, Gus had been suffering severe pain from a back injury. X-rays indicated a serious problem. Gus believed that his dancing days were over. His roles were crucial to the current repertory, especially those choreographed for him in *Scramble*, *Rainforest*, and *Walkaround Time*. There were no understudies. What was Merce to do? Much of the repertory now required three men, in addition to Merce. Gus agreed to go to Chicago, but *Place* had to be dropped from the repertory there. Jeff Slayton replaced him in *Rainforest* and *Winterbranch*.

There was only one week between the Illinois tour and the first performance at BAM to solve the Gus problem. Thanks to Peter Saul's willingness to return to take over his original roles in *Place*, *How to . . .* , and *Variations V*, and to Jeff Slayton's quick-study ability to assume Gus's other roles, we were able to perform twelve works. Gus hoped to do the three *Walkaround Time* performances in the second week, but at the last minute he called in to say he could not manage the last one. With just a brief rehearsal that day, Jeff stepped into the role. Everyone knew Jeff could move big and fast, but could he move very, very slowly, which is what was required in Gus's solo? It was technically simple, but nonetheless extremely difficult because of the stillness. The dancer must rivet the audience's attention through his absolute commitment to the material and total concentration. Jeff proved he could do it.

All of us—Merce especially—danced as though our lives depended upon it. My journals and letters record nothing about those weeks except to report that the season went well. In lieu of my own recollections, I'll let some critical voices weigh in on how it went.

[New York Times] What the season has shown is the power, prestige and sumptuous ability of Cunningham and Cunningham's dancers. Before this season he was a major talent, naturally, but a major talent with his light still hidden under a bushel. Brooklyn has removed the bushel.[28]

[New York magazine] Don't let anyone tell you Merce Cunningham's choreography has no content. . . . both kinesthetically and theatrically his work presents a point of view about the human condition. . . . this choreography, together with its ostensibly unrelated music and decor, is deeply expressive of modern life.[29]

A week after the last BAM performance of the season, Clive Barnes wrote a long piece about Merce in the Sunday New York Times, in which he quotes The Village Voice writer Jill Johnston: "I'd like to see [Merce] be real bad, I mean bad, bad, so bad we'd all love him again, indiscriminately, like in the old days. That is you know it's so bloody beautiful. I'm bored with it half the time. I'm being sentimental."[30] To this, Barnes responded: "Baby, you are being downright stupid."[31]

Three weeks after the BAM season, the company left for a four-week residency at the University of Colorado in Boulder, followed by five weeks of performances in Mexico, Argentina, Brazil, and Venezuela. Boulder, Colorado—5,430 feet above sea level—was deemed the perfect training ground for our performances in Mexico City, which rises another 2,000 feet higher. We were housed in cottages or rooms in the lodge at Colorado Chautauqua, a summer resort on the southern boundary of Boulder at the foot of the Rocky Mountains. I'd forgotten how much I loved Colorado. Every free weekend, just as Earle and I used to do, two or more of us would head into the mountains for the sheer heady joy of the rarified air and vast vistas, lush pastoral meadows, bubbling mountain streams, plunging canyons, abundant wildflowers, butterflies, hail, and thunderstorms.

The month in Boulder gave us time to teach the repertory to new company members Chase Robinson and Mel Wong. Albert Reid had decided it was time to leave. He came to Boulder for two weeks in order to teach his parts, and gave his final performance with us in Boulder on June 25. Barbara Lloyd also planned to leave, but fortunately had agreed to stay through the South American tour. Susana Hayman-Chaffey, only nineteen at the time, had been hired as an understudy and would be eased into the repertory over the course of the summer. She'd spent most of her childhood in South America, had trained at the Royal Ballet School in London, and had had some performance experience with the Brazilian Contemporary Dance Company.

Merce discovered Mel Wong while teaching a master class at the University of California in Los Angeles. In the past, new company members were chosen from students at Merce's studio, but with Peter, Gus, and now Albert all leaving, and not a single man enrolled there suitable to replace them, Merce invited Mel to join the company. Lew Lloyd sent Mel a telegram, but Mel thought it was a prank played on him by classmates and ignored it. After several days, Mel's friends convinced him to phone Lew. Mel was nine credits short of his second MFA. Throwing caution to the winds, he packed all his worldly goods into his VW Beetle, went to his choreography class to present his senior project, and then—telling no one—walked across the studio, jumped out the window, and drove nonstop to New York. "Has anyone seen Mel since he disappeared out a window at the end of senior project?" his dance professor asked some weeks later. Mel's exit has become a UCLA legend—told and retold with every passing year.

Chase Robinson did study at the studio briefly, but he came to the company as an established modern dancer, having worked in the Martha Graham, José Limón, and Lucas Hoving companies, among others. He, too, was a college graduate, having majored in psychology. In 1963, Chase and I had performed together in Grant Strate's ballet *The House of Atreus* at Juilliard.

Plus ça change, plus c'est la même chose. With the passing years, more and more time had to be spent teaching old dances to an ever-changing roster of new dancers, most of whom didn't stay longer than five or six years, some for only two or three. This was tedious for everyone involved, but it was especially discouraging for Merce, who wanted only to make new dances, not rehash old ones; and for me—then in my fifteenth year with the company—who desperately longed for Merce to make dances that would use qualities and abilities that I knew I possessed but that he apparently had yet to imagine. Despite the challenges of *Rainforest* and *Walkaround Time,* I was hungry for more and different. Of course, I was not alone in this. But the unease and dissatisfaction I was experiencing had another source as well: being away from the man I'd just fallen in love with. What a joy it had been after every performance at BAM in May to find Jim waiting at the stage door in his green Sunbeam convertible, ready to whisk me off to a late supper somewhere in the Village, where we'd talk for hours. We had such a good time together—he was so considerate, loving, fun, and funny, and now a two-month separation lay ahead. Each morning, before I was fully awake, that nagging voice of old kept asking: "What are you doing? What do you really want?"

[Boulder, Colorado—6/22/68] Dancing yesterday was work. No joy, no physical pleasure, no involvement of spirit. An awful thing to *have* to do. Felt curiously old, passé, dispirited. There must be newness, discovery, growth or it must stop.

[Boulder—6/28/68] The performance on the 25th was uninspired on my part. Again, doing my "job" but without much real pleasure.

[Boulder—6/29/68] Why did I get SO depressed in class? . . . It becomes intolerable. The situation: teacher-student. The dependency. The "by rote" do as you're told, do as I do mechanics of it. I feel no interest. No involvement. I've done it too long.

[Boulder—7/2/68] Monday of the last week in Colorado. How much I've loved the mountains, the "feel" of the land, the sun, the changing skies. How little dancing seems to mean in midst of all this.

[Midair on the way to Mexico—7/13/68] Appalled to discover how much I talk of past tours, recollecting earlier ventures with far more enthusiasm than I feel for this one. . . . I wonder a little more each day if this touring is not becoming a job to do, rather than a way of life. And yet, in the actual performing last night, the dancing was real, full, valuable to me. But the "other [company] life" has become empty. I miss Bob, perhaps more than anyone. . . . Clearly there must be a moving on—so that I live life in the present.

[Mexico City—7/14/68] Allowing myself to feel utterly miserable, lonely, even vaguely hysterical in wanting a personal, private, intimate life and feeling this rambling around the world—for all its "glamour" and excitement—leaves an enormous part of me empty. Strange, not to have felt this sooner . . .

[Rio—8/3/68] I am profoundly saddened by my dancing life. It's been happening gradually, ever since Bob and Viola left the company. It's reached alarming proportions of discontent this week in Rio. . . . We've become a commercial road company, repeating, repeating, repeating. The zest for, the belief in, the excitement of creativity is gone. Sometimes it's a dull ache I feel. Sometimes a screaming pain of protest.

All of this discontent can explain but certainly not excuse my subsequent behavior on the South American tour, which was—in a word—bitchy. I took out my frustrations and unhappiness by complaining, especially about having to perform two shows a day, back-to-back, several times. Most of my disgruntlement fell upon Lew, who was facing overwhelming financial and political problems throughout the tour. In my utterly self-involved journals and letters I seemed to have been totally oblivious of how others viewed me that summer. Thirty-odd years later I was sitting with Lew in the Beinecke Library at Yale University, sifting through his collected Cunningham company papers, and came upon these communications from Lew to Jean Rigg, our new assistant company manager, and Judith Blinken:

[7/23/68, to Jean] CB arrived in Mexico in tears. [after an 18 hour flight] . . . As a matter of fact CB's attitude about the whole week remained grim, with occasional upbeat moments, rather than the reverse which is her usual personality. . . . Things aren't very simple when one is trying to simultaneously answer questions from the press and the embassy and the dancers, move everyone through health control and passport control, collect all the bags, and get through customs, and find the bus and driver, surrounded by screaming Latins the whole time (after midnight) . . . when I snapped at Susana, Carolyn went after me again, telling me I wasn't doing my job, etc. . . . She's really at the end of her rope with this whole scene. But she isn't retiring very gracefully. . . . I'm trying my best to stay away from her since she unloads her bitterness on me.[32]

[8/4/68, to Judith:] Carolyn, as you've heard, is not touring well anymore. I don't know when she'll decide to stop, but it should be soon.[33]

It was all I could do to suppress my hoots of laughter in the hallowed halls of the Beinecke! But poor Lew, having totally forgotten these letters, was aghast. He blushed crimson with embarrassment, while I kept reassuring him that without a doubt he had been absolutely right and that I was not in the least offended. Rather, a heartfelt if belated apology was due him for my beastly past behavior.

Petulant dancers had been the least of Lew's problems. Financial calamity at least as perilous as those of the world tour loomed, complicated by the politics of the countries we visited. First and foremost among disasters was the physical well-being of the company. In Rio, Merce seriously injured his foot. He continued performing in constant pain, but was forced to rechoreograph his parts. He was unable to jump at all. As time went on, he injured his knee as well. In Buenos Aires, *Place* had to be dropped from the repertory. Chase, too, was badly injured at the very start of the tour, and he developed further problems along the way. Turista and/or a bronchial flu traveled the rounds of the company throughout the five weeks. Another problem—at least for a few of us—was feeling that with nearly half the dancers having joined the company so recently, we'd lost the commonly held aesthetic and family ethic that once so closely bound and supported us. Backbiting, little salacious scandals—shocking some, amusing others, ignored by the rest of us—buzzed through the summer months. For Merce, performing at less than one-third of his capacity was humiliating, but he remained remarkably cheerful, having learned from the 1964 experience how much his own dark moods imperiled the morale of his dancers. On this tour, he made a valiant effort to bolster our flagging spirits, despite his own misery.

As always, John wanted all of us to be happy all of the time; when we weren't, he was disconsolate. Apparently aware of my fits of ill temper, which were never directed at him or Merce, he offered spirit-lifting diversions whenever he could. Twice during our week in Mexico he hired a car with driver and invited Merce and me to join him on an excursion to Cuernavaca to visit Jasper Johns, who'd rented a house with several terraces that offered staggeringly majestic 240-degree vistas of distant mountains through roiling mist and fast-moving clouds. Cuernavaca was sunny, hot, the air delicious—blessedly free of the pollution and deafening traffic noise of Mexico City. We spent lovely, lazy hours in and out of the pool under a broiling sun and ate a delicious lunch in the shade.

Our seven performances at the Palacio de las Bellas Artes in Mexico City were part of the XIX Cultural Olympics and funded by a large fee from the Mexican government and—for the first time ever—a travel subsidy from the U.S. State Department. On the Friday and Saturday, we gave back-to-back performances with a matinee beginning at 5:30 p.m. followed by an evening show starting at nine, presenting a total of ten works on that weekend. Oxygen tanks were placed just offstage in the wings. *Place* at sea level presented endurance problems, but in Mexico City, some eight thousand feet above sea level—even with oxygen sucked in greedily between bouts onstage—it was a killer.

The fact that the Bolshoi Ballet was performing at the National Auditorium may have explained why the Palacio de las Bellas Artes was half-empty on our opening night. The Martha Graham Company had preceded us in the Cultural Olympics, and one of her dancers, a former student of mine, came to our first performance and told us our audience had been far more receptive than theirs. It had?

By week's end, we had wonderful, responsive audiences. At least seven critics—many of them came three times in order to review everything—offered diverse opinions: "We didn't understand a thing," "surprising boldness," "the strangest sounds," "daring," "intense creative imagination," "having a joke at our expense," "everything is interesting." *Winterbranch* was deeply admired by one and as passionately reviled by another. Warhol's *Rainforest* pillows were called "simply destructive, despite the most superb choreography" by one, and "Freudian" [?] by another. The *News,* an English-language paper, wrote that "Cunningham's concept, emotional stillness and depth make the Graham group seem antiquated."[34] And so it went. *Walkaround Time* was a favorite with the audience, perhaps because Gordon played Conlon Nancarrow's early rhythm studies during the entr'acte and Nancarrow, an expatriate then living in Mexico, was in the audience.

To welcome the company to Mexico on our first day there, Merce's long-time friend Nancy Oakes de Tritton (they'd studied together at the School of American Ballet in the 1940s), gave us a reception in her palatial mansion. Society photographers for the local press were everywhere; the subsequent articles filled pages of the newspapers and may have helped to fill the theater for the rest of our run. In the midst of all the picture-taking, Nancy's husband, Patrick, said to me, "I saw your performances in London in 1964"—pregnant pause—"Oh, I'm going to make a mess of this—actually I hated it, but Nancy tells me it was superb!" We both burst out laughing. An icebreaker if ever there was one.

The tour was to have included Bogotá, Colombia, and Santiago, Chile, in addition to the places where we eventually did perform, but Bogotá was dropped for lack of sponsor resources and Santiago had to be jettisoned as well. Thus the company had a week's forced "vacation" in Rio.

It was winter in Brazil, the rainy season. If the sun appeared at all it was low in the sky, and Copacabana Beach lay deep in the shadows cast by the luxury high-rise hotels and apartment buildings on its rim. Behind the high-rises and the Copacabana shopping district, favelas—jerry-built shacks of the wretched poor—jammed together in jumbled disarray, barely clinging to the steep mountainside. Nowhere, except in India, had I seen such disparity between rich and poor. In the city center one saw children begging, covered with sores; a man, slumped against a building, legs sprawled on the sidewalk, one leg swollen five times the size of the other— elephantiasis was common at the time—while a shop window next door showcased glittering jewels like those worn by the exceedingly rich women we saw on opening night of the Stuttgart Ballet in Rio's lavishly baroque theater—preposterously ostentatious, gaudily dressed women who refused to sit in their seats, despite bells ringing and lights dimming, and once in them chattered throughout the overture of *Romeo and Juliet*. At the Teatro Novo, the Brazilian Ballet, directed by Arthur Mitchell, had no such audience. The Teatro Novo, as the name indicates, was a new theater built in a working-class neighborhood. No one, not even the police three blocks away, seemed to have heard of it. One entered the backstage through a garage, and here each day during our free week Merce taught— and taught beautifully—a one-hour "therapeutic keep-it-all-together" class in the theater.

In Argentina, Brazil, and Venezuela, the political situations were alarming at best and upon occasion actually dangerous. The accumulating interference of United States business and military operations in Latin America during the fifties and sixties had set the scene for some of the difficulties we encountered.[35] In 1968 Brazil was governed by a "soft" military dictatorship and Lew, upon arrival in Rio, was informed that unless the company provided the "police censors" with a special preview on the afternoon of the opening, we could not perform. John and Merce categorically refused. The cultural attaché from the United States Embassy was called. If we refused the censorship evaluation, he said, the police could force cancellation of the entire presentation, but if the censors were convinced that there was no text in the choreography, they could waive the pre-performance requirement, and then the Cunningham company would have established an important precedent for freedom of performance and artistic activities in Brazil. According to Gordon Mumma's Brazilian musician friends, John and Merce are still remembered and admired for the stand they took. Lew arranged for the censors to attend opening night, and we waited to see what would happen. Nothing did.

Five days before our first performance the entire company was invited to attend a press conference/reception in the lobby of the Teatro Novo. Here is an excerpt of Merce's remarks, as reported in *Diário de Notícias* and translated from the Portuguese: "Our art is an artistic process and not an experience of something definite. . . . The dance we perform is realistic, but not naturalistic; in our presentations we do not protest against war or other problems of humanity, but we reject all censorship of theatre by all governments, in whatever form, accepting only the censorship or critique of the public."[36]

The company's refusal to submit its programs to the censors sparked some challenging questions about artistic freedom. John's belief in anarchy, i.e., Thoreau's "The best government is no government at all," and Merce's belief that art transcends politics with its power to open/change people's minds, was clearly articulated by them. In Mexico, Lew had decided to fight the "don't talk against the government" clause of the State Department contract, and John agreed with him. In an interview there, John attacked the State Department for including such a clause. As Lew put it, "Since when does the government *buy* your civil liberties for a lousy five thousand dollars?"[37] So, in Rio, when a reporter asked, "How could the Merce Cunningham Dance Company, as a symbol of artistic freedom, have accepted money from the United States government for this Latin/American tour?" John's response, as recalled by Gordon Mumma, was something like "Remember the country we're from." Ambiguous, at best. Of course, there was a certain irony in all this: for years, with the single exception of the five thousand dollars for travel expenses to Mexico City, no State Department financial aid had ever been given. Then came the startling announcement from John that the company was not going to accept U.S. government money. It wasn't? That statement must have given Lew apoplexy!

Despite intensive pre-publicity on our behalf, including newspaper advertisements and articles, television advertisements, and five guys walking the streets with poster sandwich-boards passing out leaflets, our audiences were small. Lew reported that our reception was very, very good—reviews, press, and applause—although we presumably didn't reach the audience who might have been the most receptive: students, artists, and, as Lew said, "the anarchists." Tickets were too expensive, and although half-price tickets were available for students, they didn't seem to know about it. In Rio, theater was the preserve of the very rich, and apparently they didn't go into working-class neighborhoods. "A disgustingly frivolous city" is how one person at the American Embassy described it.

Small audiences were only one of the company's difficulties in Rio. The most dangerous, indeed life-threatening, was the helium/hydrogen problem. For *Rainforest*, helium tanks had to be preordered at each venue.

What was delivered to the Teatro Novo were tanks of hydrogen! Here was "another wonderful example of the colonialist-imperialist aspects of Latin America. At that time, the manufacture of helium, throughout the world, was completely under the control of the United States government and its subsidiary industries. Without United States authorization, helium was not available in Brazil."[38] A consultation took place with Merce, and then with the dancers. We were told of the dangers involved. A vote was taken: we'd chance it! The pillows became objects of suspicion and were treated most carefully. No kicking, hitting. Even when brushing against them we felt threatened with imminent immolation.

The week was a financial disaster. The contract gave no guarantee, only a share of the box office which, after expenses, amounted to less than one thousand dollars for the company, a loss of nine thousand dollars. The Teatro Novo lost money as well. Still, we were told that the impact of our visit was tremendous. Oddly enough, it was with the embassy that the company seemed to have achieved its greatest success. Throughout our two-week stay, the assistant cultural attaché was extremely, and effectively, helpful. The American ambassador came to a performance. The head of USIS (United States Information Service) at the American Embassy in Rio wrote Merce and John "an absolutely florid letter praising their work and the fact that it 'upped the image' of the USA like nothing else they'd done."[39]

Unfortunately, I shall always remember the beautiful city of Rio for its abysmal poverty, cheek by jowl with its flaunting rich; police stalking the streets with machine guns; the clammy humidity, foul air, crazed taxi drivers, noisy traffic, decaying pavements. We sensed, but did not fully comprehend, how much political turmoil was seething around us. Not long after we left, a vicious crackdown led to what became known as the worst five years of Brazilian military dictatorship. The American ambassador was kidnapped. Torture was used to extract information from urban guerrillas.[40] The industrialist who had created the Teatro Novo was murdered by "unknown parties." The theater was closed.

Argentina was under a military dictatorship as well, but this time it wasn't the government that presented problems, it was our own embassy in Buenos Aires. To our astonishment, we learned that a man in the USIS section of the embassy was advising Americans to have absolutely nothing to do with the Cunningham company due to the controversial nature of the work, and citing as his authority Calvin Tomkins's *New Yorker* profile of John Cage! The representative from Pepsi, who had originally expressed the desire to support the company, met Lew Lloyd in a panic. "We cannot support these performances. We've been told that you are very avant-garde and actually show sex play on stage. The government is furious."[41] To put it bluntly, the company was sabotaged. In Buenos Aires, unlike Rio, there was no pre-publicity. The Teatro Municipal General San Martín staff claimed that no photographs ever reached their press office, and even though they admitted that our posters had arrived, they could not explain why none had been posted. Union stage crews at the San Martín refused to unload our scenery and costumes. It wasn't until we women dancers began to do the work that they were shamed into doing their job. The theater management appeared unprepared for our arrival and astounded by the size and complexity of our scenic effects, and they gave the impression of wishing we'd never come. Of whom and what were they fearful—the United States government or the Argentine junta? When the assistant cultural attaché phoned to request free tickets, Lew Lloyd told him the embassy should follow its own policies to their logical conclusion and stay away, or at the least buy their own tickets. Why, Lew asked this man, hadn't the embassy done anything for us? His answer: a decision higher up had been made that the company was to be ignored. Lew was as distraught as was I, for entirely different reasons. I continued to wrap myself in my own cocoon of despair, as this entry in my journal attests:

> And so it goes on and on—this dread of dancing. No phase, apparently—
> but a real confrontation with my life. And when I dance badly, as I did last
> night in *Walkaround Time*, it becomes unrelievably unbearable. I can't
> make myself rehearse properly; it's no wonder the results are by chance. It
> was such a relief to be out of Rio, that for two days I didn't feel depressed or
> beaten. But it overwhelmed me again, and stayed with me. . . . I cannot
> endure this deadening of the senses; I cannot endure dancing badly; I can-
> not endure not caring about something I loved.

Buenos Aires seemed less raw, more civilized than Rio, although extremely conservative. On the street, irate citizens lectured some of our very miniskirted dancers, and Michele, the company's twenty-year-old wardrobe mistress, was evicted from the theater for wearing slacks! Still we felt at ease there, probably because the city was more European than Rio; nor did we see such disparity between rich and poor. For one dollar, we ate the best steak in the world. The hot chocolate sauce—*merengue con crema con chocolate caliente*—was to die for. At the very top of the list of pleasures was the night David Tudor took Merce, Valda, and me to a tango palace to hear genuine Argentine tango, where the mostly blond audience in fancy nightclub clothes seemed straight out of a Nazi film. Every group performing had a *bandoneón* player. The most riveting was a ravaged, craggy-faced, dissolute, passionate-looking man with thick dark hair, long sideburns, sensual lips, a cleft chin, deeply etched dimples, a huge nose, and dark-ringed, intense eyes. He played the very devil out of the *bandoneón*, attacking it with savagery, tenderness, erotic sensitivity! David was in ecstasy. In fact, each one of us was captivated, both by the man and by his music. Even after four hours, at 3:30 in the morning, we could hardly bear to tear ourselves away.

> Merce has been a saint. In pain, but valiantly presenting a cheerful disposition, with flashes of dry wit. He dances nightly—is miserable at heart, says John, that he cannot dance fully and well, but he does not reveal this to us.

> A horrendous week of effort, lost money, small audiences, no publicity, Merce in pain. John was dismayed, Merce more so, to discover it cost *us* money to do this past week, to the tune of $10,500 or more! Incredible. And only the last two performances had responsive audiences. Tickets are too expensive for the audience we should appeal to. It's the same everywhere in S.A. & Mexico.

But somehow, without publicity of any kind, even with the virulent anti-Cage sentiment expressed by the American Embassy, there were those who heard about us via the underground grapevine and came from as far away as Córdoba and from Uruguay, across the Río de la Plata, obtaining tickets not from the San Martín theater but quietly, in advance, from "culturally-hip European embassies in Buenos Aires!"[42] As one critic observed, "Thanks to the prodigious reserve of the San Martín theater publicity apparatus, no notice was sent, even to editorial offices of periodicals, so that only those who detected a tiny advertisement in the daily press were able to pass the word along to their friends."[43] An excerpt from *Clarín:*

> The influence of this group will be felt, I hope, by local choreographers and dancers and the dance-loving public. If Cunningham's art were nothing more than disturbing, subtle and suggestive, it would merit the influence it exerts. But over and above that, it displays the greatest richness of ideas and the severest rigor in modern dance that we have seen in Buenos Aires.[44]

We departed Buenos Aires in the morning, and eighteen hours and five countries later arrived in Caracas, Venezuela, after "the trip from hell"—

flying over the Andes (that was spectacular) and setting down in Santiago, Lima, Guayaquil, and Bogotá. For those of us with bad colds, the five landings and takeoffs, especially the quick descent into Ecuador, caused violent, excruciating pain. By the time we fell into bed it was close to midnight, everyone nearly ill with fatigue.

Most of us stayed in the Hotel Ávila, a tropical tourist luxury palace on a mountaintop above the city. Although very expensive—it ate up our entire week's salary, and then some—it provided delicious comfort, good air, magnificent views, hot sun, a large swimming pool, and a most extraordinary, exotic symphony of insect and bird sounds from dusk till dawn. John and Merce chose to stay in the city center, and they spent their free time meeting with people, giving interviews. With no time for rest or therapy, Merce's physical condition had deteriorated. And in Caracas as elsewhere, Lew and John had to cope with political machinations that we dancers were not privy to at the time. The company was sponsored by the Comité Cultural Venezolano with the collaboration of the Creole and Neumann Foundations. Lew Lloyd wrote:

> The Rockefeller oil money (from an office called "Esso Mathematics and Systems, Inc.," deep in Rockefeller Center, and from Creole Petroleum in Caracas (barricaded behind machine guns) was to support the Caracas performances at the university theatre. . . . I was not too happy about showing up in Caracas supported by Creole Petroleum. I expressed misgivings to John. He said not to worry. Because we were performing at the university, with the great Calder mobile over the audience's heads, we would show the very best in new art and so reach the students who were the people who should see it. However, this was not to be. The sponsors in Caracas figured out what a potentially incendiary situation they might have on their hands if our work were shown at the university. We were shifted to the municipal theatre. Again we had small audiences and very few students indeed. [When] I went to Creole Petroleum to pick up our check the building was guarded by an armored personnel carrier, containing the oil company's private security forces. The entrance was guarded by men with submachine guns at the ready. As I went up in the elevator I noticed that as the door opened on each floor, a uniformed man holding a submachine gun stood facing us. It was very a depressing business.[45]

We were warned that walking the streets in the area of the beautiful (à la Fenice) Teatro Municipal was not advisable because there were street battles being waged between opposing groups and we might be caught in the crossfire, so unfortunately we saw little of Caracas. With the change of venue, the five originally scheduled performances were cut to three, plus one day devoted to televising *Rainforest*. In a letter to my mother, I reported (in contrast to Lew's remembrance quoted above) that "the audiences were marvelous. Big and appreciative. The best in South America." For the dancers, at least, cheer replaced gloom and company morale ended on a positive note, except for our sadness at losing Barbara Lloyd, who gave her final performance with the company on Sunday, August 18. Throughout the tour she had danced more beautifully than ever before. Paradoxically, this often happened when someone had once made the difficult decision to leave.

The single most important accomplishment of the Latin American tour may have been the fact that we managed to do it at all in the face of constant adversity. The work got shown to a small, determined group of people, despite obstacles at every turn. Some eyes and ears were opened, some minds at least stimulated, if not changed. The call for artistic freedom was made and acted upon. Years later, attending music conferences in South America, Gordon Mumma discovered that the 1968 Cunningham company tour was legendary and that the legend was still very much alive. No small part of the credit for this, I believe, goes to John Cage, who gave interview after interview with anyone who wanted to speak with him. "Every sentence he utters," wrote the *Daily Journal*, an English-language newspaper, "expresses revolutionary ideas," and it went on to list fifteen of them. Here's a sampling:

> Since Venezuela's oil will some day dry up, this country should devote itself to developing a new source of energy—from the sun, from the tides, from air.
>
> The space-race between Russia and the United States is ridiculous—both countries should work on the main problem of mankind, which is to relate the world's resources to the population.
>
> Men should have enough to eat before they can be asked to appreciate music—so the first problem of music is socio-economic.
>
> There are not just males and females, there are 80 kinds of males and 175 kinds of females."[46]

This was in 1968, remember, not 1998. He'd say something absolutely outrageous, smile that endearing open-mouthed, tongue-lolling smile, laugh at his own controversial, often shocking ideas, and then follow the laugh with his idiosyncratic, affirmative, "Hmmm?" He was irresistible. When he said things like, "Our proper work now, if we love mankind and the world we live in, is revolution." Or, "When you get right down to it, a composer is simply someone who tells other people what to do. I find this an unattractive way of getting things done. I'd like our activities to be more social and anarchically so,"[47] it's little wonder he was anathema to military dictatorships and big business. One of the many remarkable things about John was his ability to make friends wherever he went—with poets, philosophers, artists, journalists, scientists, psychologists, yes, but also with just plain folk. When he died, people who had met him only once said they felt they'd really connected with him, had made a true friend.

Thirty-six years later, in April 2004, at a dinner party celebrating Merce's eighty-fifth birthday, I again met Isaac Chocrón—Venezuelan writer, poet, journalist—who, like Octavio Paz and any number of other authors, had become a lifelong friend of John's. (Of course, many of these friends would become Merce's friends as well, but it was John who was the magnetic one, who made friends and kept them.) In August 1968, Isaac Chocrón wrote:

> It would be no exaggeration to say that the short season of the Merce Cunningham Group at the *Teatro Municipal* . . . was a sensational event for the Venezuelan public . . . the visit of this company has left us breathless; but the personal relations of Cunningham and Cage with Venezuelan dancers, and particularly with those responsible for the movement of dance in our country, were really splendid. It is a rare thing to find artists of such prestige who have so spontaneous a generosity and so sincere an interest in what is being done in the country they are visiting. Cunningham and Cage, and the other members of their company, sought opportunities of speaking to our creators, of visiting them and seeing what they had done; during their week in Caracas they devoted virtually all their free time to explaining what they are trying to do and what they have succeeded in doing. The most marvelous and rational thing is that they were full of questions about their work and themselves. And the most moving thing is that when they took leave of their Venezuelan friends one Monday morning on the stage of the Teatro Caracas, everyone had the feeling he had known them for a very long time.[48]

A residency in weather-perfect, sunny San Francisco in October versus a February residency in snow-blanketed, wind-buffeted, seven-degrees-below-zero Buffalo is guaranteed to produce a very happy company. Prancing around Ghirardelli Square like giddy grade-school kids let loose in a playground, we were euphoric. Ostensibly we were there to make a film for KQED television. Well, actually we *were* making a film, but having so much fun doing it that we were scarcely aware of the cameras except on those days when we worked inside in the special-effects studio (a converted garage). Everything was within a block or two of our temporary home at the Hyde Park Suites Hotel. The cable car trundled back and forth, bell clanging, just outside the hotel and took us from Ghirardelli into the city center and back again, but rarely did we feel like going anywhere else. "Are we really less harassed or is it just that it's so lovely here?" Merce asked Jean Rigg.[1]

Ghirardelli Square, an inspired urban development remake of a group of factory buildings, was comprised of Clock Tower, Mustard Building, Cocoa Building, Chocolate Building, Woolen Mill, Power House, and Wurster Building, all connected by plazas and stairways and balconies. We performed in and on as many spaces as were feasible. Everywhere—from the top of the electric sign on the highest of the handsome red brick buildings, to various rooftops on every level—a dazzling world was spread out before our eyes: San Francisco Bay, the Golden Gate Bridge, the hills of Marin County, Alcatraz, and, just below the square, the Hyde Street Wharf and Marina, with boats bobbing up and down on their moorings or scooting madly around the bay. Off the beach, hardy souls could be seen swimming in the frigid waters. Everywhere shops, restaurants, and cafés tempted tourists and locals to wander, spend money, and just hang out, and those same people became not only our ever-present live audience but an unwitting part of the film as well.

The film, called *Assemblage,* was a genuinely collaborative effort. Merce choreographed the movement modules, but the final fifty-nine-minute end product was a dense collage assembled and edited from many hours of footage by Richard Moore, the director of special projects at KQED, who had once been a dancer with the Limón company. Together they selected the locations for each segment and discussed the technical aspects of the camera, angles, focus, etc. Special effects would play a large role in what was eventually seen. For three weeks we had morning class and rehearsal in the studio garage and spent the rest of each day cavorting in the square. Merce explained the working procedure to a reporter: "The camera wanders all around and among us. Any point of view is permissible, any movement can follow any other, time is simply a thing of what you put in it or don't. Therefore, any activity is possible as a movement that could be interesting."[2]

Most of the choreographed movement material was new, but with the exception of one group phrase aptly called "Ghirardelli Square" it was not recycled into works for the stage, as so often happened with later works Merce made for film. There was much random walking, shot from above, which included the presence of whatever passerby happened along in the space. Some of what we did was improvisatory, in response to verbal directives, and this allowed for much silliness, clowning, chasing, and rushing about. In the final edit, there's a marvelous sequence when the camera follows Merce, who appears totally unhinged as he dashes madly all over the square, running, falling, careering around corners. Performing live, he appeared to have gone berserk; on screen, even more so.

The music was also a collaborative effort created while the project proceeded. Behind blue paper-covered windows of an unused store in the Cocoa Building (which also served as our on-location dressing room), John, David, and Gordon worked at long tables littered with tape machines and electronic paraphernalia, juggling a plethora of sound sources recorded mostly around San Francisco by Gordon—filtering, transforming, modulating, and editing them into a fifty-nine-minute whole. It was not composed by chance procedures but "by committee." As John explained to a reporter, "What we are trying to do basically is to get three people to work together who make each other miserable. I've gotten more interested in the social aspect of making music. If people can work together well, it is an optimistic notion of society."[3]

The three men didn't really "make each other miserable," but they did have very different "likes and dislikes," and tended to make different aesthetic, philosophical, or technical decisions. Cage, clearly abandoning his stance of "beyond likes and dislikes," was heard to say about a clear, high boat whistle tooting several times, "Isn't that beautiful? It's just gorgeous. That's perfect."[4]

As for the costumes: "Theaster [theater + easter] bunnies," Meg called us, in our blue, orange, pink, purple, and yellow sweat suits and dyed-to-match canvas shoes. Other, more stylish, very sixties costumes for the women—tight, miniskirted dresses of our own choosing and knee-high white boots—were provided by Paraphernalia, a boutique selling clothes by "Exclusive Young Fashion Designers."

My pleasure was tripled by Jim Klosty's arrival in San Francisco just one day after the company's. Until Jim graduated from New York University with an MFA in theater he had been safe from the draft, but upon graduation his draft status instantly changed to 1A. Opposing the Vietnam War but not claiming to be a conscientious objector, he had made the decision to go to jail before he would agree to serve in Vietnam. Fleeing to Canada was not an option he even considered, but another option, which he took, was to teach in the New York public school system. As luck would have it, a teachers' strike gave him a three-week break to join the company in San Francisco, where he took more than five hundred photographs during the filming and began seriously considering doing a photograph book about the company.

A week and a half into filming, on October 23 at the cocktail hour in the square, we gave a two-hour benefit for the desperately needy Cunningham Foundation, sponsored by the San Francisco Museum Performing Arts Council, with both dancers and spectators (many of them San Francisco's cultural "elite") on camera. With tickets at only five dollars it was unlikely that this substantially eased our financial straits, but it was our only San Francisco performance. Filming ended on November 3. Two days later, we headed out by bus for a two-week tour, with performances in Santa Cruz, Berkeley, Fresno, Davis, Los Angeles, and La Jolla.

The three weeks of camaraderie and fun we'd all experienced while filming in Ghirardelli Square had given birth to a "new" Cunningham company spirit, and big stages in good theaters with a large, really responsive audience—pro or con—were as stimulating as champagne. The South American disasters were forgotten. (Although not the debts.) His injuries healed, his passion to perform undiminished, Merce was back with us in full form again. In Berkeley, Meg Harper got through her first performances of Barbara Lloyd's roles in *Suite for Five, Place,* and *How to . . .* beautifully. Rick Nelson, beloved by everyone, had returned to work with us full-time once again and would remain the company's official lighting designer for the remainder of my tenure.

While we were on the West Coast, Lew Lloyd resigned from the company and went to work for Harvey Lichtenstein at BAM. In a note to me dated November 1, he wrote that he hoped his new job would help Merce and the company as much or more than he had helped before. Although I could be a pesky thorn in his side, we were actually very close friends and remain so to this day. Jean Rigg, who'd been the acting company manager in California, stepped into his shoes. Lew's attempts to book the company for as many weeks as he could had met with some confusing contradictions: John wanted Lew to try to find a way to get the company subsidized—not worked to death—so that the pace of performance was in relation to the life of creative people, not workhorses,[5] while Lew was trying to fulfill Merce's desire to perform as often as possible. One never heard Merce complain about too many performances. John understood Merce's passion to perform, but he also understood the needs of a creative life, not only his own, but Merce's. There were other strains. It hadn't helped having a very substantial European tour, still in the preliminary planning stage, vetoed by the board, who cited serious financial problems. In Lew's view this was a very shortsighted and cowardly decision. Wasn't it the board's job to come up with money to subsidize the company? And if the company didn't perform, where was any money to come from to support Merce's choreographic work? Indeed, why have a company at all? From California, Jean Rigg, genuinely baffled, wrote to Lew in New York: "What are they [the board] saying, essentially? You can be an artist, but responsible? You can be an artist, but pay your own way? Am I simply naive? Is this what I'm supposed to realize private art subsidy is like? I think it's half-assed, and I think our board should be asked to fish or cut bait. Would we be much better off without them than with them?"[6]

Earlier, in an August *New York Times* Sunday column, "Dancing on Borrowed Money," Clive Barnes, in unequivocal language, stated that American dance was virtually broke, noting that in the beginning private patrons subsidized American dance, with perhaps the greatest private patron of all the American dancer himself: "The American dancer is the lowest paid of all American artists. . . . The plight of modern dancers is worse. How some of them even survive is a miracle, and only their fierce belief in what they are doing can enable them to go on."[7]

The seriousness of the Cunningham company's financial situation had even filtered down to my own bank account. Every week in Colorado and Mexico and throughout the South American tour, I had a small part of my salary sent to my bank. The previous spring, I had reserved a large Jasper Johns lithograph (*Grey Alphabets 1968*) directly through Gemini GEL (who had generously given me a 25-percent artist's discount), and as soon as I returned in late August I finished paying for it by check with my summer savings. To my considerable embarrassment, my check was returned: insufficient funds! The Cunningham company checks deposited in my account over the summer had bounced. I don't know how many other people had a similar experience, but if the paltry (around twenty dollars a week) checks to me had bounced, then the company's need for financial assistance was desperate indeed.

On December 12, Jasper hosted a fund-raising event for the company in his converted bank building at 225 East Houston Street. In addition, he designed a poster for the company that was derived from his painting *Target with Four Faces,* except this time the four faces were Merce's. The Bank, as we always called it, had a fifty-foot-square room with a thirty-five-foot-high ceiling that served as Jasper's studio, and in this space we attempted to perform all the material that Merce had choreographed for the Ghirardelli Square film. A mob scene! Despite the studio's size, there was scarcely enough room to move, let alone dance.

That night Jeff Slayton had pneumonia with a temperature of 102. At the end of the performance, he collapsed. Upstairs in our "dressing room," he began to cry. While the party raged below, Jasper and Viola came to his aid. Eventually Merce arrived to see how he was. Jeff told me years later that he was not very nice to Merce because before the performance he had begged Merce not to make him dance, but Merce had insisted.[8] It would never have occurred to Merce, no matter how ill, not to perform. Although I'm sure he felt genuine concern, still, for him, "the show must go on" was a moral imperative. Really very ill, Jeff was also very angry. What made him even angrier was seeing all the rich "beautiful people" standing around with drinks in their hands, many of them paying no attention at all to the dancing. This kind of fund-raiser—so necessary to the company's survival then—could be demeaning, even insulting, making the dancers feel like trained monkeys or court jesters. We knew the true allure of the event was to hobnob with famous artists in Jasper Johns's studio. Fortunately, many artists—many of them our true fans—were indeed there.

In the fall of 1968, Harvey Lichtenstein, director of the Brooklyn Academy of Music, made a major commitment to dance by inviting Merce Cunningham and Dance Company and the Alvin Ailey American Dance Theater to be resident companies, offering each of them a two-week season in the BAM Opera House each year, as well as office space for the companies' managements. In 1969, Eliot Feld's American Ballet Company became the third resident dance company at the academy. At Black Mountain in 1952, Harvey's love affair with modern art and the heady ideas of the avant-garde took wing, and it was there that he first met and studied with Merce. After a series of career changes and against all odds, Harvey revolutionized the staid old Brooklyn Academy of Music when he took over as director in 1967. When the artists he invited to perform there barely filled half a house, he persisted. Asked by James Traub of the *New York Times* more than thirty years later why he hadn't switched to more popular fare, Harvey said: "I knew these were important artists. I knew Merce Cunningham was a great artist. I *knew* it. And I wouldn't stop."[9]

It was not exactly Broadway, and it was a long subway ride from midtown Manhattan, but the Brooklyn Academy of Music—or BAM, as Harvey renamed it—would provide a home base, an excellent stage for dance, the guarantee of yearly performances in New York, and a kind of security that Merce had never known. In the formal invitation letter Harvey wrote to Merce, he stated his intention to work closely with the Cunningham Foundation to raise funds necessary for the continuous operation of the company, explaining that "the Academy's self-interest is served by being closely associated with one of the world's greatest dance companies."

Prior to this spirit-lifting news, only a week after the August 4 Barnes article deploring the plight of American dance in the *Times,* the Ford Foundation announced grants to help established modern-dance groups (ours among them), and a few lesser-known ones, plus one ballet company, by funding twenty-five weeks of performances in major New York theaters: City Center, BAM, and the Billy Rose. It was the beginning—but, alas, perhaps also the apex—of New York's embrace of America's homegrown art form. "Festival of Dance 68–69" was announced with a very snappy brochure listing eight major modern-dance companies (Alvin Ailey, Merce Cunningham, Martha Graham, Erick Hawkins, José Limón, Alwin Nikolais, Anna Sokolow, and Paul Taylor), four younger groups (Meredith Monk, Yvonne Rainer, Don Redlich, and Twyla Tharp), and one ballet company (American Ballet Theatre), who would perform either at BAM or at the Billy Rose Theatre from October through the first week in February. Can one think of any other time in New York's history when so many major modern-dance companies were given this kind of exposure and support in so brief a period?

The Billy Rose performances were arranged through the auspices of Albar [Edward Albee and Richard Barr] Theatre Arts, Inc., best known for presenting the works of new playwrights. The Cunningham company opened the monthlong season at the Billy Rose Theatre on January 13, 1969 with six performances, alternating two programs. In the minds of some, being on Broadway was equivalent to making it: it meant *real* success, as opposed to merely artistic success. But surely what being on Broadway really meant for us was the opportunity to attract a new audience in midtown Manhattan. Was dancing on Broadway more fun, more glamorous, more rewarding than in other theaters in other cities? It couldn't compare with the excitement I felt dancing in the West End in London. Nor did dancing in the New York State Theatre compare with the thrill of performing in that architectural jewel La Fenice in Venice, or in the Théâtre des Champs-Élysées in Paris, the original Sadler's Wells in London, or the Royal Opera House in Stockholm. I guess that casts me as a Euro-snob. Ancient theaters have venerable ghosts and creaky floorboards where legions of artists have trod before; that knowledge—their ghosts, if you will—bestows upon those of us who follow them a respect and awe for our historical dance/theater lineage. Until very recently, America has had no sense of history. It tears down its opera houses and music halls and theaters only to put up newer, and, alas, rarely better ones. Still, there was a buzz—I do admit it—when tawdry daytime Times Square (and it was tawdry in those days) turned up the lights and everything vibrated with that curious electric energy unique to New York City.

It was the first and only time I performed on Broadway. At week's end I wrote to my mother that "I didn't dance as well as I should have—not even once! It wasn't terrible but it wasn't nearly good enough." Without coaching or instructive criticism from Merce or anyone else, growing was always an uphill task. In a ballet company, no matter how senior an artist you are, there's always a coach to advise and guide your development. In the Cunningham company it was sink or swim. Merce, included! How profoundly I valued Margaret Craske's constructive criticism in her ballet classes, which I continued to take for all my performing years, but this was not available to me when we were on the road, and of course it was never directed toward my work in the Cunningham repertory. For the next four years, neither glowing reviews nor warmly complimentary friends could ameliorate the sense that I wasn't living up to a standard I'd set for myself.

In Europe, bouquets of flowers were often presented onstage, to Merce and a few times to me, but this was verboten on American stages according to Cunningham company protocol, even when the flowers were marked "presentation bouquet," thus disappointing many an ardent fan. Jim Klosty sent flowers every night, and was determined to get around this. After *Walkaround Time,* on our closing night at the Billy Rose, he wangled it with a huge bouquet of white and lavender (they matched my costume) gladioli presented to me onstage after he'd charmed some very junior stage manager into believing the inscription on the box—"from Mr. and Mrs. C. Chaplin." Charlie, of course.

The postseason party was at Jasper's bank, although Jasper was in California, working on prints at Gemini GEL. Bob Rauschenberg, very drunk, laughing and shouting as he blew in off the street, arrived late with his entourage. When he caught sight of me, he picked me up and sat me on his shoulder in a clumsy approximation of a ballet lift, and proceeded to bite my thumb with such vigor I thought he'd bite it off. When Bob was this drunk, he scared the bejesus out of me.

Immediately after the Billy Rose, Merce began concentrated work on a new piece and on getting *Antic Meet* back into the repertory after several years' hiatus. Four weeks later we were on the road again, touring New York State and the Midwest with Merce working on *Canfield* throughout. The tour ended in Chicago with four lecture-demonstrations for bused-in black kids of all ages and five performances at the Harper Theatre.

Thank god for New Paltz! An audience receptive, responsive—wanting us as badly as we needed them! The ordeal became instead a pleasure, even a joy. Not all *Gym Events* need be deadly. Even the muscles are less weary when the audience loves us. They stood—many of them—at the end. I had almost given up that I would enjoy dancing EVER again! . . . More terrible than anything: to do something one once loved and believed in, in a state of indifference.

Several days later:

Wallowing is exactly what I have been doing. If I *can* dance well, then *that* is my responsibility. And until I actually *stop* dancing, then I must work responsibly, working to improve both technically and "spiritually," never wishing anything less, or other.

Merce enjoyed playing solitaire and had learned a game invented by a gambler named Richard Canfield, who frequented the casinos in Saratoga Springs. While playing the game at Teeny Duchamp's home in Cadaqués, Spain, on one of those extremely rare occasions when he actually took a vacation, he decided that the procedure could be used to structure a dance. To each of the fifty-two cards in a deck he assigned movement; red and black determined fast or slow; face cards appearing in succession would indicate duets or trios. Deborah Jowitt, the only critic who seemed familiar with Canfield solitaire—she'd learned it from her great-aunt—

observed that in the opening deal the initial row is nine cards long, and this was the number of dancers in the piece. Thirteen, the number of cards in a suit, comprised the total number of discrete dances in the full-length work. In an interview, Merce said: "I played the game to find the continuity of movements for each dance, thirteen games in all. Each time a card was placed it opened up different possibilities. A card game seems to me to be a formal procedure, the rules and continuity of playing being rigorously set. But in between each game there is an informal relaxed moment. So I made fourteen 'in-betweens'; one to begin the dance, the others to go just after each game, the last one to be the finale of the piece."[10]

Canfield could be presented as an evening-length piece or abridged to accommodate our usual program format of three dances in an evening. It was extremely flexible in terms of space as well as time when performed without the set, and thus it was a practical addition to our touring and Event repertory, just as *Story* had proven to be. As in *Story*, the order of the sections could change from performance to performance. The thirteen dances are sculptural, the group floor patterns and rhythms complex, the static groupings curiously dramatic, the mood contemplative. In the apt words of one critic, "Quiet relationships predominate. . . . The motion progresses and unfolds, wave-like, from stillness and concentration."[11] The in-betweens were looser, the rhythms simpler and more playful, offering some freedoms to the dancers. As we toured the college circuit from one residency to another, the choreography progressed, but even at its New York premiere at BAM on April 15 it was still incomplete.

"Cunningham Goes on without Music." "Dance: The Golden Sound of Silence." These were the headlines in the two *New York Times* articles about the evening-length version of *Canfield* that opened our 1969 BAM season. It was a night to remember. Two unions—the electricians' union and the musicians' union—haggled about who had jurisdiction over the sounds issuing from the orchestra pit of the opera house when the music used electronic instruments as well as conventional acoustic ones. When his last-minute attempts to negotiate with the unions failed, Harvey Lichtenstein made the decision to go ahead without any music. For almost any other dance company in the world at that time, this would have been an insurmountable problem. For the dancers it posed no difficulty at all, but for the musicians this union struggle could have resulted in a very serious problem indeed, since so much of the company's music involved the wedding of conventional instruments and electronic ones, and, as Gordon Mumma said, "a decision has to be made that will allow us to practice our art."[12]

The unusual situation made for much publicity. Like the *Times,* several other newspapers printed a separate news story about the unions, in addition to their review of the performance. Neither the critics nor many in our audience were troubled by the lack of sound. From the *Newark News* review: "A smashing success . . . the absence of music was never less keenly felt.[13] [and] Let it suffice to say that the unions did Cunningham a favor, and if they never settle their dispute, it would be too soon. . . . At last one could share in Cunningham's zest for life without the distraction of music . . . At last one could divine the marvelous improbabilities of indeterminism, where chance is both accompanist and governor."[14] Clive Barnes reported that on hearing the news, his wife Trish exclaimed, "Thank God!"

Patrick O'Connor, admittedly my biggest fan in all the world, had no regrets about the lack of music: "I'll just say I got my wish: I got to see the Cunningham Company dance in silence, and if that's always been your wish this is your chance. Last night, sans music, the Cunningham Company proved that it is probably the best assembly of dancers in the world, that he's a choreographer of genius and Carolyn Brown is worth a trip to Brooklyn, if not around the world . . ."[15]

If Mr. O'Connor returned, he was no doubt deeply disappointed: the union impasse was settled for the remaining performances and the sound restored, with all its acoustical/electronic infamy. *Canfield* had no musical score. The composition "In Memoriam Nikola Tesla, Cosmic Engineer" by Pauline Oliveros consisted of three pages of instructions for the musicians. Tesla once—so legend goes—adjusted an oscillator to the resonance of his studio and nearly brought the building down. In *Canfield,* the musicians' ultimate task was to discover the resonant frequency of the building in which the dance was performed but not to go so far as to bring the building down. (A most unlikely possibility.) They had a series of steps to follow, including describing—in an immediate and personal way, via walkie-talkies and the public-address system—the actual performance space, comparing it to other spaces; recording the conversation and the environment as they explored the theater, including backstage, the basement, the lobby; and finally playing back the accumulated reportage, plus the accumulated sound material along with oscillator-generated resonant-frequency sounds. However inadequate this description, it gives some idea of the aural landscape we performed in.

Robert Morris's visual design for *Canfield,* on the other hand, provided no written instructions at all. As Jasper tells it, "I asked Bob Morris to do something, and he had an idea but no interest in doing it. So he told me what had to be done, and who else was there to do it except me?"[16] In fairness to James Baird and Richard Nelson, both of whom contributed a wealth of creative and practical assistance, Jasper did not have "to do it" alone. Morris's first idea, so went the scuttlebutt, was to cover the stage floor with car grease and have the dancers perform in the buff. When that idea was nixed, he came up with the notion of having the dancers wear leotards and tights sprayed with a substance that would glow phosphorescent white when caught by a moving beam of light. Jasper dyed our leotards gray, then sprayed the reflective paint on us, while each of us stood in a makeshift plastic alcove, trying not to breathe the toxic fumes. A tall vertical beam, the full height of the proscenium arch, flat gray from the audience's perspective, had airplane landing lights installed from top to bottom. It was motorized and traversed back and forth across the front of the stage. Since there were so many variables affecting the speed of the beam, and because the sections of the dance changed from one performance to the next, we never knew when we would be totally blinded by the lights. When they caught us in their narrow beam we were meant to glow. That was the intention, but it didn't work. The "science" of the idea was faulty. As Jasper said, for the concept to fully work as intended, each person in the audience would have needed his or her own powerful flashlight. In any case, tights and leotards were washed after every performance, and with each washing a little more of the phosphorescent spray paint went down the drain. Constructing the motorized beam was Jim Baird's job. As Gordon put it, if it worked, Bob Morris got the credit; if it didn't, Jim Baird got the blame. Nonetheless, the searing lights in their relentless back-and-forth movement added a highly dramatic element to the choreography.

What did work, and added immeasurably (in my opinion) to the scenic element, was Richard Nelson's contribution. In many of his lighting designs, Rick entered fully into the Cage/Cunningham spirit and used chance processes for his lighting plots. In *Rainforest,* for example, he made charts for color, direction, and time—one chart per minute of dance time—and asked each dancer to put one dot randomly on each page. *Rainforest*'s lights were always in motion, but they moved slowly; the cues were set but nothing else was predetermined, neither their speed nor their time of completion. To create his lighting plot for *Canfield,* Rick played six hundred games of solitaire. He took photos, then made slides of Merce's notations, Pauline's notes, his own notes, and of photos of the faces of Tesla and Canfield. He had a lightbulb projecting itself: a leico with its lens arranged so that the image of the lamp and its reflector projected themselves onto the cyclorama. All of these elements were subjected to chance procedures. Arlene Croce, mistakenly crediting Morris (only the beam was his design), thought the lighting for *Canfield* and for Rick's later design for *Signals* (1971) "among the most beautiful and ingenious of late years."

Less than twenty-four hours after our final BAM performance, we were boarding an Alitalia flight to Rome. Standing in the queue, waiting to pass through security control, I became aware of a tall, curly-haired guy I hadn't remembered ever seeing before, but who seemed to be a part of the Cunningham entourage, which on this trip included Judith Blinken, my mother, and Jim Klosty. "Who is he?" I asked, sotto voce, of the person standing next to me. "Charlie Atlas, the new production assistant," I was told. Heaven knows, we needed one. Having gone from being a company that traveled light—no sets and barely any costumes—we were now burdened with literally tons of scenic and electronic apparatus. Although we gave only two performances in Rome, we took six works from the repertory, four of them—*Scramble, Canfield, Rainforest,* and *Walkaround Time*—all requiring intensive labor and setup time. The only dance Charlie had ever seen was Merce's, and he'd loved it. What he had always wanted to do was make his own films, and that desire would be fulfilled when he began filming Merce's dances two years later, the beginning of an artistically successful film career.

My most vivid memory of that trip is of our last night. I'd been fighting a miserable cold the whole week. We'd gone to the Piazza Navona to have a drink with Cy Twombly, who, after his breakup with Bob Rauschenberg, had immigrated to Italy in 1957, married an Italian (a princess, it was rumored) and lived on the Piazza Navona in an impressive house, made all the more impressive by its empty, echoing rooms. The last time I'd seen Cy was when he was virtually penniless and had sold Earle and me a large pencil drawing on paper attached to a piece of scratchy fiberboard for fifty dollars. (Over the years the paper yellowed and dried and the pencil faded to nothing.) After dinner in a restaurant, I was suddenly stricken with a violent case of turista and simultaneously had just gotten my period with a vengeance. No automobiles are permitted in the Piazza Navona. Finding a taxi anywhere near the piazza on a Saturday night in April is as likely as finding a diamond in the Bernini fountain. Jim rushed on ahead and finally hailed a horse-drawn carriage, and we set out for the hotel. No one spoke a smidgen of Italian, and Jim was unable to convey to the driver that we were in haste and not out for a leisurely tour of Rome. Adding to our difficulty was some sort of fiesta, with hordes of revelers crowding the streets. We could do no more than inch along until suddenly Jim jumped out, stopped traffic, and led the horse through the throngs of people and automobiles.

The romance and fun of the situation were completely lost on me. I started getting asthma from the sweating horses. Clenching every orifice in my body, barely able to breathe, I managed to hold on until we arrived at the hotel where, sitting on the john, in nearly hysterical relief all I could do was laugh and cry.

No more performances until mid-September. The Royal Ballet came to town in April, providing nourishment for the soul with Frederick Ashton's sublime *Enigma Variations* and inspired performances by Fonteyn and Nureyev in *Sleeping Beauty, Raymonda* (Act III), *Swan Lake, Pelléas and Melisande,* and the *Le Corsaire* pas de deux, plus the glorious dancing of Antoinette Sibley and Anthony Dowell, Monica Mason, Svetlana Beriosova, Deanne Bergsma, Alexander Grant, Brian Shaw, and Michael Coleman. My god, what a ravishing company!

The summer of 1969 felt like former years of just class and rehearsals, but with a difference: a rehearsal salary had been provided by a grant from the National Endowment for the Arts, allowing Merce time to finally complete all thirteen sections of *Canfield.* Happily, "the pace of performance in relation to the life of creative people, not workhorses" as John had requested, now seemed within reach. In the fall, another grant—through the Rockefeller Foundation to the Brooklyn Academy—made possible our longest paid-rehearsal period to date and was used for the revival of *Crises* and creation of two new dances, but that work did not begin until after a two-week residency in Minnesota's Twin Cities, subsidized in part by the National Endowment for the Arts and sponsored by the Minneapolis Walker Art Center.

In October, Merce's book *Changes: Notes on Choreography* was published by Something Else Press. For the general reader, as Clive Barnes wrote, the book is "unreadable but worth absorbing by osmosis." For those of us who have lived it however, it's readable, comprehensible, and informative, but Barnes got the right message: "Cunningham is saying to an audience: this is theatre, this is a new ritual. But much more, he is saying look at this with new eyes. Do not let your intelligence anticipate the creative act, do not let your expectation fill in the expected pattern. Delight, then, in the discord of the moment, for the discord is new in its very unexpectedness, and the newness, the freshness and the wonder, is the relationship."[17]

In June, Merce had started to choreograph new material. Upon return from the Minnesota tour he set to work in earnest. One month later, he left for Sweden to rehearse *Summerspace* and set *Nightwandering* on Birgit Cullberg's company, which was to perform at the Champs-Élysées in Paris.

He asked me to run rehearsals in his absence. A new dancer, Douglas Dunn, had to be worked into the repertory. Douglas had been invited to join the company that autumn, not to replace anyone but to augment the number of dancers. He had taken his first ballet class when a junior at Princeton in 1963, spent a summer at Jacob's Pillow, and during his senior year in college performed with Princeton Ballet Society. In the fall of 1968 he found his way to the Cunningham Studio. On the strength of his performance of Merce's part in *Rune* during the 1969 summer repertory workshop, he was invited to join the company. He's said that ten minutes into Merce's first class he understood the affinity, and after seeing the company at the Billy Rose he knew he wanted to dance like us. He told me:

> What impressed me about MC and his style was the plainness. I didn't, as with ballet, have to be a prince. And the absence of meaning in the traditional sense provided a gigantic opening in mind and body. . . . My literaryized mind let go. I was freed back to the directness of energy I had had as a child, when left alone a lot . . . where I had been quite satisfied with the simplicity of actions done for their own sake. . . . Finally the focus was where I wanted it, on movement itself: I became conscious of what had been always present as an unconscious interest.[18]

After returning from Sweden, Merce had two months to complete the new dances. He was, as ever in those days, mute and secretive about his working process, but there was a tantalizing mystery going on: the sound of recorded music or occasionally the halting sounds of someone at the piano emanated from behind closed doors of the big studio where Merce was working alone. What was he doing? Whatever it was, the rhythms seemed to be giving him trouble. The only precedent for this occurrence was in 1964, when Viola Farber and I heard the music of a jazz recording as we arrived at the studio for our rehearsal of *Cross Currents*. That time, to our delight, we actually got to rehearse with the music, but then, to our great disappointment, John refused to allow Merce to use it in performance. Everyone knew that when Merce was completely alone in the studio, he would often dance to recorded music. I always assumed it was simply for his own pleasure, but David Vaughan reminded me that one day at the Fourteenth Street Studio when Merce was at the piano playing Ravel's *Valses nobles et sentimentales*, I said, "You ought to make a dance to that music," and Merce responded, "I already have." Which of his dances was Merce's well-kept secret. Of course, the music of Satie was another matter altogether. No secrets required there: John encouraged Merce to use it. Merce claimed to love it—its mysterious, not-quite-definable quality and its formal structural inventions.[19] Erik Satie might well have been John's favorite composer in the world, and I hazard a guess that of all John's "heroes," Satie was the most influential.

Merce's first dance to Satie music was as early as 1944, with his *Idyllic Song*, set to the first movement of Satie's *Socrate*. *The Monkey Dances* in 1948, *Two Step* (1949), *Waltz* (1950), *Ragtime Parade* (1950), *Epilogue* (1953), *Septet* (1953), and *Nocturnes* (1956) followed. Now, thirteen years later, Merce went back to *Idyllic Song*, having made the decision to choreograph all three movements of *Socrate* as John had been pestering him to do for years. But there was another reason. Setting up the electronic paraphernalia for each score required more time than intermission allowed, so Gordon Mumma had requested at least one more work that would not involve any electronics.

The music emanating from behind closed doors was Satie's *Socrate*, an unusually large-scale, serious work for soprano and orchestra, very different in tone from most compositions by Satie. For *Idyllic Song*, in 1944, John had made a two-piano version. In Merce's version of the story, in 1969 John told Merce he'd begun making a two-piano transcription of the second and third movements, so that if Merce wanted to do the full work it would be available. Merce was mum but began listening to a recording of the music, and some months later, when John suggested *Socrate* once again as the solution to the electronics problem, he was surprised to learn that Merce was already at work on the choreography.[20] Communication was never Merce's strong suit, not even apparently with his closest friend and collaborator.

As the work was nearing completion, a serious setback seemed destined to cancel the project altogether: Satie's publisher refused John permission to make a two-piano version of the music, or even to use Satie's own arrangements for piano. John, not easily daunted by insurmountable obstacles, wrote a piece for one piano so that he could play it himself using I Ching chance operations with respect to seven modes and twelve transpositions of each, and then he applied these in a programmed way to his model, making a totally new composition that preserved the expressivity and replicated the exact rhythm and phraseology of Satie's original. The "melody," however, was entirely new, and thus he was able to avoid the copyright problem. Satie was known to be a great lover of puns and double entendres, and in that spirit John called his piece *Cheap Imitation* so that the title, as well as the music, would imitate Satie's sensibility. Merce responded by calling his choreography *Second Hand,* since he had worked at *Socrate* years before and had returned to it again.[21]

The primary consideration for Merce when choreographing this work was not simply the movement, as was customary with him. It was the music. He assiduously studied it, not only its phrasing and rhythm and structure and but also its *content.* The life and death of Socrates is the subject. Satie's *Socrate* is a symphonic drama; the libretto consists of fragments selected by Satie from three of Plato's Dialogues—*Symposium, Phaedrus,* and *Phaedo.* It was apparently Satie's intention that the first section be a portrait of Socrates; the second, his way of life in the form of a walk by the river with a disciple; and the third, the manner of his dying. I believe Merce's *Second Hand* mirrors Satie's intention, but in a very unspecific way.

Of course in the beginning, we dancers were not privy to any of this information. We eventually learned of the copyright problem and of John's solution, but beyond what its title might imply, we were told nothing relating to the content of Satie's music. It was Jim Klosty, a knowledgeable and passionate music lover, who enlightened me. Still, there was no reason to assume that *Second Hand* would follow the Plato libretto. Satie described *Socrate*—considered his masterpiece by many—as "a return to classical simplicity in a modern sensibility."[22] What better way to describe Merce's choreography? Descriptions of the music could as well be applied to the dance: pure line; precision; limpid texture; fluid; without *fortissimo;* austere; meditative; moving simplicity.

Part One—"Portrait de Socrate"—was a solo for Merce, in which he remained rooted in the same place throughout. Part Two—"Les bords de l'Illussus"—a duet for Merce and me, moved through the space. Part Three—"Mort de Socrate"—for the whole company (Socrates's disciples) followed a diffused circular pattern, each dancer entering and exiting separately, leaving Merce alone onstage when the curtain falls. As I wrote in Jim Klosty's book,

> At the end of our duet, just before I exit prior to Part Three, Merce and I run two full circles around the stage, arms around each other's waists. During the run in the final stage rehearsal before the premiere, Merce's expression terrified me. We'd already rehearsed *Rainforest* and *Place* that afternoon, and *Second Hand* is almost thirty minutes long, with Merce dancing the entire time. He'd always smiled at me during this run until that rehearsal, but this time he looked so anguished that my first thought was that he had injured himself or was completely exhausted. Afterwards, I expressed my

fears to John Cage. "Don't worry," John told me the next day. "Merce said it's at that moment that [Socrates] is preparing to meet death."[23]

Part Three is an elegy—pensive, reflective, the movements and phrasings mostly slow, sustained. Seeing a film of *Second Hand* more than thirty years later I was struck by the quality of profound mourning relayed simply by the movement. How did Merce manage to evoke this quality without telling us anything about the content of *Socrate*? Only recently have I come up with a possible answer. Part Three has one curious element. Merce devised sixteen different hand positions, and he gave each of us our own score and "rules" about how to use them: the changes from one position to the next were never to be abrupt, the fingers were never to be fully extended and never stiff. Merce's original score for my part lists forty sets of numbers with calligraphy representing the sixteen positions. What these signified in relation to *Socrate* remains a mystery to me. It's highly doubtful that anyone in the audience was aware of the subtle hand changes. However, what Merce accomplished by giving us this task insured single-minded, meditative concentration throughout the slow entrances. At that moment in the text, Socrates's sorrowful disciples are arriving at the prison to make their farewell and to witness Socrates being given poison and then dying. Their entrance sets the exquisitely somber, elegiac tone of the entire section.

At the premiere of *Second Hand*, there was no mention of Satie's *Socrate* in the program, and thus no way for critics or the general audience to have even the smallest clue that *Second Hand* might be what in fact it was: a programmatic ballet. In later BAM performances that season, there *was* a program note about the music, but still no one thought to connect the text of the original score with what they witnessed onstage. A bit of homework for the critics? Perhaps. In any case, no one bothered. Apparently none of them believed that Merce would ever stray from the non-narrative path, and yet, while in no way literal, *Second Hand* was in every way, in my opinion, an evocation of Satie's intention. It was mostly this critical non-comprehension of *Second Hand* that prompted Jim Klosty to write a long tirade in *Ballet Review* under the pseudonym Michael Snell called "Cunningham and the Critics." As with *Walkaround Time*, connecting the work with its inspiration might have provided the viewer with a far richer, more moving experience. There is a vast difference between knowing the processes of *how* a dance was put together (not only not necessary, but possibly a deterrent) and exploring its possible *inspiration* (not at all necessary, but possibly enriching).

Not even Jasper, who designed the costumes, was informed about the content of the Plato libretto. Satie's favorite color was white. Jasper's costumes—simple tights and leotards—were dyed using the full spectrum, which was only noticeable when we lined up to take our bows. Then, it could be noticed that the sleeve or leg on each dancer had a bit of the dominant color of the next dancer in the lineup. Viola told Jasper that we looked like a bunch of Easter bunnies—hardly what Plato or Satie had in mind. But the full spectrum is the continuum of color formed when a beam of white light is dispersed through the prism so that its component wavelengths are arranged in order. And there we were, arranged in prismatic order as Jasper had requested. One wonders: if Jasper had been told the story of *Socrate,* would he have chosen to do something different, or was this his own Satie-esque contribution to the mix? I decided not to ask him, since his own work—his painting, drawings, lithographs, and sculptures—are full of guarded secrets, mysteries, and double entendres.

Tread, the second new work, was a lighthearted, speedy romp, with antic partnering, humorous people clusters, fast spatial changes—choreography of the fun-and-games genre, danced behind a row of oscillating industrial fans (Bruce Nauman's decor), with music by Christian Wolff and performed by the dancers with much smiling and jovial interaction.

Merce taught me my *Tread* solo in about two minutes. ("I think dance only comes alive when it gets awkward again," Merce has written.) Three days later *Tread* was premiered in Brooklyn. I decided it was a dance that Merce didn't want "worked on" and so I rarely practiced it. He never made suggestions about it once he had taught it to me, and even then it was tossed off so quickly, a mere indication of shape and rhythm with only the energy of it clearly articulated. Douglas had a similar experience: he remembers not seeing anything but a bolt of energy that got from here to there when Merce demonstrated a phrase from *Tread* and he had to will himself to watch the body literally the second time so that he could learn the steps.[24] At the premiere, on the opening night at BAM, I had the flu and a high temperature. My inspiration for dancing the solo—that night and forever after—was Jeff Slayton: his fearlessness, his no-holds-barred energy and amplitude. I told myself, "Forget technique, just let it rip, go for it with total abandon." After that performance, Sara Rudner commented on how very differently I'd danced in the *Tread* solo. There is no female modern dancer I admire and respect more than Sara, so her words were always very important to me, but especially at that time, when they provided strong encouragement for a breakthrough I sorely needed to make. She delighted in seeing me make my "hell-with-technique-and-striving-for-perfection" decision, which released a new dimension worth developing further.

At BAM the *Canfield* score received universal ridicule, most of which was aimed at John, even though the score was not his. By this time John had abdicated the role and title of music director and was no longer listed on the programs in that capacity. In place of "Music Director," the program simply identified all three musicians under "Music" or "Musicians." This had little effect on the perceptions of the critics, who almost always blamed Cage for every sound emanating from the pit. While John did exercise considerable influence in selecting the people who composed for the company, often with suggestions from David and Gordon, he never—to my knowledge—interfered with the composer's work once that person had been chosen. Clive Barnes, far more than most, had tolerated the music with a certain amount of irony and good humor until we did an evening-length *Canfield,* this time *with* the Oliveros sound accompaniment, and then he lost his cool: "John Cage strikes me as more a mistake than a musician—and, at his very best, more of a joke than either. . . . Cage's score [Oliveros's score, in fact] is little more but musician-technicians working their machines in the pit and chatting interminably about sound frequencies and noise levels—reducing all music to the amiable level of noise pollution . . . Cage's whole trivial concept of music as a camp party game with knobs on."[25]

Even so, the BAM season ended on a high, with a sold-out house of 2,100 plus 196 standees viewing the two new works, *Tread* and *Second Hand,* and the revival of *Crises,* with Viola Farber returning to do her original role. A year with two more new dances and the happiest European tour of my twenty years in the company was to follow.

Rick Nelson and I were sitting in a pancake house in Tampa, Florida, one morning in mid-March 1970, talking about "the good old days," complaining about "the bad new days." To be honest, Rick wasn't complaining; I was. We'd been on the road for over a month, with performances in major cities like Boston and Washington, D.C., half-week residencies in two New England colleges, a week residency in Pittsburgh. Now, halfway through a two-week residency at the University of Florida in Tampa, the company's presence seemed an anomaly amid a largely indifferent student population. After patiently listening for a while, Rick said very seriously, "You *can* leave, you know." This was the first time I'd become painfully aware of how often I waxed nostalgic about the fifties and early sixties, the VW touring days, and the intellectual stimulation provided by long hours spent in the minibus with John, David Tudor, and Bob Rauschenberg.

In Tampa, we lived in a dormitory. Rehearsals and classes were held in a room without windows, its walls covered with dizzy-making dotted soundproofing board in four different colors. Garish bright-blue curtains draped the mirrors. The floor was shiny, sticky, treacherous—laid directly over cement. This ghastly, airless room, lit by headache-producing fluorescent lights, ill served the work Merce needed to accomplish. Outside, the sun burned bright in a pellucid blue sky. Students lolled around swimming pools. How does one study in Florida, anyway? Would we reach anyone here on any level of communication? Aside from the income to the company coffers (the point, after all), this residency struck me as absurd. Had Jim been there, at least it would have been fun. That, of course, was much of the problem. I missed him terribly and the arrival of Sara Rudner, the love of Douglas Dunn's life at the time, only reinforced my loneliness.

A young dancer named Louise Burns officially joined the company in Tampa. She'd come from her home state of Hawaii, having received a wide range of dance training in ballet, modern, and non-Western dance, and she'd also spent a year in Australia studying ballet. After a taste of Cunningham classes in Hawaii she'd gone to New York to study at the studio, was given a scholarship, and was subsequently invited to attend rehearsals. During the Florida residency she had to learn *Field Dances,* parts of *Canfield,* and *How to . . . for* Events, as well as material we all were learning for a new work. Accuracy of rhythm was of paramount importance to Merce, and he was unusually tough on Louise, especially considering that these were "open rehearsals" with spectators watching the poor embarrassed young woman struggle with so much material being thrown at her, and all of us standing around watching and trying to help. Merce had her go over one step again and again. Louise recalled: "It seemed like an eternity—and I just remember my eyes boring a hole into the floor and thinking if he would just tell what is wrong I will try to do it right. Afterwards Meg said that it had been extraordinary because I did not crack. It never occurred to me to do that—but I think that he really in some profound way embarrassed me so much that I was lost."[1]

Louise was just beginning her performing life. Mine, I felt certain, was coming to a close. For seventeen years my life had been planned and scheduled with little if any input from me. In the early years I loved not knowing what we might be doing, where we might be going—believing there was always a happy surprise just around the next corner—but as the company became more successful, the administration had to plan one, two, or even three years in advance. I began to feel suffocated. Journal notes:

[3/11/70] The "work" continues to be tiresome, irksome, dreary, repetitious, boring and frustrating. I struggle for air, for light, for wisdom, for humor, for freedom, for self-determination. Above all, yes—self-determination.

[3/13/70] Tonight I danced locked up in a cold hard lonely fury. Danced? Hardly. . . . My happiest times, dancing—be it in rehearsal or performance are those times when the dance is me and I am the dance—inseparable, one thing. The music plays freely with the time, even the space, at the whim of the dial and knob turners. The lights play freely—making beautiful sculpture of us, probably even making us look beautiful—at the whim of the lighting designer. And we—trained in a cloistered hall to do our technical feats—are put in the middle of all this freedom and told to perform like the good little trained beasts that we are. I scream resentment in every fiber. I talked to John right after the performance. He was all "there"—with me— not even slightly wined or laughing. He said it was a beautiful evening, one of the great theatrical experiences. He'd heard that I was miserable. Wanted to know why. I told him I felt like a slave, one of the slaves in the orchestra that he's always talking about; that I felt a great dichotomy in the freedom given the musicians and lighting personnel and the rigid, restrictive requirements placed on the dancers; the futility of rehearsing to accomplish technical feats when it could all be knocked to smithereens by any number of unknown elements. John nodded—said it was so beautiful though. I said I thought so too—and perhaps that is what should happen now. I should watch and enjoy it since doing it gave me no joy at all.

I had opted out of the newest dance that Merce had been slowly putting together throughout the tour. I'd told him he need not feel that he must put all of us in every dance all the time and I asked not to be in this one: "[3/15/70] Can't cope with all that movement, movement, movement. I must be involved in context, quality, dynamics—meaning too, damn it. I watch. The space and rhythms are fantastic. The dancers: facile as hell. I'm awed by [Merce's] creativity, his constant, relentless output. I want to watch it. Not do it."

The few times I'd choreographed or written articles I'd felt like a grown-up, an adult involved in a self-determining creative life, not a child whose life was always planned and scheduled months, if not years, in advance. In the VW days we rarely knew from one week to the next where we might be going, what we might be doing. Then we were (mostly) a happy, trusting little band of travelers, tucked into a small boat adrift in unknown waters, with John at the helm. Hearing an administrator call us "dancerettes"—something John would never have done—felt insulting, demeaning, above all, condescending. After choreographing *Car Lot* I had received several invitations to set my own work on small companies, but the Cunningham rehearsal-and-performance schedule did not allow sufficient time for me to accept these invitations, but if I was not in Merce's newest dance, I realized, I could accept an offer from Juilliard. I'd met with Antony Tudor and Martha Hill in November '69 to discuss the possibility. In our first conversation, Tudor had asked what music I was considering. At the first mention of Satie he said something like "too easy" or "too au courant," so I chose Elgar's *Serenade for Strings in E Minor*, which met with his approval.

As soon as we returned from Florida I began to choreograph. During April and May, I raced from ballet class with Miss Craske at Fifth Avenue and Twelfth Street to rehearsals of my ballet *West Country* at Juilliard (situated by this time at Lincoln Center), then to Merce's classes and repertory rehearsals on the other side of town at Third Avenue and Thirty-third Street, where I also taught my parts in *Rainforest* and *Canfield* to Louise.

When I had a free moment I rehearsed some Denishawn pieces I hadn't performed in years in preparation for my mother's Fortieth Anniversary Concert on April 18 in Fitchburg. I suppose I should have been exhausted; instead I felt wonderfully alive.

While in Florida, I received a phone call informing me that I was to receive a 1969 *Dance Magazine* Award. That announcement, in itself, was stunning, but more stunning by far—and utterly humbling—was to learn that the other recipients were Frederick Ashton and Ted Shawn. The award ceremony took place in the Gold and White Room at the Plaza Hotel on Fifty-ninth Street at five o'clock on Monday, May 25.

I found myself in a situation I would never have imagined. There I was, on the dais with "Papa" Shawn, my mother's teacher, whom I had known since I was five, and Sir Frederick Ashton, the ballet choreographer I most revered in all the world. On the dais with us: Agnes de Mille, Walter Terry, Bob Rauschenberg, Sol Hurok, William Como, who was the editor of *Dance Magazine,* and Jean Gordon, the magazine's associate publisher. A sea of faces filled every available space as far as one could see—including those of my mother, my brother Parker, my sister-in-law Mona, my two nieces (Robin and Rebecca), Earle (who, in June, would receive an honorary doctorate in music from the Peabody Conservatory of Music, where he was composer in residence), Jim, Merce, and present and past Cunningham company members and staff. Although Jasper said he was there, he slipped away immediately after the presentations. I never saw him. The most nerve-racking part of the occasion for some of us was having to give a speech. Bob Rauschenberg, the first to speak after Bill Como's introductory remarks, began by saying, "This is the second most impossible situation that I've been in about talking." (He said his first was speaking at his son's school at eight o'clock one morning.) By 1970, Bob had been interviewed hundreds of times; in those circumstances his words, expressing startlingly original thinking, always seemed to come easily. But this afternoon his words tumbled out in a disarray of mixed emotions. At the end he said,

I was so nervous . . . at four o'clock this afternoon I went up on my roof and just stood there, just staring out, and I said, "I can't! There's no way I can deal with the situation, presenting her award." I'm too close to Carolyn. And I'm too far away because of my respect. But *somehow*—diffusing is maybe the magic: I have plants on my roof, and there wasn't a rose there the day before yesterday. I thought, "A rose is traditional in the theatre." And at that moment I noticed that one had bloomed! And there it was!" [Rauschenberg, with a little flourish, pulls a carefully preserved rose from inside his jacket and presents it to Carolyn Brown. The audience, touched and amused by this gesture, breaks into applause.] This is home grown![2]

How earnest both Bob and I were! In my acceptance speech I expressed my gratitude to my mother—for her teaching, so full of love and devotion to dance, and her emphasis on dancing for the sheer joy of it, not necessarily with a professional career as the goal. I told of her steadfast commitment to Denishawn, which had just culminated in her Fortieth Anniversary Concert with dances she had learned from Ted Shawn and the Denishawn School in the twenties and continued to teach her students. Acknowledging my passion for ballet, most especially the Royal Ballet, I explained that I danced with Merce because I wanted to be a part of a very new experience, of what was happening today, and with Merce, John, and Bob I found that world. "We look at dancing differently today because of the three of them," I said, "and I'm very proud to be a part of that involvement."[3]

This was one of the most hectic weeks in my life: the following morning I was at Juilliard for the final rehearsal of my ballet, at a rehearsal with Merce in the afternoon, and at the first performance of *West Country* that evening, and then I dashed across Lincoln Center Plaza to catch the last two acts of *Swan Lake* with Fonteyn and Nureyev. This was Ashton's last season as the Royal's director. I had to miss the season's closing night, all vividly described to me later in a letter from David Vaughan: ovations for everything and everyone; the full-company curtain calls, the speeches, tears; Fonteyn ravishing in an orange-pink-red chiffon gown; Nureyev in putty-colored suit with matching thigh-boots; and Sir Fred's brief emotional speech, his last word strangled by a sort of sob. This kind of emotion and devotion, on both sides of the curtain, is rarely seen anymore.

West Country was my attempt at a pastoral English ballet—with the musicality of Tudor and Ashton as inspiration. A tall order. My two most recent efforts had been in the Cage/Cunningham tradition—the dance coexisting with the music (in both cases by Earle Brown) but not choreographed to it. The three informal showings of *West Country* were on a program with two works by José Limón and two by Anna Sokolow. I think Tudor was disappointed. *Car Lot,* which he'd claimed to like "uncommonly much," was edgier, more modern and more original. In the program, both Limón's *Unsung* and my ballet were called "work in progress," but mine progressed no further. At 9:30 the following morning, after its third performance, I was on a plane to Europe. Except for a letter sent to Paris from

David Vaughan ("I really liked your ballet, as did Arlene [Croce] and Pat O'Connor"), I never gave *West Country* another thought until I returned two months later and found an appreciative letter from Martha Hill suggesting that I might want to do it again with a change of cast, or perhaps set just the pas de deux for the Lincoln Center Student Program tour. In the letter she mentioned speaking with Tudor, who suggested: "Why doesn't Carolyn do another piece more in modern-dance style?" confirming my suspicion about his opinion of *West Country.*

Eighteen days, working and playing, in springtime Paris! These were the happiest days I'd ever spent in that beautiful, romantic city—in large part because Jim was there to enjoy it with me. We even managed a bit of sightseeing: Sainte-Chapelle, Delacroix's studio, museums and galleries, and a visit to the Mémorial des Martyrs Français de la Déportation de 1945, which Jim had discovered years earlier. Few Parisians seemed to know about it. Approached through a garden behind Notre Dame, on the tip of the Île de la Cité, where the Seine flows gently by and a bird can be heard to sing, it is a deeply moving, peaceful place commemorating the French citizens deported to concentration camps during the Second World War.

My dressing-room window opened onto the Luxembourg Gardens, its peace and greenery spreading behind the Théâtre de France, where we gave twelve performances. The theater was beautiful, with a steeply raked stage and a small studio at the top of the building where we could warm up. We had only one complaint: the newly laid pressed-wood floor caused floor burns and administered splinters. Our audiences varied from cool, unresponsive, fancily dressed elites on opening night, to wildly enthusiastic houses—simultaneously cheering and booing—to outright rudeness at our final performance when a strong contingent of loud hecklers—political malcontents, we were told—shouted and clapped in "political rhythms," which stood for "*Ce n'est qu'un debut. Continuons le combat!*" ("This is just a start. Let's keep on fighting!") At least they didn't throw eggs and tomatoes as they had in 1964! For us, the commotion was exciting, even fun, but for Paul Taylor, who was in the audience that night, it was alarming. He came backstage looking extremely apprehensive. His company was to open a two-week engagement in the same theater beginning the following evening. Two years earlier, during the 1968 riots, students took over the theater at the end of Paul's second performance. They asked him to give free performances for them, but he refused. (Read his book, *Private Domain,* for a play-by-play.) Jean-Louis Barrault—director of the Théâtre de France at that time—joined the students' cultural revolution and was subsequently fired by the government. A leader of the student takeover, Jean-Jacques Lebel (son of Robert Lebel, the Marcel Duchamp scholar), was a neo-Dadaist credited with being the initiator of the French Happening. Judith and Julian Beck, with their Living Theatre group, also joined the students occupying the theater in 1968. Paris was a quasi–war zone, with vast demonstrations, homemade bombs exploding helter-skelter, and thousands of *gendarmes* patrolling the streets. Anarchists and workers joined the students. Red Communist and black anarchist flags waved from the theater's rooftop. Inside, the theater was trashed. Miraculously, no one was killed.

After one of our last performances, Judith and Julian Beck waited outside the stage door to say hello, but they wouldn't enter the theater because it was again government-run. Until we arrived, many intellectuals had not been in that theater since the '68 revolution. Even two years later the scars had not healed. Our hotel, the Hôtel Odéon Michelet, adjacent to the theater in Place de l'Odéon, still bore visible evidence of the violence. The carpet in Jim's and my room had burn holes from a Molotov cocktail tossed through the window. According to Paul Taylor's account, an explosion had blown a head-sized hole in the wall of his room. Such wounds as these had been only superficially repaired. But this history, a touch of *A Tale of Two Cities,* lent the old-fashioned, rather tattered hotel an aura of romantic fiction to those of us who'd heard about the riots, not lived them. Our cheery, philosophical maid, chattering away in French about those days as she brought *petit déjeuner* each morning—ah, the luxury of warm croissants and steaming café au lait brought to one in bed!—could have been a character right out of those pages of Dickens.

On the Sunday before our opening, we'd gotten a sampling of unruly audience behavior at the Musée National d'Art Moderne. But who would have blamed them? They were packed so tightly into the small space allotted them for our museum Event that only those in front could see anything. Merce and John intended the audience to roam freely about the periphery of the space, but from somewhere in the museum's hierarchy that intention was thwarted, and Merce didn't insist. At the afternoon's rehearsal, Merce had us climbing on, dancing through, and moving around an uncredited Buckminster Fuller–ish dome near one end of a long rectangular space, but none of this was possible when the audience was herded together like cattle in a pen. The music (what Jim Klosty called the "use-what-you-find" variety), had John, Gordon, and David—each in a different room— employing cups, coins, glass tabletops, and cylindrical ashtray stands. Somehow they managed to create a kind of unearthly gamelan music, but it could scarcely be heard in the first fifteen minutes, which teetered precariously on the brink of chaos: people complained loudly, jeered, greeted a partnered lift or recognizable balletic move with mocking oohs and aahs and sarcastic applause. But after fifteen minutes the ruckus subsided as the audience engaged with whatever they were able to see and hear. At the end, no boos and many bravos could be heard.

Signals, Merce's newest work, premiered on our third night at the Théâtre de France. This brilliant, highly charged theatrical work, with its six curiously bound bodies; six metal folding chairs; a slightly menacing stick; strange audible, rhythmic exhalations from the dancers; mysterious, dramatic lighting and magical music, resembled no other Cunningham choreography, and its first performance was a smashing success. Although Merce claimed that the dance was "really like a little traveling group of players that come out, place their chairs, sit down and do their parts," and that he "tried to think of something that you could do in a very simple circumstance," but what actually happens onstage belies this simple explanation. *Signals,* as I viewed it, seemed taut with psychological tension. The dance consisted of long solos for Merce and Susana Hayman-Chaffey; a duet of ultra-cool, detached passion for Susana and Mel Wong; an intricate trio (or quartet) for Valda Setterfield, Douglas Dunn, Mel (and when a quartet, Merce), in which a slightly menacing stick was passed among the men, giving it a martial-arts quality; and finally a quintet (or sextet, with the addition of Louise Burns) that could appear sometimes playful, sometimes ominous. The costumes designed by Merce—sweatshirts and pants, the legs, arms, and torsos wound round with tape—added a mysterious gravitas to the proceedings. Although Merce claimed that the binding was merely for the purpose of delineating the body, these bodies seemed not only physically but psychologically bound as well. "Gravitas" describes Susana's very difficult solo as well: there was a regal, solemn yet voluptuous nobility about that solo as she performed it, although this quality did not transfer to others who assumed her part in later productions. Did I regret not being in *Signals?* Quite honestly, I don't believe I did, but it did put me on my mettle. The solo Merce made for Susana was not one he ever would have made for me, as much as I might have wished it. It was choreographed for her particular strengths and unique qualities, and she performed it beautifully.

The choreography had some indeterminate elements but allowed the dancers few freedoms. The musician-composers chose to do something entirely different in every performance, their choices unknown not only to the dancers, which was normal, but also to one another. At the premiere, the music was particularly beautiful, at moments even exquisite, according to the notes Jim kept of the occasion. Gordon Mumma confided to him, "Everyone's going to want it to be the same from now on, but it's not going to be." The basic rule the musicians set for themselves demanded only that each night they bring new material and not repeat themselves.

Rick Nelson's lighting also changed from night to night. As Rauschenberg had before him, he made imaginative use of the peculiarities of each theater as we toured from city to city. Just as people wanted the music to be exactly as it had been at the premiere in Paris, so did they want the lighting to be the same. Since there was no artist's decor Rick needed to consider when designing his light plot, he created his own set through technical wizardry. With the use of a laser, its beam projecting off a mirror onto the scrim, he could create innumerable designs—even the semblance of architectural structures—that had absolutely nothing to do with the choreography (he'd chosen not to watch any rehearsals), but that lent a sense of location and dramatic character. On the back wall of the stage at the Théâtre de France, foot-and-a-half-high red letters behind the scrim spelled out DÉFENSE DE FUMER above wide, arched, scenery-loading doors. Each night at a different point in the dance, these doors were opened onto the rue de Vaugirard and the Luxembourg Gardens, where anyone might be strolling by. It was hoped that, on one of the last two nights, when those doors opened, Julian Beck and Judith Malina would be standing on the street for a cameo appearance.

"Electric! Out of the ordinary! The audience was *great!*" I enthused in a letter to my mother about the second program—*Walkaround Time, Signals, Tread* (all works new to Paris). *Walkaround Time* went the best ever, we were told. Never, in two years of performing that dance, did I once feel that I'd met the challenges it proffered. But that night, and perhaps only that night, I believe I did, in the very fullest sense, and elation replaced the niggling disappointment in myself that I usually felt. The excitement of the evening continued into the wee hours with a fabulous party at Maxim's given by Michel Guy, the minister of culture. As the dancers arrived, they were all applauded. Jim and I arrived separately, having had trouble getting a taxi, so when the whole room broke into applause as we walked into the restaurant it was an overwhelming surprise. Michel Guy seated me at his table, with Merce, Teeny Duchamp, Madame Tézenas (benefactress of contemporary music), and others I didn't know. Jim was seated with Teeny's daughter, Jacqueline Matisse Monnier (granddaughter of Henri Matisse); her husband, Bernard; and Douglas Dunn and Sara Rudner, who'd flown over to join the company for our Paris season. Soon we were all table-hopping, greeting the many Paris friends—both French and American expatriates like the novelist Harry Mathews—we'd made over the years.

The morning following our raucous closing night at Théâtre de France we headed out by bus for a single performance at the Maison de la Culture d'Amiens, returning to Paris at three in the morning. Then it was *au revoir, gai Paree*! Ahead lay the Holland Festival Tour—a daunting prospect of eight one-night stands in eight cities in nine days. But first we headed south to the Loire River valley. From mid-June to mid-September, Château de Ratilly and Radiodiffusion Télévision Française (ORTF) sponsored music concerts and art exhibitions in and outside the château, which was owned by a potter. A platform had been built for our Event, but after days of relentless rain it was more like an elevated rectangular island in a sea of mud. One look, and Jean Rigg set off to find a farm store to buy mud boots for everyone. The bus had dropped off half the company at an old, charming hotel in town and taken the rest of us deep into the French countryside. An hour later—having driven past fields of wheat, oats and corn, fields of poppies and wildflowers, through woodlands and rolling hills—the bus pulled into a drive leading to a long, low ugly *très moderne* cement structure—a motel, here?—and I was heard to moan, "No! No!"

But, in Jim's words, "Disaster in front was glory behind and God knows how the French do it but the motel restaurant was magnificent." Imagine our delight to discover, hiding behind the characterless façade, spacious rooms with huge picture windows and French doors opening onto balconies and, as far as the eye could see, an ocean of wheat fields, exquisitely green, undulating in waves down to the banks of the tree-shrouded Loire. From the crew at Ratilly, word was sent back to our lodgings: "Take the day off. Rest. Rehearsal impossible today." We cheered. After a huge lunch, we climbed into our beds to nap for the entire afternoon, lulled by the soft steady rain, birds twittering and singing, insects whirring and buzzing. At eight o'clock, six of us—Merce, John, David Tudor, Sandra, Carolyn, and Jim—gathered again for dinner, a two-and-a-half-hour leisurely indulgence, where we quaffed five bottles of local Loire Valley Vouvray. How delightfully giddy and happy we all were.

Our crew—Rick Nelson, Charlie Atlas, and Jim Baird—were not so fortunate. Nor were Gordon Mumma, Jean Rigg, and Elisabeth Hayes, our lovely new young European manager, who spent the rainy afternoon and evening at the château attempting to ascertain from ORTF the plans for the following day. Upon arrival they were told to wait for a half hour, which became three and a half more hours, at which point the ORTF crew turned

Merce's company, circa 1959–1961, the early "golden years."
Left to right: Viola Farber, Judith Dunn, me, and Marilyn Wood on either side
of Remy Charlip, whom we all adored. Photo call in Rauschenberg's
Summerspace costumes and cyclorama.

RainForest: me, "the wild-cat from hell," with Chase Robinson wearing
Jasper's torn costumes amid Andy Warhol's silver pillows

More *RainForest.* A B O V E : Me with Chase
B E L O W : Merce with Barbara Lloyd and Albert Reid

Canfield with Robert Morris's blinding beam of light.
Left to right: Meg Harper, Mel Wong, Sandra Neels, Jeff Slayton,
Susanna Hayman-Chaffey, me, Chase Robinson

Event #45, Piazza San Marco, 1972

ABOVE: Merce tying my feet in *Aeon*, with Steve Paxton, 1961
BELOW: Viola Farber with Merce rehearsing for a revival of *Crises*, 1970

ABOVE: *Signals* with Susanna Hayman-Chaffey and Merce, 1970
BELOW: With Judith Dunn in our *Aeon* duet, 1961

Walkaround Time: absolute stillness

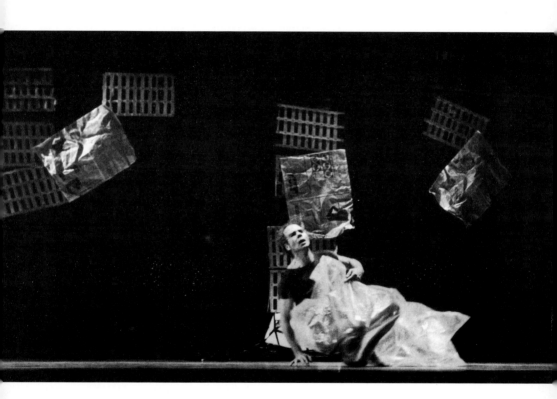

Merce in *Place:* searing passion

ABOVE: With Bob in his first choreography, *Pelican,* 1963
BELOW: Bob's *Minutiae* set. *Left to right:* Anita Dencks, Viola Farber,
the back of Remy's head, and me, 1954

Filming *Ghiradelli Square* in San Francisco, 1968

"Extended Moment" duet from *Suite for Five*

off the lights and went home without discussing anything. TV lighting requirements are rarely compatible with stage lighting. In this case, four towers had been erected, one on each corner of the stage, with two 5,000-watt lamps on each, inflicting a desert of brilliance. The stage lights belonging to Ratilly would be placed separately, with Rick in control, but under the circumstances they were fairly useless. Rick confronted the director. "You've turned off the lights and sent the crew home, yet you said I would be able to refocus them."

TV Director: "You can do it when we return tomorrow at two."

Rick: "It's impossible. We can't do it in daylight."

Director, with undisguised sarcasm: "Exactly. It's impossible. You won't be able to."

And with that, he left.

Next day the situation deteriorated. Finally the ORTF was told that either Rick must be given some semblance of control over the lights or we would refuse to perform. The company held the trump card: it had signed a separate contract with Château de Ratilly but had not yet signed with ORTF. That battle won, the director then began muttering furiously under his breath about the *"mauvais goût"* of the Frank Stella *Scramble* set, demanding to know why he hadn't been told about it. He had, a week earlier in Paris, when he hadn't bothered to attend any performances. Discovering that we would not rehearse until five o'clock in order to avoid heat exhaustion, he exploded. Gordon had problems with the director as well, but he lost his battle to provide the audience with "sonic spaces and distances" when ORTF placed the microphones directly in front of each speaker, effectively negating Gordon's intention.

These difficulties, however, in no way colored the dancers' experience. By the time we got there, after a day of hot sunshine, the mud had dried. The chateau was enchanting—like a children's book fantasy castle with turrets, the remnants of a moat (now waterless), and a courtyard full of Alexander Calder mobiles and stabiles. The platform stage was built in the fruit orchard enclosed within stone walls. Our dressing rooms were third-floor bedrooms. We danced nonstop for about seventy minutes with the chateau as our "backdrop." Loyal friends from Paris showed up for the event. From our perspective at least, the performance went without a hitch. Merce was in great spirits after the idyllic two days of rest.

The Holland Festival Tour began and ended with performances in Amsterdam. In between the schedule was: Up early / Bus to destination / Warm-up class / Rehearse / Perform / Bus to Amsterdam in the wee hours. Repeat sequence seven times.

The blur of places and events has vanished from consciousness. No journal kept, few memories retained. We were housed in a depressing modern, sterile, antiseptic tourist motel a half-hour trolley ride away from the city center. By chance, on our one day off before work commenced Jim and I discovered the Hotel Ambassade on a tree-lined street with a canal running through. We moved. For thirty-eight guilders, instead of the fifty-one paid at the dreary motel, we had a romantic aerie at the top of one of the five seventeenth-century row houses that comprised the hotel. Three windows opened into sunlit treetops overlooking the canal: the *real* Amsterdam.

Given four days off, and free to go anywhere of our choosing, eight of us flew off to play in Rome prior to a week at Gian-Carlo Menotti's Festival dei Due Mondi in Spoleto. At eight o'clock on the morning of our first performance, Jim and I were awakened by the bed shaking beneath us. Above us, the lighting fixture on the ceiling swayed ominously. Voices called out, "Earthquake! Out on the street! Out on the street!" We threw on some clothes and dashed down the stairs and out onto the sidewalk, where other startled guests gathered along with the hotel staff. Welcome to Umbria!

The Cunningham company gave six performances in a beautiful theater much like La Fenice. Spoleto's Teatro Nuovo was built in 1864—hardly seeming new, but in a town dating back to the Romans I suppose it was. Under an enchantingly painted domed ceiling, four tiers of balconies rose above an intimate red plush orchestra floor. Trouble was, we weren't allowed to rehearse in the theater because Thomas Schippers was preparing the orchestra there for an outdoor Mass to be given in the Piazza del Duomo at the end of the week. Despite the disruption of his usual work schedule, Merce remained calm, cheerfully accepting the substitute work space on the second floor of the theater, a huge, rather elegant, many-windowed room with white columns, gold fleur-de-lis, and fancy paintings. Each day he taught class and ran rehearsals there with scarcely a complaint. And not even being asked to rearrange the order of the dances— again to accommodate Mr. Schippers—appeared to distress him.

To cheer us, after the desultory reception we had received through the entire week, Merce invited seven of us to join him for a late supper and watch fireworks from a tiny restaurant tucked into a mountainside. The most spectacular fireworks I'd ever seen lit up the surrounding country, booming, roaring across the valley, ricocheting and echoing off steep mountain walls—dazzling, yet so menacing when they streaked directly at us we actually ducked for cover under the table. Had they not been so visually sensational we would have felt we'd been caught in the middle of a war zone. Sadly, Merce missed it all. The difficulties and disappointments of the week had finally taken their toll on his good spirits.

The tour was drawing to an end. Last stop: Festival International de Musique et d'Art Contemporain in Saint Paul de Vence. A certain apprehension needled its way into the minds of those of us who had been there four years earlier. Upon arrival, all seemed okay: no German film crew usurping our hotel rooms at the Marc-Hely; no lost theater luggage needing to be flown from Spain with only minutes to spare until curtain time. We arrived on Bastille Day and checked in, Jim ordered a bottle of chilled rosé and some sandwiches, and we sat on our terrace looking up toward Saint Paul de Vence, across vineyards, villas, fields, and mountains. John and Merce, on the terrace above, were doing exactly the same thing. It was a temporary respite for Merce before checking out the new theater. For several years he'd been communicating with Fondation Maeght about the design for an experimental theater to be built on Fondation grounds. In 1966 they had promised him a marvelous flexible space in which to dance the next time he came. Alas, it was not to be. From the outside it looked "quite nice," he reported on his return, but the theater itself was "fairly hopeless." The stage consisted of a small, six-sided platform of almost makeshift nature, with no place to stand when not onstage. Narrow stairs on opposite sides, in full view of the audience, provided access from the ground to the platform, and had to suffice as wings when we were not onstage. The audience-seating area was equally primitive. The experimental part of the project was solely its housing: a huge, inflated, quite handsome red-and-white plastic bubble that enclosed stage and audience like a mammoth cocoon. It's flexibility was to prove ironic indeed. During a storm that night, the electricity failed and the plastic bubble, held aloft by air constantly pumped into it, collapsed. In the morning, a strong mistral picked it up like a sail, tore holes in it, and dragged it across a light pole, which fell onto the stage and smashed electronic equipment and musical instruments for Lukas Foss's rehearsals. Only when Jim Baird and Charlie Atlas began to rescue the stuff did the Fondation workers, who'd just been standing around watching, pitch in. When we dancers arrived at noon, the wind had died down and only the wreckage gave testimony to the mayhem nature had wrought. Most of the day we just hung around, hearing dispiriting tales from American friends about the difficulties they'd encountered trying to accomplish *anything*. Lukas Foss was to open the festival the following night with an unusual music program involving a set of mirrors designed by the artist Bob Israel. Frustrated to near hysteria, Israel had been in Saint Paul for fourteen days with little result.

Next day, the bubble, having been repaired, was once again aloft. *Théâtre expérimental gonflable* was the creation of Hans-Walter Müller, a German architect who apparently had given no thought to the humans who would inhabit it, although when we spoke with him, he was, quite naturally, in a state, unhappily insisting that the theater had not been constructed according to his design. Inside the *gonflable* during the day it was suffocatingly hot, even hotter than outside under the unrelenting Mediterranean sun at midday, and the ghastly humidity—as effective as any sauna—drenched our bodies in sweat. By night, it was freezing cold, far colder inside than out with the frigid air blowing on muscles and sweating bodies. We would start out in costumes, but by the end of the evening we'd don sweat suits and ankle warmers. The musicians claimed that the acoustics were terrible, and the constantly changing temperature and humidity wreaked havoc on their musical instruments. The lighting equipment was primitive: no gels, just stark white light from poles. In order to alleviate the unmitigated ugliness of the stage, Rick chose to change the lights almost constantly, blinding us at times to the point where we couldn't see one another or the edges of the platform, affecting our balance and sense of space. From the audience's perspective, it was apparently very beautiful; from ours, it was hell. A shack built behind the *gonflable* served as a dressing room with one toilet *pour tout le monde.*

We did four Events, with excerpts from different dances every night but one; that night we performed the full *Canfield* without its set. Wonderfully enthusiastic audiences attended the first two evenings, but on the third, even before we'd danced a step, some rabble-rousers began the "Mao clap" and then during *Field Dances* began jeering and hollering: "We want sex!" "Sock it to us, Merce!" among other inanities. During my long solo in *Walkaround Time* they laughed, applauded, jeered, but instead of upsetting me it gave me a boost of adrenaline and the determination to do the dance better. I actually enjoyed the confrontation. But there was more to come: in *How to . . .* , just as we all ended skipping in a triangle, three big guys hurtled down the aisle and up onto the stage. By this time we were in the huddle, our bodies clustered together, slowly extending our arms to the side and turning our heads. The story varies as to what actually happened then. My version:

> The first thing I remember is seeing Mel's arm extend like a karate chop and then I saw Merce shove some bearded guy full force into the audience. The guy landed in Harry Mathews's lap. [He was in the front row with Maxine Groffsky and Valda's son, Ain.] Harry caught the guy Merce threw at

him, pinned him against the stage platform and held him down. No one seems to know what happened to the third guy. Mel shoved the 2nd one off the stage. Meg was horrified by the violence, not frightened, but really pained. So was I. I would have preferred to try to finish the dance. Sandra came into the dressing room and knelt down with her head in my lap and sobbed. All the women, except for Susana, who thought Merce & Mel were absolutely right, were shocked at the violent response. . . . All of us would have preferred attempting a "peaceful" response: try to finish the dance with the guys on stage. Of course, we don't know what they might have done.

Earle (as ever, our paths continued to cross) was in Saint Paul de Vence for the premiere of his *Syntagm III* to be conducted by Lukas Foss the following evening. He was sure that the intruders would have tried to dance with us, touch us, enter the activity in some way. Remy Charlip, who had arrived that very day with Burt Supree, Fance Frank, and Bénédicte Pesle after an eighteen-hour drive from Paris, said, "If you're going to do dances like that [referring to *Walkaround Time*, which he'd always hated], you deserve that kind of response. I felt like running up onstage with a bomb myself!" His reaction really shocked me.

For our final performance, Merce devised a nonviolent response should we again be besieged onstage. We were to stop whatever we were doing and begin the walking game from *Canfield*. We had no disturbances to cope with until about two-fifths of the way through, just after finishing a section of *Winterbranch*. As I stepped onto the stage to begin my solo from *Suite for Five,* a woman started to laugh, a forced, high-pitched hysterical laugh that was picked up by someone on the other side of the theater. It really got to me. It was as though I had been singled out to be jeered at and insulted. The laughter stopped almost immediately, but it had done its damage. Unlike the way I had reacted to the previous experience, I felt crushed. Bénédicte said I silenced them. Perhaps I did, but they ruined it for me. Above all else, the *Suite* solo needs meditative serenity, and I was badly shaken. The rest of the evening was uneventful except for the very end. Instead of taking a bow, Merce told us to bring all our woollies, leg warmers, socks, and blankets onto the stage and put them on in front of the audience. We got an ovation. I suppose the audience was as freezing cold as we were!

Ultimately, none of the problems mattered. The dream-world beauty of southern France made up for everything, and I was about to see much more of it in a Fiat convertible that Jim had ordered from America and picked up in Genoa. Tour over, Merce and John rented a car and drove to Perpignan, where they were met by Teeny Duchamp, who took them to her house in Cadaqués. They invited Jim and me to meet them there, but we hadn't decided what we wanted to do or where we wanted to go. On the morning of our departure, Jim found a note from John under the windshield of his spanking new, shiny dark-blue convertible:

asK
Little
autO
where it wantS
To take
You

In a leisurely four-day meander, we headed southwest along the Mediterranean coastal highway, always on the lookout for a "red rocker" hotel—what the Michelin Guide uses to indicate a "secluded, particularly pleasant and restful hotel." At the end of a dead-end road, we found one: Les Cédres de Valcros. As chance would have it, one room was available, in an ancient stone structure, recently renovated. Seclusion in full measure! When checking in, Jim mentioned to the proprietor that I was a dancer, and she said, "Really? Margot Fonteyn was here ten days ago." At which point I stumbled backward and fell down a small flight of stairs! God's truth.

We headed in the general direction of Spain—the Mediterranean on the left, the Pyrenees on the right—along the Costa Brava, its narrow roads twisting up and down the cliffs along a clear, clear ultra-blue sea edging tiny coves, rocky cliffs, and small beaches. Every spare bit of land was used to cultivate wine grapes. Crossing the border into Spain was an ordeal: long lines of cars bumper-to-bumper stalled by the Spanish customs agents. When finally it was our turn, they insisted that Jim must leave money "as ransom" to insure that he was not going to sell his many cameras while in Spain. Arriving at last in Cadaqués, we found John at the Melitón Café, as one would have found Duchamp every summer afternoon, playing chess.

John could always vacation with visible pleasure; he knew how to engage in whatever culture he found himself, how to have fun and be fun, to be amused and to amuse others in a thousand ways. Thoroughly disciplined, he could work anywhere, whether on a train or a plane, in an airport or a café. Merce did not vacation well, at least in those years. He never knew what to do with himself, since his rigorous discipline required a studio. In Spain for a dozen days, unable to dance, with no classes to teach, no company to rehearse, wouldn't he be bored and restless? But for once he actually seemed to be having a good time.

Teeny put us all up in the adorable little house she and Marcel had rented each summer for years. We took day cruises on a friend's yacht, exploring tiny, pristine coves, swimming off the boat, and lunching al fresco onboard. We swigged rioja from a wineskin on a mountaintop and picnicked near the tenth-to-twelfth-century San Pedro monastery nearby. John carried his chess set with him wherever we went. Even Merce was enticed into playing, and John began to teach Jim and me the rules of the game. Seven days flew by.

John and Merce left for New York. Jim and I headed into the Pyrenees, stretching out our vacation for sixteen more days, two of them in the tiny hamlet of Lles—pronounced "Yes!"—at another "red rocker" in a part of the world as close to paradise as I ever expect to encounter. Yet again I intoned my European refrain, "I could stay here forever." Then over the Pyrenees into France, through Andorra. Within a day's drive of Paris, Jim discovered he had to ship his car home from Genoa, so it was back to Italy, our very first taste of pesto, a plane from Nice to New York, and a rude awakening.

Between seven and eight on the evening of our return, my apartment was robbed. All my jewelry, cameras, and binoculars had been dumped into the suitcase conveniently lying open on the bed. One month later the robber returned to the scene of the crime: he came in the same window after carefully cutting the glass and breaking two window locks, leaving big black fingerprints all over the window. Having washed his hands in the bathroom—the soap and sink were filthy, a towel was missing—he left by the front door with the television. Two days later, Jim found a dirty, blood-stained acrylic brown sweater in his drawer. Missing: his blue wool one. Creepy!

Early September 1970 was unbearably hot in New York. We had invited John to dinner to celebrate his fifty-eighth birthday, but, to escape the heat, we decided to drive out to Scarsdale to dine and stay the night with Jim's parents. Perched in the tiny rear seat of the Fiat convertible, John began a rather odd conversation that I related in a letter to Earle:

On the way out he remarked that Gordon Mumma hates him. Then he said, "I think Earle hates me, too." I said I truly did *not* think so, that I didn't think Earle hated anyone. "Well," says John, "he had to deny me. So did

David Tudor. The only one who didn't was Christian [Wolff]." Jim said that Gordon didn't hate him. . . . Another oddity—he did say he hated what Gordon and David T. are doing with electronics. "It's *not* musical composition. David is *not* a composer." And then he said, "But I'll use what they've discovered."

What prompted this curious outburst was never explained. John did not demand loyalty, but he needed it. More than that, he needed love and devotion. When talking with close friends he had a difficult time distinguishing between expression of a different point of view and *refutation* of *his* point of view. To him, it appeared they were the same, a manifestation of disloyalty. His true feelings about the sounds issuing forth from the pit at Merce's performances did not surprise me, but that he expressed them quite so vehemently did. The next day, we drove John home to Stony Point. Lying on his worktable was a copy of Earle's *Folio*. Hmm . . .

O*bjects* was the last of the four dances Merce choreographed in 1970. The title derived from the structures designed by Neil Jenney: tripodal aluminum objects on wheels—somberly draped in black cloth—which we dancers pushed on and off the stage, occasionally incorporating them into the movement. Other objects existed only in the imagination, in the guise of mimed action—playing jacks, wielding a mop, looking at a wristwatch. Still unfinished on October 27, just one week before the opening of our fourth two-week season at BAM, *Objects* remained inscrutable.

Seven days before the premiere, Merce heard a taped performance of *Vespers* by Alvin Lucier, that had been suggested to him by Gordon Mumma. After hearing it he asked a few questions, then agreed to "give it a try." This flexible, live-electronics piece, which could be any length and adapted to any performance situation, had musicians moving blind through the performance space, finding their way by echolocation with the use of clicking, sonar-type instruments called "sondols."[1] The music worked well enough, but Neil Jenney's sculptures did not. They were awkward, cumbersome, and they took up too much stage space. The critic Marcia Siegel described them: "They're like some big clumsy pets without any personality. You wonder why you ever gave them house room, but you can't exactly throw them out on the street."[2] Though that's exactly where they eventually ended up.

With the exception of my very dry robotic solo in the midst of five dancers sitting on the floor miming a game of jacks, *Objects* was fun to perform. It was not, in my estimation, top-caliber Cunningham choreography. That one brief mechanistic solo—with dozens of counts that had to be memorized because the tight, sticklike movement lacked any physical kinesthetic sense I could latch on to—colored my perception of the entire dance. Douglas Dunn didn't like that section for quite a different reason. He wrote:

For the first and perhaps only time in my stint with the company, I was really offended and turned off . . . I thought, what the hell is this guy doing? I came here to dance; he has all this mythology about the steps, and I'm doing it and that's great. And all of a sudden I'm being asked to be a *mime*—something I wasn't comfortable with at all. . . . Well, we rehearsed the part for weeks . . . Then came the performance, and I was really resisting. Suddenly when the moment came to sit down in a circle, Merce *also* sat down. He'd never done this in rehearsal, *ever,* and he hadn't shown us how to play jacks, he just *told* us to play jacks. . . . we took turns. Merce was last, and I had already humiliated myself by doing my turn in resentment. But when it was Merce's turn, he did it so *beautifully* that I was very angry with myself for not realizing that here was another potential.[3]

Merce often said, "Any movement, no matter how mundane, is potentially a dance movement." I remember, with considerable embarrassment, that when Merce asked if I liked my solo in *Objects,* I nodded my head and mumbled yes when, in fact, I loathed it but didn't have the guts to say so. Never before had he asked if I liked something he'd made for me. Why did he ask? More perplexing, why didn't I ask why he'd asked? Seeing a film of *Objects* only recently proved how wrong my early assessment of the work had been. It's surprising and delightful—dance-y and spirited, with little flicks of quirky humor and mystery and humanity—different from anything else in the repertory. Don McDonagh's poetic description in the *New York Times* caught the tone wonderfully: "Mystery at the heart of merriment, playfulness surrounding loneliness, brightly costumed dancers moving around black draped tripods . . . A dance full of incongruities with laughter at times coming on the disappearing heels of sadness. . . . a dance of witty impermanence."[4]

Clive Barnes—the company's stalwart defender until the previous season, when the full-length *Canfield* with Pauline Oliveros's music soured him—began to suspect that Merce's recent creations were difficult to describe because they were basically very similar and "because of the stylistic homogeneity of Cunningham's latest choreography and the apparently deliberate blandness of its profile, the dancers tended to be interchangeable."[5] He excused Merce himself from this category and also, I was happy to note, me, but he bemoaned the loss of the company "that blazed across Europe" in 1964—Viola Farber, Barbara Lloyd, and Steve Paxton were especially missed—and compared it with the 1970 one:

This is a great company, youthful and committed, stylish and unmistakable. What is happening to it? For it is not just the troupe itself that has changed since 1964—the company itself, yes Cunningham very much included— has shifted its artistic focus in the last six years. . . . Even while I love the unity and grace of this latest Cunningham phase, as a theatre-person rather than a painter-person I regret the raw nerve-ends, surprises and ambushes of Cunningham's Rauschenberg period.[6]

He was not alone in missing the radical, very theatrical hands-on Rauschenberg approach to design versus the recent cool, hands-off artistic advising of Jasper Johns. Many of our most loyal fans, both here and abroad, keenly felt the loss of Rauschenberg, as well as the individuality of the 1964 dancers, and yes, the choreographic uniqueness of dances like *Winterbranch, Nocturnes, Summerspace,* and *Story*—all works with an inescapable Rauschenberg imprint.

However, in addition to *Signals* and *Objects,* the November 1970 repertory at BAM included *Rainforest, Second Hand, Tread, Canfield, Walkaround Time, Scramble,* and *How to . . .* "Basically very similar?" "Deliberately bland?" "Stylistically homogenous?" I think not. Nor do I believe Barnes was correct in stating, "So many of [Merce's] latest ballets are more distinguishable for their decorative realizations than from their actual choreography."[7] The movement vocabularies, the choreographic structures, the rhythms and dynamics of these dances have very real differences. Identifying them by their decor is as easy a way out as recognizing non-narrative Balanchine ballets by their music.

Merce performed, with four distinct injuries, in every dance for the entire two-week season. In seven of the BAM performances, when *Signals* was on, I danced only two of the three works. If injured or ill, I now had understudies. It was incredible to me that Merce would not make a dance without himself in it. What drove him so relentlessly? Was it his ravenous appetite to perform, or did he harbor a secret belief that the company could not sustain the interest of the audience without him?

Nineteen seventy-one was a year of sporadic touring and residencies. In January, the company performed in Chicago and toured California. The seasons at BAM did not materialize, for reasons never adequately explained. In February, by himself, Merce toured England, France, the Netherlands, and Germany, conducting classes and seminars as a Department of State "specialist." Formerly a pariah, refused State Department subsidy numerous times, Merce suddenly had become a Department of

State *specialist*? Upon his return, in March, he was appointed to the Dance Panel of the National Endowment for the Arts. It had taken twenty-seven years since his first solo concert in 1944 to receive an official, establishment stamp of approval from the United States government. In some perverse way, this acceptance was disheartening. Nineteen seventy-one was not a choreographically productive year for him. He made no new dances for the company and only one solo for himself. While he was in Europe, I taught my solos to the women in the company. I was determined, should I decide to leave, that I could do so in good conscience without jeopardizing the repertory. Teaching my solos was also a valuable learning experience for me, providing insight into these dances I might never have had without clarifying rhythms, dynamics, shapes, directions, for six very different dancers. The sixth woman in the company, Nanette Hassall—one of the dancers in my ballet for Juilliard—had been invited to join the company for the winter tour in 1971, replacing Louise Burns, who planned to leave in May to go back to college. Also new to the company, beginning with the 1970 November BAM season, was Ulysses Dove, a graduate of Bennington College where he had studied with Cunningham alumna Judith Dunn.

We performed for a week in Chicago's Civic Theatre, while next-door, in the opera house in the very same building, the Australian Ballet, with guest artist Rudolf Nureyev, was performing at the same time. Squeezing Merce's newest space-devouring dances onto the small, cramped Civic Theatre stage felt like an insult. They would have looked one hundred times better in the opera house just next door. I wrote:

> Dancing on such a tiny stage is difficult. The muscles are always contracting, holding in, pulling back. Everything gets smaller in the movement. Very unsatisfying. . . . it's like dancing in someone's living room. *Very* hard with a company of twelve. Most of Merce's dances just *DON'T* work in small spaces. Poor MODERN DANCE—almost always the poor step-child.

With just two minutes until curtain before a student matinee, as we were milling around ready to go, this gorgeous apparition—in fur hat, crotch-high soft leather boots, long leather coat—suddenly strode onto the stage, for all the world as if it owned the place. For half a second I thought it was a woman before realizing that the strikingly beautiful Tatar face and intense eyes belonged to Nureyev. Ignoring the rest of us, he made a beeline directly to Merce. They spoke briefly. Merce asked him where he'd been. He replied, San Francisco. Merce asked if he'd had fun. Nureyev looked perplexed and said he'd danced every day and had had no time to have fun.

Surely Merce was talking about having fun *dancing, his* truest notion of "having fun." One can only guess what qualified as fun for Nureyev.

After one of our performances, a radiantly beautiful, elegantly dressed Maria Tallchief, the former New York City Ballet prima ballerina and now director of the Chicago Ballet, visited Merce in his dressing room, and the Australian ballet director Peggy van Praagh came backstage to see Louise Burns, who had taken classes with her in Australia. In introducing me to Miss Van Praagh, Louise told her that I studied with Margaret Craske. I later noted the dialogue:

[Van Praagh] said she recognized my "square arabesque" as a Craske arabesque. She said I'd make a perfect Caroline for Tudor's *Lilac Garden* (. . . ah yes, well . . .). In the course of our conversation she asked if I had ever performed with a classical ballet company. When I said "no" she said "What a waste!" Ye gods! She didn't *mean* to be tactless—but it shows what ballet dancers think of modern dance.

Whatever it was that the Australian Ballet was dancing that evening, it was still going on long after we finished our show, and we'd been invited to watch from the wings of the opera-house stage. As it turned out, it was intermission when we arrived. Nureyev, who was warming up with a few spectacular practice moves, suddenly turned to us in the wings and said something like, "Soon I be modern dancer like you. This fooking feefth position is keeling me!" We hadn't the heart to tell him there was no escaping it, at least in Merce's modern dance. Did Rudi really believe it was so much easier than ballet?

While the company was on tour during January, the studio moved to the eleventh floor of the former Bell Telephone Labs building on the Hudson River between Bethune and Bank streets in the West Village. Our previous home at 498 Third Avenue was a wreck, floor sagging, plaster crumbling, paint peeling, heat unreliable, plumbing erratic. When we jumped in class, the entire building shook alarmingly. In any case, it was soon to be torn down. As chance would have it, David Vaughan had seen an article in the *New York Times* about an artists' complex to be underwritten by the J. M. Kaplan Fund and the National Endowment for the Arts. He inquired if the building had any space suitable for the company. It did, but the rent far exceeded what the company could afford. After some negotiating, a three-year subsidy was offered by the underwriters, and Merce decided to make the move to Westbeth, leaving him homeless after years of camping out in the small attic space above the 498 Third Avenue studio. Previously, Merce and John had always maintained separate living places, but in 1971 they moved into a basement floor-through on Bank Street, a block away from Westbeth, just down the street from Yoko Ono and John Lennon. This was the first time Merce and John actually lived together, yet they'd been intimate for close to thirty years!

The company gave only two New York performances in 1971: an Event in March at New York University and a performance at Brooklyn College in December. The rest of our performances took place in Washington, D.C., Illinois, Michigan, Indiana, Wisconsin, and California. Although there had been much talk about another European tour, it didn't materialize until the following year.

In May, Fitchburg State College Alumni Association presented Marion Rice Denishawn Dancers—nineteen dancers, including my mother and me—in a predominately Denishawn repertory: my mother in Ruth St. Denis's *East Indian Nautch;* my niece Robin Rice and I in *Valse à la Loïe;* the 1924 Ruth St. Denis scarf duet set to Chopin's Valse no. 14; my niece Rebecca Rice in Shawn's *Froshinn* (the Denishawn graduation dance), and I in my own solo arrangement of material from Merce's *Summerspace* with a piano version of Morty Feldman's original score for orchestra.

For five weeks in midsummer the company was in residence at the University of California in Berkeley. We'd lost Mel Wong after the spring tour. What a wonderful dancer he'd become—strong and resilient, utterly reliable as a partner, and devoted to Merce's work. His departure was very saddening to me. When Jeff Slayton left the company, Mel inherited his *Rainforest* part (originally set on Gus Solomons jr.) and he was spectacular. Mel always wanted to do his own work, be it choreography, painting, or sculpture, but at least one reason for his quitting must have been what did *not* happen in *Signals*. In the program, the solo section, *Solos for 1, 2 or 3* listed Merce, Susana, and Mel, but Merce never made the solo for Mel. The opportunity to work alone with Merce and have material choreographed specifically for one's abilities—more important, to expand one's abilities—meant a lot to each of us. Promised that experience, then denied it without explanation, even though the program continued to list his name, Mel could not help feeling disheartened. I've often wondered—was Merce reluctant to give the spotlight to another, much younger male dancer? Male solos in the repertory, other than Merce's own, were always a fleeting part of the fabric of the choreography.

In the late spring, Merce invited Edward Henkel, ballet-trained, formerly with Eliot Feld's company, to join us. Ed was worked into four of the nine dances then in the repertory, but Mel's roles in *Rainforest* and *Signals* were given to Ulysses, bypassing Douglas. Ulysses's name appeared under *Solos 1, 2 or 3*, as had Mel's, but Merce never created the third *Signals* solo. I asked Jean Rigg about this and noted her response: "She said Merce 'liked the ambiguity' or some such thing. Anyway, damn it, I think if a solo is *ever* made, Doug should have it. Doug is low low low in spirit and very withdrawn."

Beginning the previous January, the Cunningham company and the University of California at Berkeley had developed an ongoing relationship that would continue into the twenty-first century. We loved being there, loved the marvelous Zellerbach Theatre, the responsive audiences, and our hostess-with-the-mostest Joanna Harris, who never failed to give the company wonderful parties and tended to everyone's needs. And, we loved the climate!

Merce wasted no time before beginning a new dance, which would eventually develop into the four-part, fifty-two-minute work called *Landrover.*

Merce's new work seems to me closer to *Dances at a Gathering* than anything he's ever done. The section he's been working on all spring and early summer is *glorious*! It goes and goes and goes—swirling & rushing & changing & stopping & starting—but the section has breadth, a continuum unlike the brief episodic nature of most of his works (except *Second Hand*, of course). Sandy has a really jazz-y little solo that is very good for her and she's terrific in it. Now he's working on a section with Doug, Valda, Susana, Chase and me. It's hard to tell what it's like or will be like because each day he adds details, expands, etc. God Damn—he really is a genius. I know it with renewed force, as I feebly mess around with form ideas in my indeterminacy class.

John arrived five days after we did, immediately boosting morale and spreading cheer. Within minutes he'd invited a few of us to a Japanese restaurant, and afterward he took us for a drive up into the hills to see the spectacular views of the Bay, San Francisco, the Golden Gate Bridge, and the Pacific Ocean at sunset. Many of us had rented apartments on Hillegass Avenue, an easy walk from the campus. John and Merce shared the penthouse there, and it was touching to see them in their shorts, barefooted, happily cooking their dinner together, sharing domesticity.

When Merce was suddenly faced with having to present one more performance than he'd planned for, John came to the rescue by suggesting we do something in a vein similar to his own *Musicircus*. So, for our final performance of the residency, Merce turned the content of the Event over to us. He said his contribution would be to design the structure in skeleton; other than that, he would participate doing his own material as one of the eleven dancers. He organized the stage space in three separate ways, but what went on in the space and how long it went on was up to us. There was an understanding that when we exhausted material we had choreographed or chosen from his or other repertories for a particular spatial design, we would move on to the next by mutual consent—not a hard-edged ending and beginning, but an easy flow from one concept to the next. When there was hesitation or insecurity about what to do next or how to arrange our contributions in the space, Merce would offer suggestions. In the end, he contributed two or three movement ideas, more to encourage activity than to usurp control. In the company's history, this was the one-and-only truly collaborative Event in which the dancers contributed ideas and choreography. Not all of them were enthusiastic. While some jumped at the opportunity, others were intimidated, shy, even resistant. Ed and Nanette— so new to the company—were particularly uncomfortable. Although Ed never joined in the rehearsals, he took part in the performance where, suddenly, in the midst of a wild array of activities, he surprised everyone by throwing a SPECTACULAR fit, flinging himself in the air, bouncing off the floor, falling, rolling, and screaming—and I mean SCREAMING—in tortured agony and shouting karate-sounding words. The madness seemed all too chillingly real. John was blown away by it! Artaud would surely have loved it. The Berkeley audience greeted our unusual *omnium gatherum* with a standing ovation and a dozen or more curtain calls, perhaps the heartiest reception we'd enjoyed all summer. Friends commented on seeing facets of us as individuals, both as dancers and as people, quite different from those revealed in Merce's work. Although Merce acknowledged the success of the Event and even appeared to enjoy the crazy goings-on, the experiment was never repeated.

Gloom descended over the studio when the company resumed rehearsals in the fall. Chase Robinson was not among us—he'd taken a teaching job at the University of South Florida in Tampa. Then, mid-October, Ed Henkel quit. There were no possible male candidates studying at the studio to replace either of them. During his few months in the company Ed had seemed unhappy and a little out of his depth. Part of the problem was Merce's attentiveness, usually something devoutly to be wished for. The newest member of the company, male or female, traditionally received "the master's" most concentrated attention, but this time it was almost as though Merce had a crush on Ed, so smitten he was helpless to hide it—something I'd never witnessed in the past. In any case, Ed was soon gone, eventually to be replaced by Chris Komar, a graduate of the University of Wisconsin who had performed with the Milwaukee Ballet.

On December 3 at the Museum of Modern Art, Merce danced *Loops*, an Event for soloist, in front of Jasper Johns's huge *Map*—the Buckminster Fuller *Dymaxion Airocean World* version I'd seen in the American Pavilion at the Montreal World's Fair in 1966. Over his T-shirt, but under an overshirt (and thus unobtrusive visually), he wore a small belt strapped diagonally over one shoulder and under the opposite arm that captured the sounds of his breathing and heartbeat; these sounds were then monitored by Gordon Mumma and played back through loudspeakers. Gordon's sound accompaniment for *Loops* was called *Biophysical and Ambient Signals from FM Telemetry*. A similar idea would one day be used in a brilliant solo choreographed and danced by Sara Rudner called *Heartbeat* with music/electronics by Chris Janney and later performed by Mikhail Baryshnikov. For Merce's MoMA performance Gordon kept the sound level down, though still clearly audible, his intention being to complement Merce's lyrical solo in much the same way Jasper's large *Map* provided a visual complement. For Gordon,

> The extraordinary part of this occasion was learning how superbly efficient Merce was at using his performance energy. His rapid movement was not "accompanied" by rapid heartbeats or heavy breathing. The variants of increase and decrease were there, but at much lower rates-of-exchange than his physical activity. As a properly trained singer or wind-instrument performer would, Merce gently increased his air-input in advance of his more energy-consuming movement, and gradually decreased that air-input following the activity. That may well be what many skilled dancers do, even if subconsciously. So, the "musical" results of Merce's activity were gently, for me quietly lyrical, free from any "Mickey Mouse" type "sound-movement coordination," and appropriate for the MoMA *Loops* situation.[8]

Loops would reappear in Events in many guises for many years, and some of the arm and hand gestures became themes with seemingly endless variations as Merce's physical agility declined. Marcia Siegel describes one performance: "Standing in place, he describes a long rope of curlicued hand gestures. As his hand squiggles, loose-wristed, out, up, over his head, meets the other hand, gives it the gesture to continue, you get involved in all kinds of fantasies; sometimes the hands are separate creatures living a life of their own, sometimes they hold objects, or perform tasks, sometimes Cunningham seems acutely aware of them, sometimes he seems to wash his hands of them."[9]

Backstage at New York City Center on January 24, 1972, I found myself sharing a dressing room with Judith Jamison. It might be difficult to find two more disparate choreographers than Alvin Ailey and Merce Cunningham, or more disparate performers than Jamison and myself. She was about to perform her passionate, explosive signature solo, *Cry*, which Ailey had choreographed especially for her. Following her performance I would dance with Merce in his classic duet from *Suite for Five*. How strange that we were the only women representing modern dance in a gala performance to save the Dance Collection of the New York Public Library at Lincoln Center, which needed more than sixty thousand dollars to stay open for another year. Forty-two dancers, a full ballet orchestra, plus solo musicians all contributed their services to the overwhelming success of the evening's entertainment. All 2,700 seats—from the ten-dollar top balcony to the one-hundred-dollar priority seating—were sold, and the gala grossed well over one hundred thousand dollars. The crush of spectators included Mayor Lindsay, Ed Sullivan, Danny Kaye, and a who's who of the dance world. Little wonder, when Margot Fonteyn, Maria Tallchief, Carla Fracci, Natalia Makarova, Violette Verdy, Melissa Hayden, Gelsey Kirkland, Agnes de Mille, Lucia Chase, Alexandra Danilova, Erik Bruhn, Peter Martins, Helgi Tomasson, Edward Villella, John Kriza, Hugh Laing, Attilio Labis, Jack Cole, and a host of others were all on the same stage on the same night. Did a barefoot modern dancer in simple leotard and tights feel intimidated? You bet!

Once again our BAM season was in jeopardy, this time because of the sudden departure of Chase and Ed. Merce was despondent. I was sure Chase and Mel Wong would be willing to return to help out, and I suggested this to Merce. He hated having to ask them, but at the eleventh hour, that's what happened. For the two-week 1972 BAM season we had a company of six men and six women performing nine works, three of them premieres—*Landrover*, *TV Rerun*, and *Borst Park*.

Landrover, finished during the fall of '71, was given its first full-length, fifty-two-minute performance at BAM on the first of February 1972. The decor—simple tights and leotards dyed in various hues, no set—was credited to Jasper, who, like Merce, preferred the body unadorned, the choreography completely visible. The musicians chose an equally simple format: they divided the time of *Landrover* (whether we did all four parts or only one) into three equal lengths, with each part contributed by one of the three composers—John, David, and Gordon—the order changing from performance to performance so that we dancers never knew what we might be hearing. All three composers chose soft, nearly inaudible sounds, so that the dance sometimes seemed eerily silent.

There are no performance films of the dance, and still photographs have proven useless to me in trying to recapture specific kinesthetic details. Confession: the dances choreographed during my last eighteen months in the company left no residual muscle memory from which to elucidate content or qualities. One critic found *Landrover* so absorbing and imaginative a work that at the end of its fifty minutes he ached as though he had been dancing in it. I do recall a long, slow diagonal downstage crossing, with Merce leading, and me—some distance behind—following, duplicating his every move, both of us on three-quarter pointe, as high on the foot as possible, carefully negotiating the space as though we were walking on eggs, all the while solemnly gesturing with arms and hands as though partaking of some mysterious incantational rite. From reviews, I've discovered that I had a long solo, a duet with Merce, and, according to Jim, a lot of nice dancing to do. Well, you could have fooled me! Quite simply, my mind and heart were elsewhere. My only reliable personal assessment of *Landrover* is what I recorded in the heat of its creation, quoted earlier, but Clive Barnes's reviews corroborate my initial impression.

> In this new and sensuously lovely work the feel for classic ballet is exceptionally strong. It would be absurd—or at least almost absurd—to suggest that in *Landrover* Cunningham has sought to create a modern-dance *Dances at a Gathering,* but a comparison between the two might be revealing. For example, Cunningham, like Robbins in the earlier, seems to be concerned with showing a group of people in various moods and movements, without any suggestion of actual narrative, yet often with a sense of role playing. . . .
> It does seem to be Cunningham's most mature attempt to convey certain abstract visual ideals and statements with the inherent contradiction of the nonabstract human form.[10]

TV Rerun was the very antithesis of community. Each dancer followed an individual trajectory, intent, serious, without interaction of any kind despite some unison sections, and without even acknowledging the presence of the others. Except for the space-devouring bursts of energy into leaps, and fast footwork and rapid walking with complex rhythmic changes that often ended up as unison sections, the dance was insular, self-absorbed, and meditative, the focus mostly inward.

The decor, on an otherwise bare stage, consisted of one or two cameramen—Charlie Atlas and/or Jim Klosty (or, rarely, Merce himself)—filming every performance. This was Jasper's solution to Merce's expressed interest in dealing with a non-fixed focus, or an ever-shifting focus. The cameramen moved around the periphery of the stage space, filming from many angles. "Front" could be anywhere. It occurred to me, belatedly (by a few decades!), that *TV Rerun* was an answer to my complaints, expressed not to Merce, of course, but to John, that we dancers were not given the same freedoms as the composers, artists, and lighting designers, and thus became their unintended and unwitting victims. Well, in *TV Rerun* we were given freedoms galore. Spontaneously in performance we were allowed to choose phrases from the large variety of material that Merce had choreographed—any part, in any order, in any space, facing any direction, joining in unison phrases or not, indeed, choosing to perform or not. In most phrases even the tempo and speed could vary. Even with our costumes we had choices. Color: black or white leotards and tights. Style: turtleneck, V-neck, boat neck, tank top, long sleeves, short sleeves, no sleeves. One rule only: when not dancing we were to stand beside one of the cameramen. Merce's intention may have been to give the dancers more freedom, but I suspect the real reason was the continuous and devastating loss of male dancers in recent years. The dance was never jeopardized by the departure of any one dancer.

TV Rerun depended for its impact on the counterpoint and almost fugal correspondences of the choreographic material and Gordon Mumma's score. A curious addition to the costumes was three "telemetry belts" (closely related to the belt Merce wore in his solo *Loops*) that we took turns wearing. Attached to the back of each wide white belt, designed by Gordon for his accompanying score, *Telepos*, was a small box of technical gadgetry. Signals were generated in the belts by a lattice of sensors that responded to acceleration and were relayed by transmitters to Gordon in the orchestra pit. He then arranged the interactions of these signals for the audience, but any attempt to relate what one was hearing with what one was seeing was a futile exercise.

The third new dance was named after Borst Park, in Merce's hometown of Centralia, where he used to go for picnics with his family. It was of the fun-and-games variety, lighthearted, comic, with Merce playing his inimitable clown role, not much in evidence in his work for the past several years, although certainly in Berkeley the previous summer he'd played it to the hilt. As described by one critic, it was "that rare Cunningham treat—an out-and-out unobvious farce" and "zany in an honorable tradition." As I was not in *Borst Park* and never saw a performance, I remember little of it.

The Cunningham company's three-year BAM residency ended with this two-week season. With only a day to recoup energies, the company left for a five-week, rather desultory, wintry tour in the arctic cold of upstate New York, Toronto, Detroit, Minneapolis, and places in between, primarily presenting Events, giving lecture-demonstrations, and teaching master classes in colleges and universities, with few repertory performances in professional theaters. Postcard to my mother: "This tour is really a new LOW in dreariness." But despite my kvetching, I did enjoy the dancing, especially, and to my surprise, in the Events. The vast open spaces made demands on energy rather than technical precision, encouraging risk-taking and moving big.

The high point of the tour was our weeklong residency in the Minneapolis–St. Paul area of Minnesota, sponsored once again by the Walker Art Center. We'd been going to Minneapolis since the fifties, and each time it was like coming home to a warm, wonderfully supportive family. But oddly enough, it was here—after months, even years, of thinking it must be time for me to quit—that I started the ball rolling. Sitting in the Walker auditorium with John one afternoon, as we waited for an Event rehearsal to begin, I warily broached the subject. I didn't indicate any timetable for my departure; I just wanted to talk to him about the possibility, give him my reasons, and listen to what he might have to say. Less than a week later, in Philadelphia—last stop of the winter tour—Merce asked to meet with me at teatime in the Palm Court of a downtown hotel. He wasted no time, saying abruptly, "John tells me you're planning to leave the company." I was stunned. My heart flip-flopped. Yes, of course, I knew John would tell Merce about our conversation, but I didn't realize John had understood my departure to be imminent. I tried to explain to Merce that I did not love performing as he did, it did not nourish me as it always seemed to nourish him, and I wanted to leave while I could still dance at my best. He responded by saying he didn't love performing all that much, but I didn't believe him for a second, nor do I think he believed himself. So here it was, the moment had come. In a flash I realized my decision had been made, the die cast.

I told Merce only one of the reasons, but there were others: I didn't feel that I was growing as a dancer; I felt Merce was no longer able to see me freshly (after twenty years, should he be expected to?); I needed a creative challenge; and I deeply missed the good old days when, as Bob put it, "life and art were one, no separation." Behind all those reasons was the desire for a different life. In the past year Jim and I had spent most free weekends looking for a house in the country. *That* is what I truly wanted. The nagging question—"What do you really want?"—finally had an answer.

n the fall of 1971, to honor Ted Shawn and celebrate his eightieth birthday, the Dance Collection at the New York Public Library hosted a cocktail party. Among the ballet celebrities, dance historians, and critics attending were many modern dancers whose lineage traced back to Ruth St. Denis and Ted Shawn through Denishawn's principal disciples Martha Graham, Doris Humphrey, or Charles Weidman. I was a fourth-generation modern dancer via Cunningham and Graham, and directly—through my mother—a third-generation Denishawn dancer, so it's not surprising that Genevieve Oswald, curator of the Dance Collection, asked me to be one of the speakers at this occasion. But who would have expected Gloria Swanson to be among those who spoke, or to learn, in delicious detail, about the twenty-eight-second kiss a nearly naked Shawn once planted on the grape-stained lips of her supine nymph in the Cecil B. DeMille film *Don't Change Your Husband*. What a modern dancer has to do to earn five hundred dollars! Years earlier, when Shawn told this story to Ethel Barrymore, she is reported to have said, "Kiss Gloria Swanson? Five hundred dollars? Ted, my dear, not half enough!"[1]

Shawn had appeared extremely frail in October, but the news less than three months later that he had died still came as a shock. Only three days after his death, John Christian, codirector of Jacob's Pillow, called my mother to ask if she would present her Denishawn program on the opening week of the fortieth anniversary season of the Pillow's Summer Dance Festival. And so it came about that my very last performances in America would be—the circle closes—as a Denishawn, not a Cunningham, dancer.

Three generations of Rices performed together, and at age sixty-seven, my mother danced St. Denis's *Modern Nautch* (1931) "to uncanny effect," in the words of one critic, and the center part in both *Sonata Pathétique* (1919) and the St. Denis/Doris Humphrey *Soaring* (1919). In homage to Shawn, I choreographed and danced *As I Remember It*, a solo collage of bits and pieces of Denishawn phrases set to piano music by Gabriel Fauré, as well as three St. Denis pieces danced with my sister-in-law Mona and/or my nieces, Robin and Rebecca. Nothing could have pleased my mother more than Nancy Goldner's observation in her *Dance News* review that "in all the dances she did with the students of Marion Rice, she was the same Brown we see in the Cunningham Company. She also totally blended with the Rice dancers. It became obvious that her sublimely simple, unmannered style and incredible serenity descend directly from her schooling in Shawn's 'styleless style' and from her mother, Marion Rice."[2]

Barton Mumaw, who first performed with Denishawn in 1931, and with the original Men's Company from 1933 to 1940, shared the programs with us, giving "spellbinding" performances of two solos by Shawn and one of his own creation. When he saw us rehearsing *God of Our Fathers,* a dance choreographed by Mona and me in the late forties when we were teenage camp counselors and later amended by my mother, he asked if he might join us. This brief dance, which had ended all Marion Rice concerts since the fifties, reminded Barton of those works so often performed by Shawn's Men's Company that spoke to community and spirituality. It ends with the full ensemble kneeling, elbows bent, palms up, heads lifted as though in supplication, gazes fixed into the distance. At the end of each performance, Barton was in tears. Never had this simple dance seemed so appropriate or so moving. For my mother, standing on the stage of the Ted Shawn Theatre, Shawn's "temple of the dance," accepting the warm applause—with Barton Mumaw on her right, her daughter on her left, and her daughter-in-law and two grand-daughters, plus twelve of her own dancers—this had to be the pinnacle of her dancing life.

In the months leading up to Jacob's Pillow, the Cunningham company had a few single Event bookings and a week's residency at the University of New Hampshire. My last public performance in New York City was in an Event in the round at New York University's Eisener-Loeb Auditorium before a sold-out house. My journal account:

Merce in a fearful mood at rehearsal. The "black angry mood." After we all left, Charlie [Atlas] said, Merce worked for almost an hour on his parts, new parts of *Loops,* Charlie thought. Tonight's performance was an all Susana Hayman-Chaffey night: her duets with Doug from *Objects & Landrover;* her solo and duet from *Signals; Crosscurrents;* as well as bits of Sandra's parts from *Winterbranch* (double cast) . . . she was terrific all evening and the evening was hers. Merce put her solo and her duet beginning up on the stage (alone and lit). [This] really hurt Sandra, infuriated Valda (says she's ready to quit, and she says Sandra is too), and Meg looked pretty miserable.

Valda thinks it was like, "Okay, Carol is leaving, and this is how things are going to be." The funniest thing happened to me—my cue to start *Tread* was Merce dashing up to me and throwing me into the space, and then when it came time for him to catch me in the duet—no Merce. I turned and turned, realized he wasn't there. Stopped, looked around for him and by god he was up on stage, almost disappearing, clutching at his ankle in some weird fashion (dancing? hurt? who knows?) but he had forgotten (???) to do the bit with me. My own intuition—he didn't forget. The whole thing was a metaphor: flinging me into the space, and leaving me. When I saw he wasn't there, nor even seemed to be coming, I nearly broke up—I grinned like crazy and started flapping my way through [the rest of the dance]. He did brand new material, plus a solo between and sometimes during every section. *That's* what bugged Valda. All that new material (a lot from class) and HE did it all!!

My two-bit translation of what Merce was actually conveying: "The show must go on. I can do just fine without Carolyn. Susana is ready. If need be, I will continue on alone, as a soloist." He would have been right on all counts.

Fractious, disgruntled dancers did not mar the performance—we were now far too professional to let that happen, and in any case, it's Merce's choreography that always wins the day. As Deborah Jowitt put it in her review of that NYU Event, "I think that Merce is perpetually tugging people's eyeballs out of comfort and conformity. His way of making art is still way ahead of the way most people think it ought to be made, but it's so damned beautiful they don't even worry anymore about what it is."[3] I might add that he was also perpetually tugging his dancers out of comfort and conformity, which, in the moment, didn't seem so damned beautiful to us.

In preparation for a two-month tour beginning in Iran and ending in France, Merce decided to do a series of six studio performances in the last two weeks of May. On the second of these, during a full-length *Canfield*, forgetting that my new partner for a particular section was no longer Mel Wong but Chris Komar, I threw myself into a back bend with the same abandon I always had with Mel, who never failed to catch me with the resilience of a soft pillow, but Chris, new to the role, still a bit nervous and—totally unlike Mel—a very brittle dancer, caught me short without the elasticity necessary to absorb the shock. From the audience, Jim actually heard a loud crack. A searing pain shot through my back and down my leg, I got through that performance on adrenaline alone, but the injury was ultimately incapacitating. I missed two studio performances and spent the next two months suffering severe sciatic pain. Despite a nine-week company layoff, with no rehearsals or performances (although I still took class and taught), and even with two glorious weeks of ocean swimming in Tobago with Jim, the injury still had not healed. By August, I was on the chiropractor's table after every rehearsal. Sitting could be agony, and imprisonment on a plane was crippling.

In September 1972 the company included twelve dancers—including newest members Brynar Mehl and Barbara Lias, three musician/composers, three technical staff, two administrators, plus my mother and Ain Gordon. We left the East Side Terminal at 7:15 in the morning. Seventy hours later—via London, Paris, Istanbul, and Teheran—we reached our final destination, Shiraz, the "City of Roses," in a valley within the Zagros Mountains in southwestern Iran on Sunday, late afternoon.

Iran: hot, dry, dusty. The heat nearly deafening. So dry, the lips crack and the tongue runs over them again and again to no avail. Dust clogs the pores, clogs the nostrils. The skin draws tight and aches. God bless the hotel pool's tingling cold water, surrounded by oleander bushes, persimmon, and lime trees, a literally breathtaking oasis after the killing sun. Barefoot, covered from head to toe in burkas, Valda, Ain (disguised as a girl child), my mother, and I make a pilgrimage to the Shah Cheragh Shrine (902 A.D.) and enter an inverse cool-liquid world—domes and walls of mosaic mirror, gold, and silver—shimmering and utterly dazzling.

The Cunningham company definitely played third fiddle during the Sixth Festival of the Arts in Shiraz and Persepolis. The megastars were Robert Wilson and Karlheinz Stockhausen, whose works succeeded in perplexing, enchanting, irritating, and/or enraging many of those who witnessed them. Seemingly auto-intoxicated, Karlheinz strode the streets of Shiraz dressed in flowing robes of white, a latter-day Pied Piper, with hordes of local children chasing after him. Hardly the Karlheinz I'd first met fourteen years before, although perhaps the tendency toward self-aggrandizement could have been detected even then. "Stockhausen: God or Maestro?" asked the *Teheran Journal*. To the question "Does he really think he's divine?" one of his compatriots responded, "No, he just wants us to think he is."[4] As Earle said, "Karlheinz wakes up every morning and reinvents the light bulb." Although John Cage—American to the very core of his being—had "discovered" Eastern cultures and religions decades earlier and had been profoundly influenced by them, it would never have occurred to him to parade around the world in the guise of an Indian guru. In jeans and blue work-shirt, John had already become a beloved sage to legions of young and old the world over without ever having needed to act the part. In an interview with the *Kayan International,* Karlheinz is quoted as saying, "Those who are not careful about my music risk cutting their souls."[5] But perhaps Stockhausen's most outrageous statement, made twenty-nine years later, was in response to a journalist's question about the September 11, 2001, attack on the World Trade Center: "What happened there is—they all have to rearrange their brains now—is the greatest work of art ever. That characters can bring about in one act what we in music cannot dream of, that people practice madly for ten years, completely, fanatically for a concert and then die. That is the greatest work of art for the whole cosmos. I could not do that. Against that, we, composers, are nothing."[6]

The second megastar of the festival, but without the slightest hint of self-aggrandizement, was Robert Wilson—another truly American artist—whose astonishing seven-day, twenty-four-hours-a-day play, *Ka Mountain and GUARDenia Terraces,* took place all over Shiraz, inside buildings, in courtyards and gardens, and up the steep sides of a mountain. The work was an amalgam of art installation, tableau vivant, sideshow, dance, and theater, much of it in mesmerizing, excruciating, almost invisible slow motion. On the evening of our arrival in Shiraz, elated to be moving instead of sitting, we headed out to the mountain to see Part Two of Wilson's *Ka Mountain.* I later described it:

> Two camels, a small elephant, a caged lion, a caged bear, two caged monkeys [how I hate seeing animals caged!] are at the foot of the mountain. A large constructed "theatre" at base of mtn. but we ignored that and started to climb. Steep rock & rubble and spiky cactus. Nanette, Barbara [Lias], Meg, Doug and I couldn't stop climbing and it was a long hike up. We passed mysterious things: *papier mâché* fish lying in a bloody (paper) stream; cut-out little old men with canes; flamingos; flying fish; waves (painted card-board); a'top one ridge two long rows of white houses, each three sided with a window, forming a street. Small naked light bulbs dangled & twinkled in the wind. We kept climbing higher. Through a big tent. Higher. Below, the city of Shiraz spread out before us. The wind was so strong we couldn't hear each other. Our lips parched. Our skin tightened. The wind blew dry and warm. The stars looked closer. We could see over the ridge to the other valley. Cars creeping along a road. We all wanted to spend the night there. Meg started down alone. We four got lost. Treacherous, dangerous business climbing and slipping down. Crazy to have done it. What about my bad leg? My bad back? All my under-studies up there with me! None-the-less, terribly glad we did it. [on the stage platform] watched a

kind of whirling dervish dance [like one Ted Shawn used to do] Hypnotiz-ing. In the distance, a black boy in long white dress (the mute, deaf boy Wilson adopted) zig-zagged up the first part of the mtn. lighting wax flares in bowls. We left before mid-night.

The company performance schedule included two dance Events, one music concert, and two discussion sessions or debates about Cunningham and Cage work. On September 6, in Shiraz, we performed in the Théâtre de Plein-air, an open-air, recently constructed theater. Throughout the evening, we celebrated John's sixtieth birthday. He read some poetry, beautifully. During the huddle in *Canfield* we huddled around John, and when John popped the cork at the beginning of *How to . . .* David Tudor played "Happy Birthday" on a toy piano. "A Tribute to John Cage" appeared in an English-language news bulletin and gave witness to how much he had touched people in his sixty years: "The composer reveals a sense of timeless wisdom, illuminated by anecdote and the *mot juste.* He communicates a bountiful humanity which inspires listener, student, all who are fortunate enough to be in his presence. At the end of the evening's concert . . . a loyal band of followers from Iran itself and from all over the world, gathered in love to honor their mentor."[7]

The major Event for our company—also the closing event of the festi-val—was at Persepolis in the presence of the Shahbanu, Empress Farah, third wife of His Majesty Mohammad Reza, Shah Pahlavi. In 1971, Perse-polis had been the scene of the most lavish, ostentatious party in modern times, with sixty-one heads of state invited to celebrate the 2,500th anniversary of the founding of the Persian Empire by Cyrus the Great. To house the world's dignitaries, an entire tent city was built in the desert—at wildly extravagant expense—and a Hollywood film director was hired to stage the affair. Despite the Shah's many social and political improve-ments, especially regarding the rights of women, the opulence of that occasion, added to the Shah's autocratic, repressive regime and his deter-mination to quickly transform his country into a major pro-Western power, was the beginning of his downfall.

The day before the performance we were bused to Persepolis across a vast pink-beige desert, past wind-carved hills, parched riverbeds, and dusty sheep and goats, and after rehearsal bused back again to the comfort of the Park Saadi Hotel. A tiny Japanese-like pavilion served as our dress-ing room. The toilets were a long, torturous, rocky, dusty path away, their stench exceeding all others I had ever experienced. Each of us was assigned a "guide," a euphemism for the male uniformed guard with a lethal-looking gun who guarded our trips to the toilet, to the stage, to wher-ever we might need to go. For those of us backstage, the guards' weapons were visible and at the ready, but Gordon recalls that the musicians—who were, of course, in full view of the audience—were assigned guides in for-mal dress clothing, all wearing the same necktie design, their weapons placed carefully under their coats. His experience attempting to take pho-tographs tells its own story:

> My male "guide" stopped me from taking a picture of the tiered rows of seats in the amphitheater (from my view on the performance stage). Later I learned why: the central section had a "box" for the Shah [actually, only his wife and mother-in-law, the Shah did not come]. Also, every alternate seat in the theatre was "marked." The "marked" seats were for the same neck-tie-design guides who totaled half of the audience population for our perfor-mance later that day.[8]

At the performance the military was everywhere. The Shahbanu arrived by helicopter. A red carpet—literally!—was rolled out on the dusty path for her entrance into the stadium-like amphitheater where the audience, according to our crew, appeared more interested in staring at the queen and the rest of the royal entourage than they were in watching our performance.

Dancing among the ruins of Persepolis was its own reward. We re-hearsed under a scorching sun and marveled at the speed with which it slid away into the desert behind the architectural remains—stone columns and archways, sculpted horses and warriors—silhouetted against a glow-ing dusky sky. Before a move was made, a step taken, *Rainforest* silver pil-lows were let loose from their hidden moorings and floated free above the jagged pillared skyline into the atmosphere. A gorgeous, thrilling moment, with—I thought—a not-so-subtle political message! The performance had begun. Above the stage, among the ruins, everyone except Merce and me did *Field Dances,* while Merce danced his way down a flight of stone stairs with a soft-shoe Fred Astaire–like number and onto the stage, where I joined him for the duet from *Suite for Five;* then, with the full company, we went into *Scramble,* followed by *Signals,* and Part III of *Landrover,* and ending with the complete *Tread.* At 4,890 feet, the elevation in Shiraz is nearly as high as in Boulder, Colorado, but feeling tired could not mar the magic of the situation—the space, the quality, and color of the evening air, above all, the centuries of ancient history swirling around us in the desert sand and stone.

September 9, 1972—my mother's sixty-eighth birthday: breakfast in

Iran, lunch in Switzerland, dinner in Italy. The travel day began before dawn in a bare-bones military plane, the kind used by parachutists (hard benches along each side of the plane, barely high enough to stand up in, windowless and claustrophobic), and, after several changes of planes and buses, concluded in a private motor launch hired to transport us down the Grand Canal in Venice to our hotels near dawn the following morning.

We were the only dance group appearing in that year's International Contemporary Music Festival, yet an Austrian newspaper, *Salzburger Nachrichten,* stated that dance provided the most significant aspects of the Biennale di Venezia—high praise, certainly, considering the fact that many if not most of the Darmstadt/Donaueschingen music gang were represented. London's *Financial Times* music critic agreed with the Austrian, stating that "the rest of the festival rarely matched in tension and excitement the high points of the dance."

Our schedule allowed little time to attend concerts or fraternize with composer and musician friends. Earle was to be there on the sixteenth, for the world premiere of his *Loops* for chorus and orchestra, but by that time we were in Belgrade. The company had four performances, back to back, two at the Fenice. A full-length *Canfield* couldn't help looking marvelous there, but the surprise, on the second evening, was how astonishingly beautiful *TV Rerun* appeared (and felt!) on that vast, deep, wide, and steeply raked stage. A huge semicircular white scrim enclosed the dancers and photographers. The lights were un-gelled, brilliant, dazzlingly white, intensified by the close proximity of rows of light bars lowered over our heads and visible to the audience. Under them, we moved in the uncompromised glare of total whiteness. Rick Nelson had outdone himself. What a contrast with the next performance of *TV Rerun* on the stage of Teatro Toniolo—an outdoor movie theater with minimal technical equipment—in Mestre, a working-class neighborhood far removed from the romantic aura of Venice.

Our final performance—an Event in the Piazza San Marco—created quite a stir, yet somehow it fit the piazza's history. In the 1700s, it was the custom of the city to welcome visitors with bull-baiting sessions. (One might have described us as audience-baiters.) This Event, unlike any other, began in daylight at seven p.m. and ended, an hour later, under an inky sky, illuminated by lighting instruments placed on high towers that also held the loudspeakers for the electronic soundscape. Again, the three composers worked separately: John placed a microphone on a chair, and whenever he moved it, the sounds were amplified; David contributed a composed sound environment; and Gordon attempted to find a piece of classical music in the shortwave range. Merce thought the music superb. A German critic deemed it "gruesome" and the entire occasion "an embarrassment," while another felt that in the San Marco Event he was "able to participate in the immediate birth of inspiration."

We dancers entered the piazza, armed with brooms and metal folding chairs. We formed a tight circle, and then, with our chairs, moved out, pushing back (figuratively) the gathering crowds in order to form a much larger circle. The brooms came into play when some of us swept the pigeon droppings from our performance space (more theatrical gesture than useful), "scattering the dust and the tourists" before everyone began *Field Dances* followed by *TV Rerun.* At the end of one section we'd forge through the crowd to another space to form another circle. We made four circles in all, dancing sections from the repertory with an added little bit of *Grand Union* material performed by Valda and Douglas. The good-humored crowd, mixing and melding, seemed to join in the spirit of the occasion. Unsuspecting people who just happened to be strolling through the piazza also got caught up in the fun.

Jim, having cased the place earlier in the day, managed to smuggle himself into the Grand Council Chamber building opposite the Basilica di San Marco, get upstairs, and crawl out a window onto a ledge, from which he photographed the proceedings from high above the crowds. He wanted to take both still and motion pictures, but since his super-eight camera, at normal speed, could record for only three minutes without the cartridge being changed, he set the speed at two frames a second in order to concentrate on taking still photographs. The film turned out to be fast-forward Cunningham choreography with a delightful touch of Chaplinesque absurdity.

Our next three performances were in Belgrade, sponsored by the International Theatre Festival there—and according to a dispatch from the American Embassy, they were "three evenings of imaginative and thought-provoking dance,"[9] a message that must have bemused State Department officials in Washington.

The first took place on the stone floor of Belgrade's modern-art museum, where we "moved eerily among sculptures and paintings by Yugoslavia's finest contemporary artists," while "Cage's restrained interplanetary sound echoed and counterpointed body movement."[10] The following night, in Atelier 212 (a circular auditorium painted completely black), we danced a full-length *Canfield,* chosen especially because the Oliveros score is dedicated to the Yugoslav engineer Nikola Tesla. John, David, and Gordon had found some of Tesla's models at the museum and recorded their sounds, incorporating them into the evening's soundscape. A reporter for Britain's *Evening Standard* found this Belgrade performance utterly absorbing and asked these questions: "Why shouldn't modern dance break out in the same way as painting? Why shouldn't new possibilities open up? Why shouldn't music (or noise) co-exist with dance, not be subservient to it. Keep their own identities?"[11]

I remember Belgrade best as the city in which I gave myself the night off. I played truant from the last program, which included *Rainforest* and *Signals,* two dances I wasn't in. I had made the decision not to do *Rainforest* on this tour. It was a role I dearly loved, but with both my previous partners—Albert Reid and Chase Robinson—gone, I was not willing to risk further injury with a new person because of the duet section in which I must leap into my partner's arms, then fall back in a full back-bend while suspended in the crook of his elbows, and swing back and forth. I'd had one accident doing that move when Chase had forgotten to catch me, and I dared not hazard another. Susana and Douglas took over the roles. The last dance, *TV Rerun,* offered wide-open options to choose what one would or would not do. Well, I chose not to go to the theater at all! Although I had informed the stage manager, I don't think I told Merce. A brazen breach of conduct? Or was I simply taking full advantage of his use of indeterminacy? Surely it never entered his mind that any dancer would ever choose *not* to perform, and it's certain that no one ever followed my example.

Warsaw. Again we were the only dance company to appear in its International Festival of Contemporary Music. Memories of Warsaw 1964 haunted those of us who had been there before: the sense of being spied upon; the endless machinations and red tape required to accomplish anything; the heavy, suffocating totalitarian postwar Soviet architecture, and the ghastly hotel. We'd been promised a better hotel this time, but it was not to be. At midnight, we checked into the wretched, prisonlike Hotel Warsawa. At three a.m., John—finding it unbearable—decided to check out. The desk clerk warned him, "Other hotels are worse than the one you're already in!" Among other miseries, there was no hot water—*the* cardinal sin for muscle-sore dancers. To solve this mini-catastrophe, we were bused to the Opera Theatre (not the theater we performed in) for a special "Shower Event." On the Thursday, September 22, itinerary I'd jotted down: "Carol cops out. Chemical imbalance?" My aberrant behavior—irritable, teary, unconsolable—mirrored the despondency I'd felt in 1964. When John asked me what I would like for my birthday, without a second's pause, I replied "I want to go home!" Without missing a beat he responded, "Oh, I want to go home, too." Fortunately, our stay in that still-oppressive city lasted only three days, with just one performance, which Merce characterized as "incredibly pedestrian." Our post-performance party was given by the American Embassy. Welcomed by American embassies in Communist countries and all but ignored in our own democratic one?[12] How surreal is that?

We hadn't had a season in London since 1966. In the intervening years Merce had choreographed twelve new works. With a change of repertory every night, he managed to program nine of them in the one week we played the Sadler's Wells, with *How to . . .* the only work seen in London before. Our impresario was again the young and dedicated Michael White. As with past visits, the critical response was mixed, with comments ranging from "it's an epic bore" and "DANCING BAFFLES UNWARY" to "idiosyncratic, unpredictable and difficult," and peaking with "a masterpiece" (in reference to *Second Hand*) and "the most original, magical and perfectly structured choreography."[13] But there were no in-depth, perceptive articles by Alexander Bland, who seemed to miss Rauschenberg's theatrical presence in the brief overview he wrote at the end of our season, nor were there the daily soul-searching, ever-more-open-minded musings written by Clive Barnes during our first visit in 1964. Dancing and dancers were lauded: Sandra Neels, Susana, and Valda all received personal recognition for their performances. Often, in previous visits, Merce's idiosyncratic dancing—so unlike that of the *danseur-noble* of ballet—had not been sufficiently appreciated. This time it was. Rick Nelson's lighting was highly acclaimed, and even the usual antagonistic verbal battering of the music was much less severe than before. The choreography, by a few at least, was taken seriously and seriously discussed, but Cage/Cunningham aesthetic and philosophical ideas were known by this time, and they no longer shocked or surprised. It had become more a matter of like or dislike, approve or disapprove, without the buzz of excitement, the fury of outrage, or the interest in confronting, discussing, challenging, or acclaiming unconventional concepts.

However, one ballet critic, Clement Crisp, writing for the *Financial Times,* admitted that he had been "less than enchanted with what he saw" during our two previous London seasons, but now believed Merce to be "the most adventurous and uncompromising of creators."[14]

The opening-night audience was quiet, undemonstrative. *Landrover*—an hour long, with minimal music and without decor—challenged concentration, eliciting complaints of boredom, but Peter Williams, writing for *Dance and Dancers,* realized "that it was not boredom so much as there being too much for the mind to take in all at once" and "far too much to take in, in so short a time." This, I think, was—and has continued to be—a problem with Merce's lengthy, densely choreographed works, and most especially in the ninety-minute Events. Even I, who knows his work so well, can be mentally exhausted trying to digest all that "movement, movement, movement" (as Louis Horst used to mutter from his seat on the aisle). Cramming so many new works into one brief week meant that only a very few dances were repeated, and because both the Royal Ballet and the Rambert Company were performing that same week, few critics were able to see any Cunningham work twice. But Williams also found that "through all these pieces there is wonderful invention, beautiful approaches and confrontations in a manner that never seem to have been thought of before. What is so remarkable is that none of these things seem like gimmicks but a perfectly natural way of moving. . . . I found after such a concentrated dose of Cunningham that other more classical dance seemed rather trivial. The feeling passed but it was disturbing while it lasted."[15]

"Happy Last First Night in London," read the card accompanying flowers from Jim presented onstage after *How to . . .* Not even in Venice had I given much thought to the fact that these two months of performances were marking the end of a way of life for me. Suddenly it hit home hard: my last performances in London! Earle came for performances and to celebrate my birthday. Mail arrived at the theater: notes from Robin Howard and Bob Cohan (my first Graham teacher at Juilliard), a generous letter from Lynn Seymour (Royal Ballet), a letter from the poet Michael Horovitz, and a newspaper clipping, dated September 26—my birthday—calling me "one of the finest dancers in the world."[16] These lovely tributes, extra gifts of the performing life, were perhaps inconsequential compared with the deeply personal rewards experienced in the act of dancing itself, but they were meaningful nonetheless. Audience enthusiasm increased from night to night. At our final performance—*Rainforest, Second Hand,* and *Tread*—the response was wonderful, the warmest, most demonstrative of the week. Michael White hosted a marvelous farewell party in the theater with catered Indian food and champagne. Sentimental tears provided by me.

No tears were shed in Germany! We gave two single performances—a full-length, ninety-minute *Canfield* in the Cologne Opera House, and an Event in the Alten Messe restaurant in Düsseldorf. "A truly schizophrenic experience, those two performances!" Not only for Horst Koegler, who so described them in *Dance Magazine,* but for us as well. In 1964, the audience in Cologne had been lively and vocal—both booing and bravoing with equal energy—but that reception paled in comparison with the boorish behavior unleashed upon us in 1972. One critic reported "The audience laughed and shouted, barked and miowed, belched and called out 'shit'—if they hadn't already left the auditorium. All this was too much for one Cologne dance pedagogue Karl Foltz, who stood up and shouted to the upper balconies, 'Is this hospitality?' "[17]

We dancers danced on, seemingly unperturbed by the wild commotion. Koegler said we performed "with marvelous discipline under the most humiliating circumstances." In fact, I don't think any of us felt "humiliated" but instead believed the audience had managed to humiliate itself. Did we think it was damnably rude? Yes. But for the musicians, it provided more ingredients for their sonic soup. John, David, and Gordon always had a field day carrying out Pauline Oliveros's directions for *Canfield*, but never had they been the target of such malevolence. In the end, they wreaked their own not-so-subtle revenge. Of course, one can readily understand any audience's angry reaction to the pedestrian, inane chatter of the musicians as they discuss the acoustical environment of the theater and ostensibly determine the resonant frequency of the building as they roam about, talking to one another over walkie-talkies. What the audience did not know was that the bad-mouthing and obscenities had all been recorded as they occurred. Then, in the last third of the dance, it was all played back *at* the audience. Soon realizing it had been caught willy-nilly to become part of the music, the audience—according to *Der Zeit*—was silenced, embarrassed by its own aggression.

Five institutions—the American Embassy, the American Consulate, the Arts Club, the Kunsthalle, and the Steuben-Sturz Foundation—had made our Düsseldorf Event performance possible, and there was so much interest that the performance had to be moved from the Kunsthalle to the large open space of a restaurant. Nonstop dancing for nearly two hours. No decor. No theatrical lighting. With only eight spotlights to work with, "magician" Richard Nelson created constantly changing light, focusing and blurring the images or deepening the room. As one reviewer described it, "The Dusseldorf *Event* did not lose its tension at any moment . . . It is beautiful, at times disturbingly beautiful dance; the choreographer's magic works under these laboratory conditions, presenting the work like something seen under a microscope."[18]

No protests assaulted us. The young, unconventional audience used every inch of space—sitting cross-legged on the floor, in uncomfortable hard chairs or standing along three sides of our performing space, and seemed utterly absorbed throughout. No two performances could have been more different. In Cologne we felt like prisoners, locked behind a roaring seawall of hostility; on the other side of that wall, unseen, unknown people seemed to hate us. In Düsseldorf, we felt surrounded by the rapt attention of individuals we could actually see, freeing us to dance with joy.

"We must make this a day of unmitigated pleasure!" John announced at breakfast the following morning. In fact, we had not only one but two days of unmitigated pleasure, traveling through beautiful German and French countryside—from Cologne to Nancy to Grenoble—in a huge, almost all-glass bus. An engagement in Brussels had been canceled, giving us an extra gift of three idyllic days, with only one keep-it-all-together technique class scheduled. Jim and I borrowed a car, took off for the mountains, and found a romantic little chalet hotel high in Col du Cucheron. The following perfect, Indian-summer day we drove through spectacular country to Le Petit Cheveney—picnicked in some farmer's field, visited St. Pierre d'En-tremont, Gorges du Guiers Vif, and Gorges du Guiers Mort, Chartreuse, and more. A heavenly renewal of mind, spirit, and body.

Grenoble's Maison de la Culture has two theaters: the Grande Salle, a fine conventional theater where we presented three nights of repertory, and a very "avant-garde" modern theater, the Théâtre Mobile—an intriguing space with two revolving stages where we did a full-length *Canfield* and an Event. In the Event both revolves were used to great and, for the dancers, dizzying effect—disorienting, scary, challenging—and except for Merce, Sandra, and me, a new experience. It's one thing to constantly change "fronts," as we usually did in Events, but quite another to have the world turning while we were also turning, or falling, jumping, attempting to hold a balance.

In Grenoble, when most of the company was gathered in the hotel restaurant for a late supper, I was called away to the telephone—Lew Lloyd calling from New York to offer me the job of program director for dance at the New York State Council on the Arts, where he had recently become the program director for the performing arts. When I returned to the table, I related the substance of the call to Jim. John, overhearing, turned to me with near apoplectic rage—loud enough for all to hear—and said: "I shit on you if you take that job!" Silence—the silence that follows a lightning strike—electric and paralyzing! After a few seconds—it seemed like an hour—conversation resumed, muted and cautious. I don't think anyone was more shocked than John himself. Gordon Mumma recalled:

Very early the next morning (I was the only person there), John came into the breakfast room and stood silently, then quietly asked me if he could sit with me for breakfast. "Of course," I replied (with my usual open arm). He con-tinued with "I have to apologize about last night—I was so upset, and I shouldn't get upset, but it seemed impossible for Carolyn to leave Merce, and I must have got angry about it." It was one of the few times in all my years of working with John that he was so distressed, and special because he shared his review of the experience with me. In retrospect that was one of the most human real-person times I spent with John. Sharing grief, as it were.[19]

The next day John and I spoke briefly. Mortified by his own ugly words and filled with remorse, he was now apoplectically apologetic. I did understand that his astonishing outburst was issued out of anguish and dismay. How *could* I consider, even for one fleeting second, leaving Merce only to take an administrative *job* in state government? For the remaining weeks I saw little of John. When I did, he was sad and uncommunicative. This awkward estrangement from a man I adored was acutely painful, although at the time I wrote, "He doesn't understand *anything* really," but this was nonsense on my part. John's thoughts and feelings were openly, often passionately expressed, sometimes to his regret, but at least I knew what they were, and I was grateful for his honesty and generosity—if not immediately, certainly in retrospect. Merce's passion was revealed onstage, where he truly lived. Over a period of twenty years—with the exception of "dance talk" about space and time—he rarely revealed his thoughts or feelings to me in direct one-on-one, eye-to-eye communication. His thoughts and feelings found expression through actions rather than words. But how was one to comprehend their real meaning when they could be misread so easily? Merce never mentioned John's explosion of anger.

The Teatro Lirico in Milan seats 1800. Our audiences, rarely more than 150 during six performances, provided little boost to our spirits on the seventh week of the tour. The damp and cold weather in Milan aggravated the sciatica that had played games with me—here today, gone tomorrow—since August. Performances rarely began before 9:20 p.m. I dragged through the day but surprised myself by rediscovering the pleasure of dancing with renewed energy—pain or no pain.

Remy Charlip, who had been living in Paris for some months, had booked a room for Jim and me, and one for Valda as well, at the Hôtel Saint-Simon. He'd even chosen our exact rooms. It's a lovely, quiet hotel with a garden courtyard, wisteria climbing its walls, hidden away on the rue Saint-Simon in the Seventh Arrondissement, just steps away from the busy boulevard St.-Germain. Staying there was like being a guest in someone's elegant, antique-furnished home. We'd no sooner checked in than a huge bouquet of white lilac (lilac in October!) and red oak leaves arrived from Michel Guy, director of the Festival d'Automne, under whose auspices the company would appear at the Théâtre de la Ville.

The last week. I was close to tears much of the time. Memories of when dances were made or rehearsed or had special performances flooded my mind. Throughout this tour, but especially in Paris, Merce treated me with exceptional kindness. If he shared John's anger with me, he gave no evidence of it. After opening night, he and John, of course, attended the party hosted by the "French Friends of Merce Cunningham" at Bofinger, a gorgeous 1860 Belle Époque brasserie, but except for one night, when Merce was persuaded by Maxine Groffsky, the editor of the *Paris Review,* to join us, neither Merce nor John came to the post-performance restaurant gatherings I attended, which made me wonder if John was intentionally avoiding me. These suppers offered time to reconnect with loyal French friends—especially Bénédicte Pesle and the Paris gang of American expatriates: Maxine, who first saw the company with Larry Rivers at Connecticut College in 1960; Harry Mathews, who—in 1968—held down one of the assailants thrown off the stage by Merce in Saint Paul de Vence; Mark Rudkin, the man who so glamorously wined and dined me after a Paris performance in 1964 when I was totally depleted of energy and confidence; Elizabeth Hayes, our new European representative; Jacqueline Lesschaeve, who would one day write a book with Merce; Teeny Duchamp; her daughter, Jackie Matisse Monnier, who would years later join the Cunningham board of directors; her husband, Bernard Monnier; the ceramic artist Fance Frank, a friend of Bob and Jap's who had lived in the Battery in the fifties when they did; Sylvia Kim, longtime ballet chum, who'd studied with Tudor at the old Met when I did.

We played a week at Théâtre de la Ville, formerly Le Théâtre Sarah Bernhardt, where, on my first trip to Europe in 1958, Nick Cernovich and I saw the Jean-Louis Barrault Company. In the intervening years the theater had been modernized, the interior stripped clean of its history. For some reason, all the performances were billed as Events, even when we did repertory. Repertory performances were received with warmth and enthusiasm, but on two evenings—an Event on one, *Canfield* on the other—the audience was split, pro and con, their strong feelings expressed equally loudly. The audience was especially vociferous during *Canfield* and, according to my journal, created "much the biggest uproar we've had on the whole tour." (Had I forgotten Cologne, or had the French *really* been more hostile than the Germans?)

Walkaround Time was extraordinary. The audience was wild and vocal during the entre-acte and Merce's two solos after that. When I came on to do mine, the audience was still carrying on—and the music was savagely loud (a man's vocal sounds). Merce told me later that he was so worried about the music that he tried to figure out if he had time to run down to the pit to tell them to shut up or shut it off. But I went out there alone to all that cacophony and *waited*. [Utterly still, standing in fourth position on three-quarter point] It didn't stop. And I waited some more. And then I thought, "Okay—the hell with it, let's do it!" And I began. And I did silence the audience. And the "music" ceased. I felt extremely vulnerable, fragile but strangely soft and loving—not hostile at all. I've performed the dance technically better, but the quality was there. At the end, during the bows, my lip trembled and I had great difficulty controlling the welled up tears. Merce grabbed my hand very hard. He was *so* wonderful to me the whole tour, but especially that last week—so understanding and gentle and kind and generous. He saw the struggle I had to compose my face and my spirit. How precious the dancing became! And yet I know that if I were faced with months and months of it to come—the repetitious rehearsals of old works, the re-teaching, the touring, I would never have been able to love dancing so much that last week. Hard to understand why I can't do it anymore when I truly enjoyed dancing so much, so often on this tour.

Saturday night, for a wonderfully responsive audience, we did an Event. I danced my heart out, as big, as full, as totally as I could: *Scramble,* my solo from *Landrover,* and all of *Suite.* At some point I thought, "I'll never do my *Suite* solo again!" and I felt a pang of anguish as profound as though I had lost a child.

REPLAY: The taxi moved slowly along the Rue de Bac and across the Pont Royal. Hazy, late morning sunlight filtered through the remaining chestnut leaves, spilling on damp cobblestones and the darkly glinting waters of the Seine. Paris. Autumn. October twenty-ninth to be exact, a Sunday, with scarcely another automobile on the boulevard, and only an occasional pedestrian walking by the river. I held hard the hand of my friend Jim Klosty in the hope that it would relieve the thickening knot growing in my throat and quiet the fear that I wouldn't be able to control the excess of feeling which had been steadily mounting since the first day of our week long run at Theatre de la Ville. For the Merce Cunningham Dance Company, this day, with a matinee performance, was the end of the Paris season and the end of the 1972 tour begun in Iran in early September. For me, it was the end of a twenty-year way of life.

My "posh" dressing room—#8—on the fourth floor had a window opening onto the Seine with a sweeping view that included Notre Dame and the Eiffel Tower. Directly across the river was the flower market, ablaze with color. I could have opened my own mini-market with the flowers that filled every available space on my long dressing table: three white roses from Meg; a dozen peachy-pink roses from Sara Rudner, Twyla Tharp, and dancers; a dozen pale-lavender roses from Jim; a mixed bouquet with roses, iris, and spiky white flowers from Artservices (Bénédicte et al.); a bird-of-paradise for all my performances of *Walkaround Time* (again from Jim); and more. Charlie and his assistant, Monsa Norberg, had appeared the night before with a fantastic construction of small wooden brooms and brushes, absolutely drenched in fresh flowers—crazy, imaginative, and really beautiful—bringing tears, laughter, and lots of hugging.

The matinee included *Rainforest, Second Hand,* and *Tread.* As we were warming up Susana came over and embraced me and began to cry. Until then I'd been okay, but just as the smallest fissure can weaken a dam, so this moment was almost my undoing. I had to work very hard to keep the swells of intense emotion from breaking through my reserve. During the *Socrate* duet, thoughts of its meaning—Plato's, Satie's, Merce's—swam through my head. I danced it *to* Merce, with every fiber of my being focused on him. Harry Mathews said Merce and I had never looked at each other like that before. At the curtain calls, two small bouquets of flowers were thrown onto the stage. No one touched them for two curtain calls. Then Merce picked up one and Ulysses the other and presented them to me. When I got back to my dressing room I discovered that my own flowers had been scavenged, and realized, with a burst of laughter, that Jim must have taken them so that he and Harry could toss them onto the stage.

One more dance to go. I threw my entire self—EVERYTHING—into *Tread,* and then it was over. The audience was fantastic. Stamped. Clapped in rhythm. Cheered. The company made Merce and me take bows without them. Merce even stepped back and had me bow alone. "What a way to go!" said Maxine. And she was right. Everything about that week in Paris made for a terrific ending: beautiful, heartbreaking, full of tears and sadness, memories and love. My only regrets: neither my mother (who'd returned home after London) nor Earle was there. After all was over I was alone in my dressing room when there was a knock on the door: Merce had sent a bottle of champagne—a lovely, touching gesture, yet how much more it would have meant to me had he brought it himself! I went to his dressing room to thank him. He said, "It's been a wonderful twenty years. You're beautiful and I've never told you enough."

There was a company meeting onstage to which I was not invited. Nor were Nanette and Ulysses; they were both leaving the company. Ulysses had given notice in August, a total surprise to all of us. More surprising, Merce had made no attempt to have Doug, Chris, or Brynar understudy his parts. He complimented everyone individually for various performances, slowly flipping through his notebook to recall special moments, a welcome but unusual procedure. (If there were notes regarding my performances, I never got to hear them.) He told the dancers he no longer intended to teach but would meet with them in December to talk about the future. Later, at an Artservices party, I learned that both Valda and Susana felt positive about the meeting. Douglas was furious. Meg cried through the entire thing. Years later she told me, "Merce really let us know that it was over, something was over. In fact, it was an ending to a wonderful time. Nothing was ever like that again."

The finale to the day took place at La Méditerranée, our favored restaurant in 1970, across from the Théâtre de l'Odéon. *"Formidable!"* said the maître d' when Merce and John entered with their entourage—Meg, Valda, David Vaughan, Jim, and me—and then promptly brought a bottle of Vouvray in an ice bucket, compliments of the manager. It was a strange affair, friendly but not really relaxed. Merce was jolly enough. John was morose and sad, but eventually was able to pull himself together. As he and I walked down the hill together toward the boulevard St.-Germain, he said, "I will have to leave, too." "I know," I replied. "It will be all right." And then, as we hugged good-bye, he said, as he'd said so many times since his outburst in Grenoble, "I hope you'll have a good life."

Thirty years later, in a book of Merce's drawings and journals, I read his version of that afternoon.

> The backstage was an emotional trauma. At any moment there might have been torrents of tears. . . . SH [Second Hand] (its demise I guess—flowers thrown on stage. CB with eyes about to swim, mine too, but I knew if I gave in, the whole stage would have come down); *Tread* (last time too?) So many bows, so much engagement with the public. The afterward was bathed in tears, champagne too, JC unable to bear any of it. ("So beautiful," I said to her, "I never told you enough.")[20]

On a quintessentially New York—at-its-very-best spring day in April 2004, Merce had been invited to a dinner celebration in his honor at an apartment on Central Park South. What better way to get there on this exquisite late afternoon, the air redolent and delicious, than through the park? Merce grinned with pleasure as he was wheeled along the serpentine paths under a canopy of tender virginal green, past carpets of daffodils, among froths of dogwood and crabapple blossoms. While Lew Lloyd and Jim Klosty chatted with him, Sage Cowles and I skipped and danced around them, laughing like giddy schoolgirls. Appearing out of nowhere, a man cycled up beside him. "Are you Merce Cunningham?" he asked. "My name is Cunningham, too. May I read a poem in your honor?"

Only an hour earlier, as the late-afternoon sun poured through the tall, sparkling windows of the grand reception room at the French Cultural Embassy on Fifth Avenue and Seventy-eighth Street, dozens had gathered to watch Merce Cunningham receive France's highest honor, the insignia of Officier de la Légion d'honneur from the ambassador of France. It had been fifty years since the birth of his company at Black Mountain College. Merce was eighty-five. His dancer's body had failed him. Now confined to a wheelchair, one thing had not changed: neither his appetite for making dances nor his pleasure in doing so was in any way diminished.

Rewind six years—Paris: winter 1998: L'Opéra National de Paris, Palais Garnier—"A Worldly Cathedral of Civilization," in the words of Théophile Gautier—yet civilization had surely come to mean something quite unlike the Palais Garnier in the 123 years since the theater had opened. While perfect for *Swan Lake* or *The Phantom of the Opera*, would not the opulence of this Baroque/neo-Renaissance opera house ill suit the rigorously contemporary dances of Merce Cunningham, whose work was already forging ahead into the twenty-first century? Nev-

ertheless, in January 1998 the Merce Cunningham Dance Company presented a two-week season in this "temple of the bourgeoisie," the showpiece of the Second Empire designed by Charles Garnier for Napoleon III.
I couldn't miss it. Such an unlikely match, and yet how stunning Merce's
work looked on that huge, raked stage framed by the glittering gold and
plush red, under the 1964 Chagall ceiling hovering over it all like an anar-
chic angel.

Forty-nine years had passed since Merce's first visit to Paris, when Marianne Preger had hung around outside his hotel on the Île St.-Louis to tell
him she'd found a studio for him to work in. Forty-nine years since she—
along with Alice B. Toklas, Alberto Giacometti, Roberto Matta, Arthur
Gold, and Robert Fizdale had seen Merce Cunningham's very first Paris
performance on June 10, 1949, in Jean Hélion's studio in the avenue de
l'Observatoire. Forty years had passed since Nick Cernovich and I had
searched Paris in vain for a theater that Merce could afford with a stage
large enough for our duet performances. Thirty-four years since eggs and
tomatoes had been thrown at Merce and Viola Farber following their duet
Paired, in the Théâtre de l'Est in 1964. Many Paris performances had followed—at Théâtre des Champs-Élysées in 1966 and 1982, Théâtre de
l'Odéon in 1970, and Théâtre de la Ville in 1972, Centre Georges Pompi-
dou in 1979, followed by seasons at Théâtre de la Ville in 1984, '87, '88,
'90, '91, and '96, as well as innumerable performances in the provinces.
Year after year, Merce Cunningham returned to France. His audiences
multiplied. His reputation, always controversial, flourished. In 1973,
Merce created *Un Jour ou deux* for the Paris Opera Ballet. The public's
reaction was stormy. In 1977, *Summerspace* was taken into the repertory of
Théâtre du Silence, and in 1979 that company acquired *Changing Steps.*
Groupe de Recherche Chorégraphique de l'Opéra de Paris was given
Inlets 2 in 1983. At the instigation of Rudolf Nureyev, *Un Jour ou deux* was
revived in 1986. In 1990, *Points in Space* was taken into the Opera Ballet's
repertory. Two years later, Merce's own company presented a one-week
season at the Palais Garnier. As the years passed, France showered Merce
with honors: he won the Gold Medal for Choreographic Invention in 1966,
he was made a Commander of the Order of Arts and Letters in 1982, and in
1989 he was made Chevalier de la Légion d'honneur by President Mitter-
rand.

In 1998, more than two thousand people filled the Palais Garnier for
every performance of the two-week run. During the last week, people lined
the entrance stairs holding placards, begging for tickets. Marianne Preger-
Simon and I, Bénédicte Pesle, Sage Cowles, and twelve members of the

Cunningham Foundation's board of directors were among the cheering audiences during that two-week season. We saw the world premiere of *Pond Way*, a breathtakingly lyrical work costumed in flowing white silk jersey and danced before Roy Lichtenstein's sublimely simple, yet eloquent *Landscape with Boat*. I doubt that Merce had ever spent twenty-four hours, or even one hour, observing pond life, yet *Pond Way* is testament to his profound fascination with the natural world. So touching, in the midst of the adulation being heaped upon him, was Merce's murmured confession to Marianne and me on the eve of *Pond Way*'s premiere that he was as nervous about this new work as he had been before his very first concert with John Cage in New York in 1944.

So many dancers had come and gone in the forty-five years of the company's existence! Merce seemed to accept that stoically: "Well, everyone must do what they need to do," he said to Marianne and me, "You left, too, but the work has to go on." Over and over again during our Paris sojourn Merce expressed his pleasure in our presence, drawing us close to him and keeping us by his side at the party given in his honor. Marianne, hugging him, said, "It's very exciting!" "It's much, much more than that," he replied. There were tears in his eyes. It hadn't occurred to us that our being there was important to him until the company's executive director astutely observed that we were his family now, knew his history, had traveled the rocky road with him, and were there to witness his triumph and share in his joy. Without someone you love to share in your success, what meaning can it ultimately have? No one was more devoted to Merce's work than John Cage, and surely no one had loved Merce more than John. With John's death, in 1992, Merce had lost his dearest friend and closest ally.

The 1998 Paris audiences demanded curtain call after curtain call, breaking into rhythmic unison clapping, shouting bravos, and rising from their seats to pay homage to the choreographer as he hobbled slowly, painfully onto the stage at the finale of each performance. I stood, too, a lump in my throat, tears in my eyes. Emotion—hot, scalding—made it difficult to breathe. Surveying that incredible theater and the sea of applauding people, I realized that while much of my emotion was evoked by what Merce had so dazzlingly wrought in a lifetime of undiminished dedication to dance, my tears also sprang from my sadness that *he*, in the prime of his dancing career, had never had the opportunity to dance in this theater, for such an audience: two thousand applauding people, eyes riveted to the stage, honoring Merce the Merciless, Merce the revolutionary, Merce the avant-gardist!

What had happened? Merce hadn't changed. He'd never compromised, never sold out. His devotion to dance had been, still was, absolute, a daily rite, a spiritual discipline. At seventy-eight, crippled with painful arthritis, still committed to discovery, Merce Cunningham was at the absolute height of his choreographic powers, having prevailed for decades over the most abysmal odds. In Paris in 1998, in the fullness of time, the audience was ready to recognize the genius of the man. Backstage, I mumbled incoherent words about the magnificence of his choreography, the brilliance of his dancers, the overwhelming impact of the work. Choked up and teary, I finally managed to whisper: "I'm so proud to have danced in your company." With his arms around me, hugging me close, he whispered back, "I love you." And, at last, I believed it was true.

Although the content of this book comes almost wholly from my own journals and letters, I did, on occasion, seek out information from former company members and others. In this regard, I must thank David Vaughan, Cunningham archivist extraordinaire, who could be relied upon to answer almost any question put to him; Lew Lloyd, whose generosity in allowing me to quote from his 1961 world tour and 1968 Latin American tour correspondence gave me insight into the tremendous difficulties that management constantly face; and Gordon Mumma, for musical explanations, as well as his savvy political analysis of whatever country we happened to be in.

I am profoundly grateful to Merce for allowing me to quote from his letters, articles, and books; to the Earle Brown Foundation and the John Cage Trust for permission to quote from letters; to Lawrence and Nuria Schoenberg for allowing me to quote their father's letter to Earle; to Jasper Johns, who provided wonderful embellishments to stories I already knew and provided some I didn't; and to the dancers and lighting designers—Marianne Preger-Simon, Remy Charlip, Viola Farber, Paul Taylor, Valda Setterfield (and son Ain Gordon), Meg Harper, Douglas Dunn, Jeff Slayton, Gus Solomons Jr., Louise Burns, Richard Nelson, and Beverly Emmons—for sharing recollections with me.

I'm indebted to Deborah Jowitt for her hand-holding patience in answering queries about the intricacies of word processing, book publishing, and obscure dance references; Alastair Macauley for his calming reassurance in response to desperate e-mails; Alfred Stepan, who enlightened me about political realities in Brazil in the sixties; Nancy Leys Stepan, who translated a news clipping from the Portuguese; Michel Beaujour, who explained the political realities of the student uprising in France in 1968; Elizabeth Beaujour, who corrected my feeble translation from the French; Stacy Sumpman at the Cunningham Foundation, Norton Owen at Jacob's Pillow, and the staff at the Rauschenberg studio for their assistance in ferreting out photographs; and George Avakian for his generous gift of a rare photograph.

To Maxine Groffsky, my agent, who always believed I would finish the book (even when I did not), my sincere thanks for her patience. To Bob Gottlieb, kudos for his willingness to take it on after so many decades, to read all 900+ pages of the original manuscript—a heroic undertaking—and for his sage advice in how to shorten it. With abundant good humor and boundless energy he made the editing process not only educational but fun. In the words of his wonderfully helpful assistant, Alena Graedon, Bob is "a marvel," and so is she.

Last but foremost, I must express my boundless gratitude to James Klosty. Although his photographs (reflecting long hours in the dark room) will speak for themselves, his work as an astute "preliminary" editor must be fully acknowledged. Over the thirty-year period I was writing this book, Jim read every word of every version numerous times, offering suggestions and constructive criticism, even a trenchant phrase or two. Without his belief in the book's value and his constant encouragement, it would not have been completed.

All correspondence to and from Lewis Lloyd is from the Yale Collection of Western Americana, Beinecke Rare Book and Manuscript Library, cited in these notes as Yale Collection.

1 · BEGINNINGS

1 John Cage invented the prepared piano in 1938 while at the Cornish School in Seattle, Washington, at a time when he was particularly engaged in writing and performing percussion music. He'd been asked to write music for dancer Syvilla Fort's *Bacchanale*, which, he felt, cried out for percussion, but there was no space for percussion instruments—no wing space or pit—in the tiny Cornish theater; remembering Henry Cowell playing the strings inside the piano, which produced unusually interesting sounds, he consequently attempted to alter the traditional tonality of the piano by placing objects on the strings—bolts, screws, nuts, felt weather-stripping, etc.—and discovered he had created a small percussion orchestra within the piano itself that required only one musician.

2 Joseph Schillinger (1895–1943) was a Russian composer and teacher whose system of musical composition Earle had studied for four years at Schillinger House in Boston. (Earle graduated the year before we set out for Denver.) Schillinger came to America in 1928; with uncanny foresight he warned his students that orchestration was at best only a transitory discipline, that soon scientifically perfect instruments would supplant the traditional orchestra. He was the author of many books, the two most important being *The Mathematical Basis of the Arts*, completed in 1942, wherein he stated that "the space-time continuum of music consistsof the alternation of silence and sounds," and *The Schillinger System of Musical Composition*, two thick volumes in which he sought to discover the general underlying principles of the behavior of tonal phenomena—generalizations based on the properties of tonal materials themselves and on the possible combinations, permutations, and structural relations of such materials. As composer Henry Cowell expressed it, "The Schillinger System makes a positive approach to the theory of musical composition by offering possibilities of choice and development by the student, instead of rules hedged round with prohibitions, limitations and exceptions, which have characterized conventional studies."

3 Peter Yates, *Twentieth Century Music* (Pantheon, 1967), 243–4.

4 This was not quite true. In Europe, there was Olivier Messiaen's wife, Yvonne Loriod, and possibly one or two others.

2 · BLACK MOUNTAIN I

1 M. C. Richards, "Black Mountain College: A Golden Seed," *Craft Horizons*, June 1977, 21.

2 M. C. Richards, *The Crossing Point* (Wesleyan University Press, 1966, 1973), 156.

3 Ibid.

4 Duberman, *Black Mountain*, 49.

5 Myers, *Erik Satie*, 60.

6 John Cage in Kostelanetz, ed., *John Cage*, 8.

7 Just as Joseph Schillinger had done many years earlier. See chapter 1, note 2.

8 Interview with John Cage, *Tulane Drama Review* 10, no. 2 (Winter 1965).
9 Rose, *American Art*, 130.
10 Duberman, *Black Mountain*, 191–2.
11 Dick Higgins in Kostelanetz, ed., *John Cage*, 124.
12 Marcel Duchamp, "The Creative Act," in *The New Art*, ed. Gregory Battock (E. P. Dutton, 1966), 25–6.
13 Hans Richter, *Dada: Art and Anti-Art* (McGraw-Hill, n.d.), 49.
14 Cage, *Silence*, xii.
15 Artaud, *Selected Writings*, 258.
16 Interview with John Cage, *Tulane Drama Review*, 10, no. 2 (Winter 1965).
17 Artaud, *Selected Writings*, 248.

3 · NEW YORK: AUTUMN 1952

1 Cage, *Silence*, 127.
2 John Cage, *Edition Peters Catalogue* (Henmar Press, 1962), 25.
3 Cage, *Silence*, 98.
4 Rose, *American Art*, 139.
5 Antony Tudor, Interview with Jack Anderson, *Dance Magazine* (May 1966).
6 Deborah Jowitt, *The Village Voice*, October 17, 1977, 77.
7 Richard Glasstone, "Into the Future with Cecchetti," *Dancing Times*, April 1990.
8 Artaud, *Selected Writings*, 271.
9 Cunningham, *Changes*, n.p.
10 Alan Rich, "Close-Up of a Far-Out," *The New York Times*.
11 Pierre Boulez, "Music View / Donal Henahan," *The New York Times*, November 15, 1987.
12 Alan Rich, "Close Up of a Far-Out," *The New York Times*, June 9, 1963.
13 Ibid.

4 · NEW YORK: WINTER/SPRING 1953

1 Cunningham, *Changes*, n.p.
2 Cage, *Silence*, 22.
3 Ananda K. Coomaraswamy, *The Transformation of Nature in Art* (Dover n.d.), 11.
4 Cage, *Silence*, 12.
5 Ibid.
6 Botto, *Intellectual Digest*, n.p.
7 Cage, *Silence*, 174.
8 Botto, *Intellectual Digest*, n.p.
9 *Dance Observer*, August/September 1953, 107.
10 Cunningham, *Changes*, n.p.
11 Ibid.
12 *Dance Observer*, Aug/Sept. 1953, 107.
13 George Balanchine, "Marginal Notes on the Dance," in Sorell, ed., *Dance Has Many Faces*, 36.
14 Cunningham, "Space, Time and Dance," 151.
15 George Balanchine, "Marginal Notes on Dance," in Sorell, ed., *Dance Has Many Faces*, 37.
16 Frederick Ashton, "Notes on Choreography," in Sorell, ed., *Dance Has Many Faces*, 250.
17 Armitage, *Martha Graham*, 102–3.
18 Frederick Ashton, "Notes on Choreography," in Sorell, ed., *Dance Has Many Faces*, 249.
19 Cunningham, "Space, Time and Dance," 151. In a study published in the American journal, *Public Library of Science Genetics*, "Dancers Are Genetically Different Than the Rest of Us," research by Prof. Richard P. Ebstein clearly demonstrated that "the dancer 'type' expresses heightened sense of communication, often of symbolic and ceremonial nature, and a strong spiritual personality trait."
20 Cunningham, "The Impermanent Art," 73.
21 Ibid.
22 Ibid.
23 "After Hours, TV for Tomorrow," *Harper's*, Winter 1954, 93–4.
24 *The Juilliard Journal*, April 1987, 5.

5 · BLACK MOUNTAIN II

1 *Trois Morceaux en forme de poire*, according to Pierre-Daniel Templier

in his book *Erik Satie*, were probably written for Debussy. "Debussy had one day told Satie that he ought to develop his sense of form; an ambiguous smile greeted this advice. A few weeks later, Satie brought his friend the *Three Pieces in the Form of a Pear*." (MIT Press, 1969), 25–6.

2 David Vaughan, *Merce Cunningham: Fifty Years* (Aperture Foundation, 1997), 76.
3 Myers, *Erik Satie*, 75.
4 Ibid.
5 Cunningham, *Changes*, n.p.
6 Cunningham, "The Impermanent Art," 71.
7 China Altman, "Walter Grapes: A Master Architect's View of Nature," *Horticulture* LEI, no. 9 (September 1978), 45.

6 · NEW YORK: AUTUMN 1953

1 Cunningham, *Changes*, n.p.
2 John Cage, *Edition Peters Catalogue* (Henmar Press, 1962), 33.
3 Deborah Solomon, "Questions for Robert Rauschenberg," *The New York Times Magazine*, February 15, 2004, 13.
4 Horst, Louis, *Dance Observer*, February 1954, 26.
5 Armitage, *Martha Graham*, 95.
6 Margaret Lloyd, *Christian Science Monitor*, January 8, 1954, 2.
7 Rosalyn Krokover, *Musical Courier*, January 15, 1954, 19.
8 Anatole Chujoy, *Dance News*, February 1954, 10.
9 *Dance Magazine*, February 1954, 69.
10 *Newsweek*, January 11, 1954, 76.
11 Robert Sabin, *Dance Observer*, February 1954, 25.
12 Margaret Lloyd, *The Christian Science Monitor*, January 8, 1954, 2.
13 Robert Sabin, *Dance Observer*, February 1954, 25.
14 *Dance Magazine*, February 1954, 73.
15 Anatole Chujoy, *Dance News*, February 1954, 10.

16 *Dance Magazine*, February 1954, 70.
17 Robert Sabin, *Dance Observer*, February 1954, 25.
18 Marion Stevens Rice, 1954 diary.
19 Ibid.

7 · ON THE MOVE: 1954–1955

1 Paul Taylor, in written response to a series of questions I had sent to him in January 1979.
2 Cage, *Silence*, 132.
3 As mentioned in an earlier chapter, Ananda K. Coomaraswamy's books— especially *The Transformation of Nature in Art* and *Christian and Oriental Philosophy and Art*—were important influences in the development of Cage's own curiously eclectic philosophy.
4 Interview with Elaine de Kooning, in John Gruen, *The Party's Over Now* (Viking, 1972), 214–15.
5 Earle Brown, in Klosty, ed., *Merce Cunningham*, 75.
6 Ibid.
7 Cunningham, *Changes*, n.p.
8 Ibid.
9 Tomkins, *Off the Wall*, 86.
10 P. W. Manchester, *Dance News*, January 1955, 11.
11 Louis Horst, *Dance Observer*, February 1955, 24.
12 P. W. Manchester, *Dance News*, January 1955; 11.
13 Louis Horst, *Dance Observer*, February 1955, 24.
14 Ibid.
15 Cunningham company program note for the Japan Society performance at the Henry Street Playhouse in New York on May 27, 1955.

8 · THE FIRST TOURING YEARS

1 Cage, *Silence*, 99.
2 Ibid.

3 Tomkins, *Off the Wall,* 136–7.
4 *Time,* November 29, 1976, 60.
5 Russell, *Meanings of Modern Art,* 338.
6 Andrew Forge, *Rauschenberg* (Harry N. Abrams), 226.
7 Calvin Tomkins, "Everything in Sight," *The New Yorker,* May 23, 2005, 75–6.
8 Roberta J. M. Olsen, "Rauschenberg: The Extraordinary Ragpicker," *The Soho Weekly News,* March 31, 1977, 23.
9 Sandler, *New York School,* 180–3.
10 Russell, *Meanings of Modern Art,* 338.
11 John Russell, *The New York Times,* March 25, 1977.
12 By art historian Robert Rosenblum in an article by Robert Hughes, *Time,* November 29, 1976, 54.
13 John Russell, *The New York Times,* March 25, 1977.
14 Leo Steinberg, *Jasper Johns* (George Wittenborn, 1963) 15.
15 Walter Terry, *New York Herald Tribune,* July 30, 1955.
16 Gordon Anthony, *Margot Fonteyn* (Phoenix House, 1950), 7.
17 Henry J. Seldis, *Santa Barbara News-Press,* November, 1955.
18 *Musical Courier,* December 15, 1955.
19 Alexander Fried, *San Francisco Examiner,* November 17, 1955.
20 Marjorie Fisher, *San Francisco News,* November 16, 1955.
21 Alfred Frankenstein, *San Francisco Chronicle,* November 17, 1955.
22 P. W. Manchester, *Dance News,* January 1955, 11.
23 Isadora Bennett was one of the first theatrical publicity agents to champion American dance. The first dance attraction that she represented was Miriam Winslow (with whom my mother danced in Boston) and Foster Fitzsimmons—both Denishawn trained—but Bennett's longest association was with Martha Graham from 1939 to 1970.
24 "D," an English teacher, neighbor,

and friend of John's since John's move to Stony Point, began working as an unpaid booking agent. Eventually he gave up teaching entirely, and tried his hand as a vanguard impresario before becoming a documentary filmmaker, best known for his Nixon film.
25 *Tacoma Sunday News Tribune,* November 27, 1955.
26 Naima Prevost, *Dance for Export: Cultural Diplomacy and the Cold War* (Wesleyan University Press, 1998), 53–8.
27 Maxine Cushing Gray, *Dance News,* February 1956, 4.

9 · THE LEAN YEARS

1 Cunningham, *Changes,* n.p.
2 Merce Cunningham, in *A John Cage Reader* (C. F. Peters, 1982), 111.
3 Cunningham, "Space, Time and Dance," 151.
4 Cunningham, "The Impermanent Art," 71.
5 Cunningham, *Changes,* n.p.
6 Cunningham, "The Impermanent Art," 73.
7 Ibid., 71–2.
8 Margaret Craske, *The Dance of Love: My Life with Meher Baba* (Sheriar Press, 1980), 67–8.
9 Ibid., 165.
10 Walter Terry, *The New York Herald Tribune,* July 13, 1956.
11 Frederick Ashton, "Notes on Choreography," in Sorell, ed., *Dance Has Many Faces,* 249.
12 *Zen Buddhism: Selected Writings of D. T. Suzuki,* ed. William Barrett (Doubleday/Anchor, 1956), 116.
13 Meher Baba, *Life at Its Best* (1957), 65.
14 Alan Watts, *Zen Buddhism* (The Buddhist Society, 1947), 10–11.

10 · THE VW YEARS

1 John Cage, *Dance Observer,* January 1957, 10.

2 Ibid.

3 Ibid.

4 Edwin Denby was dance critic for *Modern Music* from 1936 to 1942 and for *The New York Herald Tribune* from 1942 to 1945.

5 Walter Terry, *The New York Herald Tribune*, January 20, 1957.

6 Walter Sorell, *The Providence Sunday Journal*, January 27, 1957.

7 David Vaughan, *Dance and Dancers*, April 1957, 11.

8 Ibid.

9 Walter Terry, *The New York Herald Tribune*, January 20, 1957.

10 Merce Cunningham, *Dance Magazine*, November 1957, 22.

11 *The Concise Oxford Dictionary of Ballet*, 2nd ed. (Oxford University Press, 1982), 309.

11 · THE END OF THE BEGINNING

1 The photographs appeared in *Esquire* magazine, as well as in a photography magazine and on a record jacket.

2 Tomkins, *Off The Wall*, 105.

3 This is my recollection. Other versions of the story have the greenery natural, filched from a local park by Bob and Jap, which would hardly have been "fire resistant." But as Jasper pointed out, neither was the scrim, or the costume fabric.

4 Margaret Lloyd, *The Christian Science Monitor*, December 4, 1957.

5 *Dance Magazine*, February 1958.

6 Louis Horst, *Dance Observer*, February 1958, 25.

7 *Dance News*, February 1958, 11.

8 Louis Horst, *Dance Observer*, February 1958, 25.

9 *Dance News*, February 1958, 11.

10 Ibid.

11 Louis Horst, *Dance Observer*, February 1958, 25.

12 Leo Castelli, *The Art Dealers* (Clarkson Potter, 1984), 88.

12 · CONNECTICUT: SUMMER 1958

1 Doris Humphrey, *Doris Humphrey: An Artist First,* edited and completed by Selma Jeanne Cohen (Wesleyan University Press, 1972), 218–19.

2 Ibid., 221.

3 Ibid., 32.

4 Ibid., 269.

5 Marianne Preger-Simon, journal, June 2, 1958.

6 Martha Graham was one of the mystery guests who played Miss or Mr. "Hush" on the 1947 radio program *Truth or Consequence.* See Don McDonagh's biography, *Martha Graham* (Praeger Publishers), 201–203, for further details.

7 Cunningham and Lesschaeve, *Dancer and the Dance*, 59.

8 Cunningham, *Changes*, n.p.

9 Ibid.

10 Ibid.

11 Ibid.

12 Cunningham and Lesschaeve, *Dancer and the Dance*, 132.

13 For a detailed description of the chance operations Cunningham used for *Summerspace*, see *Dance Magazine*, June 1966, 52–4, and Cunningham and Lesschaeve, *Dancer and the Dance*, 95–8 and 132.

14 *Dance Magazine*, June 1966, 52.

15 Cunningham, *Changes*, n.p.

16 *Dance Magazine*, June 1966, 52.

17 Conversation with Jasper Johns sometime in the 1990s and verified once again on April 19, 2004.

18 Some forty years later, I asked Jasper Johns if he'd worked on the backcloth and costumes. He smiled ironically, and said in mock horror, "Did I? Bob wanted *flowers* . . . the dots were mine!"

19 Nora Ephron, "On the Genesis of 'Summerspace,' " *The New York Times International Edition*, June 15, 1964.

20 I am indebted to Jasper Johns for this story.

21 Louis Horst, *Dance Observer*, August/September 1958, 102.

22 Doris Hering, *Dance Magazine*, October 1958, 34.

23 Walter Terry, *The New York Herald Tribune*, August 24, 1958.

24 Walter Sorell, *The Saturday Review of Literature*, September 13, 1958.

25 Margaret Lloyd, *Christian Science Monitor*, Aug. 23, 1958.

26 Ibid.

13 · EUROPE, AT LAST!

1 Cage, *Silence*, 37.

2 Joan Peyser, *Boulez* (Schirmer Books, 1976), 140.

3 Ibid.

4 Ibid.

5 Cunningham, *Changes*, n.p.

6 *Dance Perspectives*, no. 34 (Summer 1968), 30.

7 C.B., postcard to my parents, November 6, 1958.

8 Herbert Russcol, *The Liberation of Sound: An Introduction to Electronic Music* (Prentice-Hall, 1972), 63.

9 Ibid., 52.

10 Wilfred Mellers, *Caliban Reborn: Renewal in Twentieth-Century Music* (Victor Gollancz, 1968), 132.

11 Michael Nyman, *Experimental Music: Cage and Beyond* (Schirmer Books, 1974), 37.

14 · "SUCCESS IS DUST!"

1 Lynn Ludlow, "Chinese Poetry in Dance: Cunningham Performs 'White Stone,'" *Champaign-Urbana Courier*, March 16, 1959.

2 The four other trophies: *Trophy II* (*for Teeny and Marcel Duchamp*), *Trophy III* (*for Jean Tinguely*), *Trophy IV* (*for John Cage*), and *Trophy V* (*for Jasper Johns*).

3 *Champaign-Urbana Courier*, March 16, 1959.

4 Jean Beatty, "Cunningham Group Displays Significance of Space, Silence," *The Washington Post*, April 13[?], 1959.

5 Seymour Raven, "Dancer Shuns Random Flight," *Chicago Daily Tribune*, April 14, 1959.

6 Cunningham and Lesschaeve, *Dancer and the Dance*, 99.

7 *Dance Perspectives*, no. 34 (Summer 1968), 57.

8 Doris Hering, "The 'Good Guys' Versus the 'Bad Guys'—12th American Dance Festival," *Dance Magazine*, October 1959.

9 Cunningham, *Changes*, n.p.

15 · MOVING INTO THE SIXTIES

1 *Robert Rauschenberg*, catalogue (National Collection of Fine Arts, Smithsonian Institute, 1976), 101.

2 Barbara Haskell, *BLAM! The Explosion of Pop, Minimalism and Performance (1958–1964)* (Whitney Museum of Art, 1984), 127.

3 "How Strange," *Time*, February 29, 1960, 44.

4 Emily Genauer, "Art: Creative Parallels—This Week's Menu: Omelette of the Arts," *The New York Herald Tribune*, February 21, 1960.

5 "DANCE/Out—Way Out," *Newsweek*, February 29, 1960, 62.

6 Walter Terry, "The Dance World / Theatre Week End with the Moderns," *The New York Herald Tribune*, February 21, 1960, Section 4.

7 William Flanagan, "New Work by John Cage / A 3-Ring Circus of Lunacy Is This Musical Premiere," *The New York Herald Tribune*, March 8, 1960.

8 Ibid.

9 Eric Salzman, "By Cowell and Cage," *The New York Times*, March 8, 1960.

10 *Time*, March 21, 1960, 46.

11 Cage, *Silence*, 95.

12 A far more detailed description of the

performance and the score may be found in William Fetterman's *John Cage's Theatre Pieces—Notations and Performance* (Harwood Academic Publishers, 1996.)

13 Ibid., 111.

14 Cage, *Silence,* 47.

15 Harold C. Schonberg, "The Far-Out Pianist," *Harper's,* June 1960, 49–54.

16 Arturo Schwarz, *The Complete Works of Marcel Duchamp* (Harry N. Abrams, 1969), 527.

17 Ibid., 194–5.

16 · CONNECTICUT: SUMMER 1960

1 In the four summers that Merce Cunningham and Dance Company were in residence at Connecticut College, Merce choreographed five new works, but only *Crises* was actually commissioned by the American Dance Festival. The fifth work, *Aeon* (1961), does not qualify as an ADF premiere, however, since it was first performed in Montreal, Canada, two weeks before its American premiere at Connecticut College.

2 Cunningham, *Changes,* n.p.

3 Ibid.

4 Ibid.

5 Carolyn Brown, in Klosty, ed., *Merce Cunningham,* 26.

6 Cunningham, *Changes,* n.p.

7 Jill Johnston, "DANCE: Old Hat and New in Connecticut," *The Village Voice,* September 8, 1960.

8 P. W. Manchester, "13th American Dance Festival: The Season in Review," *Dance News,* October 1960, 7.

9 Doris Hering, "Silences and Sounds," *Dance Magazine,* October 1960, 24.

10 Ibid.

11 Emily Genauer, "Critical Summer Clearance," *The New York Herald Tribune,* September 4, 1960.

12 Ibid.

17 · EUROPE AGAIN: VENICE 1960

1 Many years later—on September 17, 1996, at the memorial service for David Tudor at Judson Church—M. C. Richards revealed the history of that poem. After one of David's piano recitals at Black Mountain College she spoke to him of her admiration for his performance and shook his hand. "It was hot! His hand was hot! And so soft, so amazingly soft—like a bird."

2 *Encyclopaedia Britannica,* 1970 edition, vol. 7, 364.

3 Peggy Guggenheim, *Out of This Century: Confessions of an Art Addict* (Universe Books, 1979), 379.

4 *Time,* October 10, 1960, 43.

5 Virgil Thomson, *The New York Times,* October 2, 1950.

18 · EUROPE, CONTINUED: 1960

1 H. W. Corten, "Berlin Festival a Great Success," *Welt Am Sontag,* October 2, 1960.

2 Werner Oehlmann, "Dada Dances in the Hebbel Theater," *Der Tagesspiegel / Feuilleton,* September 30, 1960.

3 Hedwig Muller, "Wigman and National Socialism," *Ballet Review* 15, no. 1, (Spring 1987), 65–73.

4 Horst Koegler, *Theater Heute,* October 1960.

5 Walter Kaul, "Avant-gardists as Musical Clowns," *Kurier,* September 29, 1960.

6 F.R., "The Piano Lid Played a Part; Tumult at the Dance-Duo Cunningham/Brown," *Spandauer Volksbatt,* September 30, 1960.

7 "Sense and Nonsense," *Berliner Montagsecho,* October 3, 1960.

8 Horst Koegler, "Tanz aus Mehr als einer Welt," *Theater Heute,* October 1960.

9 Earle Brown, "Planned Panichood," *An Anthology* (Heiner Friedrich, 1963).

19 · TROUBLING TIMES: 1960–1961

1 Richard F. Ahles, "Cage Cages Audience with Cagey Audiometrics," *Hartford Courant*, November 8, 1960.
2 John Martin, "The Dance: Seasonal Awards and Events," *The New York Times*, March 26, 1961.
3 Ibid.
4 "*Dance Magazine*'s Award Presentation," *Dance Magazine*, June 1961, 34–5.
5 Ibid.
6 Ibid.

20 · CONNECTICUT: SUMMER 1961

1 Cunningham, "Function of a Technique," 251.
2 Dr. Edward Podolsky, *Music for Your Health* (Bernard Ackerman, 1945).
3 The date and source of this information are unknown. It appeared in a magazine article that I had clipped out years ago.
4 Louis Horst, *Dance Observer* 28, no. 7 (August/September 1961), 101.
5 Jill Johnston, "Dance: Cunningham in Connecticut," *The Village Voice*, September 7, 1961.
6 Donal Henahan, "The Evangelical Avant-Garde at a Dead End," *The New York Times*, June 25, 1978.

21 · MOVING AHEAD

1 *Robert Rauschenberg* (Prepared in conjunction with an exhibition organized by the National Collection of Fine Arts), Smithsonian Institution, 1976, p. 104.
2 Dorothy Nichols, *Daily Palo Alto Times*, March 1, 1962.
3 Alfred Frankenstein, *San Francisco Sunday Chronicle*, February 25, 1962.
4 Jill Johnston, "Dance: New London," *The Village Voice*, August 30, 1962, 12.

22 · UPS AND DOWNS

1 John K. Sherman, "Cunningham's Ideas Extend Modern Dance Boundaries," *The Minneapolis Star*, February 14, 1963.
2 Peter Yates, "Merce Cunningham Restores the Dance to Dance," *Arts and Architecture*, November 1963, 13.
3 Cunningham, *Changes*, n.p.
4 Peter Williams, "Movement, Sound, Light: Decorenberg," *Dance and Dancers*, 15, no. 9 (September 1964), 25.
5 Peter Yates, "Merce Cunningham Restores the Dance to Dance," *Arts and Architecture*, November 1963, 13.
6 Cunningham, "Story (Part III)," 35.
7 Jill Johnston, "Dance: Cunningham, Limón," *The Village Voice*, September 5, 1963.
8 Allen Hughes, " 'Modern' Problem: 'Far Out' Dance Music Raises Protest," *The New York Times*, August 25, 1963.

23 · SOME VENTURES AFIELD

1 "The Line Up: A Glamour Exclusive," *Glamour*, June 1963, 76–9.
2 "Seven New Shows: Subtle . . . Simple . . . Sure . . . Surprising," *Newsweek*, February 18, 1963, 65.
3 Allen Hughes, "Ballet by Strate Seen at Juilliard," *The New York Times*, April 6, 1963.
4 Eric Salzman, "With the New Music Real Time's a Trouble," *The New York Herald Tribune*, October 12, 1963.
5 Alan Rich, "The Most Adventurous of Adventurous," *The New York Herald Tribune*, February 7, 1964.
6 Cunningham, *Changes*, n.p.
7 Ibid.
8 Cecily Dell, "Winterbranch . . . and hundreds of years," *Dance Scope*, Spring 1965, 20.

9 C.B., letter to Earle Brown, Paris, March 17, 1964.

24 · WORLD TOUR/PART I

1 Cunningham, "Story: Tale of a Dance," 16.
2 Although I saw this footage, it, along with reels and reels of other far more precious documentation (the full repertory in performance), ended up on the cutting room floor!
3 C.B., Paris journal, June 12, 1964.
4 Tomkins, *Off the Wall*, 7.
5 For further details read chapter 1, "Venice," in Tomkins, *Off the Wall*, 1–11.
6 Ibid, p. 9.
7 This event witnessed by David Vaughan.
8 Alexander Bland, "Farther Out Than Ever," *The Observer Weekend Review*, June 28, 1964.
9 Hans Heinz Hanl, "Sacred Poses, Earache—And Nevertheless Dance," *Arbeiter Zeitung*, June 26, 1964.
10 Otto Bruenn, "Dance in the Museum of the 20th Century," *Salzburger Nachrichten*, June 27, 1964.
11 E.A., *Volksblatt*, June 28, 1964. Translated by Susanne Zahn, revised by David Vaughan.
12 Jean-Jacques Lerrant, "Trashcans and Automobiles with the Merce Cunningham Dance Company," *Le Progrès de Lyon*, July 21, 1964.

25 · WORLD TOUR/PART II

1 C.B., letter to my parents, July 27, 1964.
2 Cunningham, "Story: Tale of a Dance," 21.
3 With this truly delightful exception—most certainly Francis's own idea—and an exhibition of Cunningham company photographs by Jack Mitchell at the American Embassy in Grosvenor Square, the U.S. State Department evinced no interest and offered no financial support for our residency in London or any other part of the six-month tour.
4 C.B., journal, Monday, July 27, 1964.
5 Edward Mason, "When Dancers Disagree," *Sunday Telegraph*, August 2, 1964.
6 Philip Hope-Wallace, "Merce Cunningham at Sadler's Wells," *The Guardian*, July 28, 1964.
7 Charles Gréville, "The New Ice-Breakers of Modern Ballet," *Daily Mail*, July 28, 1964.
8 Andrew Porter, "Merce Cunningham—I," *The Financial Times*, July 28, 1964.
9 "American Choreographer's Strangest Ballet," *The Times*, August 3, 1964.
10 Clive Barnes, "Movement, Sound and Light," *Dance and Dancers* 15, no. 9 (September 1964), 16.
11 E. S. Turner, "Onward, but Never Always," *Punch*, August 12, 1964.
12 "American Ballet's London Debut," *The Times*, July 28, 1964.
13 John Percival, "Cunningham's Impressive Dancers," *The New Daily*, August 24, 1964.
14 John Percival, "Man of Many Talents," *The New Daily*, Tuesday, August 4, 1964.
15 Clive Barnes, "U.S. Dancers Win Hearts in London," *The New York Times*, Monday August 3, 1964.
16 Alexander Bland, "The Future Bursts In," *The Observer Weekend Review*, London, August 2, 1964.
17 Ibid.
18 Oleg Kerensky, "This Joke Is Not Funny," *Daily Mail*, August 6, 1964.
19 Merce Cunningham, "Story: Tale of a Dance," 21.
20 Richard Buckle, "Invitation to the Chance," *The Sunday Times*, August 2, 1964.
21 "American Ballet's London Debut," *The Times*, July 28, 1964.
22 Clive Barnes, "Movement, Sound and Light," *Dance and Dancers* 15, no. 9 (September 1964), 21.

23 I loved it so much I borrowed the idea years later for a dance I choreographed, *Synergy II* (1974), with a sound score by Maggi Payne; decor "after" *Story* R.R. (but I changed the color scheme); costumes by the choreographer; lighting by Thomas White. A group work for nine dancers. First performance, Bay Area Repertory Dance Theatre, March 7, 1974; Zellerbach Playhouse, Berkeley, California.

24 Alexander Bland, "Farther Out Than Ever," *The Observer*, June 28, 1964.

25 Mary Clarke, "The Merce Cunningham Dance Company," *The Dancing Times* 54, no. 648 (September 1964), 620.

26 David Vaughan, *Frederick Ashton and His Ballets* (Alfred A. Knopf, 1977), 344.

27 Julie Kavanagh, *Secret Muses: The Life of Frederick Ashton* (Pantheon, 1996), 461.

28 Merce Cunningham, "Story: Tale of Dance," 21.

29 Purchased in 1970, *Story*—the painting—now resides in the Art Gallery of Ontario in Toronto.

30 John Percival, "Cunningham's Impressive Dancers," *The New Daily*, August 24, 1964.

31 Francis Mason, "London Likes American Dancers," *The New York Times*, December 27, 1964.

32 George Beiswanger, "No Dolt Can Do It—An Appraisal of Cunningham," *Dance News*, May 1965, 6.

33 Sylvia Sklar, "Theatre Limelight— Merce Cunningham and Dance Company," *This Is London*, August 14–20, 1964.

34 Clive Barnes, "It's Foolish and It's Fun," *Daily Express*, August 4, 1964.

35 Clive Barnes, "Movement, Sound and Light," *Dance and Dancers* 15, no. 9 (September 1964), 19.

36 John Percival, "Cunningham's Impressive Dancers," *The New Daily*, August 24, 1964.

26 · WORLD TOUR/ PART III

1 Cunningham, "Story (Part II)," 19.

2 Ibid.

3 Ibid.

4 Anna Greta Stahle, "Cunningham pa Operan—Protester och bra'vorop," *Dagens Nyheter*, September 10, 1964. Loosely translated.

5 *Dance Magazine*, November 1964.

6 Cunningham, "Story (Part II)," 19.

7 C.B., journal; Helsinki, Finland, September 18, 1964. In Merce's *Dance Ink* journal, he gives a slightly different version of this event.

8 Lewis Lloyd, in Klosty, ed., *Merce Cunningham*, 49.

9 Cunningham, "Story (Part II)," 20.

10 Lewis L. Lloyd, letter to Rubin Gorewitz, October 5, 1964. Yale Collection.

11 Cunningham, "Story (Part II)," 21.

12 Ibid.

13 Lewis L. Lloyd, letter to Rubin Gorewitz, October 5, 1964; Yale Collection.

14 Monique Verken, "Au sommet d'une compagnie de danse américaine les trois noms les plus insolent de l'art actuel," *Beaux-Arts*, no. 1061 (October 1, 1964), 1.

15 Cunningham, "Story (Part II)," 22.

16 Lewis L. Lloyd, letter to Rubin Gorewitz, October 15, 1964. Yale Collection.

17 Ibid.

18 Cunningham, "Story (Part II)," 22.

19 As it turned out, the painting never changed hands, but a check for $1,000 was given to Earle—one more instance of Bob and Ileana's incredible generosity. Ileana became a great fan of Earle's music in the years to follow.

27 · WORLD TOUR/ PART IV

1 "Dance Form Free of All Curbs," *The Times of India*, October 16, 1964.

2 "Cunningham Ballet: Nostalgia

Created for Normal Fare," *The Times of India*, October 17, 1964.

3 See Erikson, *Gandhi's Truth*, for more.

4 Lewis L. Lloyd, letter to Rubin Gorewitz, Bangkok, November 3, 1964. Yale Collection. This letter is primarily devoted to the dire financial circumstances of the company. In it he states that with whatever money there is, the dancers should be the first to be paid, and that other creditors must wait.

5 Lewis L. Lloyd, letter to Rubin Gorewitz, New Delhi, October 29, 1964. Yale Collection. Many of the details of our adventure in Chandigarh come from conversations with Lewis Lloyd and from his journal letters. Still recovering from "Indian flu," I kept no journals during this period.

6 Cage, John: "Essays, Stories and Remarks About Merce Cunningham," *Dance Perpectives* 34 (Summer 1968), p. 41. This is one of five versions of this story. Merce Cunningham's journal (*Dance Ink* 6, no. 3) reported the remark as, "If we had known how good your troupe was, we would have treated you better." Lew Lloyd, in a letter to Rubin Gorewitz (October 29, 1964), had a slightly different version: "If we'd known how good you were, we would have treated you properly." Yale Collection. And David Vaughan, in his book *Merce Cunningham* recorded still another: "If we had known how good you are, we would have treated you better."

7 "Dance Recital by Cunningham Group," *The Times of India*, October 30, 1964.

8 "Fantastic, Uneven, Fascinating," *The Statesman* (Delhi), October 30, 1964.

28 · WORLD TOUR / PART V

1 Hiram Woodward Jr., "Modern Ballet Did Not Invoke Responsive Chords," *Bangkok World*, November 6, 1964.

2 Cunningham, "Story (Part III)," 35.

3 Edmund C. Wilkes, "Merce Cunningham," *The Yomiuri*, November 19, 1964.

4 Cunningham, "Story (Part III)," 35.

5 Ibid.

6 Lewis L. Lloyd, letter, November 20, 1964; Yale Collection.

7 Cunningham, "Story (Part III), 35.

8 Ibid.

9 Ibid., 36.

10 Ibid.

11 Ibid.

29 · ANOTHER BEGINNING

1 Cunningham, "Story (Part III)," 36.

2 Ibid.

3 Kotz, *Rauschenberg*, 117.

4 John Cage, letter to C.B., December 17, 1964.

5 Merce Cunningham, letter to C.B. in Ashby, Massachusetts; dated only "Saturday" but written in mid-December 1964. No postmark on envelope.

6 Hubert Roussel, "Infernal Escalator," *The Houston Post*, April 15, 1965.

7 Allen Hughes, "Dance at Lincoln Center," *The New York Times*, March 5, 1965.

8 Allen Hughes, "Spotlight on Dance," *The New York Times*, March 21, 1965.

9 Horst Koegler, *The Concise Dictionary of Ballet* (Oxford University Press, 1977), 396.

10 *The Dance Encyclopedia*, rev. and enl. ed., compiled and edited by Anatole Chujoy and P. W. Manchester (Simon and Schuster, 1987), 688.

11 Grace Glueck, "Art Notes: Adventures Abroad," *The New York Times*, June 6, 1965.

12 Earle Brown, letter to C.B.; En l'Ile, Paris, January 25, 1965.

13 Jonas Mekas, "Movie Journal," *The Village Voice*, June 3, 1965.

14 Grace Glueck, "Ballet: Brides and Turtles in Dance Program," *The New York Times*, May 13, 1965.

15 Kotz, *Rauschenberg*, 117.

16 Allen Hughes, "Leaps and Cadenzas," *The New York Times*, August 1, 1965.

30 · FULL STEAM AHEAD

1 James Barber, "Dancers Are Out of Step," *The Province*, February 10, 1966.
2 Clive Barnes, "The Untamed Surge of Modern Dance," *Life*, November 12, 1965.
3 Clive Barnes, "Cunningham's Troupe Appears in Brooklyn," *The New York Times*, April 25, 1966.
4 Michael Brenson, *Visionaries and Outcasts: The NEA, Congress, and the Place of the Visual Artist in America* (The New Press, 2001), 1–2.
5 C.B., letter to Earle Brown; March 12, 1966.
6 Clive Barnes, "Dance: 'Summerspace': Cunningham, the Sea-Green Incorruptible, Triumphs with City Ballet Production," *The New York Times*, April 15, 1966.
7 Walter Terry, " 'Summerspace': Winner Almost Loser," *The New York Herald Tribune*, April 15, 1966.
8 C.B., letter to Earle Brown; April 27, 1966. Klüver's exclamation, "No!" (Buckminster Fuller didn't know what he was talking about) seems more an indication of professional jealousy than good science. In 2002, scientists in the field of nanotechnology (the science of assembling materials one atom at a time) use the names "fullerene," "Buckyball," Buckytube," and "Buckysome" as recognition of the importance of Fuller's geodesic dome, to mention only one of Fuller's contributions. See *Newsweek*, June 14, 2002.
9 Carolyn Brown, "Marshall McLuhan and the Arts," *Ballet Review* 1, no. 4 (1966).
10 Clive Barnes, "Dance: Trouble with Going Abroad—Case in Point: Trials of the Cunningham Troupe," *The New York Times*, May 21, 1966.
11 Françoise Riopelle was Jean-Paul's former wife; their daughter Yseult would become an apprentice with MCDC in the fall of 1966.
12 Lewis Lloyd, letter to David Vaughan; August 23, 1966. Yale Collection.
13 Telephone interview with Beverly Emmons; December 22, 2003.
14 Ibid.
15 Kenneth King, "Space Dance and the Galactic Matrix," in Kostelanetz, ed., 199.
16 C.B., letter to Earle Brown; Hotel Berlin, Hamburg, Germany, August 17, 1966.
17 Birgit Cullberg, letter to C.B.; Göteborg, Sweden, October 15, 1966.
18 David Vaughan, letter to Lewis L. Lloyd; Paris, November 6, 1955. Yale Collection.
19 David Vaughan, letter to Lewis L. Lloyd; Paris, November 11, 1966. Yale Collection.
20 Suzy Knickerbocker, *World Journal Tribune* (New York), December 4, 1966.
21 David Vaughan, letter to Lewis L. Lloyd; Paris, November 11, 1966. Yale Collection.
22 Ibid.
23 David Vaughan, letter to Lewis L. Lloyd; Paris, November 6, 1966. Yale Collection.
24 "The Flower Pot Hit," *Evening Standard*, November 29, 1966.
25 Mary Clarke, "The London Scene," *Dance News* 1, no. 1 (January 1967); 8.
26 J. Henry Moore, "Dance," *The International Times*, November 28, 1966.
27 Clive Barnes, "Dance: Cunningham Back After Triumphs Abroad," *The New York Times*, December 10, 1966.
28 Clive Barnes, "Dance: Paradox of a Successful Tour: Cunningham Troupe Is Back, but in the Red," *The New York Times*, January 5, 1967.

31 · WHERE FROM HERE?

1 John Gruen, "Art Meets Technology," *New York/World Journal Tribune*, October 2, 1966.

2 Grace Glueck, "Disharmony at the Armory," *The New York Times,* October 30, 1966.

3 Ibid.

4 John Gruen, "Art Meets Technology," *New York/World Journal Tribune,* October 2, 1966.

5 "The Switched-on Theatre," *Reporter Magazine* 15, no. 6 (November/December 1966), 12.

6 John Rockwell, "The Man Who Made a Match of Technology and Art," *The New York Times,* January 23, 2004.

7 Vaughan, "Fabric of a Friendship," 140.

8 "An Art Council That Works," *Saturday Review,* February 25, 1967, 68.

9 Grace Glueck, "Single-Channeled You Mustn't Be," *The New York Times,* February 5, 1967.

10 Pierre Descargues, *Tribune de Lausanne,* March 5, 1967.

11 Marcel Schneider, *Combat,* March 2, 1967.

12 Earle Brown, letter to C.B.; Paris, March 1, 1967.

13 Carla Blank, *Rediscovering America: The Making of Multicultural America, 1900–2000* (Three Rivers Press, 2003), 309.

14 Tomkins, *Bride and the Bachelors,* 272–3.

15 Ibid., 294.

16 Ibid., 277.

17 Excerpt from a hand-delivered letter from Theresa Dickinson to C.B.; Connecticut College, August 5, 1967.

18 Bruce Zumstein, "Musicircus Rocks Stock Pavillion," *The Daily Illini,* (Urbana-Champaign, Illinois), November 18, 1967.

19 Ibid.

20 Deborah Jowitt, "Dance: Brooklyn Scramble," *The Village Voice,* December 7, 1967.

21 Clive Barnes, "Dance: Cunningham's Short Season; *Scramble* Is Introduced at Brooklyn Academy," *The New York Times,* December 4, 1967.

22 Alan M. Kriegsman, "Jaunty New Dance Seems Typical of Merce Cunningham's Invention," *The Washington Post,* December 10, 1967.

32 · A PROFESSIONAL COMPANY

1 Meg Harper, letter to C.B.; March 18, 2004.

2 Cunningham and Lesschaeve, *Dancer and the Dance,* 113.

3 Jill Johnston, "Dance Journal: Okay Fred," *The Village Voice,* May 23, 1968.

4 *Jasper Johns: Writings,* 237.

5 Cunningham and Lesschaeve, *Dancer and the Dance,* 113.

6 *Jasper Johns: Writings,* 237.

7 This story is told in several interviews with Jasper Johns. In March 2004, I spoke with Jasper in order to hear it again in his own words.

8 Clive Barnes, "Dance: Premiere of *Walkaround Time*—Cunningham's Novelty Has Impressive Decor," *The New York Times,* May 23, 1968.

9 Vaughan, "Fabric of a Friendship," 141.

10 Tomkins, *World of Marcel Duchamp,* 9.

11 Ruth Foster: *Knowing in My Bones* (Adams & Charles Black, London, 1976) as quoted by David Vaughan in " 'Then I thought about Marcel . . .' Merce Cunningham's *Walkaround Time*" in Kostelanetz, ed., *Merce Cunningham,* 68.

12 However, in 2005, Paul B. Franklin's in-depth study of the work, "Walkaround Time: Merce Cunningham's Terpsichorean Tribute to Marcel Duchamp," was published in *Etant donné* 6, devoted to the relationship between Duchamp and John Cage.

13 John Mueller, "Films: Merce Cunningham's 'Walkaround Time,' " *Dance Magazine,* June 1977.

14 Clive Barnes, "Dance: Premiere of 'Walkaround Time'—Cunningham's Novelty Has Impressive Decor," *The New York Times,* May 23, 1968.

15 Patrick O'Connor, "Cunningham Lives Up to Expectations," *The Jersey Journal,* May 23, 1968.

16 Arlene Croce, *Afterimages* (Alfred A. Knopf, 1977), 339.

17 Walter Terry, "World of Dance," *Saturday Review,* July 6, 1968.

18 Tomkins, *World of Marcel Duchamp,* 171.

19 Ruth Foster: *Knowing in My Bones* (Adams & Charles Black, London, 1976) as quoted by David Vaughan in " 'Then I thought about Marcel . . .' Merce Cunningham's *Walkaround Time*" in Kostelanetz, ed., *Merce Cunningham,* 68.

20 Cunningham and Lesschaeve, *Dancer and the Dance,* 115.

21 Ruth, Foster: *Knowing in My Bones* (Adams & Charles Black, London, 1976) as quoted by David Vaughan in " 'Then I thought about Marcel . . .' Merce Cunningham's *Walkaround Time*" in Kostelanetz, ed., *Merce Cunningham,* 68.

22 Tomkins, *World of Marcel Duchamp,* 89–90.

23 Ibid., 91.

24 Kostelanetz, ed., *Merce Cunningham,* 69.

25 Cage, *Silence,* 130.

26 Tomkins, *World of Marcel Duchamp,* 89.

27 Patrick O'Connor, "A Dazzling Revelation," *The Jersey Journal,* January 9, 1968.

28 Clive Barnes, "Dance: Premiere of 'Walkaround Time,' " *The New York Times,* May 23, 1968.

29 Marcia B. Siegel, "Cunningham Here and There," *New York,* June 17, 1968.

30 Jill Johnston, as quoted by Clive Barnes in "Making It in Brooklyn," *The New York Times,* June 2, 1968.

31 Clive Barnes, "Making It in Brooklyn," *The New York Times,* June 2, 1968.

32 Lewis Lloyd, letter to Jean Rigg, July 23, 1968. Yale Collection.

33 Lewis Lloyd, letter to Judith Blinken, August 8, 1968. Yale Collection.

34 Birgitta Segerskog, "Cunningham's Magic Comes Through," *The News* (Mexico City) July 17, 1968.

35 I am indebted to Gordon Mumma and Lew Lloyd for their recollections of the political situations and particular difficulties the Cunningham company encountered on the South American tour in 1968.

36 "Protesto Tem Vez Na Arte de Cunningham: Arte Nova," *Diârio de Notícias;* July 26, 1968. (Translation from the Portuguese by Nancy Stepan.)

37 Lewis Lloyd, letter to Jean Rigg; Rio de Janeiro, July 24, 1968. Yale Collection.

38 Gordon Mumma, e-mail to C.B.; April 21, 2004.

39 Lewis Lloyd, letter to Jean Rigg & Judith Blinken; August 7, 1968. Yale Collection.

40 I am indebted to conversations with Alfred Stepan for this information. For further reference see his *The Military in Politics: Changing Patterns in Brazil* (Princeton University Press, 1971).

41 Lewis Lloyd, letter to CB; May 7, 2003.

42 Gordon Mumma, e-mail to CB; April 22, 2004.

43 *Prima Plana* (Buenos Aires), August 13, 1968. (Translated from the Spanish.)

44 Dayed (Mr. Cabrera), "Merce Cunningham: Dance Starting with Zero," *Clarín,* (Buenos Aires), August 13, 1968. (Translated from the Spanish.)

45 Lewis Lloyd to CB; May 7, 2003.

46 "Composer Cage Explains His Theories," *The Daily Journal* (Caracas, Venezuela), August 1968.

47 Cage, *A Year from Monday,* ix–x.

48 Isaac Chocrón, "Cunningham: How to Pass, Kick, Fall and Run," *Imagen: Quincenario de Arte, Literatura e Información Cultural* 31; (Caracas), August 15/31, 1968. (Translated from the Spanish.)

33 · SOME SUBSIDY AT LAST

1 Jean Rigg, letter to Lew Lloyd; San Francisco, October 16, 1968. Yale Collection.
2 Robert Commanday, "Music: Composing with Camera," *This World,* November 10, 1968, 31–2.
3 Ibid., 31.
4 Ibid., 32.
5 John Cage, letter to Lew Lloyd; April 8, 1968. Yale Collection.
6 Jean Rigg, letter to Lew Lloyd; San Francisco, California; November 3, 1968. Yale Collection.
7 Clive Barnes, "Dancing on Borrowed Money," *The New York Times,* August 4, 1968.
8 Jeff Slayton, e-mail to CB; July 29, 2004.
9 James Traub, "The Alt-Lincoln Center," *The New York Times Magazine,* April 25, 2004, 40.
10 Cunningham, *Dancer and the Dance,* 115–16.
11 Thomas Willis, "Cunningham Show Lacks Zip," *Chicago Tribune,* March 26, 1969.
12 Louis Calta, "Cunningham Goes on without Music," *The New York Times,* April 16, 1969.
13 Joseph Gale, "Discord from the Unions," *Newark News,* April 20, 1969.
14 Joseph Gale, "Music Isn't Missed," *Newark News,* April 16, 1969.
15 Patrick O'Connor, "Cunningham Sans Music, Magnificent," *The Jersey Journal,* April 16, 1969.
16 *Jasper Johns: A Retrospective,* 136.
17 Clive Barnes, "May I Talk About Indians?" *The New York Times,* October 26, 1969.
18 Douglas Dunn, e-mail to CB; September 10, 2004.
19 Cunningham, *Dancer and the Dance,* 93.
20 Ibid., 88.
21 Ibid., 88–9.
22 Ornella Volta, *Satie: Seen Through His Letters* (Marion Boyars Publishers, 1989), 152.
23 Klosty, ed., *Merce Cunningham,* 25.
24 Douglas Dunn, e-mail to CB; September 10, 2004.
25 Clive Barnes, "Dance—Theater Event," *The New York Times,* January 16, 1970.

34 · MIXED SIGNALS

1 Louise Burns, e-mail to CB; January 12, 2005.
2 Robert Rauschenberg, quoted in "*Dance Magazine* Awards: Recognition of a World Community," *Dance Magazine,* August 1970, 59.
3 Carolyn Brown, quoted in *Dance Magazine,* August 1970, 60.

35 · THE BEGINNING OF THE END

1 Gordon Mumma, "From Where the Circus Went," in Klosty, ed., *Merce Cunningham,* 70–1.
2 Marcia B. Siegel, "More Than the Music," *Boston Herald Traveler,* November 29, 1970.
3 "Cunningham and His Dancers: A Symposium with Carolyn Brown, Douglas Dunn, Viola Farber, Steve Paxton, Marianne Preger Simon, Valda Setterfield, Gus Solomons, and David Vaughan," *Ballet Review* 15, no. 3 (Fall 1987).
4 Don McDonagh, "New Dance Limns Joy and Sadness," *The New York Times,* November 11, 1970.
5 Clive Barnes, "Is Cunningham Too Restricted?" *The New York Times,* November 29, 1970.
6 Ibid.
7 Clive Barnes, "Dance—New Cunningham," *The New York Times,* November 7, 1970.
8 Gordon Mumma, e-mail to CB; February 3, 2005.
9 Marcia B. Siegel, *Watching the Dance Go By* (Houghton Mifflin, 1977), 237–8.

10 Clive Barnes, "Dance—New Cunningham: Debut of 'Landrover,'" *The New York Times,* February 2, 1972.

36 · LAST CHAPTER

1 Walter Terry, *Ted Shawn: Father of Modern Dance* (Dial Press, 1976), 93.
2 Nancy Goldner, "Marion Rice's Denishawn Dancers, Carolyn Brown, Guest Artist, and Barton Mumaw—Jacob's Pillow, Lee, Mass., June 22–24," *Dance News,* October 1972, 16.
3 Deborah Jowitt, "Dancelog—Impertinent Entries," *The Village Voice,* April 20, 1972.
4 James Underwood, "Stockhausen: God or Maestro," *The Teheran Journal,* September 2, 1972.
5 "Stockhausen," *Kayan International* (Teheran), September 9, 1972.
6 "Attacks Called Great Art," *The New York Times,* September 19, 2001. After the uproar in the press, Stockhausen issued a clarification. See his Web site: http://www.stockhausen.org/message_from_karlheinzhtml
7 "A Tribute to John Cage," *6th Festival of Arts Shiraz Persepolis* bulletin, September 8, 1972.
8 Gordon Mumma, e-mail to CB; March 2, 2005.
9 Unclassified document from American Embassy in Belgrade to American.
10 "A Strange, Strange Night in Belgrade," *Evening Standard,* September 22, 1972.
11 Ibid.
12 Among the voluminous pre-tour correspondence each of us received from our administrator, Jean Rigg, was the note, "We are dissuading sponsors and friends from arranging social activities for us on tour. However, as the tour is assisted with State Department funds, we feel obligated to accept invitations from the American Embassies. We will try to see that these are scheduled reasonably and that other people we might want to meet or see again will be invited." At long last the Cunningham company had received some State Department support! One has to wonder what changes took place in Washington to bring this about!
13 Fernau Hall, "Cunningham in Magical Masterpiece," *The Daily Telegraph,* September 27, 1972.
14 Clement Crisp, "Cunningham's Dances," *The Financial Times,* October 2, 1972.
15 Peter Williams, "Medium Without the Message," *Dance and Dancers,* November, 1972, 30.
16 Fernau Hall, "'Landrover' Dancing Baffles Unwary," *The Daily Telegraph,* September 26, 1972.
17 Klaus Bauer, "Barking and Miowing for U.S. Ballet," *Kolnische Rundschau,* October ?, 1972.
18 Jochen Schmidt, "Cunningham the Magician," *Frankfurter Allgemeine Zeitung,* October 11, 1972.
19 Gordon Mumma, e-mail to CB; April 18, 2005.
20 Cunningham, *Other Animals,* 68.

Armitage, Merle, ed. *Martha Graham: The Early Years.* Da Capo Press, 1978.

Artaud, Antonin. *Antonin Artaud: Selected Writings.* Edited and with an introduction by Susan Sontag. Farrar, Straus and Giroux, 1976.

Botto, Louis. Interview with George Balanchine. *Intellectual Digest,* June 1972.

Cage, John. *Silence.* Wesleyan University Press, 1961.

————. *A Year from Monday.* Wesleyan University Press, 1967.

————. "2 Pages, 122 Words on Music and Dance." *Dance Magazine,* November 1957.

————. "Essays, Stories and Remarks About Merce Cunningham." *Dance Perspectives* 34 (Summer 1968).

Cunningham, Merce. *Changes: Notes on Choreography.* Edited by Frances Starr. Something Else Press, 1968.

————. *Other Animals: Drawings and Journals.* Aperture, 2002.

————. "The Function of a Technique for Dance." In *The Dance Has Many Faces,* edited by Walter Sorell. The World of Publishing, 1951.

————. "The Impermanent Art." In *Seven Arts #3,* edited by Fernando Puma. Falcon's Wing Press, n.d.

————. "Space, Time and Dance." *Transformation* 1, no. 3 (1952).

————. "Story: Tale of a Dance and a Tour." 3 parts. *Dance Ink* 6, no. 1 (Spring 1995); no. 2 (Summer 1995); no. 3 (Fall 1995).

Cunningham, Merce, and Jacqueline Lesschaeve. *The Dancer and the Dance.* Marion Boyars, 1985.

Duberman, Martin. *Black Mountain: An Exploration in Community.* E. P. Dutton, 1972.

Erikson, Erik H. *Gandhi's Truth: On the Origins of Militant Nonviolence.* W. W. Norton, 1969.

Jasper Johns: A Retrospective. The Museum of Modern Art, 1996.

Jasper Johns: Writings, Sketchbook Notes, Interviews. The Museum of Modern Art, 1997.

Klosty, James, ed. *Merce Cunningham.* Saturday Review Press / E. P. Dutton, 1975.

Kostelanetz, Richard, ed. *John Cage.* Documentary Monographs in Modern Art series. Prager Publishers, 1970.

————. *Merce Cunningham: Dancing in Space and Time.* Da Capo Press, 1998.

Kotz, Mary Lynn. *Rauschenberg: Art and Life.* Harry N. Abrams, 1990.

Myers, Rollo H. *Erik Satie.* Dover, 1968.

Rose, Barbara. *American Art Since 1900.* World of Art series. Praeger, 1975.

Russell, John. *The Meanings of Modern Art.* Museum of Modern Art / Harper and Row, 1981.

Sandler, Irving. *The New York School: The Painters and Sculptors of the Fifties.* Harper and Row, 1978.

Sorell, Walter, ed. *The Dance Has Many Faces.* World Publishing Company, 1951.

Tomkins, Calvin. *The Bride and the Bachelors: Five Masters of the Avant-Garde.* Rev. ed. Viking, 1968.

————. *Off the Wall: The Art World of Our Time.* Doubleday, 1980.

————. *The World of Marcel Duchamp.* Time-Life Library of Art series. Time-Life, 1974.

Vaughan, David. "The Fabric of a Friendship: Jasper Johns in Conversation with David Vaughan." In *Dancers on a Plane: Cage, Cunningham, Johns.* Alfred A. Knopf, 1990.

————. *Merce Cunningham: Fifty Years.* Aperture, 1997.

Grateful acknowledgment is made to the following for permission to reprint previously published material:

Richard Glasstone: Excerpt from "Into the Future with Cecchetti" by Richard Glasstone (*Dancing Times*, April 1990). Reprinted by kind permission of Richard Glasstone.

Jill Johnston: Excerpts from "Dance: Cunningham in Connecticut" (*The Village Voice*, September 7, 1961), "Dance: New London" (*The Village Voice*, August 30, 1962), and "Dance: Cunningham, Limón" (*The Village Voice*, September 5, 1963). Reprinted by permission of Jill Johnston.

John Mueller: Excerpt from "Films: Merce Cunningham's 'Walkaround Time' " by John Mueller (*Dance Magazine*, June 1977). Reprinted by permission of John Mueller.

The New York Times Agency: Excerpt from "Cunningham's Troupe Appears in Brooklyn" by Clive Barnes (*The New York Times*, April 25, 1966), copyright © 1966 by The New York Times Co.; excerpt from "Dance: Trouble with Going Abroad—Case in Point" by Clive Barnes (*The New York Times*, May 21, 1966), copyright © 1966 by The New York Times Co.; excerpt from "Critical Summer Clearance" by Emily Genauer (*The New York Herald Tribune*, September 4, 1960), copyright © 1960 by The New York Times Co.; excerpt from "A Mania for All Seasons" by Walter Terry (*The New York Herald Tribune*, August 25, 1963), copyright © 1963 by The New York Times Co. Reprinted by permission of The New York Times Agency.

Robert Rauschenberg: Excerpted material by Robert Rauschenberg from "*Dance Magazine* Awards: Recognition of a World Community" (*Dance Magazine*, August 1970). Reprinted by permission of Robert Rauschenberg.

Frontispiece: Hans Wild, courtesy of
Archives of the Cunningham Dance
Foundation

INSERT 1

Radford Bascome: pages 10 and 11
Arnold Eagle, courtesy of Archives of the
Cunningham Dance Foundation:
page 3, top
James Klosty: page 1; page 2, top left; page
5; pages 6 and 7, top and bottom; page 8,
top; page 9, top and bottom; page 12
Jun Miki: page 8, bottom
© Jack Mitchell: page 4, top and bottom
Richard Rutledge, courtesy of Archives of
the Cunningham Dance Foundation:
page 2, bottom
Hans Wild, courtesy of Archives of the
Cunningham Dance Foundation:
page 3, bottom

INSERT 2

Author's collection: page 1, top and bottom
left; page 7, bottom
Oscar Bailey: page 7, top
Carolyn Brown: page 4, bottom
© Hervé Gloaguen/Rapho: page 5, top and
bottom left
Kay Harris, courtesy Robert Rauschen-
berg Studio: page 6, bottom left
Kate Jennings/Estate of Bob Cato: page 6,
top left

James Klosty: page 1, top right; pages 2
and 3, top and bottom; page 5, bottom
right
© Hans Namuth, Ltd.: page 8
John Van Lund, © Jacob's Pillow Dance
Festival Archives: page 1, bottom right
Whitestone Photo: page 4, top

INSERT 3

Air France Photo: page 1
Author's collection: page 6, top right;
page 7
Carolyn Brown: page 3, top
James Klosty: page 2; page 3, bottom; page
4, top and bottom; page 5; page 6, left
topmost and bottom; page 8, top left, top
right and bottom
Marion Rice: page 6, middle left

INSERT 4

Archives of the Cunningham Dance
Foundation: page 10, bottom
Oscar Bailey: page 3, bottom
James Klosty: page 2; page 3, top; pages 4
and 5; page 6, bottom; page 7, top;
pages 8 and 9; page 11
Elizabeth Novick, courtesy Robert
Rauschenberg Studio: page 10, top
John G. Ross: page 12
Richard Rutledge, courtesy of Archives of
the Cunningham Dance Foundation:
page 1; page 6, top; page 7, bottom

A NOTE ON THE TYPE

This book was set in Bodoni Book, a typeface named
after Giambattista Bodoni (1740–1813), the celebrated
printer and type designer of Parma. The Bodoni types of
today were designed not as faithful reproductions of any
one of the Bodoni fonts but rather as a composite,
modern version of the Bodoni manner. Bodoni's
innovations in type style included a greater degree of
contrast in the thick and thin elements of the letters and
a sharper and more angular finish of details.

COMPOSED BY
North Market Street Graphics,
Lancaster, Pennsylvania

PRINTED AND BOUND BY
Berryville Graphics
Berryville, Virginia

DESIGNED BY
Iris Weinstein